UNIVERSITY LIBRARY
UW-STEVENS POINT

READINGS
IN
FEDERAL TAXATION

By

FRANK E. A. SANDER
Professor of Law, Harvard Law School

And

DAVID WESTFALL
Professor of Law, Harvard Law School

Mineola, New York
THE FOUNDATION PRESS, INC.
1970

Copyright © 1970
By
The Foundation Press, Inc.
All rights reserved

Library of Congress Catalog Card Number: 76–133299

Sander & Westfall Fed.Tax Pamph.

KF
6289
.A2
S3

PREFACE

For some time we have had a growing feeling that we should do more to introduce our students to materials that sought to raise some of the fundamental questions of tax policy. Should capital gains be taxed differently from ordinary income? How valid is the case for permitting the deduction of charitable contributions? Should trusts be treated as separate entities for tax purposes, or should they be viewed merely as intermediaries for the individual taxpayers who have the paramount interest in the trust income? As each tax act brings with it a new encrustation of detail and refinement, there seems to be an increasing need to stand back and consider some of these basic issues.

We conceive that the book might be used in a variety of ways to supplement the traditional materials in the basic taxation course. With respect to some topics (e. g., the process of tax legislation), the relevant portions of the book could simply be assigned as independent background reading. Some of the specific proposals (such as those of Professors Brazer and Slawson, pp. 187, 495) might usefully be subjected to class discussion. Others—like the Treasury's proposal to treat the transfer of appreciated property at death as a realization (p. 547)—could form the basis for an instructive drafting exercise. Finally, there are some subjects (such as revenue sharing) that most teachers never reach; here again an assignment of outside reading might be appropriate.

Every anthology is bound to disappoint some readers who do not find in it their favorite pieces. Although we have no expectation of avoiding this fate, it may be in order for us to indicate the general principles that have guided our selections. By and large we have given preference to provocative pieces over "balanced" pieces. We have felt under no obligation to include the "classics" in the field if we thought that a later piece was more lucid or more concise. If we have placed heavy reliance on the report of the Canadian Royal Commission on Taxation (Carter Commission), it is because we regard it as the most comprehensive reexamination of a national tax system in any major English speaking country in recent years.

Needless to say the process of choice was often a difficult one. There was a strong temptation to err on the side of over-inclusion, but our firm resolve to produce a book of reasonable size and cost compelled us to keep within stringent bounds. That same consideration underlay the choice of a photographic method of reproduction, with the consequence that our editing has had to be of very limited proportions. Thus, occasionally we have had to leave in cross-references to omitted portions in order to facilitate the reproduction process, and any updating has had to be confined to brief references in our introductory comments to some of the major intervening statutory changes.

We acknowledge with gratitude the suggestions we have received from a number of colleagues and friends in the course of putting together this book. We look forward to receiving additional suggestions in the hope that we might be able to reflect some of these in a future edition.

FRANK E. A. SANDER
DAVID WESTFALL

Cambridge, Massachusetts
August, 1970

TABLE OF CONTENTS

324635

†

READINGS IN FEDERAL TAXATION

Chapter I

AN OVERVIEW

A. Tax Legislation and Administration

Most students of taxation do not take long before they experience an acute sense of frustration at a tax code that appears at times to be overly intricate and virtually incomprehensible. Even the redoubtable Judge Learned Hand confessed to some such feelings when he wrote:

> In my own case the words of such an act as the Income Tax, for example, merely dance before my eyes in a meaningless procession: cross-reference to cross-reference, exception upon exception—couched in abstract terms that offer no handle to seize hold of—leave in my mind only a confused sense of some vitally important, but successfully concealed, purport, which it is my duty to extract, but which is within my power, if at all, only after the most inordinate expenditure of time. I know that these monsters are the result of fabulous industry and ingenuity, plugging up this hole and casting out that net, against all possible evasion; yet at times I cannot help recalling a saying of William James about certain passages of Hegel: that they were no doubt written with a passion of rationality; but that one cannot help wondering whether to the reader they have any significance save that the words are strung together with syntactical correctness.[a]

The causes and cures for this malaise are less obvious. The first two pieces that follow explore the role played by so-called "special provisions"—a term defined by Professor Blum as any provision that allows a taxpayer "to accumulate wealth or en-

[a] L. Hand, the Spirit of Liberty 213 (Dilliard ed. 1952).

joy personal consumption without paying the full tax." (p. 41).[b] Although Professor Surrey's article was written thirteen years ago, and there have been some obvious changes of detail in the interim,[c] a contemporary reader is bound to be struck with the fact that, as the French say, "plus ça change, plus c'est la même chose." Many of the questions raised by Professor Surrey—particularly those relating to private bills—were raised anew by Senator Edward Kennedy in connection with the 1969 Tax Reform Act. See 115 Cong.Rec. S 16099 (daily ed. Dec. 8, 1969).

It is instructive to compare Professor Surrey's essentially institutional analysis with Professor Cary's focus on the type of statute we are trying to create. To what extent, Cary might well have asked with equal relevance to the 1969 Act, is our present plight traceable to our persistent disregard of the bold, simple solution in favor of an overrefined compromise? According to Eisenstein, who has contributed the next to last excerpt, the compromise solution may be an inevitable concomitant of our political system. The final excerpt explores the proper allocation of responsibility for decisionmaking between the Treasury, the Congress and the courts.

[b] Those special provisions that are in effect designed to accomplish certain social objectives are explored from another vantage point by Professor Surrey in Section C of this chapter where he compares the tax route with the subsidy route for accomplishing such objectives. As is apparent from Professor Bittker's article in Section B, he rejects altogether the concept of a "special provision."

[c] For example, we do now have a system of comprehensive averaging, and the top rate is considerably below the 91% of 1957.

SURREY, THE CONGRESS AND THE TAX LOBBYIST—HOW SPECIAL TAX PROVISIONS GET ENACTED *

70 Harv.L.Rev. 1145 (1957).

THE development of a proper tax structure for an economy as large and as complex as ours is a task of the first magnitude. Given the dimensions of the task and the political arena in which it must be undertaken, the Congress has performed the essential work successfully. It has shown remarkable collective wisdom in shaping our federal tax structure, and its accomplishment in this field may be measured favorably against the tax systems of other countries. Since we live in an era when both professional learning and public opinion regard a progressive income tax as the most appropriate method of raising governmental revenue,[1] and since the progressive income tax is the mainstay of our tax structure, this accomplishment is remarkable. For a progressive income tax is also the most complicated and difficult of taxes to maintain. It places a premium on sensitivity to economic changes and to public attitudes. It demands high technical skills on the part of those who shape the legislative structure, who administer and interpret its provisions, who advise the public how to order its business and family affairs under the tax. It requires a literate citizenry with a respect for law and a willingness to shoulder

[1] For a recent discussion, see DeWind, *Law and the Future: Federal Taxation*, 51 Nw. U.L. REV. 227 (1956).

* Copyright © 1957 by The Harvard Law Review Association. Reproduced with permission.

fiscal burdens. Our over-all successful record in relying on the progressive income tax is thus a noteworthy achievement in public finance.

The continuation of this success with our federal-tax structure demands, however, constant alertness to the correction of faults as they appear. Recently there has been considerable criticism directed against the existence in our tax laws of provisions granting special treatment to certain groups or individuals. This criticism is aimed at both the increasing number of new provisions of this kind and the continuation of old provisions the significance of which has become far more important with passage of time. Some, it is true, have irresponsibly resorted to criticisms of this character as a justification for discarding the income tax.[2] But nearly all who have voiced objections to special-treatment provisions have done so in the hope that a consideration of the problem would result in a strengthening of the income tax.[3]

The criticisms on the whole involve these assumptions: (1) that it is essential under a progressive income tax, and also progressive estate and gift taxes, to adhere as far as possible to the criterion of equity or fairness. Stated simply, this criterion demands that the income-tax burden should as far as possible apply equally to persons with the same dollar income; (2) that

[2] See, *e.g.*, Andrews, *Let's Get Rid of the Income Tax!*, The American Weekly, April 22, 1956, p. 6, reprinted in 102 CONG. REC. A3331 (daily ed. April 24, 1956); *Why the Income Tax Is Bad*, U.S. News & World Report, May 25, 1956, p. 62 (interview with T. Coleman Andrews); *cf.* Hawley, *Our Tax Laws Make Us Dishonest*, 27 PA. B.A.Q. 230 (1956).

[3] For some of the recent literature, see Harriss, *Erosion of the Federal Estate and Gift Tax Bases,* in NATIONAL TAX ASSOCIATION, PROCEEDINGS OF THE FORTY-EIGHTH ANNUAL CONFERENCE ON TAXATION 350 (1955); Hellmuth, *Erosion of the Federal Corporation Income Tax Base*, in *id.* at 315; Pechman, *The Individual Income Tax Base*, in *id.* at 304; Atkeson, *The Economic Cost of Administering Special Tax Provisions*, in JOINT COMMITTEE ON THE ECONOMIC REPORT, FEDERAL TAX POLICY FOR ECONOMIC GROWTH AND STABILITY 276 (1955); Blum, *The Effects of Special Provisions in the Income Tax on Taxpayer Morale*, in *id.* at 251; Eisenstein, *The Rise and Decline of the Estate Tax*, in *id.* at 819; Groves, *Special Tax Provisions and the Economy*, in *id.* at 286; Paul, *Erosion of the Tax Base and Rate Structure*, in *id.* at 297; Cary, *Pressure Groups and the Revenue Code: A Requiem in Honor of the Departing Uniformity of the Tax Laws*, 68 HARV. L. REV. 745 (1955); DeWind, *supra* note 1; Surrey, *"Do Income-Tax Exemptions Make Sense?,"* Colliers, March 30, 1956, p. 26, reprinted in 102 CONG. REC. A3053 (daily ed. April 16, 1956); Bulletin of the Tax Section, American Bar Association, Oct. 1956, p. 3 (remarks of Congressman Wilbur D. Mills); *"Keep the Income Tax But Make It Fair,"* U.S. News & World Report, July 27, 1956, p. 68 (interview with Congressman Wilbur D. Mills); 102 CONG. REC. A3696 (daily ed. May 8, 1956) (remarks of Congressman Daniel A. Reed).

the Congress has not always followed this criterion in tax legislation; and (3) that there are a good many instances in the income, estate, and gift taxes in which the failure to follow this criterion is not properly justified by the requirements of other criteria. As illustrations, the critics point to such matters under the income tax as the present exceedingly preferential treatment of capital gains and especially its application to employee stock options, pension-trust terminations, coal and timber royalties, patent royalties, growing crops, livestock, and so on; percentage depletion; the exemption of interest on state and local obligations; the continual expansion of deductions for personal expenses unrelated to profit-seeking activities; the provisions for the blind and the aged; and the exemption of certain fringe benefits. In the estate-tax area, reference is made, for example, to the exemption of employee annuities and of transferred life insurance. In addition to these provisions involving certain groups in our society, the criticisms are of course directed against those special provisions which can affect only a handful of taxpayers, or even only one or two, such as the so-called "Louis B. Mayer amendment."[4]

---

[4] INT. REV. CODE OF 1954, § 1240. Sections of the 1954 Code will hereinafter be cited only by section number. The history of § 1240 is related in Cary, *supra* note 3, at 747–48. Under this provision amounts received from the assignment or release by an employee of over twenty-years employment of his rights to receive, after termination of his employment and for a period of not less than five years, a percentage of future profits or receipts of his employer are taxed at capital-gains rates if the employee's contract providing for those rights had been in effect at least twelve years. Clearly the blueprint for compliance with this section is quite detailed. It is generally assumed that the amendment at the time covered only two persons, Louis B. Mayer, retired vice-president of Loew's, Inc., and one other executive in the company, and that the amendment saved Mayer about $2,000,000 in taxes. Mayer, as a vice-president, had been in charge of Metro-Goldwyn-Mayer motion-picture studio for many years. He had received a compensation contract under which he was to receive 10% of the net proceeds from every picture made at that studio between April 7, 1924, and the day he left the company. On his retirement in 1951, Mayer released his rights under the contract in return for, apparently, $2,750,000. The 1954 Code, while continuing the provision, which had been adopted in 1951, underscored its special character by restricting its application to contracts entered into prior to the 1954 Code.

For other highly personalized provisions, see Cary, *supra* note 3, at 749–54. See also the following recent provisions:

(a) Section 2055(b)(2), added by Pub. L. No. 1011, 84th Cong., 2d Sess. (Aug. 6, 1956), treats as an exempt transfer to charity by a decedent property later transferred to charity by the spouse of the decedent under a power of appointment given to her by the decedent and exercisable at her death, subject to such conditions as that the spouse must be more than eighty years old at the decedent's

Often these provisions are spoken of as "loopholes" or "special tax privileges." Of course, the use of the appellation "loophole" is a matter of viewpoint. What is a "tax loophole" to a CIO or an ADA meeting is merely "relief from special hardship or intolerable rates" to an American Bankers Association or NAM meeting — and vice versa. Obviously we do not all feel the same way about each of the examples mentioned above. But despite an absence of consensus on any particular list of provisions there seems to be considerable agreement that Congress in its tax legislation has adopted provisions favoring special groups or special individuals and that these provisions run counter to our notions of tax fairness. Moreover, the tendency of Congress to act this way seems to be increasing.

---

death and must have executed an affidavit under certain conditions one year after his death proclaiming her intention to exercise the power in favor of charity. The provision was enacted August 6, 1956, but made retroactive to August 16, 1954.

(b) Section 106 of the Internal Revenue Code of 1939, as amended, 70 STAT. 404 (1956), applies a 30% income-tax rate to amounts received under a claim against the United States arising under a contract for the installation of facilities for any branch of the armed forces, remaining unpaid for more than five years from the date of the claim, and paid prior to January 1, 1950. The conference report stated that "it is the understanding of all the conferees that the action taken with respect to this amendment is not to be considered a precedent for future legislative action." H.R. REP. No. 2253, 84th Cong., 2d Sess. 5 (1956). Apparently the provision was designed solely to cover the taxpayer involved in Sanders v. Commissioner, 225 F.2d 629 (10th Cir. 1955), *cert. denied,* 350 U.S. 967 (1956), since the facts of the case fit precisely under the provision.

(c) Section 1342, added by 69 STAT. 717 (1955), provides for retroactive exclusion of damages received under a court decision in a patent-infringement suit and later repaid because of the subsequent reversal of the court decision on the ground that it was induced by fraud or undue influence. Apparently this provision grew out of the litigation reported in Universal Oil Products Co. v. Root Refining Co., 328 U.S. 575 (1946).

(d) Section 152(a)(10), relating to the deduction for "dependents," covers a cousin receiving institutional care for physical or mental disability if prior to being institutionalized the cousin was a member of the same household as the taxpayer. Section 152(b)(3) excepts from the exclusion of noncitizens a child born to or adopted by a member of the armed forces in the Philippine Islands before January 1, 1956. See Act of Aug. 9, 1955, c. 693, 69 STAT. 625, making this provision retroactive to 1946 and substituting the January 1, 1956, date for the July 5, 1946, date formerly contained in § 152(b)(3).

(e) Section 24(c) of the Internal Revenue Code of 1939, as amended, 67 STAT. 617 (now § 267(a)) allowed the deduction of an accrued expense if the related payee included the amount in income within two-and-one-half months after the close of the year and applied the change retroactively to 1946. The retroactive aspect, and perhaps the proposal, appear to be a consequence of the litigation in L. R. McKee, 18 T.C. 512 (1952), *rev'd per curiam,* 207 F.2d 780 (8th Cir. 1953), in which the taxpayer had been unsuccessful in the Tax Court under the previous provisions.

Against this background, the purpose of this article is to consider the question of why the Congress enacts these special tax provisions, to use a fairly neutral term. Not being a congressman, I cannot of course really answer the question. Nor can I hope to enumerate all of the factors that might influence a congressman in this area. But it may be useful to speculate about some of these factors and to see if there are ways in which the consideration of tax legislation could be altered for the better. It may help first to sketch some of the major factors that are operative in tax legislation. I propose to do this only briefly, since these factors are generally well recognized.

I. Some Major Factors

(*1*) *High Rates of Tax.* — The high rates of the individual income tax, and of the estate and gift taxes, are probably the major factor in producing special tax legislation. This is, in a sense, a truism, for without something to be relieved of, there

---

(f) Section 2053(d), added by 70 Stat. 23 (1956), was enacted February 20, 1956, but was made retroactive to cover decedents dying after December 31, 1953. It allows charitable deduction from the gross estate for the amount of state inheritance taxes imposed on a bequest to charity. This provision reportedly was adopted to affect the problem of a particular estate under the interaction of the Pennsylvania tax laws and the federal estate tax.

(g) Section 166(f) treats as a business-bad-debt loss a payment by the guarantor of a noncorporate obligation. The provision reportedly was designed to meet the problem of a Texas father who had made advances to his son's business. This *ad hoc* amendment obviously does not fit with the rest of the provisions respecting losses and bad debts, as is evidenced by the difficulty which it gave the Supreme Court in Putnam v. Commissioner, 352 U.S. 82 (1956). The dissent there labors long to gather an intelligible legislative history from the provision, but fails to realize that the provision has all the earmarks of an *ad hoc* resolution of a particular situation.

(h) Section 1235(d) provides that capital-gain treatment on the sale of a patent shall not apply to a sale between an individual and a related person, but then excepts brothers and sisters. Apparently this was inept phrasing to exclude a sale to a corporation owned by a brother, since the Joint Committee on Internal Revenue Taxation, Proposed Technical Amendments Bill of 1957, § 28 (CCH Stand. Fed. Tax Rep., Oct. 26, 1956), and the accompanying summary involve an amendment to make it clear that the protection was intended for the brother's corporation. For a statement by a taxpayer's representative questioning the justification for this special treatment for a brother, see *Hearings on Technical Amendments to the Internal Revenue Code Before a Subcommittee of the House Committee on Ways and Means,* 84th Cong., 2d Sess. 1 (1956).

(i) Section 1361, a complicated provision with many problems unsolved, which permits a proprietorship or partnership to elect corporate tax treatment, apparently received its main impetus and perhaps the only real reason for its existence from the situation of a particular Georgia partnership.

would be no need to press for relief. The point is that the average congressman does not basically believe in the present rates of income tax in the upper brackets. When he sees them applied to individual cases, he thinks them too high and therefore unfair. Any argument for relief which starts off by stating that these high rates are working a "special hardship" in a particular case or are "penalizing" a particular taxpayer — to use some words from the tax lobbyist's approved list of effective phrases — has the initial advantage of having a sympathetic listener. Put the other way around, an advocate of the "Louis B. Mayer amendment" would simply make no headway with a congressman who firmly believed in a ninety-one-per-cent top tax rate. But most congressmen apparently do not believe in such a rate — certainly not in the concrete and perhaps not even in the abstract. Since they are not, however, willing to reduce those rates directly, the natural outcome is indirect reduction through special provisions.[5]

The United States is not unique in this regard. Students of the British tax system, for example, state that the very high rates of that system are considerably ameliorated in a number of ways through which the wealthy can escape the full impact of those rates.[6] The exclusion of capital gains is one broad method. The estate tax offers a number of avoidance possibilities. Indeed, it may be said that both here and abroad, as various pressures have driven tax rates to top levels, the refuge of the wealthy has been in the brains of their tax lawyers and in the technicalities of the tax law. Governments are generally aware of these escape routes but are reluctant to close them and enforce with vigor the excessively high tax rates. In effect, a sort of political paralysis appears to be forming in countries relying strongly on income taxation, under which no clear way has appeared to move away from the combination of high rates tempered by many avoidance possibilities. The obvious solution would seem to be simultaneous lowering of the rates and closing of the escape routes. But con-

---

[5] See Surrey, *supra* note 3.

[6] The text statements are based on impressions obtained from a conference on the British tax system held in New York on January 4–5, 1957, under the joint auspices of the Harvard Law School Program in International Taxation, and the American Branch, International Institute of Public Finance. See also Wheatcroft, *The Anti-Avoidance Provisions of the Law of Estate Duty in the United Kingdom*, (paper to be published in NAT'L TAX J. (1957)). Professor Carl Shoup, an informed observer of the Japanese tax system, asserts that the same trend is evident in that country.

servative governments fear the political consequences of rate reduction for the wealthy although their effective tax burden would not be lessened. They may also fear that, once the system were tightened and stabilized at a lower tax-rate level, political pressures might drive the rates up again, this time with a much more severe effect. Liberal governments fear that they cannot persuade their supporters to accept tax-rate reductions for the wealthy in such clear terms as reduction of a ninety-per-cent rate to fifty per cent or sixty-five per cent, especially when the starting rates are high and the compensating factor is merely the closing of a number of loopholes which the public cannot understand. This is obviously a dilemma which the income tax must solve in the years ahead.[7]

(2) *Tax Polarity.* — The existence of two rate structures in the income tax and of two types of taxes on the transfer of wealth permits a congressman to favor a special group by placing its situation under the lower rate structure or the less effective tax. Thus, the presence of the twenty-five-per-cent capital-gains rate enables Congress to shift an executive stock option from the high rates applying to executive compensation to the lower capital-gains rate. If there were no special capital-gains rate, or if we did not tax capital gains at all, this shift could not be made, since a congressman would not completely exempt the stock option. Similarly, the presence of a gift tax permits certain transfers of wealth, such as transferred life insurance, to be shifted from the higher estate tax to the lower gift tax. As a consequence,

[7] Spokesmen on this subject in both political parties appear to recognize the need for solving the dilemma. As regards the Democrats, see Stevenson, *The New America, Where is the Money Coming From?*, N.Y. Times, Oct. 29, 1956, p. 22; U.S. News & World Report, July 27, 1956, p. 68 (remarks of Congressman Wilbur D. Mills). As regards the Republicans, see 103 CONG. REC. 697 (daily ed. Jan. 17, 1957) (statement of Secretary of the Treasury Humphrey); 102 CONG. REC. A3696 (daily ed. May. 8, 1956) (remarks of Congressman Daniel A. Reed); *Hearing on H.R. 4090 and H.R. 4091 Before the House Ways and Means Committee*, 85th Cong., 1st Sess. 4, 7–9 (1957) (testimony of Secretary Humphrey).

The dilemma should not be solved solely in the context of the income tax, but must be considered in the light of the entire tax structure. Thus, those who believe that stabilizing the income tax at levels of 50–65% does not leave a sufficient over-all burden on the wealthy would urge a concomitant strengthening of taxes on capital. In other countries this may mean a resort to net-worth taxes restricted to the upper levels and further development of estate taxes. In this country constitutional requirements may restrict the effort to a strengthening of the estate tax. Looking further ahead, there may be experimentation with expenditure taxation for the upper brackets, as contrasted with the current sales taxes that reach all levels but with greater impact at the lower ranges.

given this congressional tendency, we reach the paradox that having a gift tax as well as an estate tax may, given the present lack of proper co-ordination of the two taxes, result in less effective taxation of certain transfers of wealth than if we relied only on an estate tax.

(3) *Technical Complexity.* — The high rates of tax, the complexities of modern business, the desires of the wealthy and middle-income groups for clear tax charts to guide their family planning, the Government's need for protection against tax avoidance, the claims of tax equity, and various other factors have combined to make the income, estate, and gift taxes exceedingly complex in technical detail. These technicalities involve the drawing of countless dividing lines. Consequently, a case on the high-tax side of a line may closely resemble the cases on the other side receiving more favorable tax treatment. The result is a fertile ground for assertions of inequity and hardship as particular taxpayers desire legislation to bend the dividing lines and thereby extend the favorable treatment to their situations. Also, faulty tax planning, ill-advised legal steps, or transactions concluded in ignorance of tax law can produce severe tax consequences. These "tax penalties" could have been averted under an informed tax guidance that would have taken the taxpayer safely through the technical tax maze. In these circumstances, the taxpayer facing severe monetary hurt because of a "mere technicality" (to use the phrase that will be pressed on the congressman) is quite likely to evoke considerable sympathy for his plight.

(4) *History and Politics.* — The accidents of tax history also play a major role in the existence of special provisions. Tax-exempt securities in large part achieved their favored status through the vagaries of constitutional interpretation and not through any special desire to relieve the wealthy. Percentage depletion for oil and gas and the deduction of intangible drilling expenses have their roots in legislative compromises and administrative interpretation which for the most part do not appear to have been planned as special-interest relief.[8] It is only later that the extent of the tax generosity inherent in such provisions is comprehended. But by then they are in the law, the problem of the group benefited is one of defense rather than attack, and the

[8] For the history of these provisions, see Freeman, *Percentage Depletion for Oil — A Policy Issue*, 30 Ind. L.J. 399 (1955).

strategic advantages are all with that group. This is especially so when the area involved touches on major political matters, as in the case of percentage depletion and tax-exempt securities.

Political considerations naturally overhang this whole area, for taxation is a sensitive and volatile matter. Any major congressional action represents the compromises of the legislator as he weighs and balances the strong forces constantly focused on him by the pressure groups of the country. Many special provisions — capital gains, for one — are caught in these swirling pressures. The response of the legislator to issues raised by these provisions is, like his response to the general level of tax rates or to personal exemptions, a political response of considerable significance. It is an important part of the fabric of political responses which determines whether he will remain a congressman and whether his party will control Congress. In this group of provisions highly affected by political considerations are those "tax relief" provisions which have a broad public appeal and are thus likely to be regarded by the congressman as useful "vote-getters" — a "baby-sitter" deduction, the exclusion of "retirement income," or an extra exemption for the "aged." The political appeal of favorable action on these issues is quite likely to outweigh what a congressman would regard as "technical" tax arguments to the contrary.

(5) *Separation of Executive and Legislative Branches of Government.* — But many of the tax provisions we are considering do not lie at this political level. They are simply a part of the technical tax law. They are not of major importance in their revenue impact. But they are of major importance to the group or individual benefited and they are glaring in their departure from tax fairness. The inquiry, therefore, must here be directed toward some of the institutional features in the tax-legislation process which may be responsible for special provisions of this technical variety. Lacking direct knowledge, I must leave to others the task of describing the types of pressure from constituents or other groups which may be operative in a particular case. While these pressures may explain why the congressman who is directly subject to the pressures may act and vote for a special provision, they do not explain why other congressmen, not so subject, go along with the proposal. We must look for reasons beyond these pressures if we are to understand the adop-

tion of these special tax provisions. A number of these reasons lie in the institutional aspects of the tax legislative process.

Basic to a consideration of these institutional aspects are the nature of our governmental system and the relationship between the Congress and the executive. A different governmental structure might give the legislator little or nothing to say about tax provisions. Under a parliamentary government, the revenue department retains tight control over the statutory development of tax law. It is responsive only to the broad political issues that require decisions of a party nature. Beyond these, the governmental tax technicians mold the structure, so that the tax lobbyist pressing for special legislative consideration or the legislator seeking to ease a constituent's problem by special tax relief is not a significant part of the tax scene. Thus, under the British practice, finance bills are framed by the Treasury and the Board of Inland Revenue. The bills are debated in the Committee of Ways and Means — the entire House of Commons sitting under another name and with different rules of procedure. Here is an opportunity for anyone sufficiently concerned, who can persuade a Member of Parliament to voice his proposals, to have these proposals considered in the debates on the bill. Such discussion may focus attention on weaknesses in the bill or law, and if the proposal is considered meritorious by the minister in charge of the bill a change will be made. But if the government does not accept a member's amendment, party discipline is such that the minister is always supported and the amendment defeated. In practice, consequently, finance bills generally emerge in about the same form as introduced.[9]

The United States picture is quite different, for here Congress occupies the role of mediator between the tax views of the executive and the demands of the pressure groups. This is so whether the tax issue involved is a major political matter or a minor technical point. The Congress is zealous in maintaining this position in the tax field. A factor of special importance here is article I, section 7, of the Constitution, which provides that "All Bills for raising Revenue shall originate in the House of Representatives." The House Committee on Ways and Means jealously guards this clause against possible inroads by the Senate. It also

[9] These statements are not the result of any intensive examination of the British procedure, but are based on correspondence and discussion with British officials and practitioners.

protects its jurisdiction over revenue legislation from encroachment by other House committees. When senators and other congressmen must toe the line, the executive is not likely to be permitted to occupy a superior position. Further, a legislator regards tax matters as politically very sensitive, and hence as having a significant bearing on elections. It is no accident that the tax committees are generally strong committees, whose membership is carefully controlled by the party leaders.

The Congress, consequently, regards the shaping of a revenue bill as very much its prerogative. It will seek the views of the executive, for there is a respect for the sustained labors of those in the executive departments and also a recognition, varying with the times, of the importance of presidential programs. But control over the legislation itself, both as to broad policies and as to details, rests with the Congress. Hence a congressman, and especially a member of the tax committees, is in a position to make the tax laws bend in favor of a particular individual or group despite strong objection from the executive branch. Under such a governmental system the importance to the tax structure of the institutional factors that influence a congressman's decision is obvious.

II. Some Institutional Factors

(*1*) *The Congressman's Desire To Be Helpful.* — A congressman's instincts are to be helpful and friendly. If it were otherwise, he would not be in Congress. When a constituent, or some other person who is in a position to claim attention, seeks legislative action, the congressman likes to respond within reason. If the proposal presented to him is at all rational he will, in all probability, at least introduce it in bill form so as not to offend the constituent. If the congressman is not a member of one of the tax committees, that may end the matter — but it may not, for the proposal has been launched and lies ready to be pushed ahead by whatever pressures may be generated in its behalf.

The desire — sometimes the need — of a congressman to be useful often places a congressman who sits on one of the tax committees, the House Committee on Ways and Means or the Senate Committee on Finance, in a difficult position. A fellow congressman who sits on the Public Works Committee, for example, can respond to constituent pressure by approving the project involved; a member of the Appropriations Committee can respond by a favorable vote on a specific appropriation. But a congressman on a tax committee can respond only by pushing through a special tax provision. His legislative stock in trade, so to speak, is special tax treatment. This difficulty is especially acute in the case of those congressmen who come to sit on a tax committee only after they have been members of other committees and have become so accustomed to using their committee powers in helpful ways that the habit persists. And after all, the congressman who sits on a tax committee is frequently regarded as a powerful personage at home, in part because the fact of membership is often used by the congressman as an argument to support continued re-election. The congressman must be able to live up to this stature and obtain successful action on a proposal — as a senator on the Senate Finance Committee once put it, "What's the good of being on this committee if you can't get through a little old amendment now and then?" Sometimes, however, a senior congressman on a tax committee has enough influence and personal friendships around the Congress so that he can, when necessary, take care of his constituents in legislative ways other than tax proposals; if so, he is more likely to be quite objective when it comes to tax problems.

In view of all this, it is a credit to the congressmen on the tax committees that our tax laws are not in far weaker shape. Congressmen have withstood political pressures more staunchly than most people assume. Knowing the intensity of these pressures, the party leaders have tended to appoint members from relatively safe districts to these committees. But the institutional factors are such that some yielding to pressure must occur, and there is concern that the situation is slowly worsening. I believe that this concern is present inside the Congress as well as out, and that those congressmen subject to pressures would welcome reexamination of the institutional aspects of tax legislation if it would lead to a lessening of these pressures.

(2) *Lack of Congressional Appreciation of Departure From Fairness.* — In many cases the congressman considering a special tax provision may not realize that tax fairness is at all involved. He sees only the problem of the particular constituent or group concerned. The case in this focus may be very appealing, for human beings are involved with human problems. The income tax, always an impersonal, severe, monetary burden, becomes an

oppressive force bearing down on men in difficulty. The congressman may therefore not even appreciate that arguments of over-all fairness and equity have any relation to the question, or may very well think them too intangible and remote. Provisions for the relief of the blind and the aged are perhaps illustrations. Or the congressman, moved simply by a desire to help a constituent, may not understand the ramifications of the proposal. He is not a tax technician and he may view the proposal in isolation rather than perceive its relationship to the intricate technical structure of the revenue code. The proposal, so viewed, becomes merely a "little old amendment" which helps a constituent and does no harm. His brother congressmen are quite willing to be good fellows and go along, especially if the congressman urging the proposal is well-liked. After all, they too from time to time will have "little old amendments" to propose. Thus, in 1955 the Ways and Means Committee decided that in the initial consideration of members' bills dealing with technical matters it would allow each member one bill to be considered and then reported by the full committee if the bill met with unanimous agreement.

The attitude that the proposal does no "harm" needs explanation. "Harm" to most congressmen considering a tax proposal means "revenue loss" — if the provision is enacted it will cost the "Treasury" so many dollars in revenue. (Note that the cost is to the "Treasury" and not the United States or the public. This attitude, which views the bureaucratic Treasury as the obstacle, is quite important, and I shall consider it later.) If the dollar cost is high, the proposal faces a severe obstacle. The friendly congressman can now say to his constituent that the proposal is fair, that everyone agrees it has merit and that it is appealing, but that it simply costs too much at this time when the federal budget is so large and so on. But for a great many special proposals the cost is not high, perhaps at most a few millions. Therefore in these situations no "harm" is done. For "harm" does not include the fact that special treatment is afforded, that special treatment here breeds special provisions elsewhere, that once a foothold is obtained the special treatment expands and becomes costly. All this can seem quite remote to the congressman when measured against an appealing situation. When the immediate cost is high but the special provision has a reasonably broad application — the aged, the blind, and the like — the immediate-loss-of-revenue argument is far less persuasive and the result will depend on other considerations. These considerations may be difficulties of governmental administration or, more important, of securing taxpayer compliance, the potentialities for greater revenue loss if the provision is likely to be expanded, and even the merits of the proposal as a tax matter. But when a limited special provision is involved, the absence of "cost" gives the provision a significant advantage.

(*3*) *The Treasury Department's Presentation.* — The congressman's failure to recognize that tax fairness is at all involved may often be due to the inadequacy of the Treasury Department's presentation of the issues. This is not said critically, but by way of explanation. The problem facing the Treasury in these matters is formidable. The interested constituents or groups are generally skillful in presenting their cases in appealing form. Their energies are concentrated on one matter; they have time and money to devote to it; they may have the advantage of personal acquaintance, directly or through intermediaries, with the congressman; they can obtain skilled counsel informed on the ways of the Congress. The Treasury's tax staff must tackle all of these problems; its members are usually not chosen for skill in the presentation of issues or in handling congressmen; although on the whole remarkably good, considering the compensation, they are rarely among the ablest in the tax field, nor do they usually have the needed experience.

Further, private groups concentrate on making the best case possible and in so doing gloss over or forget the unfavorable aspects. They present the proposal in its simplest form and often avoid the complications involved in embodying the proposal in statutory drafts. At times a congressman is misled by this simple but convincing presentation and commits himself before he is aware of the full implications of the proposal. The treasury staff, on the other hand, feels compelled to present the pros and cons and to point out the complications. It is both explaining and criticizing — not just attacking — and its presentation may seem confusing rather than informative to the congressman. When he compares the complex, technical, "on the one hand, but on the other hand" explanation of the treasury staff with the deceptively simple and certainly forceful description of the problem presented by the private group, the latter is bound to achieve a considerable advantage. Congressmen, and even most congressmen on the tax committees, are laymen in tax matters; they are not tax technicians. Again this is not said critically. A congressman has a great many tasks to perform and decisions to make, so that he cannot — and really should not — be immersed in the technicalities of everything. After all, how skillful in tax law is the average lawyer?

Under these circumstances, the treasury type of explanation may at times be not really helpful. Yet if the treasury staff resorts to oversimplification, it is subject to the criticism from the committee members that it is not performing its proper role. This is especially so when the oversimplification may appear to be a one-sided attack on the proposal; the treasury staff is there to advise and inform, not to decide. The term "treasury staff" in this context refers to the treasury tax technicians. Their stock in trade before the committee is fairness and completeness of explanation — they are the "tax experts." If there are any departures from integrity in this regard, then the expert's usefulness is ended. The function of a top treasury policy-maker, usually an under or assistant secretary, is quite different. He is there to present the policy point of view of the executive branch and to use what talents he has to persuade the Congress to accept that point of view. The committee members can take his view or leave it, and their attitude toward the policy-maker depends on the imponderables of personal reactions and the ponderables of political forces. While the newspapers and the party news releases may praise this treasury official as a tax expert, he is not so regarded by the congressmen. He is operating at their level and not the technical level, and the congressman can readily appreciate the difference.

The treasury tax technicians are the "treasury experts." But as any skilled lawyer knows, it is not easy for an expert to explain complex matters to the uninitiated. Any tax lawyer who has faced the task of presenting extremely technical material to a tax-institute audience of nontax lawyers will readily appreciate the problem. Even this analogy is far from complete, for the treasury expert faces an audience which is sympathetic to the proposal under discussion, demands a complete presentation of the issues, and establishes standards under which any departure or even suspected departure from fairness is well-nigh fatal. Under these conditions, it is understandable that the explanation of an expert who values his integrity is often in the end likely only to confuse and not to enlighten. In this setting, the congressman struggling to perform his legislative task will often find the way to a decision lighted only by his sympathies.

Also, the treasury staff is usually not well known to the congressman. Its members, not being political, ordinarily do not mix with him at the same level, nor do they meet him socially. Hence the congressman is generally not in a position to act on the assumption that, although he doesn't fully understand all of what they say, he knows them to be good fellows and they are probably right. Nor do they spend with an individual congressman the amount of time needed to develop the problem fully. Thus in a committee meeting, the congressman must often decide an issue after only a minimum amount of discussion and before his biases and preconceptions have been replaced by a real understanding of the issues. The interested groups and the tax lobbyists, on the other hand, have the time to brief the various congressmen on their proposals. They are pushing one proposal and can concentrate on it. The treasury staff is faced with considering all of the proposals, and the time and personnel needed for an adequate informal discussion on each proposal with the necessary congressmen are not available.

Of course, if the interested group does not carry out its lobbying task carefully, the treasury staff has an easier time. It may point out that the proposal, especially if it is in legislative form, gives unintended benefits — will open up a "loophole." While this may be only the result of faulty drafting and could be corrected, it may be enough to stop the proposal at the time. Thus, it has been said that the tax lobbyist's task is to prepare a draft of an amendment simple enough so that a person who is not a tax expert can understand it, yet sufficiently precise that the treasury staff cannot demolish it. Or the congressman explaining a proposal in committee executive session may not have been briefed on the arguments involved or on the details of the proposal. Perhaps the lobbyist failed to point out how far the proposal really goes, so that the proposal if enacted would have a considerably greater effect than the congressman thought. If so, the Treasury's task — and its application of the term "loophole" — is considerably eased. Or the tax lobbyist may have failed to explain his proposal to enough congressmen on the committee or to the "key members," so that the particular congressman pushing the proposal is left without friendly support from other members. But all of this simply means a less-than-skillful lobbying performance. Just as cases can be lost in court through inadequately prepared briefs or poorly developed oral arguments, so can they be lost before the legislature.

(*4*) *Lack of Omniscience on the Part of the Treasury.* — The treasury tax staff is not omniscient. Yet understanding approaching omniscience is needed to do its job. A lack of knowledge on any particular matter, a failure of skill at any moment, can be fatal. The approach of the average congressman is to hear the private group, find out in general what it wants, react sympathetically for a variety of reasons, and then ask the Treasury whether there is any objection to the proposal. If the Treasury is off its guard and acquiesces, the proposal becomes law. If the Treasury is unprepared and presents a weak case, the proposal becomes law. Equally serious is the in-between situation in which the Treasury acknowledges that some hardship is present in the particular situation, but points out that the difficulty is but a phase of a general problem and that it has not yet been able fully to analyze the general area. It therefore urges that the particular proposal be postponed until further study is given to the whole matter. But recognition of some hardship and of some merit in his particular proposal is all that the congressman needs. His constituent wants relief from that admitted hardship now, and not years later when the whole matter has been thought through and his case fitted into a solution appropriate for many cases. Hence the congressman will seek approval of the proposal in the limited form necessary to solve the particular problem presented to him — and a special tax provision is thereby born.

It is obvious, given the vast number of proposals to which it must react, that the Treasury must sometimes fail. The failure rate will vary with the competence of the treasury staff at any particular time, and there is a considerable variation in that competence. It will vary, moreover, with the degree of importance which the treasury policy-makers attach to research on tax matters, and here also differences in attitude are marked. But even when competence is at a high general level and there is a proper appreciation of the need for extended staff research, errors in judgment or gaps in knowledge are inevitable. The whole matter of capital gains for pension-trust terminations,[10] for example, started with

[10] §§ 402(a)(2), 403(a)(2). These sections were derived from Int. Rev. Code of 1939, § 165(b), added by 56 STAT. 863 (1942).

an error in judgment on the Treasury's part in 1942 when it acquiesced in capital-gain treatment as a solution for the bunched-income problem present in this area. It so happened that the problem was presented in the context of a pension trust in which only the lower-bracket taxpayers received lump-sums distributions, and as an *ad hoc* solution the result was not too objectionable. But there was a failure to think through the problem, a failure caused by lack of time and lack of knowledge about the provisions respecting termination of pension trusts. Thus the provision got its start — and the rule of the camel's nose is cardinal in the field of tax privileges.[11]

Lack of omniscience may disclose itself in the drafting process. Inadequate drafting can result from lack of knowledge of the ramifications of the problem, from failure to analyze the problem in detail, or from failure to scrutinize closely the words used. The effect, again, may be that a special benefit is unintentionally granted. In the process of time, however, rationalizations as to the "intent of Congress" gradually transform this drafting carelessness into a major tax policy which the special-interest group benefited will defend with a loftiness of argument far removed from the origins of the benefit. There is much of the Daughters of the American Revolution in tax privileges.

An example of this phenomenon is the Western Hemisphere-trade-corporation provision.[12] The application of that provision to simple export operations, its principal application today, resulted from insufficient knowledge on the part of the draftsmen of the general tax background for this area, and lack of recognition of the problem to be covered and of the significance of the words used in the draft. Yet the provision has traveled far from this humble origin.

Many special provisions represent acute instances of a general difficulty. If there has been adequate study of the general problem, the Treasury is then in a position either to solve the general problem as well as the aggravated example or to demonstrate convincingly that the general problem cannot be solved by means consistent with the larger demands of our tax

[11] In a sense the "Mayer amendment," see note 4 *supra*, is traceable to this type of error.

[12] Now § 922. Its legislative history and current application are described in Surrey, *Current Issues in the Taxation of Corporate Foreign Investment*, 56 COLUM. L. REV. 815, 834–38 (1956).

structure so that relief for a particular taxpayer alone is unfair and undesirable. But unless the Treasury has had the time or made the effort to study the problem as a whole it is in a difficult position to deal with the particular situation. For, as stated earlier, the congressman is faced with the issue of relief now for a particular hardship. Consequently, the Treasury, once it sees defeat ahead on the issue of relief for the particular constituent or group involved, will then, in self-defense and fear of the unknown, attempt to reduce the problem to its narrowest boundaries. Generally these boundaries are determined simply by what is needed to meet the particular situation presented to the congressman. He will scarcely object to having only his case solved, and both sides will therefore acquiesce in a legislative solution confined in terms to that case. This is in large part the explanation for many of the special provisions that clutter up the tax law. Sometimes the general problem is later solved, and the special provision disappears. In other instances the special provision remains, its immediate task accomplished and the revenue cost and administrative difficulties that are involved in a solution of the general problem avoided. Sections 1301–04 of the Code, relating to bunched income attributable to prior years, are an example of a general solution growing out of a special provision previously adopted,[13] and even they represent instances of the unsolved

[13] These sections are a good instance of how tax law grows: A lawyer who works years on a case receives a large fee in one year, so that most of the fee goes in taxes in contrast to the result of spreading the fee over the years worked. A sympathetic Congress in 1939 adopts a provision to cover the situation, confined to bunched income from employment. Int. Rev. Code of 1939, § 107, added by 53 STAT. 878 (1939) (now § 1301). An author, said to be Ernest Hemingway, runs into a similar problem with respect to the royalties on a book which has taken a number of years to write, and Congress in 1942 adds a provision to spread back royalties from both artistic works and patents. Int. Rev. Code of 1939, § 107(b), added by 56 STAT. 837 (1942) (now § 1302). Parenthetically, Hemingway's royalties over several years were so large that it was said he could not come within the conditions of the sections. Some Ford Motor Company employees receive a large back-pay award under the National Labor Relations Act, again a bunched-income situation, and Congress in 1944 adopts a throwback provision to meet this situation. Int. Rev. Code of 1939, § 107(d), added by 58 STAT. 39 (1944) (now § 1303). In 1955 Congress adds a limited provision to cover another bunched-income situation, compensatory damages for patent infringement. § 1304, added by 69 STAT. 688 (1955). The American Law Institute has recommended extension of these provisions to cover back interest, back dividends on cumulative preferred stock, back rent, and damages for loss of profits and earnings. ALI FED. INCOME TAX STAT. § X350(c) (Feb. 1954 Draft). And, of course, lying ahead are the suggestions from various sources for an over-all averaging system.

broader problem of averaging. Section 303, removing dividend taxation from corporate distributions in redemption of stock to enable the payment of death taxes by the estate holding the stock, is another example.[14] The "Mayer amendment" in the field of deferred compensation, the various *ad hoc* benefits in the capital-gain field, and section 1342 in the transactional-accounting field,[15] remain as isolated resolutions of particular situations in areas in which the general problem has not yet been faced.

(*5*) *Lack of Opposition Apart From the Treasury Department to Proponents of Special Tax Provisions.* — The critical importance that attaches to the level of treasury competence and the fatal consequences of any slip on its part derive from its unique position in tax legislation. The question, "Who speaks for tax equity and tax fairness?," is answered today largely in terms of only the Treasury Department. If that department fails to respond, then tax fairness has no champion before the Congress. Moreover, it must respond with vigor and determination, and after a full explanation of the matter it must take a forthright stand on the issues. A Treasury Department that contents itself with explaining the issues and then solemnly declaring the matter to be one for the policy determination of Congress abdicates its responsibility. The congressman understands aggressiveness and a firm position. He is often in the position of the small boy inwardly seeking parental bounds for his conduct while outwardly declaiming against them. He may not accept policy guidance from the treasury policy spokesman, but he wants it presented. He will invariably interpret a treasury statement that the matter is one

---

[14] This provision appeared in its original form as Int. Rev. Code of 1939, § 115(g)(3), added by 64 STAT. 932 (1950). It was apparently adopted to meet the problem of the *Boston Post* and to make unnecessary the sale of that paper by an estate in order to meet estate taxes. Interestingly enough, the paper was nevertheless sold not long afterward. Section 472, relating to the last-in-first-out inventory method, is another example of a general solution replacing a special provision. See Int. Rev. Code of 1939, § 22(d), 53 STAT. 11, which originated in a limited form in the Revenue Act of 1938, § 22(d), 52 STAT. 459.

[15] Added by 69 STAT. 717 (1955). As originally introduced, this provision had a broad and sensible application to the transactional situations involving the inclusion of an income item and its later repayment. The provision was, however, confined to the particular case treated in § 1342 at the Treasury's request, since it had not yet studied the basic problems. Section 1304, added by 69 STAT. 688 (1955), relating to a throwback for compensatory damages recovered in a patent-infringement suit, is another illustration of a provision specially limited at the Treasury's request.

for his own policy decision as a victory for the seeker of the special provision.

Thus, in the tax bouts that a congressman witnesses the Treasury is invariably in one corner of the ring. Assuming the Treasury decides to do battle, which is hardly a safe assumption at all times, it is the Treasury versus percentage depletion, the Treasury versus capital gains, the Treasury versus this constituent, the Treasury versus that private group. The effect on the congressman as referee is inevitable. He simply cannot let every battle be won by the Treasury, and hence every so often he gives the victory to the sponsors of a special provision. Moreover, the Treasury is not an impersonal antagonist — it is represented before the Congress by individuals. These individuals are constantly forced to say that enactment of this proposal will be unfair, and the same of the next, and the next. The congressman, being only human, is bound from time to time to look upon these individuals as the Cassandras of the tax world. To avoid this dilemma, the Treasury in a close case will sometimes concede the issue if the proposal can be narrowly confined. It feels compelled to say "yes" once in a while simply to demonstrate that it maintains a balanced judgment and possesses a sense of fairness. A special provision is thus enacted simply because it happens to have somewhat more merit than the numerous other special proposals before the committees and because an affirmative answer here by the Treasury will protect negative responses to the other proposals.

At another level, what should the Treasury reply to a congressman who says, "I have fought hard in this committee for your position on all of the major issues. Yet when I introduce a minor amendment to take care of a problem of one of my constituents, you take a self-righteous stand and tell me and the committee that the amendment is inequitable and discriminatory. Is that any way to treat your real friends on the committee?" Faced with such a protest, a treasury policy official with a major program hanging in the balance before the committee may well look the other way when a special provision comes up for discussion. Once again a dilemma is raised by the fact that to the congressman the Treasury appears as one protagonist before the committee rather than as a representative of taxpayers in general.

But all this really takes us to the question why the Treasury, representing the executive branch, stands in the open before the

Congress virtually alone as the champion of tax fairness. The main reason is obvious. When the issue is a special provision for one group as against the taxpaying public as a whole, what pressure group is there to speak for the public? Other legislation — labor laws, natural-gas prices, farm legislation — brings forth strong and opposing pressure groups. But what pressure group fights against capital-gain treatment for employee stock options? Which group sees itself harmed by a "Mayer amendment"? When the tax issues are at a major political level, as are tax rates or personal exemptions, then pressure groups, labor organizations, the Chamber of Commerce, the National Association of Manufacturers, and the others, become concerned. But when the tax issues are technical, the pressure groups act only as proponents and not as opponents. Since most special provisions benefit the wealthier taxpayers, labor should certainly take a more direct interest. But labor is largely uninformed in these matters, and its presentation stereotyped and unskilled. Moreover, some special provisions are to its own benefit, such as the exclusion of fringe benefits. In sum, there are no private pressure groups actively defending the integrity of the tax structure.

As a consequence, the congressman does not see a dispute over a special provision as one between a particular group in the community and the rest of the taxpaying public. He sees it only as a contest between a private group and a government department. He begins to think of the government department as representing only itself and as having no identification with the public and with taxpayers in general. Far too often this picture passes swiftly into that of a hard-pressed, struggling group of citizens engaged in worthy endeavors only to be opposed by an unsympathetic bureaucracy. When this image appears, victory for the special tax provision is inevitable.

(6) *The Congressional Tax Staff.* — The description of the Treasury as the principal and often the sole defender of tax fairness calls for a consideration of the role of the congressional tax staff. Most of the congressional tax technicians are members of the staff of the Joint Committee on Internal Revenue Taxation and as such serve both the House Ways and Means Committee and the Senate Finance Committee. There are a few technicians attached to the separate committees, and the clerks of the committees can play a very important role if they are personally so

inclined. But institutionally the chief guidance given to Congress by its own employees comes from this joint committee staff.

The members of this staff work closely with the treasury tax technicians. Their work on the details of proposals and drafts is highly important, but the task of policy formulation and policy guidance to the congressmen appears to be reserved exclusively to the chief of that staff. His role is a difficult and unenviable one. Many congressmen pass along to him the tax proposals that they are constantly receiving from their constituents. Undoubtedly, the Chief of Staff discreetly but effectively blocks many of these proposals from proceeding further. But he also, whatever his inclinations may be, cannot in his situation always say "no." Perhaps inevitably on the crucial issues his role tends to be that of the advocate of the congressman advancing a particular proposal on behalf of a special group. The special-interest groups cannot appear in the executive sessions of the committees, and the congressman sympathetic to their point of view is not technically equipped to present their case; he tends to look to the Chief of Staff to assume that task. Further, he looks to the Chief of Staff to formulate the technical compromises which will resolve the dispute between the special-interest group and the Treasury. The Chief of Staff must therefore work closely with the congressmen and be "brilliantly sensitive to their views." [16] He must necessarily be able to gauge the degree of interest that a congressman may have in a proposal and weigh that in the consideration of the guidance he will give.

Because of these institutional pressures the Chief of Staff is very often the opponent of the Treasury Department before the tax committees. As a result, the difficulties for the average congressman on the tax committees become even greater. The issues get more and more complex as the "experts" disagree, and the congressman can hardly follow the technical exchanges. He is quite often content to fall back on the comfortable thought that, since the congressional expert appears to disagree with the treasury experts, there is adequate technical justification for voting either way. Hence the congressman is free to be guided by his own sympathies and instincts. Since generally these sympathies are in favor of the private groups, their proposals obtain his vote.

---

[16] Darrell, *Internal Revenue Code of 1954 — A Striking Example of the Legislative Process in Action*, in U. OF SO. CALIF. SCHOOL OF LAW, 1955 TAX INST. 1, 6.

Unfortunately agreement between the congressional Chief of Staff and the Treasury can sometimes present just as difficult a problem. When the two disagree, at least the congressman who is seeking to discover the real issues may find them exposed at some time through this disagreement of experts. But if the experts agree, the effect is often to foreclose any real committee consideration of the issues. The congressman may be lulled into thinking that no significant issues are involved, and the proposal therefore become law. But if the government experts have erred, or if they have incorrectly gauged the congressional sentiment, special benefits may well result which the congressman would not have sanctioned had he understood what was involved. Many of the proposals in the 1954 House bill appear to have had their origin in this situation. It was largely the response of the bar and accounting groups which saved the Congress — and the government experts — from much unsatisfactory legislation.

The staff arrangements for the tax committees of Congress and the procedures of these committees do not seem well adapted to acquainting the congressmen with the facts of tax life. The recent hearings by the Subcommittee on Tax Policy of the Joint Committee on the Economic Report [17] are in sharp contrast to the usual procedure. At these recent hearings the proponents of special legislation were in effect pitted directly against economists and lawyers, mostly from the universities, who presented their individual views and did not represent any pressure group. The congressmen present thus had an opportunity to test the assertions of those favoring special legislation, an opportunity not usually available to the members of the tax committees. The usual hearings of those committees consist of an almost endless parade of witnesses seeking tax benefits for themselves or the groups they represent. There is no effective analysis or rebuttal at the time this special pleading takes place, no questioning by committee counsel to develop a rounded picture of the issue. This is not to say that the committees should hear only the professors and others testifying *pro bono publico*. Certainly the proponents of particular legislation and their supporters from the ranks of

---

[17] *Hearings Before the Subcommittee on Tax Policy of the Joint Committee on the Economic Report*, 84th Cong., 1st Sess. 1, 6 (1955). See also JOINT COMMITTEE ON THE ECONOMIC REPORT, FEDERAL TAX POLICY FOR ECONOMIC GROWTH AND STABILITY (1955), the accompanying volume of papers on which these hearings were based.

business, labor, farming, and the like are entitled to present their case before the legislature. But the committees, in turn, must have procedures adequate to a full exploration of the issues thus presented. Moreover, it is not sufficient that the pros and cons be debated only in executive sessions. The various faults should be developed as far as possible in the public hearings so that the congressman at the outset obtains an appreciation of both sides of the problem and does not leave the hearings with only a hazy impression of a situation sympathetically presented.

It is also debatable whether reliance on a single staff is preferable to the more usual arrangement under which the corresponding Senate and House committees each has its own staff. The Joint Committee on Internal Revenue Taxation is composed of five members from the Senate tax committee and five from the House tax committee, selected by party seniority on the respective committees. This Joint Committee, apart from controlling the staff and its studies and considering refund claims agreed to by the Treasury but required to be presented to the Joint Committee, has little to do.[18] Its members act on substantive tax matters in their capacity as members of the House and Senate committees. Since the Joint Committee is composed of the most senior members of those committees its membership is less responsive to the electoral swings which affect the composition of the tax committees. As a consequence, the scope and course of the staff activities are less affected by changing political considerations. The more traditional system of separate staffs does not involve this situation to the same degree. Further, the absence in the tax field of separate staffs makes it difficult for the tax committee of one chamber to question as closely as is desirable the work of the tax committee of the other. The separate staff work in other legislative areas appears to produce a greater exploration of the issues, more research activity, and a resulting diversity of considerations likely to achieve better legislation.

Some, however, believe that the present unified character of Joint Committee staff work tends better to control the demands for special tax legislation. They feel that separate staffs for the tax committees would simply tend to give the proponents of such legislation more chance of finding support within the Congress. At the very least, however, reconsideration of the present institu-

---

[18] For its organization and powers, see § 6405; §§ 8001–05; §§ 8021–23, as amended, 69 STAT. 448 (1955).

tional arrangement in the tax field would seem to be warranted, especially since that arrangement is a departure from the usual pattern. Moreover, the idea of a joint committee exercising jurisdiction over administration of the tax law was adopted in 1926 as an *ad hoc* solution to the problem of sidetracking a special investigating committee, the Couzens Committee, whose continuing activities were not viewed favorably by some senior congressmen. But all this occurred before the present-day concern with the problems of staffing congressional committees and concentration on administrative supervision by all of the regular committees. Hence the solution of 1926 should be re-examined in the light of subsequent developments in the functioning of congressional committees.

(7) *Lack of Effective Aid From the Tax Bar.* — The lack of any pressure-group allies for the Treasury in its representation of the tax-paying public could have been remedied in part by effective aid from the tax bar. Yet for a good many years the vocal tax bar not only withheld any aid but very often conducted itself as an ally of the special pressure groups. Many a lawyer representing a client seeking a special provision could without much difficulty obtain American Bar Association or local-bar-association endorsement for his proposal. He could then appear before Congress and solemnly exhibit the blessing of the legal profession. In fact, the activity of the Bar Association in this respect became so obvious that it seemingly boomeranged — many a congressman began instinctively to smell mischief when presented with a Bar Association tax proposal or endorsement.

The pendulum is beginning to swing, however, and there is some hope for a more objective attitude on the part of the bar. The Council and the committees of the Tax Section of the American Bar Association are becoming far more appreciative of the public interest.[19] The signs of a growing maturity in the Tax Section on these matters are constantly increasing. But so far this change in attitude has been negative and limited to self-restraint and refusal to join with the proponents of special tax provisions. The change has not carried the Tax Section to the point of appearing affirmatively before Congress to oppose the particular proposals of special-interest groups or to urge the elimination of existing provisions. The Tax Section is becoming less and less a protago-

[19] The Federal Income Tax Committee of the Association of the Bar of the City of New York has also made helpful analyses of technical matters.

nist against the Treasury Department, especially on the more extreme proposals, but it has not yet become a vocal ally of the Treasury in defending the integrity of the tax system before the tax committees. In this respect it appears to be lagging behind the other chief professional group in the tax field, the accountants. Over one-third of the items in the 1955 statement of tax proposals of the American Institute of Accountants are recommendations urging the elimination of tax provisions which it considers to constitute unjustified favoritism for special groups. Yet one can scan report after report from the American Bar Association without finding a single similar recommendation.

This does not mean that the bar will not some day provide objective guidance to the Congress in these matters. In this regard the corporate provisions of the House version of the 1954 Code may be a harbinger. For perhaps the first time we find bar associations going before Congress and pointing out that proposed legislation will open up unjustified tax loopholes. True, the bar, and also the accountants, were not opposing other special groups, but they were seeking to save the Congress from the weaknesses of the particular measures. The bar in this instance deserves much credit for its affirmative guidance on the side of intelligent and fair tax legislation.

There are obvious obstacles to affirmative action by the legal profession in opposing special tax provisions. The Council of the Tax Section of the American Bar Association can speak publicly only on matters which have been approved by votes at annual meetings held in different geographical areas. The absence of a continuous group, with the consequence of shifting viewpoints and the lack of opportunity for sustained and informed consideration over the years, injects considerable instability and fortuitous results into the formal actions of the Tax Section. For, as discussed later, lawyers as a group need considerable discussion and education on these matters before objectivity replaces biases. Further, matters approved by the Tax Section must in turn be approved by the House of Delegates. A body that has regularly approved a proposed constitutional amendment to limit income-tax rates to twenty-five per cent [20] is

[20] See *Hearing on S.J. Res. 23 Before a Subcommittee of the Senate Committee on the Judiciary*, 84th Cong., 2d Sess. (1956). See also Cary, *The Income Tax Amendment: A Strait Jacket for Sound Fiscal Policy*, 39 A.B.A.J. 885 (1953); Dresser, *The Case for the Income Tax Amendment: A Reply to Dean Griswold*,

not likely to understand the problems of special tax provisions. The Council of the Tax Section, whatever its inclinations might be, is thus largely circumscribed by the institutional framework of the American Bar Association. The accountants, on the other hand, are able to speak through their Committee on Federal Taxation of the American Institute of Accountants, a group free from corresponding institutional forces. This may well account for the more aggressive stand against special tax provisions taken by that Committee.

One of the chief problems here is that most tax lawyers have hardly any conception of what is involved in approaching a tax issue from the over-all legislative standpoint. They can readily perceive the adverse effect of the tax laws upon a particular client or transaction. They can then phrase the legislative solution they think necessary to remove the claimed tax obstacle or burden. But they are usually quite incapable of standing off from the problem and their proposed solution and viewing both from the perspective of the general public interest. The difficulty is largely one of lack of experience, not lack of judgment or moral values.

Moreover, policy insights in the tax field are hard to come by. Here a large responsibility rests upon the Treasury. Unless its technical tax staffs are charged with utilizing their experience and information by engaging in research on current tax issues, and unless that research is made public, those interested in tax issues face great difficulties in obtaining the full picture. The government tax experts, both in the Treasury and in the Congress, must also be encouraged to write for the professional journals and to make available the insights they have reached through experience. The papers and hearings presented recently by the Subcommittee on Tax Policy of the Joint Committee on the Economic Report are another excellent illustration of what can be done to increase understanding of tax issues.[21] The professors of tax law and the tax economists in the universities also bear a responsibility here, for they have more freedom from the pressures of time and situation which the bar faces. There is significance in the fact that when the Subcommittee on Tax Policy of the Joint Committee on the Economic Report desired objective analyses of

---

39 A.B.A.J. 25 (1953); Griswold, *Can We Limit Taxes to 25 Per Cent*, Atlantic Monthly, Aug. 1952, p. 76, reprinted in Mass. L.Q., 1952, p. 50.

[21] See Joint Committee on the Economic Report, *op. cit. supra* note 17.

various tax issues it went for the most part to the economists and law professors in the universities.

After all, most members of our tax bar are really opposed to "special privileges." They have a respect for the tools of their trade. They know that in the long run the pendulum may swing and that a "loophole" may be closed with a vigor that pushes the cure too far. Even when their legal business requires them to lobby directly for a special tax favor for their clients, I doubt that most lawyers relish the task. The door may open for them, but it may open wider for the next attorney, and who knows where the game will end? Hence a bar association's advocacy of any particular special tax provision is in most cases traceable to the lawyer's sympathy for the welfare of his clients and to a lack of understanding of the basic tax issues involved. If the lawyer is exposed to those issues and if he is not acting simply as an outright advocate for a particular client — that is, as a tax lobbyist on the particular measure — he will generally emerge with the correct answer. Hence the importance of forcing a bar association to see the issues and face up to them.[22]

Tradition also plays a role. Lawyers as a profession are deeply conscious of a duty of loyalty to their clients. In his day-to-day relations with other lawyers and with the business world a lawyer does not act contrary to his clients' interests. These attitudes of loyalty and protection are ingrained in the profession; their roots lie deep in the past. Can they be reconciled with speaking out in the public interest against special tax provisions? The problem is of course more acute as the particular provision comes closer to the client's situation. But it must have been presented in one way or another to almost every lawyer who has considered the situation. The same problem arises in a different form when a client asks his lawyer to seek a legislative change in favor of the client. Should the lawyer apply different standards to his client's case in deciding whether to represent him before

[22] The task here, however, lies mainly with the members of the tax bar themselves rather than the law school professors. I am sufficiently realistic to understand that an academic tax professor talking "equity" and "loophole" and "special privilege" rarely if ever sways a bar association meeting. "He doesn't have any clients!" But nothing is more effective in bringing up short the advocates of a special proposal than to hear other lawyers, whose fees are as high as theirs and whom they otherwise respect, point out that the proposal is an unwarranted special privilege. The arguments used may be no better than those of the professor, but they sound infinitely more persuasive when presented by a lawyer with clients — and this is proper and understandable.

a tax committee than he does in deciding whether to represent him in litigation? Must a lawyer seeking a legislative change believe the change to be in the public interest? And if he does not, should he still represent his client before the legislature? Or need the lawyer as legislative advocate have no more belief in the fairness of his client's cause than when the matter is in litigation? In short, how does a lawyer adjust the considerations of private interest and public interest in the area of legislation? Clearly, these matters are difficult. Some lawyers manage to find a way through the difficulties and speak openly and positively against special provisions.[23] Others write, or speak in bar-association meetings. Others meet the situation by neither publicly opposing special provisions nor seeking them on behalf of clients; in effect, they turn away from the problems entirely and simply practice law. And others act as legislative advocates, with varying degrees of belief in the proposals they present and with stress on the view that a person is entitled to have his case presented to the legislature just as he is entitled to his day in court.

Given these problems, it is hard to say whether the tax bar can take a position of leadership in this area. Yet here also there is room for development. The work of the American Law Institute in its Tax Project has had a significant effect in educating a number of tax lawyers to the many facets that must be examined in the legislative exploration of a tax proposal.[24] Further, its drafts of proposed solutions to technical tax problems stand as a benchmark against which to measure other proposals. It is significant that much of the criticism of the corporate provisions of the House bill in 1954 was based upon the inadequacy of those provisions when measured against the standards hammered out in the work of the Institute. Moreover, the close co-operation between the Institute and the American Bar Association Tax Section has had an important effect on the content of tax legislation in a number of areas, for it represents a genuine working merger of the criteria of tax fairness and practical sense.[25] The

---

[23] The late Randolph Paul was a shining example. But his outstanding position in this respect so approached uniqueness that one is given pause in thinking about the problem. See his reflections on the problem in PAUL, TAXATION IN THE UNITED STATES 771–74 (1954).

[24] See Darrell, *supra* note 16, at 17–25; Surrey, *The Income Tax Project of the American Law Institute*, 31 TAXES 959 (1953). The last article also appears in N.Y.U. 11TH INST. ON FED. TAX. 1049 (1953).

[25] See Darrell, *supra* note 16, at 17, 27.

most significant consequence of the Institute's Tax Project is the demonstration that lawyers working under procedures such as those of the Institute can on most technical tax matters develop constructive proposals which balance fairly the interests of the "Government" and the "taxpayer." [26]

(*8*) *Lack of Public Knowledge of Special Tax Provisions.*— Perhaps the most significant aspect of the consideration of special tax provisions by the Congress is that it usually takes place without any awareness of these events by the general public. Almost entirely, these matters lie outside of the public's gaze, outside of the voter's knowledge. The special provisions which are enacted lie protected in the mysterious complex statutory jargon of the tax law. This technical curtain is impenetrable to the newspapers and other information media. The public hears of debate over tax reduction or tax increase and it may learn something about the general rate structure. But it seldom learns that the high rates have no applicability to much of the income of certain wealthy groups. Nor does it understand how this special taxpayer or that special group is relieved of a good part of its tax burden. All of these matters are largely fought out behind this technical curtain. Hence the congressman favoring these special provisions has for the most part no accounting to make to the voters for his action. He is thereby much freer to lend a helping hand here and there to a group which has won his sympathy or which is pressing him for results.

It is true that under our governmental system we have given to the Congress, subject to presidential veto, the responsibility of deciding what is "fair" in the federal sphere from our collective standpoint. Its decision is our democratic answer. But all this presupposes that the congressman's decision will be known to the

---

[26] Recently the Subcommittee on Internal Revenue Taxation of the House Ways and Means Committee has sought the aid of the tax bar through special advisory committees selected by it to present proposals for changes in various parts of the Code. While there are facets of the present situation which have led to this *ad hoc* solution, it is doubtful whether it represents an appropriate line of growth. At the very least, reliance on such advisory committees calls for sustained and informed government technical activity so that short-run solutions do not distort long-run developments. Further, there are many fortuitous elements in the process, as the selection of the particular members of the advisory committees, the time available, and the like. The procedures of the American Law Institute, and in some respects those of the Tax Section of the American Bar Association, have the merit of a wider participation in and testing of tax changes as they pass through the various stages of their formulation.

voters and that he will have to account to them for his view. In the tax field this accounting does not exist, so that the presuppositions that on most matters stamp final congressional action as "fair" in a democratic sense are here lacking.

The task of educating and informing the public is formidable. To begin with, the educators are a very limited group. Most of them are in the executive branch, and hence perhaps the prime responsibility should fall on them. The treasury officials and technicians, as stated earlier, should be charged with continued research on these issues and, more important, with making public their observations. The Treasury Department has published — in the 1940's especially — many useful research papers. But in recent years that department has shown little disposition to inform the public about tax problems or to engage in continuous and far-ranging research inquiries. Some of the prospective educators are in the universities. But academic knowledge and learned writing are not the keys to public education of this nature — more writing at the public-information level is clearly needed. Beyond this there is the matter of leadership and the stamp of importance. Here again the major responsibility should rest with the executive branch. A vigorous program directed to meeting these problems, led in public by the President or the Secretary of the Treasury, with whatever aid can be obtained from the Congress, is perhaps the only effective answer. But one does not yet see this on the horizon.

(9) *The Relationship of Special Tax Provisions to Private-Relief Bills.* — Some of these special provisions represent simply private-relief claims for the particular individual benefited. While phrased as amendments to the tax law, they are only money claims against the Government based on the equities asserted to exist.[27] Thus, it is said of a senator skilled in congressional ways

[27] See, for example, the discussion in 102 CONG. REC. 13395 (daily ed. July 26, 1956), of an amendment designed to relieve a particular individual in Vermont from an asserted tax hardship growing out of the conjunction of the severity of Vermont winters and the vagaries of § 270, the hobby-loss provision. The senator pressing the amendment stated that while it was basically designed for the relief of a particular individual, he had originally hoped to generalize the language but the Treasury had pointed out defects in the generalization. The amendment did not prevail, the chairman of the Senate Finance Committee solemnly stating that "it would establish a very dangerous precedent, and we would be attempting to pass a general law for one specific purpose." The day before, the chairman had reported out the bill allowing an estate-tax deduction in a situation

that he would ask the legislative draftsman preparing the draft of a particular tax provision to make the amendment as general in language and as specific in application as was possible. The tax committees and the Treasury have not solved the problem of how to handle these special bills. Curiously enough, some tax situations do come through the judiciary committees as private-relief bills along with other private-relief bills involving claims against the Government. These bills may involve, for example, a removal of the barrier of the statute of limitations in cases thought equitable, or the recovery of funds spent for revenue stamps lost in some fashion.[28] Here they are subject to the criteria developed

---

involving an eighty-year-old widow who had taken certain action specified in the bill. See note 4, para. (a), *supra*.

[28] The following private-relief bills involving tax situations were enacted by the 84th Congress:

(a) Priv. L. No. 206, 84th Cong., 1st Sess. (July 14, 1955). This act reimbursed the taxpayer for the $900 he lost when his beer-tax stamps were stolen or lost. See H.R. REP. No. 259, 84th Cong., 1st Sess. (1955); S. REP. No. 484, 84th Cong., 1st Sess. (1955).

(b) Priv. L. No. 661, 84th Cong., 2d Sess. (May 19, 1956). This act granted $1620.09 to a taxpayer who had paid a tax on alcoholic products which were exported and for which drawback claims were rejected because the products were not originally bottled for export. The taxpayer had been ignorant of the requirement and the government representative who supervised the packaging had acquiesced in the manner in which it was done. See H.R. REP. No. 1715, 84th Cong., 2d Sess. (1956); S. REP. No. 1948, 84th Cong., 2d Sess. (1956).

(c) Priv. L. No. 663, 84th Cong., 2d Sess. (May 22, 1956). This act permitted the taxpayer to file an election to claim the benefit of Int. Rev. Code of 1939, § 112(b)(7), as amended, 67 STAT. 615 (1953) (now § 333), which he had originally filed one day late due to inadvertence arising from the pressure of taking office as Mayor of Houston. See H.R. REP. No. 263, 84th Cong., 2d Sess. (1956); S. REP. No. 1957, 84th Cong., 2d Sess. (1956).

(d) Priv. L. No. 728, 84th Cong., 2d Sess. (June 29, 1956). This act granted $6896.14 plus interest to the estate of a deceased member of the armed services after the estate had sued for that amount under the forgiveness provisions of Int. Rev. Code of 1939, § 421, added by 57 STAT. 149 (1942), repealed by 64 STAT. 947 (1950), and had lost, Allen v. Bickerstaff, 200 F.2d 181 (5th Cir. 1952). The Supreme Court had overruled that decision in a subsequent case, Marcelle v. Estate of Lupia, 348 U.S. 956 (1955), *affirming* 214 F.2d 942 (2d Cir. 1954). The Treasury stressed that its favorable report on this private bill should not be regarded as precedent for a policy of changing the result of decided cases by legislation. See H.R. REP. No. 1914, 84th Cong., 2d Sess. (1956); S. REP. No. 2202, 84th Cong., 2d Sess. (1956).

(e) Priv. L. No. 764, 84th Cong., 2d Sess. (July 11, 1956). This act permitted the taxpayers to file refund claims involving an amount in the vicinity of $380,000, although the period of limitations had expired and an agreement with the Government had been executed. The committees appeared to be convinced that the taxes and penalties involved had been erroneously paid. See H.R. REP. No. 2127, 84th Cong., 2d Sess. (1956); S. REP. No. 2277, 84th Cong., 2d Sess. (1956).

over the decades by those committees in the handling of private-claims bills.[29] These criteria are reasonably strict, and few of the bills pass the Congress. Of those that do succeed, a number are vetoed, and a veto is customarily regarded as a final disposition of the bill.

Many situations come before the tax committees that are quite comparable, in that the tax proposal is equivalent to a money claim against the Government, equal to the tax to be saved, sought for a specific taxpayer on equitable grounds. This is especially true in the case of proposals of a retroactive character.[30] In the tax committees these special proposals tend to take on the coloration of an amendment to the tax code of the same character as all the various substantive tax matters before these committees. In essence, all amendments to the tax laws that private groups push on their own behalf are designed to lower taxes for the proponents and thereby relieve them from a tax burden to which

---

(f) Priv. L. No. 800, 84th Cong., 2d Sess. (July 24, 1956). This act granted to an estate a refund of $1793.10 representing a credit for death taxes paid to the state, although the period within which a claim for such a refund must be filed had elapsed. The executor had relied on an erroneous statement in a letter from the district director as to the permissible filing period. See H.R. REP. No. 2224, 84th Cong., 2d Sess. (1956); S. REP. No. 2499, 84th Cong., 2d Sess. (1956).

The Treasury Department had objected to the bills involved in Private Laws 663 and 764, but not to the other bills; all bills were approved by the President.

[29] See Gellhorn & Lauer, *Congressional Settlement of Tort Claims Against the United States*, 55 COLUM. L. REV. 1 (1955); Note, *Private Bills and the Immigration Law*, 69 HARV. L. REV. 1083 (1956). See also HOUSE COMMITTEE ON THE JUDICIARY, 85TH CONG., RULES OF SUBCOMMITTEE NO. 2, WHICH HAS JURISDICTION OVER CLAIMS (1957).

[30] See, *e.g.*, Code sections cited note 4, paras. (a)–(f), *supra*. See also Pub. L. No. 901, 84th Cong., 2d Sess. (Aug. 1, 1956); Pub. L. No. 414, 84th Cong., 2d Sess. § 4 (Feb. 20, 1956).

One recent special provision, Act of Aug. 12, 1955, c. 878, 69 STAT. A166, took in part the formal course of a private-relief bill but proceeded in a somewhat unusual fashion. On July 30, 1955, Congressman Curtis of Missouri introduced a private bill for the relief of the Cannon Foundation, which had been established by Congressman Cannon of Missouri. H.R. 7746, 84th Cong., 1st Sess. (1955). That foundation was established in 1950 as a charitable foundation, but its charter, though apparently not its activities, ran afoul of § 503(c). The bill, as passed, made this provision inapplicable for 1950–56, and apparently charter amendment in 1955 took care of future years. The bill had originally been referred to the Ways and Means Committee, but on August 1, 1955, it was referred to the House Judiciary Committee, and then reported and passed that day. It was reported by the Senate Finance Committee the same day, S. REP. No. 1283, 84th Cong., 1st Sess. (1955) (which does not explain the particular problem involved — in fact it is not explained in any of the public documents), and it then passed the Senate on August 2, 1955, with an amendment concurred in that same day by the House. The Congress adjourned on August 2, 1955.

they are subject. The special proposals thus become simply one more amendment in the long list of changes to be considered. The proponents of these special proposals are thereby able to cloak the fact that they are presenting private-relief claims against the Government. This is especially so when the proposal is considered as merely one more item in a general revenue bill. Here it is also protected from the threat — and fate — of a presidential veto. Even when the proposal is considered as a separate bill, the fact that it is merely one of the bills before a tax committee that is considering a great many substantive bills involving amendments to the tax code generally produces the same result. The committee will tend to focus on the proposal as curing a substantive defect in the law and lose sight of the fact that the special proposal is essentially a private-relief bill.

The tax laws are not perfect and cannot be. They will affect some taxpayers more seriously than others, and hardships and inequities will certainly occur. But every hardship and every inequity cannot be corrected; and this is even clearer when the correction must be retroactive. Some standards must be evolved against which a claim for relief may be judged, or chaos will result. Tax lobbying will grow by leaps and bounds — it is already doing that. But what standards may be formulated, what procedures should be adopted, what institutional changes may be necessary — these are still unstudied topics.

There is another curious but highly important aspect of casting private-relief claims as amendments to the tax code. In the case of most other private-relief bills involving claims against the Government, the Congress is concerned with the amount of the fee paid to the attorney representing the claimant and the relationship of that fee to the services performed by the attorney. Often the bill when passed will carry a proviso that no part of the amount awarded be paid to the attorney for his services, or that the amount so paid be limited to 5 per cent or 10 per cent of the sum awarded.[31] But there is no such concern when the tax committees are passing on special tax provisions. The legal fees involved in legislation of this character can be quite large, especially when the special provision operates to open the way

[31] See HOUSE COMMITTEE ON THE JUDICIARY, 85TH CONG., *op. cit. supra* note 29, rule 16; NEWMAN & SURREY, LEGISLATION: CASES AND MATERIALS 156 (1955). For a summary and discussion of statutory and administrative restrictions on practitioners' fees, see Committee on Administrative Practitioners, Administrative Law Section, A.B.A., *Report*, 8 AD. L. BULL. 137 (1956).

for a successful refund claim. Yet the services performed may be far less demanding than would be required if the same fee were earned in other phases of legal work. This would seem to be a matter requiring exploration along with those suggested earlier.

At present, under the Legislative Reorganization Act, the House and Senate Judiciary Committees have jurisdiction over all "measures relating to claims against the United States." It may not be appropriate to have special tax measures presented to these committees, since these measures should be co-ordinated with the rest of the tax code. But it would seem proper for the Congress to require that all retroactive tax proposals limited in application to one person or to a small group be presented as private-relief bills to be considered by the tax committees. The bills would name the individuals concerned and specify the amounts involved. The reports on the bills would state the equities present and the reason for granting relief, if that is the action urged. Each matter would be handled as a separate bill, subject to presidential veto. The amounts granted need not be the complete tax to be saved by retroactive change, since the equities may point to a lower figure. The tax committees would have to develop procedures and criteria for handling these measures — presumably they would go to special subcommittees. Rigorous standards would have to be evolved lest the committees be engulfed. It may be that naming the particular individual involved will result in congressional action on some measures being influenced one way or the other not so much by the merits as by an identification with the particular individual. Hence, it might be thought that these special bills should be anonymous as far as possible. Yet the beneficiaries of other relief bills are identified. Anonymity would only provoke intense curiosity on the part of the press and others, and probably could not be preserved. Thus, despite the disadvantage indicated, identification of the beneficiary would seem proper.

If the above procedure were adopted, it may well be that it could be extended to those special provisions for a particular person or a limited group which are prospective in operation. After all, a proposal that for the future a cousin in a mental institution who was formerly in the taxpayer's household,[32] or a

[32] See § 152(a)(10).

child adopted in the Philippines by an army officer,[33] be classified as a dependent, is really a petition for a private-relief bill. Nor is there any reason why the "Louis B. Mayer amendment" should not have been handled as a "bill for the relief of Louis B. Mayer" and the amount of the relief stated in a precise dollar figure. If the particular proposal presented is only an example of a general problem, it should be handled as such and relief denied if the general problem is not to be solved, unless the equities for special treatment are overwhelming. If it is an isolated situation, its equities could be judged in that light. If special relief were granted, and the consequent publicity indicated that others were similarly situated, then the relief could be extended. But the particular claim would be highlighted for what it is — an appeal to the generosity of the Congress to be exercised in the particular situation. In time, experience may indicate that certain of these matters may be handled by the Treasury Department, perhaps with the assistance of a special board of advisors.[34] The essential task is to separate special situations from the broader substantive problems that represent the basic work of the tax committees, and thereby to judge them on their particular merits. Also, and equally as important, treatment as a private bill would permit full public understanding of the particular case and an awareness of the relief involved. The technical curtain referred to earlier would thus be lifted to a considerable extent from legislative consideration of special provisions.

III. Conclusion

The consideration of any legislation is a complex matter and tax measures are no exception. But the institutional factors in the tax legislative process do differ from those in other legislative areas, and the differences have affected the end product. The growing concern with the integrity of our tax system may well

---

[33] See § 152(b)(3), as amended, 69 Stat. 626 (1955).

[34] The British have a system of "extra-statutory concessions," adopted and made public by the Board of Inland Revenue, which represent in effect administrative relief granted when the statutory law is working in an unintended way with harsh effect. There are between fifty and one hundred of these concessions outstanding; they are generally used when the matter is minor and often when it also would be difficult to draft a complete legislative solution. There are also unpublished "office practices" under which the rigor of the law is not pushed too far. In effect, the more important of these office practices are published as extra-statutory concessions.

force a substantive re-examination of many of the special provisions now in the law. This concern should also extend to the tax legislative process itself. The situation is a serious one, and the solutions are far from clear.

It is suggested that the executive branch take affirmative action to attack the problem through a strong program led by the President or the Secretary of the Treasury designed to focus public consideration on special provisions and their interaction with the rate structure. The Treasury's tax officials and technicians should engage in intensive research on these matters and the results of their studies should be made public. In the Congress, consideration should be given to changes in the methods of obtaining information on tax problems, to improvements in the conduct of hearings, and to a re-examination of the staff arrangements. Procedures should be adopted under which proposals for amendment of the tax laws limited in application to a single person or a small group, especially when retroactive in nature, would be treated as private-relief claims. These claims should be considered by the tax committees under special procedures similar to those applicable to private-relief bills generally. In respect to the bar, both bar associations and lawyers generally should consider how, consistently with the traditions of the profession regarding the protection of a client's interests, the wisdom and experience of the tax bar can be made available in the public interest to aid the Congress by objective guidance. The sum total of these suggestions is that the Congress, the Treasury Department, and the tax bar equally bear a responsibility to reappraise their roles and activities in the tax legislative process.

BLUM, THE EFFECTS OF SPECIAL PROVISIONS IN THE INCOME TAX ON TAXPAYER MORALE

Joint Committee on the Economic Report, Federal Tax Policy for Economic Growth and Stability 251 (1955).

I. Definition of Preferential Tax Treatment

To discuss preferential or special provisions under our income tax, it is first necessary to define them. This is difficult in part, because taxpayers who benefit from special provisions commonly insist that these do not give them an advantage over the rest of the taxpaying public, but merely put them on a par with everyone else by recognizing that their situations are in fact somewhat different. Thus it can be made to appear that no provision in the law prefers any taxpayer and that all special legislation merely adjusts for special circumstances. To avoid this dead end the problem of determining what provisions result in preferential treatment must be separated from the problem of deciding whether such preferences are justified.

While theorists may argue about what constitutes preferential treatment, sophisticated taxpayers have not experienced a similar difficulty. Instead they have been guided by this single principle: It is more advantageous to accumulate wealth or enjoy personal consumption in ways calling for the payment of less total income tax than if the savings and consumption were financed only by money received in the form of ordinary income and if that money were spent on consumption or saved only in ways which did not give rise to deductions for tax purposes. There is no reason why we should depart from this realistic principle. Legislation is preferential to the extent it allows any taxpayer to accumulate wealth or enjoy personal consumption without paying the full tax. And the full tax is that which would be due if all of the taxpayer's economic enhancement were financed by cash received as ordinary income and if he did not qualify for any nonbusiness deductions or extraordinary exemptions or credits in the course of saving or spending his income.

The wholly nonpreferred taxpayer thus is the man who receives everything in fully taxable forms, who satisfies his personal consumption and accomplishes his savings in nondeductible ways, and who does not otherwise qualify for special exemptions or credits. To the extent that any taxpayer fares better than this yardstick he is being preferred. In this sense many if not most taxpayers today enjoy some degree of preferential treatment under the law. But this does not impair the utility of the yardstick, for it nevertheless puts us in a position to know precisely how much and in what respects various taxpayers are being preferred. Such information is just what is needed before starting to discuss the consequences of special legislation.

II. Perspective

In my opinion the primary case for or against any preferential provision should turn on its impact on the fairness of the distribution of the income-tax burden. This aspect of special legislation is the subject of other papers. I mention it only to put my own presentation in proper perspective and to record my view that there should be a strong presumption that it is fairer to treat any receipt which is capable of financing a dollar of savings or consumption like every other dollar received, to treat every dollar spent on personal consumption like every other dollar so spent, and to treat every dollar saved like every other dollar saved. The dollar is a common denominator for measuring the relative incomes of taxpayers. When we differentiate taxwise between dollars on the basis of how they were received, or how they were spent on personal consumption, or how they were saved, we undermine the common unit of measure. As this happens it becomes increasingly difficult to form reasoned judgments as to whether the income-tax burden is being distributed fairly. We have yet to discover a substitute for the dollar as a common denominator in measuring ability to pay income taxes.

The case for many preferential provisions often is rested heavily on grounds of some asserted public policy, usually economic policy. The economic implications of various special provisions, as well as the economic consequences of all such provisions taken as a whole, are also matters which are explored in other papers. Here I again only seek perspective by noting my view that there should be a strong presumption against subsidizing a particular economic activity through the income-tax system. When one focuses attention on a particular economic activity it is only too easy to conclude that it should be encouraged. Of course there is a great deal to be said for encouraging the production of, say, oil; and of course a comfortable supply of oil is important for national defense. But in our society there is also a lot to be said for encouraging virtually every kind of legitimate investment and enterprise; and the production of many different commodities is important for national defense. The preferred treatment of one economic activity necessarily translates itself into a penalty on those not favored. For this reason, in legislating taxes it is especially important not to confine attention to any particular activity but to consider the whole of our economic system. And even if it be decided to subsidize a certain activity, we should be hesitant about administering the subsidy by way of a tax preference. Subsidies in this form vary directly in amount with the tax brackets of the recipients; they are invariably hidden in technicalities of the tax law; they do not show up in the budget; their cost frequently is difficult to calculate; and their accomplishments are even more difficult to assess. Partly for these very reasons they are likely to become fixtures which are not easily removed.

But while the most significant aspects of preferential tax provisions are thus outside the scope of my presentation, the consequences with which I shall deal are not unimportant. Anything which has a bearing on the morale of taxpayers and their advisers deserves attention because it may have an impact on the health and strength of our income-tax system.

III. Special Provisions Complicate the Income Tax

Probably the most nearly universal quality of preferential provisions is that they complicate the job of determining the proper amount of tax to be paid. To create a preference the law must draw a distinction between that which is and that which is not to be accorded the special benefit. Thereafter this distinction becomes relevant in computing the tax liability of anyone who possibly might qualify for the preference. If a taxpayer wants to take advantage of every preference to which he is entitled—and it is right that he should do so, regardless of how many dollars are involved—attention will have to be paid to the applicability of each special provision for which he conceivably might qualify.

Thus, preferential provisions place a burden on the community as a whole. Those taxpayers who attempt to make out their own returns will obviously have to devote more time and effort to this task. Each added distinction, moreover, will afford additional occasions for error, and it therefore is to be expected that the total volume of mistakes will increase. At the same time the increased complexity of the tax is likely to cause larger numbers of taxpayers to seek expert assistance, either from Government officials or from private practitioners. It has been argued that wider use of private tax experts is desirable because errors would thereby be avoided and the workload of the Revenue Service would correspondingly be reduced. No doubt numerous errors would be eliminated, but it would not be surprising to find that many who now hold themselves out as tax experts actually add to the burden of the Revenue Service in the course of trying to show their patrons how useful they are in minimizing tax assessments. In some circles a tax expert is little more than one who thinks he knows how to cut the corners. But even if all tax experts were more mindful of the revenues, it seems clear that on balance the net effect of additional complexity in the law can only be to increase the total cost of administration to the individual taxpayers or the Government, or both.

Preferential provisions may also cause some taxpayers to become hostile—a potentially dangerous attitude in a system which depends to a high degree on voluntary cooperation by the public. Such resentment can develop in a number of ways. A taxpayer simply might react against having to turn to a professional in making out a return, or he might rebel when he discovers that at some past time he did not obtain the benefit of a special provision because its complexities resulted in his failure to understand its application, or he might become upset in finding that a preferential rule just barely misses fitting his case, even though his situation seems to him to be indistinguishable from others covered by it. This occurrence is made more likely when, as is often the case, the theory behind the preferential provision is not obvious or where the line which it draws is largely arbitrary, or the resentment may come about in a more indirect fashion. Special provisions which are widely publicized and usually associated with wealthier taxpayers (such as those concerning percentage depletion and capital gains) might lead people to underestimate greatly the amount of taxes generally paid by those with high incomes. Discontent flowing from this kind of misunderstanding can be particularly serious. Since it goes to the fairness or unfairness of the distribution of the whole income-tax burden, it might take hold deeply and be contagious.

The complexities of the law, aided perhaps at times by accompanying feelings of hostility, may encourage some taxpayers to relax their consciences in assessing themselves. Probably in most instances such a result is due merely to the usual give-yourself-the-benefit-of-the-doubt attitude. But in some cases it seems to have more disturbing roots. We have heard about taxpayers who knowingly winked at the law because they thought that a special relief provision should in all justice have been written more broadly to cover their circumstances. We have known of taxpayers who deliberately erred and excused themselves on the ground that their friends were in a position lawfully to take advantage of some special provision which did not quite reach their case. And there has been talk of taxpayers who willfully erred because they figured that a preferential provision would be too complicated for the Government to police effectively.

This is not to say that the preferential features now in the law have engendered wholesale resentment or cheating by taxpayers. It is likely that many of those who are now discontented or are inclined to cheat would be that way in the absence of special provisions. It is possible, moreover, that taxpayers as a whole would be more hostile and more lax in conscience if we were to adhere tenaciously to a tax law without preferences of any kind. It is even conceivable that taxpayers on the average would be more cooperative in a system which intentionally went out of its way to accord at least some kind of preferential treatment to everybody, so that each person could feel that the legislators were not unmindful of his particular circumstances. The plausibility of this is increased where, as in the case of our income tax, the whole set of rules is so complex that very few persons are aware of or understand the benefits bestowed upon others. In the face of these untested possibilities, one cannot be certain how the average taxpayer will react to a maze of preferential provisions in the law. But at the very least, a strong caution is in order. Preferences do burden the system. And while they might please their beneficiaries, they might well have a seriously adverse effect upon the attitude of other taxpayers.

IV. Special Provisions Increase Tax-Motivated Conduct

Other considerations enter the picture when we center attention on the sophisticated taxpayer who is personally knowledgable taxwise or who regularly receives professional counsel in tax matters. The most glaring is that preferential provisions usually result in time and talent being devoted by the principals and their advisers to planning designed to maximize the tax benefits. There probably is no way of reasonably estimating the quantity of energy which has been spent this year in manufacturing capital gains, splitting income, deferring income, and so forth, but surely the total must be tremendous. To the effort given over to such planning must be added that devoted to learning the ropes and to transmitting the know-how to others in the field. In these days there might be more than well-meant humor in the warning that the golden opportunity of this decade could be lost to us because our top talent was consecrating itself to the invention of new and better capital gains.

Tax planning, which eventually rests on preferential provisions, not only consumes time and skill but it can also have the effect of channeling transactions into molds which are wasteful or otherwise undesirable. This might be true from two distinct points of view. The individual taxpayer himself might not have set up the transaction as he did in the absence of the tax benefit. Often a tax-conscious person is willing to arrange business transactions, or investments, or family estate plans in a relatively inefficient manner because the tax advantages thereby gained seem to make the inferior plans worthwhile. In effect the preferential rules subsidize particular forms or practices. From the view of society as a whole, the resulting arrangements might be less desirable than alternatives which would have prevailed if the tax inducements had not been present. And the very fact that tax considerations tend to freeze transactions into rigid patterns may be a loss to a society which develops and moves forward through experimentation. Unfortunately it is only future generations who will be in a position to gage the extent of such a loss.

In inviting tax planning, preferential provisions also multiply the volume of litigation and of controversy at the administrative level, and thus are a further drain on the talent resources of our society. Virtually all statutes of course require interpretation and application, and the doubtful points must be resolved by administrators or courts or subsequent legislatures. But a tax statute is especially likely to be fruitful in this respect since dollars turn on every substantive distinction it draws. There will always be some persons (and no criticism of them is intended) who will seek to probe for the limits of a tax rule in their favor; to a large degree, tax planning for these taxpayers consists in arranging their affairs so as to come as close as possible to these limits without crossing over them. Such efforts continually put the statutory language into issue and thus call for administrative or judicial determinations. When a preferential rule is added to the statute, it usually provides another area within which this process can go on anew. While the capacity of a special provision to produce controversy varies with its nature, those now in the law certainly have left, and are still leaving, a monumental trail of controversy in their wake.

The evolution of our present income-tax statute is powerful testimony that there is no inherent limitation on the development of preferential provisions. On the contrary, it seems patent that one special enactment breeds pressures for others, especially among sophisticated taxpayers and their counselors. At any time in recent years it would have been easy to locate hundreds of preferential proposals which were with varying degrees of intensity being readied for presentation to Congress. In most instances the proposal in some respect copied a preferential provision already in the law; and usually the chief argument advanced in its behalf was that some other taxpayers already were enjoying a comparable benefit. This is a contention which any legislator will find hard to ignore or resist since our generally accepted major premise of tax justice is that equals should be treated equally. But the very fact that the argument frequently is persuasive serves to underscore why preferential provisions have a propensity to multiply. No matter how compelling the case for special relief may be in one situation, there will almost always be other taxpayers who can demonstrate that their situation is comparable if not identical. Congress then has two avenues for treating equals equally: it can revoke the preference which it has already granted or it can give a comparable preference to those in comparable situations. No great research is needed to show which of these ways is likely to be chosen. We all know that there is a reluctance to withdraw a preference once granted, that a sudden revocation might disturb plans made in reliance upon it, and that the unraveling process might itself cause new complications and discriminations. A legislator's freedom of action is thus hedged about by the largess or sympathy or mistakes of his predecessors in office. But nevertheless there can only be one of two results if the original preferential treatment is retained in the law. Either the pleas of taxpayers with comparable cases will have to be turned down, or comparable preferences will have to be written into the statute.

It is generally agreed that simplification of the income tax is a goal to which we should aim. Simplification may well mean different things to different persons. It should be obvious, however, that a compounding of preferential provisions must in the long run serve to increase the complexity of the tax. Conversely, real simplification can be achieved only through the elimination of preferences now in the law.

V. Effects of Special Provisions on Tax Advisers

Some mention has already been made of the impact of preferential provisions upon professional tax advisers—that is, lawyers and accountants. It is clear that as the law grows in complexity, more taxpayers consult them and they work under heightened pressure to arrange for their clients the maximum tax advantages available. Moreover, as special legislation expands in volume, the professional adviser tends increasingly to become a lobbyist on behalf of his clients. These happenings have not been without consequences for the professions involved.

It has repeatedly been observed in recent years that the general lawyer or accountant is often no longer in a position to supply adequate advise on tax matters. Gradually a more or less well defined group of tax men has been emerging to cope with the complexities of our tax system. It may be questioned whether this development is of itself desirable or whether it is inevitable in a society which is almost everywhere putting a premium on specialization. Whatever be one's opinions on these issues, the fact is that the creation of the tax specialist itself represents another major cost of the tax system for our society. Furthermore, this development has affected taxpayers as a whole because for many years the usual lag in the production of competent specialists existed. There is abundant evidence that many taxpayers received inadequate tax advice at a time when general practitioners were not in a position to master the complexities accompanying the special provisions, and when specialists were either not available or their role was not recognized. In effect a whole range of new discriminations could be said to have come into existence between taxpayers who did and those who did not or could not obtain competent advice.

The development of a group of tax specialists has paralleled and perhaps has affected the role of the professions in tax legislation. To what seems to be an increasing extent, members of the tax bar have become special pleaders for preferential legislation on behalf of their clients. In and of itself such activity calls for no reproach. Through the years in many situations lawyers have traditionally served their clients in presenting views to the legislature, and this is entirely proper in the tax field even though in the end it may turn out that tax lawyers are incidentally the prime beneficiaries of an increase in preferential tax rules. Lately, however, leaders of the tax bar themselves have begun to express uneasiness that many of their fellow specialists have moved so far in the direction of special pleading that they are in danger of losing all capacity to judge proposed legislation objectively from the point of view of our tax system as a whole. Such an occurrence would indeed be a significant loss. A high degree of skill is required to write our tax laws and regulations in a sound manner, and the available supply of talent is definitely limited. If any large share of it were indifferent or actively hostile to the public interest, or if, as some have cynically predicted, the organized tax bar became an organized taxpayers' lobby, it is certain that our tax system would suffer.

While there is no way of demonstrating decisively that the attitude of taxmen toward legislation has been affected by the high incidence of preferential enactments, it appears most likely that the two things are related. Surely the successes of special pleading in the past have encouraged further efforts along the same line. Certainly the ease or strategems with which various preferences were secured has caused not a few taxmen to become cynical about notions of justice in taxation. The very fact that Congress has frequently been willing to overturn Supreme Court interpretations of the statute favorable to the Government has itself augmented this attitude. It is indeed a sad commentary on our system to have leading taxmen confidently boast that, "If we can't win in court, we can always win in Congress."

In brief, the pyramiding of preferential provisions in our tax law is slowly but surely likely to make inroads on the public morality of professional taxmen. Of course, it will not directly influence them to countenance loose practices or wink at frauds on the revenues. It is very likely, however, to weaken their will to serve the public interest and to undermine their convictions about the justice of our system. What this might eventually lead to is anyone's guess. But it is safe to predict that the cynicism of tax advisers is almost certain to be communicated to their clients and to infect them as well.

VI. Special Provisions and the Administration of the Tax Law

Preferential provisions might also have an effect on taxpayer morale through their impact on the administration of the tax law. It has already been noted that the complexities introduced by the accumulation of special provisions in the law greatly burdens the administration of the income tax. Taxpayers on the average are more likely to request assistance from revenue officials; controversy and litigation are almost certain to expand; and there is virtually bound to be an increase in errors committed by taxpayers. Moreover, the revenue officials will be in need of more extensive training so as to be able to advise taxpayers and properly administer the provisions. As professional tax counselors become more specialized, their counterparts in Government service are likely to feel pressure for comparable specialization. And, as the number of distinctions drawn by the law increases, the lag in learning is apt to be experienced inside of Government service as well as by taxmen on the outside.

All of these items have one thing in common: They tend to divert the drive of revenue officials away from the central task of checking up on the accuracy of returns and taxpayer compliance with the law. Unless the size and quality of the administrative staff is kept abreast of the additional workload generated by special provisions, a vicious cycle can be set into operation. As enforcement proficiency declines, more and more taxpayers get by with improprieties in their returns. This in turn encourages them to repeat or enlarge their questionable practices and, as word gets around, tempts other to follow suit. The result is likely to be an even heavier handicap for the administrators, coupled with a shrinking chance that the improprieties of taxpayers will be detected. And so the administrative process is in danger of running downhill steadily, and increasing great efforts will be required to convince the taxpaying public that the Revenue Service had stepped up its enforcement activities to close the breach.

That this unpleasant picture of taxpayer response to ineffective administration is not more fancy is shown by some reactions to new preferential provisions introduced by the 1954 code. To many taxmen, for example, it is a familiar story that not a few taxpayers last year helped themselves to an undeserved retirement-income credit because they reasoned that it would be years before the Revenue Service would be in a position effectively to police the provision. Others for the same reason knowingly enlarged the dividend credit to which they were entitled by showing a relatively larger portion of their dividends as having been received in the months that counted for the credit. Whether the total of such indiscretions is large or small is beyond the immediate point. The fact is that in the thoughts of some taxpayers the efficiency of administration was downgraded because of the new complications in the law, and these views have been and are being spread to others.

VII. Broad Versus Narrow Special Provisions

So far all preferential provisions have been lumped together in commenting upon their consequences. However, it sometimes is argued that, wholly apart from their merit on grounds of equity or economic effects, special provisions which are fairly general in their application are less obnoxious than those whose applicability is restricted to only a few taxpayers. The thought here is simply that in our tradition the rules of taxation ideally are to be general rules, and a more general preference seems to be closer to the ideal than a less general one.

Certainly a special dispensation for which only one or a handful of taxpayers can qualify is most undesirable. Our sense of fairness is apt to be irritated by what virtually amounts to the incorporation of a private bill in public law. The more private the bill the more likely it is to offend against our ideal of government by rule of law. But fairness (and economic considerations) to one side, special legislation of limited applicability probably has fewer undesirable consequences than special relief of a broader nature. The private bill variety of preference hardly can be said to complicate the tax system to any appreciable extent inasmuch as so few taxpayers need be concerned with it. In all probability, the more limited the scope of the preference, the less likely it is that any sizable number of taxpayers will know about it at all. Moreover, because of its minuscule reach, neither private tax advisers nor Government administrative officials need give much thought to the private bill type of preference. Similarly it is not likely that such legislation will stimulate much tax planning or maneuvering to come within its terms. For the same reason a narrow preference usually does not have much potential to produce controversy or litigation. And by and large it is probable that the tightly circumscribed character of the private bill variety of preference does not lend itself readily to spawning new preferential provisions by suggesting analogous situations which seem to merit comparable treatment. In all these respects it is easier to live with special legislation of restricted applicability.

* * *

VIII. Conclusion

These, then, are some of the secondary consequences affecting the morale of taxpayers which might stem from the adoption of preferential provisions. That they could have a bearing on the health and strength of our income tax is patently clear. It is also plain that, despite the large number of special provisions which have found their way into the law, these consequences have not yet appeared in alarming proportions. This is high testimony to the ability of our income-tax system to absorb considerable punishment before it reaches the danger point. If we could be sure that we have seen the end of the growth of special legislation, the secondary consequences perhaps could be regarded as unimportant and attention could then be confined to the merits of the special provisions now in the law. But one of the secondary consequences, as we have seen, is the propensity of preferential provisions to produce progenies. Should preferential legislation continue to mushroom in the future as it has in the past, the secondary consequences could seriously impair the workings of our income-tax system. From our vantage point of today, it would be highly imprudent to overlook them.

CARY, REFLECTIONS UPON THE AMERICAN LAW INSTITUTE TAX PROJECT AND THE INTERNAL REVENUE CODE: A PLEA FOR A MORATORIUM AND REAPPRAISAL *

60 Colum.L.Rev. 259–68 (1960).

Notwithstanding the spate of articles concerning the American Law Institute Tax Project and the Internal Revenue Code of 1954, no one has openly ventured to question the basic premise on which both were drafted.[1] In both instances the policy of the draftsmen seems to have been that tax statutes should be as specific, detailed, and inclusive as possible. Apparently the quest for certainty among tax lawyers is as overpowering an impulse as is the quest for security in society as a whole. The philosophy—SPECIFICITY AT ALL COST—appears to have been embraced by the American Law Institute, the American Bar Association, most distinguished teachers of taxation, the leaders (and the leaders in reform) of the tax bar, and Congress. Challenging such a phalanx would seem to involve not merely the risk of rout but even possible loss of respectability.

Nevertheless, a minority position does exist and has much broader support among active practitioners than this dissent would indicate. It is therefore

1. It should be noted that in early 1957, Mr. Norris Darrell, a distinguished member of the American Law Institute, dispassionately reassessed the 1954 Code and raised some of the points elaborated here. See Darrell, *Law School Graduates Seeking Opportunities To Specialize in Taxation Law Problems*, 25 Hennepin Law. 103, 107-09 (1957) (reprinted as *Whither Federal Income Taxation*, pp. 11-14). Also, just before completion of this paper, it was found that many of the points made respecting "intricate formulation" of statutes had been discussed with perception by Professor Ernest J. Brown in his presentation to the Ways and Means Committee. See Brown, *An Approach to Subchapter C*, 3 Tax Revision Compendium 1619.

* Copyright, 1960, By Directors of The Columbia Law Review Association, Inc. Reproduced with permission.

high time that existing doubts be aired. My own position is essentially the conservative one: we are legislating far too much. The Ways and Means Committee is becoming the forum for the decision of tax matters whether great or small, general or particular. The Senate in turn has become a sort of appellate body that initiates legislation. Increasingly involved in technical revision, Congress has had little time for considering matters of policy—the only responsibility it should even contemplate assuming. It is performing the role formerly left to the Internal Revenue Service, the Treasury, and the courts, and at the same time has no thorough understanding of what it is enacting.

Furthermore, certainty has not been achieved. Indeed, the more that Congress strives for certainty the farther away it seems to withdraw. And unlike Theseus, we have no hope of retracing the path taken into the labyrinth. Addressing himself principally to subchapter C, Professor Ernest J. Brown has noted this current tendency in the formulation of statutes and has pointed out that "as deficiencies and anomalies appear, a continuation of this method requires even more intricate elaborations . . . ."[2] With reference to certain subchapter C proposals he indicates that many, if not all, of them seem sound if taken in isolation and evaluated against the statute that called them forth. However, he says, "one may be confident that if these proposals are accepted, still further elaboration will become necessary as the limitations and questionable results . . . begin to appear. There is an element of irony as well as of warning in the frequency with which amendatory statutes known as technical changes acts have appeared in recent years."[3] Indeed, this continuous revision process makes it impossible for even an experienced practitioner to keep a truly firm grasp upon any principles underlying the Code.

This is not a wistful plea for Hellenic simplicity in revenue statutes. Nor is it a repetition of the time-honored brief favoring general over specific legislation. One must face the fact that in a complex commercial setting such simplicity is probably as unattainable as certainty.[4] Furthermore, it would be absurd to challenge every section of the 1954 Code, or many of the provisions of the ALI draft. For example, some of the structural ideas relating to partnerships[5] represent an improvement. At the same time, it is possible to demonstrate the extreme lengths and incredible detail to which the ALI-1954 Code philosophy has driven us. Perhaps the Institute project was a necessary preliminary in order to demonstrate conclusively that tax problems cannot be thus resolved, even by superior craftsmen. Nevertheless, there is

---

2. *Id.* at 1619.
3. *Id.* at 1619-20.
4. See Blum, *Simplification of the Federal Income Tax Law*, 10 TAX L. REV. 239 (1955); Paul, *Simplification of Federal Tax Laws*, 29 CORNELL L.Q. 286 (1944).
5. See especially INT. REV. CODE OF 1954, §§ 708, 751.

cause for disenchantment indeed when a distinguished member of the bar, presently acting as a senior advisor to the Ways and Means Committee, says publicly that we have reached the point in tax legislation where Congress has no notion of what it is deciding upon.

The thesis of this paper—restated another way—is that our Institute Tax Project was erroneously conceived but well executed, and that the Internal Revenue Code was both erroneously conceived and poorly executed—an inevitable result of hasty draftsmanship. It may be too late to turn back, for we have already created a Frankenstein monster. Yet, if congressional action is to be taken, I believe we should, for the most part, return to the 1939 Code, or even earlier provisions, in drafting new tax legislation.

Before developing this thesis, it may be appropriate to indicate why the ALI project and the 1954 Code are here linked so closely together. Although there are many differences between the two, the influence of the Institute's draft income tax statute upon the Code is unmistakable. In fact, the Institute speaks proudly of its contribution.[6] The Code covers a wider policy area than the Institute attempted to touch. For example, dividend tax relief, child care expenses, retirement income credit, and other relief measures were said to be outside the scope of the Institute's project. On the other hand, while the Code covers the great majority of problems identified and dealt with in the Institute's draft, it does not cover many technical areas as fully and extensively as the latter. By and large, however, the Code follows in the Institute's footsteps—though carelessly and inconsistently. As the Rococo succeeding the Baroque, it not only embraces, but carries to an extreme, the philosophy of elaboration and specificity. In the words of one distinguished Institute spokesman, "There is little relationship between the two in arrangement of the sections, language used or drafting techniques. But, generally speaking, the technical objectives of the two and many of the solutions chosen are similar. . . . Indeed, it seems fair to say without the Institute's groundwork we would not now have the new Code."[7]

I. THE AMERICAN LAW INSTITUTE TAX PROJECT

As might be anticipated, the draftsmanship of the ALI Tax Project is of high quality, within the premises adopted. Nobody can entertain any doubts as to the intellectual capacity or the public spirit and motives of those in the

6. See Darrell, *Internal Revenue Code of 1954—A Striking Example of the Legislative Process in Action*, U. So. CAL. 1955 TAX INST. 1, 17-25.

A letter to the members of the American Law Institute from the Director, dated January 27, 1955 and sent with the Darrell article said, "You will be interested to read this paper . . . about the 1954 tax law and what contribution the work of The American Law Institute made to it."

7. Darrell, *Internal Revenue Code of 1954—A Striking Example of the Legislative Process in Action*, U. So. CAL. 1955 TAX INST. 1, 20-21.

Institute who devoted time and thought to the task. Rather the problem lies in the direction in which all this talent was directed. For six years, unhappily, the combined labor of the ablest and most enlightened elements of the tax bar was upon detail.[8]

A. *Failure To Examine Basic Premises*

Some may say that this talent has been focused upon an elaborate tapestry without first examining the pattern. That is not the main thrust of this paper. To some extent, however, it is true that the "restatement" approach, adopted by the ALI in the criminal field notably, has not been consistently applied in the Tax Project. Whereas in the drafting of the Model Penal Code, policy questions are constantly being subjected to intensive scrutiny,[9] the basic premise of the Institute was that no major question of tax policy should be examined.[10] This premise is vulnerable in two respects. First of all, taxation is public law and literally bristles with policy issues all down the line. Thus, unconsciously the Institute was making policy decisions, though of lesser magnitude. Secondly, by "avoiding" (major) policy questions, the ALI actually accepted and lent massive prestige to a pre-existing policy. It was the *status quo*. With a disavowal of all policy considerations, we members of the Institute adopted innumerable propositions that had already become embedded in the law. Thus, the very best tax talent in America was largely diverted from fundamental inquiries, whether they related to capital gains, tax exemption, percentage depletion, or something that appears as prosaic as deductions.

Immense learning was poured into an analysis and codification of existing law and cases, and an intricate and elaborate superstructure was built on a foundation that was not fully tested. No consideration was given at the outset to limiting the proliferation of capital gains[11] (assuming they should receive some special treatment), or providing for correlation and integration of the

---

8. Happily, not all their energy was diverted, for individual members at the same time contributed probably the best discussions of basic tax problems that appeared in legal literature since the war. See, *e.g.*, Surrey, *Definitional Problems in Capital Gains Taxation*, 69 HARV. L. REV. 985 (1956); Surrey, *The Congress and the Tax Lobbyist—How Special Tax Provisions Get Enacted*, 70 HARV. L. REV. 1145 (1957); Darrell, *Law School Graduates Seeking Opportunities To Specialize in Taxation Law Problems*, 25 HENNEPIN LAW. 103, 107-09 (1957) (*Whither Federal Income Taxation*, pp. 11-14); Griswold, *Percentage Depletion—A Correspondence*, 64 HARV. L. REV. 361 (1951); Griswold, *The Mysterious Stock Option*, 2 TAX REVISION COMPENDIUM 1327. See also ADVISORY COMMITTEE TO THE TREASURY DEPARTMENT, FEDERAL ESTATE AND GIFT TAXES, A PROPOSAL FOR INTEGRATION AND FOR CORRELATION WITH THE INCOME TAX (1947).

9. See Wechsler, *The Challenge of a Model Penal Code*, 65 HARV. L. REV. 1097 (1952).

10. See Miller, *The Law Institute's Tax Project: An Answer to the Challenge*, 37 A.B.A.J. 191-92 (1951).

11. See Surrey, *Definitional Problems in Capital Gains Taxation*, 69 HARV. L. REV. 985 (1956).

estate, gift, and income taxes[12]—subjects on which individual ALI participants have written with vigor and brilliance—or to other problems of comparable importance. It might be argued that a tax-exempt institution cannot take policy positions, and thus influence legislation, without endangering its exempt status.[13] If this is true, then the answer is that the project was not of the type which the Institute should have considered undertaking in the first place.

In demonstrating that the Institute failed to examine the underlying structure of the tax laws, typically one might start with capital gains. Instead, let us take a narrower illustration involving the gift tax. Since this tax was passed in large part to prevent estate tax avoidance,[14] the question of integrating the gift and estate taxes might have been re-examined; but it was not. Furthermore, the Institute took no position as to the exact amounts of the exemption and exclusion, but the split gift was assumed.[15] The latter in turn foreclosed any re-examination of the marital deduction principle adopted in 1948. As a result, a gift made by a married transferor to a third person could be treated as made one-half by him and one-half by his spouse; exclusions and exemptions were for all practical purposes doubled.

As to the amount of the annual per donee exclusion, the present $3,000 was accepted.[16] As is well known, Congress originally intended to make the exclusion sufficiently liberal to cover wedding and Christmas gifts.[17] When tax rates moved up, the amount of the exclusion was lowered from $5,000 (1932-1938), to $4,000 (1939-1942), to $3,000 (1943 to date).[18] Yet in 1948 the split gift provision—practically speaking—raised it to an all-time high of $6,000.[19] Now it is a standard practice among counsel advising clients

---

12. See ADVISORY COMMITTEE TO THE TREASURY DEPARTMENT, *op. cit. supra* note 8.

13. See INT. REV. CODE OF 1954, § 501(c)(3).

14. Note, however, that the report of the Committee on Ways and Means contained the following statement as to the 1924 gift tax provisions: "[T]he gift tax was passed not only to prevent estate tax, but also to prevent income tax avoidance through reducing yearly income and thereby escaping progressive surtax rates." See WARREN & SURREY, CASES ON FEDERAL ESTATE AND GIFT TAXATION 6 (1956 ed.); Harriss, *Legislative History of Federal Gift Taxation*, 18 TAXES 531 (1940); Magill, *The Federal Gift Tax*, 40 COLUM. L. REV. 773 (1940).

15. See ALI, Federal Income, Estate and Gift Tax Statute, Discussion of Tentative Draft No. 10, May 19, 1955, at 20.

16. *Ibid.*

17. See H.R. REP. No. 708, 72d Cong., 1st Sess. 29 (1932), 1939-1 CUM. BULL., pt. 2, at 478:

> By subsection (b) a gift or gifts to any one person during the calendar year, if in amount or of the value of $3,000 or less, is not to be accounted for in determining the total amount of gifts of that or any subsequent calendar year. Likewise, the first $3,000 of a gift to any one person exceeding that amount is not to be accounted for. Such exemption, on the one hand, is to obviate the necessity of keeping an account of and reporting numerous small gifts, and, on the other, to fix the amount sufficiently large to cover in most cases wedding and Christmas gifts and occasional gifts of relatively small amounts. The exemption does not apply with respect to a gift to any donee to whom is given a future interest.

18. See LOWNDES & KRAMER, FEDERAL ESTATE AND GIFT TAXES 759 (1956).

19. See INT. REV. CODE OF 1954, § 2513.

of substance to suggest an annual program under which the husband and wife jointly give $6,000 per year to each child. This is conventional estate planning.

As practitioners, all of us find the exclusion useful, but even with inflation, is there not some question whether $6,000 per year per person exceeds even the traditional concept of American open-heartedness at Christmas? (The $6,000 is, of course, available also for each grandchild.) It is to be noted, then, that the basic proposition of $6,000 was left untouched. It was only upon detail that the Institute concentrated. Under existing law the exclusion was only available with respect to the gift of a present interest,[20] so one important question before the Institute was to define the term "future interest." At that time there was a substantial controversy in the courts as to what gifts to minors, including gifts in trust, would be considered gifts of a future interest.[21] The Institute formulated a concept that certain gifts in trust for minors "shall not be treated as future interests."[22] Thus the generic function of freeing Christmas bounty from gift tax was, by acceptance of premises presently in the Code,[23] transmuted into a device for providing an annual $6,000 exclusion for a special kind of trust for the benefit of minor children. So that donors might take advantage of the exclusion in this manner, a complicated new property arrangement had to be improvised; and enabling legislation was enacted in most jurisdictions.[24]

The foregoing illustrates in detail how a distinguished body of lawyers can weave a new corner of the tapestry and leave features in the basic design unexamined. An immense intellectual investment has been made in the

---

20. See INT. REV. CODE OF 1939, § 1003(b)(3), 56 Stat. 953 (1942) (now INT. REV. CODE OF 1954, § 2503(b)).

21. See Caplin, *How To Treat Gifts to Minors*, N.Y.U. 13TH INST. ON FED. TAX 193 (1955).

22. ALI FED. INCOME TAX STAT. § X1009(a) (Tent. Draft No. 10, 1955).

23. See ALI, Federal Income, Estate and Gift Tax Statute, Discussion of Tentative Draft No. 10, May 19, 1955, at 28-30.

> . . . [W]hat happened to the suggestion that we discard entirely the future interest concept and go to my favorite, the per donor exclusion? . . .
>
> . . . [T]he group did not know how to figure out the per donor exclusion and some of them argued for some flat figure determined in some fashion. Some argued for a figure based on X dollars times the number of children that the donor had, or the number of dependents in certain categories, while the majority voted for a flat figure.
>
> At that point a number of those who had expressed interest in the per donor exclusion said that their interest might wane because they felt that the figure would not be high enough and, therefore, would be smaller than the present effective benefit of a per donee exclusion, which is $3,000 times the number of children, times the number of dependents, times anything else. So, that is about where the matter stood and we got the sense of the group that this was not the most fruitful line to consider, at least until you had exhausted more consideration of a per donee exclusion.

24. See, *e.g.*, N.Y. PERS. PROP. LAW §§ 265-70. Either the Model Gifts of Securities to Minors Act or the Uniform Gifts to Minors Act is now in effect in more than forty jurisdictions. See Miller, *Appropriate Forms of Gifts to Minors*, N.Y.U. 16TH INST. ON FED. TAX 765 (1958).

status quo. There are other examples available—innumerable in the field of capital gains—but let us return to the main theme of this paper without further diversion.

B. *The Sanctification of the Statutory Solution*

Whether or not the ALI should have first re-examined some of the premises underlying the existing tax law, the basic criticism of the Institute's project (quite independent of the failure to examine underlying premises) centers on its general philosophy that every conceivable transaction can and must have a statutory solution. Carrying the analytical approach to its logical dénouement, the ALI seems to have adopted the principle of never letting the existing statute alone if it can be broken down, or has been broken down by judicial decisions, into several component parts. This is the restatement method carried over into an ever-proliferating tax code.

In its own defense, the Institute can say—quite truthfully—that its emphasis on specificity is as nothing by comparison with the 1954 Code. Indeed, the Code is like a shadow grossly exaggerating the design of the ALI Tax Project. The latter, however, seems to have provided an intellectual base, and the imprimatur, for the philosophy of elaboration so warmly embraced by Congress from 1954 to date.

One of the best illustrations of the ALI philosophy lies in its approach to the keystone section, old section 22(a) of the 1939 Code, now sections 61(a)(1)-(15) of the 1954 Code. Was there anything fundamentally wrong with this long-standing definition of income? It was a brief statute of general language. Actually, by 1954 the theory of income under section 22(a) was still growing, developing in such a way as to encompass receipts generally.[25] Constitutional barriers were becoming almost vestigial.

Here, indeed, one might suggest leaving well enough alone. In all fairness the Institute accepted section 22(a) for all practical purposes. But not exactly. A few words were omitted, and subsection (b) was added. The latter was an enumeration of everything the courts had already held to be income. There were twenty new statutory subdivisions, in part as a means of reference to later sections, in part for the sake of completeness. The preamble stated that the twenty items were "among those included in gross income. This enumeration shall not restrict the scope of subsection (a) . . . ."[26]

If the ALI chose to allow the definition of income to grow in the traditional way, then why did it tinker with it? The official comments upon the ALI draft make the following statement: "While paragraphs (1) through

25. See Wright, *The Effect of the Source of Realized Benefits Upon the Supreme Court's Concept of Taxable Receipts,* 8 STAN. L. REV. 164 (1956).
26. 1 ALI FED. INCOME TAX STAT. § X105(b) (Feb. 1954 Draft).

(17) either enumerate obvious items of income or items whose substantive treatment is specifically determined in later sections, paragraphs (18) through (20) prescribe the inclusion of items whose status without such enumeration might under certain circumstances have to be determined by litigation."[27] Paragraph (18) refers to awards and prizes, which are explicitly covered by a separate subsection under the section heading "Items Excluded from Gross Income."[28] The last two paragraphs (19 and 20) relate to the taxability of winnings from gambling and the like, and of proceeds from bribery, blackmail, extortion, embezzlement, theft, or other illegal acts. In both instances the case law was already pushing toward the inclusion of these two classes of receipts as income. Paragraph (20), in fact, might be regarded as little more than the extrapolation of the latest Supreme Court decision.[29]

Even though the draftsmen have attempted an enumeration of items falling within the ambit of income, there will still be questions involving novel forms of receipt. A list may be useful if it is exclusive, but, as already noted, the American Law Institute explicitly rejected exclusivity. Again, it may be helpful as guidance—in the application of the principle of *ejusdem generis*, but in this case there is no similarity among the items specified, and hence no basis for correlation. Under these circumstances no satisfactory function was served by meticulously cataloguing the various kinds of receipts that the courts have thus far held to be income. Despite the general disclaimer that "this enumeration will not restrict the scope of subsection (a)," the possibility exists that taxpayers will rely upon the maxim *inclusio unius est exclusio alterius*. Thus, it would seem that the proliferation of statutes sometimes generates, rather than clarifies confusion. Despite the breakdown into twenty parts, one still has to come back to the general definition of income to arrive at fundamental conclusions.

Another illustration of the Institute's ultra-analytical approach is its handling of the field of corporate distributions. Under the 1939 Code the principal issue before the courts in the area of stock redemptions was whether the distribution was "essentially equivalent to a dividend."[30] The cases in turn broke the problem down into two separate compartments. In general, a distribution was treated as a dividend unless there had been either a corporate contraction or a disproportionate redemption.

One clear illustration of contraction was the case of a company engaged in the business of retinning and soldering metals and of renting excess space

---

27. 1 ALI FED. INCOME TAX STAT. § X105, comment B(2) (Feb. 1954 Draft).

28. 1 ALI FED. INCOME TAX STAT. § X107(m) (Feb. 1954 Draft).

29. See Rutkin v. United States, 343 U.S. 130 (1952).

30. See Bittker & Redlich, *Corporate Liquidations and the Income Tax*, 5 TAX L. REV. 437-61 (1950).

in buildings that it owned. Fire destroyed the two upper floors of the seven-story main building, which was covered by insurance. In 1942 the company recovered $28,000 as insurance proceeds. Finding that there was a shortage of building materials and that the cost of rebuilding was prohibitive, the company decided to remove the two floors that had been burned out and to place a roof over the fifth floor, at the cost of $15,000. With the excess cash the corporation reacquired about half of its outstanding shares at par for $15,000, more or less proportionately from its shareholders. Upon these facts it was held that the redemption of the stock was not essentially equivalent to the distribution of a taxable dividend among the shareholders and hence should receive capital gain treatment.[31]

In the ALI 1954 draft the conclusion was reached that redemptions on the "contraction" theory should not be entitled to capital gains. A general—as distinguished from specific—approach was characteristic of this early draft. Subsequently, however, there was a noticeable shift. In its 1958 report the staff of the Institute withdrew from the earlier position, saying, "basically, it is felt that where a substantial part of the business operation is liquidated, the resultant distribution, even though pro rata, should receive capital gain treatment."[32] In the phraseology of the report, "the problem thus becomes one of finding a workable statutory definition of partial liquidation embodying this approach."[33] But why did they seek a new definition? What was wrong with the original one? It is true that out of the existing cases a few more situations can be distilled into statutory language, but there will be others of which the draftsmen never dreamed. In the definition finally recommended there was agreement among the ALI Tax Advisory Group upon an objective test: *i.e.*, there must be a fifty per cent reduction in net worth.[34] A corporate liquidation, thus, would not qualify if the reduction amounts only to forty-nine per cent.

In addition, at the 1958 meeting of the Tax Advisory Group the members voted by a small margin for retention of the "five-year-separate-business-test" provided in section 346(b) of the present Code:[35] *i.e.*, the benefit of capital gains would be available where a trade or business was terminated which had been actively conducted throughout a five-year period before the distribution.

---

31. Joseph W. Imler, 11 T.C. 836 (1948).

32. ALI, Federal Income, Estate and Gift Tax Project, Income Tax Problems of Corporations and Shareholders 100 (1958).

33. *Ibid.*

34. *Id.* at 126. See *id.* at 123 (ALI Fed. Income Tax Stat. § 302(b) (5)).

35. With a percentage of net worth limitation. See Surrey, *Income Tax Problems of Corporations and Shareholders: American Law Institute Tax Project—American Bar Association Committee Study on Legislative Revision*, 14 Tax L. Rev. 1, 8 n.8 (1958).

Along with these precise formulations the "essentially equivalent to a dividend" test was retained as a general standard—to be relied on to reach exceptional situations warranting capital gains treatment.[36]

If the Institute found it impossible to discard the generic test, a question arises as to the value of additional filigree. Under any circumstances there seems to be no justification for exact formulation. I should like to suggest that the thirst for certainty—which has admittedly not been satisfied, as demonstrated by the decision to retain the old (general) test—simply adds immensely to the verbiage and thus to ultimate confusion.

The above illustrations of multiplying statutory standards dramatize the fact that the Institute tended to become entangled in the sophisticated learning of its members. One almost questions whether they cared how complicated a provision was so long as it covered the subject. "Only experts will be working upon it." Yet, as demonstrated by the new and expanded definition of income, as well as by the "essentially equivalent" test, detailed statutes and formulae never do seem to cover the subject; they usually have to be supplemented by general provisions. Further, the policy of covering a matter in detail demonstrates the stress upon finding a "solution," like the holy grail, when probably none exists. Through 1958, members and the staff of the ALI were still trying to discover an "answer" to such imponderables as thin incorporation and collapsible corporations, as to which there will be further discussion below. Undoubtedly some committee will still be worrying about these problems decades hence—when each of them may well occupy at least twenty pages of the code.

Finally, the attitude seems to pervade that no simple lawyer in a small community will ever have to (or be able to) handle even a garden variety problem. In this respect the partnership provisions are noteworthy. Designed by skilled lawyers representing in some instances complicated oil syndicates and brokerage firms, the ALI and 1954 Codes offer no elemental ground rules for all the small businesses that are generally conducted in partnership form. Unable to afford special tax counsel, these businesses may well throw up their hands or perhaps incorporate under the provisions of subchapter S as the lesser evil! Before the partnership subchapter (K) was enacted, at least it had been said that "if application of known principles created an unrealistic result, there was a tendency on the part of both the Government and the taxpayer to disregard them in favor of a more practical rule of reason."[37]

---

36. *Id.* at 4.
37. See *Preface* to WILLIS, HANDBOOK OF PARTNERSHIP TAXATION at iii-iv (1957).

EISENSTEIN, SOME SECOND THOUGHTS ON TAX IDEOLOGIES *

N.Y.U. 23rd Inst. on Fed.Tax 1–4 (1965).

* * *

Several years ago I wrote an essay on "The Ideologies of Taxation." This modest work was primarily concerned with our so-called progressive income tax. "Our taxes," I stated, "reflect a continuing struggle among contending interests for the privilege of paying the least." They "are a changing product of earnest efforts to have others pay them." [1] I then indicated, with the help of James Madison, that there are various kinds of competing interests, both major and minor. Now, in a democracy reasons must be given for the tax proposals made by different interests or groups. The mere virtue of enlightened self-interest is not enough. These reasons must, at the very least, express some universal good that transcends private gain.

The ideologies of taxation provide the required reasons. They are the modes of thought to which groups resort in order to obtain tax laws to their liking. In short, they are the verbal means of conducting fiscal warfare. But they are more than that. They are also the ways in which men justify their fiscal aspirations to themselves as well as others. Even when one is asking for a lower tax, he must feel ennobled by a higher principle.

A tax ideology, like other ideologies, has certain distinctive characteristics which are easily recognized. In the first place, it rationalizes the fiscal position taken by the group that it serves. Second, it performs this vital function by justifying the position in terms of certain values. Third, these values are expressed as dispassionate principles rising above partisan preferences. The desires of the particular interest are transformed into a profound and impartial concern for everybody. What is good for the group is good for the country. Fourth, since an ideology is designed to persuade, it is armed with an appropriate rhetoric. Sentences speak eloquently of the public interest, the

1 The Ideologies of Taxation 3–4, 11 (1961).

* Copyright © 1965 by New York University. Reprinted by permission from the *Proceedings* of The New York University Institute on Federal Taxation, published by Matthew Bender & Co.

general welfare, or anything else which conveys a similar sense of achievement. Fact and logic are not too important. What counts is plausibility. Finally, an ideology is emotionally satisfying. Its words and phrases afford the exhilarating experience of fulfilling a significant moral purpose.

As I see it, there are three basic tax ideologies. I call them the ideology of ability, the ideology of barriers and deterrents, and the ideology of equity. These provide a framework of reason and rhetoric in which the contending interests operate.

I will now briefly summarize the three ideologies by indulging in the unfortunate practice of quoting oneself.[2] "The ideology of ability declares that taxes should be apportioned in accordance with the ability to pay them; and that ability to pay is properly measured by income or wealth." As income or wealth rises, it can more easily be spared. "Since the ability to pay is the ability to do without, the more dispensable dollars are the more taxable dollars." Hence, "the ideal levies are a progressive income tax and a progressive death tax."

The ideology of barriers and deterrents views things differently. According to this ideology, progressive taxes "dangerously diminish the desire to work; they fatally discourage the incentive to invest; and they irreparably impair the sources of new capital. Our economic system must come to an untimely end if private capital cannot accumulate and private initiative is destroyed." These melancholy insights end in a grim prediction of impending disaster. Progressive taxes are "barriers and deterrents to the economic growth and stability of the nation. Even if the system is not on the verge of collapse, the barriers and deterrents must be rapidly removed. Otherwise the system must eventually decline and decay, since neither capital nor ambition will be available to sustain it." Needless to say, the ideology of barriers and deterrents is closely concerned with our economic well-being.

We now come to the third ideology—the ideology of equity. This mode of reasoning is devoted to the noble theme of equality among equals. "It maintains that those who are similarly situated should be similarly treated and those who are differently situated should be differently treated." Of all three ideologies, the ideology of equity is the most obliging. It supplies the answer to almost any prayer. However, as this ideology is commonly applied, equity consists largely of two principles. The first principle is that equity is special relief for certain taxpay-

[2] Id. at 13, 15, 23–24, 176.

ers who are differently situated from all other taxpayers. The second principle is that equity is the privilege of paying as little as somebody else. Since someone is always paying less, it is always possible to ask for equity.

If my analysis is correct, then it follows that, under our economic and political arrangements, our tax laws must reflect the pressures of competing interests or groups operating through the various ideologies. The relevant question is not whether such pressures can be overcome, but which ones shall prevail. Another conclusion also readily follows. The power to tax is the power to reallocate the distribution of worldly goods among different groups in our society. Every tax system necessarily affects that distribution, whether or not it is expressly designed to do so. Therefore, our income tax is doomed to be an elaborate hodgepodge as long as it represents an uneasy compromise among contending interests.

The difficulty with such observations is that they are unpleasant. As a result, several scholarly experts have been deeply shocked and taken me to task. One of these experts summarizes my views as a "nihilistic analysis." [3] Another repeatedly accuses me of indulging in cynicism. But in the end he confuses me by finding some "nobility" amid such behavior.[4] A third troubled expert has left me still more bewildered. He calls me both a cynic and a social reformer. To make matters worse, he even suggests that I may be "an adventurer without scruples," and then kindly concludes that I am "a deeply moral man." [5] One of the lesser benefits of writing a book is that the author discovers various things about himself through discerning critics.

Why are these thoughtful experts so sorely disturbed? The answer seems fairly clear. They all yearn for some objective standard of right and wrong—the revelation of some dispassionate and automatic principle—which will redeem our tax laws from the corruption of interests and groups. In other words, they are awaiting some magical solution which will remove taxes from the realm of politics. This approach to salvation is beyond my grasp. But while it fails to impress me, I can still understand why these experts find it so attractive. Each is a professor of law engaged in the worthy pursuit of instructing the young in federal taxation. Obviously, it would be rather dis-

[3] Sander, Book Review, 77 Harv.L.Rev. 1183, 1186 (1964).

[4] Blum, Book Review, 56 Ill.L.Rev. 692, 700–701 (1961).

[5] Sneed, Book Review, 71 Yale L.J. 186, 188–189, 193–194 (1961).

tressing to concede that this intricate jurisprudence is an elaboration of partisan ideologies which have prevailed from time to time. The effect on the young might even be more serious if they were exposed to such disconcerting facts. They might then fail to develop an appropriate reverence for what they are taught. A stout belief in redemption through dispassionate principles helps to maintain a respectful attitude in the classroom.

NOTE, TOWARD NEW MODES OF TAX DECISION-MAKING—THE DEBT-EQUITY IMBROGLIO AND DISLOCATIONS IN TAX LAWMAKING RESPONSIBILITY *

83 Harv.L.Rev. 1695–96, 1704–21 (1970).

It is a familiar rule of tax law that while interest costs payable by corporations in return for the use of borrowed funds are properly deductible as business expenses, dividends paid to shareholders constitute distributions of profit, and as such are taxable to both corporation and shareholder as income.[1] Neither interest deductibility [2] nor double taxation of corporate dividends [3] has escaped criticism on the merits. Yet once the difference in treatment has been accepted, it becomes necessary for purposes of determining the deductibility of payments made in return for the use of capital to distinguish between debt and equity.[4] Although the problem raised by dubious "loans" made to close corporations by stockholders and related persons is by no means new,[5] the approach taken to its resolution in the Tax Reform Act of 1969 [6] suggests a new direction in the allocation of tax lawmaking functions. Rather than attempting fully to resolve the problem for itself, Congress has expressly delegated the job to the Treasury.

Specifically, section 415(a) of the Act amends the Internal Revenue Code of 1954 to add a new section 385. Subsection (a) of

---

[1] *See* INT. REV. CODE OF 1954, §§ 163, 301(c)(1); Treas. Reg. § 1.163–1(c) (1966). *See also* INT. REV. CODE OF 1954, § 316(a)(1).

[2] For an economically oriented criticism of the deduction for interest payments, see Lent, *Bond Interest Deduction and the Federal Corporation Income Tax*, 2 NAT'L TAX J. 131 (1949).

[3] The problems which inhere in double taxation of corporate profit distributions are discussed in 3 HOUSE COMMITTEE ON WAYS AND MEANS, 86TH CONG., 2D SESS., TAX REVISION COMPENDIUM 1537–1609 (Comm. Print 1959).

[4] Actually, litigation with respect to the differential treatment of debt and equity has tended to concentrate in three major areas: (1) in determining the basis of exchanges of property for securities, generally pursuant to incorporation, under section 351 of the Internal Revenue Code of 1954, (2) in determining whether payments made to security holders are interest distributions deductible to the corporation under section 163, or nondeductible dividend payments, and (3) in determining whether recapture of principal in excess of adjusted basis constitutes a capital gain or a "disguised dividend." *See generally* B. BITTKER & J. EUSTICE, FEDERAL INCOME TAXATION OF CORPORATIONS AND SHAREHOLDERS § 4.02, at 121 (1966). The problem is discussed in text with reference to interest deductibility, but the problems of definition are common to all three areas.

[5] *See* Lent, *supra* note 2, at 131.

[6] Pub. L. No. 91–172, § 415(a), 83 Stat. 613 (1969) (codified at INT. REV. CODE OF 1954, § 385).

* Copyright © 1970 by The Harvard Law Review Association. Reproduced with permission.

section 385 delegates to the Treasury authority to prescribe "such regulations as may be necessary or appropriate to determine whether an interest in a corporation is to be treated . . . as stock or indebtedness." Subsection (b) lists five factors which the Treasury may, but need not in all cases,[7] take into account in formulating the regulations.[8] However, what is unique in section 385 is not that specific authority is delegated to the Treasury to prescribe regulations. In addition to section 7805 of the Code, which grants the Treasury general power to "prescribe all needful rules and regulations," specific delegations of rulemaking power are found in no less than 1338 places in the 1954 Code.[9]

* * *

[7] The Senate Report on the bill makes clear that the factors listed are merely suggestive, and are to be given special weight neither by the Treasury in formulating its guidelines, nor by the courts in interpreting the guidelines formulated:

> It is not intended that only these factors be included in the guidelines or that, with respect to a particular situation, any of these factors must be included in the guidelines, or that any of the factors which are included by statute must necessarily be given any more weight than other factors added by regulations.

S. REP. NO. 552, 91st Cong., 1st Sess. 138 (1969).

[8] The factors are:

> (1) whether there is a written unconditional promise to pay on demand or on a specified date a sum certain in money in return for an adequate consideration in money or money's worth, and to pay a fixed rate of interest, (2) whether there is subordination to or preference over any indebtedness of the corporation, (3) the ratio of debt to equity of the corporation, (4) whether there is convertibility into the stock of the corporation, and (5) the relationship between holdings of stock in the corporation and holdings of the interest in question.

Tax Reform Act of 1969, Pub. L. No. 91-172, § 415(a), 83 Stat. 613 (1969) (codified at INT. REV. CODE OF 1954, § 385).

[9] 1 K. DAVIS, ADMINISTRATIVE LAW TREATISE § 5.04, at 129 (Supp. 1965).

B. The Courts and the Regulations Problem

Was section 385 necessary? Inasmuch as the Treasury had general power to prescribe "all needful rules and regulations," to implement the Internal Revenue Code,[49] could it not have defined "debt" and "equity" without the explicit congressional authorization contained in section 385? It could, but such a regulation would merely have been "interpretive"; that is, the Treasury's interpretation of the statute, and as such liable to have been disregarded by the courts if not in accord with their own interpretation of the statute.[50] On the other hand, a specific delegation of rulemaking power from Congress such as that contained in section 385 permits promulgation of "legislative" regulations, which are binding on the courts so long as within the granted power, issued pursuant to proper procedure, and reasonable.[51] Thus, section 385 is at once a congressional prod to

---

[49] INT. REV. CODE OF 1954, § 7805.

[50] *See* Alvord, *Treasury Regulations and the Wilshire Oil Case*, 40 COLUM. L. REV. 252, 257 (1940). *See generally* 1 K. DAVIS, ADMINISTRATIVE LAW TREATISE § 5.03, at 300 (1958). Greater weight has, on occasion, been accorded interpretive regulations if the section under which they were originally promulgated has been reenacted. The theory is that Congress has "approved" or "adopted" the interpretation in reenacting the statute. *See, e.g.*, Helvering v. R.J. Reynolds Tobacco Co., 306 U.S. 110 (1939). Of this doctrine Randolph Paul once wrote:

> Among the innumerable fictions which have formed a part of the science of law, that which holds the record for unrealism is the doctrine that where a statute has been reenacted in the same form after an administrative construction, Congress has silently approved and incorporated the existing ruling.

Paul, *Use and Abuse of Tax Regulations in Statutory Construction*, 49 YALE L.J. 660, 663–64 (1940). The basic objection to the doctrine is that Congress almost invariably is totally ignorant of the administrative construction. *See* Griswold, *A Summary of the Regulations Problem*, 54 HARV. L. REV. 398, 401 (1941).

[51] 1 K. DAVIS, *supra* note 50, at 299. While it is generally assumed that an explicit grant of rulemaking power with respect to a given subject operates invariably to narrow the scope of judicial review of regulations promulgated pursuant to it, there is some disagreement as to whether legislative regulations may be promulgated *without* such a grant of power. Some commentators have argued that an explicit grant is always required. *See, e.g.*, Alvord, *supra* note 50, at 253. But there have been cases which suggest the contrary. *E.g.*, National Broadcasting Co. v. United States, 319 U.S. 190 (1943). If the distinction between

the Treasury and a warning to the courts: the debt-equity problem must be resolved, and it must be resolved through Treasury rulemaking, not adjudication.

The congressional intention to limit judicial review under section 385 [52] is rather understandable after thirty years of judicial inability to provide adequate guidelines in the area. More importantly, though, analysis of the reasons for judicial failure to provide guidelines suggests a principle inherent in the contours of what would constitute a successful resolution of the debt-equity imbroglio which points to a far narrower role for judicial review in the administration of the tax law than that played currently. The problem of distinguishing debt from equity may yet be far from final resolution, but the broad outlines of a successful answer can be suggested. What is needed is not an all-embracing definition of the terms "debt" and "equity" by identification of their essential characteristics. Nor may the dilemma be resolved by compiling a list, no matter how exhaustive, of factors relevant in making case by case determinations. Rather, nonlitigious taxpayers should be offered a "safe harbor" — a nonexclusive, arbitrarily defined area of debt — by reference to which, together with their lawyers, they could plan the capitalizations of closely-held corporations in confidence that certain payments would be deductible as interest. For the adventurous taxpayer the law may leave the possibility of litigation in the fringe areas of debt and equity, but tax law should not compel taxpayers to be adventurous.

This kind of arbitrary technical rule required to create the safe harbor is precisely what the courts are not equipped to provide. Giving due consideration to shared social goals, courts in deciding cases must formulate and apply principles of general applicability to factual contexts in such a way that only those facts relevant to application of the principle control the result.[53] A safe harbor cannot be created in this way; by definition it requires an arbitrary elevation of selected factors from mere relevance to controlling status.

"legislative" and "interpretive" rules requires an explicit grant of rulemaking power, it may be justified as a judicially imposed policy of clear statement, requiring Congress expressly to manifest an intention to narrow the scope of judicial review. If an explicit statement is not required, then the distinction is merely a make-weight used to describe, after the fact, differences in treatment of different regulations. Whatever may be the propriety of strict judicial adherence to the dichotomous characterization of regulations, however, the fact remains that Congress did intend clearly to limit the scope of judicial review of the regulations promulgated under the new section 385. *See* note 52 *infra*.

[52] See the excerpt from S. Rep. No. 552, 91st Cong., 1st Sess. (1969), quoted note 7 *supra*.

[53] *See* H.M. Hart & A. Sacks, *supra* note 48, at 160–61.

But more basically, there is really no principle by reference to which a court may distinguish debt from equity. It is true that different outcomes in different cases are normally based on reasoned distinctions which may be called rules of law,[54] but it is also true that if such rules take the form of statements that certain factors are relevant in making a given determination, wide discretion is necessarily delegated in the weighting of those factors and in their application to future factual contexts. Absent some definitive principle which requires the choice of some factors over others as controlling, that discretion remains essentially unfettered.[55]

Interest on debt and dividends on equity both represent payments made in return for the use of capital, and while it might not be wrong or particularly imprudent to tax distributed earnings twice, it would not be wrong or imprudent to tax them once either. The statutory decision to allow a deduction for interest and not for dividends is not a principled one; it is based on discretion.[56] This sort of discretionary choice is within the appropriate sphere of congressional power.[57] But when Congress makes a difference in treatment turn on a distinction which is inherently one of form or degree, there is no way the courts can fill the interstices with detail derived from principle unless they create the principle themselves. Normally, when there is no statutory

---

[54] Paul, *supra* note 29, at 782.

[55] *Cf.* Jaffe, *supra* note 12, at 249.

[56] It is possible to argue that certain principles in income taxation may be deduced from widely accepted definitions of economic income. *See, e.g.*, Surrey, *Tax Incentives as a Device for Implementing Government Policy: A Comparison with Direct Government Expenditures*, 83 HARV. L. REV. 705, 706 (1970) ("special provisions" in taxation can be identified as those which result in taxation of a quantity not corresponding to "widely accepted definitions of income"). Economic income may have relevance in the quest for a comprehensive income tax base — that is, as a model for basic legislative income tax reform. *See, e.g.*, Musgrave, *In Defense of an Income Concept*, 81 HARV. L. REV. 44 (1967). *But see* Bittker, *A "Comprehensive Tax Base" as a Goal of Income Tax Reform*, 80 HARV. L. REV. 925 (1967). Nevertheless, it can be of little aid to the courts in filling the interstices of a tax statute such as our own which, as written, deviates widely from taxation of economic income. Most deviations from taxation of economic income are justified in terms of other economic and social goals. *See* Surrey, *supra* at 711–13. Consequently, for courts to construe such provisions so as to further taxation of economic income as widely defined may thwart their very purposes. Moreover, in some areas of tax law, the definition of economic income provides no assistance. One such area, the appropriate taxable entity, lies at the bottom of the debt-equity imbroglio. *See* Pechman, *Comprehensive Income Taxation: A Comment*, 81 HARV. L. REV. 63, 65 (1967) (Haig-Simons definition of income is neutral with respect to "the proper unit of taxation").

[57] *Cf.* H.M. HART & A. SACKS, *supra* note 48, at 171–72. Some discretionary choices may, of course, be better than others for policy reasons. *See* note 56 *supra*.

principle to apply, one may yet be derived from the broadly shared goals of the society generally.[58] But when there are no broadly held societal views on a subject, such as is likely to be the case in many areas of tax law,[59] the courts are left completely without a meaningful *ratio decidendi.* Thus, the one "great principle" to emerge from all the wasteful litigation in regard to debt and equity was precisely the wrong one: that form should never be exalted over substance. When there is no principle to be found, form — that is, an aspect of a transaction which does not call into play the operation of a governing principle — must always control substance if there is to be any rule at all. But the courts are not equipped to make the requisite formalistic rules. In the tentative formulation of principle, the courts, faced with specific facts, are likely to issue broad dicta covering wide varieties of analogous situations which may in fact have no applicability in those situations at all.[60] Although when confronted with analogous situations demonstrating the inappropriateness of their prior dicta, the courts will disavow them, the interim effect on tax administration and planning may be chaotic. There is a danger of confusion in all such broad statements, but the probability of inaccuracy is unusually high when the probability a principle can be found is low and when the court is unfamiliar with the general body of law with which it is dealing. Both these conditions are likely to obtain in questions of tax law.

Further, exactly because there is likely to be no general agreement on where the ultimate lines should be drawn in taxation, no serious objection to the taxpayer's quest for certainty in the law can be maintained. Certainty is of enormous practical desirability because of the financial reliance which is placed upon the existing content of tax rules,[61] and this reliance cannot be dismissed as

---

[58] *See* L. Fuller, The Forms and Limits of Adjudication, Nov. 19, 1957 (unpublished paper presented to a group of Harvard University faculty members) reproduced in part in H.M. HART & A. SACKS, *supra* note 48, at 421–26 (in the absence of a statute it is only by reference to the principle of reciprocity of obligation or to shared goals that a court may enunciate a principle determinative of the case *sub judice* which predates the case, and thus render its decision acceptable to the parties).

[59] This is at the heart of the oft-expressed notion that it is more important to settle tax questions than to settle them right. *See, e.g.*, Burnet v. Coronado Oil & Gas Co., 285 U.S. 393, 406 (1932) (Brandeis, J., dissenting); Eisenstein, *supra* note 33, at 524; Griswold, *supra* note 30, at 1159.

[60] *Cf.* Eisenstein, *supra* note 33, at 525. Hort v. Commissioner, 313 U.S. 28 (1941), provides a good illustration of the erroneous enunciation of a principle in taxation. *Compare* United States v. Dresser Industries, Inc., 324 F.2d 56, 61–62 (5th Cir. 1963) (concurring opinion) (recognizing the principle to be overly broad).

[61] *Cf.* Paul, *supra* note 50, at 665 (maintaining the status quo is of special value in tax law).

unjustifiable, for there is nothing wrong in relying on an arbitrary tax rule which is arbitrary precisely because there is no general agreement as to the applicable principle. It will not do to recite that certainty permits tax avoidance as did the Senate in rejecting clarifying legislation in 1954.[62] The goal of all tax planning is tax avoidance, albeit more often termed tax minimization. The real task is to draw lines in such a way that widely shared economic and social goals may be achieved. If the problem does not admit of immediate definitive resolution, interim guidelines can be established enunciating conduct which is thought clearly acceptable.[63] In the meantime, definitive resolution of a problem when there is no agreement on goals must begin with a search for an informed consensus as to those goals. The search is not aided when the problem is obfuscated in uncertainty.

Certainty in tax law is not promoted by permitting courts to judge the propriety of Treasury regulations, whether they are denominated "legislative" or "merely interpretive." Not only do such decisions operate retroactively, thus destroying expectations built on reliance,[64] but they tend to create protracted uncertainty because appeals may be heard from the ninety-five courts of original jurisdiction in eleven courts of appeals,[65] none of the decisions of which need be accepted by the Government or the tax-

---

[62] *See* note 38 *supra.*

[63] *Cf.* Eisenstein, *supra* note 33, at 504–05 n.161 (making the analagous point with reference to grantor trusts following Helvering v. Clifford, 309 U.S. 331 (1940)).

[64] It is somewhat surprising to note that although the American Bar Association Section of Taxation's Special Committee on Legislative Regulations has recommended that amendments of Treasury regulations operate prospectively only, it has seemed not to have appreciated the extent to which frequent judicial invalidation of regulations perpetrates the same evils as does retroactive amendment. *See* ***Report of the Special Committee on Legislative Regulations***, 20 BULL. A.B.A. SEC. TAXATION 105 (July, 1967), reprinted as a final resolution in 21 TAX LAWYER 973–79 (1968). A reading of the Committee's explanation of its recommendations makes clear that it has failed to distinguish between legislative and interpretive regulations, perhaps on the assumption that legislative regulations always involve broad delegations of power and interpretive regulations narrow ones. *See id.* at 978 (1968) (separate opinion of Prof. Bittker). It is impossible to tell whether the Committee approves the current scope of judicial review.

[65] *Cf.* R. MAGILL, THE IMPACT OF FEDERAL TAXES 209 (1943) (large number of courts of original jurisdiction and courts of appeals secures "a state of complete uncertainty in tax jurisprudence"). Aside from litigation in the Tax Court, the ninety-three federal district courts have general jurisdiction to entertain taxpayer actions for refunds under 28 U.S.C. § 1340 (1964). Additionally, the Court of Claims has jurisdiction under 28 U.S.C. § 1491 (1964) to hear claims for refunds. Moreover, appeals from judgments of the Tax Court, in which most tax cases are heard, as well as appeals from the district courts, may be heard in all eleven courts of appeals. INT. REV. CODE OF 1954, § 7482.

payer.[66] Conflicts between the circuits may be resolved only by the rare grant of certiorari from the Supreme Court, which is neither equipped nor inclined to devote much of its valuable time to tax questions. Once a given application of a regulation has been invalidated, nothing is immediately substituted for it, since one court's resolution of the problem need not be another's. Until the Supreme Court has decided the question, "there is virtually nothing that the taxpayer or his counsel — or the government — can rely on," [67] and ultimate resolution by the Supreme Court will take eight or nine years from the time the controversy arises.[68] Nor is there any assurance that the Supreme Court's disposition of the case will dispose of the problem; the debt-equity dilemma is but one example of a situation in which it did not.[69]

Finally, the mere presence of the Treasury in the pyramidal structure evidences a congressional recognition that an institution is required at the level of initial administration with technical expertise to answer specific questions, and to answer them with reference to an overview of a body of law perhaps unique in its interrelated complexity [70] and need for certainty.[71] Judicial restraint is thus appropriate in recognition not only of limitations inherent in the judicial process, but of a limitation of the judicial function inherent in the tax institutional structure itself.

All these considerations point to a limited supervisory role for the courts in the tax institutional structure. The optimal decision-making pyramid would have three tiers rather than the present four: Congress, the Treasury, and the taxpayer aided by counsel would remain in the pyramid. The courts would stand astride it to assure that each decisionmaker maintained his proper position. Thus, the courts would invalidate regulations only if beyond the power delegated by Congress, although then, as now, it would be assumed that Congress did not intend to delegate the power to issue blatantly unreasonable rulings.[72] But all problems cannot

[66] The Commissioner can and does disregard adverse decisions in hopes of achieving a conflict between the circuits which the Supreme Court will resolve with a grant of certiorari. Nor need taxpayers accept the decision of a single court either, due to the large number of courts which hear tax cases. *See generally* Griswold, *The Need for a Court of Tax Appeals*, 57 HARV. L. REV. 1153, 1154–57 (1944).

[67] *Id.* at 1156.

[68] Traynor, *Administrative and Judicial Procedure for Federal Income, Estate, and Gift Taxes — A Criticism and a Proposal*, 38 COLUM. L. REV. 1393 (1938). *See also* Paul, *supra* note 50, at 664. John Kelley Co. v. Commissioner, 326 U.S. 521 (1946), provides a good illustration: the taxable years in issue were 1937, 1938, and 1939.

[69] For another notable example, see Helvering v. Clifford, 309 U.S. 331 (1940).

[70] *Cf.* Eisenstein, *supra* note 33, at 524–25.

[71] *See* Paul, *supra* note 50, at 665.

[72] *See* 1 K. DAVIS, *supra* note 50, at 299.

be anticipated in advance. Questions would still arise under the statute for which the Treasury had failed to provide answers in the regulations; and questions would arise in the interpretation of the regulations themselves. In such cases the courts would still be required to fill the gaps, drawing principle from the statute or analogous regulations where possible, deciding cases on grounds of general fairness where impossible. Yet hopefully the gaps would not be so wide, nor the unresolved policy questions so broad, as they are currently.[73]

C. Congress and the Regulations Problem

Having relegated the judiciary to a supervisory role in the tax lawmaking superstructure, the crucial issue remains: which questions should be answered by Congress and which delegated to the Treasury for resolution. Part of the answer is suggested by the structure of the pyramid itself — by the existence in the Treasury of an administrative agency with technical expertise and specialized function,[74] and by the democratic responsibility of Congress to decide questions of basic policy.[75] And, part of the answer is suggested by the efficiency which results from the creation of clear, unambiguous tax rules which may readily be applied by the taxpayer and his counsel to individual factual contexts uniquely well known to them.[76] But a more precise answer requires reference to the tax legislative process itself.

While custom,[77] following the Constitution,[78] requires that tax legislation be drafted in the House, detailed recommendations typically come from the administration.[79] This was, for example, the case with the Tax Reform Act of 1969.[80] In the executive, primary responsibility for preparation of recommendations resides in the Treasury, which employs a fairly large staff of experts

---

[73] *See* p. 1719 *infra.*

[74] *See* p. 1703 *supra.*

[75] *Cf.* Jaffe, *An Essay on the Delegation of Legislative Power: II*, 47 COLUM. L. REV. 561, 592–93 (1947).

[76] *See* p. 1703 & note 45 *supra.*

[77] *See* Note, *Tax Adjustments for Economic Stability and Growth: Proposals for Reform of the Legislative Process*, 5 HARV. J. LEGIS. 265, 267 (1968).

[78] U.S. CONST. art. I, § 7.

[79] Of course, recommendations may also come from outside sources and from the tax committees themselves. *See* J. PECHMAN, FEDERAL TAX POLICY 33–34 (1966).

[80] Impetus for the Tax Reform Act originally came from the outgoing Johnson Administration Treasury Department, which formulated a series of proposed reforms. See U.S. TREAS. DEP'T, 91ST CONG., 1ST SESS., TAX REFORM STUDIES AND PROPOSALS (Comm. Print 1969).

for that purpose.[81] Once introduced, tax recommendations are referred to the House Committee on Ways and Means, which generally holds hearings on tax recommendations at which the Secretary of the Treasury is traditionally the first witness, and the only witness who represents anything akin to the broad public interest.[82] The hearings are rapidly taken over by spokesmen for various special interest groups [83] seeking advantageous tax treatment, and attendance by Committee members declines precipitously as testimony becomes repetitious.[84] Shortly after the hearings are closed, the Committee goes into executive session to hammer out a draft bill. At this time, the Committee, aided by staff of the Joint Committee on Internal Revenue Taxation and representatives of the Treasury will, together with the House Legislative Counsel, transform their several views into workable statutory compromise.[85]

Debate of tax legislation in the House is typically conducted under a "closed rule" limiting amendment and debate.[86] The Tax Reform Act of 1969 provides a good illustration. It was debated under a rule providing that the entire bill, a document of 631 pages, was to be discussed without amendment for a total of six hours, three controlled by the chairman and three by the ranking minority member of the Committee on Ways and

---

[81] The Treasury's tax legislative staff consists of some thirty-five economists and statisticians attached to the Office of Tax Analysis, and about twenty tax lawyers and an accounting adviser working through the Office of Tax Legislative Counsel. Technical assistance may also be obtained from the Bureau of Internal Revenue, the Bureau of the Budget, and the Council of Economic Advisers. J. PECHMAN, *supra* note 79, at 33–34.

[82] *See* R. BLOUGH, THE FEDERAL TAXING PROCESS 62, 67–68 (1952). The Democratic membership of Ways and Means comprise their party's Committee on Committees which makes all committee assignments. The ranking majority and minority members of Ways and Means are invariably among the House leadership. *See id.* at 62. This coincidence of leadership is no doubt a factor of considerable aid in obtaining closed rules for House debate.

[83] While there are serious problems in attempting to define "special tax provisions," and hence "special interest groups," *cf.* Bittker, *supra* note 56 *passim*, for purposes of this Note it will be sufficient to define these provisions in terms of the arguments used in support of them by their proponents. *Cf.* Surrey, *supra* note 56, at 707. When used in text, the term, "special tax provision" means one advocated for reasons other than its tendency accurately to tax gains in net worth plus consumption during the taxable period. *See* Musgrave, *supra* note 56, at 47. "Special interest groups" are those which advocate "special tax provisions."

[84] R. BLOUGH, *supra* note 82, at 70: "[M]any witnesses present their testimony before half a dozen or perhaps even only two or three members" of the twenty-five member committee.

[85] *Id.* at 71–73. As the bill takes shape, the Chief of Staff of the Joint Committee, aided by Treasury staff, will prepare a report to accompany it to the floor. *Id.* at 75–76. *See also* note 99 *infra*.

[86] R. BLOUGH, *supra* note 82, at 76; J. PECHMAN, *supra* note 79, at 39.

Means.[87] Despite some traditional [88] outcry,[89] the membership of the House was well aware that a defeat for the rule would have doomed the bill,[90] and after a prearranged hour's debate, the rule was approved by a wide margin on a roll call vote.[91]

Tax legislation passed by the House is sent to the Senate where it is referred to the Committee on Finance.[92] Consideration in the Senate follows much the same pattern as that in the House, with two relevant differences. First, committee action in the Senate is focused on a draft bill, and consequently is more specific.[93] Second, and more important, debate in the Senate is unlimited, and tends to concentrate on specific provisions affecting special interest groups with substantial pecuniary stakes in the content of these provisions.[94] While many proposed floor amendments are voted down at the instance of the Finance Committee leadership,[95] some are carried into conference where the ranking members of the Senate Finance and of the House Ways and Means Committees compromise the Senate and House versions of the bill.[96]

Immediately suggested by even such a truncated description of the tax legislative process is the essential role of expertise in tax lawmaking. At virtually every stage of the process, with the exception of Senate floor debate — where it has been suggested

---

[87] H.R. Res. No. 513, 91st Cong., 1st Sess., 115 Cong. Rec. H6968 (daily ed. Aug. 6, 1969).

[88] *See* R. Blough, *supra* note 82, at 77.

[89] Debate of the resolution is in 115 Cong. Rec. H6968–77 (daily ed. Aug. 6, 1969).

[90] *See id.* at H6970 (remarks of Representative O'Neill):

> [I]f we ever have an open rule on this bill you will be here not only until Christmas but the year after Christmas, and probably beyond. This bill would never be enacted.
>
> Furthermore, we would be deluged with vans bringing in all the lobbyists from all over the United States who were working on this legislation.

[91] The vote was 265 to 145. *Id.* at H6977.

[92] R. Blough, *supra* note 82, at 78.

[93] *See id.* Attendance at committee hearings also tends to be more sporadic in the Senate. *Id.* at 79.

[94] No doubt a part of the reason for the influence of the Finance Committee leadership in this regard is that, since the ranking members will take the bill to conference, amendments they disfavor will likely be dropped anyway.

Unlimited debate is possible in the Senate due to the smaller size of the body — less than one-fourth the size of the House. Moreover, because basic tax policy is not generally formulated in the Senate initially, debate can often concentrate on more technical and less interesting subject matter, no doubt tending to shorten it considerably.

[95] *See* J. Pechman, *supra* note 79, at 41.

[96] *See* R. Blough, *supra* note 82, at 81–86.

that many tax loopholes are added due to the lack of it [97] — there is constant reliance on Treasury and Joint Committee staff expertise. Further, while major policy decisions are made by committee members, the mere attempt to eliminate ambiguity in drafting bills involves "the necessity for making policy refinements that are not clearly covered in the Committee's decision." [98] This in turn suggests that whether Congress explicitly delegates power to experts or not, experts will of necessity be making those decisions which committee members initially, and members of Congress ultimately, do not insist on making for themselves. The extent to which this factor of "automatic delegation" operates is further enhanced by the fact that most major tax legislation originates in recommendations coming not from the congressional tax committees, but from the executive administration, where the role of Treasury experts is once again conspicuous.[99]

In light of this process of automatic delegation, it becomes relevant to inquire what sorts of decisions the present tax legislative process encourages Congress to insist on making for itself through the tax committees. The answer is not comforting to traditional notions of democratic representation, for all constituent pressure [100] and almost all testimony presented at hearings [101] is directed for or against specific, often highly technical provisions of pecuniary interest to special groups. The public interest is represented only by a staff of nonelected experts from the Treasury.[102] In this atmosphere, where the average constituent is unlikely to appreciate the merit of positions taken by his elected representative, the system is placing enormous reliance on the extent to which a relatively small number of congressmen who sit on the tax committees are motivated to act in the public interest. While they may often be so motivated, a number of

---

[97] *See, e.g.*, 115 CONG. REC. H6975 (daily ed. Aug. 6, 1969) (remarks of Representative Anderson):

> [M]any of the inequities that have crept into our Tax Code . . . have taken place because of [unlimited Senate debate]. We might be far better off today if we had tax laws that had been carefully drafted by the Finance Committee . . . and were not subject to the kind of Christmas tree decoration . . . that has taken place on so many occasions . . . .

[98] R. BLOUGH, *supra* note 82, at 74.

[99] The role of Treasury expertise in the preparation of tax legislation and accompanying committee reports also suggests the absurdity of judicial insistence on de novo determinations of questions of tax law in disregard of Treasury regulations. There is little reason for relying on Treasury prepared committee reports and not Treasury promulgated regulations interpreting the statute.

[100] *See* R. BLOUGH, *supra* note 82, at 32.

[101] *See* p. 1711 *supra*.

[102] *See* R. BLOUGH, *supra* note 82, at 42. *See also* Surrey, *supra* note 46, at 1158–60.

factors have combined to produce a situation in which these few congressmen, and consequently the taxing process itself, have become insulated from the need to respond to political pressure for basic reform in the public interest. First, due to the tremendous amount of pressure from special interest groups to which members of tax committees are continually subject, there is a tendency to appoint individuals from "safe districts"; that is, individuals who it is anticipated will be rather routinely reelected notwithstanding unpopular positions they may have to take on special tax matters.[103] Regrettably, committee members insulated from the need to respond to special interest group pressure are a fortiori insulated from a need to respond to political pressure from the unorganized public whose interest they in theory serve. Second, "the tax laws are too complicated, and the consequences of changes too uncertain and potentially far reaching for anyone to intervene effectively without skilled help."[104] In Congress, specialized knowledge with respect to taxation is concentrated in the staff of the Joint Committee on Internal Revenue Taxation, and the members of the staff of that Committee "keep their loyalties exclusively" for the senior members of the House Ways and Means and Senate Finance Committees who comprise the Joint Committee.[105] This exclusive access to necessary expertise results in a further concentration of power in the hands of a few senior members from safe districts. Extreme concentrations of power in these hands serve to accentuate representative imbalance in two ways. First, it grants disproportionate power to older, often unrepresentatively conservative men. Second, it enhances the power over issues of national concern of congressmen accountable only to regional constituencies with often unrepresentatively parochial interests.[106] It has been suggested, moreover, that the continued need to compromise specific provisions and to forestall unwanted change leaves senior committee members little time to examine questions of basic tax policy,[107] which is theoretically the appropriate congressional function.

Yet if the preceding discussion of the tax legislative process has iconoclastic implications, the icon need merely be an outdated conception of the democratic congressional function in tax lawmaking, not the function itself. A more modern approach to the proper role for Congress in the taxing process requires enthu-

---

[103] *See* Surrey, *supra* note 46, at 1156.

[104] Mansfield, *The Congress and Economic Policy*, in THE CONGRESS AND AMERICA'S FUTURE 121, 138 (D. Truman ed. 1965) [hereinafter cited as TRUMAN].

[105] *Id.*

[106] *See generally* Huntington, *Congressional Responses to the Twentieth Century*, in TRUMAN, *supra* note 104, at 5, 12–16.

[107] Mansfield, *supra* note 104, at 138.

siastic exploitation, not grudging acceptance of the essential role of expertise. This in turn requires recognition that the congressional function has already shifted from legislation to ratification of committee responses to administration initiatives.[108] Since both the executive branch and congressional tax committee already rely heavily on the nonelected expert, more expansive delegations of power to the Treasury would not be open to substantial attack as undemocratic. While it is true that the current Treasury contribution to the content of tax rules is subject to congressional review, an explicit delegation of rulemaking power need not omit this control. Indeed, if the democratic primacy of Congress is not itself to be submerged in a quagmire of undigested fact, the congressional function in regard to tax legislation must undergo the further shift from ratification of committee action to supervision of administrative rulemaking. Not only do congressional attempts to fashion tax legislation out of whole cloth often fly in the face of the need for continued expert administration and rapid responses to developing problems in the course of that administration,[109] but also because of the existing tax committee structure, they do not even assure legislation which is responsive to broadly felt public needs. It follows that a solution to the problem of allocating tax legislative functions in something close to an optimal fashion requires broader delegations of authority to the Treasury, and closer congressional scrutiny of Treasury lawmaking functions.

It is genuinely impossible to suggest a principle which will in each case yield the correct decision as to whether resolution of controversy should be delegated to the Treasury or attempted through the existing tax legislative process. The democratic responsibility of Congress to decide legitimately disputed questions of basic policy [110] provides an approach, but the definition of basic policy is inherently elusive. To the extent the term refers to issues affecting large numbers of people, it can be defined only in terms of degree; to the extent it refers to the intensity of feeling aroused by the issue, the problem of measurement may be added to that of definition. But since at any given time, law must be made by some institution, at a minimum it is fair to say that so long as Congress is in fact failing to decide questions, thus in effect delegating their resolution — to the courts under the current system [111] — the relative abilities of courts and Treasury to decide questions of tax

[108] *See* Huntington, *supra* note 106, at 22–23.

[109] *See, e.g.*, Note, *supra* note 77, at 280 (broader delegations to the executive branch are necessary if quick countercyclical fiscal responses to economic activity are to be made).

[110] *See* Jaffe, *supra* note 75, at 593.

[111] *See* p. 1702 *supra*.

law invariably suggests a delegation to the Treasury of undecided questions. Furthermore, to the extent that Congress legislates on tax subjects so technical that the operative decisions are actually being made by technicians behind the scenes, an explicit delegation, subject to more stringent oversight, is preferable. Delegation in this situation would reflect a more nearly optimal use of scarce institutional time by permitting the Treasury to experiment with various approaches to the problems involved, leaving Congress free to focus on asserted dislocations resulting from specific provisions in actual operation. Additionally, it would permit more general statutes enunciating basic policy, however defined, more clearly. Finally, it would at least offer the possibility of isolating taxing decisions from a political arena overdominated by special interest group pressure.

In establishing a system of delegated authority, however, the substantial problem remains that Congress characteristically responds to strong differences of opinion within its membership by failing to act,[112] a fact which flows from the need to align not merely a majority of congressmen, but a series of majorities in various committees of both Houses if affirmative action is to be taken.[113] Since a delegation requires affirmative action, Congress may not delegate rulemaking power precisely when it should. Consequently a viable solution to the problem of allocating tax lawmaking functions optimally may require that Congress confer a general interstitial rulemaking power upon the Treasury, much like that now contained in section 7805, before it is faced with a particular problem with which it is not prepared to deal. But any meaningful resort to use of such a power would require a recognition on the part of Congress, Treasury, and courts alike that lawmaking power, not merely power to "interpret" the statute, was in fact being delegated.

Broader delegations of authority by definition involve more important policy issues, and thus suggest more stringent controls of the power delegated. One method of assuring closer congressional scrutiny of Treasury regulations would be a "laying plan" such as that used in Britain.[114] The statute delegating power to

---

[112] *Cf.* J. PECHMAN, *supra* note 79, at 30–31.

[113] Thus, for example, passage of a tax bill requires not only a majority vote on the floors of both houses, but additional majorities in the House Ways and Means, House Rules, and Senate Finance Committees. As a practical matter it often requires no more than two or three, or perhaps even one powerful member's disapproval to bury a provision forever.

[114] *See, e.g.*, Schwartz, *Legislative Control of Administrative Rules and Regulations: I. The American Experience*, 30 N.Y.U.L. REV. 1031 (1955); Carr, *Legislative Control of Administrative Rules and Regulations: II. Parliamentary Supervision in Britain*, 30 N.Y.U.L. REV. 1045 (1955); Note, *"Laying on the Table" — A Device for Legislative Control over Delegated Powers*, 65 HARV. L. REV. (1952).

promulgate regulations could reserve the right of Congress within a specified period of time to invalidate any proposed regulation by joint resolution. Under a variant plan, the statute might require affirmative congressional approval by joint resolution before the regulations could become effective. A joint committee, perhaps a newly constituted Joint Committee on Internal Revenue Taxation, provided with an adequate staff, could screen regulations and make recommendations to Congress.[115]

Alternatively, and perhaps preferably,[116] continuous watch could be kept through a joint committee staff on Treasury regulations in actual operation. This method would avoid requiring a congressional staff to undertake the formidable and somewhat redundant task inherent in the "laying" procedure of attempting to second guess the Treasury in identifying potential problem areas before the regulations had gone into effect. The easiest way to keep watch would be to concentrate staff oversight on the most heavily litigated areas, litigation being symptomatic of systemic inefficiency from the inability of taxpayers to predict consequences.[117] Even if it is assumed that nothing approaching complete oversight of Treasury rulemaking could be provided in this way, special interest groups would no doubt continue to inform Congress of what they considered to be inequities in the law, thus permitting concentration of staff oversight on regulations affecting unorganized groups, including the least organized group of all: individual taxpayers.[118]

It is true that a system of legislative supervision of agency lawmaking contains the potential for ill-considered, ad hoc congressional invalidation of regulations, but that is present now.[119] It would be far more efficient, moreover, for members of Congress to examine inequities complained of by constituents in light of

---

[115] This is not a new suggestion; Roswell Magill proposed something akin to it in 1949. Magill, *The Never Finished Tasks of Federal Tax Revision*, 93 PROC. AM. PHIL. SOC'Y 283, 288 (1949).

[116] Aside from various constitutional difficulties, which are discussed at length in Ginnane, *The Control of Federal Administration by Congressional Resolutions and Committees*, 66 HARV. L. REV. 569 (1953), a "laying procedure" would inevitably permit political clashes to paralyze tax administration if an affirmative resolution were required, and probably would provide no greater check than that of the alternative procedure suggested in text if it involved selective invalidation of regulations.

[117] *See* p. 1700 *supra*. A more elaborate, but far more quickly responsive variant of this plan would be to establish a computerized reporting system. All deficiencies assessed by the Commissioner, and the reasons for each assessment, could be fed into a computer programmed to flag recurrent problem areas.

[118] *See generally* R. BLOUGH, *supra* note 82, at 27–32.

[119] *See generally* Cary, *Pressure Groups and the Revenue Code: A Requiem in Honor of the Departing Uniformity of the Tax Laws*, 68 HARV. L. REV. 745 (1955); Surrey, *The Congress and the Tax Lobbyist — How Special Tax Provisions Get Enacted*, 70 HARV. L. REV. 1145 (1957).

administrative experience than to attempt to assess the potential for asserted inequities by writing the rules to begin with. Indeed, a transition from legislation to examination of purportedly unfair regulations would give recognition to existing congressional priorities which generally favor constituency service.[120]

D. The Treasury and the Regulations Problem — Essential Institutional Reliance and the Need for Responsibility

The arguments advanced in this Note in support of the need for broader reliance on the Treasury as a tax lawmaking institution have been of two major types: those deriving from the nature of our institutional lawmaking pyramid itself,[121] and those deriving from the idiosyncratic strengths and weaknesses of particular institutions in making law on the subject of taxation.[122] While it is true that certain idiosyncratic weaknesses of the courts [123] and of Congress [124] could be shored up through procedural reforms, it is equally true that others could not be. Among the latter are the unique inability of the courts definitively to resolve tax disputes due to the absence of governing principle,[125] and the undesirability of extensive congressional legislation on tax subjects due to the needs for expertise, ongoing administra-

[120] *See* Huntington, *supra* note 106, at 25.

[121] Conclusions flowing from arguments of this type include (1) that self-applying rules are most efficient since they utilize familiarity with operative facts and low cost institutional time found at low levels of the tax institutional pyramid and (2) that since law must be made somewhere within the institutional structure, the inquiry of an institution when called upon to decide a question is properly not whether the question should be decided, but whether it should be decided at a given level of the institutional pyramid. The first conclusion implies rulemaking is preferable to adjudication. The second combined with the first suggests explicit congressional delegation to the Treasury rather than implicit delegation to the courts.

[122] Several examples of idiosyncratic weaknesses of Congress are the representative imbalance inherent in the committee structure, and the large number of members. Additional idiosyncratic weaknesses of the courts include the large number of courts of original jurisdiction and of appeals, and the long time lags between the origin and resolution of conflict.

[123] For example, the long delays in tax litigation might be shortened by the creation of a court of tax appeals. *See generally* Griswold, *The Need for a Court of Tax Appeals*, 57 HARV. L. REV. 1153 (1944). Additionally, delay in the resolution of conflict over regulations might be shortened by amending the Supreme Court's rules to add conflict between a judicial decision and a Treasury regulation as a ground for the grant of certiorari. *See, e.g.*, Paul, *supra* note 50, at 684; Griswold, *supra* note 50, at 419.

[124] For example, the problem of representative imbalance might be eliminated by abolishing the seniority system; a step of lesser magnitude would be to give all members of the taxing committees free access to information by giving them seats on the Joint Committee on Internal Revenue Taxation.

[125] *See* pp. 1705–07 *supra*.

tion, and rapid responses to developing problems in the course of that administration.[126] Thus, despite its current weaknesses, the Treasury is the only existing institution capable of playing the predominate role in an optimum tax lawmaking system, even assuming all other institutions function optimally.

Basic reform of the taxing process must therefore begin with basic reform of the Treasury's role in it. There can be little argument but that the Treasury has sometimes in the past preferred the role of unpredictable party litigant to that of responsible lawmaker.[127] But a good many of its irresponsible past practices, such as failing to issue regulations[128] and attacking its own regulations in court once issued,[129] can be traced directly to the lack of respect shown Treasury regulations by courts, and consequently by taxpayers, and the failure of Congress to rectify the situation.[130] This is not to suggest the Treasury does not bear a part of the blame. In the debt-equity area, to mention but one example, a policy of selective allowance of interest deductions enunciated in clear regulations was no doubt within the power of the Treasury all along.[131] Hopefully, though, a recognition by Congress and courts of the Treasury's status as an administrative agency with legislative rulemaking power would go far toward restoring lost confidence and resulting lost initiative.

Indeed, given appropriate precautions, the Treasury might prove as well to be a clear voice for the public interest audible above the din of special interest group spokesmen. While it seems safe to assume that roughly the same resources would initially be expended to influence the content of a given rule whether the content were to be determined in Congress or in the Treasury,[132] several factors suggest the problem of over-responsiveness to organized pressure might be mitigated in the Treasury. First, the Treasury has traditionally assumed a posture hostile to special

---

[126] *See* p. 1715 *supra.*

[127] *See* Eisenstein, *supra* note 33, at 524.

[128] *See* note 131 *infra.*

[129] *See* Eisenstein, *supra* note 33, at 508.

[130] *See id.* at 506–07.

[131] Such a regulation, operating exclusively to the benefit of taxpayers, could not have been attacked by them even if technically beyond the "interpretive" power conferred by section 7805 as currently construed by the courts. *See* p. 1704 *supra.*

[132] The amount a group will be willing to expend in order to influence the content of rules may be expected to vary directly with the strength of its interest in that content and the prospects it perceives for the success of its lobbying efforts. This suggests that unless a group anticipates a greater chance for successful lobbying efforts in the Treasury, which seems unlikely due to the Treasury's traditional opposition to special interest groups in the tax legislative process, the amount expended will be no greater than had Congress determined to resolve the issue itself.

tax provision proponents in the tax legislative process,[133] and it is not unreasonable to suppose that increased responsibility might reinforce the tendency. Second, since most tax decisions cut across industry boundaries, the Treasury as lawmaker, unlike some other administrative agencies, would more likely be confronted by lobbying coalitions which form and disperse ad hoc than by the type of continuous concerted industry group pressure which might be expected to pose the most serious control problems. Third, while it is not necessarily in the congressional interest to investigate and expose unethical practices by congressional lobbyists and fellow congressmen, the same consideration does not obtain when the investigation is to focus upon administrative practices. Finally, it is true that delegation to administrative agencies eliminates the institutional check of the ballot box. But as has been suggested previously, the technicality of tax law [134] and the composition of the congressional tax committees [135] both indicate minimum effectiveness for ballot box control of congressional acquiescence in unreasonable special interest group demands. In fact, it may be the high cost of running for reelection which renders congressmen as receptive to lobbying pressures as they are currently.[136]

The pressure which may be applied by special interest groups is not the only danger inherent in a delegation of increased lawmaking responsibilities to the Treasury. In the past "there has perhaps at times been a tendency on the part of the Treasury, when it did not get what it wanted from Congress, to try to reach its goal through an ambitious regulation." [137] But scrutiny of this sort of overreaching is precisely what judicial review would guard against in the optimal tax institutional structure.[138] Moreover, inasmuch as the provisions of the Administrative Procedure Act [139] currently require publication of, and hearings on, pro-

---

[133] *Cf.* Surrey, *supra* note 46, at 1164:

> The question, "Who speaks for tax equity and tax fairness?," is answered today largely in terms of only the Treasury Department. If that department fails to respond, then tax fairness has no champion before the Congress.

[134] *See* p. 1713 *supra*.

[135] *See* p. 1714 *supra*.

[136] *See, e.g.*, P. STERN, THE GREAT TREASURY RAID 295 (1965) (quoting a ranking member of the Senate Finance Committee as admitting that selective support for special tax provisions was "the way we finance our campaigns"); *cf.* D. PEARSON & J. ANDERSON, THE CASE AGAINST CONGRESS 309 (1968) ("most Congressional campaigns have become financed mainly by the special-interests and pressure groups"). *See also* J. DEAKIN, THE LOBBYISTS 98–102 (1966).

[137] Griswold, *supra* note 50, at 407.

[138] *See* p. 1709 *supra*.

[139] 5 U.S.C. § 500 *et seq.* (Supp. IV, 1969). The Administrative Procedure Act, *id.* § 553(b)(3), exempts from the procedural requirements with respect to prior publication and hearings, "interpretive rules, general statements of policy, or

posed Treasury regulations of a "legislative" character, any extension of the Treasury's power to issue such regulations would automatically carry procedural safeguards along with it.

Yet while judicial review, congressional oversight, and the Administrative Procedure Act can guard against flagrant overreaching, irrationality, and acquiescence in special interest group demands, only a responsible and competent Treasury staff can guarantee complete and unambiguous regulations furthering a clear and rational Treasury policy. Whether the present Treasury is capable of performing the task remains to be seen. But the regulations issued under the new section 385 may provide the beginnings of a long sought answer.

---

rules of agency organization, procedure, or practice . . . ." In the past, however, it has been Treasury policy to hold hearings on all proposed regulations.

B. The Tax Base

There is no small measure of irony in the fact that shortly before the publication of Professor Bittker's provocative piece questioning the very existence of a "comprehensive tax base," the Canadian Royal Commission on Taxation (Carter Commission) issued its massive report which, if adopted, would go very far towards the statutory embodiment of the comprehensive base concept. It is altogether fitting, therefore, that this Section should be devoted to an exploration of these two contrasting viewpoints.[a]

The Bittker article gave rise to a vigorous debate which can be found at 81 Harvard Law Review 44–67, 1016–43 (1967–68). The entire discussion, along with some additional comments, has been conveniently reprinted in a paperback, Bittker et al, A Comprehensive Income Tax Base?—A Debate (Federal Tax Press 1968).

3 REPORT OF THE ROYAL COMMISSION ON TAXATION (CANADA) 22–25, 54–57 (1966) *

In order to allocate taxes in accordance with the equity principles we espouse, we must specify a tax base that would estimate consistently the economic power of each individual and family relative to others. There is, of course, a variety of methods by which economic power, the ability to command goods and services for personal use, can be estimated. Some are conceptually pure but impossible to administer; others are readily administered but depart significantly from the spirit of the concept. The problem is to specify a tax base that maintains the integrity of the concept without creating insuperable administrative difficulties.

At a point in time, a person's economic power can be measured by the market value of his net assets. The money he holds and the money he could obtain by exchanging his other assets for money, determines his personal command over goods and services (given prevailing prices).

[a] See also Proceedings, Canadian Tax Foundation 36 (Nov. 1967), for Prof. Bittker's specific comments on the comprehensive tax base recommendations of the Carter Report.

* Reproduced with the permission of the Queen's Printer for Canada. Some footnotes have been omitted.

But this is not a useful measure in our context. If the tax base of each taxable unit were measured by the market value of the unit's assets, excluding human capital,[6] on a given date each year, the units that derived all of their income from personal effort could easily arrange their affairs so that they received and spent large sums between these dates but yet had no marketable assets on these dates. Such a tax-planning prodigal who received employment income could arrange to have little if any economic power on the crucial date if such a measure were used, despite the fact that he had exercised economic power whenever he consumed goods and services during the year. The financial or physical assets of the saver would, however, be taxed year after year.

These problems can be avoided by measuring all changes in economic power over a period of time rather than economic power at a particular point in time. The choice of any time period is inherently arbitrary. The conventional choice is, of course, the calendar year. Using this unit of time, a tax unit's economic power can be measured as the sum of the following:[7]

1. The market value of the goods and services used up by the tax unit during the year to satisfy its own wants (consumption).
2. The market value of the goods or services given to other tax units during the year (gifts).
3. The change over the year in the market value of the total *net* assets held by the tax unit (current saving = change in net worth = change in wealth). This may be either a positive or a negative figure in any time period.

Given our definition of economic power there can be no doubt that item 1, consumption, should be included in the annual tax base. This measures the goods and services that the tax unit actually commanded over the year. The value of gifts made by the tax unit to other tax units, item 2, are included because they represent consumption goods and services the tax unit could have commanded in the year had it chosen not to transfer this command to someone else. The making of a gift is a form of exercise of economic power. Inclusion of item 3, the *change* in the market value of the unit's net assets over the year, would result in

[6] For all practical purposes it is impossible to measure the market value of each man's human capital, that is, the present value of his future net earnings arising from his strength, skill and knowledge.

[7] This is a modification of the definition of income advocated by H. C. Simon, *Personal Income Taxation*, Chicago; University of Chicago Press, 1938, p. 41, following the definition of R. M. Haig.

taking the *change* in the potential command over goods and services after taking into account the command actually exercised during the period.

By taxing in each year the actual consumption plus the change in potential consumption over the year, rather than the potential at some point of time during the year, the tax base given above avoids the valuation of human capital and avoids the repeated taxation of the same net assets year after year. This is not to deny that taxing this base involves taxing additions to assets and also taxing the returns that may later be earned by these assets. By taxing the change in net assets each year, from the beginning to the end of each person's life, the system would succeed in taxing all the tax unit's wealth once, but only once.

It is not suggested that this concept of the tax base should be written into the Canadian taxing statute. For a number of reasons that we discuss in Chapter 8, this concept must be reformulated and modified to arrive at an administratively feasible tax base. But if these practical problems are ignored for the moment, one of the main points we want to make can be seen. The proposed tax base must of necessity take into account all of a person's net gains over the year. All gains, after meeting the expenses necessary to generate them, must be reflected in the base because all of them must be disposed of in one of the three ways we have specified in the tax base. The distinction between wages, interest, dividends, business income, gains on shares, bequests, sweepstake winnings, and so on, all would disappear. Because it encompasses more than the present tax base, we have called our new concept the "comprehensive tax base".

We believe that the comprehensive tax base would measure the relative economic power of individuals and families on a consistent basis. Its very consistency would in fact produce a radical change from the present income tax base. Whether one wishes to consider it as a great broadening of the concept of income or as a fundamentally different tax base is of little consequence. Certainly we do not think that anything is to be achieved in this context by a debate about the meaning of words. It ultimately does not matter whether capital gains, gifts and bequests are or are not called "income". What does matter is that these things increase the economic power of those who are fortunate enough to receive them, and therefore should be taxed like wages, salaries, rent, dividends, interest and so on. If economic power is increased it does not matter in principle whether it was earned or unearned, from domestic or foreign sources, in money or in kind, anticipated or unanticipated, intended or inadvertent, recurrent or non-recurrent, realized or unrealized. When we use the term "income" in the context of the tax system we are proposing, we mean the comprehensive tax base as we have just described it.

Our acceptance of the comprehensive tax base is an implicit rejection of the allocation of taxes in accordance with either wealth or consumption.

* * *

CONCLUSIONS AND RECOMMENDATIONS

NET GAINS FORMULATION

1. We have defined the comprehensive tax base as the market value of goods and services consumed or given away in the taxation year by the tax unit, plus the annual change in the market value of the assets held by the unit. This definition must be reformulated in terms of net gains to make compliance and enforcement possible. Our general conclusions with respect to this reformulation are set out in this chapter, to be developed in more detail in subsequent chapters.
2. Under the net gains formulation, the tax base of each tax unit would include the annual net gains less net losses from the provision of personal services, the disposal of property, the receipt of gifts and legacies, windfall gains, the ownership of property, or any combination of the foregoing.
3. Gross gains can take the form of cash, the acquisition of rights to, and interests in, property, benefits in kind or changes in the value of property held.
4. Expenditures (in cash, or transfers of rights to, or interests in, property) made in the expectation of acquiring a net gain should be deductible from the gross gain in determining the net gain or loss.
5. In the case of transactions between persons not dealing at arm's length net gains and losses should be determined on the basis of fair market value.

PERSONAL EXPENDITURE

6. No personal consumption expenditure should be deducted from gross gains. In particular:
   a) general living expenses should not be deducted as expenses;
   b) the net losses of operating a business should not be deducted from other income if there is no expectation of generating a net gain;
   c) gifts are personal expenses and should not be deducted.

VALUATION OF BENEFITS IN KIND

7. Gross gains that take the form of benefits in kind, rather than cash or rights to, or interests in, property, should be taxed in the same way as other forms of gain. When benefits in kind have an established market value, including them in the tax base is a relatively simple matter; but in many cases there are difficult valuation problems. More stringent reporting requirements for benefits in kind are required, and it will be necessary to adopt arbitrary standards where valuations cannot be made consistently and objectively. We recommend the following general rules:
   a) Ordinarily the recipient of a non-cash benefit should bring into his tax base the market value of the benefit.
   b) It should be assumed that the recipient of the benefit chose it in preference to the cash required to buy the benefit in the market.
   c) When goods and services are received in the performance of one's work the tax base should take into account:
      i) the extra cost of providing goods and services of a greater quantity or better quality than would be purchased by the recipient;
      ii) the reduction in personal expenditures made possible by the consumer goods and services provided by others;
      iii) the extent to which the goods and services were provided to satisfy the individual rather than to produce income.
   d) Where a common facility provides a benefit in kind to several people simultaneously, the value of the benefit should be apportioned among them or a special tax should be imposed on the provider of the benefit.

TRANSACTIONS NOT AT ARM'S LENGTH

8. When the parties to a transaction do not have conflicting interests, the prices at which goods and services are exchanged may provide a gift from one party to another. Because gifts are not deductible to the donor it will be necessary to apply the test of reasonableness to expenses to prevent any element of gift from being deducted. In addition, transactions which take place at other than fair market values should generally be adjusted to prevent the understatement of net gains.

IMPUTED INCOME

9. In principle, the income forgone through the personal use and enjoyment of one's own property and services should be brought into the tax base. Experience in other countries suggests that taxing most forms of imputed income, and in particular the imputed rental income of owner-occupied homes, is impracticable because of valuation problems. To fail to tax imputed income of owner-occupied homes, that is, the income foregone by not renting the house, discriminates against the individual or family that rents accommodation. To allow the deduction of mortgage interest or property taxes would compound this inequity.

REALIZATION OF GAINS

10. To be consistent with the principle of the comprehensive tax base net gains on assets should in principle be brought into income annually, whether the gains were realized or not. This would preclude tax postponement, and if time were provided to pay the tax on the gains, serious liquidity problems could be avoided. Taxing gains on a realized basis allows for tax postponement and may induce holders of property not to realize their gain in order to avoid the tax. Furthermore, if gains were taxed annually, whether realized or not, the postponement of tax through the retention of income in corporations, trusts and mutual organizations would not pose a problem. There would be no reason to collect tax from these organizations except to obtain tax from non-residents and to prevent tax avoidance.

11. We are convinced, however, that the annual valuation of all property is not practical at this time, and therefore, that property gains should be taxed on realization. However, to prevent permanent deferment we recommend that a realization be deemed to occur on making a gift of property or on giving up Canadian residence. In addition, we recommend that a realization be deemed to take place when an individual dies, except in the case of property passing to a surviving member of his family unit. There should also be a deemed realization to a family unit with respect to property which a child takes with him on leaving the unit.

TREATMENT OF INTERMEDIARIES

12. To prevent tax postponement when only realized property gains are taxed we will recommend that the income of intermediaries, such as corporations, co-operatives and trusts,

should ordinarily be taxed at the top marginal personal rate. However, resident tax units should be given a full credit for the taxes collected from the intermediary, when the income of the intermediary is distributed or allocated to them. Accordingly, the tax system would be neutral with respect to the form of business organization, there would be no tax advantage in the retention of earnings, and progressive rates of tax would apply to all income.

BITTKER, A "COMPREHENSIVE TAX BASE" AS A GOAL OF INCOME TAX REFORM *

80 Harv.L.Rev. 925 (1967).

SINCE World War II, our ablest commentators on federal income taxation have repeatedly attacked the "exceptions," "preferences," "loopholes," and "leakages" in the income tax provisions of the Internal Revenue Code and have called upon Congress to reverse the "erosion of the income tax base" caused by these "special provisions." It is no exaggeration to say that a "comprehensive tax base" (hereafter CTB) has come to be the major organizing concept in most serious discussions of our federal income tax structure. This theme dominated the *Tax Revision Compendium* published in 1959 by the House Committee on Ways and Means and the hearings based on this collection of papers; it inspired the "optional simplified method" recently proposed by Senator Long; its exploration is a major task of the Special Committee on Substantive Tax Reform of the ABA's Tax Section; it was a major *Leitmotiv* in the responses of economists and others when the Joint Economic Committee in 1965 asked them to comment on the "fiscal policy issues of the coming decade"; and discussions of federal income taxation written for, or by, the nonexpert but interested citizen have brought it to the attention of a wider public.[1]

[1] HOUSE COMMITTEE ON WAYS AND MEANS, 86TH CONG., 1ST SESS., TAX RE-

* Copyright © 1967 by The Harvard Law Review Association. Reproduced with permission.

Some of this discontent with "preferences" and "leakages" has focused on the economic or social shortcomings of the particular provision under discussion; but increasingly a different line of argument has become popular. This approach accepts the rationale advanced in defense of the "preference," at least arguendo, but goes on to assert that equally persuasive arguments may be offered in support of virtually all other "preferences," including many that are still embryonic. Moreover, it is argued, a tax concession is a poor way to distribute a government bounty or to encourage activities that are in the public interest: the value of the concession varies with the beneficiary's tax status, the impact of the program may be erratic and unpredictable, its cost cannot be accurately estimated or budgeted in advance, and its operation is covert rather than open to public inspection and criticism.[2] The only road to a simplified and improved tax structure, it is contended, is to eliminate "preferences" ruthlessly, no matter how persuasive or seductive their individual appeals may be, and to impose the tax on the resulting CTB. The broader base will per-

---

VISION COMPENDIUM OF PAPERS ON BROADENING THE TAX BASE (Comm. Print 1959) [hereinafter cited as 1959 COMPENDIUM]; House Committee on Ways and Means, *Panel Discussions on Income Tax Revision*, 86th Cong., 1st Sess. (1960) [hereinafter cited as *1959 Panel Discussion*]; S. 3250, 88th Cong., 2d Sess. (1964) (Long proposal), *reprinted in* Bittker, *An Optional Simplified Income Tax?*, 21 TAX L. REV. 1, 37–51 (1965); *Report of the Section of Taxation on Substantive Tax Reform*, 90 ABA REP. 289 (1965); Galvin, *Progress in Substantive Tax Reform*, U. SO. CAL. 1965 TAX INST. 1; JOINT ECONOMIC COMMITTEE, 89TH CONG., 1ST SESS., FISCAL POLICY ISSUES OF THE COMING DECADE (Comm. Print 1965); D. BAZELON, THE PAPER ECONOMY 144–68 (1963); J. HELLERSTEIN, TAXES, LOOPHOLES, AND MORALS (1963); P. STERN, THE GREAT TREASURY RAID (1964).

[2] An offsetting advantage of tax concessions is that they leave taxpayers with greater freedom than some governmental programs; it was this, I take it, that led some advocates of a CTB in 1962 to favor the investment credit rather than a subsidy as a means of encouraging economic growth. Another premise that seems to be buried in the CTB approach is that "preferences" are not nullified by the market; a corollary is that the revenue gain to be achieved by eliminating preferences can be estimated without adjusting for changes in the pretax income to be received under the new tax structure.

It is odd that so many economists are advocating a "neutral" income tax base in the classroom at the same time that they are striving to persuade Congress that the income tax should be used as a flexible fiscal tool. This is not entirely a paradox; something can be said for the view that fiscal ends are best accomplished by changing the rate structure rather than the tax base. In the end, however, this effort to distinguish between legitimate and illegitimate fiscal uses of the tax system is likely to founder. Indeed, the 1962 depreciation guidelines and investment credit have been hailed as triumphs of a discretionary fiscal policy, though neither changed the rate structure. *See* Statement of Gardner Ackley, Chairman, Council of Economic Advisers, in *Hearings on Fiscal Policy Issues of the Coming Decade Before the Subcommittee on Fiscal Policy of the Joint Economic Committee*, 89th Cong., 1st Sess., at 3 (1965).

mit rates to be reduced, and with lower rates the benefit to be reaped by the restoration of any one "preference" will be lessened; this will let some of the steam out of efforts to renew the process of "eroding" the base. Alternatively, Congress could tax the augmented base at rates that will produce additional revenue, using the surplus to finance directly the programs that are now covertly financed by tax concessions. In either event, Congress will be willing and able (it is argued) to resist attempts to "erode" the new tax base since it will be armed with an argument — "one exception inevitably breeds another" — that now lacks persuasive force because today's Code is already riddled with "preferences" and "exceptions." [3] The aim, in short, is a reformed Internal Revenue Code with a "correct" tax base, to which all men of good will can and will rally when it is threatened by "exceptions," "special provisions," "preferences," "loopholes," and "leakages."

In trying to come to grips with the CTB approach to income taxation, I have encountered a distressing vagueness in the use of terms like "preference." Sometimes we are offered a goal no more precise than "an income-tax system which refuses special benefits to some taxpayers because their income comes from particular sources, and which taxes alike all dollars of income." [4] Of the more elaborate conceptual frameworks, the following are a fair sampling:

> "[S]pecial Tax Provisions" . . . means any and all provisions of tax law which are designed to afford significant preferential treatment within each of the normal basic taxpayer categories.
>
> . . . .
>
> Thus, this runs the whole gamut of taxpayer differentiation affected by type of entity, size of income, time and nature of receipts and

---

[3] *See* Blum, *Federal Income Tax Reform — Twenty Questions*, 41 TAXES 672, 679 (1963):

> There is nothing about the combination of rate reduction and base broadening which dictates that all preferential provisions be eliminated, but there are potent reasons for leaning over backwards before allowing any of them to remain . . . . [The] existence of any one special dispensation makes it easier to argue on behalf of others. . . . [T]he fewer gaps left in the base, the more rates can be cut without affecting revenue yields. . . . [A] Spartan attitude toward defending the integrity of the base will aid in creating the impression that the reform plan is intended to improve the system as a whole, with the chips falling as they may, and is not calculated to benefit certain identifiable groups possessing political strength.

[4] Paul, *Erosion of the Tax Base and Rate Structure*, in JOINT COMMITTEE ON THE ECONOMIC REPORT, 84TH CONG., 1ST SESS., FEDERAL TAX POLICY FOR ECONOMIC GROWTH AND STABILITY 297, 310 (Comm. Print 1956) [hereinafter cited as 1955 COMPENDIUM]; *see* note 10 *infra*.

expenses, geographical location, age, state of health, and family status.[5]

While theorists may argue about what constitutes preferential treatment, sophisticated taxpayers have not experienced a similar difficulty. Instead they have been guided by this single principle: It is more advantageous to accumulate wealth or enjoy personal consumption in ways calling for the payment of less total income tax than if the savings and consumption were financed only by money received in the form of ordinary income and if that money were spent on consumption or saved only in ways which did not give rise to deductions for tax purposes. There is no reason why we should depart from this realistic principle. Legislation is preferential to the extent it allows any taxpayer to accumulate wealth or enjoy personal consumption without paying the full tax. And the full tax is that which would be due if all of the taxpayer's economic enhancement were financed by cash received as ordinary income and if he did not qualify for any non-business deductions or extraordinary exemptions or credits in the course of saving or spending his income.

The wholly nonpreferred taxpayer thus is the man who receives everything in fully taxable forms, who satisfies his personal consumption and accomplishes his savings in nondeductible ways, and who does not otherwise qualify for special exemptions or credits. To the extent that any taxpayer fares better than this yardstick he is being preferred.[6]

Reference to a tax provision as "preferential" or "special" does not connote opposition to the social or economic objective which Congress has used the tax law to support. It does mean the provision deviates from a norm. Implicit in the reference is the idea that the income tax has an essential integrity; that there is a fundamental standard for determining the tax base and the applicable rates; that maintenance of the standard (restoration where it has been eroded) is important to society, high on its scale of values; that the proponent of a measure which deviates — which creates a preference — has a burden of proof which goes as much to the use of the tax system as the means of accomplishment as to the measure's specific social or economic objective.[7]

---

[5] Atkeson, *The Economic Cost of Administering Special Tax Provisions,* in 1955 COMPENDIUM 276, 279.

[6] Blum, *The Effects of Special Provisions in the Income Tax on Taxpayer Morale,* in *id.* at 251–52.

[7] Wolfman, *Federal Tax Policy and the Support of Science,* 114 U. PA. L. REV. 171, 173 (1965).

To determine the extent of erosion, we must first have some notion as to what the tax system ought to be. Since this is to a large extent a matter of equity, and since equity judgments are highly personal, no single standard will meet everybody's approval. Economists have defined the term "income" as consumption plus (or minus) the net increase (or decrease) in value of an individual's assets during the taxable period. I propose to use this definition with two modifications: First, capital gains will be included in income when realized or when transferred to others through gifts or bequests; second, gifts and inheritances are to be excluded from income. The first of these modifications is made because it is probably impractical to include capital gains in income until they are realized or transferred. The second accepts the present status of estate and gift taxation as separate from income taxation. As a working approximation, this concept of income is equivalent to gross receipts in cash and in kind (other than gifts and inheritances) received by the taxpayer during the taxable period less the expenses necessary for the production of such receipts, plus the net rental value of owner-occupied homes and net capital gains transferred at gift or death.[8]

Most provisions leading to erosion [of the corporate income tax base] . . . represent favorable treatment granted with the intention of promoting objectives deemed to be more important than revenue and equity considerations. The dominant consideration may be to provide an incentive to some highly desirable activity such as defense-plant expansion, to relieve a depressed area or industry such as coal, to help small business, or to remove existing discrimination by extending special tax treatment to comparable industries or types of income. . . .

. . . .

Two standards are used in this paper to identify preferential provisions. First, taxes should be neutral between different types of economic activity. Tax neutrality is used here in the sense that taxes be levied without discrimination and without favor between different forms of income, between different categories of expenditure, and between different industries. . . .

. . . .

Secondly, taxable income in most cases should correspond to commonly accepted business measures of net income consistently followed.[9]

---

[8] Pechman, *What Would a Comprehensive Individual Income Tax Yield?*, in 1 1959 COMPENDIUM 251, 259.

[9] Hellmuth, *The Corporate Income Tax Base*, in *id.* at 283, 284, 285, 286.

Some briefer statements are quoted below.[10]

When writers turn to the task of listing the sources of "erosion," the bill of particulars almost always begins with such exclusions as state and municipal bond interest, sick pay, foreign source income earned by citizens abroad, and social security payments. As the extracts set out above suggest, however, their authors are not exclusively concerned with items that are totally excluded from the tax base. Thus, the concept of "erosion" embraces deductions (percentage depletion), differential tax rates (the long-term capital gain rate),[11] rules relating to timing (postponement by qualified pension plans), and other provisions, regardless of the technical form in which they appear in the Code.

So far as I know, however, no one has attempted to list all the sources of "erosion" to be found in existing law,[12] although the

---

[10] Brazer, in *1959 Panel Discussion* 201: "[I]ncome is essentially equal to the value of rights exercised in consumption expenditure plus the change in one's capital position over the course of the year. Now, you have a loophole under this definition if you allow a deduction or an exclusion that is not justified under the terms of this definition." Sneed, in *id.* at 12: "[E]ach dollar of income to a taxpayer should be fully included in the tax base, irrespective of its source, except where administrative convenience requires otherwise. The Simons definition of income should be used as the ideal." For other statements see Surrey, *The Congress and the Tax Lobbyist — How Special Tax Provisions Get Enacted*, 70 HARV. L. REV. 1145, 1146–48 (1957); Blum, *Tax Policy and Preferential Provisions in the Income Tax Base*, in 1 1959 COMPENDIUM 77, 84; *see* Ture, *The Costs of Income Tax Mitigation*, 49 NAT'L TAX ASS'N PROCEEDINGS 51, 52 (1956); note 86 *infra*.

[11] The relationship of the CTB movement to differential rates is puzzling. Although the tax base might initially be regarded as independent of the rate structure, excluding an item is in effect interchangeable with putting a zero rate on it; and the capital gain provisions disclose a similar link between deductions and special rates. Percentage depletion can also be regarded as a device to moderate the tax rate applicable to a specified type of income. The advocates of a CTB regularly describe the capital gain provisions as a source of "erosion" that must be closed to achieve a CTB, and they sometimes apply the same label to the special rates applicable to joint returns. However, Pechman, *supra* note 8, at 276, calculates the yield of a comprehensive income tax both with and without income-splitting, asserting that this rate issue involves a value judgment that "cannot be resolved on a priori grounds." This may imply that some (but not all) special rates are inconsistent, on definitional grounds, with a CTB, for instance those that differentiate on the basis of the *source* of income, such as the capital gain provisions and the rate reduction applicable to Western Hemisphere Trade Corporations.

[12] The most extensive examination seems to be R. GOODE, THE INDIVIDUAL INCOME TAX 99–152 (1964). In my opinion, as will be seen, Goode's list is not exhaustive. In Pechman's estimates, the references to "all" eroding features were probably intended to refer only to those "leakages" that he was able to quantify. *Erosion of the Individual Income Tax*, 10 NAT'L TAX J. 1, 2 (1957); *What Would a Comprehensive Individual Income Tax Yield?*, in 1 1959 COMPENDIUM 251; *see* p. 929 *supra* for his definitions. Surrey has compiled a list of "principal income exclusions and preferences," but some of its inclusions are as surprising as some of its omissions, and I do not know how vigorously he would defend it. Thus, the ex-

philosophy of "treating all income alike" in order to achieve a CTB, with no seeds from which new "exceptions" can grow, is premised on our ability to identify the provisions to be eliminated. For this task we need more than a compilation of everyone's favorite complaints.[13]

From the rhetoric of the broad base approach to tax reform,[14] one might get the impression that its advocates (or at least the lawyers among them) would compute the taxpayer's gross income by using section 61(a) as a starting point, discarding as

---

clusion of the income of state and local governments is cited, but not the exclusion accorded to the income of tax-exempt institutions. Surrey, *The Federal Income Tax Base for Individuals*, in 1 1959 COMPENDIUM 1, 15. Heller acknowledges that "a consensus on a detailed definition may be difficult to achieve" and addresses himself only to provisions or omissions "which have received considerable attention as inroads on the equity of the income tax." He does not disclose whose blackballs were counted in this election, or how they were weighted; but I judge from his list that the criterion was not one-man, one-vote. Heller, *Limitations of the Federal Individual Income Tax*, 7 J. FINANCE 185, 192–93 & n.14 (1952).

Efforts to compute "effective" income tax rates, as distinguished from nominal rates, are necessarily premised on an "adjusted" taxable income figure, and thus require the author to offer his alternative to the Code's version of "taxable income." Here again, however, I know of no alternative definition that purports to eliminate all "preferences." *See, e.g.*, Musgrave, *The Incidence of the Tax Structure and Its Effects on Consumption*, in 1955 COMPENDIUM 96. For macroeconomic analysis, Musgrave's adjusted "broader income concept" may be adequate, but it would hardly qualify as a no-preference base for taxing purposes. *See also* Musgrave, *How Progressive is the Income Tax?*, in 3 1959 COMPENDIUM 2223; White & White, *Horizontal Inequality in the Federal Income Tax Treatment of Homeowners and Tenants*, 18 NAT'L TAX J. 225 (1965). Attempts by welfare economists to measure "income inequality" also require the scholar to devise an adjusted income base if he thinks that taxable income is a misleading or inadequate concept. *See* STAFF OF JOINT ECONOMIC COMMITTEE, 88TH CONG., 2D SESS., THE DISTRIBUTION OF PERSONAL INCOME 106 (Comm. Print 1964); J. MORGAN *et al.*, INCOME AND WELFARE IN THE UNITED STATES ch. 20 (1962); Lampman, *The American Tax System and Equalization of Income*, 49 NAT'L TAX ASS'N PROCEEDINGS 271, 277–78 (1956).

[13] *See* Blum, *Federal Income Tax Reform — Twenty Questions*, 41 TAXES 672, 691 (1963): "So long as comprehensive reform is only a slogan, referring generally to rate reduction and base broadening, and not a concrete program for action, an assessment of its chances is premature. . . . Until a specific program has been developed, we cannot expect that the merits of the idea will get an adequate airing."

[14] In the absence of an authoritative membership list, I have treated all who profess faith in a CTB as though they were full-fledged members of the club, although I recognize that they may not feel this way about each other. My concern is not to measure degrees of loyalty to the CTB rhetoric, but to see what it means and where it leads. The scholar whose professional work focuses on taxation may brush the rhetoric aside as a crude label for a program, the details of which he can consider on their individual merits. As the no-preference, comprehensive tax base concept moves into the larger world, however, it is bound to lose some of the qualifications that the experts tucked away in footnotes and appendices; and a fortiori it will lack those that were never made explicit.

a "preference" any provision which alters the result that would be reached if section 61(a) stood alone, whether it does so by excluding an item from gross income, by assigning it to a different year or to a different person, or otherwise. Having computed gross income by looking solely to section 61(a), we would then convert it into taxable income by deducting the expenses, losses, bad debts, and depreciation incurred in the taxpayer's business or profit-motivated transactions — but nothing else. A rigorous application of the "comprehensive base" approach, then, seems to imply that sections 61(a), 162, 165, 166, 167, and 212 are the only operative provisions needed for an ideal computation of taxable income.

Another answer to the same question — how can we arrive at a comprehensive base, devoid of all "preferences"? — that is suggested or implied by the commentators, especially the economists, is use of the Haig-Simons definition of income as the touchstone. Haig defined personal income as "the money value of the net accretion to one's economic power between two points of time," a formulation that was intended to include the taxpayer's consumption, and that was thought by Simons to be interchangeable with his own: "Personal income may be defined as the algebraic sum of (1) the market value of rights exercised in consumption and (2) the change in the value of the store of property rights between the beginning and end of the period in question." [15] At times, the "broad base" commentators seem to imply that a "true" or rigorous CTB would be achieved if Congress enacted the Haig-Simons formulation. It is always admitted, to be sure, that valuation difficulties or administrative problems require some departures from the ideal (for example, with respect to unrealized appreciation, imputed income from assets, and domestic services by the taxpayer or his wife); but I take it that these concessions assume that the departure *is* a preference, albeit an unavoidable one. Such concessions, in other words, are adjustments to practicality, rather than an integral part of the definition.[16]

[15] THE FEDERAL INCOME TAX 7 (R. Haig ed. 1921), *reprinted*, READINGS IN THE ECONOMICS OF TAXATION 54 (R. Musgrave & C. Shoup eds. 1959) (emphasis omitted); H. SIMONS, PERSONAL INCOME TAXATION 61–62, 206 (1938). When it came to a program for action, Simons was more latitudinarian than his definition; indeed, he said: "If one accepts our definition of income, one may be surprised that it has ever been proposed seriously as a basis for taxation." *Id.* at 103.

[16] If a concession to practicality is thought to be unavoidable, is it quibbling to call it a "preference" rather than a definitional criterion? I think not, for two reasons: (*1*) Whether practicality requires the concession is always a matter of

Still another criterion that has been tendered as the starting point in achieving a CTB, especially in the last few years, is the concept of personal income as employed by the National Income Division of the Department of Commerce in its national income statistics. Comparisons between the amount of taxable income as reported on tax returns and personal income as computed by the NID are sometimes efforts to estimate the amount of illicit underreporting of items that may be more accurately estimated by the NID than by taxpayers' admissions on tax returns. I detect, however, an incipient tendency to move beyond this use of the NID's conceptual framework, and to hold it up (with some modifications, primarily the inclusion of capital gains and losses and personal contributions for social insurance) as a normative model.[17]

I do not suggest that the advocates of the "broad base" approach have explicitly asserted that the way to extirpate all "preferences" and thus to "restore" the tax base is to repeal all substantive parts of existing law except section 61(a) and the business expense and loss provisions, or to enact the Haig-Simons or National Income Division definition. These seem to me the directions in which they point, however, and I have found in their writings no other standards by which "preferences" can be infallibly identified.

Against this background, I have set for myself the task of ex-

---

judgment; thus, to admit that the item is "income" within the Haig-Simons definition invites debate on the possibility of solving the practical problem — a debate which a whole-hearted supporter of a CTB ought to enter with an eagerness to be shown that inclusion *is* feasible. If the concession is buried in the definition, on the other hand, this debate is foreclosed. (*2*) As I will suggest later, one who thinks the item *ought* to be (but for practical reasons cannot be) included in income may want to make other adjustments in the tax base to counterbalance this unavoidable departure from principle.

[17] For the use of NID statistics as a test of underreporting see Holland & Kahn, *Comparison of Personal and Taxable Income*, in 1955 COMPENDIUM 313. For their normative use (explicitly or implicitly) see, *e.g.*, Surrey, *supra* note 12, at 16–17; Cohen, *Substantive Federal Tax Reform*, U. SO. CAL. 1964 TAX INST. 711, 716; Galvin, *supra* note 1, at 3–4; *Resolutions on Substantive Tax Reform*, BULL. ABA SECTION OF TAXATION, July 1963 (Annual Report), at 4, 10 ("it may be that as a matter of equity the spread [between NID personal income and IRC taxable income] should be severely narrowed"); R. GOODE, THE INDIVIDUAL INCOME TAX 6 (1964) (supporters of income tax "are disturbed by special provisions allowing much income to escape taxation, the ingenuity of taxpayers in finding loopholes, the reluctance of Congress to repair the erosion of the tax base, and incomplete compliance with the law. In 1960, for example, the amount of income actually taxed equaled only about two-fifths of total personal income . . . .").

amining the major substantive areas of income tax law to see what changes would be required if our overriding legislative aim is to be a CTB without "preferences," "exceptions," or "special provisions." In some of these areas, CTB commentators have already specified a number of provisions that in their view constitute "preferences," and I have sought by extrapolation from these certified items to identify provisions that are equally deserving of the same label. In other areas, I have had to strike out largely on my own, since the possibility that "preferences" exist in these areas seems to have gone unnoticed.

For reasons that will be set out in more detail hereafter, I have concluded that a systematic and rigorous application of the "no preference" or CTB approach would require many more sweeping changes in the existing tax structure than have been acknowledged. I also believe that many of these changes would be quite unacceptable, despite their conformity to the Haig-Simons definition, to many of those who are attracted, in the abstract, by the idea of a CTB. At the same time, there are in my view many more ambiguities in the concept than have been acknowledged, and at these points it sheds less light than some of its supporters seem to claim. Some alleged "preferences," in other words, are as compatible with the Haig-Simons definition as their elimination would be. Finally, those who continue, in defiance of all experience, to hope for a simplified tax structure in a complex society are doubly deluded, in my view, if they believe that a CTB will make a significant contribution to simplification. Most of our troublesome complexities concern issues that are either independent of the definitional criteria or unavoidable once we accept the departures that even the most committed believers in a CTB accept as desirable or necessary.

I. Exclusions from Gross Income

Because tax differentials among taxpayers based on the *source* of their income are inconsistent with the Haig-Simons emphasis on consumption and net accretions to wealth as the proper measures of income, lists of "preferences" almost invariably begin with items that are now excluded from gross income, such as interest on tax-exempt bonds and social security payments. Indeed, although the concept of "erosion" takes in such tax concessions as deductions, credits, and differential rates, it has at its very core the idea that many items properly belonging in the income tax base have been excluded from it by statutory or administrative fiat. It is appropriate, therefore, to begin with the statutory and other exclusions from gross income in analyzing the implications of a CTB.

A. Social Security, Welfare, and Other Public Transfer Payments

An important theme in the literature of "erosion" is that social security payments are earned by the taxpayer's personal services and increase his wealth just as much as receipts from traditionally taxable sources. Since these payments are not geared to the taxpayer's financial needs, it is argued that their exclusion from gross income is a poor way to protect a minimum subsistence level and that direct public aid to the poor would insure that any given amount of governmental assistance would reach those who deserve it, rather than being wasted on less needy claimants. Including social security payments in gross income (with an adjustment to permit the taxpayer to recover his contributions [18]) along with analogous benefits like railroad retirement and veterans' pensions, therefore, has been a favorite way of "restoring" the tax base.

Social security, railroad retirement, and veterans' benefits are nominated for inclusion in the proposed CTB because they increase the taxpayer's net worth in the Haig-Simons sense and because if excluded they will have a differential value depending on his tax bracket and will not be openly reflected in the federal budget-making process. These characteristics are shared, however, by many other federal, state, and local government benefits, such as soil conservation and reforestation grants, subsidies to attract industrial plants, scholarships and fellowships, aid to the blind and other disabled persons, meals, clothing, and shelter supplied to patients and inmates of hospitals, prisons, and other public institutions, veterans' readjustment allowances, Medicare protection, and unemployment compensation. Some advocates of a CTB are prepared to tax these benefits (and those who eschew this responsibility impair their credentials as consistent enemies of "preferences"); but it must be noted that this route soon

---

[18] The employee's contributions — his tax payments — amount on the average to 10–20% of benefits, and a similar share comes from his employer's tax payments. *See* Deran, *Income Redistribution Under the Social Security System*, 19 NAT'L TAX J. 276, 281 (1966). The balance is often described as a gift from the Government. As suggested below, however, if gifts from private persons are to be excluded from the CTB, it is not clear why the exclusion of gifts from the public would be a "preference."

brings one face to face with the fact that every modern nation — even if it does not call itself a welfare state or a Great Society — provides its citizens with a variety of benefits through programs that involve no transfer of cash or identifiable "property." [19] This means that the "comprehensive tax base" must either measure the benefit derived by the taxpayer from *all* governmental services, or grant a "preference" to those who benefit from indirect government programs.

Thus, to tax the student who receives a federal or state scholarship, while exempting the one who can attend a public institution without charge, is a "preference" — as that term is used by the advocates of a CTB — to the latter; and the same can be said of an exemption for the businessman whose plant is made more accessible and valuable by public improvements while his competitor is taxed on a grant of land which was given him to induce a change of location; of an exemption for the farmer who benefits from a flood control project while his neighbor is taxed when a public agency plants trees on his land to check erosion; and of rental allowances vis-à-vis public or subsidized housing. Other troublesome areas are the services of welfare workers, county agricultural agents, and the like; the net deficit of the postal service; and government guarantees of loans to homeowners and businessmen. Even if we look only to public programs providing benefits that are susceptible to valuation and can be accepted or refused at the recipient's option, a policy of rigorously taxing direct grants would inevitably discriminate in favor of indirect benefits.

To be sure, a decision to tax all direct grants while exempting indirect benefits in order to avoid a valuation quagmire [20] is not

---

[19] Federal subsidy programs aggregating $8.5 billion (excluding veterans' benefits, public assistance, public health and school lunch grants, and aid to Indians) for fiscal 1967 are listed in U.S. BUREAU OF THE CENSUS, STATISTICAL ABSTRACT OF THE UNITED STATES 394 (1966), many of them providing indirect rather than direct benefits to individuals and business firms. *Cf.* R. TITMUSS, ESSAYS ON "THE WELFARE STATE" 44 (1959), arguing that state intervention in the economy in the interest of social policy did not commence in Britain with the "welfare state" of 1948, but with the introduction of progressive taxation in 1907.

[20] *See* MEASURING BENEFITS OF GOVERNMENT INVESTMENTS (R. Dorfman ed. 1965), which assesses the difficulties of measuring the *social* benefits from some public programs; to allocate these benefits, when measured, to individual taxpayers would compound the difficulties, to put the matter mildly. For an attempted allocation to various income classes see Gillespie, *Effect of Public Expenditures on the Distribution of Income*, in ESSAYS IN FISCAL FEDERALISM 122 (R. Musgrave ed. 1965); *see also* Conrad, *Redistribution Through Government Budgets in the United States, 1950*, in INCOME REDISTRIBUTION AND SOCIAL POLICY 178 (A. Peacock ed. 1954); Adler, *The Fiscal System, The Distribution of Income, and Public Welfare*, in FISCAL POLICIES AND THE AMERICAN ECONOMY 359 (K. Poole ed. 1951).

unreasonable; but it would require an admission that the aim of "taxing all income alike" and extirpating all "preferences" had been compromised. And once this is acknowledged, it is only a short step to the conclusion that public policy is not necessarily served by a single-minded effort to tax all grants that *can* be measured, and that it might be better to decide, program by program, which should be taxed and which should be exempt. To take just three examples, the exclusions granted by existing law to combat pay, unemployment compensation, and prizes for notable public achievement may reflect an intuitive sense of fairness or public pride. Assuming the irrationality of this feeling, what is gained by including these items in a tax base that will inevitably exclude a host of noncash benefits under public programs?

For a fully committed enemy of "preferences," governmental benefits belong in the CTB even if the recipient must pass a means test to qualify; thus, the exclusion allowed by existing law for public assistance is a hidden subsidy to local welfare programs, and it creates geographical disparities since it is worth more to the residents of a city that is generous in its welfare allowances or lenient in disregarding outside earnings than to those whose city is more strict in these respects. Pechman, for example, would include such payments in the tax base, relying on the personal exemptions (raised above the existing level, if necessary) and on increases in the welfare payments themselves to prevent the income tax from encroaching on the taxpayer's ability to feed, clothe, and house himself.[21] Even if every welfare recipient received a federal subvention precisely equal to the tax burden resulting from including his welfare payments in his gross income, I presume that this reform would be viewed as an improvement over existing law by a thoroughgoing enemy of "preferences" because it would bring the federal grant into the open and compel it to pass through the budgetary process. Some advocates of the CTB may falter at this point,[22] opening themselves to the charge of being "soft on preferences"; but even they, presumably, would favor including welfare payments in gross income if, as with social security payments, the recipient is not subjected to a means test. If so, they

[21] Pechman, *Erosion of the Individual Income Tax,* 10 NAT'L TAX J. 1, 12–14 (1957).

[22] L. Shere, Federal Tax Revision To Promote Economic Growth and Stability 10 (mimeo 1956), *reprinted, Hearings on 1957 Economic Report of the President Before the Joint Economic Committee,* 85th Cong., 1st Sess. 424 (1957), offers a list of objectionable exclusions that is identical with Pechman's, save for public assistance.

may reach the same practical result as Pechman (despite their rejection of his logical rigor) as the means test comes increasingly to be rejected as degrading and self-defeating in the administration of welfare programs.

In the foregoing discussion, I have accepted arguendo the theory that public assistance, veterans' benefits, scholarships and free tuition at public educational institutions, and the like are "subsidies" in their entirety and that social security payments are "subsidies" to the extent that they exceed the recipient's OASI payments. This premise is not unassailable, however; its validity depends upon the kind of cost accounting one chooses to use. If we take account of *all* taxes paid by the recipients of these public programs over their lifetime, it may be that they pay *in full* for what they get. Another possibility is that the price they pay cannot be estimated with reasonable accuracy; and that the case for excluding the benefits from income in order to make sure that the recipients are not taxed on a return of their contributions is as good as the case for treating the benefits as "subsidies." The CTB is to take no account of police, fire, and military protection, I assume, because there is no feasible way of comparing the taxpayer's benefits with his payments.[23] In the case of public assistance and social security, the cash receipts can be measured, but it takes an act of faith to come to a firm conclusion about the amount paid by the recipient for these benefits. Perhaps the exclusion of these items does not "erode" the base after all.

B. Charity and Other Private Transfer Payments

Government agencies were not the first to distribute welfare benefits, nor have they yet preempted the field. If grants from the public treasury to needy persons are to be included in gross income, is there any justification for permitting gifts by charitable institutions (which, in any case, are increasingly viewed as having a quasi-public status) to be excluded? If veterans are to be taxed on their G.I. benefits, can an exclusion be justified for scholarships

---

[23] Perhaps the rationale is that the "recipient" of police, fire, and military protection is society, not its individual members. In the case of public elementary and secondary school education, it might again be argued that the "recipients" of the expenditures are not the school children or their parents but society as a whole. (But Gillespie, *supra* note 20, at 146, allocates expenditures for education to school children.) Perhaps the same can be said of free college and university education. If so, what is the predicate for the conclusion that welfare, unemployment compensation, and social security programs provide individual, rather than social, benefits?

and fellowships awarded by Harvard or the Ford Foundation? If welfare checks are to be included in income, why not the amounts received by the *New York Times*'s Hundred Neediest Cases or the beggar on the streets? I presume that the CTB is to include charitable grants of all types in gross income, but I do not recall any explicit discussion of the issue; and I suspect that some who are attracted by the CTB concept will not be happy if it taxes private charity along with public transfer payments.

Workmen's compensation, military disability benefits, and sick pay, which are included in Pechman's list of unwarranted welfare-oriented exclusions, substitute for or supplement the taxpayer's wages when his earning capacity has been impaired by illness or accident; but these are not the only sources of such assistance. Existing law also excludes amounts received as damages for personal injuries in automobile and industrial accidents, payments under accident and health policies, and similar receipts. The ABA Committee on Substantive Tax Reform (in conjunction with its study of proposals to "broaden the tax base" by "including in gross income items not now included") recently asked the Treasury to estimate the revenue effect of including items of this type in gross income "to the extent that such amounts are in the nature of replacement of income rather than recovery of capital, with provision, however, for tax free recovery of cost of such items." [24] The terms of this inquiry imply that such receipts might continue to enjoy an exemption if they compensate the taxpayer for medical expenses, pain and suffering, and loss of limb or bodily function but not if they compensate him for loss of earnings or, perhaps, for a diminution in his earning capacity.

Aside from difficulties in administering this distinction, especially as respects lump-sum settlements of tort claims, it cannot be easily reconciled with a "no-preference" tax base. If the deduction for extraordinary medical expenses in existing law is a "preference," why is not the proposed tax-free recovery of medical expenses from a tortfeasor also a "preference"? In the same vein, if existing law is "eroded" by the extra 600 dollar exemption for the blind (and if, as argued, it would be preferable to bring assistance to the blind out into the open by direct government subsidies to those who need financial aid), is it not equally a "preference" to exempt the damages received by a blind taxpayer from the tortfeasor who caused his misfortune? If the pain

[24] *Report of the Section of Taxation on Substantive Tax Reform*, 90 ABA Rep. 289, 292–93 (1965).

of daily labor and the exhaustion of the taxpayer's body during his occupational career are not to be reflected in any tax concession, is it not a "preference" to exempt the compensation he may receive for pain and suffering or permanent injury caused by an automobile or industrial accident? The ABA Committee's request for a Treasury estimate does not mention the miscellaneous personal injury recoveries that are excluded by administrative practice or case law rather than by explicit statutory provisions (for instance, damages for libel of personal reputation); but a rigorous attack on "erosion" would, I presume, nullify these exclusions as well.

Here again, I suggest that a CTB devoid of "preferences" has ramifications that have seldom been explicitly acknowledged and that will be repellent to many persons who are attracted by the rhetoric of the broad base approach.

C. *Personal and Dependency Exemptions*

Although conditioned on the taxpayer's family status rather than on the source of his income, the personal and dependency exemptions "erode" the tax base on a grand scale. The 64 million individual income tax returns filed for 1963 claimed 183.5 million exemptions, removing 110 billion dollars from taxable income and thus reducing tax revenue by about 18.8 billion dollars.[25] If the purpose of the exemptions is to protect a minimum level of subsistence against income taxation, the unvarying allowance of 600 dollars for the taxpayer, his spouse, and each dependent is objectionable because much of the benefit goes to persons who are above the specified plateau. A "vanishing" exemption — diminishing rapidly for income above the subsistence level — or a credit of a fixed amount would be free of this defect; [26] but even a vanishing exemption or a credit would perpetuate another feature of the personal exemption: it is "inefficient" by welfare standards because it can be claimed by wealthy persons who are only temporarily in low brackets, as well as by the children and other dependents of high bracket taxpayers.[27]

---

[25] U.S. INTERNAL REVENUE SERVICE, STATISTICS OF INCOME — 1963: INDIVIDUAL INCOME TAX RETURNS 30 (1966).

[26] *See generally* M. LEVY, INCOME TAX EXEMPTIONS (1960); Note, *A Proposed Flexible Personal Exemption for the Federal Income Tax*, 18 STAN. L. REV. 1162 (1966).

[27] Perhaps an averaging system could be devised to prevent wealthy taxpayers with fluctuating incomes from getting "unnecessary" exemptions, but this would take some ingenuity. As to children and other dependents of high bracket

Since the advocates of a CTB argue that a direct government subsidy to the needy is preferable to the tax concessions of current law for taxpayers who are blind or over sixty-five, receive social security payments, or incur extraordinary medical expenses or casualty losses, one would expect them to ask that the personal and dependency exemptions also give way to federal public assistance to qualified persons. This expectation is borne out by their criticism of the extra exemptions allowed taxpayers who are over sixty-five or blind; [28] but they appear to accept the personal and dependency exemptions as an appropriate way of preserving a minimum level of income from encroachment by the tax. Yet if we convert the 183.5 million personal and dependency exemptions claimed for 1963 into a hypothetical federal subsidy of 18.8 billion dollars, it can hardly be disputed that the circle of persons to whom Congress would be prepared to allocate this subsidy would overlap only in part the circle of taxpayers claiming the exemptions.

For this reason, one might have expected the advocates of the CTB to argue that it is inconsistent with their approach to exempt entirely a family with three children having 3,699 dollars of income, if indigent families of this size are getting only (say) 2,500 dollars of public assistance. Why not tax the first family, and let Congress appropriate — as part of the open budgetary process — such "subsidies" as are appropriate to aid *all* needy families (including the 3,699 dollar family, if the imposition of an income tax pushes it below the subsistence level)? The arguments that

---

taxpayers, exemptions could be denied to them if we taxed family units as aggregates; but unless this (or the abolition of all personal exemptions) is a necessary concomitant of a CTB, it seems to follow that the CTB is thought by its supporters to be compatible with these "unnecessary" exemptions.

[28] *E.g.*, Shere, *supra* note 22, at 9, *Hearings*, *supra* note 22, at 429:

> Unfortunately the blind are only one of many disability groups that suffer from handicaps in life. Chronological age is not a satisfactory measure of fitness, and fitness is not an acceptable measure of taxable capacity under the income tax. . . . The benefits under . . . [the social security] system can be better adjusted to meet some rational standard than can the hidden benefits under the graduated income tax which are progressively scaled to income. The public would be in a better position to evaluate the sum total of benefits that are desirable for older and disabled persons if they were kept together in one place under the social security system . . . .

Pechman, *supra* note 21, at 19, adduces a different objection to these exemptions: "The aged and the blind would have a valid claim for an additional exemption if it could be shown that they are required to spend more out of a given income than other taxpayers. There are no data on the expenditures of the blind, but the available evidence indicates that a family headed by an individual over 65 years of age does not on the average spend more than other families in the same income group."

are adduced against the exclusion of public assistance from gross income seem to me equally applicable to the exemptions. Conversely, if the welfare function of the personal and dependency exemptions is compatible with a comprehensive tax base even though their benefits are "inefficiently" distributed, other welfare-motivated tax allowances (like the exclusion of unemployment compensation and social security benefits) can hardly be opposed on the ground that the tax law is the wrong forum for advancing social ends. Here again, I do not suggest that all preferences must be preserved if any are preserved, but only that we will not make much headway by unwarranted claims of logical rigor.

The exemptions are sometimes defended as devices for keeping unproductive tax returns off the administrative rolls, rather than for protecting a minimum subsistence level from taxation. This aim might account for the taxpayer's own exemption, but it does not explain those allowed for his wife and dependents; and it would suggest a "vanishing" exemption or credit rather than a constant amount that can be claimed even though the return is above the nuisance level and must be filed and audited in any event. Moreover, with the advent of the withholding system, administrative convenience became a less tenable ground for exemptions of any kind. Many taxpayers whose taxable income is completely offset by their exemptions must file returns to obtain refunds of withheld taxes; and these unproductive returns are thus part of the administrative load in any event. And now that we have automatic data processing, it may be less costly and troublesome to keep *all* potential taxpayers on the rolls at all times than to search annually for nonfilers to make sure that they are not subject to tax.

Another rationale for the exemptions is that they adjust the tax burden to the taxpayer's familial responsibilities. (They do this only at low levels of income, of course; for taxpayers in the middle or upper reaches, the 600 dollar exemption bears no sensible relationship to the cost of maintaining a wife, child, or other dependent.) But if the reduced rates applicable to taxpayers filing joint, head-of-household, and surviving spouse returns are objectionable because family expenses are costs of living that should be defrayed from after-tax income — as contended by some proponents of a CTB — the exemptions allowed for the taxpayer's spouse and dependents would seem objectionable for the same reason.

Finally, exemptions are the principal source of progressivity at low brackets and can be viewed as the equivalent of a zero rate of tax on the bottom bracket. So viewed, are exemptions consistent with a CTB? In one sense, yes; one might rationally argue for a CTB coupled with a rate schedule that (for example) imposed a zero rate on the first 25,000 dollars of income and a fifty percent rate on amounts above that level. But when a zero rate is imposed on amounts that vary with the size of the family and that are regularly discussed in terms of subsistence-protection (sometimes by advocates of the CTB themselves, in proposing an increase in exemptions to offset the burden resulting from taxing welfare and other transfer payments [29]), it seems to me that the "welfare" function of the exemptions is paramount. If so, the "nonbudgeted subsidy" argument of the CTB enthusiasts is not easily reconciled with preservation of the personal exemptions.

D. Proceeds of Life Insurance

If the war on preferences compels us to include in gross income the amounts received by a deceased wage-earner's family under the federal social security system, I suppose it also requires us to tax anything the family may receive from a tortfeasor for their decedent's wrongful death: in both cases, the payments increase the family's net worth and replace wages that would have been taxed as earned. At this point, however, consistency requires the advocates of a CTB to reconsider their apparent tolerance of section 101(a)(1), which excludes the proceeds of life insurance paid on the death of the insured. This is no doubt an unpalatable suggestion, but there is unfortunately no way to be comprehensive except by being comprehensive.

Death benefits of 4 to 5 billion dollars are received annually by the beneficiaries of life insurance policies, and almost all of this amount "leaks" from the income tax base through the exclusion of section 101(a)(1), although it comes within the Haig-Simons concept of income. To the extent of the policy's cash surrender value (if any), this "preference" bears a resemblance to the exclusion of gifts and bequests from gross income; but the theory that the income tax exclusion merely compensates for a federal

[29] *See* Pechman, *supra* note 8, at 267:

> The exemptions in effect provide a zero rate for that part of an individual's income which is below the minimum levels. Apart from the obvious humanitarian reasons, this zero rate is supported on the ground that taxation below the minimum levels will reduce the health and efficiency of the lowest income strata of the community and will eventually result in lower economic vitality, less production, and possibly higher Government expenditures for social welfare purposes.

gift or estate tax burden is flimsy. Decedents' estates filing taxable federal estate tax returns in 1963 included only about eighteen percent of the life insurance death benefits paid in 1962,[30] and the gift tax is even less of an obstacle to the tax-free transfer of life insurance. Moreover, some insurance proceeds are received in a business setting — for example, "key man" insurance — where the analogy to a bequest is not persuasive.

The inclusion of life insurance savings (imputed interest on the terminal reserve or increases in the cash surrender value) in gross income would be a palliative but not a corrective, since it would not affect pure term insurance, payments under double indemnity and other accidental death clauses, or mortality "gains" resulting from early death.[31] These payments (for instance, death benefits of 50,000 dollars under flight insurance purchased for a few dollars at an airport) are similar to gambling profits: without making the nation richer, they transfer wealth from long-lived insureds to the beneficiaries of short-lived insureds.

Let me make clear that I am not advocating the inclusion of life insurance proceeds in taxable income. I am simply recording my conviction that the exclusion of these receipts is a "preference" as that term is used by the advocates of a CTB, that it may promote the purchase of life insurance just as percentage depletion encourages the discovery and draining of oil wells, and that it invites the exclusion of other items that are functional substitutes for insurance. If I am wrong in thinking that the war on preferences requires repeal of section 101(a)(1), however, why do its com-

---

[30] Life insurance included in 1963 taxable returns totaled $680 million; death benefits paid in 1961 and 1962, the years of death for estate tax returns filed in 1963, were $3,581 and $3,878 million respectively. U.S. INTERNAL REVENUE SERVICE, STATISTICS OF INCOME — 1962: FIDUCIARY, GIFT, AND ESTATE TAX RETURNS 51 (1965); INSTITUTE OF LIFE INSURANCE, LIFE INSURANCE FACT BOOK 1966, at 37. Part of the amount included as "life insurance" in tax returns no doubt represents values other than death benefits (policy dividends, cash surrender values of insurance on persons other than the decedent, and so on); if these were taken into account, the proportion of death benefits included in taxable estates to aggregate benefits paid would be even smaller than 18%.

[31] A good deal of attention has been devoted to the "interest" component of life insurance, of course, but the beneficiary's tax-free receipt of the proceeds has elicited less criticism. *See, e.g.*, Irenas, *Life Insurance Interest Income Under the Federal Income Tax*, 21 TAX L. REV. 297, 314–18 (1966); Goode, *Policyholders' Interest Income from Life Insurance Under the Income Tax*, 16 VAND. L. REV. 33 (1962). Vickrey argues that it would be "theoretically correct" to require the beneficiary to report "that part of the benefit which consists of insurance proper, but not that part which is paid from the reserve," the latter being excluded, evidently, as a gift from the policyholder. W. VICKREY, AGENDA FOR PROGRESSIVE TAXATION 66 (1947).

manding generals have so much enthusiasm for repealing section 101(b) (the 5,000 dollar employee death benefit) and for taxing death benefits paid under the social security system?

E. Gifts and Bequests

Both Haig and Simons, who might be regarded as the spiritual forefathers of the CTB, believed that gifts and bequests constituted "income" as they defined the term. The theory that these items should be excluded from gross income because we have separate transfer taxes on gifts and bequests — which take no account of the recipient's other income — was characterized by Simons as "one of the most spurious and naïve types of argument in the literature." [32] To his rebuttal at the theoretical level one might add that only about one-eighth of inherited property finds its way into the taxable estates of decedents subject to the federal estate tax.[33] Most amounts received by bequest, in other words, bear no federal estate tax burden; and for those that do, the death tax burden is often less than the income tax that would be imposed on the recipient if this "leakage" were eliminated. As to gifts, the existence of a federal gift tax is an even weaker reason for excluding them from a CTB. The statistics on inter vivos transfers are fragmentary, but experience tells us that the donor who pays a gift tax is a *rara avis.*

Although advocates of a CTB sometimes call attention to this issue, the dominant mood is acquiescence in existing law. I do not know whether they have steered clear of section 102 (excluding gifts and bequests from gross income) because they think it is a "good" preference or out of political realism. Bunching of income would be a problem, of course, if section 102 were repealed; but the advocates of a CTB almost always favor income averaging rather than an exclusion as the appropriate remedy for this

---

[32] Simons, *supra* note 15, at 126–127.

[33] In the absence of a more authoritative estimate, I offer the following computation. R. LAMPMAN, THE SHARE OF TOP WEALTH-HOLDERS IN NATIONAL WEALTH 1922–56, at 23 (1962), estimates that about 30% of "personal sector wealth" was held in 1953 by "top wealth-holders" (persons with gross estates of $60,000 or more). Let us assume that the wealth owned by top wealth-holders who died in 1953 was 30% of the wealth owned by all 1953 decedents. Federal estate tax returns filed in 1954 reported net estates of $7 billion ($7.4 gross, less debts of $0.4). U.S. INTERNAL REVENUE SERVICE, STATISTICS OF INCOME — 1962: FIDUCIARY, GIFT, AND ESTATE TAX RETURNS 81 (1965). If these returns reflected 30% of the wealth owned by all 1953 decedents, the aggregate wealth transferred by death in 1953 was $23.3 billion (100/30 times $7 billion). Taxable estates aggregated $3 billion, or 13% of the aggregate amount transferred by death.

phenomenon, and sometimes they promise rates so low that timing will be unimportant. There are other reasons for excluding gifts and bequests from the income tax base, such as the distortions in family transfer patterns that would result from efforts to bypass as many generations or intermediate donees as possible, and the difficulties in taxing the beneficiaries of discretionary trusts. These, however, are no more self-evident or compelling — to me, at any rate — than the reasons that led Congress to enact many of the other "preferences" of existing law. Nor can gifts and bequests be excluded from gross income without inviting the exclusion of many other items that share some of their characteristics — scholarships and fellowships, prizes, some employee death benefits, life insurance proceeds, public assistance, social security payments, unemployment compensation, and so on.

F. Support, Dower, and Similar Rights

If a gold digger strikes it rich, would a CTB require the present value of her right to be supported by her wealthy husband to be included in her taxable income in the year of marriage, along with the estimated value of her dower rights? If this mode of improving one's economic status is to be granted a "preference" by being excluded from gross income because of valuation difficulties, should the amount actually spent by the husband on his wife's support be reported by her annually during the continuation of the marriage? As to wives, this refinement would be of little significance *if* the husband were allowed to deduct the amounts included in the wife's tax base (as with periodic alimony under existing law) and *if* the joint return of existing law were preserved in the reformed tax structure; but if support payments "belong" in a CTB, they ought to be accounted for by children as well as by the wife. Absent a "family" return aggregating the income of parents and children, however, the tax structure would be much altered by including support in the taxable base of children and other dependents. And even as to the wife, the advocates of a CTB ordinarily assert that family responsibilities are merely a form of personal consumption that are not legitimately reflected in a tax base — an approach implying that the husband should not be permitted to deduct the expense of maintaining his wife even if she is required to account for the support in *her* income.

A committee of the ABA Tax Section recently recommended that the Internal Revenue Code be amended to provide explicitly that the wife does not realize taxable income "from the acquisition of support rights or dower rights either on marriage, or annually thereafter."[34] Although this proposal merely codifies the administrative practice of the day, it implies that section 61(a) of existing law is broad enough, at least in theory, to require these items to be included in taxable income. Is the ABA proposal one of those "special exceptions" that would "erode" the tax law, to be resisted at all cost lest it serve as a precedent for more "preferences"? I put the question not entirely in a spirit of *Schadenfreude*, because genuine problems *do* arise if support is excluded from a CTB. Support is a next door neighbor of gifts and bequests; if wives and children are not taxed on the support they receive from the head of the family but are required to include gifts and bequests from him in their taxable income, some mighty fine distinctions will have to be drawn. This painful task may be avoided by excluding gifts and bequests, support payments, and life insurance death benefits from the proposed CTB. But the resulting disloyalty to the Haig-Simons definition will then be so monumental that I am baffled by professions of faith in that touchstone when the issue is the proper treatment of other types of transfer payments by individuals, private institutions, and public agencies.

G. Imputed Income from Taxpayer's Assets

The exclusion from gross income, as presently defined, of the net rental value of owner-occupied residences has been a common target of commentators, and some have also criticized the failure to tax imputed income from other assets, for example, the net rental value of household furnishings and the value of bank services provided in lieu of interest on idle balances in checking accounts.[35] Acknowledging that it would not be easy to value these

---

[34] BULL. ABA SECTION OF TAXATION, July 1965 (Annual Report), at 59. Thus far, the ABA Tax Section has not turned its attention to another danger that looms on the horizon if the tax base is broadened to take all economic enhancement into account. I mean the possibility that a wealthy bachelor may realize income on marriage equal to the present value of the tax savings resulting from filing joint returns until his death or divorce. For a calculation of this increase in his net worth see Hellborn, *Uncle Sam's Dowry*, 44 NAT'L TAX ASS'N PROCEEDINGS 310 (1951).

[35] It has been reported that a private bank proposes to provide its depositors with "a highly trained staff that will translate letters and documents, carry out personal secretarial assignments, get theater tickets and travel reservations and advise on investments," in the manner of "an exclusive private club where privileges and services will be extended only to properly sponsored and approved members." The bank would require minimum balances of $25,000 in personal checking accounts and $50,000 in business accounts. N.Y. Times, Aug. 12, 1965, at 29, col. 1.

economic advantages or to enforce compliance, most advocates of a CTB would evidently be satisfied with taxing the imputed rent of owner-occupied residences and willing to exempt imputed income from other assets. I presume that they would agree, however, that this tolerance, even if impelled by the pain and suffering that consistency would require, would "erode" the tax base.[36] I do not know the order of magnitude of the "special exception" that is thus to be granted to the owners of personal property, but it must be at least as substantial as many "preferences" that we are asked to nullify.

H. Income from Vicarious Enjoyment

Under existing law, the income from property transferred by gift is ordinarily taxable to the donee, not to the donor; but in some circumstances (as with so-called grantor or Clifford trusts), the income is imputed to the donor on the ground that he continues to enjoy it, though vicariously. It is often suggested that the tax base is "eroded" by excessive concessions to donors, and that the income thrown off by transferred property, family partnerships, and the like should be taxed to the donors whenever they vicariously enjoy it, not merely in the limited circumstances defined by existing law.[37] As the expression of an attitude, this is all very well; but it hardly constitutes a program for reform. Is it proposed that a taxpayer who makes a gift of stock to his ten year-old son be taxed on the dividends even if they are accumulated in a bank account rather than spent currently? — even if the parents are divorced and the mother rather than the taxpayer gets custody of the child? — even after the child reaches his majority? If the CTB requires inclusion in all these circumstances, what of the income generated by stock (or the reinvested proceeds thereof) that is donated by the taxpayer to adult children, friends, and charitable institutions?

The Haig-Simons definition seems to seize upon *legal* rights rather than vicarious enjoyment as the measure of income; but, as is true whenever we encounter an issue that is worth arguing about, it is sufficiently flexible, or ambiguous, to support either approach.

---

[36] *See* note 16 *supra.*

[37] Of course, the income generated by donated property, transfers in trust, and family partnerships is taxed to *someone*; it does not drop out of the income tax base entirely. Hence the claim that these income-splitting arrangements conflict with a CTB implies that the CTB concept dictates, or helps to determine, the taxpayer by whom a given item of income should be reported. This is, at best, a debatable theory. *See* pp. 974–77 *infra.*

If the CTB is to look solely to the taxpayer's legal rights, it will achieve consistency at the expense of realism, while if it accepts vicarious enjoyment as a determinant of income, it will plunge us into the same morass that the income-splitting practices of existing law create. Unless *all* donors are taxed on *all* income from property transferred by gift, distinctions will have to be based — just as under existing law — on the relationship between the donor and donee, the character of the property, the mode of transfer, and other factors thought to be relevant. No matter where these lines are drawn, they will grant "preferences" to those on the nontaxable side. Here again, there is no formula that will give us a tax base devoid of "exceptions," "loopholes," and "leakages."

I. Miscellaneous Exclusions

If the aim is to eliminate *all* exclusions of existing law so that *all* income is included in the CTB, what are we to do about such tax-exempt persons and institutions as the British ambassador, the Girl Scouts, the local Baptist church, the City of Boston, the Port of New York Authority, the Benevolent and Protective Order of Elks, the Teamsters, the Yale Club of New York City, and so on? There are occasional intimations that some of these exemptions are "preferences," [38] but I know of no authoritative list of those marked for extinction; and I suspect that even the most hardy advocates of a CTB will find reasons for keeping the list rather short. Still, as Blum says, one preference leads to another; [39] there is surely no magic in the line drawn by existing law between exempt and taxable institutions. Conversely, if we can have a CTB even though churches, universities, labor unions, and other socially useful institutions are tax-exempt, I do not see why the CTB is not also consistent with the partial tax-exemption, special deductions, or special rates that are available to cooperative societies, mutual savings banks, insurance companies, Western Hemisphere Trade Corporations, and other organizations. Once these provisions are accepted, in turn, it is but a small

[38] As pointed out in note 12 *supra*, Surrey's list of exclusions and preferences includes § 115, exempting the income of state and local governments. Hellmuth, *supra* note 9, at 312–13, says that "the possibility of including net income of Government-owned commercial enterprises, such as electric powerplants, could be raised." I do not know whether the question to be raised is whether the existing exclusion is a "preference," or whether the "preference" should be eliminated. If the exemption of governmental revenue is threatened by a CTB, I suppose that a fortiori § 501(c) is in jeopardy.

[39] *See* note 3 *supra*.

step to many other "preferences" that we are asked to eliminate in order to achieve a CTB. Thus, if Harvard's investment income is to be exempt from income tax because its activities are socially useful, is it persuasive to assert that a deduction must be denied to contributors to Harvard in order to keep the income tax structure "neutral"? Conversely, if the exemption of state and municipal bond interest is an illegitimate, because hidden, federal "subsidy," what is the proper label for section 115, exempting all income derived by a state or political subdivision from operating a public utility or exercising an essential governmental function? No doubt many if not most of our tax-exempt institutions operate at a loss, but some do not. For these, an exempt status can be predicated only on value judgments of the type that the CTB is supposed to avoid.

II. Personal Deductions

Advocates of a CTB are ordinarily hostile in theory to the personal deductions of existing law, arguing that the taxpayer's disposable income is the ideal tax base no matter how he may choose to spend it. But they do not cleave consistently to this theory. Thus, Pechman would preserve the deductibility of state income taxes to encourage use of these taxes at the state level [40] and to minimize interstate tax differentials, and he favors or would accept deductions for large charitable contributions, extraordinary medical expenses, and major casualty losses.[41] Senator Long's "optional simplified tax method" [42] is more hostile than Pechman's proposal to personal deductions, rejecting all of the "preferences" that Pechman favors or is willing to accept; but it makes its own "exceptions" to the tax base: alimony, bad debts, and section 212(3) expenses. Galvin would preserve the same personal deductions as Pechman (charitable contributions, medical expenses, and casualties) and would add the interest deduction to this list of acceptable "preferences," but only to the extent that these items amount in the aggregate to more than twenty percent of the taxpayer's adjusted gross income.[43] Some other enemies of "prefer-

---

[40] *Cf.* the suggestion that inclusion of interest from state and municipal bonds in the federal income tax base might cause the states to rely more heavily on regressive taxes, in Bronfenbrenner, *Economic Effects of the Taxation of Government Securities*, 35 Ill. L. Rev. 293, 305–07 (1940).

[41] Pechman, *supra* note 8, at 273–74.

[42] S. 3250, 88th Cong., 2d Sess. (1964).

[43] Galvin, *Tax Reform — What? Again?*, 17 Sw. L.J. 203, 219–20 (1963).

ences" find virtually all of the personal deductions acceptable, but want dollar or percentage floors to be established so only extraordinary amounts will qualify; in some cases, they also favor the imposition of ceilings to insure that extraordinary amounts will not qualify if they are *too* extraordinary.

I think it is fair to say of these proposals that they cannot be reconciled with the generalization ("no preferences") that we are often urged to accept as the prime criterion of a sound tax structure. They *can* be reconciled with other criteria, however, which might be verbalized as follows: The base to which the tax rates are to be applied should take account of costly catastrophes in the taxpayer's personal life and should offer him an incentive to make charitable contributions. It should also (some would say) allow him to deduct state income taxes in order to encourage, or refrain from discouraging, the levy of this type of tax by the states. Some other items such as interest and bad debts should be deductible to avoid the abrasive administrative burden of separating those that are business-oriented from those that serve only a personal purpose. Finally, the difficulty of verifying claims for personal expenditures and the fact that all taxpayers incur some items of this type as part of the normal cost of living, justify the imposition of a nondeductible floor on these expenses.

The principles that govern — as distinguished from those that are *said* to govern — the tax programs offered to us by their authors strike me as (*a*) sensible, and (*b*) familiar. I describe these principles as sensible because they involve an examination of each deduction to see what can be said for and against it, and as familiar because they do not depart in any significant sense from the principles embodied in every revenue act since 1913. Many of the proposed changes seem meritorious to me, but they stem from relatively minor differences in judgment; and they do not begin to resemble the dramatic leaning over backward against "exceptions" and "preferences" that is prescribed by Blum as the only posture capable of protecting the tax system against further "erosion." [44] In short, the proposals summarized above would invite — precisely as existing law invites — the proliferation of other personal deductions on the ground that they too deserve a boost from the tax structure or result from unexpected or catastrophic events in the taxpayer's personal life; and they also would invite the same process of refining, elaborating, and individualizing the concept of a "proper" deduction that has resulted in the

[44] *See* note 3 *supra*.

preposterous detail of the charitable contribution and medical expense provisions of existing law. On balance, however, I would prefer to amend or even to retain the personal deductions and face the troubles they inevitably spawn rather than abolish them. Evidently the enemies of "preferences" have come to the same conclusion.

III. The Personal-Business Borderline

Since the ideal of the advocates of a CTB is a tax on "net" income, they retain the distinction between the cost of living, which is not to be deductible, and the cost of *earning* a living. They cannot be blamed for the haziness of this distinction, of course, but they have blithely bestowed the pejorative terms "preference," "erosion," and "special exceptions" in the erroneous belief that the CTB concept is a useful tool of analysis in this area. In point of fact, however, it is of no assistance in separating personal from business expenditures, or in deciding whether or how to allocate the cost of items that inextricably confer personal benefits on the taxpayer at the same time that they serve his business purposes.

Thus: should taxpayers be allowed to deduct the expense of driving to and from work, of clothing or grooming themselves in the manner required by or suited to their jobs, of liberal or professional education,[45] of moving to new business locations, of curing or insuring against occupational diseases or job-related injuries, of entertaining customers and other business associates, or of maintaining themselves on business trips? The deduction of travel and entertainment expenses is so frequently denounced as a "preference" as to imply that the proposed CTB is not to make allowances for any borderline expenditures; but perhaps this hostility to "T & E" is an ad hoc or moral judgment that does not apply to moving expenses, work clothes, or accident insurance. Similarly, the ability of business executives and self-employed professionals to squeeze a variety of personal benefits out of their deductible expenditures — the lawyer who can use his secretary on personal errands; the physician who reads the *National Geographic* before putting it in his waiting room; the executive whose family occupies empty seats on a company plane — is often cited as a source of "erosion" in the tax base; but here again we are

[45] *See* Goode, *Tax Treatment of Individual Expenditures for Education and Research*, 56 Am. Econ. Rev. 208 (1966).

assailed by labels rather than offered an analysis.[46] Like it or not, our lives are not so compartmentalized that these borderline items can be readily classified.

The child care deduction of existing law, section 214, is a good example of this troubled area, and it nicely illustrates the irrelevance of the CTB concept to the problem of borderline expenditures. If the mother of small children takes a job outside the home, she may have to hire a nurse or baby-sitter; thus, section 214 is a plausible way to reflect the fact that the working mother's salary is not all gravy. But if section 214 is not a "preference" and does not "erode" the tax base, would it deserve these pejoratives if it were amended (*a*) to eliminate the family income limit of section 214 (b)(2)(B), thus permitting upper bracket families to qualify; (*b*) to permit all two-job families to deduct the increase in their living expenses resulting from the housewife's absence from the home (such as the extra cost of cleaning the house and of preparing meals or eating in restaurants); or (*c*) to permit bachelors to deduct the extra cost of living alone? Finally, what is the difference — so far as the concept of a CTB is concerned — between allowing the working mother to deduct her child care expenses and allowing the business executive to deduct the extra cost of custom-tailored clothing? If the answer is that the business man works in order to be able to live well, rather than the reverse, it is also true that some mothers do not hire a nursemaid in order to work, but work in order to hire a nursemaid.

A ground for eliminating provisions like section 214, and resisting the enactment of others, is that the business necessity of borderline expenditures is hard to prove or disprove, while their personal component is usually clear, with the result that deductions in this area cannot be adequately policed and will therefore breed exaggeration, fraud, and public discontent.[47] This is a plausible reason for restricting such deductions, but it is different from one-dimensional insistence on a CTB. Moreover, it leaves

---

[46] I have heard no clarion call for denying the academic community the right to deduct living expenses incurred while teaching away from home for the summer or traveling on sabbatical leave, or for taking into income such fringe benefits as free tuition for faculty children and personal use of university facilities; but perhaps these "preferences" are "desirable as means of carrying out supervening economic and social policy" rather than tainted by "mere submission to private interest groups and political expediency" (to use Heller's dichotomy, *supra* note 12, at 193).

[47] On the possibility of allocating such expenses see Klein, *The Deductibility of Transportation Expenses of a Combination Business and Pleasure Trip — A Conceptual Analysis*, 18 STAN. L. REV. 1099 (1966).

room for deciding that some borderline expenditures should qualify for deduction because their business function can be either established with reasonable certainty or properly assumed without proof, or because the personal benefit they confer is usually modest. In an analogous area — interest and bad debts — some advocates of a CTB, acknowledging that it may be difficult to say whether the taxpayer's payment or loss is personal or profit-oriented, have favored an unlimited deduction rather than an attempt to separate the business items from the personal ones or a Draconic denial of any deductions for interest and bad debts. This is a plausible approach (and it can with equal plausibility be applied to the business-personal expenditure area), but it is a judgment that derives no support from, because it is irrelevant to, the CTB concept.

IV. Business Deductions

If there is such a thing as a "classic" preference, percentage depletion heads so many lists that it surely qualifies for this accolade. In allowing the taxpayer to deduct more than his financial outlay in the interest of stimulating investment, however, percentage depletion has much in common with the investment credit. The former is more selective, to be sure, because limited to the mineral industries; but the investment credit is by no means "neutral" either. It is intended to prefer investment over consumption, and it distinguishes among competing investment opportunities: foreign investment, short-lived and nondepreciable assets, and most buildings do not qualify, and public utilities are treated less generously than other taxpayers.

I assume, therefore, that the investment credit has been less frequently described as a source of "erosion" only because it was unveiled too late to be included in most lists of "special provisions," not because it is consistent with a "no preference" tax system.[48] This impression is strengthened by the fact that percentage depletion and the investment credit were evidently bracketed by the ABA Committee on Substantive Tax Reform when it requested Treasury estimates of the impact on revenue of a variety of tax reforms, since one of its assumptions was that business and investment outlays would be capitalized and "the basis of such assets [would be recovered] over the useful life of

[48] Some proponents of a CTB no doubt regard the credit as a "good" preference because of the contribution it makes to economic growth.

the assets in accordance with any one of several methods of capital recovery used by the business and investor community."[49] This statement eschews explicit mention of percentage depletion, but it seems (and was understood) to be a roundabout way of asking the Treasury to assume that depletion deductions would be restricted to the taxpayer's cost; and it also seems to exclude the investment credit from the hypothetical tax structure whose revenue results were to be estimated by the Treasury.

In contemplating the depreciation or amortization of business assets by "any one of several methods of capital recovery used by the business and investor community," moreover, the ABA committee may also have been implying that a CTB is inconsistent with the recent statutory trend toward speeding up the write-off of a wide range of expenditures that under conventional accounting principles would either be written off more slowly or be held in abeyance and applied to reduce taxable income only on a sale or abandonment of the asset. These statutory provisions, some of them inspired by the allowance of accelerated amortization for wartime productive facilities, include: section 169 (grain storage facilities); section 173 (newspaper and magazine circulation expenditures); section 174 (research and experimental expenditures); sections 175, 180, and 182 (expenditures by farmers for soil and water conservation and for clearing and fertilizing land); section 177 (trademark and trade name expenditures); section 179 (additional first-year depreciation deduction for small business); section 248 (corporate organizational expenditures); and sections 263(c), 615, and 616 (expenditures for exploring, drilling, and developing mineral properties). To these statutory "preferences," we might add the administrative practice of allowing the taxpayer to deduct the cost of small tools and institutional advertising, when capitalizing these expenditures would be more appropriate,[50] as well as the 1962 depreciation guidelines, to the extent that they permit the taxpayer to assign shorter useful lives to his assets than an independent examination of his business practice would warrant.[51]

---

[49] *Report, supra* note 24, at 294.

[50] For 1964, it is estimated that $1.4 billion of "producers' durable equipment" (primarily tools) was charged to current expense. U.S. DEP'T OF COMMERCE, SURVEY OF CURRENT BUSINESS, Aug. 1965, at 12.

[51] Double declining balance depreciation was proposed as a practical substitute for "correctly-computed realistic depreciation" by G. TERBORGH, REALISTIC DEPRECIATION POLICY 149 (1954), but empirical evidence on loss of value through time (which should be controlling to those who hold to the Haig-Simons defini-

Such statutory and administrative provisions for the "expensing" or rapid amortization of capital outlays are usually proposed either as incentives to investment or as devices to avoid difficulties in allocating the expenditures in question to specific years; but voices are also sometimes raised in favor of allowing *all* capital outlays to be deducted in computing taxable income when incurred or over whatever period of time the businessman chooses to designate. One such proposal is based on the claim that existing practices sanction the current write-off of virtually all expenditures for intangible assets even though they have a protracted useful life, so that it is pointless to blow the whistle on outlays for tangible property. This suggestion might be regarded as a "no-preference" approach to the write-off of capital investments.[52]

It is also argued that technological developments in a dynamic economy "make any capital expenditure of certain benefit only for the present accounting period," so that expensing such outlays (with the exception, perhaps, of real estate improvements) would accurately reflect economic reality.[53] Though it may appeal to our vision of an America on the move, this theory cannot be reconciled with the fact that the average attained age of business equipment in use today is about ten years, a figure that has not varied more than a year or two in either direction for any year since 1920, and that is, of course, less than the anticipated *useful* life of the equipment. Moreover, equipment with an average attained life of five years or less accounted for about thirty-five percent of all business equipment in 1920 and for about the same percentage in 1965. As for business plant, as distinguished from equipment, its average attained age in our "dynamic" society is about twenty-four years, while it was only about twenty years in the period 1920–1930.[54] These macroeconomic estimates are confirmed by experience: few taxpayers have attempted to prove useful lives for their equipment shorter than those in the 1962

tion of income) is, by the author's own admission, totally inadequate. *Id.* at 39. Rapid depreciation may also be viewed as a rudimentary method of compensating for inflation; indeed, "expensing" of capital outlays would eliminate the complaint that depreciation does not provide an adequate replacement fund in an inflationary economy. The advocates of a comprehensive tax base, however, would presumably not find this a persuasive argument.

[52] Dean, *Four Ways To Write Off Capital Expenditures — Can We Let Management Choose?*, in 1955 COMPENDIUM 504, 509–11; Dean, *Capital Wastage Allowances*, in 2 1959 COMPENDIUM 813.

[53] Galvin, *supra* note 43, at 220. This argument implies that published financial statements overstate income on a monumental scale.

[54] *See* CAPITAL GOODS REV., Sept. 1964 (Machinery & Allied Prods. Inst.).

"guidelines"; and the vigorous complaints that we hear about the reserve ratio test stem from the fact that equipment is not being replaced at the rate implied by the 1962 guidelines, let alone at the rate that would be implied by a general expensing policy.

When all is said and done, then, statutory provisions and administrative practices that permit capital outlays to be deducted when incurred, or over periods shorter than their useful lives, are properly seen as "preferences" by the taxpayer who must depreciate his productive facilities over their useful economic lives and who cannot amortize any part of his investment in land, goodwill, and similar assets because their economic life is not reasonably predictable. Since they take no account of the taxpayer's net worth, such provisions are not easily reconciled with the Haig-Simons definition.

Indeed, one who is seeking to eliminate all "preferences" cannot avoid questioning the propriety — from the point of view of "treating all income alike" — of the rapid methods of depreciation that entered the Code in 1954 or that were approved earlier by administrative practice. The statutory methods are not permissible for used or short-lived assets; these limitations acknowledge an intent to stimulate investment rather than to "clearly reflect income," and this nonrevenue purpose would presumably require their ouster from a purified tax system.[55] Finally, one might go so far as to ask whether straight-line depreciation, though sanctioned by long usage, would be consistent with the CTB or would accurately reflect "the taxpayer's economic enhancement"[56] unless limited to the annual decline in the market value of the depreciable property. We are told, to be sure, that depreciation "is a process of allocation, not valuation,"[57] but if there is no decline in value, what is there to allocate?

It is obvious that these implications of a systematic program

---

[55] The debate among accountants and security analysts over the proper way — "flow-through" or "normalization" — to reflect the tax savings generated by the investment credit, the 1962 depreciation guidelines, and the 1954 accelerated depreciation methods springs from a candid acknowledgment that these write-offs are less "realistic" than the depreciation deducted for financial statement purposes.

[56] *See* p. 928 & note 6 *supra.*

[57] AMERICAN INSTITUTE OF CERTIFIED PUBLIC ACCOUNTANTS, ACCOUNTING TERMINOLOGY BULLETIN NO. 43, at 76 (1961). *But see* Detroit Edison Co. v. Commissioner, 319 U.S. 98, 101 (1943): "The end and purpose of it all [depreciation accounting] is to approximate and reflect the financial consequences to the taxpayer of the subtle effects of time and use on the *value* of his capital assets" (emphasis added).

to "treat all income alike" would be highly unpalatable to many who profess to be attracted by the principle of eliminating "preferences" of every variety. In an effort to avoid these implications, they are likely to urge that tax "incentives" to invest in productive facilities will pay us dividends in increasing output, an improved growth rate, and less unemployment — forgetting that wholehearted devotion to a CTB leaves no room for such "special provisions." They may even argue that the CTB is compatible with the expensing or "fast" depreciation of capital outlays because these are mere matters of timing — forgetting that they have insisted on the importance of "mere timing" in criticizing other "preferences."

V. Problems of Timing

The Simons definition of income does not specify the period of time to which it is to be applied: that is left to the person who uses the definition, which refers only to "the beginning and end of the period in question." Similarly, Haig's definition refers to the accretion in the taxpayer's economic power "between two points of time." [58] Simons himself was not much concerned with the problems of the taxable period, or with the effect on the Treasury of moving income from one taxable period to another; and he had little patience for "those who persist in deploring long postponement of tax payment and the consequent interest cost to the Treasury," [59] referring to the issue as "this mosquito argu-

[58] *See* p. 932 *supra*.

[59] H. Simons, Federal Tax Reform 127 (1950); *see id.* at 155. Simons argued that the elimination of the special rate for capital gains, coupled with realization at death, would make the income tax virtually independent of time; taxpayers could then be allowed to depreciate assets at their discretion, to deduct losses on "wash sales," and so on. *Id.* at 44–52. But if time *really* does not matter, a carryover of basis generation after generation would be as satisfactory as realization at death, except for transfers to tax-exempt institutions. It would be interesting to know if Simons was so tolerant of postponement that he would have accepted "Yankee storekeeper" accounting: deduct inventory costs when incurred, but take sales into account only when the customer pays. For a proposal along this line see Carson, *An Investment-Recovery-First Concept of Taxable Profit*, 26 Accounting Rev. 456 (1951).

Simons's tolerance of tax postponement was not a peripheral aspect of his tax theory. The taxing system, he argued, "must not require or presuppose sharp allocations of income among short accounting periods . . . tax legislation calling for definitive annual determinations means awful complexity, difficult administration, expensive compliance, endless litigation, and bad taxpayer and Bureau morale," as well as — perhaps this was the worst of all — a "pestilential multiplication" of tax lawyers. "Income taxation has simply never faced squarely the axiom that an-

ment." His disciples, however, have not inherited his insouciance; they have condemned devices by which taxpayers can postpone the recognition of taxable income from one taxable year to another as "preferences" that are inconsistent with a CTB. Since these items do not drop out of the tax base entirely, the assertion that these "preferences" have the effect of "eroding" the tax base must mean that a CTB is a function of time, as well as of scope. Even if the tax base includes all appropriate items, then, it is not "comprehensive" if some of the items are included in the "wrong" period. As will be seen, however, this concern with timing is not pursued consistently; if it were, it would require changes in the existing structure of a far more sweeping character than has been acknowledged or, perhaps, recognized.

Before we proceed, however, a curious aspect of this area should be noted. The achievement of a CTB, it is often argued, is desirable because it will afford an opportunity to reduce the upper bracket rates and thereby mitigate the degree of progression. And one of the virtues claimed for a less progressive rate structure, in turn, is that it will reduce the importance of timing. The chain of reasoning seems to amount to this: postponement devices must be eliminated in order to create a CTB, which will in turn make possible a rate structure under which postponement devices will be innocuous. Notwithstanding this involuted way of returning to Simons's view that objections to the postponement of income are no more bothersome than mosquitoes, I intend in the discussion that follows to accept the contrary premise that timing *is* important.

The postponement of tax liabilities by the astute selection of an accounting method, contractual arrangement, or other device is often analogized to an interest free loan by the Government to the taxpayer. Translated into dollars, the value of postponing for five, ten, or twenty years the payment of a liability of 1,000 dollars is set out in the following table, depending upon whether the taxpayer discounts the future at five, ten, fifteen, or twenty percent:

Years	*5%*	*10%*	*15%*	*20%*
5	$216	$379	$503	$598
10	386	614	753	838
20	623	851	939	974

---

nual-income accounting is and should be tentative and provisional." H. SIMONS, *supra* at 58–60. The trouble with this line of argument is that no foreseeable income tax rate structure or general interest rate will make the timing of tax liabilities irrelevant or unimportant.

It is often argued that the same aggregate tax burden should be imposed over a period of time whether income is realized early or late in the period selected; and proposals have been made to neutralize the taxpayer's time preference by averaging income over the period and imputing interest on early tax payments.[60] This would reduce the importance of timing, but postponement would retain some of its charms if the interest rate were inadequate in the eyes of the individual taxpayer. A rate of five percent, for example, might seem satisfactory to a conservative fiduciary or to a public utility; but for many businessmen, a rate of ten or fifteen percent would be required to take the advantage out of postponement. And for taxpayers — there must be millions of them — who are perpetually in debt to personal finance companies, a rate of twenty-four or thirty percent might be necessary to achieve the desired result. On the other hand, a rate that is tailored to the needy or leverage-minded taxpayer would be so high that other taxpayers would be tempted to adopt devices to *accelerate* the realization of income.[61] And if an average rate were to be selected, the Government would be "borrowing" from some taxpayers (those who accelerate their liabilities) at too high a rate, at the same time that it was "lending" to others (those who postpone their liabilities) at too low a rate. I do not mean to suggest that averaging coupled with interest on early payments would not mitigate the importance of timing, but I do assert that the issue would continue to be of major importance. I see no possibility, with high income tax rates, of reducing the issue to the mosquito level to which Simons thought it belonged.

The continued importance of timing, even with averaging and imputed interest on early payments, is further assured because the "loan" that is obtained by postponing a tax liability has features that are overlooked by the academician but critical to the businessman. Loans from banks and other nongovernmental lenders can be procured only if the lender is satisfied with the debtor's financial ability, and are often accompanied by restrictions on the borrower's freedom; in the case of loans to corporations, for example, the salaries to be paid to shareholder-employees may be limited, dividends may be restricted beyond the limits imposed by state law, and the major shareholders may be required to

---

[60] *E.g.*, W. VICKREY, *supra* note 31, at 164–97.

[61] For some accounting ramifications of the phenomenon of "prepaid" federal income taxes see H.A. BLACK, INTERPERIOD ALLOCATION OF CORPORATE INCOME TAXES 72–74 (1966).

endorse the corporation's notes. The loan that results from a postponement of tax liabilities, by contrast, is obtainable at the borrower's will, regardless of his financial condition, and entails no restrictions on his freedom. Moreover, it does not appear on his balance sheet as a liability, and hence does not reduce his power to get other loans. Finally, an ordinary loan carries a fixed maturity date, imposed by the lender, and is subject to extension only at his sufferance. Postponed tax liabilities, on the other hand, become "due" only if the taxpayer takes whatever step (sale of property, reduction of inventory, change of accounting method, withdrawal of funds, or liquidation) is required to realize the income in question. Thus, even if interest is imputed on early tax payments at the same rate that would be paid by the taxpayer for a commercial loan, he would be well advised to "borrow" from the Government by postponing his tax liability whenever possible rather than to borrow from a private lender.[62]

A. The Taxable Period

Income must be measured chronologically. The unit of time selected by the Internal Revenue Code is the twelve month taxable year, not the month, triennium, or decade; and this decision, though conforming to business custom, is by no means neutral in its impact, since tax rates are progressive and taxpayers have a variety of earning cycles. Although the twelve month taxable year is controlling for most purposes, it is modified by a variety of carryover provisions, which in turn specify their own chronological limits. These include section 170(b)(5) (five year carryforward of individual taxpayer's excess charitable contributions), section 172 (three year carryback and five year carryforward of net operating loss), and section 1212(b) (unlimited carryforward of individual's capital loss).[63]

---

[62] One can usefully compare the wide-open "loan" that is obtained by postponing the realization of income with the more conventional terms that will be imposed on a taxpayer by the Collection Division of the IRS if he has incurred a tax liability but wishes to pay it in installments or at a later time. It is also instructive to note the extent to which financially pressed businessmen are tempted to "borrow" government funds by failing to pay over taxes withheld from their employees' wages on the due date, despite the severe penalty on this practice. *See* Stutsman, *The Penalty for a "Withholding" of Withholding Taxes*, U. So. CAL. 1964 TAX INST. 657.

[63] Income averaging under §§ 1301–05 is another exception to the annual accounting principle. For the differential advantages to various categories of taxpayers resulting from averaging see Steger, *Averaging Income for Income Tax Purposes*, 1 1959 COMPENDIUM 589, 614–15.

I do not recall any suggestion that these modifications of the twelve month taxable year are "preferences," but I am not sure why they have escaped these labels. Can it be that existing law — so deficient, we are told, in so many other ways — has somehow succeeded in defining the taxable period in a way that is consistent in every respect with a CTB? Or are we to conclude that the concept of a CTB is independent of time, and that (as Simons argued) it requires only that all items of income be taken into account at some time or other, no matter when? If so, what are we to make of the assertion that the employee who recognizes income from a qualified pension plan at retirement rather than when his employer makes contributions is receiving a "preference"?

Perhaps the advocates of a CTB object to the delayed recognition of income from qualified pension plans only because it seems inconsistent with the twelve month taxable period that usually controls in computing taxable income. If the accretion in the taxpayer's economic power (Haig's criterion of income) is normally measured by comparing his wealth on December 31 with his wealth on January 1 of the same year, it may be asserted that the same two points in time ought to be used in measuring the economic growth resulting from his participation in a qualified pension plan. This is a persuasive, though perhaps not irrefutable, argument; but it would carry the advocates of a CTB into territory that they have hitherto not attempted to invade. Our network of statutory rules governing tax-free exchanges, as well as the statutory and nonstatutory rules of "tax accounting," will require agonizing reappraisal — as I will show in a moment — if consistency in applying the twelve month taxable period is a prerequisite to achieving a CTB. Moreover, the many carryovers and other exceptions to the twelve month taxable period that are to be found in existing law are not easily reconciled with the notion that the same two points in time must invariably be used in measuring the accretion in economic power that is to be the new measure of taxable income.

B. Averaging

The effect of the twelve month taxable period may be modified in the case of income that was earned or accrued over a longer period of time (as with back pay awards under section 1303 of pre-1964 law) or that substantially exceeds the taxpayer's average income during a specified base period (as with sections 1301–05 of existing law). If the averaging device applies only to a limited category of income, however, it is not easily squared with the demand, frequently voiced by advocates of a CTB, that income be taxed "without regard to its source." The "preference" accorded to capital gains is a rough and ready kind of averaging; neither the deduction allowed by section 1202 nor the alternative special tax rate takes account directly of the tax that would have been paid had the appreciation been measured and taxed in the earlier years, to be sure, but they are often defended as a simple way of mitigating the effect of bunching. This claim would be strengthened if the holding period were longer, as it was before 1942. By contrast, the income averaging provisions of current law do not even purport to deal with slowly maturing income, and they resemble the capital gain provisions in modifying the tax rate applicable to the computation year without regard to the tax that would have been payable if the averageable income had been received during the base period.

I have seen no analysis of the implications of the Haig-Simons definition for income averaging. In the case of income that is earned over a period of time, there may be a corresponding increase in the taxpayer's net worth to be accounted for annually under the definition; but if the accretion cannot be measured or is dependent upon successful completion of the project, the income would not be reflected in the taxpayer's net worth until the final year. Tempering the rate of tax in that year to take account of the income-maturing process seems consistent with the Haig-Simons formulation (indeed, it might be regarded as an optional retroactive adoption of accrual accounting), but only if all forms of slowly maturing income are entitled to this benefit. I am not sure, however, whether the averaging contemplated by some advocates of a CTB is to apply to all slowly maturing income regardless of its source, or only to capital gains.

Averaging that takes account of the income-maturing process does not necessarily do anything for the taxpayer with fluctuating income, since an "abnormal" amount of income in a given year may reflect nothing more than that year's activities. A reduction in the tax rate to mitigate this kind of "bunching" may be consistent with the Haig-Simons definition, but here again it would seem to be a "preference" — as that term is used by advocates of a CTB — if only a limited category of income qualifies for the rate reduction. The income averaging rules of the current Code (sections 1301–05) are not applicable to capital gains or to income from property received by gift or bequest during the computation year or base period. Perhaps these disqualifications can be excused as atoning in some measure for the "preferences" accorded to these types of income; otherwise, they would seem to be objectionable because they turn on the "source" of the taxpayer's income.

C. Accounting Methods

Aside from a few peripheral issues, the advocates of a comprehensive tax base have not directed their attention to accounting methods, possibly on the assumption that "exceptions" and "preferences" are not to be found in this area. In point of fact, however, accounting methods are composed of conventions, primarily governing the time when items are to be taken into account, that are often indistinguishable from "substantive" statutory provisions that are thought to deserve pejorative labels. The cash receipts and disbursements, accrual, installment, completed contract, and percentage of completion methods of reporting income can produce very different results in any given taxable period, and these divergencies may continue for many years — possibly for the full span of the taxpayer's natural or business life.

To illustrate the impact of accounting methods on the CTB concept, one example will suffice. The installment method of accounting (section 453) permits the taxpayer's gain on a sale of property to be spread out over the period of collection, even if the buyer is highly solvent and his obligation to pay is evidenced by promissory notes or other negotiable instruments. The rationale of this method of accounting, which an authoritative committee of the American Accounting Association considers too misleading for financial statement purposes,[64] was recently explained as follows by the Internal Revenue Service: [65]

> The method of reporting income on the installment basis was enacted by Congress as a relief measure, the idea being that it would enable merchants to actually receive in cash the profit arising out of each installment before the tax was paid. In other words, the tax could be paid from the proceeds collected rather than be

[64] Committee on Concepts and Standards Underlying Corporate Financial Statements, American Accounting Association, *Accounting Principles and Taxable Income*, 27 ACCOUNTING REV. 427, 429 (1952); *see* SEC Securities Act Release No. 4811, 3 CCH FED. SEC. L. REP. ¶ 72,124 (Dec. 7, 1965) (proper reporting of deferred income tax liability resulting from use of installment basis of computing income).

[65] Rev. Rul. 65-185, 1965-2 CUM. BULL. 153, 154.

advanced by the taxpayer. . . . It is this "ability to pay" concept which underlies the privilege of reporting income on the installment basis.

If the cash flow theory that underlies this method is acceptable to the proponents of a CTB, why is it a "preference" to permit employees to exclude from their gross income the contributions made by an employer to a qualified pension plan that will not pay any benefits in cash for many years? If all income is to be treated "alike," I see no escape from either repealing the installment method of accounting or extending it to all taxpayers.[66]

The installment method of section 453 is by no means the only accounting method that permits the taxpayer to reflect income in a later year than would be required by a consistent application of the Haig-Simons principle for measuring the taxpayer's economic gain, or that is available to some taxpayers but denied to others similarly situated. The completed contract and percentage of completion methods of reporting income can be used, under section 1.451–3(a) of the Regulations, only for building, installation, and construction contracts. Surely the systematic elimination of "preferences" would require either the abandonment of these accounting methods or their extension to all contracts taking more than one year to complete.

Even more basic is the fact that the cash receipts and disbursements method of accounting permits the taxpayer to control the timing of income by accelerating or postponing the receipt and payment of many items. Deferred compensation arrangements have been criticized by proponents of a CTB, who recommend that cash basis taxpayers be put on an accrual basis in this limited area; but a consistent application of this approach (which also underlies proposals to include the interest component of life insurance savings in the CTB as it accrues) would collide on a grand scale with the assumptions of cash basis accounting. Deferred compensation arrangements are a dramatic illustration of the "creative" use of cash basis accounting principles by the tax planner, but they do not begin to exhaust the possibilities.[67]

---

[66] For its limited applicability to income from personal services see W.W. Pope, 34 P-H Tax Ct. Mem. 1198 (1965) (carpenter-dealer allowed to use installment method for houses built and sold by him).

[67] *See* Goetz, *The Myth of Special Tax Concessions for Qualified Pension Plans*, 51 Iowa L. Rev. 561 (1966), arguing that the cash method of accounting, rather than "special" legislation, is responsible for the exclusion from the employee's current income of employer contributions to qualified pension plans and of the investment income thereon. Compare the right of cash basis taxpayers to exclude the

Indeed, a rigorous application of accrual accounting principles would require some items and transactions to be taken into account even earlier than the advocates of a CTB have proposed in their war on "preferences." For example, if social security benefits are to be stripped of their tax immunity, why wait until benefits are paid to the employee before requiring him to take them into account? If his employer bought an annuity for him, the contribution would be taxable when made under existing law, and we are asked to extend this rule to qualified pension plans as well. If this extension is required to achieve a "no preference" tax base, should not the employee be required to report, *when earned*, the present discounted value of social security benefits to be paid in the future? [68] If Medicare benefits are to lose their immunity, should not the taxpayer be required to report annually the value of the protection that is conferred on him, just as he would be taxed if his employer bought him an accident and health policy as compensation? There are, to be sure, reasons for not imposing the tax at this time, but they are not easily squared with the "no preference" approach.

Not even the pitiless suppression of all accounting methods other than accrual accounting, however, would give us a tax system devoid of "preferences" and "exceptions." In support of this dismal conclusion, let me simply remind the reader of the many variations of accrual accounting that are to be found in the Treasury Regulations, rulings, and judicial decisions.[69] Which ones are

---

interest component of U.S. savings bonds until redemption or maturity, despite the annual increase in redemption value.

[68] Of course, the scale of benefits might be revised later, but that can be taken into account when it occurs; surely few would contend that a *downward* adjustment of benefits is so likely that the fully insured employee has not experienced an accretion in net worth. The Tax Adjustment Act of 1966, § 302(a), 42 U.S.C.A. § 428 (Supp. July 1966), provides that persons previously outside the social security system are to receive monthly benefits of thirty-five dollars for life on reaching the age of seventy-two. Would a CTB require such a person to include in income the fair market value of a comparable annuity (about $5000) as soon as he qualifies? *See* United States v. Drescher, 179 F.2d 863 (2d Cir.), *cert. denied*, 340 U.S. 821 (1950) (employee must include in gross income the present value to him of a nonassignable annuity contract purchased and held for him by his employer).

[69] Consider, for instance, the pricing of inventories. LIFO was used in valuing 20% of total closing inventories on tax returns filed for fiscal 1963. 25 J. TAXATION 267 (1966). If it is a "preference" that ought to be purged from the comprehensive tax base (as Hellmuth, *The Corporate Income Tax Base*, in 1 1959 COMPENDIUM 283, 312, suggests), it would broaden the base far more than many targets that are frequently mentioned. Other ambiguities in the term "accrual accounting" are reflected by the recent debates regarding prepaid income, reserves for estimated expenses, accrual of vacation pay, dealers' reserves, and disputed liabilities.

"exceptions," and to what general rule, I leave to scholars more skilled than I in this type of taxonomy.

One final thought: if for some reason that escapes me we can achieve a tax base that is devoid of preferences without hacking away at accounting methods, it will be necessary to define just what it is that is to enjoy this immunity from reform. The difficulty, of course, is that many statutory provisions that bear on the timing of income could be dressed up as "accounting methods" and transferred to Subchapter E (Accounting Periods and Methods of Accounting). Among these are most if not all of the business deductions mentioned earlier (research and development expenses, depreciation, and so on), the nonrecognition provisions discussed below, and such more esoteric provisions as section 77 (commodity loans), section 165(h) (disaster losses), and section 165(e) (theft losses).[70]

D. Unrealized Appreciation

Appreciation in the value of the taxpayer's assets is not included in gross income under existing law until it has been "realized" by sale or other disposition. None of the proponents of a CTB, so far as I know, wants to substitute an annual net worth computation to take account each year of the taxpayer's increase or decrease in wealth.[71] I do not quarrel with this exemption of unrealized appreciation, but it unquestionably tolerates a "preference" and is inconsistent with the hope of achieving a tax base unsullied by human compromises. Although Henry Simons acknowledged that a yearly computation of the taxpayer's net worth was implied by his definition of income, and called the realization concept a "professional conspiracy against truth," [72] he thought that

[70] Compare the problem of distinguishing among "accounting method," "accounting practice," and "error" under sections 446 and 481. *See* Boughner, *Change in Accounting Method, Practice, or Correction of Error? The IRS Position*, 23 J. TAXATION 264 (1965).

[71] In 1937, however, an eminent committee that included the president of Equitable Life Assurance Society and a partner of Sullivan and Cromwell recommended an annual accrual of capital gains and losses; curiously, only the former chairman of the National Labor Relations Board objected to the taxation of "paper profits." TWENTIETH CENTURY FUND, INC., COMM. ON TAXATION, FACING THE TAX PROBLEM 476 n.15, 477, 490 (C. Shoup ed. 1937). Compare the stress on "realizable profits" and "realized cost savings" in E. EDWARDS & P. BELL, THE THEORY AND MEASUREMENT OF BUSINESS INCOME (1961).

[72] H. SIMONS, PERSONAL INCOME TAXATION 81 (1938). Referring to Seligman's insistence on realization as a condition to recognizing income while simultaneously favoring depreciation deductions (to which inventory write-downs and bad debt reserves might have been added), Simons said: "Surely no definition of income

no "workable scheme" could be devised to reach the theoretically correct result. He was not explicit about his reason for this conclusion, however, except for the statement that income taxation "simply must follow, in the main, the established procedures of accounting practice."[73]

Perhaps this source of "erosion" in the CTB is to be tolerated because of the difficulty of valuing the taxpayer's assets each year. In point of fact, of course, we somehow manage to value assets of almost every description in computing the gain or loss on taxable in-kind exchanges and in applying gift and death taxes; and Simons, like many other advocates of a CTB, wanted transfers by gift and at death to be treated as taxable realizations of gain, thus accepting the responsibility of valuing the assets at that

---

which admits 'mere value changes' only in one direction can well escape the fate of appearing ridiculous." *Id.* at 88. As to the phrase "inchoate income," coined by Seligman as a label for unrealized appreciation, Simons said that it "deserves prominent place among the curiosities of economic terminology." *Id.* at 87.

[73] *Id.* at 208. Thus, Simons in the end joined the "professional conspiracy against truth," or at least abdicated in favor of accounting procedures that he profoundly distrusted: "The reputable accountant never loses sight of the fact that his income statements are influential in matters of dividend policy. Income, for him, is perhaps only what may be reported safely to unsophisticated directors as income. He aims, it would seem, never to ascertain what income is, in any really definable sense, but rather to devise rules of calculation which will make the result a minimum or at least give large answers only in the future." *Id.* at 81. In point of fact, although some accountants may try to protect "unsophisticated directors" by refusing to count chickens before they are grandparents, others are told by their clients whether an optimistic or pessimistic income statement is wanted. *See* Briloff, *Needed: A Revolution in the Determination and Application of Accounting Principles*, 39 ACCOUNTING REV. 12 (1964); Cohen, *Accounting for Taxes, Finance, and Regulatory Purposes—Are Variances Necessary?*, 44 TAXES 780 (1966). Accounting principles often come in pairs or sets, from which management can select those that will yield the most useful financial statements. Consistency from year to year is about all that can be expected, and even this is not essential if the inconsistency is disclosed in a footnote.

As to the treatment of unrealized appreciation by accountants, it is interesting to compare the vigorous assertion that appreciation and depreciation in market values must be recognized in order to measure net revenue in W. PATON & R. STEVENSON, PRINCIPLES OF ACCOUNTING 238–43, 451–69 (1918), with Paton's equally firm assertion twenty years later that "appreciation in its various forms is not income." W. PATON & A. LITTLETON, AN INTRODUCTION TO CORPORATE ACCOUNTING STANDARDS 46, 62–63 (American Accounting Ass'n Monograph No. 3, 1940); *see Income Measurement in a Dynamic Economy*, in FIVE MONOGRAPHS ON BUSINESS INCOME 57 (S. Alexander ed. 1950) ("the accountant's use of realized rather than accrued gain is based principally on convenience"); Litherland, *Fixed Asset Replacement a Half Century Ago*, 26 ACCOUNTING REV. 475 (1951); AIA, STUDY GROUP ON BUSINESS INCOME, CHANGING CONCEPTS OF BUSINESS INCOME 23–24 (1952). For a contemporary proposal to take unrealized appreciation into account currently see E. EDWARDS & P. BELL, *supra* note 71, at 276–77.

time.[74] Moreover, once the giant step of taxing unrealized appreciation was taken for the first year, it would produce a grand list of values, and later changes in value might be satisfactorily approximated by index figures based on economic trends (subject to rebuttal evidence at the taxpayer's option). The first year, in other words, would be the hardest. At the very least, before accepting the "special exception" or "loophole" that is created by the exclusion of unrealized appreciation from gross income, the advocates of a CTB might be expected to examine the possibility of applying to this area the principle used elsewhere in the tax field: value those assets that *do* have an ascertainable market value, and hold the others in abeyance until valuation becomes feasible. This is what the proposed taxation of life insurance savings by requiring the annual increase in the policy's terminal reserve or cash surrender value to be reported would amount to.[75] If the exclusion of this type of unrealized appreciation erodes the tax base, what is the rationale for excluding other readily measurable appreciation?

Perhaps unrealized appreciation is to be excluded from the proposed CTB not because of anticipated difficulty in valuing assets but because "paper profits" produce no cash to pay the tax and may be wiped out in a later year. These are not untenable grounds for exempting unrealized appreciation, but they furnish equally persuasive support for other exclusions as well. One example: employees get no ready cash when their employer contributes on their behalf to a qualified pension or profit-sharing plan, and they will be involuntarily at the the risk of the market until the benefits are paid in cash. Why not, then, preserve the employee's right under existing law to exclude the employer's contribution from gross income; it is a "preference," to be sure, but so is the exclusion of unrealized appreciation. Indeed, if lack of cash and continued risk of the market are legitimate grounds for taking appreciation into income only when it is realized, why should we not amend existing law to allow employees to deduct or exclude from gross income their contributions to pension plans and their social security taxes? [76] The employee's claim is not properly answered by the assertion that he wants a "prefer-

---

[74] H. SIMONS, *supra* note 72, at 167.

[75] *See* Irenas, *Life Insurance Interest Income Under the Federal Income Tax*, 21 TAX L. REV. 297, 314 (1966).

[76] In computing "personal income," the National Income Division excludes *both* employee *and* employer contributions for social insurance. U.S. DEP'T OF COMMERCE, *supra* note 50, at 8.

ence" while the investor is getting only what natural law requires. The employee, in fact, is in the usual case asking only for postponement; under existing law, the investor's unrealized appreciation will be excluded from income permanently if he holds the property until death.

E. Realization of Gain or Loss on Transfer at Death or by Gift

Advocates of a CTB ordinarily propose to take account of unrealized appreciation and depreciation when property is transferred by gift or at death. In this way, they would convert the outright exemption enjoyed by such appreciation under existing law into a postponement provision. For a taxpayer who is fifty years old, a current increase in net worth would not be reported for twenty-four years if his life conforms to the 1958 Standard Ordinary Mortality Table; for thirty-five and sixty-five year-old taxpayers, the corresponding figures are thirty-seven and thirteen years. The value of postponing payment of a tax liability of 1,000 dollars for these periods of time, assuming various interest rates, is set out in the following table:

Years	*5%*	*10%*	*15%*	*20%*
13	$470	$710	$838	$906
24	690	898	965	988
37	836	971	994	999

If it is an unwarranted "preference" to allow employees to postpone the recognition of currently earned pensions and annuities until they start to receive payments on retiring from active service, realization at death also deserves the label "preference" even though it would constitute an important reform of existing law.

One need hardly add that the only version of realization at death that has been so far unveiled — the 1963 proposal of the Kennedy Administration — was a mere sieve when measured by the criterion of "treating all income alike." [77] Even this proposal,

---

[77] Some property was excluded entirely and granted a basis equal to its fair market value at death (personal residence and household effects); a carryover basis was provided for one-half the assets transferred to a surviving spouse; life insurance was not included; no provision was made for recapturing percentage depletion deductions in excess of the property's basis; and there was a minimum exemption (with a stepped-up basis) for $15,000 of unrealized appreciation. *Hearings on the President's 1963 Tax Message Before the House Committee on Ways and Means*, 88th Cong., 1st Sess., pt. 1, at 128–40 (1963). I do not quarrel with these ex-

however, encountered such heavy weather that it was replaced by a plan for a carryover of the decedent's basis, so that the gain would go untaxed until the taxpayer's heirs sold or exchanged the property in a market transaction. This modest suggestion — a "preference" proposed as a substitute for a "preference" that in turn would have only diluted a more formidable "preference" [78] — also failed to survive the House Ways and Means Committee's examination. Resistance to change in this area is so great that any reform, even a carryover of basis for inherited property, may be seen as a victory for the CTB ideal, justifying a ruthless elimination of "preferences" in other areas. A clear-eyed view of the landscape, however, would disclose that neither a carryover of basis nor realization at death would be more than a halfway house on the road to a truly comprehensive base.

F. Tax-Free Exchanges and Similar Transactions

In addition to exempting appreciation in the value of the taxpayer's property from his gross income if it is not realized by a sale or other disposition, existing law is riddled with provisions for the nonrecognition of the gain even if it is realized. These nonrecognition provisions, which may be regarded as "exceptions" in the sense that their repeal would result in taxability of the taxpayer's realized gain under section 61(a), are usually mandatory, but some are optional with the taxpayer. Among the most important are the following:

(*1*) section 351 (transfer of property to a controlled corporation);
(*2*) section 354 (exchange of stock or securities in a corporate reorganization, such as a merger or stock-for-stock acquisition);
(*3*) section 1031 (exchange of business or of investment property other than stock, securities, or inventory assets for other property "of a like kind," *e.g.*, an exchange of industrial equipment or of investment real estate);
(*4*) section 1033 (replacement of property lost by "involuntary conversion," such as condemnation or fire, with other property "similar or related in service or use"); and

---

emptions, but I should think they would be intolerable to anyone who worries about the erosion of the tax base resulting from the exclusion of welfare payments.

[78] Although it has been asserted that a carryover of basis "would accomplish the same result" as constructive realization at death, Somers, *The Case for a Capital Gain Tax at Death*, 52 A.B.A.J. 346, 347 (1966), they can be regarded as equivalents only if one assumes with Simons, *see* p. 958 & note 59 *supra*, that timing does not matter.

(5) section 1034 (sale of the taxpayer's principal residence at a gain if another residence is acquired within one year).

In addition to nonrecognition provisions, of which the foregoing are merely a sample, the Code contains a number of other provisions that operate similarly, though not under the same technical label. Examples are section 305, excluding stock dividends from gross income, and section 108, permitting the taxpayer to exclude income realized on the cancellation of his indebtedness for less than its face amount if he agrees to reduce the tax basis of his assets.

The policy underpinnings of these provisions are several in number, and they overlap in part. Some nonrecognition transactions are forced on the taxpayer, and some of these he may regard as misfortunes rather than profitable events. Whether the transaction is voluntary or not, he ordinarily either receives no cash or promptly uses any cash received to replace the assets that were disposed of, so that the imposition of a tax might compel him to sell other assets, to borrow, or to take some other inconvenient or uneconomic step. Often he does not wholly liquidate his economic interest in the assets given up, or he acquires an interest in similar property, so his profit is arguably a paper one. Another rationale for the nonrecognition provisions is a Congressional intent to encourage, or to eliminate barriers to, business adjustments, labor mobility, or other economic or personal behavior.

These all strike me as legitimate reasons for the nonrecognition provisions, and as to some transactions I find them persuasive or conclusive; but to those who envision a tax base without "preferences" or "exceptions," this attitude must seem fuzzy-minded if not downright pusillanimous. To be sure, the taxpayer's gain usually goes unrecognized only at the expense of a carryover of his basis, so that the unrecognized gain will be taken into account if he disposes of the property in a taxable transaction at a later date; but this postponement of income is itself a "preference." Moreover, nonrecognition in today's tax structure often leads to the exclusion of gain by reason of the stepped-up basis conferred on the property at death. Even if this "super-preference" were eliminated by a watertight requirement of realization of gain at death, however, the nonrecognition provisions would remain as an important source of "erosion."

Curiously, however, the nonrecognition provisions have been

little assailed by the advocates of a CTB. Criticism of details has been plentiful, but there has been no parallel in this area to the vigorous and nearly unanimous assault on such "preferences" as the exclusion of wage supplements or social security benefits. The economists, viewing the nonrecognition provisions from macroeconomic heights, may have thought them of minor importance; but it can be confidently predicted that their repeal would be as unpopular as restricting percentage depletion.[79] Even if the tax base were expanded by rules for realization of gain at death, the nonrecognition provisions would surely retain much of their appeal; indeed, given a choice, many individual taxpayers (as well as corporations and trusts) would undoubtedly prefer realization at death to a repeal of the nonrecognition provisions.

VI. The Taxable Unit

Before we can measure the "economic accretion" to which the "broad base" income tax is to be applied, we must specify the taxpaying unit whose economic betterment we want to measure. The "individual" income tax of existing law is not quite what its name implies; it is imposed on some income of trusts and estates, as well as on the income of individuals. Moreover, of the 64 million "individual" returns filed during 1965, 38 million were joint returns of married persons reporting their combined incomes.

For some purposes, the taxpayer is regarded by existing law as an isolated unit; thus, he must report gain realized on a sale of property even if the buyer is his wife or child. For other purposes, however, account is taken of the taxpayer's marital and family relationships: witness the separate rate structures for married couples, surviving spouses with dependent children, and heads of households; the dependency exemptions; the deductions allowed for medical expenses of the taxpayer's dependents and for alimony payments; the disallowance of losses on intrafamily transactions; and the effect of marriage on the numerous dollar and percentage limitations on deductions and other allowances. Our tax structure is similarly ambivalent as regards relations between the taxpayer and business or other economic entities in which he is financially interested. Sometimes the income of such entities is im-

[79] Since the average holding period for capital assets is probably longer for high bracket taxpayers, L. Seltzer, The Nature and Tax Treatment of Capital Gains and Losses 142–44 (1951) (1934–1937 statistics), the value of the realization concept, tax-free exchange provisions, and other postponement opportunities no doubt increases as we go up the economic ladder.

puted to the individual, sometimes his income and the entity's are computed as though they had nothing to do with each other, and sometimes there are separate computations that partially reflect an identity of economic interest. Although statutory provisions taking account of, or disregarding, family or economic relationships are sometimes said to "erode" the tax base, I think these claims stem from an inadequate analysis of the problem and that in reality the concept of a CTB is quite independent of the choice of taxpaying units.

A. *Family Relationships*

To begin with, I find nothing in the CTB concept that leads inexorably, or even points vaguely, to the conclusion that the income of individuals should be taxed, rather than the income of married couples, families, or households, or that tells us anything about the extent to which tax rates should take account of marriage bonds or family responsibilities. Since the tax base could be enlarged to include every item that constitutes "income" under the Haig-Simons definition even though the rate structure differentiated between single persons and married couples, why is the income-splitting joint return of existing law classified as a "leakage" or source of "erosion" by some advocates of a CTB? [80]

[80] *E.g.*, Pechman, *Erosion of the Individual Income Tax*, 10 NAT'L TAX J. 1, 21 (1957); Heller, *The Federal Income Tax and the Working Man*, in CIO CONFERENCE ON TAXATION 21, 23 (1953). Pechman, however, points out that the income-splitting issue "cannot be resolved on a priori grounds," and hence offers alternative calculations of the revenue yield obtainable by eliminating leakages, dependent on whether income-splitting is permitted or not. *What Would a Comprehensive Individual Income Tax Yield?*, in 1 1959 COMPENDIUM 251, 276. As pointed out in the text, however, an admission that the Haig-Simons definition is compatible with a structure that reduces the tax liability when a wealthy bachelor gets married is a dangerous concession for the advocates of a CTB. It clearly implies that the Haig-Simons definition is equally compatible with other adjustments of the tax liability to the taxpayer's marital or family status.

Simons himself was ambivalent on this issue. He asserted that "it would be hard to maintain that the raising of children is not a form of consumption on the part of parents" and that consequently no more should be allowed than "small, fixed credits" for minor children and other dependents who are incapable of self-support. H. SIMONS, *supra* note 72, at 140, 141. At the same time, however, he conceded, *id.* at 137–38, that:

> It seems reasonable enough that the credits for, at least, minor dependents should vary directly with the family income. This might be arranged — as indeed was done under the German *Reichseinkommensteuer* — by providing minimum and maximum credits per child, together with a credit expressed as a percentage of income between those limits. It may also seem reasonable that adult members of a taxpayer's household should be taxed with respect to that part of the joint consumption expenses attributable to them (less contributions by them), with deduction of the amounts so imputed in determining the taxable income of the householder. Consistency, of course, would

Although they are not as explicit on this point as one would wish, their objection to income-splitting evidently is that it violates their theory that the income tax should not take account of the way taxpayers choose to spend their income. In this view, I take it, a single man's tax should not be reduced by his acquisition of a wife any more than by his acquisition of a yacht.

This is one way of looking at life, of course, but it is surely not the only one, and others might conclude that tax distinctions based on marriage or other family responsibilities are of a different order from those based on the taxpayer's other expenditure choices. And if it be admitted that a CTB does not forbid taking account of family responsibilities by variations in the rate structure, I perceive no reason why a CTB is not equally consistent with the use of exclusions, deductions, or credits as the means of achieving the desired differentials.

In fact, even those who find it difficult or impossible to distinguish between the taxpayer's support of his wife and children and his other "personal" expenditures should not, in my opinion, move directly to the conclusion that all tax variations based on family responsibilities must be extirpated. An intervening question must be answered: *whose* income is being used for the "consumption" we are talking about? It is at least arguable that what we choose to call the husband's income is not "his" to the extent that he is required by law to use it for the support of his wife or children — that he is merely a conduit pro tanto, so that this portion of his earnings should be reported by, and taxed to, the wife or child. If married couples think of themselves as equally entitled to their combined income, how do the tax rates applicable to joint returns "erode" the tax base? If the husband's income is 25,000 dollars and the wife's zero, their tax on a joint return is less than a single person must pay on 25,000 dollars; but it is the same as the tax on two single persons with 12,500 dollars of income each.

Some commentators compare the husband with 25,000 dollars of income to the bachelor with the same income, saying that they have merely chosen to spend their money in different ways, and that their choices are irrelevant to a tax on *disposable* income. Others may find it more persuasive to compare the married couple to two unmarried persons with 12,500 dollars of income each; whether the couple resides in a community property state or not,

require the authorization of generous deductions with respect to amounts contributed to the support of persons outside the household.

marriage creates emotional, social, and legal claims so that the husband's salary is not "his" in the same sense that the salary of an unmarried taxpayer with no close relatives belongs to him. On this theory, if there are children, part of the husband's income "belongs" to them, not to him. Laymen are usually more legalistic than lawyers, and this bias may lead them to emphasize the husband's "right" to his salary and other income; but the insights of domestic life ought to dispel this preoccupation with legal concepts.

So far as I can tell, its advocates think that a CTB is consistent with allowing alimony to be deducted by the husband and reported by the ex-wife. If this is not a "leakage," would it be equally consistent with the Haig-Simons definition to allow a taxpayer to deduct amounts paid for the support of his wife and children, provided these amounts were reported by the recipient? Like alimony, these obligations stem from the fateful, but voluntary, decision to marry; and in both cases the taxpayer may have married in haste only to repent at leisure. Perhaps the tolerance shown toward alimony reflects the fact that the amount to be paid — the cost of support — has been fixed by an arm's-length agreement or by a court, while there is no such reliable basis for allocating a part of the husband's income to his wife or children during the pendency of the marriage; this ground would imply that some of the husband's income *ought* to be deductible by him and taxed to his wife or children, if only a satisfactory measure of the obligation of support were at hand. If so, it might be better to do what we can to allocate something (whether by a formal deduction coupled with inclusion in the recipient's income, as with alimony, or by some other means, such as a manipulation of the rate structure, exemption, or credit) rather than do nothing at all. In any event, tolerance of the alimony deduction suggests a sound, if unacknowledged, lack of assurance in the family-as-consumption theory — an implicit admission that support of one's family, though undertaken voluntarily,[81] should not be classed with the taxpayer's other consumption expenditures.

I do not mean to suggest that the joint return rate schedule, the dependency exemption, or any other structural provision of this area is immune to criticism or preferable to alternatives. What I do assert, however, is that the concept of a CTB is of no assistance in selecting the taxpaying unit. A decision to include every dollar

[81] It might also be noted here that a legal duty of support may devolve involuntarily on the taxpayer, for example in the case of indigent parents.

of economic betterment in someone's gross income does not help us to designate the appropriate someone. And a statutory provision can be an "exception" or a "preference" only if we have an agreed-upon standard.

B. Partnerships, Corporations, and Trusts

The ambiguity of the term "income" is encountered again when we ask if a taxpayer enjoys a "net accretion to" his "economic power" (Haig's formulation) when a partnership, trust, corporation, or other entity in which he is financially interested engages in profitable transactions. In the case of partnerships, the Internal Revenue Code requires each partner to report his share of the firm's profits, whether it is distributed to him or not. Ordinarily, of course, he has the legal right to compel a distribution, but an exercise of this right would often disrupt the business and his relations with his partners; and sometimes the partnership agreement permits a distribution of profits only by majority or unanimous vote of the partners. Since the Internal Revenue Code takes no account of practical or legal restrictions on the partner's right to withdraw his share of the firm's income, he is in effect taxed on "economic enhancement" rather than on the amount available to him for personal expenditures.

A shareholder of a corporation, however, is not taxed on its income until it is distributed to him, and this means no tax at all at the shareholder level if he holds the stock until death. (The corporation, of course, is taxed on its income as realized; but the aggregate burden of a corporate tax on the corporation's income and a personal tax on such gains as are distributed or otherwise realized by the shareholder may exceed or fall short of, but will almost certainly not correspond to, the tax that would have been paid if the same income had been realized by a partnership or individual proprietorship.) In contrast to the partnership, then, the corporation shields the shareholder against the individual income tax so long as the income is accumulated. And it does this even if the shareholder owns all of the stock and can withdraw the profits at will; spendable receipts are what count, not economic enhancement or even legal control over the profits. Natural law does not dictate this distinction between partnerships and corporations; in the case of two categories of corporations — foreign personal holding companies and foreign corporations realizing Subpart F income — the shareholder *is* taxed on his share of the corporation's undistributed income. Moreover, the existence of section

531 is a constant reminder of the intimate relationship between a corporation's profits and the tax status of its shareholders.

Trusts and estates fall between partnerships and corporations as respects the tax treatment of accumulated income: sometimes it is taxed to the beneficiaries even though not distributed to them (as with partners), but sometimes it is not taxed to them until distribution (as with shareholders). There are also circumstances in which trust income is taxed to the grantor of the trust, even though it cannot be distributed to him, because of the "non-economic" satisfactions he obtains by dedicating the income to the beneficiaries of the trust.[82]

In short, in its treatment of the taxpayer's financial interest in business and other entities, existing law wobbles between spendable receipts and economic enhancement as the criterion of income, and occasionally it fixes instead on vicarious enjoyment as controlling. We are sometimes told that some minor threads in this tangled web of rules are "preferences" that "erode" the tax base, the implicit premise being that the CTB concept implies a set of rules governing the attribution of entity income to the persons beneficially interested. Despite these fragmentary announcements, I know of no attempt to explain why a CTB is consistent with some attribution rules and not with others, nor any effort to spin out the implications that are thought to reside in this concept by systematically identifying the provisions in today's tax law that would have to be changed to achieve a CTB.

If corporate stock owned by the taxpayer were to be valued at the beginning and end of each taxable period in order to take the net accretion in unrealized gain or loss into account, as the Haig-Simons formulation seems to require, no other steps to reflect the taxpayer's interest in the corporation would be required. If unrealized appreciation or depreciation is to be disregarded, however, we might expect the advocates of a CTB to explore the milder measure of imputing the realized corporate income to the shareholders. There are obstacles in the way of doing so, of course, and the separate corporate tax may be viewed as rough compensation for failing to tax the shareholders; but this apology is just another way of saying that a CTB can be no more than a faintly flickering, far-off ideal. As to trusts, I presume (in the absence of an unequivocal statement by the CTB experts) that beneficiaries are to be taxed on income that is allocated to them, whether distributed or not. The status of the undistributed income of dis-

[82] *See* pp. 946–47 *supra* on the relationship of vicarious enjoyment to a CTB.

cretionary trusts, under the Haig-Simons formulation, is less clear. Perhaps it is income without a taxpayer, to be held in abeyance until the beneficiary who will receive it can be identified and taxed. There is little justification for taxing it to the fiduciary except as an interim measure, to be followed by an adjustment (additional tax or refund) when the real party in interest becomes identifiable. To the economists, this may seem obvious enough; but I suspect that the ABA Tax Section's Committee on Substantive Tax Reform will not be very comfortable with this application of the principle of "taxing all income equally."

Without claiming prescience, I venture to predict that many advocates of a CTB will draw back from the logical consequences of the idea that "economic enhancement" should be taxed wherever it can be identified, and will propose or acquiesce in an exception for the undistributed income of corporations and trusts. The justification that is likely to be offered for this exception is that the undistributed income of these entities is not presently available for expenditure by their shareholders or beneficiaries (except by selling or borrowing against their interests), and that it may never be distributed to them because it remains at the risk of the entity's activities. Fair enough. But cannot the same be said of the employer's contribution to a qualified pension plan, or even of the employee's own contribution if it is mandatory? And would the enemies of preferences be equally complacent if the personal holding company provisions were amended to permit the personal service income of movie stars — or of law professors and factory workers — to be accumulated in a corporation free of the individual income tax? My bones are not sensitive to the threat of rainy weather, but they tell me that *this* proposal would "erode" the tax base. But why would it, if an incorporated storekeeper is not taxed on *his* corporation's earnings until they are distributed to him?

Although the CTB concept thus implies a group of changes in the individual tax structure that are much more far-reaching than its advocates have acknowledged, it leaves us without guidance in a closely related area of the "taxable unit" problem, the separate corporation income tax. Just as the Haig-Simons formulation requires the taxable period to be specified without shedding any light on the criteria to be used in fixing a period, so it seems to require the taxable unit whose economic accretion is at stake to be prescribed by criteria that are not part of the definition of income. If the unit is selected on the basis of such "outside" criteria, however, it evidently follows that we can have a CTB whether corporations are taxed as separate entities or not. If so, the assertion that the dividends-received exclusion erodes the tax base [83] is puzzling: why is it not a partial nullification of a separate corporate tax that was not a necessary part of a CTB to begin with?

More important, is the tax base "eroded" if corporations are classified into categories (ordinary business corporations, personal holding companies, insurance companies, commercial banks, and so on) with the income of each category being computed and taxed in a manner — and at a rate — thought to be suited to its function in the nation's economy? If all incorporated taxpayers must be treated alike in order to achieve a CTB, today's rules will have to be drastically reformed at a variety of points that have not yet been identified for us by the CTB advocates. If, on the other hand, the aim of "taxing all income alike" is compatible with separate taxing systems or separate rate structures for insurance companies, personal holding companies, mutual savings banks, and commercial banks, I do not see why this aim is not equally consistent with taxing mining corporations differently from manufacturers, business executives differently from ministers, and married persons differently from bachelors.

VII. Conclusions

This attempt to work out the implications of the "no preference, comprehensive base" approach in a systematic way, and thus to ascertain where it would take us if it were converted from a slogan into a program for action, has led me to these conclusions:

(*1*) The systematic elimination of "preferences" in order to achieve a truly "comprehensive" base would require many more fundamental changes in existing law than are usually acknowledged. Among the areas that would be drastically affected by a whole-hearted use of the Haig-Simons definition are: mortality gains on life insurance; governmental benefits furnished in kind or in services; recoveries in suits for personal injury or death; charitable gifts to individuals; personal and dependency exemptions; tax-exempt organizations; the investment credit; deduction or rapid amortization of business assets; depreciation below

---

[83] *E.g.*, Pechman, *Erosion of the Individual Income Tax*, 10 NAT'L TAX J. 1, 12 (1957). I mean to imply not that the dividend exclusion is a desirable provision, but that the CTB concept sheds no light on the issue.

market values; inventory pricing; accounting methods; and tax-free exchanges. Some of these areas seem to have been disregarded by the proponents of the CTB, and others have not received the attention their importance deserves.

(2) At many points, the most enthusiastic proponents of a CTB have drawn back from its implications: they almost always advocate the exclusion from gross income of unrealized annual net worth increases, gifts and bequests, and imputed income from personal services, and support allowances for such personal expenditures as charitable contributions and medical care; and some also favor provisions to encourage investment, such as the investment credit or rapid depreciation. Their reasons for departing from the Haig-Simons definition are, in my opinion, no different from the reasons that are offered in support of all of the "preferences" of existing law: the necessity or desirability of avoiding difficulties in valuation or enforcement, of stimulating economic growth, of encouraging behavior thought to be socially useful, of alleviating economic hardship, of retaining the freedom of choice that results from use of tax concessions rather than some other governmental mechanism, or of pursuing other social policies. I dare say that they would give similar reasons for favoring perpetuation of many other preferences of existing law if they were required to express an opinion on all of those mentioned in this article.[84] In short, they harbor, in my opinion, the same attitude

---

[84] *See* L. Eisenstein, The Ideologies of Taxation 193, 197–98 (1961):

> Scholars who are hot for certainties . . . . must have answers if they are to be happy, and the answers must derive from some uniform standard which is objectively applied. Besides, the term "loophole" has become too charged with emotional overtones for the staid world of tax scholarship. . . . And so the scholars have turned to other words that are supposedly less partial and hence more informative.
>
> There are enough words to please everybody who wishes to appear impersonal and detached. Instead of loopholes the enlightened now speak of "erosions" of the tax base. Or they refer to special treatments and special provisions, special deductions and special exclusions, special exceptions and special accommodations, differentials and preferentials, discrepancies and discriminations, openings and leakages, tax shelters and tax havens, tax favors and tax advantages, tax mitigations and tax concessions. All these words, as well as others now in fashion, disclose a marked capacity for devising polite synonyms. They produce an air of impartial judgment. To call percentage depletion a loophole is to indulge in a personal prejudice. To call it an erosion is to make an objective appraisal . . . .
>
> My inquiry into loopholes confirms anew a familiar truth. Better answers require wiser questions. Ultimately dispensations for certain taxpayers are condemned, not because they conform to some definition of a loophole, but because they are considered undesirable for various reasons. . . . We cannot learn very much by asking what is a loophole. The only meaningful questions are those which focus on the precise purposes and effects of a dispensation. Of course, the answers will vary, for they will reflect different standards of good and evil . . . . No larger wisdom is discernible.

The following extract from *Report Supporting Resolutions on Substantive Tax*

toward the Haig-Simons definition of income that Congress is said to exhibit toward our progressive rate schedule: a declaration of faith, combined with advocacy or tolerance of numerous exceptions, each of which inures to the benefit of a "special" group of taxpayers.

(*3*) If I am right in asserting that most professed supporters of the CTB concept favor a host of important departures from the Haig-Simons standard, there ought to be an equally drastic revision of their rhetoric, including a renunciation of the claim that we can or should eliminate all, or even most, "preferences" and "special provisions" from the Internal Revenue Code. This means not that all provisions of existing law are equally good, but rather that we cannot avoid an examination of each one on its merits in a discouragingly inconclusive process that can derive no significant assistance from a "no preference" presumption that would at best be applied only on a wholly selective basis. Put another way, there are "preferences" and "preferences"; some are objectionable, some are tolerable, some are unavoidable, and some are indispensable. A truly "comprehensive" base, in short, would be a disaster.

It may be argued that the rhetoric of the CTB approach does not matter; we are used to political slogans and exhortations that contain a kernel of truth and do no harm even though they promise more than they can deliver. What concerns me is that the rhetoric

---

Reform, BULL. ABA SECTION OF TAXATION, July 1963 (Annual Report), at 5, 12–13, would have been admirable grist for Eisenstein's mill:

> There can be no wavering from a resolute determination that what is really income must be taxed without exception. Once there is a compromise with principle or a yielding to pressure to admit a special exception, the hole in the dike widens. All efforts at real reform go for nought. Having stated this broad proposition, however, one should note certain possible exceptions: for example, certain tax exempt organizations could continue their exempt status as under present rules; there could be a deferment of recognition of income in certain exchanges and corporate reorganizations; and such deferment might be extended to cover sales of property followed by reinvestment in comparable property.

I suspect that much of the enthusiasm for rigorous "broad base" reform among academicians would prove equally evanescent if subjected to cross-examination. Take, for example, these recommendations in JOINT ECONOMIC COMMITTEE, 89TH CONG., 1ST SESS., FISCAL POLICY ISSUES OF THE COMING DECADE (Comm. Print 1965): "broad-based, flat tax on all gross income" (Brown, in *id.* at 11, 14); "an adjusted gross income tax if possible" (Buchanan, in *id.* at 19, 21); "a general broadening of the tax base to include all forms of income" (Eisner, in *id.* at 42, 44); "[a tax] preferably on adjusted gross income with minor exemptions" (Groves, in *id.* at 61). I suggest that these shorthand expressions would, if expanded, translate into a somewhat broader tax base than we now have, but with a host of major and minor exclusions and deductions retained, rather than into a rigorous application of the Haig-Simons definition.

will foster changes in the tax structure not because they are desirable in themselves, but merely because they will broaden the base. Since I am convinced that a full-fledged CTB will, and should, remain miles away, I see no automatic advantage in moving a few feet in its direction. It is a truism that existing law bears more heavily on earned income than on income from investments, and I venture the judgment that the base-broadening provisions that are most likely to be enacted in the pursuit of a CTB would enlarge rather than narrow this disparity.

(*4*) To the extent that a departure from the Haig-Simons definition is compelled by administrative difficulties (valuation, enforcement, and the like) rather than by its contribution to a social or economic goal, the advocates of the CTB have given too little attention to the paradox of the "second best." [85] I take it that one of the virtues they see in the Haig-Simons definition is that its rigorous application would lead to an "ideal" distribution of the tax burden, by measuring the ability to pay that arises from "income" in the most accurate way.[86] If this is their view, it would be appropriate to quantify the tax burden distribution that would result from a rigorous application of the definition by taking into account, at the best estimates available, such difficult items as annual increases in net worth, imputed income from personal assets, housewives' services, and gifts and bequests. Even if the valuation problems are too formidable to justify inclusion of these items in the tax structure itself on a taxpayer-by-taxpayer basis, a rough and ready estimate would be better than nothing

[85] Lipsey & Lancaster, *The General Theory of Second Best*, 24 REV. ECON. STUDIES 11 (1956).

[86] *See* H. SIMONS, *supra* note 72, at 105–06: "Since the devices of accounting and tax legislation contemplate only very rough approximation to income, it is decisively important to see behind these methods of calculation an 'ideal income,' calculable by different and less practicable methods. Only on the basis of some broader conception is it possible to criticize and evaluate merely practicable procedures and to consider fruitfully the problem of bettering the system of presumptions." *Accord*, R. MUSGRAVE, THE THEORY OF PUBLIC FINANCE 165 (1959). (But Musgrave, *id.* at 165, refers to the "excellent analysis" of the income concept in N. KALDOR, AN EXPENDITURE TAX (1955), which concludes, at 70, that "the problem of *defining* individual income, quite apart from any problem of practical measurement, appears in principle insoluble.") *See* White, *Consistent Treatment of Items Excluded and Omitted from the Individual Income Tax Base*, in 1 1959 COMPENDIUM 317 ("Aside from practical difficulties in administration, the base of the individual income tax ought never, or hardly ever, to be determined on any criterion other than that of consistency with the economic [Simons] definition of personal income"); H. BRAZER, A PROGRAM FOR FEDERAL TAX REVISION 7 (1960); Blum, *Federal Income Tax Reform — Twenty Questions*, 41 TAXES 672, 680 (1963); authorities cited note 10 *supra*.

for the kind of macroeconomic model that I am suggesting. Having worked out in this way an approximation of the "ideal" distribution of the tax burden, it would be possible to test alternative reform programs to see which comes closest to the "ideal." [87] The "best" practical program, on this theory, would not be the one that eliminated the *most* "preferences," but the one whose tax burden distribution was closest to the ideal.

This method of judging the proximity of a proposal to the professed ideal would recognize that unavoidable preferences (those compelled by limitations in valuation techniques, anticipated problems in compliance, and similar factors) might be offset by deliberately preserving (or even creating) other preferences. It has often been pointed out that the elimination of an exclusion would serve no purpose if it is so equally distributed that the tax burden would be unaffected by the tidier system resulting from the change. I am suggesting nothing more than a generalized application of this well-known principle. If the tax base is to continue to exclude gifts and bequests, annual net worth increases, and imputed income from personal property, for example, the continued exclusion of unemployment compensation, social security payments, and similar items may distribute the tax burden more equitably (using the Haig-Simons definition as the touchstone) than a reform program that adds the latter category of items to the base.

---

[87] Such a study would employ the computer techniques pioneered by J. Pechman and described in his A NEW TAX MODEL FOR REVENUE ESTIMATING (1965), and applied in B. OKNER, INCOME DISTRIBUTION AND THE FEDERAL INCOME TAX (1966). The study proposed by the ABA Committee on Substantive Tax Reform of the Section of Taxation, 90 ABA REP. 289, 295 (1965), will be a step in the right direction if it is rigorous enough in its conception of a "broad income tax base." The proposed study ought to examine the effect of "preferences" on both "horizontal" and "vertical" equity (that is, within each income bracket and as among brackets, respectively). There may be "preferences" that, taken in combination, produce a distribution of tax liabilities within certain brackets comparable to the burden that would result from a more rigorous application of the Haig-Simons definition; and other combinations of "preferences" may have a similar effect as among income brackets. Finally, there may be more elaborate combinations that would perform the same function simultaneously for both the horizontal and vertical planes.

I do not wish to minimize the difficulties; to satisfy everyone, the study would have to offer a series of "ideal" distributions of the tax burden, each based on its own assumptions about the proper way to resolve the definitional issues in the concept of income. Moreover, since we lack information on the size and distribution of many items that are not now reflected on tax returns, a good deal of estimating ingenuity would be required. One of the dangers, of course, in the availability of *some* information in a form that permits easy computer use is that items that are not "machine-handleable" will be disregarded. *See* Spengler, *Machine-Made Justice: Some Implications*, 28 LAW & CONTEMP. PROB. 36, 44–45 (1963).

(*5*) There are many problem areas in which the search for "preferences" is doomed to fail because we cannot confidently say which provisions are "rules" and which are "exceptions." In these areas, we cannot comply with Blum's advice to "lean over backward" to avoid "preferences" [88] because, in the absence of a generally acceptable or scientifically determinable vertical, we cannot know whether we are leaning forward or backward. The central source of difficulty is the fact that the income tax structure cannot be discovered, but must be constructed; it is the final result of a multitude of debatable judgments.

If we were dealing not with an income tax but with a tax whose label described its reach with greater precision, an "exception" would be easier to identify. For example, in constructing a poll tax, we would have at the outset a consensus on what constitutes a natural person whose "head" is to be taxed. To be sure, even here there would be marginal cases — conceived but unborn children, persons who have been legally declared dead but who reappear, Siamese twins, and so on. These peripheral cases aside, a consensus on the base to which the tax is to be applied would be feasible, and it would warrant the use of terms like "exception" and "preference" to describe proposals to exempt from the tax such persons as children, foreign tourists and diplomats, or incompetents. And one could say of proposals to exempt soldiers on combat duty, Boy Scout leaders, or persons over the age of sixty-five or blind that, however meritorious such "preferences" might be when considered individually, there would be no satisfactory criteria for exempting one group of meritorious persons while refusing to exempt other persons such as Peace Corps workers, nurses, or the unemployed. Under these circumstances, it could be persuasively argued that a "pure" tax base would be a fortress that could be effectively defended against all comers, no matter how appealing their claims. When we turn to the field of income taxation, however, we do not begin with a consensus on the meaning of income, but with a myriad of arguments about what should be taxed, when, and to whom. The CTB concept is simply irrelevant to many of these issues — the taxable unit, the taxable period, the personal-business borderline, and others — and hence, notwithstanding the contrary assumption of some commentators, it can make no contribution to the elimination of "preferences" from these areas.

C. Taxation and Social Policy

Increasingly we tend to look to the tax law to serve as a cure for all of society's ills. The first article in this section explores some of the implications of achieving any particular social objective through a tax provision rather than a program of direct governmental grants. The student of taxation may well wish to ask himself how the considerations advanced by Professor Surrey apply to particular "nontax" provisions encountered by him in the course of his study.[a]

One specific case in point is the desire to distribute additional funds to the poor. As the article by Professor Brazer makes clear, this can be readily done outside the income tax. But either such a scheme takes the form of a demogrant (i.e., distribution to every individual, or every child, or every family, regardless of need)—which is prohibitively expensive at any realistic payment level—or else it gears the payments to need (in effect a negative income tax). Professor Brazer's scheme seeks to avoid the complications inherent in the latter type of proposal,[b] while looking to the tax law to recoup most of the unneeded benefits of a demogrant from the rich, so as to bring its cost within reasonable bounds.

[a] This assumes, of course, that we can readily identify a "nontax" use of the tax law. Professor Bittker, in a piece that echoes many of the points made in his "comprehensive tax base" article contained in Section C of this chapter, contends that we cannot. See Bittker, *Accounting for Federal "Tax Subsidies" in the National Budget*, 22 Nat.Tax J. 244 (1969), and the various replies at *id.* pp. 528 and 538.

[b] The major difficulties are the framing of an appropriate tax base, tax unit and tax rate—issues that raise very similar considerations as their counterparts in the positive income tax. See, e. g., A Model Negative Income Tax Statute, 78 Yale L.J. 269 (1968).

SURREY, TAX INCENTIVES AS A DEVICE FOR IMPLEMENTING GOVERNMENT POLICY: A COMPARISON WITH DIRECT GOVERNMENT EXPENDITURES *

83 Harv.L.Rev. 705 (1970).

SUGGESTIONS are constantly being made that many of our pressing social problems can be solved, or partially met, through the use of income tax incentives. Moreover, the present federal income tax is replete with tax incentive provisions. Some were adopted to assist particular industries, business activities, or financial transactions. Others were adopted to encourage non-business activities considered socially useful, such as contributions to charity. This article will deal with the question of whether tax incentives are as useful or efficient an implement of social policy as direct government expenditures, such as grants, loans, interest subsidies, and guarantees of loans. The discussion will be in terms of the federal income tax, but it is intended to be helpful for other jurisdictions and other forms of taxation as well.

* Copyright © 1970 by The Harvard Law Review Association. Reproduced with permission.

I. The Nature and Extent of Existing Tax Incentives

The term "tax expenditure" has been used to describe those special provisions of the federal income tax system which represent government expenditures made through that system to achieve various social and economic objectives. These special provisions provide deductions, credits, exclusions, exemptions, deferrals, and preferential rates, and serve ends similar in nature to those served by direct government expenditures or loan programs. In any specific functional area the Government may use direct expenditures, interest subsidies, direct federal loans, and federal insurance or guarantee of private loans as alternative methods to accomplish the purposes which the special tax provision seeks to achieve or encourage.

The use of the phrase "special provisions" clearly involves a major definitional question: which tax rules are special provisions and therefore tax expenditures, and which tax rules are just tax rules; simply part of the warp and woof of a tax structure? The description and analysis of tax expenditures contained in the fiscal 1968 report to the Secretary of the Treasury used these guidelines: [1]

> [The analysis] lists the major respects in which the current income tax bases deviate from widely accepted definitions of income and standards of business accounting and from the generally accepted structure of an income tax . . . .
>
> * * *
>
> The study does not attempt a complete listing of all the tax provisions which vary from a strict definition of net income. Various items that could have been added have been excluded for one or more of several reasons:
>
> (a) Some items were excluded where there is no available indication of the precise magnitude of the implicit subsidy. This

[1] 1968 Sec'y Treas. Ann. Rep. on the State of the Finances 326–30; *see* Statement of Joseph W. Barr, Secretary of the Treasury, in *Hearings on the 1969 Economic Report of the President Before the Joint Economic Comm.*, 91st Cong., 1st Sess. 8–44 (1969) (containing a "Comparison of Budget Outlays and Tax Expenditures by Function Fiscal Year 1970"). *See also* Statement by Stanley S. Surrey on the Tax Expenditure Budget, in *Hearings on Economic Analyses and Efficiency in Government Before the Subcomm. on Economy in Government of the Joint Economic Comm.*, 91st Cong., 1st Sess. (Sept. 16, 1969). For a discussion of the definitional task, see Bittker, *Accounting for Federal "Tax Subsidies" in the National Budget*, 22 Nat. Tax J. 244 (1969), and Surrey & Hellmuth, *The Tax Expenditure Budget — Response to Professor Bittker*, 22 Nat. Tax J. (to be published). The latter article also discusses the relevance of the tax expenditure concept to taxes other than the income tax. *See also* Wolfman, *Federal Tax Policy and the Support of Science*, 114 U. Pa. L. Rev. 171, 173–74 (1965).

is the case, for example, with depreciation on machinery and equipment where the accelerated tax methods may provide an allowance beyond that appropriate to the measurement of net income but where it is difficult to measure that difference because the true economic deterioration or obsolescence factor cannot be readily determined.

(b) Some items were excluded where the case for their inclusion in the income base stands on relatively technical or theoretical tax arguments. This is the case, for example, with the imputed rent on owner-occupied homes, which involves not only a conceptual problem but difficult practical problems such as those of measurement.

(c) Some items were omitted because of their relatively small quantitative importance.

Other features of our income tax system are considered not as variations from the generally accepted measure of net income or as tax preference but as part of the structure of an income tax system based on ability to pay. Such features include personal exemptions and the rate schedules under the individual income tax, including the income splitting allowed for married couples filing joint returns or for heads of households. A discussion of income splitting and the dependent's personal exemption is thus considered outside the scope of this study on tax expenditures.

It must be recognized that these exclusions are to some extent arbitrary . . . . The immediate objective, however, of this study is to provide a list of items that would be generally recognized as more or less intended use of the tax system to achieve results commonly obtained by government expenditures. The design of the list seems best served by constructing what seemed a minimum list rather than including highly complicated or controversial items that would becloud the utility of this special analysis.

* * *

. . . The assumption inherent in current law, that corporations are separate entities and subject to income taxation independently from their shareholders, is adhered to in this analysis.

These guidelines readily identify a significant number of provisions in existing law which we can all agree are "special" and represent tax expenditures: tax benefits for the aged, natural resources provisions such as percentage depletion allowances, the investment credit, excessive real estate depreciation. These provisions are identifiable as tax expenditures for the additional reason that they have been defended, either by their beneficiaries or by Congress in adopting them, on the grounds that they achieve a particular purpose, claimed to be desirable, other than the measurement of net income under an income tax.

On the basis of these guidelines, the Treasury analysis identified a long list of tax expenditures, with estimates in terms of fiscal year 1968. The expenditures were classified according to the functional categories of government expenditures used in the budget, with the addition of two special categories: Aid to State and Local Governments, and Capital Gains: [2]

---

[2] Statement of Joseph W. Barr, *supra* note 1. Footnotes are here omitted. The Tax Reform Act of 1969, Pub. L. No. 91–172 (Dec. 30, 1969), cut back a number of these expenditures, and added a few new ones. *See* p. 713 and pp. 736–37 nn. 39–41 *infra*.

No significant tax expenditures are made in the budget categories of Space, Interest, and General Government.

The Treasury analysis contained the following comments on revenue estimates:

> All estimates of tax expenditures resulting from special tax provisions represent revenues lost on an annual basis. The estimates of revenue foregone are, in general, based on the assumption that such provisions never existed, or, alternatively, that such provisions have been withdrawn sufficiently long ago that we are now beyond the period needed to permit an equitable transition to a new tax situation.
>
> The revenue cost estimated for these special provisions is not in many cases the revenue change which would result in the first full year if these provisions were withdrawn. Replacement of some or all of these provisions by direct expenditures or lending programs might change the level and composition of economic activity. The revenue cost of each special tax provision presented for 1968 would, of course, generally vary over time with growth in the economy and changes in various parts of the tax base. Also, a realistic approach to any change in these provisions would provide in many situations transition arrangements which would effect the revenue change gradually over a period of years.
>
> Another key assumption is that economic activity for the year would not have been affected by the absence of these special provisions. This, of course, is a simplifying assumption for tax expenditures undoubtedly have significant effects on the composition and perhaps the level of economic activity. Also, in the absence of these tax benefits, there would doubtless have been changes in Government direct spending and net lending to accomplish some of the objectives of the existing provisions. No attempt has been made to speculate how the budget and the economy might differ if none of these provisions were in the law.

Statement of Joseph W. Barr, *supra* note 1, at 34. Thus, in effect the estimating techniques used are similar to the "first effect" estimates typically given by the Treasury to indicate the revenue effect of any proposed change.

Professor Henry Aaron has compiled another inventory of existing tax incentives, arranged according to the types of economic decisions which the tax provision influences. Aaron, *Inventory of Existing Tax Incentives: Federal*, in TAX INSTITUTE OF AMERICA, SYMPOSIUM ON TAX INCENTIVES (to be published) [hereinafter cited as INCENTIVES SYMPOSIUM]. He uses the term tax incentive to denote any tax provision which is "defended or advocated primarily because it so alters resource allocation as to improve economic efficiency." He excludes "tax provisions defended primarily because they are alleged to have favorable effects on the distribution of income by income class, family status, age groups or other socioeconomic categories." Thus, he would exclude tax expenditures for the aged and the blind. His tax incentives fall into three main categories: those influencing *household behavior* — spending patterns (for example the charitable contributions deduction), place of employment (for example the exemption of certain income earned abroad), or portfolio choice (for example capital gains); *business behavior* — investment in capital (for example the investment credit), composition of the wage offer (for example the exclusion of employer contributions to pension plans), industrial composition (for example the tax benefits to agriculture and natural

TAX EXPENDITURES BY BUDGET FUNCTION	REVENUE COST MILLIONS OF DOLLARS
National Defense	
Exclusion of Military benefits and allowances	$500
International Affairs and Finance	
Individual taxation:	
Exemption for certain income earned abroad by U.S. citizens	40
Exclusion of income earned in U.S. possessions	10
Corporate taxation:	
Western Hemisphere trade corporations	50
Exclusion of gross-up on dividends of less developed country corporations	50
Exclusion of controlled foreign subsidiaries	150
Exclusion of income earned in U.S. possessions	70
Total	370
Agriculture and Agricultural Resources	
Farming: Expensing and capital gains treatment	800
Timber: Capital gains treatment for certain income	130
Total	930
Natural Resources	
Expensing of exploration and development costs	300
Excess of percentage over cost depletion	1,300
Capital gains treatment of royalties on coal and iron ore	5
Total	1,605
Commerce and Transportation	
Investment credit	2,300
Excess depreciation on buildings	500
Dividend exclusion	225
Capital gains: Corporations (other than agricultural and natural resources)	500
Excess bad debt reserves of financial institutions	600
Exemption of credit unions	40
Deductibility of interest on consumer credit	1,300
Expensing of research and development expenditures	500
$25,000 surtax exemption	1,800
Deferral of tax on shipping companies	10
Total	7,775
Community Development and Housing	
Owner-occupied homes, deductibility of:	
Interest on mortgages	1,900
Property taxes	1,800

resources), business location (for example the Western Hemisphere Trade Corporations provision); and *state and local government behavior* — sources of finance (for example deductibility of state and local taxes).

For an inventory of incentives in state and local taxes, see Slater, in INCENTIVES SYMPOSIUM.

Tax Expenditures by Budget Function	Revenue Cost Millions of Dollars
Rental housing–excess depreciation	250
Total	3,950
Health and Welfare	
Aged, blind, and disabled:	
Additional exemption, retirement income credit and exclusion of OASDHI for aged	2,300
Additional exemption for blind	10
Exclusion for sick pay	85
Exclusion of unemployment insurance benefits	300
Exclusion of workmen's compensation benefits	150
Exclusion of public assistance benefits	50
Exclusion for employee pensions	3,000
Deduction for self-employed retirement	60
Exclusion of other employee benefits:	
Premiums on group term life insurance	400
Accident and death benefits	25
Medical insurance premiums and medical care	1,100
Privately financed supplementary unemployment benefits	25
Meals and lodging	150
Exclusion of interest on life insurance savings	900
Deductibility by individuals of charitable contributions (other than education) including untaxed appreciation	2,200
Deductibility of medical expenses	1,500
Deductibility of child and dependent care expenses	25
Deductibility of casualty losses	70
Standard deduction	3,200
Total	15,550
Education and Manpower	
Additional personal exemption for students	500
Deductibility of contributions by individuals to educational institutions	170
Exclusion of scholarships and fellowships	50
Total	720
Veterans Benefits	
Exclusion of certain benefits	550
Aid to State and Local Government Financing	
Exemption of interest on State and local debt obligations	1,800
Deductibility of nonbusiness State and local taxes (other than on owner-occupied homes):	
Individual income tax	1,350
General sales taxes	775
Gasoline taxes	400
Personal property taxes	150
Other taxes	125
Total	2,800

TAX EXPENDITURES BY BUDGET FUNCTION	REVENUE COST MILLIONS OF DOLLARS
Property taxes on owner-occupied homes (included under community development and housing)	1,800
Total, all State and local nonbusiness taxes	4,600
Capital Gains — Individual Income Tax	
Special provisions (increase in basis at death; exclusion of one-half of long-term gains; maximum tax rates of 25% on long-term gains)	5,500–8,500

The analysis also showed the relationship of tax expenditures to direct expenditures for these budget categories. In some cases the tax expenditures exceeded or were close to budget expenditures (Community Development and Housing, 204%; Commerce and Transportation, 114%; Natural Resources, 90%; Health and Welfare, 37%) (fiscal 1969 figures). In none of the categories listed above except for National Defense and Veterans were the tax expenditures less than 10% of budget expenditures. The total of the estimated tax expenditures, in a round number, was $45 billion.

If we take as our definition of tax incentive a tax expenditure which induces certain activities or behavior in response to the monetary benefit available, almost all of the tax expenditures included in the above analysis can be considered tax incentives. Many of the tax expenditures were expressly adopted to induce action which the Congress considered in the national interest. For example, the investment credit was intended to encourage the purchase of machinery and equipment; excessive bad debt reserves for some financial institutions were allowed to encourage the growth of savings and loan associations and mutual savings banks; the charitable deduction was intended to foster philanthropy; the preferential tax treatment of qualified pension plans was intended to foster broad pension plan coverage; and the corporate surtax exemption was intended to foster small business.[3] Other tax expenditures whose origins are cloudy are now defended as incentives to home ownership, as in the case of the deduction for mortgage interest and property taxes, or as aids to state and local governments' tax bases, as in the case of the deduction for state and local taxes. Other tax expenditure pro-

[3] Other tax expenditures in this class include the treatment under the foreign tax credit of dividends paid by the corporations of less developed countries, capital gains treatment in general, the exemption of credit unions, the special treatment of timber capital gains, the hundred dollar dividend exclusion, and the deduction for one-half of medical insurance premiums, group term life insurance, and income earned abroad. Accelerated depreciation on real estate probably is another example, although it was adopted largely as a happenstance along with accelerated depreciation provisions designed to encourage investment in personal property.

visions were adopted as relief provisions to ease "tax hardships," or were adopted to simplify tax computations. Some of these provisions have come to be defended on the basis of their incentive effects: for example, the intangible drilling expenses deduction, the percentage depletion allowance, the Western Hemisphere Trade Corporation preferential rate, and the research and development expense deduction.[4] Moreover, to the extent that such tax relief — *i.e.*, tax treatment that is special and not required by the concept and general standards of a net income tax — is granted for an activity that is voluntary, the relief is in effect an incentive to engage in that activity, even though the provisions may not be defended on incentive grounds. For example, if meals and lodging furnished an employee on the premises of an employer are not taxed, the effect is to make employees more likely to choose such employment. If coal and iron royalties receive capital gains treatment and other royalties do not, investment preferences will be affected.[5]

The only tax expenditures that are not tax incentives, as we are using the expression, are expenditures related to involuntary activities of taxpayers. Most such provisions are designed to provide tax reduction in order to relieve misfortune or hardship — situations involving "personal hardships," as contrasted with the "tax hardships" that have brought about other special tax provisions, chiefly for business activities. The extra exemption for the blind is one example. The extra exemption for the aged is another — we can't grow old any faster because of the exemption.[6] Special provisions of this character are relatively few in

[4] Additional examples include the bad debt reserves for banks, the cash method of accounting for farmers, and the special personal exemption for students.

[5] Incentive effects are also produced by the exemption of military pay earned in combat zones.

[6] Perhaps the other tax benefits for the aged — the retirement credit and the social security exemption — also fall in this non-incentive category, though this is not so clear. The retirement credit provides some incentive to retire. Also, favoring retirement income may encourage saving for retirement. The employee sick pay exclusion may be in the non-incentive class, since sickness is presumably involuntary, yet the provision can have the incentive effect of inducing employers to provide such plans or unions to negotiate for such plans. The general medical expense deduction similarly has non-incentive characteristics, yet the presence of the deduction does tend to induce the purchase of health insurance and the greater use of medical services and equipment. The exclusion of unemployment insurance and public assistance benefits also has non-incentive characteristics, if we regard unemployment and need for public assistance as essentially involuntary conditions. Yet for some individuals the generality will not hold, and the tax result will add to the monetary inducement which makes the condition acceptable. The casualty loss deduction is also generally not an incentive, though in particular cases it may induce certain action that would otherwise be too risky, such as self-insurance, or ownership of a house in a hurricane area.

number. By and large, therefore, the classification guidelines in the Treasury Analysis which separate tax expenditures from other tax provisions also serve to identify existing tax incentives.

The recently considered tax expenditures are all in the tax incentive category. They include pollution control machinery credits, manpower training credits, educational expense credits, tax benefits for investing in low income housing, and tax benefits for business investment in central cities or rural areas. In all these situations the direct purpose of the proposed tax change is to provide monetary assistance or benefit through the tax laws so as to make the desired course of action financially more palatable to taxpayers involved, and thereby induce them to take that action. Whatever the purpose of the economic benefit involved — be it to make an expensive activity less costly, to reduce its risk, or to increase the rate of after-tax profit — the incentive effect is the desired effect.

II. Comparison of Tax Incentives with Direct Expenditures

This section of the discussion is concerned with criteria for evaluating the use of tax incentives as compared to the use of direct government expenditures. This evaluation does not involve the issue whether we should seek to achieve the particular goals for which tax incentives are now used or suggested. We can assume it is understood that each incentive must serve purposes which the nation wants to achieve and is willing to finance, rather than let the marketplace determine the extent to which the result will obtain. This is not to say that every proposal for a tax incentive is presented or defended with a careful analysis along these lines. Far from it — many sponsors of tax incentives simply assume that if the benefit sought is helpful to them in reaching a desired result, the incentive is in the public interest. But this discussion assumes that these issues have been decided. Therefore, we are assessing the use of tax incentives as a technique to provide the government assistance. The discussion is applicable to those tax expenditures intended to alleviate personal hardships, although we have indicated that they might not be classified as tax incentives.

There are, of course, as stated earlier, a variety of ways to provide government financial assistance — direct grants, loans, interest subsidies, guarantees of loan repayment or interest payments, insurance on investments, and so on. These methods are here called budgetary or direct expenditures. Skilled tax technicians and budgetary experts can take any tax expenditure and devise a budgetary expenditure approach to serve the same goals as a direct expenditure.[7] For example, the British for some years used an approach under their tax law somewhat similar to our 7% investment credit to encourage the acquisition of machinery and equipment. They subsequently dropped the tax technique and substituted direct cash payments.[8] The existing tax incentive for charitable giving could also be structured as a direct expenditure program, under which the Government would match an individual's contribution to charity with a proportional contribution of its own to the same charity.[9] Tax credits to an employer for manpower training could be structured as grants or contract payments to the employer. Tax benefits to the aged can be structured as cash to the aged. And so on.

It follows that a meaningful comparison between the tax incentive technique and the direct expenditure technique must involve *similar substantive programs.* There is no point to saying that in a particular situation a tax incentive is a more useful approach because it involves no government supervision over the details of the action to be induced, whereas a direct expenditure involves detailed supervision. To say so is not to compare a tax incentive with a direct expenditure but simply to compare a loosely controlled method of paying out government funds with a tightly controlled method. Direct expenditures can involve loose as well as tight supervision. Once we decide which substantive program we want then we can go on to decide which technique, tax incentive or direct expenditure, is preferable for that program.

The matter of what type of substantive program is best calculated to achieve the desired goal lies in the fields of cost-benefit and cost-effectiveness analyses. These methods are being used more and more to devise and test direct expenditures, and they should a priori be equally applicable to programs using a tax in-

---

[7] *See* Stone, *Tax Incentives as a Solution to Urban Problems*, 10 WM. & MARY L. REV. 647, 651–53 (1969) (describing possible assistance devices for urban housing). *See also* Slitor, *Tax Incentives and Urban Blight*, in INCENTIVES SYMPOSIUM (generally defending tax incentives). For other discussions of tax incentives, see Blum, *Federal Income Tax Reform — Twenty Questions*, 41 TAXES 672 (1963); Kurtz, *Tax Incentives: Their Use and Misuse*, U. SO. CAL. 1968 TAX INSTITUTE 1.

[8] The tax provision was the Finance Act of 1954, 2 & 3 Eliz. 2, c. 44, § 16, repealed by the Finance Act of 1966, c. 18, § 35. Direct grants were instituted by the Industrial Development Act of 1966, c. 34, § 1.

[9] Where the charity was a religious institution, a direct government contribution would raise serious questions under the establishment of religion clause of the first amendment. But such a direct subsidy should be considered constitutional if the present tax provision is, since there is no practical difference between the two.

centive technique.[10] For present purposes I am assuming that the substantive analysis, as respects methodological approach, use of econometric techniques, and the like, should be of the same order whether a tax incentive or a direct expenditure is involved. This is not to say that this has been true with regard to tax incentives in the past. Far from it — and therein lie many of the problems with tax incentives. Nor can we say that it will be true as to future tax incentives, nor can we say that all direct expenditure programs are carefully thought through.

A meaningful comparison between the two techniques must also be *realistic*. Thus, it must recognize that a tax incentive does involve the expenditure of government funds. It is often said that a tax incentive is more useful than a direct expenditure because people do not like or will not respond to "subsidies." Such statements always assume that the direct expenditure is the "subsidy," whereas the tax benefit obtained in the tax incentive — the lower tax — is not so regarded. Perhaps we may find that this fiscal illusion has its usefulness, but we should at least be aware of what is the reality and what is the illusion.[11]

A. Some Asserted Virtues of Tax Incentives — Falsely Claimed

Against this general background we can now consider some of the virtues and defects generally claimed for tax incentives and, on the other side of the coin, for direct expenditures. The first level of consideration relates to virtues claimed for tax incentives, but, in light of the above background, falsely claimed.

1. Tax Incentives Encourage the Private Sector to Participate in Social Programs. — Frequently a tax incentive is urged on the ground that the particular problem to be met is great and that the Government must assist in its solution by enlisting the par-

---

[10] For recent examples of such studies applied to tax incentives relating to natural resources, see Consad Research Corp., *The Economic Factors Affecting the Level of Domestic Petroleum Reserves*, in HOUSE WAYS & MEANS COMM. & SENATE COMM. ON FINANCE, 91ST CONG., 1ST SESS., UNITED STATES TREASURY DEPARTMENT, TAX REFORM STUDIES AND PROPOSALS (Comm. Print 1969); Mid-Continent Oil and Gas Association, Analysis and Comment Relating to the Consad Report on the Influence of U.S. Petroleum Taxation on the Level of Reserves, April 25, 1969; Consad Research Corp., *Comments on Mid-Continent (MC) Oil and Gas Association Critique*, 115 CONG. REC. S14290–91 (daily ed. Nov. 13, 1969). As to buildings, see Taubman and Rausche, *The Income Tax and Real Estate Investment*, in INCENTIVES SYMPOSIUM; Taubman and Rausche, *Economic and Tax Depreciation of Office Buildings*, 22 NAT. TAX J. 334 (1969). As to the investment credit, see Brannon, *A Requiem for the Investment Tax Credit*, in INCENTIVES SYMPOSIUM (describing existing studies on the credit).

[11] Sneed, *The Criteria of Federal Income Tax Policy*, 17 STAN. L. REV. 567, 602–03 (1965).

ticipation of the private sector — generally business. The need for Government to participate can be fulfilled by a tax incentive, and this is asserted as a virtue of tax incentives — they provide government assistance. Thus, a tax incentive for manpower training proposed in the Senate was defended in these terms: [12]

> Tax incentives [are proposed] to encourage the fullest participation of the private sector in employment, upgrading, and training of less skilled people.
>
> . . . .
>
> . . . A tax incentive program should [make] . . . it economically possible for American business to play an important role in our manpower program.
>
> . . . .
>
> . . . .
>
> I understand the objections that are at times put forward to the use of the tax system for social purposes. However, I think it is time we realized that in order to encourage business to participate in programs of this nature, Government must be willing to meet business half way. The most convenient form for subsidizing a businessman is through his income tax.
>
> . . . [This bill] enlists the job-creating potential of private enterprise by realistically recognizing the high initial costs involved in hiring, training, and providing supportive services for low-skilled individuals.

But all this is a non-sequitur; it points not to the virtue of tax incentives but to the need for government assistance. The existence of that need has no relevance to the question whether the need should be met by an incentive or by a direct expenditure.

2. *Tax Incentives Are Simple and Involve Far Less Governmental Supervision and Detail.* — A whole swirl of virtues claimed for tax incentives is summed up in the general observation that they keep Government — that is, the government bureaucracy — out of the picture: that they involve less negotiation of the arrangements, less supervision, less red tape, no new bureaucracy, and so on. The manpower proposal referred to above was supported by this argument: [13]

> The advantages to a tax credit approach are numerous. The most important, however, is that the program can go into effect immediately upon enactment. Employment programs in the past have taken months and years to become operative. . . . Employers who participate in the program will receive a tax credit of 75 percent of the wages paid to the employee for the first 4

[12] 115 CONG. REC. S5329, S5330 (daily ed. May 16, 1969) (statement of Senator Percy). The bill is S. 2192, 91st Cong., 1st Sess. (1969).

[13] 115 CONG. REC. S5329, S5330 (daily ed. May 16, 1969) (statement of Senator Percy).

> months of employment, 50 percent for the next 4 months, and 25 percent for the balance of the individual's first year of employment. This is an uncomplicated program with the minimum of redtape. Any employer who hires a certified employee is eligible for the tax credit — it is as simple as that.

But this merely comes down to saying: "Let's have a manpower program under which the Government pays an employer who hires a certified employee an amount calculated as a percentage of the employee's wage." There is nothing so far that indicates whether the payment should be by way of a tax credit or a direct expenditure. If the employer can obtain government funds (*i.e.*, a reduction in tax through the tax credit) for his employment activities by filling out a schedule on a tax return, a manpower program could be devised instead under which he would receive the same monetary assistance by filling out the exact same schedule on a piece of paper that had "Department of Labor" at the top in place of "Internal Revenue Service."

A government that decides it is wise to pay out tax credit money via a simple tax schedule would be highly irrational if it also decided that it would be unwise to pay the same amount directly on the same basis. A dollar is a dollar — both for the person who receives it and the government that pays it, whether the dollar comes with a tax credit label or a direct expenditure label. Nor is a new bureaucracy needed to pay out these amounts as a direct expenditure — a check-writing process is all that would be needed in keeping with the parallel to the tax credit. Nor, similarly, must there be long negotiations, complex contracts, and the like. It is not the tax route that makes the program simple — it is a substantive decision to have a simple program. In many cases, it is true, direct expenditure programs are probably overstructured and the urging of tax incentives is a reaction to, and a valid criticism of, badly designed expenditure programs. The cure lies of course in better designed expenditure programs.

It should be added, parenthetically, that the alleged simplicity of tax incentives is likely to be illusory. Thus, the argument quoted above states that "[a]ny employer who hires a certified employee is eligible for the tax credit — it is as simple as that." But this is not really so, because the legislation actually proposed would have required the employer to be certified by the Secretary of Labor, and to be eligible for certification an employer would have had to prove that the employment program would not impair or depress the wages, working standards, or opportunities of present employees; that the business was not affected by strike, lockout, or similar conditions; that the employees in the program would be afforded an equal opportunity for full-time employment after the expiration of the credit period; that a formal on-the-job training program would be available; and that there would be no discrimination on account of race, color, religion, or national origin. Further complexities were involved in the proposed system for determining the creditable wage base, which was to be defined as the higher of the minimum wage or the wage customarily paid by the employer for such services.[14] Similarly, the low income housing tax incentive legislation discussed in 1967 and 1968 was studded with requirements of "approval by the Secretary of Housing and Urban Development."

The tape was thus present in the tax credit program and its color was red. This is not to criticize the particular programs, but rather to observe that those who design tax incentive programs, just as those who design direct expenditure programs, may find that complex requirements become desirable.

3. Tax Incentives Promote Private Decisionmaking Rather Than Government-Centered Decisionmaking. — It is said that better progress will be made towards the solution of many social problems if individual decisionmaking is promoted, and that since tax incentives promote this they should be preferred to approaches that underscore government-centered decisionmaking. Senator Ribicoff, for example, has expressed the view that "[r]ecognition that tax incentives can account for real Federal expenditures should not obscure the fact that such programs can eliminate the need for additional bureaucratic apparatus while promoting the use of private capital and initiative toward socially useful projects." [15]

We need not discuss the merits of private enterprise as a device for solving social problems, except to note in passing that many business groups who in urging tax incentives stress the virtues of private enterprise overlook the fact that they are really stressing private enterprise *plus* government assistance. But wise or unwise, the contention that private enterprise should be allowed free play, without government interference, tells us nothing as to the choice between tax incentives and direct expenditures, given the same substantive program. This contention is really a variant of the previous "red tape" argument. Just as we could design a direct expenditure program that provides for reduction of red tape, so we could design one that provides more flexibility for private decisionmaking and less scope for government control.

---

[14] S. 2192, 91st Cong., 1st Sess. (1969). *See* p. 716 *supra*.

[15] JOINT ECONOMIC COMM., 1969 JOINT ECONOMIC REPORT, H.R. REP. NO. 142, 91st Cong., 1st Sess. 20 (asterisk footnote). *See also id.* at 80 (views of Senator Talmadge); 3 CITY, April, 1969, at 5 (quoting Norman Ture to the effect that "incentives can bring into play previously unused or under-utilized resources most efficiently").

For example, the deduction for charitable contributions is sometimes cited as a method of government assistance that promotes private decisionmaking — the taxpayer, and not the Government, selects the charity and determines how much to give. But a direct expenditure program under which the Government matched with its grants, on a no-questions-asked and no-second-thoughts basis, the gifts of private individuals to the charities they selected, would equally preserve private decisionmaking. Similarly, the freedom of choice that states and local governments have as to how to use the funds they borrow with the assistance of the tax exemption for the interest on their bonds can be preserved by a direct expenditure program in which the federal government pays a part of the interest cost.[16]

It is true that many of the existing tax incentives are less structured than direct expenditure programs. But in part this reflects lack of scrutiny and foresight when the tax incentives were being planned or considered. If after a careful consideration it is decided that a simple structure is wise, then it would assume considerable irrationality to say that the simple structure will necessarily be kept if a tax incentive is used but scrapped in favor of a more complicated structure if a direct expenditure is used.

B. Some Asserted Defects of Tax Incentives

1. Tax Incentives Permit Windfalls by Paying Taxpayers for Doing What They Would Do Anyway. — It is generally argued that tax incentives are wasteful because some of the tax benefits go to taxpayers for activities which they would have performed without the benefits. When this happens, the tax credit or other benefit is a pleasant windfall, and stimulates no additional activity. With respect to many existing and proposed incentives this criticism is well taken, and indeed it is often difficult to structure a tax credit system which avoids this problem without increasing complexity and introducing arbitrariness. But this also is a problem not unique to the tax incentive technique. A direct expenditure program similarly structured would be equally open to the charge. For example, grants or contract payments made to employers who hire unskilled employees as part of a manpower program may go to employers who for one reason or another would have hired those employees anyway.

---

[16] *See* Surrey, *Federal Income Taxation of State and Local Government Obligations*, 36 TAX POLICY, May-June 1969, at 3; Healy, *The Assault on Tax-Exempt Bonds*, 36 TAX POLICY, July-August, 1969, at 2; Surrey, *The Tax Treatment of State and Local Government Obligations — Some Further Observations*, 36 TAX POLICY, Sept.-Oct. 1969.

It may be desirable in particular programs to tolerate this inefficiency or windfall. Or it may be desirable to attempt to eliminate it, perhaps by constructing a program under which taxpayers bid for the government assistance needed and the assistance goes to the lowest bidders if otherwise qualified, just as in direct government purchasing. It may be that such a substantive program is difficult to operate through the tax technique, but other ways of reaching only the marginal decision could be built into a tax incentive. The significant question is what sort of substantive program is desired.

2. *Tax Incentives Are Inequitable: They Are Worth More to the High Income Taxpayer than the Low Income Taxpayer; They Do Not Benefit Those Who Are Outside the Tax System Because Their Incomes Are Low, They Have Losses, or They Are Exempt from Tax.* — This criticism of tax incentives in terms of their inequitable effects is properly levied against most of the existing tax incentives, and probably most of the proposed incentives. The existing incentives were never really carefully structured and in many instances just grew up, without serious thought ever having been given to the question whether they were fair in these terms. The entire process was molded by the fact that the positive tax structure was being affected, and within that structure tax benefits — deductions and exclusions — had these effects as a matter of course. The deductions and exclusions of the tax incentive provisions and their inequitable effects took on the protective coloration of the deductions and exclusions that were a part of the basic tax structure.

The fact that tax benefits for the aged and the sick provide no benefits for those aged or ill who are too poor to pay income taxes was not even thought of as a difficulty, since the focus was, as in any positive tax system, on writing the rules for *taxpayers*.[17] The problem was sometimes thought about in the context of an individual who fell outside the tax system because of current losses, and at times a carry-forward of incentive benefits was provided. Thought was occasionally given to the fact that the deduction of mortgage interest or charitable contributions is worth more to the top bracket taxpayer than the low bracket taxpayer, but the disparity was generally dismissed on the grounds that all deductions had that effect. Sometimes this matter was regarded as worrisome, and a tax credit was used instead

---

[17] The fact that deductions and exemptions benefit only taxpayers is, to take the large view, a product of the fact that we have only a *positive* income tax system. If we had a *negative* income tax as well, then direct expenditures would benefit those whose incomes were below the level of positive tax, and a continuum in treatment would prevail.

of a deduction, as in the case of the retirement income credit for the aged.

This unfairness persists even in recently proposed tax incentives. The proposed tax credit for educational expenses [18] would not have helped poor families with incomes below the taxable level. The proposed manpower training credit [19] would not help a new business experiencing initial losses and struggling to stay alive, or it would help only by deferring into the future, through a carry-forward provision, benefits needed at once.[20] No assistance is provided to a tax-exempt organization or local government incurring added expenses under its participation in manpower training activities.[21]

Thus, the lesson is hard to learn. The recent tax reform legislation contained a tax incentive for the rehabilitation of low income housing, using the device of five-year amortization of capital expenditures [22] which otherwise would be depreciated over a longer period. This device, which was proposed by the Treasury Department, has these interesting effects for individual taxpayers: for a taxpayer in the 70% bracket, the benefit is the equivalent of a 19% investment credit (assuming an expenditure with a 20-year life and discount rate of 10%); for a taxpayer in the 20% bracket it is the equivalent of a 5% credit. In terms of interest costs on a loan made for rehabilitation purposes, the benefit of five-year amortization is equivalent for the 70% bracket taxpayer to reducing an 8% interest charge to 3%; for the 20% bracket taxpayer it is equivalent to reducing the 8% charge to 7%. The inequitable effect of this tax incentive device is not mentioned either in the proposal or in the committee reports explaining it.[23]

It is thus clear that most tax incentives have decidedly adverse effects on equity as between taxpayers on the same income level, and also, with respect to the individual income tax, between taxpayers on different income levels. As a consequence of these inequitable effects, many tax incentives look, and are, highly ir-

---

[18] Tax Reform Bill of 1969, H.R. 13,270, 91st Cong., 1st Sess. § 917 (1969). The provision was not retained in the final legislation.

[19] A similar unfairness existed in the proposed deduction for transportation expenses of handicapped persons. Tax Reform Bill of 1969, H.R. 13,270, 91st Cong., 1st Sess. § 915 (1969). This provision was not retained in the final legislation.

[20] S. 2192, 91st Cong., 1st Sess. (1969).

[21] Canada appears to be shifting from tax incentives to direct expenditures in providing government assistance to regional economic expansion. Regional Development Incentives Act of 1968–69, c. 56. One reason given is the ineffectiveness of tax incentives when new ventures are involved.

[22] Tax Reform Act of 1969, Pub. L. No. 91–172, § 521(a) (U.S. CODE CONG. & AD. NEWS No. 12 (Dec. 30, 1969)), *amending* INT. REV. CODE OF 1954 § 167.

[23] *See Hearings on H.R. 13,270 Before the Senate Comm. on Finance*, 91st Cong., 1st Sess., pt. 5, at 4903–08 (1969) (statement of Charles Davenport).

rational when phrased as direct expenditure programs structured the same way. Indeed, it is doubtful that most of our existing tax incentives would ever have been introduced, let alone accepted, if so structured, and many would be laughed out of Congress. What HEW Secretary would propose a medical assistance program for the aged that cost $200 million, and under which $90 million would go to persons with incomes over $50,000, and only $8 million to persons with incomes under $5,000? The tax proposal to remove the 3% floor under the medical expense deductions of persons over 65 would have had just that effect.[24] What HEW Secretary would introduce a program under which Social Security benefits would be unaffected if the recipient's total income including the benefit were under $900, would be automatically increase by 14% if the recipient's income were between $900 and $1,400, by 15% if between $1,400 and $1,900, and so on up to 70% if over $100,000? That is the effect of the present exclusion from income of Social Security benefits. What HUD Secretary would suggest a housing rehabilitation subsidized loan program under which a wealthy person could borrow the funds at 3% interest but a poor person would have to pay 7% or 8%? That is the effect of the five-year amortization of rehabilitation expenditures contained in the recent Tax Reform Act.[25]

This criticism — that tax incentives produce inequitable effects and upside-down benefits — is valid as to the general run of tax incentives.[26] It demonstrates why tax incentives make

---

[24] Tax Reform Bill of 1969, H.R. 13,270, 91st Cong., 1st Sess. § 914 (1969). The provision was not enacted.

[25] Tax Reform Act of 1969, Pub. L. No. 91-172, § 521(a) (U.S. CODE CONG. & AD. NEWS No. 12 (Dec. 30, 1969)).

Professor Henry Aaron uses this example:

> Yesterday on the floor of Congress, Senator Blimp introduced legislation to provide cash allowances for most of the aged. Senator Blimp's plan is unique, however, in that it excludes the poor. The largest benefits, $70 per month, are payable to aged couples whose real income exceeds $200,000 per year. The smallest benefits, $14 per month, would be payable to couples with income between $1,600 and $2,600. Widows, widowers, and unmarried aged persons would receive half as much as couples. No benefits would be payable to those with very low incomes.

Professor Aaron states this is a way of describing the (then) additional $600 personal exemption for the aged. Aaron, *Tax Exemptions — The Artful Dodge*, TRANS-ACTION, March, 1969, at 4.

[26] In the case of the corporate income tax, the absence of the progressive rate structure of the individual income tax makes the tax incentive less inequitable than in the individual income tax situation. Nevertheless, inequities do exist when a tax incentive deduction is used, since the larger corporations receive a 48% benefit (absent the surcharge) and the smaller corporations only a 22% benefit. Corporations incurring losses may receive no benefit. The use of a tax credit rather than a deduction would eliminate the first aspect, but would probably leave the loss corporation without assistance, since tax incentive credits in excess of tax liability typically are not paid out.

high-income individuals still better off and result in the paradox that we achieve our social goals by increasing the number of tax millionaires. The marketplace does not work this way — for the individual who earns his profits, even high profits, by meeting a need or desire of society, finds his rewards subject to the progressive income tax. The economic system is thus functioning as it is intended it should, and the tax system, which acts as a control, is also functioning as intended. But when rewards are in the form of tax incentives, the latter control is eliminated, and tax millionaires are produced.

The financial assistance afforded by the incentive, with the purpose of making profits high enough to induce the desired action by the taxpayer, is not itself included in income. The tax incentive thus provides both financial assistance and freedom from taxation. That freedom itself means much more to the well-to-do individual than to one in the lower brackets. The tax incentive is thus a method of reward and assistance that is just upside-down from the way the country decided — when it adopted a progressive income tax — that the rewards of the marketplace should operate in combination with the income tax. The use that has been made — and is being made — of tax incentives is thus destructive of the equity of a tax system. This is illustrated by the Treasury Department's first proposing a housing rehabilitation tax incentive and then having to suggest that the incentive is a tax preference which must be guarded against by including it in a minimum tax structure designed to prevent the wealthy from escaping all tax burdens.[27] The use of the direct expenditure route would have prevented this particular undermining of the tax system.

In some cases, however, the tax incentive could be fashioned to avoid this criticism, though the result would be a different program and one structured more closely along direct expenditure lines. For example, suppose in the case of the exclusion of Social Security benefits, that a uniform tax credit was used instead of the exclusion, the tax credit was included in taxable income, and any unused credit was paid to the taxpayer. This would be the equivalent of a direct expenditure program for all aged on a per capita basis, with positive taxpayers receiving a diminishing final share depending on their tax bracket, and those aged outside the tax system receiving their full share. The elements of inequity would be removed and the tax incentive technique would

---

[27] *See* article by Eileen Shanahan in N.Y. Times, Dec. 22, 1969, at 25, col. 4 ("There are four other major new tax preferences in the bill: tax incentives (which is what preferences always are at their birth) aimed at stimulating . . . the rehabilitation of old residential housing . . .").

be on the same footing as a direct expenditure under which each aged person received the same per capita amount. Indeed, this is how tax incentive programs *should* be structured if they are to be equitable and not involve the unfairnesses described. But this approach may only rarely be feasible given its novelty and the difficulties involved in convincing the business community and others who are the beneficiaries of tax incentives, let alone the policymakers in Government, of the appropriateness of making such changes as including the tax incentive amount itself in taxable income.[28]

As an aside, we can here see the importance of distinguishing tax expenditures and tax incentives — so-called special tax provisions — from those provisions considered a proper and necessary part of the structure of an income tax. If an item is *properly* deductible in the latter sense, it does come off at the taxpayer's top tax rate, and its benefits are confined to those who are taxpayers. Given the decision to have an income tax at all, the result is equitable, within the concept of an income tax. An income tax is a tax on *net* income and not a tax on gross receipts; therefore the deductions from gross income required to produce the net income base must be allowed. Those deductions, generally speaking, are the expenses and costs incurred in the process of producing or earning the gross income received by the taxpayer.

Thus, consider the deduction for moving expenses: it is a deduction and so benefits a taxpayer (reduces his tax) in accordance with his marginal tax rate. It also benefits only taxpayers; an employee who incurs moving expenses, but whose income is so low as not to leave him taxable, does not obtain any benefit or assistance. This is the correct result under a positive income tax system if the moving expense should properly be taken into account in the measurement of net income, as it should be if it is an expense in earning income rather than a personal expense. If it is the latter, the deduction is a subsidy or tax expenditure, inequitably cast, to induce labor mobility. Actually, the moving expense deduction is at the frontier of the positive income tax structure; a gradual shift is occurring, and such ex-

---

[28] Where the tax incentive amount is similar to a contribution to capital, it would not be included in income but would reduce the basis of property related to the contribution. *Compare* INT. REV. CODE OF 1954 §§ 118, 362(c).

There are other ways to structure a special tax provision to eliminate inequities. For example, the system of special bad debt reserves for financial institutions could be handled by allowing the deduction of the special reserve but then requiring the tax savings to be invested in special federal bonds that do not carry interest. This approach is now used in the tax treatment of special reserves for mortgage insurance companies. *See* HOUSE WAYS & MEANS COMM., 91st Cong., 1st Sess., UNITED STATES TREASURY DEPARTMENT, TAX REFORM STUDIES AND PROPOSALS, pt. 3, at 467 (Comm. Print 1969).

penses are coming to be regarded as a factor proper and necessary to the measurement of net income.[29]

3. Tax Incentives Distort the Choices of the Marketplace and Produce Unneutralities in the Allocation of Resources. — This criticism is in one sense always valid, because that is what the tax incentive is designed to do. Generally, the critic is also saying or implying that the distortion introduced by the particular incentive is undesirable for various reasons. In large part this criticism is true of many existing incentives for reasons earlier described. The criticism has relevance because the distorting effects of tax incentives often pass unnoticed. But the criticism is of course equally applicable to direct expenditures, some of which certainly are unwise. Again, we are not here concerned with the overall role of government or the extent to which and under what circumstances financial assistance is desirable to induce private action different from what the marketplace would provide. This criticism thus does not per se tell us when one or the other technique should be used.

It is interesting to note that even within the area sought to be benefited by the tax incentive, the design of the incentive may push or pull in unneutral directions, which may or may not be desirable. Thus, a tax credit for pollution control facilities focuses on expenditures for machinery as the method of control to the exclusion of other methods, such as a different choice of materials involved in the manufacturing processes.[30] A tax credit for businesses located in urban slums may focus concentration on monetary assistance to the neglect of the provision of technical assistance.

4. Tax Incentives Keep Tax Rates High by Constricting the Tax Base and Thereby Reducing Revenues. — This criticism of tax incentives states a fact that many overlook in their advocacy of tax incentives. The lack of an explicit accounting in the federal budget for the tax expenditures involved in tax incentives

---

[29] *See* Tax Reform Act of 1969, Pub. L. No. 91–172, § 231 (U.S. CODE CONG. & AD. NEWS No. 12 (Dec. 30, 1969) (expanding the deduction and extending it to include self-employed individuals). There is a hazy line between business expenses properly deducted from income for the purpose of an income tax, and personal expenses, which should not be deducted. Thus, commuting expenses are personal, but the expenses of providing comfortable working conditions in an office are business; wearing nice clothes at work is a personal expense but wearing uniforms is a business expense. The borderlines that evolve are a part of the "generally accepted structure of an income tax" that is used as a standard to identify tax expenditures. We sometimes speak of tax changes designed to provide incentives for taxpayers when what is really involved is the removal of imperfections in the design of a proper tax structure that inhibit their activities. *See, e.g.*, the discussion of the Foreign Investors Tax Act of 1966, in Stone, *supra* note 7, at 648.

[30] *See* Wilson, *Tax Incentives and Pollution*, in INCENTIVES SYMPOSIUM.

and the lack in most cases of an accounting in the tax statistical data combine to cause many to forget that dollars are being spent. As a consequence, the criticism that is made against direct expenditures — that they keep our tax rates high — is often lost sight of when tax incentives are involved. This criticism of tax incentives is thus a useful reminder that government funds are being spent, and that therefore whatever degree of scrutiny and care should be applied to direct expenditures should also be applied to tax incentives.[31] Tax incentives are usually open-ended: they place no limit on how much tax benefit a taxpayer can earn. Hence it is difficult to foretell how much will be spent by the Government through a particular incentive. It is difficult in the nature of things to structure most tax incentives in order to provide a limit on their use. Thus, tax incentives are much like the uncontrollable direct expenditures in the budget.

In the end, the issue is whether, as to any particular area, we want direct government provision of services or goods, government financial assistance (subsidies) to encourage and assist private action to provide the services or goods, or reliance on private action unaided by the Government. If we choose government provision or assistance, then dollars must be spent, and whether they are dollars forgone through lost tax revenues or dollars spent directly through direct expenditures, the effect on tax rates will be the same. So also will the effect on the economy if the government program succeeds, and the resultant effect on the revenue base and tax rates of the increased economic activity that such success may mean.

C. Summary of Asserted Virtues and Vices of Tax Incentives

This description of the virtues and vices of tax incentives yields these conclusions: the *asserted disadvantages* — waste, inefficiency, and inequity — are true of most tax incentives existing or proposed because of the way they are structured or grew up. The whole approach to tax incentives — one of rather careless

---

[31] Senator Percy's statement on the manpower training bill included, in the section claiming that the proposed program was uncomplicated, the sentence: "This bill would require no Federal appropriations." 115 CONG. REC. S5330 (daily ed. May 16, 1969). If this is intended to convey the idea that government funds are not being used, it is subject to the criticism on this page of the text. If it is intended to convey the thought that such legislation can be passed more quickly than direct expenditure legislation because no appropriation bill is needed, it is really an attack on the whole process of appropriation bills. If it is intended to convey the thought that the Congress will spend tax expenditure dollars but not direct expenditure dollars, it appears to charge the Congress with being irrational, as to which see pp. 732–33 *infra*.

or loose analysis, failure to recognize that dollars are being spent, or to recognize the defects inherent in working within the constraints of the positive tax system — has produced very poor programs. But *if* the problems were recognized and *if* care were taken to design tax incentive programs that one would be willing to defend in substantive terms were the programs cast as direct expenditure programs, then these disadvantages would not be involved, except to the extent that they are inherent in government assistance itself. These are large conditions, and in some cases would be hard to bring about. For example, it would not be easy to give tax benefit assistance to groups outside the tax system but performing desired activities, such as local governments or tax-exempt organizations hiring the disadvantaged — direct payments outside the tax system would be needed. And it would not be easy to design tax incentive programs which were not inequitable as between taxpayers in high and low brackets and between taxpayers and nontaxpayers. Indeed, there is no tax incentive in existence or proposed that meets the above standards. But for purposes of comparison we are here assuming that the standards could be met under some tax incentive programs.

Similarly, the *asserted advantages* of tax incentives — greater reliance on private decisionmaking and less detailed requirements — to the extent that they are true in fact (and they are often only illusory) are really criticisms of the complications and supervision built into direct expenditure programs, or else a reflection of the structural weaknesses of the tax incentive program, depending on the amount of detail and supervision appropriate to the particular program. In a rational world, one should assume that if after careful study it is considered that certain complexities and details are not needed and can be left out of a tax incentive program, then they should and can simply be dropped from the direct expenditure program. Again, this may be a more difficult condition than appearance suggests, but it is probably less difficult to bring about than the conditions for repairing tax incentives, or at least no more difficult. Again, for purposes of comparison, we are also here assuming it can be done in direct expenditure programs.

D. What Is Lost by Using a Tax Incentive Rather Than a Direct Expenditure

Given, under the assumptions just made, the same substantive program, under which government assistance in the same amount is being given in ways and to persons that would be equally acceptable whether tax incentives or direct expenditures were used, what factors should determine the choice of framework for a particular program? We can approach this question by asking: what is lost if the tax incentive technique is used? There are several answers.

1. Tax Incentives, by Dividing the Consideration and Administration of Government Programs, Confuse and Complicate that Consideration in the Congress, in Administration, and in the Budget Process. — Let us start with the congressional consideration of tax incentive programs. By definition, such programs are designed to induce action to meet a particular social goal — manpower training of the disadvantaged, education, housing, pollution control, or business location in desired areas, to use some recent examples — and would not be a part of the tax structure were they not deliberately cast as tax incentives. Such governmental programs would normally be considered by the appropriate congressional committee charged with the legislative area involved: the House Education and Labor and Senate Labor and Public Welfare Committees, the House and Senate Banking and Currency Committees, the House and Senate Interior and Insular Affairs Committees, the House Interstate and Foreign Commerce and Senate Commerce Committees, and so on. These committees are responsible for overseeing and developing legislation in their jurisdictional fields, and so are able to coordinate the Government's programs and policies. Tax legislation, however, goes to the House Ways and Means Committee and the Senate Finance Committee. These committees would normally not consider the substantive areas involved in tax incentive programs. Tax incentives suddenly charge them with acting on substantive matters outside their fields of responsibility simply because the program uses the tax system. Although tax committees are highly competent in tax matters, they do not have as much insight into these programs as the legislative committees normally handling the programs. A similar situation would prevail if the latter committees were suddenly to legislate on technical tax matters. Moreover, the tax incentive program considered by the tax committees would be isolated from the regular flow of legislation and activity in the field involved, and this isolation would make coordination and the consideration of priorities difficult. The purpose of the congressional committee system is to distribute expertise among the members of Congress. To cast solutions to social problems as tax measures and exchange expertise in those problems for unfamiliarity is, to say the least, both disruptive and unproductive.[32] Moreover, the jumbling of a number of different incentive

[32] The 1969 tax reform act is an example of the hasty judgments that may result from this system. Without any study at all the Ways and Means Committee, in dealing with that measure, committed the Government to an expenditure of nearly

programs in the tax committees would inevitably set in motion a "log-rolling" process, in which careful consideration would be displaced by trading for support among members. Such a process is difficult to control once a committee is operating outside of its area of expertise and with no clear limits of subject matter to restrain it.

These difficulties could perhaps be overcome. Tax committees might refer incentive proposals to the appropriate legislative committees and accept their judgments, or both groups of committees could consider the matter jointly. Approaches like these are sometimes used in areas where a trust fund having earmarked taxes exists. But the system is awkward and leaves unanswered questions — for example, which committee would exert continuing oversight over the program? Given all the trouble and care that must be taken to patch up an arrangement basically at variance with the normal practice, what is gained by choosing that arrangement in the first instance and thereby dividing the governmental consideration of the program?

Much the same can be said about the parallel effect at the administrative level. Social programs are normally administered by executive departments such as Labor, HEW, HUD, and Interior. Taxes are administered by the Internal Revenue Service. A social program cast in tax terms must in the first instance be administered by the IRS, whose expertise does not extend to these other areas. Problems of lack of coordination with other substantive programs would also arise because of the isolation of tax incentive programs. Again, these difficulties could be patched up to some extent — and probably would have to be — by having the appropriate executive department provide some guidance to IRS. But why the divided arrangement in the first place?

At the budgetary level such a division of responsibility makes oversight and control more difficult. Budgetary problems exist even where several relevant executive departments have a hand in the same program or area. The difficulties are compounded when one of the agencies (IRS) really doesn't belong there in the first place, and when it distributes the funds by tax reduction rather than direct expenditure.[33] Our present budgetary process

---

half a billion dollars for pollution control facilities installed by industry. Without any study at all the Treasury induced the committee to commit the Government to an expenditure of over $300 million for the rehabilitation of rental housing. Neither action was taken with any regard to the overall priorities in the pollution control and housing areas. *See* Surrey, *Federal Tax and Fiscal Policy: Some Aspects of Future Developments*, 48 TAXES 49 (1970).

[33] One defect in the administration of tax incentives by the IRS is that the IRS agents are "income oriented" and tend to look askance at deductions and credits having no relation to the measurement of income. This attitude could re-

badly compounds these difficulties by giving no recognition or accounting to what is being spent on existing tax expenditures. Until 1968, when the Treasury Department published its analysis of tax expenditure programs and a Tax Expenditure Budget, there was no accounting for the existing tax incentives. The necessary data were not available to the public and not comprehended within the Government. No one really knew what was being spent through the tax system or for what purposes.[34]

An additional problem is the difficulty of coordinating the treatment of tax incentives with the overall handling of direct expenditures. For example, when overall expenditure limits are directed by the Congress or when the President decides to cut expenditures it is essentially impossible to apply the restrictions to tax incentives. So far none of the various expenditure control
tax incentives. So far none of the various expenditure control
devices, such as those voted in recent years by the Congress, have in any way affected tax expenditures. Yet had these tax programs been structured as direct expenditures, they would have had no such immunity. In substantive terms they do not merit that immunity any more than the direct expenditures, yet their tax clothing shields them. For similar reasons, tax incentives are not covered by the annual budgetary review process; the Bureau of the Budget doesn't even know about many of them, or how much they cost. We do have "uncontrollable" areas in the budget, such as interest on the public debt, and since they can play havoc with a budget, an effort is made to keep them to a minimum, and

---

sult in uneven administration of incentive programs. The agents, not seeing the purpose behind the deductions and credits, since they are not tax purposes and so are outside the general expertise and background of the agents, are likely to view the benefits as too generous and to raise audit problems for claimants. This is less likely to occur in the administration of a direct expenditure program since it would be in the hands of an agency interested in the success of the program. Thus the existence of an IRS audit system is not necessarily, contrary to the claim sometimes made, an argument for using tax incentives. Moreover, other agencies, such as the Department of Labor, have inspection or audit systems, and still others could develop them.

[34] *See Hearings on Economic Analysis and Efficiency in Government Before the Subcomm. on Economy in Government of the Joint Economic Comm.*, 91st Cong., 1st Sess. (1969) (statement of Stanley S. Surrey on the Tax Expenditure Budget).

It is sometimes said that a tax incentive has the advantage of "permanency" since tax provisions generally are only infrequently reexamined, whereas direct expenditures are usually reviewed annually, and that some programs to be effective require such permanency. However, if, as a general matter, periodic review of government expenditures is considered desirable, no program should be removed from that scrutiny except for compelling reasons. If in a particular case such reasons are determined to exist, then devices to postpone review are available under the direct expenditure route: for example, longer appropriations and trust funds. There need be no resort to the tax system simply to prevent periodic review.

at least to identify them and try to estimate their effect. But in the budget process this is not done for tax incentives.

Overall, therefore, a resort to tax incentives greatly decreases the ability of the Government to maintain control over the management of its priorities. This is true both as to the substantive programs to be introduced, modified, or dropped and as to the amounts to be spent in particular programs and areas. These consequences run counter to the whole thrust of our concerns with the ordering of national priorities and with the wise allocation of our resources, which we have come to see as limited and therefore in need of careful management.

Some of these difficulties could be met. Tax incentives could be identified, amounts estimated, and the data incorporated in the budget. Unless this is done, comparisons of tax expenditures and direct expenditures must be comparisons of hidden programs with open ones. But even after such clarification, further difficulties would remain. Perhaps the President could be given authority to treat the tax incentive funds as direct expenditures for budgetary control purposes, and the incentives could be structured as far as possible to have them fall in the controllable rather than the uncontrollable expenditure pattern. Perhaps the tax incentive programs could be given yearly or biannual expiration dates, so that they could be reviewed in the same way as direct expenditures under the appropriation and budgetary procedures.

But these solutions, like those available for the problems of congressional consideration and administrative operation, raise the question, what is gained by turning what would normally be a direct expenditure program into a tax incentive program and then trying to structure the program so that it can nevertheless be handled as a direct expenditure program? Why the detour through the tax system? Why inject the tax system into the program, when the program can be effectively structured without it?

2. *Tax Incentives Will Not Improve the Tax System and Are Likely To Damage It Significantly.* — Certainly the tax system does not gain when expenditures are made through tax incentive programs. We have already seen that tax incentives are inimical to the equity of a tax system — indeed, in a sense that is necessary to their purpose and function. Moreover, the tax system is complex enough as it is, and to have a large number of tax incentives side by side with the provisions making up the structure of the tax itself can only cause confusion and a blurring of concepts and objectives.[35] Tax incentives make it more and more

[35] It has been pointed out that phrasing the assistance in terms of tax benefits may in some cases make it so difficult for potential beneficiaries to determine their

difficult to distinguish between what is subsidy and what is proper structure. This is especially so where the tax incentive is not identifiable as such but is merged into a provision that has a genuine relationship to the measurement of net income — as is, for example, the subsidy involved in accelerated depreciation for real estate, since some degree of depreciation is appropriate.

It is no answer to say, as do some cynics, that since the tax system today has so many special provisions there should be no objection, when worthwhile programs are involved, to adding still more to the heap. Rather, the effort should persist to contract those existing special provisions that are improper and wasteful. We know from long experience that provisions can be enshrined in tax laws far past their usefulness and long after their defects become clear. We should not, when alternatives are present, freeze in more special provisions, especially since programs in the complex areas of social policy to which many tax incentive proposals relate are essentially experimental in nature.

E. What Is Gained — Allegedly — by Using a Tax Incentive Rather Than a Direct Expenditure

Thus, a great deal is lost when tax incentives are used. What is to be gained by that approach compared with the direct expenditure approach? Some have advanced answers which are essentially political in nature, and, I think, rooted in illusions or irrationalities. Professor Aaron has observed that the popularity of the tax devices "derives from a peculiar alliance among conservatives, who find attractive the alleged reduction in the role of government that would follow from extensive use of tax credits, and liberals anxious to solve social and economic problems — by whatever means — before it is too late." [36] We have already discussed the illusion that tax credits for social purposes are simple and removed from the bureaucratic hand. The second illusion in the above argument is that the Congress will vote dollars through tax incentives that it refuses to appropriate through expenditure programs. Just why a Congress that focuses on the matter should be so inconsistent is not explained. Certainly many members of tax committees, such as Chairman Mills, have recognized that tax incentives do involve expenditures — "back-door expenditures" in his words — and that a legislator concerned with expenditure levels and expenditure control should not, while holding the front door shut, let hidden expenditures in through the back door. But perhaps irrationality will govern; perhaps administrators and

rewards that they will fail to take advantage of them. *Cf.* Stone, *supra* note 7, at 654.

[36] Aaron, *supra* note 25, at 5.

legislators will devise and accept programs structured as tax provisions which they would reject as direct expenditures, or will refuse to improve direct expenditure programs, or will spend money through tax incentives that they would not appropriate as direct expenditures. In that event, rational consideration will not change matters.

There is another answer, which also appears to be irrational or illusory. This is the claim that businessmen respond to tax credits but not to other forms of government assistance; that there is a glamour and magic possessed by dollars of tax reduction that will attract the businessman who would pass up dollars offered through direct expenditures. To the extent that this answer rests on the belief that tax incentives are really simpler, or that complexities can be sheared away only if tax incentives are used, it rests on beliefs already discussed and found either unrealistic or true only if the underlying government policies are themselves irrational. To the extent that the answer rests on the claim that business regards tax incentive dollars as "clean dollars" — just part of a tax computation — but sees direct expenditure dollars as somehow unclean because they are a subsidy, one can only answer that business probably does not respond this way, or that if it does, it is behaving irrationally. Experience with direct subsidies — the SST program for example — suggests that business firms are willing to and do calculate profit prospects in the light of government subsidies. Similarly, the argument that business is familiar with tax credits — though until the investment credit there were no credits widely used in the corporate tax system — but not with other forms of government assistance is certainly not always true. Lack of business familiarity could be overcome by publicizing direct subsidies. The manpower training credit proposal quoted earlier suggested that "the Department of Labor . . . be required to make [the proposal's] provisions known to the unemployed and potential employers in the business community." [37] Such a duty could equally well be placed on that Department if it were administering a direct expenditure program.

There may be an aspect of this asserted preference for tax incentive programs that is not illusion or irrationality, but more serious. It may be that legislators and the beneficiaries of tax incentive programs — businesses receiving accelerated depreciation or percentage depletion, state and local governments receiving tax exemption on their bonds — fear that once the public is fully aware of the amounts involved and can weigh expenditure costs against benefits received by the nation, the tax incentives

[37] 115 CONG. REC. S5329, S5330 (daily ed. May 16, 1969).

will be found wanting in many respects. In this view, the deeper the incentive is buried in tax technicalities and tax terminology, the more it looks like any other technical tax provision, the more it partakes of the protective coloration of the tax law that can be obtained by such outward similarity to ordinary tax provisions, then the more desirable the tax incentive becomes. The public must dig hard and deep to find the subsidy and evaluate it. But such an approach to government expenditures — the preference for the hidden subsidy over the open subsidy — is contrary to all experience with budgets, and to efforts to achieve a rational use of resources. If this is the argument for tax incentives, it should not be accepted.

III. Conclusion

What, then, is the balance sheet regarding these two methods of government assistance, direct expenditures and tax incentives? I conclude from the above observations that, as a generalization, the burden of proof should rest heavily on those proposing the use of the tax incentive method. In any particular situation — certainly any new situation — the first approach should be to explore the various direct expenditure alternatives. Once the most desirable of these alternatives is determined, if one still wishes to consider the tax incentive method for the same substantive program, the question must be what clear advantages can be obtained by using the tax method. Again, as a generalization, I think it unlikely that clear advantages in the tax incentive method will be found. Moreover, I stress strongly that the advantages must be clear and compelling to overcome the losses that accompany the use of the tax incentive, even the well-structured incentive. The problems of achieving a well-structured incentive are in themselves formidable. Even assuming that such problems as unfairness and windfalls are overcome, there are still the losses and drawbacks we have described: confusion and divided authority in the legislative and administrative processes, difficulties in maintaining budgetary control, confusion in perceiving and setting national priorities, and dangers to the tax structure itself.

It could be that a program of government assistance that is broadly based, relatively simple, and properly structured can be more readily administered if joined to the tax system. Some have defended the deductions for charitable contributions and personal interest and taxes on this ground, though pointing to the need to correct abuses and recognizing that the corrections would make the tax incentive more like a direct expenditure program. Others have defended the investment credit for the same reasons, again with a recognition that improvements can be made.[38] But none of these incentives has had to meet the test of comparison with a carefully structured direct expenditure program. Only after that is done can we reach the point of well-informed choice.

These are general guidelines; there may be particular cases to which they do not apply because special considerations are involved. Even so, care must be taken to look hard at special considerations advanced as reasons for an exception to be made "in this particular case." The legislative halls are crowded with advocates skilled in tying their problems to the last exception and in devising techniques to make each step from the last precedent appear to be only short, logical, and harmless. Our gaze can thus be averted from the constantly widening gap between proper tax structure and each additional special provision.

One question raised by this discussion especially merits more research and thought. Just why is it that in many cases legislators appear willing, with hardly any thought, to accept an expensive tax incentive program when they would just as quickly reject a similar direct expenditure program, even a much smaller one? Why do they require lengthy study and analysis of direct expenditure programs before legislative and appropriation committees while they are ready to enact tax incentives on no more than generalizations and hunches? Is it that they do not realize, or stop to think, that dollars are spent by tax incentives? Is it that tax bills are so complicated that hardly anyone studies them unless prodded by an industry or taxpayer that is hurt, in his tax pocketbook, and that therefore provisions dispensing largesse slide by — although this would be a case of the proper concession of tax expertise to the tax committees papering over their lack of expertise in the areas involved in tax incentives. Is it that the legislators know full well what is involved, despite the complexity of tax bills, but believe the public will not perceive what is being done because of the complexity of tax bills and because tax expenditures do not show up in the budget? To claim this would almost be to claim that any expenditure of funds is acceptable to a legislator — the more money to constituents the better — but most legislators do not follow this principle.

We could ask similar questions about administrative agencies. Just why do administrators of direct expenditure programs allow tax incentive proposals to be pushed when the funds involved

---

[38] Indeed, the relative simplicity of the investment credit, which is applied with very little supervision, may have misled businessmen into thinking all tax credits are simple in structure. Yet, as stated earlier, the tax credit proposals in social areas have far more details and complexities. On the investment credit generally, *see* Brannon, *supra* note 10.

in such programs could be used, and probably much better used, as coordinated parts of the direct expenditure programs? Is it that their policy is to accept gratefully contributions from any source? Is it that they will not face up to the need either to improve the direct expenditure program or squarely demonstrate the erratic and wasteful character of the tax incentive proposal? Is it that they are sometimes negligent in their legislative intelligence and are simply left at the legislative starting gate when the tax incentive is adopted? And why should a Treasury Department which is charged with preserving the integrity of the tax system ever willingly propose or accept a tax incentive solution except in the unusual and rare situation when a tax credit may possibly be properly tailored, and better suited to the purpose — conditions which do not appear to exist as to any of the recent proposals?

With *new* situations — that is, new or expanded government programs — we are in a position to follow a rational course in choosing between these methods. During the 1960's, as attention turned increasingly to government financial assistance to meet urgent social problems, almost every problem brought proposals of a tax incentive as the solution; often the tax incentive was the first solution to be advanced. The Treasury Department responded by pressing the White House staff and other agencies to devise, with the Treasury, non-tax alternatives for comparison on a cost-effectiveness basis. For example, the Treasury, with HEW, developed the federal guaranteed student loan program and expanded scholarship and work programs, so that they could be pushed in opposition to a tax credit for college tuition. In the manpower field, the Treasury urged strong and expanding federally-supported training programs which could be advanced instead of a tax incentive. The skepticism with which specialized tax incentives for social problems were regarded by the Treasury together with a realization that a negative answer to proposals of tax incentives did not solve the problems, thus led the Treasury to be a strong force within the Government in developing and pushing direct expenditure programs, both to counter tax incentive proposals and to move forward to meet the problems in other ways.

With *existing* tax incentives, the task is one that falls in the category of "tax reform," where progress is difficult and slow.[39]

[39] The 1969 TAX REFORM STUDIES AND PROPOSALS, *supra* note 10, related in the case of the income tax almost entirely to tax incentives and involved varying degrees of scaling down and restructuring. Only a few of the proposals related to defects in the fitting together of the tax structure proper (for example, multiple corporation provisions and mineral production payment provisions) or changes in the application of that structure, such as elimination or reduction of tax for those

This is especially so with incentives which have long histories. We do learn as the tax years pass by: the newer tax provisions are in general more carefully tailored with an eye to many of these problems than their predecessors. For example, compare the moving expense and medical expense deductions with those for personal interest and taxes as originally adopted. Or compare the structure of the 7% investment credit with the provision for accelerated depreciation for real estate as it appeared in 1954.[40] Unfortunately, we also can forget what we have learned, as the earlier discussion of the upside-down structure of the new five-year amortization for housing rehabilitation expenditures indicates.[41]

It seems likely that tax reform for many existing incentives will be in the direction of contracting the area of incentives by reducing the number of those eligible for benefits, reducing the extent of the benefits, and removing the undue advantages granted upper income groups. The degree of change will presumably vary with the breadth of the incentive: those that involve specific areas and provide tax benefits for a restricted group — for example, accelerated depreciation for real estate and the natural resource provisions — will, or at least should, be subject to serious cutbacks in scope and benefit, whereas incentives with broad reach — for example, the charitable, interest, and tax deductions — will be scrutinized for particular abuses. This, in general, is the tenor of the Tax Reform Act of 1969.

Once we begin to recognize that the existing tax incentives represent expenditures of funds that in many cases should be dispersed directly, we must develop legislative and administrative techniques to move the funds involved — to the extent that government assistance is still considered desirable — from the tax

---

below or around poverty income levels. This helps place in perspective the whole matter of tax reform. The 1969 tax reform act also follows this pattern, and most of its major reforms consist of reducing the scope of existing tax incentives, such as those relating to real estate, financial institutions, capital gains investment, natural resources, and farm activities.

[40] The investment credit structure itself pointed to problems, such as the precedent effect of a credit of this nature.

Another problem involved under the investment credit is related to the difficulties caused by confining the credit to taxpayers and placing a limit on the credit in terms of tax liabilities, thereby inducing concerns which could not use their credits to "barter" them to others and enlarge the tax abuses in leasing syndicates and similar arrangements. While the "bartering" may have widened the use of the credit by avoiding the limitation based on tax liability and thus corrected what may have been the undesirability of the limit, the detour too generously compensated the middleman lessor.

[41] The 1969 Act introduced other undesirable tax incentives, also using the five-year amortization technique: the provisions for pollution control facilities, railroad cars, and mine safety equipment.

expenditure budget to the regular budget. The tax committees or the Bureau of the Budget could indicate to the Congress and the administrative agencies concerned the amounts involved in particular tax incentive programs. A period of time would then be allowed for the appropriate legislative committees and administrative agencies to develop direct expenditure programs, and a time limit could be put on the duration of the tax incentive programs. At the end of this period the tax incentive would be ended and the new direct expenditure program funded with the dollars returned to the revenue side of the budget. Certainly, new tax incentive programs, if any are to be adopted, should have a time limit set on their operation, to permit such a shift to a direct expenditure program, or at least to permit evaluation of the effectiveness and operation of the tax incentive.[42]

For the present, a de-escalation of existing particular incentives would be progress, though it would leave a set of tax incentives that probably would not be used at all if we were able to treat the problems fully as new problems. But this is the path of tax history and indeed all legislative history. Knowing all this, let us at least attempt not to repeat past mistakes in future solutions.

---

[42] The 1969 tax reform act puts five-year termination dates on the new five-year amortization incentives for pollution control facilities, rehabilitation of low income housing, railroad cars, and mine-safety equipment. Tax Reform Act of 1969 Pub. L. No. 91–172–4 § 70, (INT. REV. CODE OF 1954, § 169), § 521 (INT. REV. CODE OF 1954, § 167(k)), § 705 (INT. REV. CODE OF 1954, § 184), § 707 (INT. REV. CODE OF 1954, § 187) (U.S. CODE CONG. & AD. NEWS NO. 12 (Dec. 30, 1969)). The more generous provision for recapture of depreciation of federally assisted housing projects also has a five-year termination provision. *Id.* § 521, *amending* § 1250(a)(1)(c)(ii).

BRAZER, THE FEDERAL INCOME TAX AND THE POOR: WHERE DO WE GO FROM HERE? *

57 Calif.L.Rev. 422 (1969).

In American society being poor and being among the "disadvantaged" mean essentially the same thing. Being poor places one in a position in which his various rights are more likely to be impaired than if he is not poor, simply because, in protecting his rights against infringement, one typically incurs substantial costs. This paper is concerned, therefore, with the position of those who may be classified as "poor" or "near-poor," and whether the federal individual income tax is or may be used as an appropriate and effective instrument for alleviating or even eliminating poverty. Clearly the elimination of poverty will not, in itself, ensure equal access to justice for all. It will, however, bring us closer to realization of that goal. While some will always, by reason of their greater affluence, be more advantaged than others, we must set limits on the degree of economic disadvantage that we are willing to tolerate.

This Article will first review some of the facts of poverty and then consider the case for redistributing income in favor of the poor. It will examine the role of the federal individual income tax in its present form in relieving poverty, and, finally, present and evaluate what appear to be the more promising ways of using the machinery of the income tax to combat the basic disadvantage suffered by people in this country—being poor.

I

THE NEED FOR A PROGRAM OF DIRECT GOVERNMENT INCOME TRANSFERS

A. A Definition of Poverty and the Poverty Gap

Poverty may be defined in either relative or absolute terms. If we define the poor as those whose incomes fall, say, below the 20th

* Copyright ©, 1969, California Law Review, Inc. Reprinted by permission.

percentile when all families and unrelated individuals are arrayed according to size of income, we have arbitrarily declared that approximately 40 million of our population are poor, and the poor, in this sense, shall always be with us. Our policy objective then becomes that of raising the standard of living of the poor. Alternatively, we may define poverty in terms of a target level of income per family or per person which, though arbitrarily selected, represents a minimum that the conscience of an affluent society is willing to tolerate. This target or poverty benchmark is useful as a policy objective. It should be understood, however, to be only an interim objective at best; the specified "poverty line" would then be subject to regular upward adjustment as prices and productivity rise. A definition of poverty in absolute terms seems preferable, as a policy objective or reference point, because it lends itself to a more readily meaningful calculus in terms of costs and provides a yardstick for progress. It nevertheless remains useful and relevant to pose questions periodically as to the welfare of those who are within the bottom fifth, or quarter, or half of the income distribution. And surely, there can be no room for complacency until all Americans are able to live "decently," with dignity and freedom from deprivation.

A measure of poverty that has come into wide use has been developed by the Social Security Administration.[1] It is based on the cost per day per family member of an "economy" food plan designed by the Department of Agriculture to be "nutritionally sound." This cost for a nonfarm family of four is approximately 75 cents per person.[2] Assuming that a poor family should be expected to spend no more than one-third of its income on food,[3] the minimum income requirement for such a family at 1966 prices is $3,335. The figure is adjusted for size of family, age of children, sex and age of head, farm and nonfarm residence, and so forth. The poverty line range for nonfarm families goes from $1,560 for a single female under the age of 65 to $5,440 for a family of "7 or more" members headed by a male. For farm residents the figures are just under one-third lower.[4] This poverty index is far from generous, as may be seen from the fact that in 1966 the median income of all four-person families was

---

1. The Social Security Administration's measures of poverty and low-income are described in detail in Orshansky, *Counting the Poor: Another Look at the Poverty Profile*, SOCIAL SECURITY BULL. Jan. 1965, at 5-10, and *Who's Who Among the Poor: A Demographic View of Poverty*, SOCIAL SECURITY BULL. July 1965, at 3-10.
2. Orshansky, *The Shape of Poverty in 1966*, SOCIAL SECURITY BULL. March 1968, at 5.
3. *Id.*
4. For a table of weighted average poverty level incomes for 1966, see *id.* at 4.

$8,340,[5] slightly more than 2½ times the $3,335 poverty line for non-farm families of that size. Nevertheless, more than 15 percent of the total noninstitutionalized civilian population, 29.7 million out of 193.4 million, were, by this austere standard, classified as poor in 1966.[6] Of the 29.7 million people 4.8 million were "unrelated individuals," and 24.9 million, 12.5 million of whom were children under 18 years of age, lived as members of two-or-more-person families.[7]

In the aggregate the difference between money income received by the poor in 1966 and income sufficient to bring all families and unrelated individuals to a level of income equal to the "poverty line"—the so-called poverty gap—has been estimated at $11 billion.[8] This represents an average of over $1,000 for each of the more than 10 million[9] poor families and unrelated individuals in the United States. In Table 1 we present data on the size of the poverty gap in 1965[10] by number of related children in the family and for unrelated individuals, separately for whites and nonwhites. Two facts stand out most sharply. The median poverty gap for nonwhite families, most of whom are black, at $1,165, is almost $300 larger than it is for white families. And the size of the poverty gap generally increases as the number of related children in the family rises. For both whites and nonwhites the gap ranges from about two to 2 1/2 times as large for families with four or more children than it is for those without children. Thus less than $1,000 of additional income per family would bring almost three-quarters of the white and two-thirds of the nonwhite childless families above the poverty threshold, but amounts of this size would accomplish this objective for less than one-third of the largest white families and substantially less than one-quarter of the largest nonwhite families.

B. The Face of the Poor and the Need for a Multifaceted Approach

The years 1959 to 1966 comprised a period of unprecedented growth in the American economy. During this period progress was

5. *Id.* at 6.

6. *Id.* at 6.

7. U. S. Bureau of the Census, *The Extent of Poverty in the United States: 1959 to 1966*, CURRENT POPULATION REPORTS 12 (Series P-60, No. 54, 1968).

8. Tobin, *Raising the Incomes of the Poor*, in AGENDA FOR THE NATION 104 (K. Gordon ed. 1968). Mollie Orshansky reports a poverty gap of $11 billion for 1965. Orshansky, *The Shape of Poverty in 1966*, SOCIAL SECURITY BULL. March 1968, at 19. If the same figure is applicable to both 1965 and 1966, it may be implied, because the number of poor persons declined between the two years, that the poor in 1966 were somewhat worse off than those considered poor in 1965.

9. See Table 1, *infra*.

10. The latest year for which the details are available.

TABLE 1

AMOUNT OF ADDITIONAL INCOME NEEDED TO RAISE INCOMES OF POOR FAMILIES AND UNRELATED INDIVIDUALS TO THE POVERTY LINE, 1965

	Total families (thousands)	*Number of related children under 18 years of age* None	1	2	3	4	5	6 or more	Unrelated individuals (thousands)
				(thousands of families)					
White	4,590	1,844	680	579	566	424	248	249	3,935
Size of poverty gap				*(percent of total)*					
Less than $500	30.7	41.6	22.3	27.4	25.8	25.6	18.5	14.4	38.4
500 to 999	25.3	32.6	27.0	17.8	18.6	17.9	20.6	17.7	38.1
1,000 to 1,499	16.2	14.4	20.6	16.9	16.5	13.2	19.4	15.6	13.7
1,500 to 1,999	10.9	6.7	13.7	15.4	14.7	13.9	7.6	14.8	9.6
2,000 to 2,499	7.7	2.4	12.6	12.3	9.0	8.5	14.5	11.7	0.1
2,500 to 2,999	3.3	0.5	1.0	6.6	6.4	7.8	4.8	7.2	0.0
3,000 and over	5.9	1.9	2.9	3.7	9.1	14.2	14.5	18.5	0.3
				(dollars)					
Median gap	$ 872	616	1,016	1,108	1,202	1,333	1,250	1,586	621
				(thousands of families)					*(thousands)*
Nonwhite	1,861	359	276	241	270	206	202	307	831
Size of poverty gap				*(percent of total)*					
Less than $500	20.4	33.4	27.8	22.6	16.3	11.2	11.3	13.1	34.6
500 to 999	21.0	34.8	24.6	21.4	19.7	20.9	9.9	9.1	37.6
1,000 to 1,499	22.2	24.2	25.2	27.9	26.0	17.5	13.8	17.9	17.2
1,500 to 1,999	11.5	5.9	9.8	9.8	15.5	15.5	15.8	12.0	10.2
2,000 to 2,499	11.1	1.4	11.9	11.1	9.3	18.4	16.3	14.7	0.0
2,500 to 2,999	5.3	0.0	0.0	4.9	6.7	3.9	12.4	11.7	0.2
3,000 and over	8.5	0.3	0.7	2.0	6.7	12.6	20.3	21.6	0.1
				(dollars)					
Median gap	$ 1,165	736	910	1,095	1,211	1,518	1,955	1,919	679

Source: U. S. Bureau of the Census, *The Extent of Poverty in the United States: 1959 to 1966*, CURRENT POPULATION REPORTS, 32 (Series P-60, No. 54, 1968).

made in reducing the number of people living in poverty as we have defined it.[11] In seven years that number was reduced from 38.9 million to 29.7 million, from 22.1 to 15.4 percent of the total population.[12] But some groups fared much better than others. At the extremes, we find that the number of poor people living in families headed by a white male, the largest single category shown in Table 2, fell by almost 40 percent beteeen 1959 and 1966, whereas the number living in families headed by a nonwhite female *increased* by almost one-quarter. As may be seen in Table 2, the reduction in the number of children living in poverty was somewhat greater, at 24.8 percent, than for all persons, but the contrast among groups of children was striking. Reflecting improved employment opportunities and the very low level of unemployment experienced by married men in 1966, the number of related children who were members of poor families headed by *males* dropped over 36 percent and by almost 40 percent in the case of whites. For children of families headed by *females*, however, the picture was very different: a net increase of 11 percent made up of a decline of 13 percent with respect to whites and a *rise* of 44 percent in the case of nonwhites. Thus rapid growth and high employment in the economy, together with public and private training programs and other measures introduced since 1959, appear to have lifted a substantial proportion of the poor above the poverty line. But nearly half of the poor are still members of families headed by a white male, only 117,000 of whom were unemployed as of March, 1967.[13] And nonwhites, particularly those who are in families headed by a female, have gained little since 1959 or have actually lost ground. The hard fact remains that over 60 percent of all persons and more than 75 percent of children in nonwhite families headed by a female were classified as poor in 1966. These proportions are only slightly lower than they were in 1959.

Under present economic circumstances few people are poor because, although able to work, they cannot find a job. Poverty among the gainfully employed, and such persons comprise fully half of all heads of poor families, stems from inadequate training or education, personal disabilities of a physical, mental, or emotional nature, large size of family relative to earning capacity, and, un-

11. In subsequent sections of this paper data on the characteristics of the poor are drawn from Orshansky, *The Shape of Poverty in 1966*, SOCIAL SECURITY BULL., March 1968, at 3-32, unless other sources are specifically cited.

12. These figures do not take into account the rise in the cost of living.

13. See Table 2 and source cited.

TABLE 2

INCIDENCE OF POVERTY, BY FAMILY STATUS AND COLOR OF HEAD, 1966 AND 1959

	1966	*1959*	*Change: 1959 to 1966 (percent)*
	(thousands of persons)		
Total	29,731	38,940	—23.6
White	20,126	28,231	—28.7
Nonwhite	9,605	10,709	—10.3
In families with male head	17,644	26,885	—34.4
White	12,264	19,867	—38.3
Nonwhite	5,380	7,018	—23.3
In families with female head	7,267	6,979	+ 4.1
White	3,836	4,205	— 8.8
Nonwhite	3,431	2,774	+23.7
Unrelated individuals	4,820	5,076	— 5.0
Male	1,276	1,565	—18.5
White	1,007	1,161	—13.3
Nonwhite	269	404	—33.4
Female	3,544	3,511	+ 0.9
White	3,019	2,998	+ 0.7
Nonwhite	525	513	+ 2.3
Related children under 18 total	12,503	16,637	—24.8
In families with male head	8,045	12,627	—36.3
White	5,294	8,756	—39.5
Nonwhite	2,751	3,871	—28.9
In families with female head	4,458	4,010	+11.2
White	2,011	2,311	—13.0
Nonwhite	2,447	1,699	+44.0

Source: U. S. Bureau of the Census, *The Extent of Poverty in the United States: 1959 to 1966,* CURRENT POPULATION REPORTS 14 (Series P-60, No. 54, 1968).

doubtedly for many Negroes and other deprived minorities, limited opportunity and occupational choice. Approximately one-sixth of all poor persons are members of families headed by people aged 65 or over, or are aged unrelated individuals most of whom are no longer in the labor force. Another large group among the poor not in the labor force are the approximately one million female heads of families who are under 65 years of age.

This brief overview of some of the salient characteristics of the poor should suffice to make the point that realization of even so modest a goal as raising the incomes of all families and unrelated individuals to a level above the very spartan poverty line will require a multifaceted approach. The earning capacities of those who can work can be improved by elimination of discriminatory practices in hiring and promotion, by job training programs, by improving worker mobility and placement efforts, by better health care, and by continued economic growth at "capacity" rates accompanied by national unemployment levels of less than 4 percent. Others who are not now in the labor force would be freed to find jobs if child care facilities were vastly expanded and appropriate training provided.

But the earning capacity of many of the poor, particularly those who are already well beyond school age, and even many of those who are still in school but who are growing up under economically and culturally deprived circumstances, is not likely to rise to levels that will permit an escape from poverty. In 1966 more than one-third of all poor families consisted of five or more persons, and for these larger families poverty may be due as much or more to the number of children dependent on the breadwinner as to the inadequacy of his ability to earn income. In addition there are those poor who cannot or should not work, including mothers of young children for whom adequate care cannot be provided, the aged, and those too disabled to work.

Thus even if we could accomplish at once all that might be done to raise the earning capacity of the working poor, elimination of poverty would still require a major program of direct governmental transfers or grants in cash and/or in kind. Without such transfers grinding poverty and its attendant miseries would continue for great proportions of the aged, the disabled, broken families, and families whose heads are industrious but limited in their skills. Moreover, children in these families would be tied to the treadmill of poverty transmitted generation to generation. Children who are inadequately fed, clothed and housed, who grow up with their physical and mental faculties impaired by ill health, without hope or dignity, are likely to suffer from insurmountable handicaps on entry into the educational system. Even if that system were all that its critics believe it should be,[14] these children might be incapable of acquiring an education that would enable them to escape from poverty and dependency. Income transfers or supplements to earnings are required simply because education, training and other aspects of what Professor Tobin has called the "structural approach" in antipoverty policy,[15] take a good deal of time to produce results. The poor have no private resources to draw on until employers revamp hiring and promotion policies and procedures, or while training or learning new skills. An educational system divided into 20,000 school districts and structured by teacher training institutions to serve the needs and aspirations of the white middle class will not be fully prepared for at least another generation to cope with the problems involved in imparting to poor children—and especially poor minority group children—the skills enabling them to climb out of poverty.

C. The Operation of a Successful Income Supplement Program

Income transfers may take the form of cash or transfers in kind. The latter have been advocated as a means of ensuring that low income families will have adequate housing, health care and nutrition.[16] They play a major role in current transfers under public assistance and are justified on the ground that funds paid out would otherwise be wasted through unwise spending by their recipients. It is this attitude, however, that most severely stigmatizes the "welfare family," that most clearly sets it apart as incapable of making its own decisions. Without cash to spend as one pleases there can be little dignity or self-respect in our society, and little prospect for development of a rational consumer mentality. Thus transfers to the poor should take the form mainly or exclusively of cash, supplemented by medicaid and consumer counseling. The failures of public housing, food distribution, and so forth, argue strongly in favor of this position.

Supplements to income, whatever their specific form, should meet several basic criteria. Most important, perhaps, they should be

14. See, *e.g.*, the provocative and insightful essay on the shortcomings and need for reform of our public schools by Ralph W. Tyler, entitled *Investing in Better Schools*, in AGENDA FOR THE NATION 207-36 (K. Gordon ed. 1968).

15. Tobin, *supra* note 8, at 90.

16. In the broad sense transfers in kind may be defined to include education, police and fire protection, sanitation services, recreation, and other public services. To the extent that these services are provided to the public in general, without regard to individual or family income, however, I prefer to exclude them in the present context.

regarded as a matter of right, without the stigma of public charity attaching to present forms of public assistance. Means or income tests should be based on self-declarations similar to those applicable to income tax returns and, as in the case of the income tax, the individual should be presumed to be honest until proven otherwise. This implies, of course, the abandonment of the kind of means test now generally used.

Income transfers or grants should not discourage efforts to earn income. Transfers should, therefore, be so structured that they improve the relative income position of the recipient but do not change his rank ordering in the income distribution.[17] That is to say, within a particular family size group, in order to change his rank in the distribution, a person would have to receive some form of earnings in addition to income transfers.

Abandonment of eligibility requirements, including the means test, as now apply with respect to AFDC[18] will in itself do much to encourage people to seek jobs, free of the fear that if the job is found and then soon lost, the individual may be worse off than if he had never made the effort to earn income. The form of and conditions attaching to grants should serve to strengthen rather than destroy family ties. Unlike present practices under public assistance, there should be no income premium associated with the breaking up of the family group.

The transfer program should be efficient in the sense that the portion of the cost attributable to benefits accruing to the poor and near-poor should be as nearly equal to the entire amount of the program's cost as is compatible with avoiding effective marginal tax rates[19] on low-income people so high as to discourage work effort. Obviously no fine line can be drawn here. The income level at which net benefits should fall to zero or below is bound to be arbitrary. Given that the objective of income transfers is to support structural policies designed to eliminate poverty, however, it is this writer's judgment that that level should be somewhere below the median income for each family size.

Poverty, therefore, must be attacked on many fronts. Complementing other policy measures, income supplements will continue indefinitely to comprise a major part of the national effort.

---

17. In other words, if there are three people, and the poorest of them receives transfer payments, he should remain third in rank after their receipt.

18. Aid to Families with Dependent Children.

19. The marginal tax rate is merely that rate of income tax that one pays on each increment to income.

Such supplements can eliminate most or all of poverty as soon as we are willing to implement them adequately. Their supportive role could then be expected to decline for as long as two generations, after which they would be paid primarily to the aged, the disabled, and large, broken families.

II

THE PRESENT STRUCTURE OF THE INCOME TAX AND INCOME DISTRIBUTION

The federal individual income tax has been at the center of the stage in most recent discussions of measures designed to supplement the income of the poor.[20] In its present form the income tax is widely viewed as a major instrument of income redistribution. Its actual achievement on this score, however, is surprisingly small. The "Gini coefficient"[21] is the most convenient measure of inequality in the

20. For a recent summary of the literature, see C. GREEN, NEGATIVE TAXES AND THE POVERTY PROBLEM (1967). Among other contributions that have been added since Green's book appeared are: Rolph, *The Negative Income Tax*, 59 NAT'L TAX ASS'N PROCEEDINGS 147 (1966); Tobin, Pechman and Mieszkowski, *Is a Negative Income Tax Practical?* 77 YALE L.J. 1 (1967); Tobin, *supra* note 8; Brazer, *Tax Policy and Children's Allowances*, in CHILDREN'S ALLOWANCES AND THE ECONOMIC WELFARE OF CHILDREN (E.M. Burns ed. 1968); and SELTZER, THE PERSONAL EXEMPTIONS IN THE INCOME TAX (1968).

21. Defined as the ratio of the area between the Lorenz curve (depicting the cumulated proportion of total income accruing to the cumulated proportion of income recipients arrayed in ascending order by level of income from lowest to highest) and a diagonal line representing full equality in income distribution to the entire area under the diagonal.

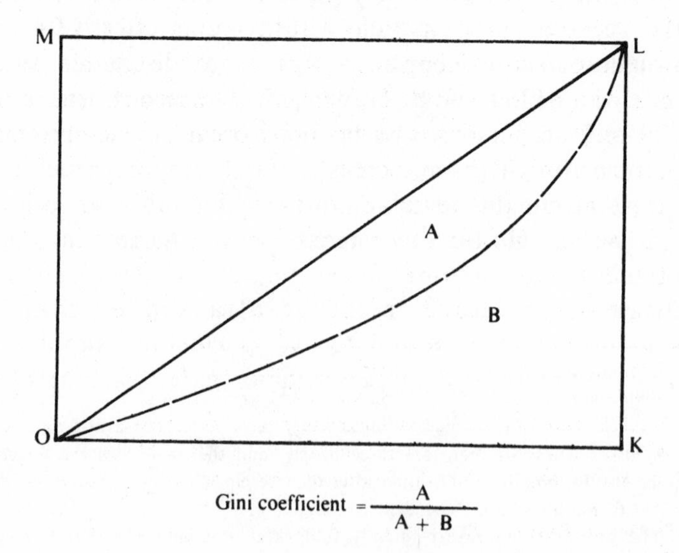

$$\text{Gini coefficient} = \frac{A}{A+B}$$

distribution of income. Its limits lie between 0, when income distribution is fully equal, and 1, when all income is received by one unit. For 1966 it has been estimated that for all income tax units the before-tax Gini coefficient was equal to .446. Its after-tax value was .409, a reduction in the degree of inequality of 8.3 percent.[22] Thus the *relative* income position of low-income individuals and families who filed income tax returns in 1966 may be said to have been modestly improved. But the income tax currently adds nothing to anyone's income and therefore accomplishes no improvement in the *absolute* level of well-being of the poor and near-poor. Moreover a large proportion of poor persons are not accounted for on tax returns,[23] so that the Gini coefficients cited actually understate inequality in the distribution of income.

There is, however, at least one sense in which the individual income tax, given the structure of tax rates, provides benefits for the poor and near-poor. This is accomplished by means of the tax savings that accrue as a consequence of the existence of the personal exemptions, nonbusiness deductions, the optional or minimum standard deduction, and various allowable exclusions. But except for the minimum standard deduction, the benefits realized by the poor in each instance are but a small fraction of total revenue foregone by the government. In the case of the personal exemptions, for example, in 1966 a total of $117 billion was deducted on all returns, $96.3 billion on taxable and $20.7 billion on nontaxable returns.[24] If the $96.3 billion had been taxed at an average rate of 20 percent (somewhat higher than the average of 19.6 percent on actual taxable income), the increase in revenue realized would have been $19.3 billion. Disallowance of the exemptions claimed on nontaxable returns, and addition of the $400 to $500 million in tax that might have been paid by the 20 million persons who do not appear as exemptions claimed on tax returns, might have increased this figure to about $21 billion. To what extent did this reduction in tax liability accrue to low-income people? If we assume that all returns which reported less than $3,000 of adjusted gross income were filed by poor persons we can approximate an answer. On taxable returns with less than $3,000 of

22. Pechman and Okner, *Application of the Carter Commission Proposals to the United States: A Simulation Study*, NAT'L TAX J. Vol. XXII (forthcoming).

23. For 1963 an estimated 20.8 million persons were not represented in income tax returns filed. *See* A. Ott, D. Ott and J.S. Turner, Simulation of Costs of a Negative Income Tax Plan and its Implications for the Poor 3, December, 1968 (unpublished manuscript on file with authors).

24. INTERNAL REVENUE SERVICE, U.S. TREASURY DEP'T, STATISTICS OF INCOME 1966: INDIVIDUAL INCOME TAX RETURNS 7 (1968).

adjusted gross income $7.5 billion was deducted for personal exemptions. At an average tax rate of 15 percent the tax saving would have amounted to $1.1 billion. At the outside we might add $1 billion in tax that would have been paid if the $14.4 billion in exemptions claimed on non-taxable returns with adjusted gross income of less than $3,000 had not been allowed, plus perhaps another $400 million to take into account tax that might have been due from those not now required to file because their adjusted gross income falls below $600 or, for the aged, below $1,200.[25] Thus $2.5 billion seems a generous estimate of the benefits accruing to the poor. It would seem, therefore, to "cost" the federal government more than $8 in order to save the poor $1 through this route.

Similarly, an increase in the level of the personal exemption appears to be a most costly and unpromising way to improve the well-being of the poor. Those who either do not file returns now or who file nontaxable returns would, obviously, gain nothing. For taxable returns with adjusted gross income of up to $3,000 a $100 increase in the personal exemption would reduce taxable income by less than $1 billion and tax liability by about $150 million. The revenue loss associated with the increase in exemptions would amount to some $3 billion, so that only one-twentieth of the tax saving would accrue to the poor.[26]

Similar analysis with respect to deductions and exclusions would show that the gains in tax saving realized by low-income individuals and families are only a small fraction of the total revenue cost. The one exception, as already noted is the minimum standard deduction of $200 for the taxpayer plus $100 for each exemption (including his own), up to a maximum of $1,000.[27] The $350 million cost of this provision accrues largely to those with incomes under $5,000. But even this route will not take us very far. In fact if all taxable returns with adjusted gross income reported in 1966 of less than $3,000 were relieved entirely of all tax liability the gain in disposable income would be only $1.2 billion, about 6 percent of reported income.[28]

Nor do there appear to be significant gains to be realized by the poor through bold reforms that would broaden the tax base by curtailing or eliminating deductions and exclusions and thus permit major reductions in tax rates. One must conclude, rather, that income tax reform that stops short of providing substantial net *payments* to

25. INT. REV. CODE of 1954, § 151.

26. Estimates derived from STATISTICS OF INCOME, *supra* note 24, Table 2.

27. INT. REV. CODE of 1954, § 141.

28. STATISTICS OF INCOME, *supra* note 24, at 6.

the poor and near-poor is simply incapable of making any appreciable inroads on the poverty problem. It certainly cannot do so efficiently, in the sense in which efficiency was suggested[29] as one important criterion to be met by measures designed to alleviate poverty.

III

ALTERNATIVE FORMS OF NEGATIVE INCOME TAXATION

This brings us to consideration of the "negative" income tax and the various forms that it might take. Negative income tax is, perhaps, a misleading term, because for most present taxpayers the individual income tax would continue to function as it now does. The tax becomes "negative" only in the sense that the liability of the lowest income recipients becomes negative; that is, they receive a net payment from the Treasury. Most plans would include all persons who met the low income test, some would require major reform of the tax base while others would not, and there are variations as well in the extent to which existing public assistance and social security programs would be supplanted. Space will permit the examination of only two of the plans that have been offered and a somewhat more elaborate version of my earlier proposal that limits the negative income tax to families with dependent children. Most other proposals are, however, essentially variants of the first two.

A. The Credit Income Tax

Earl Rolph has suggested a form of negative income tax which he calls the "Credit Income Tax."[30] As he describes it, "The plan has two main ingredients: (1) a system of flat-sum credits to which every person in the country would be entitled, and (2) a general proportional income tax with zero exemptions."[31] Actually Rolph would provide uniform credits for adults and smaller credits for children which would vary with age, presumably higher credits for older than for younger children. He expressed the view that the adult credit might equal "about $400," although recognizing that this would ameliorate but not eliminate poverty.[32] Thus for a family of two adults and two children the credits might total perhaps $1,200 to

---

29. See text accompanying note 19 *supra*.
30. Tobin, *supra* note 8.
31. *Id.* at 147.
32. *Id.* at 149.

$1.400. But this is only about 40 percent of the "poverty line" income,[33] and credits of the suggested size would be too small to supplant AFDC, aid to the blind, the disabled, and the aged in all but the states with the lowest benefits. Nevertheless, even at the suggested level of the credit, it would make substantial inroads into the poverty gap, particularly with respect to the working poor.

If we assume a credit of $400 for each adult and an average of $300 for each child under the age of 18, the aggregate amount of credits allowed would be approximately $52 billion for adults plus $21 billion for children, a total of $73 billion. If the net yield to the government from the individual income tax is to be, say, $67 billion, then a proportionate tax on income as comprehensively defined, with no exemptions, exclusions, or deductions would have to raise a total of $140 billion. Suppose that personal income, broadly defined, is equal to $700 billion. Then the uniform tax rate would be 20 percent. Of the gross yield of $140 billion the Treasury would receive $67 billion and credits would absorb the rest. The effect of the credit income tax on a family of two adults and two children, at various income levels, is illustrated in Table 3. Net benefits begin at $1,400 when income before tax or credits is zero and fall off as income rises until they disappear when income reaches $7,000. Beyond that level a

TABLE 3

EFFECTS OF CREDIT INCOME TAX ON DISPOSABLE INCOME, FAMILY OF FOUR, VARIOUS INCOME LEVELS

Income before tax and credits	*Credits*	*Gross tax (20 percent proportionate rate)*	*Net benefit or tax (-)*	*Disposable income*
		(*dollars*)		
0	1,400	0	1,400	1,400
1,000	1,400	200	1,200	2,200
2,000	1,400	400	1,000	3,000
3,000	1,400	600	800	3,800
5,000	1,400	1,000	400	5,400
7,000	1,400	1,400	0	7,000
10,000	1,400	2,000	— 600	9,400
20,000	1,400	4,000	— 2,600	17,400
50,000	1,400	10,000	— 8,600	41,400
100,000	1,400	20,000	—18,600	81,400
200,000	1,400	40,000	—38,600	161,400

33. See text accompanying note 3 *supra*.

net tax is paid that approaches but never quite reaches an average effective rate of 20 percent. Fairly steep progression is achieved through the relevant range by means of the credit, while the marginal rate is constant at 20 percent throughout the income scale.

The credit income tax would achieve vast simplification of the income tax by doing away with the differential treatment of income that is now provided on the basis of differences in sources and disposition, timing of receipts, splitting among taxpaying units, including trusts and minor children, and so forth. Improvements in terms of horizontal equity and efficiency in resource allocation are obvious consequences. If the income base is defined so as to include capital gains in full, including gains constructively realized upon gratuitous transfer of assets, presently exempt interest, social security and related benefits, and imputed net rental income on owner-occupied homes, and if depletion charges were limited to historical cost, few glaring inequities would remain. Moreover, it is even likely that vertical equity, defined in terms of egalitarian objectives, would be better served as well. And, as described, the credit income tax would not provide incentives to break up families.

Obviously, however, the scheme would involve a major redistribution of tax liabilities, particularly toward those whose incomes are now wholly or partially exempt, or who are entitled to large nonbusiness deductions. This clearly suggests that reform on as bold a scale as is here indicated would face extremely difficult political obstacles. If the present income tax base were to survive the reform effort, a proportionate tax rate of about 40 percent would be needed. This might not be an excessively high price to pay in exchange for the gains made available to low-income families and individuals, but it would mean sharply higher taxes in the upper middle income range.[34] Compromises are clearly possible. A credit income tax need not require an "ideal" income tax base; in fact, one that would include all imputed income and even place a value on leisure is undoubtedly not administratively feasible. Nor is there anything at all sacrosanct about the suggested size of the credit—it might be substantially higher or even lower. But, given the net revenue

34. For example, a family of four with adjusted gross income of $10,000 would pay about $830 under present law, $600 under the credit income tax illustrated, and $620 if the present tax base were retained but a credit of $400 per adult and $300 per child were introduced and a proportionate tax rate of 40 percent were to replace the present rate structure. But for a family having $20,000 adjusted gross income, the tax liability, now at $2,910, would more than double, to $5,840, compared with $2,600 under the Rolph-type plan. (Calculations of tax liability under present law assume nonbusiness deductions of 15 percent of adjusted gross income and ignore the temporary surtax).

objective, there is an inescapable interdependence between the definition of the tax base, the amount of the credit, and the required tax rate. If the Administration or the Congress pursues the scheme it will need to establish acceptable limits with respect to all three variables and present alternative sets of values within the limits.

B. The "Standard" Negative Income Tax

The credit income tax is, of course, but one of a "family" of negative-type income taxes. Such proposals provide a minimum allowance or credit which establishes the lowest income that any individual or family with no other income may have, at the same time imposing a tax on other income over and above the regular income tax. Typically they retain the existing individual income tax, with or without reform of the base, and allow the taxpayer to elect not to receive the basic allowance when it, coupled with his offsetting tax, produces a negative net benefit. The Tobin-Pechman-Mieszkowski negative income tax proposals[35] provide for alternative high and low schedules of basic allowances and the option of a 50 or 33 1/3 percent offsetting tax rate. For illustrative purposes we shall consider their high schedule coupled with a 50 percent tax rate. The basic allowance, which is the income received by an individual or family with no income from other sources, is $800 for a single adult, $1,600 for a two-adult family, $2,100 for three persons ($1,800 if only one adult), $2,600 for four persons ($2,300 if only one adult), an additional $400 for each of the fifth and sixth persons and $200 for the seventh and eighth. The maximum allowance is, therefore, $3,800, irrespective of family size. With the 50 percent offsetting tax, when other income is equal to double the amount of the basic allowance the "break-even point" is reached. The effect is the same as if no allowance had been received and no taxes paid. At somewhat higher income levels, ranging from $1,876 for one person to $8,359 for a two-adult, eight-person family, the tax break-even point is reached. At or above this point the individual or family is better off not receiving the allowance, not paying the offsetting tax, and simply paying the regular income tax.

The effects of the Tobin-Pechman-Mieszkowski high allowance plan with a 50 percent offsetting tax rate are presented in Table 4 for families of two, four, and six persons. When other income is zero the basic allowance provides a minimum income of $1,600, $2,600, or $3,400, amounts which equal roughly three-quarters of the poverty line income for nonfarm families headed by a male adult. In each case

35. Tobin, Pechman and Mieszkowski, *supra* note 20, at 4-6.

it takes between $1,000 and $2,000 of other income to close the poverty gap, the amount increasing with the size of the family. Unlike the Rolph-type credit income tax, the Tobin-Pechman-Mieszkowski plan imposes heavy budgetary demands. Its cost is estimated at $26 billion before taking into account the revenue gained from including social security benefits, veterans' pensions, unemployment compensation, imputed rental income on owner-occupied homes, the value of food consumed on farms, a fraction of gifts received, exempt interest, and other items in the negative income tax base, and before calculating the savings of a large part of public assistance costs. The net cost is expected to be about $20 billion.[36] The income base for the offsetting tax would be radically different from the positive income tax base. As indicated, the offsetting tax, but not the ordinary income tax, would apply to a wide range of sources of income excluded from the concept of adjusted gross income, and exemptions and nonbusiness deductions would not be allowed for purposes of the negative income tax.

Under both the credit income tax and the Tobin-Pechman-Mieszkowski-type negative income tax it would seem fairly simple to provide for monthly or biweekly distributions of payments to those who expect to receive net benefits. Both plans appear to be entirely workable, but both may be expected to encounter formidable political opposition. The negative income tax, at the level of benefits suggested, involves a major budgetary commitment, one that can readily be scaled down, but only at the expense of making the plan inadequate as a means of alleviating poverty. It will be argued as well that it would provide a strong incentive to break up families. For example, a family of two adults and six children would, if they had no other income, receive benefits of $3,800, compared with $4,600, or $800 more, if they split into two families of four. The authors appear correct, however, in their contention that "Amounts of this size do not seem to be large in comparison with the other considerations that are ordinarily significant in the decision to maintain or split a family unit."[37] The logic of that part of the proposal denying any benefits to children beyond the sixth appears more questionable. This provision is designed to give some incentive to limit family size. The obvious response to this is that "other considerations that are ordinarily significant in the decision"[38] determining family size are likely to outweigh the desire to gain an extra $200 (the incremental allowance

36. *Id.* at 24-26.
37. *Id.* at 9.
38. *Id.*

TABLE 4

EFFECTS OF TOBIN-PECHMAN-MIESZKOWSKI NEGATIVE INCOME TAX ON DISPOSABLE INCOME, FAMILIES OF TWO, FOUR, AND SIX PERSONS, VARIOUS INCOME LEVELS

(dollars)

Income before allowance and taxes	*Allowance*	*Offsetting 50 percent tax*	*Ordinary income tax*[a]	*Net benefits or tax (-)*	*Disposable income*
		Family of two adults			
0	1,600	0	0	1,600	1,600
1.000	1,600	500	0	1,100	2,100
2,000	1,600	1,000	0	600	2,600
3,000	1,600	1,500	0	100	3,100
4,000	0	0	354	— 354	3,646
		Family of two adults and two children			
0	2,600	0	0	2,600	2,600
1,000	2,600	500	0	2,100	3,100
2,000	2,600	1,000	0	1,600	3,600
3,000	2,600	1,500	0	1,100	4,100
4,000	2,600	2,000	0	600	4,600
6,000	2,600	3,000	0	— 400	5,600
8,000	0	0	772	— 772	7,228
		Family of two adults and four children			
0	3,400	0	0	3,400	3,400
1,000	3,400	500	0	2,900	3,900
2,000	3,400	1,000	0	2,400	4,400
3,000	3,400	1,500	0	1,900	4,900
4,000	3,400	2,000	0	1,400	5,400
6,000	3,400	3,000	0	400	6,400
8,000	0	0	552	— 552	7,448
10,000	0	0	886	— 886	9,114

[a]Assumes the higher of optional or minimum standard deduction is taken. Surtax and F.I.C.A. are ignored.

for the fifth and sixth child) by having an additional child. Moreover, and far more important in the short run, is the fact that children already living in families of more than eight persons are far more likely to be impoverished than are children in smaller families.[39]

C. The Children's Allowance

If the budgetary demands of the negative income tax impose a major barrier to its acceptance, and if the opposition of those who view the proposal as a threat to the social security system or to continued privileged treatment of various forms of income is insurmountable, a well designed children's allowance plan could provide an attractive and feasible alternative.[40] The social security system, with appropriate amendments, can readily be made into an effective instrument for alleviating or even eliminating poverty among the aged and the disabled. Federalization of the unemployment compensation system, together with extension of the benefit period and improvement in the level of benefits, plus integration of the system with ongoing and improved manpower training programs, could take care of another large part of the population counted as poor. The remainder of the poor population would then consist largely of the working poor who are poor because their earnings are too small to support, even at minimum standards, the number of children dependent upon them, and members of families headed by a female who is not a breadwinner. The case for focusing a major part of antipoverty efforts on the needs of children has been well stated by Professor Tobin:

> The acute problem is the inability of many employable males to earn enough to support their children. The result is usually a family in poverty unrelieved by public assistance. With increasing frequency, however, the mother and children are left on their own and 'go on welfare.' The basic solution in the long run is to build up earning capacities by education and work experience. *Meanwhile, people are*

39. In 1966 the proportion of families that were poor was more than twice as great for families with six or more children than for families with four children. Orshansky, *The Shape of Poverty in 1966*, SOCIAL SECURITY BULL. March 1968, at 19.

40. Most advocates of children's allowances favor universal allowances of modest amount such as are found in virtually every industrialized nation in the world except the United States. *See, e.g.*, J. VADAKIN, CHILDREN, POVERTY, AND FAMILY ALLOWANCES 183-200 (1968), for a description of children's allowances and advocacy of a plan to distribute $10 per month per child under age 18 to all families in the United States. But a plan of this kind can be no more than a minor palliative, although if the allowance were set at the level of $10 per month per child the cost would be about $7.3 billion per year. *Id.* at 197. Far preferable, it seems, is a children's allowance plan under which, at no greater budgetary cost, much higher benefits are made available to the poor within the framework of a universal system.

poor and their children are raised under handicaps that may destine them to be poor too.[41]

The children's allowance plan has three essential elements. The present exemption for dependent children under the individual income tax[42] would be discontinued. It is essentially a children's allowance that carries a value ranging from $0 for those at the bottom of the income scale to $420 for those at the top.[43] The second element consists of a children's allowance of $1,400 for the first child, $900 for the second, $600 for the third, and $400 for the fourth and subsequent children. These allowances would not be included in taxable income, but they would give rise to a "children's allowance tax" (CATAX) so structured as to be a function of other income and the number of children in the family. The base of the CATAX would be adjusted gross income as presently defined. The tax schedule applicable to a two-adult family, with rates ranging from 15 to 56 percent, is set forth in Table 5.[44] The major constraint imposed in the construction of the schedule is that for a taxpayer with up to four children the combined marginal tax rate, including CATAX, income tax, and social security tax, is not permitted to exceed 65 percent for all but very high income taxpayers. The CATAX reaches a maximum total equal to 95 percent of the amount of children's allowances received. Thus the effect is to provide credits for children, in lieu of the present exemptions, in amounts that range from $1,400 to $70 for the first child, $900 to $45 for the second, $600 to $30 for the third, and $400 to $20 for the fourth and all additional children beyond the fourth. The full allowances are retained only when other income is $0, while the minimum net allowance applies when other income is $8,000 or more. When the additional income tax attributable to the discontinuation of the dependents' exemptions is taken into account, however, the actual net change in after-tax income ranges from gains equal to the full amount of the allowances to reductions that reach maximum levels of $350, $375, $390, and $400 when the marginal income tax rate is 70 percent. The break-even point is reached when adjusted gross income is approximately $7,450 for a faimily of two adults and two children. It is somewhat higher for a family with one child and lower for larger families.

---

41. Tobin, *supra* note 8, at 114 (italics added).

42. INT. REV. CODE of 1954, § 151.

43. The tax saving attributable to the exemption ranges from $0 when the marginal tax rate is zero to $420 when the marginal tax rate reaches 70 percent.

44. A second schedule is required for one-adult families. It takes account of the higher income tax rates paid by "heads of households" and thus provides for somewhat *lower* CATAX rates.

TABLE 5

CHILDREN'S ALLOWANCE TAX RATE SCHEDULE, MARRIED TAXPAYER

Adjusted gross income	*Number of children*					
	1	2	3	4	5	6
Not over $2,000	15%	25%	32%	36%	40%	45%
Over $2,000— but not over $6,000	$300, plus 19% *of excess over $2,000	$500, plus 31% *	$640, plus 40% *	$720, plus 45% *	$800, plus 50% *	$900, plus 56% *
Over $6000— but not over $8,000	$1,060, plus 13.5% † of excess over $6,000	$1,740, plus 22.2% †	$2,240, plus 25.7% †	$2,520, plus 30.7% †	$2,800, plus 35.7% †	$3,140, plus 37.7% †
Over $8,000	1,330	$2,185	$2,755	$3,135	$3,515	$3,895

The operation of the plan is illustrated in Table 6 for two-adult families with one, two, and four children, with other incomes ranging from $0 to $10,000. In the case of the one-child family with no other income the allowance of $1,400 is equal to 54 percent of poverty line income for a nonfarm family of three. At $2,300 for a family of four 69 percent of poverty line income is received. For a family of six, three-quarters of the poverty gap is removed, and that proportion is approximately maintained for larger families. When other income exceeds zero the net allowances fill increasingly large proportions of the poverty gap and bring a substantial fraction of all poor families above the poverty line. In the case of a family with two children and other income of $1,000, for example, the initial poverty gap of $2,335 is reduced to $285, or by almost 88 percent, and when other income reaches $2,000 and the net allowances raise disposable income to $3,772, or $437 above the poverty line. Net benefits decline as other income rises, the implicit marginal tax rates approaching 65 percent and then falling off to equal the marginal individual tax rate when adjusted gross income is $8,000, the point at which the marginal CATAX becomes zero. Gains continue to be realized until other income exceeds $7,000, so that the program assists not only the poor but low-income families generally.

Estimates based on data supplied by the Social Security Administration provide interesting insights into the cost components of the program and its impact on poverty among families with dependent children under 18 years of age. The gross cost of the children's allowances is $68.5 billion. Of this amount $7 billion is recovered in the form of additional income tax revenue resulting from the discontinuation of exemptions for dependent children. The children's allowance tax (CATAX) is estimated to yield $52.1 billion, thus reducing the net cost to $9.4 billion. If it is assumed that the receipt of children's allowances will reduce AFDC payments dollar for dollar, the reduction in such payments would amount to $1.8 billion and the net cost of the program to all levels of government would be $7.6 billion. For federal budgetary purposes the cost would be about $8.6 billion, while state and local governments would save approximately $800 million.

The total poverty gap for families with children is estimated at $6.2 billion for 1966. Some 13 million children, members of over 4 million families, lived in poverty in that year. The children's allowance program outlined here, if it had been in effect in 1966, would have reduced the poverty gap for families with children by 81 percent and more than half of all poor children would have been lifted

TABLE 6

EFFECTS OF CHILDREN'S ALLOWANCE PLAN ON DISPOSABLE INCOME, TWO-ADULT FAMILIES WITH ONE, TWO, AND FOUR CHILDREN, VARIOUS INCOME LEVELS

(dollars)

Income before allowances and taxes	*Allowance*	*CATAX*	*Net allowance*	*Increase in income tax due to loss of dependents' exemptions*	*Net benefits or cost (—)*	*Income tax*[a]	*Disposable income*
Family with one child							
0	1,400	0	1,400	0	1,400	0	1,400
1,000	1,400	150	1,250	0	1,250	0	2,250
2,000	1,400	300	1,100	42	1,058	42	3,058
3,000	1,400	490	910	87	823	185	3,725
4,000	1,400	680	720	93	627	338	4,382
6,000	1,400	1,080	320	106	214	658	5,662
8,000	1,400	1,330	70	114	— 44	1,000	7,070
10,000	1,400	1,330	70	114	— 44	1,342	8,728
Family with two children							
0	2,300	0	2,300	0	2,300	0	2,300
1,000	2,300	250	2,050	0	2,050	0	3,050
2,000	2,300	500	1,800	28	1,772	28	3,772
3,000	2,300	810	1,490	170	1,320	170	4,320
4,000	2,300	1,120	1,180	182	998	322	4,858
6,000	2,300	1,740	560	208	352	658	5,902

TABLE 6—(continued)

Income before allowances and taxes	Allowance	CATAX	Net allowance	Increase in income tax due to loss of dependents' exemptions	Net benefits or cost (—)	Income tax[a]	Disposable income
			(dollars)				
8,000	2,300	2,185	115	228	— 113	1,000	7,115
10,000	2,300	2,185	115	228	— 113	1,342	8,773
			Family with four children				
0	3,300	0	3,300	0	3,300	0	3,300
1,000	3,300	360	2,940	0	2,940	0	3,940
2,000	3,300	720	2,580	0	2,580	0	4,580
3,000	3,300	1,170	2,130	140	1,990	140	4,990
4,000	3,300	1,620	1,680	290	1,390	290	5,390
6,000	3,300	2,520	780	390	390	620	6,160
8,000	3,300	3,135	165	448	— 283	1,000	7,165
10,000	3,300	3,135	165	456	— 291	1,342	8,823

[a]Assumes the higher of optional or minimum standard deduction is taken. Surtax and F.I.C.A. are ignored.

out of poverty. Moreover, at the net cost of $7.6 billion, the disposable income of those who were initially poor would have been increased by $6.4 billion, or 84 percent of the net increase in the disposable income of all families. The $6.4 billion represents an increase of more than 70 percent in the income of those who were initially poor. Thus the program appears to satisfy the test of "efficiency,"[45] in the sense that the net benefits are heavily concentrated among the poor. At the same time marginal tax rates, especially for smaller families (one and two children) are not so high as to discourage work effort. While they do exceed 65 percent for high income families with more than four children, incentives to work outside the home, in the case of families headed by a female, are unlikely to be strong under any circumstances. For families headed by a male, incentives to work are not likely to be dependent on marginal tax rates as long as such rates are substantially below 100 percent.

Administration of the program would not present major difficulties. All families with children would receive children's allowance checks once or twice a month and the CATAX can readily be built into withholding schedules. Those whose incomes are not subject to withholding would be expected to report and pay the CATAX along with their quarterly payments of income tax. Verification of the number and eligibility of children and of income would fit readily into a somewhat enlarged Internal Revenue Service audit program. The force of incentives to break up families would be somewhat stronger than under the Tobin-Pechman-Mieszkowski negative income tax plan.[46] If this were regarded as a major problem the differential in the allowances for successive numbers of children could be reduced. But this would place serious hardships on one- and two-child families. On balance it seems preferable to rely on the dominance of other factors governing decisions as to family unity.

Another issue that arises involves the relationship between aid to families with dependent children and the proposed children's allowances. At most this issue concerns only the one-third of all poor children who are now beneficiaries under AFDC.[47] For them the children's allowance benefits suggested are substantially larger than AFDC payments per child in all but one-quarter of the states.[48] The

45. See text accompanying note 19 *supra*.

46. For example, a family with six children would receive gross allowances in the amount of $4,100, whereas two families with three children would each receive $2,900. Thus splitting the large family in two would yield a gain of $1,700 if no other income were received.

47. Orshansky, *The Shape of Poverty in 1966*, SOCIAL SECURITY BULL. March 1968, at 20.

48. *See* SOCIAL SECURITY BULL. November 1968, at 44.

most appealing approach is one that would permit the states to supplement children's allowances under continued federal aid. The children's allowances would then establish a floor under support levels available to families with children, one that would reduce drastically the influence of state residence on the welfare of children.[49]

The children's allowance proposal, being essentially a proposal for a negative income tax confined to families with dependent children, necessarily encounters the same kinds of problems with respect to the definition of income subject to the offsetting tax that so much concerned Tobin *et al.* Because the aged would rarely be affected, social security benefits and other nontaxable pensions received by them are not at issue. But almost 3 million children do receive survivors' benefits under OASDHI, and all other excludable income, such as municipal bond interest, imputed rental income on owner-occupied homes, food consumed on the farm, half of long term capital gains, and unemployment compensation, should, ideally, be taken into account in arriving at net benefits. Otherwise inequities obviously would arise as between renters and homeowners, for example, inequities that, given the relatively high marginal rates required under the CATAX, are more serious than those presently in existence under the income tax. The added complexities in compliance and administration that would ensue must be considered together with the desirability of a comprehensive redefinition of income for purposes of the CATAX. It seems advisable to accept the inequities with respect to the CATAX until or unless the Congress is willing to remove them and adopt a comprehensive income tax base. This is, of course, a matter for political judgment.

CONCLUSION

The individual income tax does not presently serve as a major instrument for redistribution of income. Nor is it capable, in its present form, of providing substantial help for the near-poor. For those who are living in poverty the income tax can assume significance only by incorporating a substantial negative element. The negative factor would enable the government to make payments to people having very low or zero incomes and it would reduce appreciably the net contribution to the Treasury of many with incomes that are low but above the poverty line as defined by the Social Security Administra-

49. Average monthly payments per child now range from as low as $9.42 and $10.34 in Puerto Rico and Mississippi to $77.09 in New Jersey and $96.96 in New York. Derived from SOCIAL SECURITY BULL. Nov. 1968, at 44.

tion. Once this general approach is accepted in principle, and the income tax extended so that it provides for net payments to part of the population as well as demanding upwards of $80 billion per year from its more affluent members, it can become a major means of alleviating or even eliminating poverty and deprivation. Education, training, work experience, the elimination of racial barriers to jobs, and access for all to decent housing and health services are undoubtedly the prerequisites for any ultimate solution to the problem of poverty in an affluent nation. But income maintenance programs will always be needed for some groups in the population, and the poor are no longer complacent about being poor while awaiting the results of programs designed to raise their earning capacities. For some, such as female heads of large families and male family heads with limited abilities to acquire the skills needed to enable them to escape poverty, such efforts are likely to bring results only in the next generation. There can be hope for that next generation only if, while growing up, it is supported by a level of income that will insure decent nutrition, adequate housing, protection of health, and some sense of dignity.

As a benevolent dictator, one would be strongly moved toward adoption of a credit income tax with credits set high enough to remove substantially more than half of the total poverty gap of about $11 billion, but not so high as to dissuade large numbers of people from seeking gainful employment. The credit income tax, however, seems a long way off in a representative democracy. Its prospects are poor in the political arena because it encroaches on strongly entrenched vested interests; presently allowed exclusions and deductions would have to be abolished in order to broaden the tax base sufficiently to permit the tax rate to remain within reasonable bounds.

The negative income tax of the kind advocated by Tobin, Pechman, and Mieszkowski is far less radical than the credit tax, but it too may demand too much, in terms of budgetary costs and the authors' insistence on including major elements of income in the base of the offsetting tax which presently represent privileged exclusions.

Both the credit income tax and the negative income tax could be made more acceptable from a political standpoint if the credit or basic allowances were offered at very low levels while, at least initially, a narrower tax base was adopted. But this approach would offer far more than it is capable of delivering. It would not permit discontinuation of any of the public assistance programs that now accentuate the affliction of poverty. And at the same time it could once more lead to the frustration of thwarted expectations.

If recourse must be had to a modest program, a children's allowance of the dimensions and properties described above has enormous appeal. It requires only a comparatively minor change in the individual income tax. The exemptions for dependent children need simply be replaced by what amounts to a dependents' credit that varies inversely with the number of children in the family and income. Instead of the accretion to after-tax income resulting from the dependents' exemption, which varies in amount from nothing at very low income levels to as much as $420 at the highest levels of income, the combined children's allowance and children's allowance tax would add as much as $1,400 to income at the lowest level and as little as $20 (for the fourth and succeeding children) through the middle and high range of the income scale.

The children's allowance approach gains its appeal in part from the fact that children constitute the largest unaided portion of the existing poor population. Existing social security and unemployment compensation programs are capable, if appropriately improved, of alleviating poverty among the aged, the disabled, and the unemployed. But programs of education and training aimed at breaking the cycle of intergenerational transmission of poverty are doomed to failure if the children to be educated are without adequate food, clothing, shelter, and health services and are living under circumstances that cannot foster hope, dignity, or pride.

D. Progression

A consideration of progression—Undoubtedly one of the most basic and troublesome issues in the income tax—must distinguish between two separate questions—the "is" and the "ought". At the outset, it should be borne in mind that as recently as 1965, only $5 billion—about ten percent of the total revenue raised by the individual income tax—was produced by rates in excess of 20%.[a] Moreover, progressive rates undoubtedly account for a good part of the complexity of our present tax system (through the encouragement of controversies over questions of timing and income shifting). Nevertheless, we seem to be rather firmly committed, at least in principle, to a progressive rate structure.[b]

The commitment is only partially carried out in practice. As is dramatically evident from the chart[c] that immediately follows this introduction, as well as from the subsequent excerpt, there is only the remotest relation between the marginal rates that are specified in Section 1 of the Code and the actual effective rates of tax.

One consequence of this disparity has been an effort to narrow the gap. Various provisions of the 1969 Tax Reform Act—such as the new "minimum tax for tax preferences" (see Sections 56–58 of the Code) and the limitations imposed on the use of the 25% alternative tax for long term capital gains—were addressed to the attainment of that objective. A rather different suggestion has been to impose a flat rate tax on a much broadened base, raising anew the debate over progression but in the context of a more comprehensive tax base, as discussed in Section B.[d] The next two excerpts deal with that issue.[e] Finally,

[a] U. S. Treasury Dept., Tax Reform Studies and Proposals, 91st Cong., 1st Sess., pt. 1, at 106 (1969).

[b] For the classic analysis of the issue, see Blum and Kalven, The Uneasy Case for Progressive Taxation, 19 U.Chi.L.Rev. 417 (1952) (also available in paperback).

[c] This chart is taken from Goode, The Individual Income Tax 236 (1964).

[d] See, e. g., the assertion of Dean Charles Galvin (based on the work of the American Bar Association Substantive Tax Reform Committee) that a 13% flat tax on a fairly comprehensive base could raise the same revenue that is now obtained. Galvin and Bittker, The Income Tax: How Progressive Should It Be?, p. 4 (American Enterprise Institute for Pub. Policy Research, Wash., D.C. 1969).

[e] For another comment on the Carter Commission's "discretionary income" approach to progression, see Bittker, Income Tax Reform in Canada: The Report of the Royal Commission on Taxation, 35 U.Chi.L.Rev. 637 (1968).

in response to the oft-heard complaint that high progressive rates stifle incentives, there is included a piece that explores the impact of high rates on work effort. See also page 534, infra, concerning the effect of tax rates on investment.

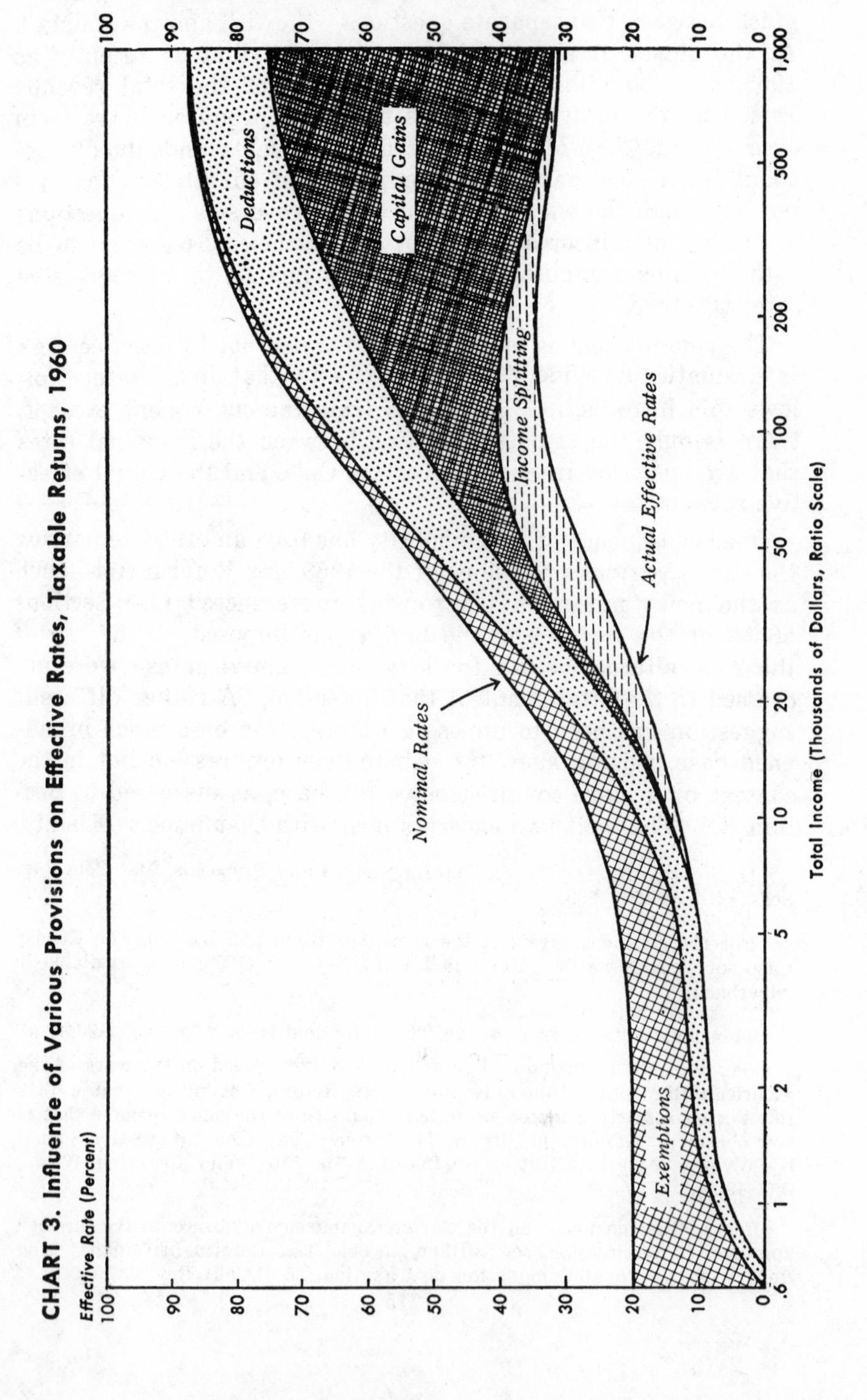

CHART 3. Influence of Various Provisions on Effective Rates, Taxable Returns, 1960

PECHMAN, THE RICH, THE POOR, AND THE TAXES THEY PAY *

The Public Interest, Fall 1969, pp. 21, 32–33.

Summary of the National Tax System

It is not easy to arrive at an accurate estimate of the impact of the whole tax system at various income levels. Taxes are reported to different federal, state, and local government agencies. No single agency has the responsibility to compel reporting of taxes on a meaningful and consistent basis. A number of isolated attempts have been made by students of public finance to piece together from the inadequate data estimates of the distribution of all taxes by income classes. These studies were for different years, make different assumptions for the incidence of the various taxes, and use different statistical sources and methodologies to correct for the inconsistencies in the data. Nevertheless, they all arrive at similar conclusions regarding the relative tax loads at different income levels.

The most recent estimates were prepared by the Council of Economic Advisers for the year 1965. They show the distribution of taxes by the income classes of families and unattached individuals, income being defined exclusive of transfer payments. The estimates for taxes and transfers separately, and in combination, are summarized in Table 5.

The following are the major conclusions that can be drawn from these and previously published estimates:

1. Since at least the mid-1930's, the federal tax system has been roughly proportional in the lower and middle income classes, and clearly progressive for the highest classes. Federal income tax data suggest that the preferential rate on capital gains, and the exclusion of interest on state and local bonds and other items from the tax

* © 1969 by National Affairs, Inc. Reproduced with permission.

base, have produced some regressivity for the very small group at the top of the income pyramid, say, beginning with incomes of $100,000 or more.

2. State and local taxes are regressive throughout the income scale.

3. The combined federal, state, and local tax burden is heaviest in the very bottom and top brackets, and lowest in the middle brackets. This statement is, of course, based on averages for each group and there are wide variations around these averages for specific individuals, depending on the sources of their incomes, the kind of property they own, and where they live.

4. The poor receive numerous transfer payments (e.g., social security, unemployment compensation, public assistance, etc.) that are financed by this tax system. The net effect of transfers as against taxes is distinctly progressive, because transfer payments make up such a large proportion of total income at the bottom of the income distribution—56 per cent for those with incomes of less than $2,000 in 1965. (To some extent, this progressivity is overstated because the transfers do not always go to the same people who pay taxes, the best example being social security retirement benefits that are received only by retirees—many of whom are not poor—while $1.5 billion of the payroll tax levied to pay for these benefits are paid by the poor.) There is no reason in the abstract, why a nation should not levy taxes on and pay transfers to the same groups; but while the nation wages a war on poverty, it is surely appropriate to consider the possibility of providing additional financial assistance to the poor by *tax reduction* as well as through transfer payments.

TABLE 5. *Taxes and Transfers as per cent of Income, 1965*

	Taxes				
Income Classes	Federal	State and Local	Total	Transfer Payments	Taxes Less Transfers
Under $2,000	19	25	44	126	–83*
$ 2,000 - 4,000	16	11	27	11	16
4,000 - 6,000	17	10	27	5	21
6,000 - 8,000	17	9	26	3	23
8,000 - 10,000	18	9	27	2	25
10,000 - 15,000	19	9	27	2	25
15,000 and over	32	7	38	1	37
Total	22	9	31	14	24

Source: *Economic Report of the President,* 1969. Income excludes transfer payments, but includes realized capital gains in full and undistributed corporate profits.
*The minus sign indicates that the families and individuals in this class received more from federal, state, and local governments than they, as a group, paid to these governments in taxes.

3 REPORT OF THE ROYAL COMMISSION ON TAXATION (CANADA) 3–12, 20–22 (1966) *

For centuries men have been seeking some general principle that could be used to apportion the burden of taxation in an equitable manner. Two streams of thought have emerged from this great debate. The benefit approach postulates that equity is served if taxes are apportioned according to the benefits derived from government by particular individuals, or groups of individuals. Under this approach, taxes are treated as a payment for the goods and services provided by the government. If these goods and services reflect the wishes of the people, so goes the argument, the imposition of taxes on those who benefit can be treated as a fair exchange, similar to the exchanges that take place in the market. The other train of thought, the ability-to-pay approach, largely ignores what the government provides to the members of society by way of goods or services, and takes the position that taxes are equitable when they are levied according to a defined tax capacity, or ability to pay, of individuals or groups.

It will be amply evident from earlier statements made in this *Report* that we favour very strongly the ability-to-pay approach. The benefit approach in our view has very serious practical and theoretical deficiencies. In a few areas of public expenditure where a very close relationship can be established between outlay and benefit, a specific levy may be appropriate. The most obvious example is that of the gasoline tax imposed to support highway expenditure, and to some extent the real property tax where some of the services provided by a municipality are of direct benefit to the owners of property. But the list of such instances is short. A careful examination of the goods and services provided by government or government enterprises does not suggest that greater emphasis should be placed on the benefit approach in Canadian taxation. We base this conclusion on three considerations:

1. The redistribution of purchasing power, which we believe to be an important function of government, would be precluded if all public expenditures were financed by taxes

* Reproduced with the permission of the Queen's Printer for Canada. Some footnotes have been omitted.

levied according to the benefits received, if benefits are narrowly defined. It is the people with the least economic power who are most in need and benefit most from public expenditures. If the benefit approach were applied exclusively, the more the government did to help this group, the more it would have to pay in taxes. The whole transfer process would thus be frustrated.

2. There are many expensive government services that bestow benefits that cannot be allocated to specific individuals in a generally accepted manner. For example, to assert that a particular individual must pay a certain proportion of the nation's defence bill, because it had been decided that he had enjoyed that proportion of the benefit, would be outrageously high-handed.

3. Some government goods and services, such as education, provide benefits that accrue partly to the users and partly to society as a whole. There is no problem in assigning *some* of the benefits to the actual users of such government services, but there are serious problems in trying to determine the relative importance of the direct and indirect benefits. Furthermore, the allocation of the indirect benefits among all the people would pose the same problems as the allocation of the benefits from such things as defence expenditures. Any assignment of indirect benefits would be completely arbitrary and, we believe, capricious. Indeed, because some of the indirect beneficiaries may live outside our tax jurisdiction altogether, the complete allocation of the indirect benefits would be futile.

The other concept, taxation according to ability to pay, is inherently as arbitrary as the benefit approach, in the sense that the fundamental propositions on which it is based cannot be proved or disproved. There is, however, an important difference. We do not believe there is an equitable method of allocating taxes according to the benefits of government expenditures. There are, however, principles that we believe provide a fair basis for the allocation of taxes according to ability to pay. We can do no more in designing a tax system than found it upon these principles.

In a democracy, equity questions ultimately must be resolved in terms of the shared values of the people. There is no higher authority. It is our earnest hope that the ability-to-pay principles in which we believe, and from which we have derived our major recommendations, commend themselves to most Canadians.

DEFINITION OF ABILITY TO PAY

In our judgment taxes should be allocated among tax units in proportion to their ability to pay. We believe this would be achieved when taxes were allocated in proportion to the discretionary economic power of tax units. This statement is only meaningful if the term "discretionary economic power" is defined. For this purpose we have found it useful to think of discretionary economic power as the product of the tax unit's total economic power and the fraction of the total economic power available for the discretionary use of the unit. By "tax units" we mean families and unattached individuals. By "total economic power" we mean the power of a tax unit to command goods and services for personal use, whether the power is exercised or not. By the "fraction of the total economic power available for discretionary use", we mean the proportion of the unit's total economic power that does not have to be exercised to maintain the members of the unit. Maintenance is not synonymous with bare, physical subsistence. Rather, it denotes the provision of the services necessary to maintain the appropriate standard of living of the family or unattached individual relative to others.

Later in this chapter we discuss the concept of total economic power. But to be able to derive the major implications of our ability-to-pay principles, we can anticipate that discussion and say that we believe the total economic power of tax units, relative to one another, can best be measured over time by the adoption of what we have called a comprehensive tax base. This base would constitute a great broadening of the present income tax base, but for expository convenience we call the base "income". It should be borne in mind, however, that our concept of "income" encompasses much more than the present tax base.

To be more explicit about the concept of ability to pay, we believe the allocation of taxes in accordance with ability to pay requires adherence to five fundamental principles:

1. Families and unattached individuals should be treated as the basic tax-paying units, that is, the entities with potential ability to pay.
2. Taxes should be allocated among tax units in proportion to ability to pay. Specifically, the tax allocated to unit A should bear the same relationship to the tax allocated to unit B, that the ability to pay of A bears to the ability to pay of B.
3. The ability to pay of a tax unit should be assumed to be proportionate to its discretionary income. In other words, the

ability to pay of unit A should be assumed to bear the same relationship to the ability to pay of unit B, that the discretionary income of A bears to the discretionary income of B.

4. The discretionary income of a tax unit should be assumed to be equal to the total income of the unit multiplied by the fraction of that income available for the discretionary use of the unit.
5. It should be assumed that, other things being equal, the greater the income of a tax unit the larger will be the fraction of that income available for discretionary use.

The meaning of these principles can be clarified by a simple hypothetical example. Suppose that tax unit A has an income of \$10,000, and that one tenth of this income can be spent or not spent at the discretion of A. Suppose further that B has an income of \$20,000 and two tenths of this income is available for the discretionary use of B. According to our ability-to-pay principles the relative taxes imposed on A and B should be as follows:

$$\frac{\text{tax on A}}{\text{tax on B}} = \frac{\text{income of A} \times \text{fraction available for discretionary use of A}}{\text{income of B} \times \text{fraction available for discretionary use of B}}$$

$$= \frac{\$10{,}000 \times 0.10}{\$20{,}000 \times 0.20}$$

$$= \frac{\$1{,}000}{\$4{,}000}$$

From this calculation it follows that the tax on B's income would be four times the tax on A's income. If a total revenue of \$1,000 is to be raised from A and B, the rate of tax on the discretionary income of each unit should be 20 per cent (that is, 20 per cent of \$1,000 and \$4,000).

This example perhaps gives a misleading impression of precision of the principles we espouse. To apply these principles, the concept of income must be defined and applied on a consistent basis. Furthermore, the fraction of a tax unit's income available for discretionary use is not an objective phenomenon. It can only be determined on the basis of judgment. But the foregoing principles have the virtue that they make our fundamental beliefs explicit and provide a framework within which judgments can be made.

Once an income tax base is established that measures the relative total economic power of tax units, an equitable allocation of taxes among units would be achieved when fair and reasonable judgments were made about the relative differences in the fractions of income available for discretionary use in different circumstances. In our opinion the following three factors should be recognized:

1. Differences in income.
2. Differences in family responsibilities.
3. Differences in certain specific non-discretionary expenditures.

We will briefly discuss how each of these circumstances should be taken into account.

Recognition of Differences in Income

As stated above in the fifth ability-to-pay principle, we believe that the level of a tax unit's income and the proportion of that income available for discretionary use are not independent. Other things being equal, the greater the income of the unit the greater is the fraction available for discretionary use. As illustrated in the foregoing example, we believe a tax unit with an income of $10,000 has a smaller proportion of that income available for discretionary use than an identical family with an income of $20,000.

This general principle must be supplemented by two additional assumptions in order to derive precise rules for allocating taxes among tax units in proportion to their respective abilities to pay. We believe that the following assumptions give fair and reasonable results:

1. All income of a tax unit in excess of some amount is assumed to be available for discretionary use. We have taken this amount to be $100,000.[2]
2. Below this limit, equal proportionate differences in income are associated with equal absolute differences in the fraction of income available for discretionary use.

The first of these assumptions constitutes an implicit rejection of the belief that non-discretionary expenses are those necessary for physical subsistence, for the subsistence approach would imply that non-discretionary expenses do not change with income. This in turn would call for the application of a constant rate of tax to a base consisting of total income less a fixed exemption. We believe that most non-discretionary expenses increase, although not proportionately, as income rises.

[2] This limit is obviously arbitrary.

The second assumption is the simplest we could make that was consistent with our belief that the fraction of income available for discretionary use rises rapidly at the lower end of the income scale, and that upper middle income tax units have a substantial fraction of their income available for discretionary use.

Although there are various methods that could be adopted to allocate taxes in accordance with the foregoing principles and assumptions, one method of achieving an equitable result under an income tax would be to establish an ascending schedule of proportions of income that would represent discretionary economic power, and then subject these to a proportional tax. However, a more familiar method to achieve the same result would be to apply to a base that measures the total economic power of each tax unit a schedule of progressive rates of tax. We believe this schedule of rates should have the following characteristics:

1. The top marginal rate of tax is reached at an income of $100,000.
2. Brackets encompass equal percentage differences in income.
3. Marginal rates rise by equal amounts from bracket to bracket.
4. The top marginal rate is consistent with revenue requirements.

In Table 7-1 we have drawn up a hypothetical rate schedule consistent with our ability-to-pay principle to illustrate what is involved. The following assumptions are contained in the table:

1. The assumed rate of tax on discretionary income equals the top marginal rate of tax.
2. The marginal rate of tax on the income in each bracket equals the top marginal rate of tax multiplied by the assumed fraction of income in that bracket available for discretionary use.
3. The marginal rates are predetermined once the rate of tax on discretionary income, the lower limit of the top bracket, the number of brackets, and the discretionary income fraction for each bracket have been established.
4. It should be stressed that this rate schedule is hypothetical and is intended only to show the operation of the principles we have developed concerning ability to pay. A number of other objectives and constraints must be taken into account. These are discussed and proposed rates schedules are presented in Chapter 11.

TABLE 7-1

A HYPOTHETICAL RATE SCHEDULE CONSISTENT WITH OUR ABILITY-TO-PAY PRINCIPLES

Income Bracket $	Assumed Fraction of Income in the Bracket Available for Discretionary Use	Discretionary Income: From Bottom to Top of Bracket $	Discretionary Income: Cumulative Total to Top of Bracket $	Tax on Discretionary Income at an Assumed Rate of 50 per cent: From Bottom to Top of Bracket $	Tax on Discretionary Income at an Assumed Rate of 50 per cent: Cumulative Total to Top of Bracket $	Marginal Rate of Tax on Income in the Bracket [a] %	Average Rate of Tax on Income at Top of Bracket [b] %
	(1)	(2)	(3)	(4)	(5)	(6)	(7)
0 - 195	0.0	0	0	0	0	0	0.0
195 - 390	0.1	20	20	10	10	5	2.5
390 - 781	0.2	78	98	39	49	10	6.3
781 - 1,562	0.3	234	332	117	166	15	10.6
1,562 - 3,125	0.4	626	958	313	479	20	15.3
3,125 - 6,250	0.5	1,562	2,520	781	1,260	25	20.2
6,250 - 12,500	0.6	3,750	6,270	1,875	3,135	30	25.1
12,500 - 25,000	0.7	8,750	15,020	4,375	7,510	35	30.0
25,000 - 50,000	0.8	20,000	35,020	10,000	17,510	40	35.0
50,000 - 100,000	0.9	45,000	80,020	22,500	40,010	45	40.0
100,000 - 200,000	1.0	100,000	180,020	50,000	90,010	50	45.0

a Column (4) divided by width of the bracket or, alternatively the assumed rate of tax on discretionary income multiplied by column (1).

b Column (5) divided by the top of the bracket.

It can also be seen from Table 7–1 that taxes can be allocated in accordance with our ability-to-pay principles in any of the following ways:

1. By the application of a uniform rate of tax to a base that measures the discretionary income of each unit (columns 4 and 5).
2. By the application of an average rate of tax to a base that measures the total income of the unit, where the average rate is greater the greater the total income of the unit (column 7).
3. By the application of progressive marginal rates of tax to a base that measures the total income of the unit (column 6).

The distinction that is often made between systems that impose tax at a constant rate, method 1, and systems that impose tax at progressive rates, methods 2 and 3, is not fundamental. By adjusting the base it is possible to achieve the same result in either way. The important distinction is between systems that assume that discretionary income is a constant fraction of total income throughout most of the income range and those that do not. We are firmly convinced that the latter assumption is valid. We therefore reject proportionate taxation except for income in excess of a generous limit.

We stressed in Chapter 6 the great importance we attach to the redistributive function of the fiscal system. The adoption of a tax system that would subject a base that measures the total economic power of each unit to a schedule of progressive marginal rates with the attributes we have just specified would ensure that the costs of government transfers and expenditures were allocated among Canadians in proportion to their abilities to pay. Such a tax system, when combined with a progressive transfer-expenditure system that provided relatively greater benefits to low income families and individuals, would achieve the following results:

1. Low income families and individuals would become net beneficiaries of government.
2. Middle and upper income families and individuals would become net contributors to government.
3. The lower the income of the family or individual the greater the relative net benefit obtained from government.

These results are as they should be in a society committed to providing greater equality of opportunity and improving the well-being of those who have the least economic power.

* * *

BASIC EXEMPTIONS

In arriving at the income levels at which tax liabilities should begin, we have taken into account, as far as possible, the redistributional effects of other taxes, government transfer payments, and government expenditures. We have not tried to exclude from personal income tax an absolute amount that purports to be the income necessary to maintain a minimum standard of living. The idea that income taxes should not reduce income below "subsistence" is laudable in its intention but, we believe, misconceived. Subsistence has no absolute meaning. It is the relative positions of individuals and families that are important. Furthermore, neither exemptions from tax nor credits against tax can ensure that every Canadian has a minimum income. This objective can only be achieved through increased government transfer payments including, for example, refundable credits against taxes. The income tax system as such cannot be used to help people without income—those who most need the help.

We are convinced, however, that the first dollars of income should not be subject to tax. Clearly the fraction of income available for discretionary use is extraordinarily small for a family with an income of, say, $2,000. Moreover, such a family bears sales and property taxes that are disproportionately large relative to its ability to pay. To reflect our belief that those with low incomes have little if any discretionary power, and to compensate for these other taxes, we recommend two zero brackets: one for unattached individuals and one for family tax units. These zero rate brackets are equivalent to the adoption of exemptions equal to the zero brackets, or schedules of rates that tax income in the first bracket but allow credits that just offset the tax on the first bracket.

It is sometimes argued that exemptions should reflect regional differences in living costs. There is no doubt that in some remote areas of Canada living costs are extremely high because of high transportation costs. In order to attract workers to these areas employers have to pay high wages and salaries. To exempt a higher proportion of the incomes of people living in these remote areas would be, in effect, to subsidize their employers. We think it would be most unwise to hide the real costs of the development of remote areas through a personal income tax exemption. To introduce regional differences into the tax system would, moreover, produce an endless factious debate. If it is government policy to accelerate such development, we would recommend that subsidies be granted openly and explicitly.

BLUM, PROGRESSIVE TAXATION RECONSIDERED—NORTH OF THE BORDER *

45 Taxes 718 (1967).

ONE OF THE MOST INTRIGUING ASPECTS of the *Report of the Canada Royal Commission on Taxation* is the case it makes for a steeply progressive rate structure in taxing income.[1] The matter deserves close analysis, not only because the subject is of central importance in taxation, but also because the treatment of it may be disarming.

An old observation underlies the Commission's position in favor of progressive taxation. People generally provide for necessities before buying luxuries. Those with small resources ordinarily spend almost all their income on necessities and therefore have no funds which can be used in a "discretionary" manner. When offered as a foundation for taxing income at progressive rates, the point has long been recognized to have certain weaknesses. On the one hand, if the level of income at which there are no discretionary funds is equated with a minimum standard for physical existence, the most that follows is that a very small amount of income ought to be exempted altogether from tax. On the other hand, as the level of income which precludes discretionary use is moved upward toward some conception of a minimum satisfactory standard of living, there will be diminishing agreement on what elements of consumption ought to be included in defining the standard. The fact is that the distinction between necessities and other goods or services tends rapidly to lose sharpness once a rigorous view of the minimum standard is rejected.

Even if we reached agreement on defining a comparatively generous minimum satisfactory standard of living, the usual discretionary income reasoning would lead only to a fixed, single pattern of progression having a strictly limited thrust. All the progressivity in this so-called "degression" pattern comes about by virtue of exempting the nondiscretionary income from tax, resulting in ever-larger effective

[1] *The Report,* released on February 24, 1967, is an outstanding piece of work. It is indispensable reading for anyone concerned with improving our own federal tax system. Unless otherwise stated, all references hereafter are to this *Report.*

* © 1967, Commerce Clearing House, Inc. Reproduced with permission.

rates of tax on total income as the taxpayer crosses the exemption line and moves up the income scale. In effect, as total income increases, an ever-growing percentage of it exceeds the exempted amount and is thus subject to tax. What needs to be underscored here is that there is nothing in the usual version of the distinction between discretionary and nondiscretionary income that supports taxing additional amounts of discretionary income at rates which are graduated upward. The degression pattern, in brief, is a combination of a zero rate of tax on the exempted amount of income and a constant positive rate on all income in excess of the exemption. Such a rate structure redistributes income between those with exempted incomes and all others, but it has little potential for redistributing income among the others.

Commission's Approach

The Commission's approach to progression bypasses these difficulties and limitations. Its starting place is the slogan: "Taxes should be allocated among tax units in proportion to ability to pay." [2] The next step is an assumption that is common to all discretionary income conceptions in taxation: "The ability to pay of a tax unit should be assumed to be proportionate to its discretionary income." [3] This relationship is then modified by another very important assumption: "It should be assumed that, other things being equal, the greater the income of a tax unit the larger will be the fraction of that income available for discretionary use." [4] A caution is introduced here: " . . . the fraction of a tax unit's income available for discretionary use is not an objective phenomenon. It can only be determined on the basis of judgment." [5]

The Commission explicitly divides its judgment into three elements in recommending a steeply progressive rate structure: (1) No income below some small floor amount (placed at a few hundred dollars) is assumed to be available for discretionary use. (This judgment, it might be noted, does "not purport to exempt a minimum subsistence income from tax.") [6] (2) All income in excess of some large amount (taken to be $100,000) is assumed to be available for discretionary use.[7] (3) Below this upper limit it is assumed that "equal proportionate differences in income are associated with equal absolute differences in the fraction of income available for discretionary use." [8] This last assumption is especially significant. It appears to be dictated by and is obviously consistent with the Commission's more general belief that "the fraction of income available for discretionary use rises rapidly at the lower end of the income scale and that upper middle income tax units have a substantial fraction of their income available for discretionary use." [9]

The effect of these assumptions is illustrated in the *Report* by a comparison of the treatment accorded tax unit *A* having a $10,000 income and unit *B* having a $20,000 income.[10] Income of $100,000 forms a kind of baseline for the calculations inasmuch as all income above that mark is assumed to be available for discretionary use. *A*'s income of $10,000 is 10 per cent of $100,000, and under the assumptions it follows that $1,000 (10 per cent) is discretionary. *B*'s income of $20,000 is 20 per cent of $100,000, and it follows that $4,000 (20 per cent) is avail-

[2] Vol. 3, p. 6.
[3] Vol. 3, p. 6.
[4] Vol. 3, p. 6.
[5] Vol. 3, p. 7.
[6] Vol. 3, p. 35.
[7] Vol. 3, p. 8.
[8] Vol. 3, p. 8.
[9] Vol. 3, p. 9.
[10] Vol. 3, pp. 6-7.

able for discretionary use. Since *B* has four times as much discretionary income as *A*, it follows from the assumptions that *B*, who has only twice the total income of *A*, should pay four times as much tax as *A*. Pursuing this formula further, it is seen that a tax unit with an income of $50,000 (which is 50 per cent of the $100,000 baseline) would be regarded as having $25,000 (50 per cent) available for discretionary use, and therefore should pay a tax 25 times that levied on *A*, although its total income is only five times as great.

The key question that arises is simple: How strong a justification can this approach provide for steeply progressive taxation?

The *Report* does little to define discretionary expenditures or to establish the plausibility of the assumption that the proportion of nondiscretionary expenditures decreases sharply as income rises. It does note that "what constitutes a 'necessity' and what constitutes a 'luxury' is essentially subjective. The wealthy man's necessities are the poor man's luxuries; what was once a luxury becomes a necessity." [11] The only follow-up on this observation, however, is the familiar point that "attempts to reflect the diminishing relative importance of non-discretionary expenses as income rises can only reflect a judgment of what is fair and reasonable." [12]

The Commission, it is submitted, did not push its thinking far enough.

Discretionary Use of Income

Attention first should be focused on the idea of a discretionary use of income. What, for example, is meant by asserting that a tax unit with $10,000 of total income has $1,000 available for discretionary use? To simplify the problem let us assume that for many years the taxpayer has had a $10,000 income and anticipates no change soon. Several possible interpretations of the Commission's basic notion readily come to mind.

One is that the Commission believes that such a taxpayer *should* budget his income so that one-tenth of it is not specifically committed but remains available to satisfy whatever desires might develop as events unroll. A difficulty with this concept is that it tells us nothing about how $10,000 taxpayers actually view their situation. At best it only informs us that the Commission thinks that people should react in certain ways, whether or not they in fact so do. Other experts are likely to advocate different guidelines.[13]

Another possible interpretation is that the Commission believes that the typical taxpayer with a static $10,000 income does budget resources on this pattern. Maybe so, but not one bit of supporting evidence is offered. Surely many people do not budget their whole income much in advance, and among those who do, there is not apt to be a significant "to-be-determined-later" category.

Still another interpretation is that the Commission believes that the typical static $10,000 taxpayer feels "compelled" by his life circumstances to spend in certain ways all but $1,000 of his income, and that the forces which determine his living pattern have a smaller hold on this 10 per cent residual amount. Individuals and families usually can or do place rough priorities on their own expenditures, and therefore it is possible for each tax

[11] Vol. 1, p. 20.

[12] Vol. 1, p. 20.

[13] In distinguishing between income available for discretionary use and other income, the Commission does not urge that, from the viewpoint of society, expenditures of the discretionary variety are less important than nondiscretionary outlays. One may, however, detect slight overtones of this notion in the *Report*.

unit to arrange the purchases in some rank order of "importance." Items in the bottom $1,000 bracket could then be viewed as reflecting the satisfaction of wants (or needs) of lesser "urgency" than all the other entries on the list. Such an exercise, however, would in no way show that acquiring the bottom items was more discretionary than acquiring those immediately above in the ratings or even those in the middle of the range. Merely because a particular $10,000 man would buy beer before buying tickets to the opera does not make either expenditure any more discretionary than the other.[14]

A variant of this interpretation is that expenditures for items lowest on the list involve a greater element of choice or discretion in the sense that the variety of entries in a low priority bracket is likely to far exceed the number in high priority categories. This seems to be merely another way of stating the obvious point that once top priorities have been assigned, every other possible expenditure has a lower priority, so of course more entries are to be expected in the low brackets. But the point can be turned around. In deciding on his top priorities, the taxpayer makes his selection from among all possible items, including those he placed at the top. When the process is so viewed, there is less rather than more choice at the bottom, as compared with the top, of one's own scale of expenditures.

Suppose, however, we concede that there is a sort of folk-wisdom to the effect that people generally feel that certain of their expenditures are less demanded while others are more demanded by their circumstances. Attention then should be turned to those persons whose incomes have been rising or falling. If 10 per cent of the income of a taxpayer sticking at the $10,000 level is thought to be under low pressure from circumstances, the same proportion is not likely to hold for those experiencing income changes. The man slipping down the income ladder could well feel highly pressured into committing every cent in order to maintain his earlier pattern of consumption. Similarly, the man on the way up might feel that the pressures on his new increments of income are relatively minor. Thus even the folk-wisdom is not likely to equate the discretionary component in the income of three $10,000 taxpayers, one of whom previously had lived within a $5,000 income, one of whom had enjoyed a $15,000 income, and one of whom had experienced no income change. A comparable limitation on the folk-wisdom is probably also called for where anticipated incomes rather than past incomes differ among those whose present incomes are identical.

Very likely some will urge that the folk-wisdom can ignore these qualifications because the upward moving people are balanced out by the ones headed downward, leaving the stationary taxpayers as an "average" in each income bracket. And it can be argued that in most brackets the taxpayers with static incomes predominate by far and hence are "typical." Let all this be granted for the moment. Attention then needs be turned to the assumption that the fraction of total

[14] The *Report* contains some indications of what types of expenditures the Commission regards as nondiscretionary. ". . . some specific nondiscretionary personal expenses are made by some tax units but not by others. The allocation of taxes in accordance with ability to pay requires that tax units with these expenses should pay lower taxes than units with the same family responsibilities and the same income who do not have the same special expenses. At least some part of the following expenses are, we believe, nondiscretionary: (1) Extraordinary medical expenses. (2) Gifts to close relatives to provide them with support. (3) The special expenses of working mothers with young children." Vol. 3, p. 19.

income available for discretionary use increases roughly in the proportion that total income increases, until a ceiling is reached. If, in short, we concede that a $10,000 man has $1,000 of discretionary income, how plausible is it to think that a $20,000 man has $4,000 of such income?

Difficulty of Making Interpersonal Comparisons

Here we confront the old difficulty of making interpersonal comparisons —a difficulty which has long snagged efforts to justify progressive taxation on the basis of the assumption that the marginal utility of money for a person declines, meaning that the use of additional incremental units of money yields ever-smaller amounts of satisfaction to the user. (It is worth noting that there is a strong mathematical resemblance between the assumption that an increasing fraction of income is available for discretionary use and the assumption that the utility of money declines proportionately more than income increases.) The crux of the trouble is that while introspection possibly might tell someone how another in his position feels about money, it cannot provide a means of comparing the feelings of those differently situated. Suppose that in spending their last increment of income the $10,000 man and the $20,000 man both feel subjected to less pressure from circumstances than they feel in making their other expenditures. Consider how very restricted the reach of this supposition turns out to be. It does not imply that as each spends the last $1,000 increment of his income the richer man feels less pressure of circumstances than does the other fellow. And all the more clearly it does not imply that the relief from pressure which the less wealthy man feels regarding his last $1,000 increment is a relief which the wealthier man feels regarding the last $2,000 of his income, to say nothing of the last $4,000.

It may be true that the $10,000 man believes that if he had $20,000, he would feel less pressure of circumstances in spending the additional resources than in spending his present income. But the $20,000 man might "know" better. Innumerable signs in our society indicate that many $20,000 men feel as much pressure in accommodating to their circumstances as the $10,000 men do in reacting to theirs. Witness the fact that great numbers of the former, as well as of the latter, stay almost constantly in debt to finance their style of living.

In this context it should be recalled that one cannot establish the premises for a progressive tax by assuming that the $20,000 man has merely twice as much "low pressure" resources as does the $10,000 man. To reach progression on this basis it must be assumed that the wealthier man has more than double such resources, and to reach the steep progression advocated by the Commission it must be assumed that he has four times such "low pressure" resources.

One fact might on quick thought suggest that the Commission's view on the distribution of discretionary income is nevertheless sound. Among those who are comfortably situated, savings by individuals or families on average does tend to increase proportionately more than income. This relationship, however, presents an ultimate challenge to the whole idea of income available for discretionary use. Would we agree that a man who saves by building up an equity in the home he occupies is making a highly discretionary use of his funds? And would we agree that such an expenditure is more discretionary than purchasing a vacation or fine wines? And would we agree that a man who invests in his own business feels under less pressure of circumstances than the wine buyer, the vacationist or the homeowner? Reflection on these questions is likely both to underscore the frailty of the entire conception of income available for discretionary use and to highlight the difficulty in comparing individuals or families on the basis of it.

Conclusion

In examining the case which it makes for steeply progressive taxation, I perhaps have been somewhat unfair to the Canada Commission. Harry Kalven and I observed in *The Uneasy Case for Progressive Taxation* that a "progressive tax on income necessarily operates to lessen the inequalities in the distribution of that income," and we urged that "any consideration of progression must at some time confront the issue of equality." [15] The fact is that the Commission did address itself to the redistribution issue at length. Its treatment of the subject, however, does almost nothing to support a central feature of its position on progression.

"In our opinion," states the Commission, "there is a consensus among Canadians that the tax-expenditure mechanism (including transfers) is equitable when it increases the flow of goods and services to those who, because they have little economic power relative to others, or because they have particularly heavy responsibilities or obligations, would otherwise not be able to maintain a decent standard of living." [16] To implement this viewpoint, the Commission recommends "reducing effective tax rates on those with low incomes, broadly defined" [17] and instituting a study of transfer payments, including consideration of "negative income taxes" and "cash tax allowances." [18] Obviously it is the redistribution goal which leads the Commission to advocate a tax system that is highly progressive as between those with low incomes (however broadly defined) and all other taxpayers. Judged by the *Report*, however, the concern with economic inequality apparently is not the basis for advocating steeply progressive taxes among the well-to-do—those, say, with total incomes of $10,000 and over. On this score all that the Commission concludes is: "Without a progressive tax system . . . the net contribution of those with relatively large incomes would be approximately a constant proportion of income. We believe that this would be unfair. The greater the income the greater should be the relative net contribution of the family or individual." [19]

Perhaps the argument for reducing economic inequalities among the well-to-do is weak or has little popular appeal today. Or perhaps when all is said and done the heart of this issue turns out to be an unanalyzable subjective judgment that it is always fairer to take proportionately more from the very rich than from the rich. But whatever the strength of the case for progressive taxation *among* the wealthy may be, it is not buttressed by recourse to an assumption that nondiscretionary expenditures are proportionately less as income is greater.

[15] Blum and Kalven, *The Uneasy Case for Progressive Taxation* 70 (1st Phoenix ed., 1963).

[16] Vol. 2, p. 6.

[17] Vol. 2, p. 271.

[18] Vol. 2, p. 272.

[19] Vol. 2, pp. 271-72.

BREAK, THE EFFECTS OF TAXATION ON WORK INCENTIVES

Joint Committee on the Economic Report, Federal Tax Policy for Economic Growth and Stability 192 (1955).

The point of view that high income-tax rates such as have prevailed in this country since World War II seriously sap the work incentives of the American people and thereby deter economic growth has been presented with great vigor and persistence. Typically the conclusion is treated as self-evident or as so reasonable, given a little thought, as to eliminate the need for direct empirical evidence. One may admire the strategy of this line of attack, but further investigation shows the forces involved in it to be largely illusory.

The first three sections of this paper are concerned with the economic factors which determine the influence on work incentives of the taxation of earned income. It will be seen that there are at least as good reasons for believing that such taxation will have a net incentive effect as there are for believing it will have a disincentive effect. In the next two sections a similar analysis is applied to income taxes on property incomes and to excise and sales taxes. Finally, the findings of a number of recent empirical studies of worker behavior are examined briefly. The results are likely to surprise those who have accepted the disincentive argument as conclusive. High income taxes, it would appear, have as yet not had any serious disincentive effects. It is true that some workers have been led to contract their efforts, but at the same time others have been induced to work both harder and longer. Whatever the merits of fiscal policies aimed at lowering income-tax rates may be, the encouragement of greater productive activity on the part of workers does not appear to be one of them.

Incentive and Disincentive Effects of Income Taxation

To many taxpayers the disincentive proposition given at the beginning of this paper probably appears realistic enough. They may reason that "with tax rates as high as they are now it is not worth my while to do any extra work because the income from it after taxes is inadequate." The implication, of course, is that at lower tax rates the additional work would be undertaken. In reaching this conclusion, however, the taxpayer is likely to be thinking in terms of a given base income to which a larger reward from a given amount of extra work is added when tax rates are lowered. This argument overlooks an important fact—that lower tax rates would increase the taxpayer's base income—and at higher income levels, as empirical studies have shown, people typically want to take more leisure time rather than less. A lowering of income-tax rates, in short, exerts two opposing influences on work incentives: a stimulating one because after-tax rates of pay are higher, and a discouraging one because for a given amount of work taxpayers have more money. Conversely, an increase in tax rates, by lowering wage rates, tends on the one hand to induce greater effort because taxpayers find themselves with less money to spend, but, on the other, makes added effort less attractive by reducing the reward.

Some workers may react to higher taxes by simply tightening their belts, preferring to economize on consumer goods and services and on saving rather than on leisure time. Others may work more, thereby economizing on leisure as well as on other things. Still others may work less, illustrating the disincentive effects of tax increases. These people, it may be noted, show a marked lack of attachment to the rewards from productive activity, since they are led by a fall in earned income as a result of taxation to cut their incomes still further by reducing their efforts. Such a reaction is, of course, possible. To elevate possibilities of this sort to the rank of inevitabilities, as some of the more ardent critics of income taxation are prone to do, seems, however, more than a little extreme.

Another way of describing the effects of income taxes on work incentives is in terms of the value to the worker of the disposable income obtainable from the last unit of work he does. "Value" in this case does not refer simply to the number of dollars earned but more fundamentally to the usefulness of those dollars to the worker and his family. When tax rates rise the value received from a unit of effort is reduced since fewer dollars are brought home to the family coffers, but the usefulness of each dollar is increased since the family has fewer total dollars to spend. If, on balance, the value of the income earned by the last unit of effort decreases, the worker will tend to work less as a result of the increased tax rates; if, on the other hand, the value increases he will continue to work as much as before and may well wish to expand his supply of labor. Opposite results occur when tax rates are lowered. Again we note the existence of opposing lines of influence and the indeterminacy of the final outcome at this level of analysis.

High income taxes, then, do not necessarily have important disincentive effects. Some workers, it is true, may work less hard because of the influence of high tax rates. Others, however, may be led to increase their efforts, and a good many people may be virtually unaffected. Additional evidence is needed before any useful conclusions can be drawn. Fortunately, both theory and observation can help provide that evidence.

The Effects of Inflexible Monetary Commitments

Most of us have more than a nodding acquaintance with relatively fixed monetary commitments of one kind or another. Monthly payments on a home mortgage or rental to a landlord, life-insurance premiums, contributions to pension and annuity funds or to prepaid medical plans, union or professional dues, and other fixed costs of earning income, periodic payments incurred when consumer durables are bought on time, the obligation to support and educate children or to care for elderly relatives—all fall in this category. Possession of such commitments tends to make the taxpayer react to an increase in income taxes by increasing his efforts to earn income. The disincentive effect of lower take-home rates of pay is more than offset by the incentive push of a lower level of income when living expenses are not easily contracted.

High income taxes, therefore, are likely to have incentive effects on workers with large families, on young people who are setting up homes and acquiring their stock of consumer durables, and upon all who, for whatever reason, have become heavily indebted to others. A period following a rapid rise in consumer and mortgage debt, when higher taxes may well be called for because of strengthening inflationary pressures, is relatively favorable to the imposition of higher income taxes since their incentive effects will be intensified and their disincentive effects lessened by the previous growth in fixed-debt obligations. For similar reasons, a high and rising birthrate is favorable to high income taxes. On the other hand, Government policies which reduce the pressure of fixed monetary commitments on the worker, such as baby bonuses, provision for old age and retirement, for temporary periods of unemployment, or for sickness and injury tend, by themselves, to strengthen the disincentive effects of income taxation. These adverse tendencies, however, will be offset to the extent that Government benefits of this sort are closely matched by contributions on the part of the beneficiary.

A worker is also effectively committed to the maintenance of a given level of living in the face of an increase in income taxes if that level of living represents the minimum necessary for continued physical existence in his society. On the lowest income groups, therefore, income taxes may be expected to have incentive effects. At higher income levels the purely physical pressure of minimum subsistence is absent, but it may be replaced by equally effective social pressures—well-defined modes and standards of living which the workers feel they must maintain.

Fixed monetary commitments of various kinds, therefore, exist at all income levels. Together they provide an important set of factors which strengthen the incentive effects of high income taxes at the expense of the disincentive effects.

The Effects of Changes in Personal Exemption Allowances

A raising or lowering of personal exemption allowances has a powerful effect upon income-tax revenues because of the large proportion of income taxed at the lowest bracket rates. Such changes are also likely to affect work incentives. Unfortunately we can specify the result definitely only for those who remain in the same tax bracket both before and after personal exemptions are altered. For them the marginal rate of tax, and hence take-home rates of pay on the last units of work done as well as on any additional units that might be done, remains constant, while disposal incomes rise or fall as exemption allowances rise or fall. The sole effect on incentives, therefore, comes from the changes in disposable income, larger exemptions tending to reduce effort and smaller exemptions to increase it.

A large number of taxpayers, however, will be shifted into a different tax bracket when personal exemptions are changed. For them both marginal and average tax rates—i. e., take-home rates of pay and disposable incomes—change, and opposing influences on work incentives are again set in motion. Increased exemptions, for example, stimulate desires for more leisure time as a result of increased disposable incomes, but increased rates of pay at the margin make work more attractive. The strength of the latter effect will differ at different points on the income scale since rate changes from one tax bracket to the next are not uniform. By far the largest change, of course, occurs at the bottom of the tax scale where the rate plummets from 20 percent to zero for the income receiver who moves down out of the first bracket.

The net incentive or disincentive effect of a given change in personal exemptions, therefore, will depend upon the extent to which taxpayers are concentrated at the boundaries of the various tax brackets rather than at the centers. For those at the boundaries the effect may go either way, but those at the centers will be induced to work harder by reduced exemption allowances and to work less by greater exemptions. A relatively even distribution of taxpayers over the various tax brackets, therefore, would create the presumption that lower exemptions are favorable to work incentives and higher exemptions unfavorable. On the other hand, a significant concentration at the bracket boundaries, especially at the bottom of the lowest bracket, could easily produce exactly the opposite result.

The Tax Treatment of Property Incomes

Another relevant issue to be taken into consideration in studying the incentive effects of any income tax is the treatment of incomes which are more or less independent of any labor services rendered by the income receiver. At given levels of yield—and this is the only important comparison to make—a general income tax which treats all types of income equally will be more favorable to work incentives than one which exempts some property incomes entirely and taxes others only partially.

As compared to the selective tax, the general one taxes certain kinds of property income more heavily but all other types of income less heavily. Since the two taxes are equally productive, taxpayers as a group have the same total disposable income in each case, but under the general tax they realize higher rates of take-home pay from the rendering of labor services. This acts as an incentive to still greater effort. The fact that this kind of tax treats some kinds of property income more severely has little or no effect on work incentives since little or no labor is involved in the creation of these incomes. On the average, therefore, the general tax is more favorable to productive activity. It has the further virtue, of course, of being more equitable since it treats all types of income the same way.

For these reasons policymakers should scrutinize closely proposals which would have the effect of narrowing the base of the individual income tax. If the incomes involved are largely of the property type, the influence of the income tax at given yields is shifted in the disincentive direction. Present provisions concerning capital gains and losses, tax-exempt bond interest, percentage depletion, certain allowable deductions (such as those for meals and the like, which to a large extent are personal consumption on the part of the taxpayer rather than costs of earning income) all tend to make the individual income tax less favorable to work incentives than it would otherwise be.

The Incentive Aspects of Excise and Sales Taxes

One of the traditional tenets with reference to the relative merits of different kinds of taxes is that excise and sales taxes are more favorable to work incentives than are income taxes. Let us examine this assumption for a moment.

Consider first the probable effects on work incentives of the price changes induced by sales and excise taxes. A general increase in consumer good prices, for example, makes consumers with relatively fixed money incomes worse off and thereby tends to induce more effort.

The rewards from that effort, however, have undergone a reduction in their buying power and so the effort itself is less attractive than it once was. When considering the extra work the worker finds himself both pushed toward it (by his lower real income) and repelled (by the lower real rates of pay) at the same time, and he may in the final analysis expand his labor supply, contract it, or leave it unchanged.

It is true that many consumers may fail to perceive the price changes induced by changes in excise taxes,[1] but they are likely to be much more aware of what it costs them to maintain their accustomed standard of living and what happens to the level of their cash balances in the process. Some evidence of the effects of high prices on worker behavior is provided by a recent British investigation which found that approximately 40 percent of the workers interviewed regarded high prices as a factor which deterred their productive efforts and some 70 percent thought they were also a factor making for greater incentive.[2]

Taxpayers may, of course, do more work not in order to buy additional things but primarily to raise their level of saving. Even in this case, however, the tax-induced price increases are by no means irrelevant. The saving may be specifically earmarked for a future purchase of a taxed good or service. Unless the tax is believed to be temporary, the incentive effect is likely to be the same here as in the case of a person who works in order to consume. Even the person who saves in order to accumulate a certain amount of capital may adjust his goals upward when prices rise.

Finally, excise and sales taxation will affect work incentives in still another way. Such taxes reduce the money incomes of certain income receivers below the levels which would otherwise prevail. An excise tax on watches and clocks, for example, will lower the earning power of workers who are highly skilled in watchmaking, and these effects are likely to spread to all who do the same type of high-precision, fine-scale work. As we have already seen the incentive effects on these people may go either way. Lower income levels induce more effort, but reduced rates of pay have the reverse effect. Until we know more about the types of workers whose incomes are reduced by different kinds of sales and excise taxes and the extent to which these reductions take place—and this whole area of analysis is currently undergoing extensive reexamination [3] we cannot formulate a complete picture of the incentive-disincentive effects of sales and excise taxation.

---

[1] Cf. Robert Ferber's conclusion that "* * * awareness of reductions in Federal excise taxes or in selling prices on particular items 6 to 8 weeks after the fact was quite limited. Judging by the general tenor of the replies, most people were aware that some changes in excise taxes had been made, but few were able to identify specific changes." (How Aware Are Consumers of Excise Tax Changes? National Tax Journal, VII (December 1954), p. 358).

[2] Royal Commission on the Taxation of Profits and Income, Second Report, CMD 9105 (London, 1954), sec. 87.

[3] See in this regard: Earl R. Rolph, A Proposed Revision of Excise-Tax Theory, Journal of Political Economy, LX (April 1952), 102–17; R. A. Musgrave, General Equilibrium Aspects of Incidence Theory, American Economic Review, Proceedings, XLIII (May 1953), 504–17, and On Incidence, Journal of Political Economy, LXI (August 1953), 306–23; J. F. Due, Toward a General Theory of Sales Tax Incidence, Quarterly Journal of Economics, LXVII (May 1953), 253–66; J. A. Stockfisch, Excise Taxes: Capitalization-Investment Aspects, American Economic Review, XLIV (June 1954), 287–300; H. P. B. Jenkins, Excise-Tax Shifting and Incidence; A Money-Flows Approach, Journal of Political Economy, LXIII (April 1955), 125–49; and Paul Wells, A General Equilibrium Analysis of Excise Taxes, American Economic Review, XLV (June 1955), 345–59.

The Effects of Labor Market Rigidities

So far we have not concerned ourselves with the extent to which the worker if free to satisfy his own preferences with regard to the amount of labor services he supplies to the market. The great majority of workers, of course, must either have a full-time job or none at all. We cannot, however, count on this fact to neutralize, for such workers, the potential incentive or disincentive effects of income taxation. For one thing, their preferences may be only temporarily frustrated. Future bargaining with employers may restore the balance. In addition, workers typically have ways of changing their labor supply other than by altering the number of hours worked a week or the number of weeks worked a year. Overtime opportunities may be available and be refused or exploited more fully, other members of the family may enter or leave the labor force, proposed ages of retirement may be altered, or absenteeism on a day-to-day basis may change. These possibilities must be kept in mind in evaluating the results of empirical studies. In flexible behavior in one area or disincentive effects in another do not necessarily imply either insensitivity or reduced incentives as far as the labor supply as a whole is concerned.

Empirical Studies of Work Incentives

Since the pioneering work of Senator Paul H. Douglas [4] in this area, a number of empirical studies of the reactions of workers to changes in their rates of pay have been made. The results, to be sure, are incomplete. We still lack detailed information about the behavior of a number of important worker groups, especially independently employed professional and business people at the middle- to high-income levels, who are both strongly affected by income taxes and able to vary their labor supply more freely than wage earners or salaried personnel. Wage and salary workers, as noted in the preceding section, may vary their supply of labor in a number of different ways, and full information on these various possibilities is not always available even for groups that have been studied rather extensively. In addition, it has frequently been difficult to be certain that the behavior actually observed was due to changing pay rates rather than to other factors which also exert an influence on work incentives. Nevertheless, the evidence so far compiled warrants careful consideration because it is both extensive and consistent as to the direction in which it points.[5] For the most part it appears that income taxes exert relatively little influence on work incentives, and that when they do they induce greater effort as frequently as they deter it.

Thomas H. Sanders, for example, concluded, on the basis of an extensive postwar study of executive behavior, that—

> the cases in which the evidence showed executives to be working harder were at least equal in number to those indicating less effort, and the former were more definitely recognizable as a tax influence.[6]

---

[4] Paul H. Douglas, The Theory of Wages (New York, 1934).

[5] A more detailed summary of the results of studies of the United States labor market up to 1953 is included in the author's Income Taxes, Wage Rates, and the Incentive To Supply Labor Services, National Tax Journal, VI (December 1953), 350–1. More recent investigations are noted in the text below.

[6] Thomas H. Sanders, Effects of Taxation on Executives (Boston, 1951), p. 20.

In addition, there was evidence that high taxes induced more wives of business executives to enter the labor force and, in general, led the executives themselves to postpone their dates of retirement from active participation in the business. Offsetting these tax incentives, however, was a tendency for some to refuse promotions and advantageous offers from other companies when the change meant greatly increased burdens and relatively little increase in net compensation. Finally, it was noted that a good deal of executive effort was being diverted into a study of tax laws and of ways of reducing tax burdens.

Another study of a small sample of 7 surgeons with incomes between $36,000 and $115,000 led the author to conclude "* * * we would judge that increased taxes have not reduced the surgeons' incentive." [7] He also noted that 4 of the 7 doctors planned, at the time of interview, to retire later than they had previously planned (before World War II) because they had been unable to accumulate sufficient capital. These reactions might be attributed to the influence of higher taxes or higher prices, or both.

It is interesting to note that in a recent British study, although over two-thirds of the male workers interviewed believed that as a general matter income taxes discouraged productive effort, less than one-third of them felt that taxes had affected their own personal effort adversely, and almost as many thought the effect was to induce them to work harder.[8] When workers who had turned down an opportunity to work overtime were asked why they had done so, only 5 percent or less of them cited high taxes in reply.[9] The National Coal Board, as a result of a number of studies of absenteeism in the British coal mines, concluded that "Tax considerations were * * * responsible for only one-third of 1 percent of the shifts lost.[10] The Royal Commission itself reached the general conclusion that "the levels of taxation within present limits do not inhibit or induce any significant proportion of the working population to modify their attitudes to their working behavior.[11]

These findings are the more significant since the pressure of taxation is in general greater in Britain than in the United States, the income tax starts at lower levels of income and its rate structure rises more steeply, and British workers are provided with comprehensive low-cost medical and dental services which, alone, might be expected to push the influence of income taxes in the disincentive direction. In addition, a recent study shows that central government tax and expenditure programs have carried the redistribution of income further in Britain than in the United States.[12]

---

[7] Robert Davidson, Income Taxes and Incentive: The Doctor's Viewpoint, National Tax Journal, VI (September 1953), p. 297.

[8] Royal Commission on the Taxation of Profits and Income, op. cit., secs. 74 and 81. A similar result for the United States appears when we contrast Kimmel's 95 percent affirmative response to the question: "Do you believe that the higher the tax rate the less the incentive to work and save?" with the results of Sanders' study of executive behavior. Cf. Lewis H. Kimmel, Taxes and Economic Incentives (Washington, 1950), pp. 101–102.

[9] Royal Commission on the Taxation of Profits and Income, op. cit., secs. 74 and 81.

[10] Ibid, sec. 39.

[11] Ibid, p. 115.

[12] Allan M. Cartter, the Redistribution of Income in Postwar Britain—A Study of the Effects of the Central Government Fiscal Program in 1948–49 (New Haven, 1955), especially pp. 91–92.

CONCLUSIONS

Human motivation is a complex phenomenon no matter what the area of study. People who are keenly interested in their jobs are not likely to be much deterred by even significant changes in taxes. Strong personal ambitions may also push even very high income taxes into the background. Workers in a society that is alert and active and progressing rapidly may not be deterred in their efforts by taxation, whereas workers in a stagnant and disillusioned society might well be. Strong public support for what the Government is doing and a widespread belief that it is accomplishing its objectives in an efficient and honest manner may tend to impart favorable incentive aspects to taxation. Cultural and religious patterns, by imposing on the individual certain habits of thought and action, may govern his reactions to taxation of various kinds, and so on.

In spite of the complexities, we are by no means completely at sea. Careful empirical studies have been made and, incomplete as the results still are, it is encouraging to note that neither in Great Britain nor in the United States is there any convincing evidence that current high levels of taxation are seriously interfering with work incentives. There are, in fact, as indicated above, a number of good reasons for believing that considerably higher taxes could be sustained without injury to worker motivation should the need arise. Conversely, the social and economic need for strong work incentives does not, at the moment, make imperative a reduction in Government expenditures or an expansion in the role of excise and sales taxation in order to bring about a reduction in income taxes.

E. Alternatives to the Income Tax

Although the income tax is likely to remain the mainstay of the federal tax system, other types of taxes may have to be increasingly considered, at least by way of supplementation, in order adequately to meet the fiscal needs of the national government.[a] The excerpt from Dr. Pechman's book canvasses some of the most common types of consumption taxes;[b] the net wealth tax is considered in the subsequent excerpt from the Canadian Royal Commission on Taxation (Carter Commission). Finally, there is a brief reference to the federal payroll tax on employees —a levy that is largely ignored by tax experts despite its increasing importance to low and lower middle income taxpayers.[c]

[a] These needs may include some support to state and local governments. See Chapter X.

[b] For the classic discussion of the expenditure tax, see Kaldor, An Expenditure Tax (1955).

[c] But see Pechman, Aaron, and Taussig, Social Security—Perspectives for Reform (1968).

PECHMAN, FEDERAL TAX POLICY 141–61 (1966) *

CONSUMPTION TAXES are not very popular in the United States. It is true that general sales taxes are used by state and local governments (see Chapter 9), but even when they are taken into account, consumption taxes are less important here than anywhere else in the world (Chart 6-1). In fiscal year 1967, excise taxes and customs will account for only about 10 percent of federal cash receipts, and this proportion will decline somewhat as the excise tax reductions scheduled for later years take effect.

There is a bewildering variety of consumption taxes. An *expenditure* tax is levied on the total consumption expenditure of the individual; a *sales* tax is levied on the sales of goods and services; and a *value added* tax is levied on the difference between a firm's sales and purchases. Expenditure taxes can be proportional or progressive; sales and value added taxes are imposed at a uniform rate on all commodities or at several rates on various groups of commodities. Expenditure taxes are collected from the consumer, while sales and value added taxes are collected from the seller. Sales taxes are in widespread use throughout the world; the value added tax is used only in France, but seems to be gaining in popularity; the expenditure tax has been used—without much success—only in India and Ceylon.

* © 1966 by The Brookings Institution. Reproduced with permission.

CHART 6-1. Importance of Consumption Taxes and Customs in Selected Countries, 1961[a]

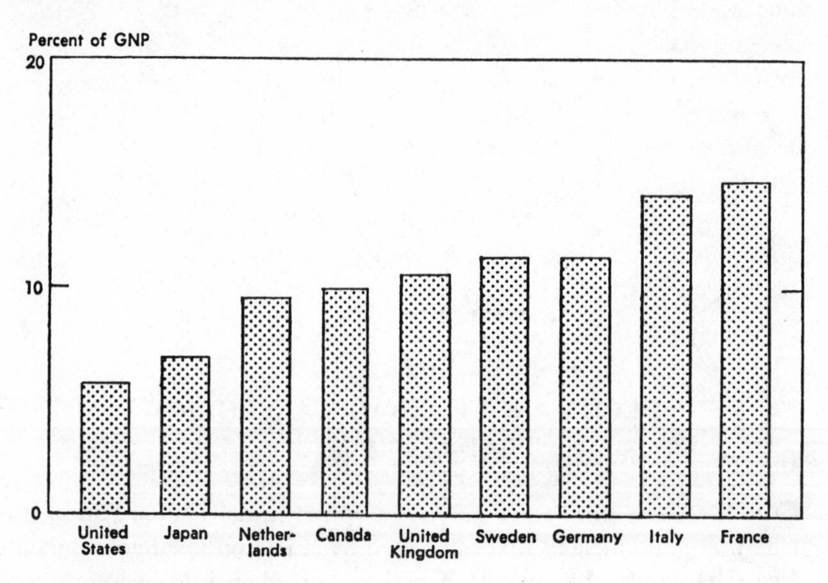

Source: Appendix Table C-4.
[a] Includes state and local taxes.

The sales tax can be a single or multistage tax. Canada levies its sales tax at the manufacturers level; Great Britain at the wholesale level; and United States state and local governments at the retail level. Italy levies a *turnover* tax, which derives its name from the fact that the tax is levied every time a commodity "turns over" from one firm to another. The value added tax is also a multistage tax, but it is figured on the *net* value added by each firm.

A common form of consumption tax is the *excise* tax on the sale of a particular commodity or group of commodities. Excise taxes are levied almost everywhere on alcoholic beverages and tobacco products, but they apply to many other products as well. They are also employed as "user charges" to collect part or all of the cost of government services enjoyed by specific groups of taxpayers. Gasoline taxes and taxes on automobiles and automotive products are used in this way to pay for highway construction and maintenance. Appendix Table A-5 summarizes the major excises used by the federal government since 1913.

Customs duties, which are levied on imports, are used in this country primarily to protect domestic industries against foreign competition. The policy of the United States Government is to reduce trade barriers in the interest of promoting world trade, but the size and pace of the reductions depend on international negotiations, which are complicated and time-consuming. The negotiations are concerned with the role of customs duties in the nation's foreign economic policy, rather than with their role as taxes to produce revenue. Customs duties will therefore not be discussed in this book.

The major issue regarding consumption taxes in this country is equity. Because the poor consume more of their income than the rich, the burden of a flat rate sales tax falls as incomes rise. The sales tax also bears more heavily on families who have larger expenditures relative to their incomes than others, such as families with a large number of children or families who are just beginning a household. Some excise taxes may be progressive, but they are usually levied on mass consumption items and tend to be regressive on balance.

Sales and excise taxes are also criticized on economic grounds. Consumption taxes are never levied at a uniform rate on all goods and services, so that they interfere with the freedom of consumer choice and misallocate the nation's resources (except, as will be noted below, when they are employed as user charges or to discourage consumption of items, such as narcotics, that lead to increased social costs). They rank low as automatic stabilizers, because they respond no more than in proportion to changes in income. Moreover, purchasers may be charged more than the amount of the tax through *pyramiding* when markups are applied to the same goods as they move through the channels of production and distribution. On the other hand, sales and excise taxes are often supported for their relative stability of yield, a characteristic which commends itself for financing state-local activities, but not federal.

As a result of the equity and economic shortcomings of sales and excise taxes, other forms of consumption taxation have been proposed as substitutes. Some economists have been partial to a graduated expenditure tax, but this tax is generally regarded as too difficult to administer. Value added taxation, on the other hand, is beginning to spread, particularly among countries that have relied heavily on turnover taxes and have come to recognize their economic deficiencies.

In this country, the allocation of consumption taxes as a source of revenue between the federal and state-local governments has been stabilized and is not a major issue. Federal consumption taxes are restricted to selective excises, while the state and local governments levy general sales taxes (and, in one case, a value added tax) as well as excises. In 1965, all but a few major federal excise taxes were eliminated. Substitution of a value added tax for part or all of the corporation income tax has been suggested, but Congress has not shown interest in such a trade. Forty-two states and many local governments levy retail sales taxes, and the trend is toward greater use of this tax at the state and local levels.

Issues in Excise Taxation

The imposition of heavy taxes on particular commodities substantially alters the results of the market mechanism. Such interference should be avoided, but there are circumstances under which excise taxes are useful and even necessary.

Economic Effects of Excise Taxes

The immediate effect of an excise tax is to raise the price of the taxed commodity. The consumer's response will be to consume less of the taxed commodity, and to purchase other commodities or to save more. The burden of the tax is thus borne in part by consumers and in part by producers (and distributors) of the taxed commodity. If demand is relatively inelastic (that is, if the consumer does not reduce his consumption very much as the price of the article increases), most of the burden is borne by the consumer. On the other hand, if supply is relatively inelastic (if the producer does not or cannot reduce his production as price declines), the burden is borne mainly by the producer.

In general, the objective of excise taxation is to place the burden of the tax on consumers; and most excise revenues are derived from taxes imposed on articles for which the demand is relatively inelastic. For example, taxes on alcohol, tobacco, and gasoline accounted for almost 60 percent of excise revenues in the year before the 1965 tax cuts went into effect, and will account for almost 85 percent when the cuts become fully effective in 1969 (Table 6-1).

TABLE 6-1. Federal Excise Tax Revenue Before and After the Enactment of the Excise Tax Reduction Act of 1965, by Major Source

(Dollar amounts in millions)

Major Source	Revenue Prior to the Enactment of the 1965 Act[a]		Revenue After the Enactment of the 1965 Act[b]	
	Amount	Percentage of Total	Amount	Percentage of Total
Liquor	3,855	25.2	3,855	36.4
Tobacco	2,240	14.7	2,222	21.0
Highway and auto taxes	6,163	40.4	4,213	39.8
Gasoline	2,800	18.3	2,800	26.4
Other	3,363	22.0	1,413	13.3
Retailers' excise taxes	550	3.6	—	—
Communications	1,075	7.0	—	—
All other	1,387	9.1	304	2.9
Total	15,270	100.0	10,594	100.0

Source: Treasury Department, Office of Tax Analysis (mimeograph). Figures are rounded and may not necessarily add to totals.

[a] Based on consumption levels in fiscal year 1966.

[b] Rates to be effective January 1, 1969. The Tax Adjustment Act of 1966 delayed tax reductions for automobiles and telephone service scheduled for 1966 and 1967, but did not affect the final rates for January 1, 1969, enacted under the 1965 Act.

Furthermore, supply is generally so highly elastic in the taxed industries that, even where demand is relatively elastic, very little of the burden of consumer taxes is borne by the producers.

BURDEN OF EXCISES. The effects of excise taxes on the allocation of economic resources depend on the sensitivity of consumption to a rise in price. If consumption is not much reduced by increased price, the consumer responds by cutting his consumption of other commodities as well as the taxed commodity. The effect is much like that of an income tax which reduces disposable income and causes the consumer to reduce consumption of a wide range of commodities. There is little incentive for labor and capital to move out of the taxed industry, and the allocation of resources elsewhere in the economy is not altered significantly.

When consumption is quite sensitive to price, however, production and employment in the industry producing the taxed commodity will decline. Demand for other products increases at the expense of the taxed industry, and over time the labor and capital will move to other industries (assuming full employment is maintained). In this case, the tax substantially alters the pattern of production and consumption in the private economy. It also may create hardship for the employees and owners of capital in the industries affected.

Thus, an excise tax imposes a burden on the economy because consumers are not as well off as they would have been if the same revenue had been raised by another tax that did not change patterns of consumption. The loss due to this distortion is called the *excess consumer burden* of the excise tax. The amount of the excess burden is the difference between (a) the value placed by consumers on the consumption they give up and (b) the yield of the tax. Excess burden is, in other words, the loss in economic efficiency caused by the imposition of the tax.

This analysis holds only in a world in which the allocation of resources before imposition of the commodity tax is optimum. In the real world there are substantial departures from the conditions necessary for this optimum for reasons other than taxes, and there is no *a priori* basis for making the judgment that a new excise tax necessarily involves a loss in consumer welfare. Consumers may value additional items of the newly taxed commodity less highly than other items which they consume in its place after the tax is imposed, particularly if the imposition of the new tax leads consumers to shift their consumption to commodities that are already heavily taxed.

Nevertheless, the case for selective excise taxes is weak. Conceivably there are excise taxes that would not reduce consumer welfare, but there is no basis for making such a selection. Excise taxes should be avoided unless there is a compelling reason for altering the allocation of resources, and for discriminating among individuals and families on the basis of their consumption preferences.

EXCISE TAXES IN WARTIME. One situation in which the government has a definite interest in changing the pattern of resource use is in wartime or in a similar national emergency. Numerous materials that are in short supply are needed for production in war industries. In extreme cases, as in the two World Wars, the government is forced to replace the market mechanism with direct rationing and to halt production of items that conflict with the war effort. During a more limited emergency, such as the Korean War, it may not be necessary to take such drastic steps. In such circumstances, excise taxes may be helpful both as a rationing device and as a selective method of reducing consumer demand. By increasing prices of the taxed commodities, the government can reduce demand and divert it to other commodities in more plentiful supply, or to saving.

Excises are among the first taxes to be raised in a national emergency. Criticism of such use usually develops on the legitimate ground that the taxes chosen are hard to justify on economic and equity grounds. Further, the rationale of discouraging consumption on a selective basis is quickly forgotten once excises are imposed, and the revenue objective becomes paramount. Even in wartime, use of excise taxes as a major revenue source should be avoided; first, because there are better ways to raise general revenues and, second, because the wartime taxes are apt to linger on—and do considerable damage—for many years. For example, the excises levied by the federal government on many electric, gas, and oil appliances in 1941 were not repealed until 1965.

USER CHARGES. Selective excise taxes may be used to good advantage as a method of obtaining payments from individuals who benefit from particular public services. When public programs lower the cost of a particular activity, that activity will be artificially stimulated and too many resources may be used in its performance. An excise tax, or other method of charging for the service, is needed to maintain economic efficiency.

Despite the sound theoretical justification for such "user charge" excise taxes, they are not employed nearly enough for this purpose at any level of government in the United States. Since 1956, when the Federal Highway Trust Fund was set up to pay for the interstate highway system, Presidents Eisenhower, Kennedy, and Johnson have recommended adoption of a wide range of special taxes as user charges, including payments for the use of federal air and inland waterway transportation facilities, recreation facilities, and numerous other federal services. Pollution of water and air by private individuals and businesses imposes heavy costs on society which should not be borne by the general taxpayer. Adoption of user charges to pay for such benefits and costs would ease the burden of other taxes, promote equity, and improve economic efficiency. But successive administrations have had little success in persuading Congress to accept this approach. User charges are strongly resisted by the groups that would be required to pay, and past experience suggests that their resistance is politically potent and difficult to overcome.

SUMPTUARY AND REGULATORY TAXES. Excises on commodities or services which are considered socially or morally undesirable are known as *sumptuary* taxes. The best examples are the excises on liquor and tobacco. The rationale for sumptuary taxes is that the use of some articles for consumption creates additional costs to society which are not costs the producers bear and are not reflected in the prices they charge. For example, mass consumption of liquor involves costs in the form of losses of working time, accidents, broken homes, and increased delinquency; and consumption of cigarettes has been shown to be associated with higher frequencies of a wide range of illnesses. An excise tax raises prices on such commodities to a level that more nearly reflects total social costs as well as private costs.

In some cases, the costs imposed by certain items are so great that society prohibits their consumption entirely. This is true, for example, of narcotics and gambling. The federal government prohibits the sale of narcotics except under very strict rules, while most states either outlaw or regulate gambling. Taxes are imposed on these items largely to aid in regulation and law enforcement.

In a democratic society, complete prohibition of the use of any one commodity or service requires virtually unanimous agreement that its consumption is harmful or immoral. Where such unanimity does not exist, the majority expresses its view by levying a heavy tax that will discourage consumption without eliminating it entirely. Those who place a high value on the consumption of such items are allowed to purchase them but at a differentially higher price. This explains why gambling is illegal in some states and is subject to regulation and to special taxes in others. Similarly, since opinion on the harmful effects of alcoholic beverages and cigarettes is not unanimous, purchases of these items are permitted but are heavily taxed by the federal and state governments and even by some local governments. The main effects of the taxes levied in the United

States are to tax smokers and drinkers heavily without curtailing their consumption very much and to introduce an element of regressivity into the system.

Another type of regulatory tax, introduced only recently in the United States, is the "interest equalization tax." This excise applies to purchases by United States residents of foreign securities issued in industrial countries (except for new Canadian bond issues), and to loans abroad with maturities of one year or more. The tax is levied on common stock at a rate of 15 percent and on foreign bonds and loans at rates that are equivalent to an interest rate increase of about one percentage point. The purpose of this discriminatory tax is to improve the United States balance of payments by discouraging the flow of capital abroad. The tax was applied to purchases after July 18, 1963, and is now scheduled to expire on July 31, 1967.

Equity Considerations

Excise taxes rank low in terms of equity on a number of grounds. First, consumers probably bear the major burden of the excise taxes which have been employed in the United States. How this burden is distributed depends on the proportion of income allocated to consumption of these items at the various income levels. For example, excise taxes on beer and cigarettes are highly regressive, while those on furs and some consumer durables are progressive. On balance, the post-World War II excise tax structure was regressive throughout the income scale (Table 6-2).

Second, excise taxes are unfair as among different people with the same income. Families whose preferences for the taxed commodities are high are taxed much more heavily than those who prefer other ways to consume their income. This violation of horizontal equity is not justified unless there are overriding social reasons for discouraging the use of particular goods or services. However, where there are special costs or benefits associated with the production or distribution of a particular commodity which are not borne or paid for by the individuals and firms creating the costs or receiving the benefits, imposition of a selective excise tax will improve horizontal equity.

Third, while most of the pre-1965 excise taxes were levied on goods and services used by consumers, some applied to items that were used primarily or exclusively by business (such as business and

TABLE 6-2. Effective Rates of Federal Excise Taxes and Customs, 1954, and of a Hypothetical Wisconsin General Retail Sales Tax, 1956

Money Income Class (Dollars)	Federal Excise Taxes and Customs, 1954[a] (Percentages)	Wisconsin Retail Sales Tax, 1956[b] (Percentages)	
		Including Food[c]	Excluding Food[d]
0– 1,000	7.3	4.9	4.8
1,000– 2,000		2.4	2.5
2,000– 3,000	4.8	2.0	2.1
3,000– 4,000	4.3	1.8	2.0
4,000– 5,000	4.1	1.7	1.9
5,000– 6,000	3.8	1.7	1.8
6,000– 7,500		1.6	1.8
7,500–10,000	3.5	1.4	1.7
10,000 and over	2.0	1.0	1.3
All classes	3.6	1.6	1.8

Sources: Federal excise taxes and customs: R. A. Musgrave, "The Incidence of the Tax Structure and Its Effects on Consumption," *Federal Tax Policy for Economic Growth and Stability*, Joint Committee on the Economic Report, 1956, p. 98. Retail sales tax estimates: Daniel C. Morgan, Jr., *Retail Sales Tax: An Appraisal of New Issues* (University of Wisconsin Press, 1964), p. 32.

[a] Effective rates are based on money income, including transfer payments and capital gains, plus retained corporate earnings and unshifted portion of the corporation profits tax attributed to individual stockholders.

[b] Effective rate on adjusted gross income; based on 1956 Wisconsin incomes and expenditures, assuming the tax is borne by Wisconsin residents.

[c] At a 2 percent rate.

[d] At a 3 percent rate.

store machines, lubricating oils, long distance telephone, and trucks). Taxes levied on such items enter into business costs and are generally reflected in higher prices for consumer goods. Since low income persons spend a larger proportion of their income than those in the higher income classes, taxes that enter into business costs are by nature regressive. Furthermore, they often create unfair competitive situations by discriminating against firms that use the taxed commodity or service and distort the choice of production methods. The classic example of a bad excise tax is the one on freight since it discriminates against firms that are distant from the market. The freight tax was eliminated in 1958.

The Excise Tax Reduction Act of 1965 eliminated most federal excises, except for a few regulatory taxes and highway taxes that recover the costs of services or facilities directly benefiting individuals and business firms. The Act reduced the tax on passenger cars in stages from 10 percent to 1 percent on January 1, 1969, and also reduced the 10 percent telephone tax in stages until it is completely eliminated on January 1, 1969. The scheduled reductions were suspended by the Tax Adjustment Act of 1966 until April 1, 1968, but the 1 percent automobile tax and the repeal of the telephone tax will be effective as originally scheduled on January 1, 1969.

A General Consumption Tax?

The major drawback of selective excise taxes is that they are not neutral, that is, they discriminate among different consumption items. A broad-based tax is a much more appropriate method of taxing consumption. The three broad-based taxes mentioned most often are the general sales tax, the value added tax, and the expenditure tax.

The General Sales Tax

Sales taxation has been used extensively throughout the world, and there is almost no limit to the variations in the structure of these taxes. On the whole, experience suggests that a single-stage tax is preferable to a multistage or turnover tax, and that the scope of the tax should be as broad as possible. Among single-stage taxes, the retail sales tax is to be preferred on economic and equity grounds, but it is somewhat more costly to administer than either a manufacturers' or wholesalers' tax.

SINGLE-STAGE VERSUS MULTISTAGE TAXES. The advantage of the multistage tax is that any particular revenue goal can be realized at the lowest possible rate. This makes the turnover tax politically attractive, but highly objectionable on other grounds. A turnover tax levied at a uniform rate will result in widely varying total rates of tax on different goods, depending on the complexity of the production and distribution channels. This means that the total tax burden will differ among commodities, much as it does under a selective excise tax system. Moreover, the multistage tax provides a strong incentive for firms to merge with their suppliers and contributes to greater concentration in industry and trade.

Even the uniform rate turns out to be a will-o'-the-wisp whenever the turnover tax is tried. The discriminatory effects of the uniform rate soon become very serious and the government finds it difficult to resist pressures to moderate the tax load where it is demonstrably out of line. Once introduced, modifications of the uniform rate proliferate and the tax becomes a maze of complications and irrational distinctions. Thus, a tax that was originally intended to be relatively simple turns out to be an administrative monstrosity and highly inequitable.

WHOLESALERS' AND MANUFACTURERS' SALES TAXES. Administrative complications are reduced if the tax is levied at the wholesale or manufacturing level. The number of firms is smaller, their average size is larger, and their records are more adequate. These advantages are offset, however, by the difficulty of identifying taxable transactions and of determining the price on which the tax is charged.

The most troublesome feature of the wholesalers' tax involves the determination of wholesale values when manufacturers sell directly to retailers. This problem is usually handled by raising the manufacturers' prices to allow for the normal wholesalers' markup. The adjustment goes the other way in the case of the manufacturers' tax: the price charged by a manufacturer to a retailer must be lowered to eliminate the value of the wholesale services.

Both taxes are subject to the criticism that the rate tends to be pyramided as goods move to the retail level. Thus, a 10 percent manufacturers' tax may become a 20 percent tax at the retail level, after the wholesaler and retailer have applied their customary markups. There is less pyramiding under a wholesalers' tax, but the problem is by no means avoided. In time, competition will tend to wipe out the effect of pyramiding, but the adjustment process may be slow.

On balance, there is little to choose between the wholesalers' and manufacturers' tax. The wholesalers' tax is more practical when the wholesale and retail stages are fairly distinct; on the other hand, complications arise if there is a substantial degree of integration between manufacturers and retailers. The manufacturers' tax is more practical when there is either a high degree of integration in most consumer lines or none at all; the mixed situation raises the most difficulties.

RETAIL SALES TAX. A retail sales tax is intended to apply uniformly to most goods and services purchased by individual consumers, and is basically much less complicated than a wholesalers' or manufacturers' tax. However, retail sales taxes are rarely completely general, although they are usually imposed on a broad base. It is difficult to reach many consumer services, although it is possible to include such services as admissions, repairs, laundry, and dry cleaning. The retail sales tax does not apply to housing—the largest service in most consumer budgets—but housing is subject to the property tax. Many state sales taxes in the United States exempt food and other commodities that are regarded as necessities.

Although the retail sales tax often falls short of complete generality, it has much to commend it over the taxes levied at earlier stages of the production or distribution process. Its most important advantage is that there is little or no pyramiding. For goods purchased by consumers, wholesale and retail markups are not inflated by the tax since it applies only to the final price. An attempt is sometimes made to exempt investment goods purchased by business firms from the retail sales tax, but taxes on business purchases often run as high as a fifth of sales tax receipts. Such taxes enter into business costs and are probably pyramided, but the extent of pyramiding must be only a small fraction of that which occurs under a manufacturers' or wholesalers' sales tax.

The broader base of the retail sales tax permits the use of lower rates than other single-stage taxes to yield a given amount of revenue. The difference in rates is not small, since prices may be 50 or 100 percent higher at the retail level. Thus, a retail tax of 5 percent may be the equivalent of a manufacturers' tax of 7.5 or 10 percent.

On administrative grounds, the retail sales tax has both advantages and disadvantages. It is more difficult to deal with the large number of small retailers than with the less numerous and more sophisticated manufacturers or wholesalers. On the other hand, the problems of defining a transaction and of determining the base of the tax are more easily handled at the retail level, although even at this level the problems are not insignificant. The state governments have had retail sales taxes for many years, and most of them have learned that the tax is not easy to administer and enforce.

The introduction of a retail sales tax by the federal government would involve duplication of existing state and local taxes. The state and local governments would interpret this as an unwarranted interference with their freedom of action in regard to rates and coverage of their own taxes. At the minimum, some effort would have to be made to coordinate the definition of the tax bases and perhaps also to administer collection of the taxes on a cooperative or joint basis.

The strongest objection to a retail tax, which also applies to wholesale and manufacturing taxes, is its regressivity. It has been estimated that a 2 percent sales tax in Wisconsin on all tangible commodities, including food, but excluding all services except gas, electricity, admissions, and communications, would amount to 4.9 percent of income for families below the $1,000 level and only 1.0 percent for those above $10,000 (Table 6-2). These figures, based on income and consumption in a one-year period, probably overstate the regressivity of the sales tax, since persons temporarily in the lower income classes do not reduce their consumption by the entire reduction in their income and those temporarily in higher classes do not raise their consumption by the entire increase in their income. Some economists have suggested that the burden of the sales tax should be measured against income over a longer time period. On this basis, a retail sales tax might be proportional, but it is unlikely that it would turn out to be progressive in any significant degree, regardless of the time period used.

Many units of government have exempted food and other items of consumption from the sales tax to alleviate its burden on the poor. Such exemptions moderate, but do not eliminate, its regressivity (Table 6-2). As an alternative, experts have long suggested refunding the estimated tax paid by individuals with low incomes. This suggestion was disregarded until 1963 when Indiana introduced a retail sales tax and adopted a small tax credit against the income tax as a relief measure for the sales tax paid by low income recipients. Since then, Colorado, Hawaii, and Massachusetts have adopted the same device and other states are considering it.

The Value Added Tax

The value added tax, first proposed in 1918 by a German industrial executive, was discussed sporadically for another three decades before it was actually put to use. A modified version was adopted in 1953 by the state of Michigan; in the following year, the central government of France imposed such a tax. Other countries are now considering it as a substitute for other forms of consumption taxes. Some have advocated the addition of a value added tax to the federal tax system to provide a revenue source that could be raised or lowered in the interest of stabilization policy.

FORMS OF VALUE ADDED TAXATION. Conceptually, the value added tax is a general tax on the national income. For any given firm, value added is the difference between receipts from sales and the amounts paid for materials, supplies, and services purchased from other firms. The total of the value added by all firms in the economy is equal to total wages, salaries, interest, rents, and profits and is therefore the same as the national income.

In practice, there are two types of value added taxes that differ only in the way outlays for investment purposes are treated. The first type permits business firms to subtract purchases of capital goods in computing the tax base. Total value added is thus equal to total retail sales of final consumer goods. In the second type, purchases of capital goods are not deducted; instead, firms are permitted to deduct an allowance for depreciation over the useful life of the asset. Thus, only the second type is equivalent to a tax on the national income; the first, which is proposed most often, is a general consumption tax.

There are two methods of computing the allowance to be made for purchases from other firms. Under the "tax credit" method, the tax rate is applied to the total sales of the firm and the tax paid on goods purchased is then deducted. Where this method is used, the tax on all goods shipped must be shown separately on each invoice. Under the second, so-called "calculation" method, purchases are subtracted from sales and the tax rate is then applied to the net figure. Both approaches amount to the same thing, but some administrators believe that the tax credit method is easier to control, because it automatically provides an accounting of the tax to be remitted on exports (the standard practice to avoid putting domestic firms at a competitive disadvantage in foreign markets), and solves some of the problems raised by the inclusion or exclusion of various items such as charitable contributions that are troublesome under the calculation method.

ECONOMIC EFFECTS OF THE VALUE ADDED TAX. The value added tax reduces or eliminates the pyramiding that would occur under the turnover tax or manufacturers' and wholesalers' sales taxes. Since a firm receives credit for the tax paid by its suppliers, it is not likely to apply a markup to its purchases in computing the price to be charged. For example, suppose a retailer who pays $52.50 for an item (including $2.50 tax) wishes to apply a markup of 100 percent. Under the tax credit method, he will charge his customer $105 ($100 plus $5 tax) and take a credit of $2.50 in computing the amount to be paid to the government, leaving a net tax of $2.50. If the calculation method is used, the retailer deducts from the $100 the $50 paid to his supplier and then applies a tax rate of 5 percent to the remainder to obtain the same $2.50 net tax. The customer pays the same total price of $105, which consists of the $100 price net of tax, the $2.50 tax paid by the supplier, and the $2.50 tax paid by the retailer.

The base of the consumption-type value added tax is equivalent to that of a retail sales tax with the same rate, and confined to consumption goods. On the other hand, the income-type value added tax is equivalent to a proportional income tax. Whether the patterns of burden distribution of the income-type and consumption-type value added taxes are equivalent is in dispute, reflecting a difference of opinion regarding the impact of a proportional income tax and a general tax on consumption. The income-type value added tax is paid on capital goods at the time the purchase is made and the tax is presumably recovered as it is depreciated. Under the consumption-type value added tax, purchases of capital goods are free of tax. Thus, at any given time, the income-type value added tax imposes an extra tax on net investment. Some argue that prepayment of the tax under the income-type of tax reduces the return on capital; others believe that it is reflected in higher prices for final consumption goods and has no effect on the rate of return. The difference is not likely to be significant, however.

THE VALUE ADDED TAX VERSUS THE RETAIL SALES TAX. The consumption-type value added tax and the retail sales tax are similar on both economic and equity grounds. Both taxes are, for all practical purposes, taxes on general consumption. The retail sales tax involves fewer administrative problems because determination of tax liability is less complicated and the number of taxpayers is smaller. But in practice retail sales taxes always omit many items of consumption, while a value added tax could probably be levied on a more general basis.

The Expenditure Tax

The expenditure tax has long been discussed in the economic literature, but was not seriously considered until the U.S. Treasury Department recommended it during World War II. It was also advocated by the minority of the British Royal Commission on the Taxation of Profits and Income in 1955. Although neither recommendation was accepted, the tax has since come to be regarded as a respectable possibility.

Unlike the consumption taxes already discussed, the expenditure tax is levied on the individual consumer rather than on the seller of goods and services. In practice, there is little difference in the method of administration between the expenditure tax and the individual income tax. The individual taxpayer submits a form at the end of the year estimating the amount of his expenditures. Deductions for selected expenditures may be allowed, as well as personal exemptions. The rates may be proportional or graduated; usually, however, the expenditure tax is suggested in its graduated form.

Expenditure taxation is intended either to replace or to supplement the income tax. It is supported strongly by those who believe that the income tax has an adverse effect on investment and saving incentives (see Chapter 4). It is also supported as a useful supplement to income taxation when capital gains and other incomes are either not taxed or are taxed at a preferential rate. While capital gains are not reached by the expenditure tax as such, the tax does apply to consumption financed out of capital gains.

Some believe that the income tax is inequitable because it taxes income when it is saved and then again when the savings earn additional income. It is now generally agreed that this double taxation argument is sterile. Both the expenditure tax and the income tax may be progressive and redistributional in effect. If one considers income the better measure of ability to pay, the expenditure tax is inferior. If expenditures are considered the better measure, the income tax is inferior.

The expenditure tax is not more widespread primarily because of difficulties of compliance and administration. It is impractical to ask taxpayers to estimate their expenditures directly, since almost no one keeps adequate expenditure records. Thus, expenditures must be estimated by subtracting saving from income received during the year. This requires the taxpayer to provide balance sheet information (to estimate saving) as well as an income statement. Some proponents of the expenditure tax have pointed out that the requirement to supply balance sheet information should be regarded as a major advantage and not as a disadvantage of the expenditure tax, since the information would be helpful in administering the income tax. However, it is generally agreed that the administrative and compliance problems of an expenditure tax are formidable and that it would be very difficult for most countries to enforce such a tax with the present state of administrative know-how.

Consumption vs. Income Taxes

Until recently, the major argument for adoption of a general consumption tax by the federal government was the arbitrariness of the excise tax system. Except for sumptuary and benefit taxes, the excises which were in effect between 1945 and 1965 could hardly be defended on rational grounds. If revenues from consumption taxes were permanently needed, it would have been better to replace the miscellaneous excises by a general low rate tax on consumer goods.

This argument was eliminated by enactment of the Excise Tax Reduction Act of 1965. For all practical purposes, it can be said that the federal government has reduced consumption taxation to a minimum. The appeal of a general consumption tax must now rest on the substantive ground that it would be better national policy to replace part of the income tax by a general consumption tax.

Heavier reliance on a general consumption tax by the federal government is opposed for several reasons:

First, the shift from income taxes to a consumption tax would impair the built-in flexibility of the tax system. The automatic reductions in income tax revenues during the four postwar recessions were of major importance in moderating the declines of disposable income, and made a major contribution to the brevity and mildness of the recessions. Although the United States has avoided a recession for more than five years, the business cycle has not been eliminated. Maintenance of built-in flexibility is good insurance against the possibility of a serious business contraction in the future.

Second, the use of a general consumption tax would involve federal entrance into a field that is now the most important source of state revenue, and is also becoming important at the local level. Federal use of this tax source would almost surely restrict its use by the state and local governments, which would impair their fiscal capacities at a time when they face large financial responsibilities.

Third, because of the opposition of the state and local governments, any general consumption tax enacted by the federal government would probably be a tax at the manufacturers' or wholesalers' levels. As has been seen, such taxes tend to be pyramided through conventional markups and thus to burden the consumer by more than the amount of revenue collected. Moreover, experience in other countries has shown that there are numerous difficulties in defining the tax base to avoid serious inequities.

Fourth, taking federal, state, and local taxes together, the tax load on low income recipients is already heavy. The increases in state-local taxes in the years immediately ahead will be obtained largely from sources that are most burdensome on these low income groups. Additional consumption taxes at the federal level would make the combined structure at the lower part of the income scale even more regressive. Such a policy would be particularly inappropriate at a time when the federal government has just begun a major effort to moderate the impact of poverty in the United States.

On the other hand, several arguments are advanced supporting greater use of consumption taxes by the federal government:

First, even though income taxes were reduced in 1964, the income tax rates are still too high, particularly for individuals with high incomes. These high rates may reduce incentives and the willingness and capacity to save.

Second, built-in flexibility does not require that all elements of the federal tax system be highly sensitive to changes in income. Furthermore, large automatic growth of tax receipts has the undesirable by-product of promoting higher federal expenditures. If these tax receipts were not so easily obtained, federal expenditures might be much lower.

Third, the federal government need not impair the fiscal capacities of the state and local governments in order to build up its own consumption tax revenue. Use of a value added tax would avoid duplication of state-local revenue sources by the federal government. Since practically all business enterprises already file income tax returns, the administrative and compliance problems of a value added tax should not be insurmountable.

Fourth, adoption of a general consumption tax in lieu of part of the corporation income tax would improve the United States balance of payments position. This substitution would either improve the trade surplus, if the corporation income tax is shifted in the form of higher prices, or the capital account, if the tax is borne by the owners of capital (see Chapter 5). Even a modest improvement in the nation's balance of payments would be a contribution, since the problem has not been easy to solve.

While there are a number of important peripheral considerations, the major issue in the income tax versus consumption tax controversy concerns the degree of progression. Proponents of a general consumption tax rarely recommend a graduated expenditure tax as an alternative to income taxation. Their concern is to reduce progression, and they propose a flat rate sales or value added tax as a method of accomplishing this objective. On the other hand, those who oppose a general consumption tax either defend the present degree of progression or believe it is inadequate. Most of them would support a graduated expenditure tax if a new consumption tax were necessary, but would oppose adoption of a sales or value added tax.

Summary

The federal government has relied exclusively on selective excises for consumption tax revenues. These taxes were increased during every major war, and were subsequently de-emphasized as the need for revenue declined. The cycle lasted somewhat longer during and after World War II, but the last vestige of the wartime excises was eliminated by the 1965 Excise Tax Reduction Act. Under this law, which will become fully effective January 1, 1969, the only excise taxes remaining in the federal revenue system will be the sumptuary taxes on alcohol and tobacco, the benefit taxes for highways, airways, and some recreational activities, and certain regulatory taxes.

Sumptuary taxes help to offset the additional cost imposed on society by the consumption of certain commodities; taxes imposed on those who benefit from particular government services are needed to prevent excessive use of such services; and regulatory taxes are used primarily to assist law enforcement rather than to raise revenues. Otherwise, excise taxes are bad taxes: they discriminate arbitrarily against the consumption of the taxed commodities and distort the allocation of resources in the economy.

If consumption taxes are needed for revenue purposes, economic and equity considerations suggest that a general consumption tax would be more appropriate than a series of selective excise taxes. A general tax does not discriminate against particular forms of consumption and therefore produces less distortion in the economy.

Among general consumption taxes, manufacturers' and wholesalers' sales taxes are probably easiest to administer, but they are pyramided through the markup of prices as goods go through production and distribution channels. Retail sales taxes and the value added tax involve much less pyramiding, if any. All these taxes are either regressive or, at best, proportional. Progression can be achieved by the adoption of a credit for sales taxes paid against the individual income tax, or by taxation of consumption through a graduated expenditure tax. The expenditure tax has a number of attractive features, but it is generally regarded as too difficult to administer.

Consumption taxes are more burdensome on the low income classes than income taxes, and have less built-in flexibility. Adoption of a general consumption tax by the federal government would also interfere with a revenue source that has become a mainstay of state and some local tax systems. Consumption taxes are vigorously supported, however, by those who believe that the federal tax system is too progressive and that income taxation has impaired economic incentives. More recently, some have been supporting the adoption of a value added tax as a replacement for part of the corporation income tax to help improve the United States balance of payments.

3 REPORT OF THE ROYAL COMMISSION ON TAXATION (CANADA) 27–32 (1966) *

Wealth as a Tax Base

We have suggested earlier in this chapter one of the reasons why we reject wealth as a tax base. If it were practical to define wealth to include human assets, and if human assets were traded in the market on the same basis as physical and financial assets, we acknowledge that wealth would be a good indication of economic power *at a point in time.* But in a free society human assets are not treated like other assets. The problems of valuing such assets are great and they cannot be "liquidated" to satisfy a tax liability. Yet to ignore human assets would grossly understate the ability to pay of those who earn and immediately spend employment income.

Furthermore, even if human capital could be included with other assets, to tax both additions to assets (saving), and then to tax repeatedly the stock of assets, while failing to tax consumption, would seriously discriminate against one disposition of the income generated by assets relative to another. For example, suppose there are two men each of whom has a net worth (including human capital) of $200,000. Suppose that no taxes have been paid by either in the past. If the government had to raise $10,000 from them now, it would seem reasonable that each should pay an equal tax of $5,000. Let us suppose that over the following year each earns $10,000 in cash, but one consumes the whole $10,000, while the other spends $5,000 on consumption and saves $5,000. The larger spender ends the year with a net worth of $195,000; the saver ends the year with a net worth of $200,000. If wealth were used as the index of ability to pay the spender would have less ability to pay than the saver. But we can hardly ignore the fact that both received the same increase in economic power during the year. On equity grounds we cannot justify exempting the dollar destined for consumption any more than we can justify exempting the dollar destined for saving.

* Reproduced with the permission of the Queen's Printer for Canada.

While we do not think it would be appropriate to recommend exempting savings from tax by placing greater weight on consumption taxes relative to income taxes, we are equally opposed to taxing saving more heavily by imposing taxes on wealth as such. Such a wealth tax would, we believe, not only be inequitable but would also tend to reduce the rate of domestic saving and thus reduce the rate of capital formation or, alternatively, increase Canada's reliance on foreign saving.

Imposing taxes on the comprehensive tax base each year, as we propose, would tax all additions to wealth. Over time, all of a man's wealth would be taxed, but only once. This is substantially more stringent than the present system under which increases in economic power from some sources are not taxed at all.

There are, we acknowledge, some legitimate grounds that can be advanced for taxing wealth as such. First, by levying a low rate of tax on all net worth at regular intervals, the owners of property would be put under pressure to hold assets that yield a high cash return. If administratively feasible, it also would tend to compensate for the exclusion from the comprehensive tax base of imputed income derived from owner-used property. Secondly, a net worth tax could be imposed to increase the redistributive effect of the tax system.

It may be thought by some that a top personal rate of 50 per cent would not result in a sufficiently progressive tax system despite the great broadening of the base that we recommend. If still greater progressiveness in the tax system were desired, a net worth tax at a low rate, say, 2 per cent, levied on net assets over $1 million every few years would probably be administratively feasible and would increase the redistribution effects of the tax system while retaining the 50 per cent top personal rate.[8]

We do not recommend such a net worth tax because we do not want to penalize saving and because we are convinced that the comprehensive tax base with the rate structure we recommend would achieve an adequate degree of progressiveness in

[8] Retaining the top personal rate of 50 per cent is highly desirable because only if the top personal rate is approximately equal to or less than the tax rate levied on corporate income is the full integration of corporate and personal income taxes feasible. We could not countenance an increase in the rate of tax levied on corporations, both because of its depressing effects on domestic investment and because of the international ramifications.

the tax system. On the other hand, if more progression were required, we would prefer to see the imposition of such a net worth tax rather than the acceptance of a top marginal personal rate that was much above 50 per cent.

Consumption and Wealth Taxes as Methods of Collection

Acceptance of the comprehensive tax base as the best indicator of economic power does not mean rejection of all taxes on wealth and on consumption. Property taxes and retail sales taxes, to name but two important variants of wealth and consumption taxes, have sufficiently useful attributes to justify their continued existence. In particular, we think it is important that each of Canada's three levels of government have a tax source over which it has primary control, although we do not mean to suggest that each level of government should rely exclusively on one type of tax. The present arrangement under which the municipalities rely extensively on property taxes and the provinces rely extensively on retail sales taxes has a great deal of merit because it gives each level of government a degree of fiscal autonomy and hence fiscal responsibility. While we think it important that there should be more joint decision making between the federal and provincial governments with respect to sales taxes and income taxes, this is not inconsistent with the idea that each level should administer one major tax.

From the point of view of equity, however, we believe that wealth and consumption taxes, other than those imposed on a fee-for-service basis, should be methods of collecting taxes rather than independent levies. Ideally, therefore, taxpayers should be given full credit for some portion of consumption and wealth taxes against their tax liabilities determined by a progressive rate structure applied to the comprehensive tax base. These credits for consumption and wealth taxes should be refundable to the extent that they exceed income tax liabilities. The credits would have to be arbitrary in amount for two reasons. First, it would be impossible to measure the actual consumption taxes paid by a particular taxpayer or the proportion of property taxes levied on a fee-for-service basis, or the property tax component of residential rents. Second, the federal government should not be put in the position of having to raise its taxes every time a province or municipality raises its own, thereby increasing the federal credit required.

We have decided not to recommend this arbitrary refundable credit for sales and property taxes. To do so would be to recommend, in effect, the adoption of a negative income tax. As we have suggested earlier, we strongly recommend that the transfer system as a whole be reviewed. The present system is cumbersome and has important gaps and there is some overlapping. The advantages and disadvantages of a negative income tax can only be appraised in this wider context.

It must be recognized that the full integration of all of these taxes would require a dramatic increase in marginal rates. These higher rates might have substantial disincentive effects that would have to be weighed against the improvement in equity that would be attained.

There is, however, a middle ground between complete integration and no integration of these taxes. By gradually reducing the relative weight of consumption and property taxes in the system, by reducing or compensating for the regressive features of sales taxes, and by reducing the weight of personal income taxes on the lower income brackets, Canada can move closer to the objective of allocating taxes according to ability to pay. We are recommending that a start should be made on all of these fronts. Subsequently, more could be done by increasing the width of the individual and family unit zero rate brackets, or by adopting a system of refundable tax credits in lieu of these zero brackets so that those in the lowest income brackets would obtain a refund (admittedly arbitrary in amount) of sales and property taxes.

We want to emphasize that either course of action would be consistent with our basic approach. Certainly implementation of the second alternative would represent the natural evolution of the tax system we are proposing.

The Income of Organizations as a Tax Base

It is sometimes argued that legal entities and institutions such as corporations and trusts which we will call intermediaries, have tax-paying capacity. With our concept of ability to pay this cannot be so. For us, tax-paying capacity arises from discretionary economic power, and intermediaries cannot have discretionary economic power—the residual power to command goods and services for personal use. Consumption is a strictly human trait. But the question is not simply definitional; all the assets and net receipts of intermediaries are ultimately held by, or accrue to the benefit of, natural persons. What happens to intermediaries necessarily affects the interests of natural persons whatever the intention. Here too, taxing intermediaries is a convenient collection technique but the ultimate burden is on people. Because there are good and sufficient reasons why income taxes on resident organizations cannot be abandoned (as discussed in Chapter 19), we are convinced that the taxes levied on the incomes of resident organizations and resident individuals should be fully integrated through the provision of a refundable tax credit for the tax paid by corporations and other intermediary organizations against personal income tax liabilities.

Our principles concerning ability to pay relate primarily to residents of Canada and our recommendations reflect this. It is not ordinarily possible or appropriate to measure the tax liabilities of non-residents with respect to Canadian source income by reference to this ability to pay.

Accordingly, for a variety of reasons outlined in Chapter 26, we recommend that, in general, income derived from Canadian sources by non-residents should be subject to withholding taxes at arbitrary rates and that non-residents should not receive refundable tax credits for taxes paid by corporations or other organizations in which they hold interest. However, we believe that in some specified circumstances it is feasible and appropriate to give non-residents the opportunity to have their tax liabilities determined by reference to their ability to pay. We recommend in Chapter 26 that in these circumstances they be given the option to file tax returns as Canadian residents.

PECHMAN, THE RICH, THE POOR, AND THE TAXES THEY PAY *

The Public Interest, Fall 1969, pp. 21, 36.

The Payroll Tax

Much has been said about the need for removing the poor from the income tax rolls, and Congress seems to be prepared to remedy this anachronism. But the more urgent problem is to remove the much heavier payroll tax burden of the poor. The federal income tax bill of the families and individuals who are officially classified as poor is only $200 million a year, as compared with the $1.5 billion they pay in payroll taxes. In addition, the regressive feature of the payroll tax at the higher income levels should be moderated immediately and ultimately eliminated entirely.

Several different approaches might be taken to achieve these objectives.

First, part or all of the payroll tax could be converted into a withholding tax for income tax purposes. No formal change in the payroll tax need be involved; at the end of the year, individuals would receive credit against their income taxes (or a refund if they are not income tax payers) for the amount of payroll taxes paid.

Second, contributions from general revenues might be made, on the basis of a fixed formula, to the social security and other trust funds. Such a possibility was foreseen in the earlier days of social security.

Third, the social security system might be combined with a liberalized and modernized public assistance system or some variant of a negative income tax. The negative income tax payments to the aged in such a system would be financed out of general revenues.

But whatever is ultimately done about the payroll tax as the basic revenue source for social security financing, the poor should be relieved of paying this tax as soon as possible. The principle of a minimum taxable level under the income tax—soon to be raised to the poverty levels—should be carried over into the payroll tax. The Internal Revenue Service is already proficient at handling tens of millions of refunds per year under the income tax; the additional payroll tax refunds would not be an excessive burden.

* © 1969 By National Affairs, Inc. Reproduced with permission.

Chapter II

INCOME

In this chapter, as in the next, we have selected a few prototypical income and deduction items that seemed to us to raise especially noteworthy policy issues. Some other items are considered in Professor Bittker's Comprehensive Tax Base article in Chapter I, Section B.[a]

A. Gifts

The present income tax from its inception in 1913 has not applied to "property acquired by gift, bequest, devise, or inheritance" (Code § 102); interestingly enough, the Income Tax Act of 1894 (which was subsequently held unconstitutional in the famous *Pollock* case) did tax gifts and inheritances of money and personal property. Are there valid reasons for the exclusion today? The excerpt from the Canadian Royal Commission on Taxation that follows answers this question in the negative, at least with respect to transfers outside the family.[b]

The Royal Commission's recommendations concerning the taxation of the family that are briefly alluded to in the ensuing excerpt are more fully discussed in Chapter IV of this book.

[a] See also the consideration of retirement benefits in Chapter IV.

[b] An omitted portion of the Royal Commission's report contains more detailed discussion concerning different types of gifts, valuation issues, etc. See also Klein, An Enigma in the Federal Income Tax: The Meaning of the Word "Gift," 48 Minn.L.Rev. 215 (1963).

3 REPORT OF THE ROYAL COMMISSION ON TAXATION (CANADA) 465–69 (1966) *

The allocation of taxes according to ability to pay requires the imposition of progressive rates of tax on a tax base that measures the change in the economic power of each individual and family. No one can doubt that gifts increase the economic power of those who receive them, for they either "save the pocket" or provide an asset that can be exchanged for consumer goods and services. We recommend that gifts from one tax unit to another should be brought into the comprehensive tax base of the recipient in the same way as wages, business income, dividends, interest, rents, property gains and windfall gains. As we have stressed, the source of a gain and the expectations and intentions of the recipient of a gain are completely irrelevant. Anything that increases an individual's or a family's capacity to command goods and services should be included in the tax base. However, in order to simplify administration, by reducing the need to value and account for many small gifts, we will propose that there should be certain annual exemptions, as well as a lifetime exemption, for gifts received.

While this chapter is primarily concerned with gifts from the point of view of the recipient, we want to emphasize that the inclusion of gifts in the tax base of the donee would not mean that gifts should be deducted from the tax base of the donor. The only deductions we recommend are expenses which are reasonably related to the earning of income, and certain special types of deductions such as charitable donations within specified limits. *Inter vivos* gifts are a voluntary exercise of the donor's economic power. They are personal expenditures that should be treated in exactly the same way as personal consumption expenditures. Neither *inter vivos* gifts nor testamentary gifts are related to the earning of the donor's income. Indeed, as we have said in Chapter 15, a gift from one tax unit to another is a disposition of property and the gain, if any, calculated on the basis of the fair market value, should be brought into the tax base of the donor. In other words, gifts should be made only from tax-paid income.

To prescribe that gifts must be made from the tax-paid income of the donor and that they are income to the donee does not in our opinion involve "double taxation". We simply recommend

* Reproduced with the permission of the Queen's Printer for Canada.

that all income be taxed once to each unit that received it. No one thinks that the taxation of a worker's wages and the taxation of a merchant's profit derived from selling goods and services to the worker is "double taxation". The merchant must include the price of the goods or services in his income, while the worker cannot deduct that amount, because it is a personal or living expense. Our approach to gifts is basically the same.

We have taken the position in this *Report* that consumption and savings should be taxed on the same basis. This means that changes in the taxpayer's *capacity* to command goods and services for personal use should be taxed, and not only the command actually exercised. On the basis of this test, the donee should be deemed to have received a gift when he has received the right to it rather than when he exercised the right. Any other approach would make it possible to arrange gifts in such a way as to achieve an unwarranted deferment of tax. As we have said, postponed taxes are less onerous taxes and are unfair taxes because the ability to postpone is not available to everyone to the same extent.

The family unit concept that we recommend in Chapter 10 has important implications for the taxation of gifts. The recommendations set forth in this chapter are predicated on the adoption of the family unit concept. Under that concept, transfers of wealth within a family unit would not be subject to tax, just as a transfer of cash from one pocket to another is outside the scope of the present system. Only transfers of wealth between tax units would have tax consequences. By recommending that spouses and their dependents should form a family unit for tax purposes, and by stipulating that it should continue until the death of the last surviving spouse or until all children have lost their dependant status, whichever comes later, the tax system we recommend would probably exempt from tax a large proportion of all gifts. Professor Carl Shoup, in his study of death and gift taxation in the United States, has estimated that well over one half of all transfers are among persons who fall within our definition of the family unit.[1] While comparable data are not available for Canada, we expect that a similar proportion prevails here.

[1] C. S. Shoup, *Federal Estate and Gift Taxes*, Washington: The Brookings Institution, 1966.

In Chapter 10, we explain why we recommend that transfers between spouses and between parents and dependent children should not have tax consequences. It is our view that the property is accumulated by a family as a result of joint decisions and a common effort of both husband and wife, either in earning or in refraining from spending. Accordingly, it should be possible to transfer property freely and without tax consequences within the family unit. Children should be included in this unit during the period when they are the financial responsibility of the parents and unable to support themselves. In some circumstances the income of children increases the economic power of families; and when this occurs the income of dependants should be aggregated with the income of the family. We believe it would be neither desirable nor feasible to differentiate between the expenses of parents that are legal or social obligations, and expenses that are essentially gifts from parents to their children. For these and for other reasons relating to the need to aggregate family income, we believe that the consumption of dependants should be treated as family consumption; and the money saved by children, unless kept outside the family unit through the deposit system we suggest, should be treated as family saving.

There comes a point in the life of most children when they both want and need independence. They are capable of making their own way. Because this point is difficult to define, we have specified a number of conditions and have provided certain options to accommodate the diverse circumstances that exist. It is our approach that prior to reaching this point in their lives children have no ability to pay taxes except as members of a family unit. But having become independent, they immediately acquire an ability to pay taxes. As in the case of other individuals and families, their ability to pay depends on what property they receive in the form of gifts, on what they earn, and on their own obligations and responsibilities. Accordingly, we propose that when a child leaves a family unit, he, or his new family unit if he has married, should include in income the market value of all property taken from the original unit. This would be subject to the lifetime exemption for gifts to each individual in the amount of $5,000 that we recommend later in this chapter. The smaller annual exemptions which we propose should also apply and the averaging provisions which we discuss in Chapter 13 should be available with respect to this income.

When a new tax unit is established, its biggest asset will often be the health, strength and knowledge of the new taxpayer; but because we do not propose to tax human capital, this is not taxable to the new tax unit. Apart from the administrative exemptions referred to above, this would be the only net gain of the new tax unit that should not be subject to tax. All of the money and other property brought into the new tax unit should be taxable to that unit as income. This applies to property taken from the child's original family unit on termination of his dependant status and anything subsequently received from the original unit, as well as income subsequently earned by the child or other members of his new unit.

Some children will have greater material advantages than others because their families are more affluent. The proposed system ensures that well-to-do parents who support their children lavishly can do so only by spending income taxed to the family at progressive rates. Some children will receive substantial gifts from their parents either before or after losing their dependant status. The proposed system would not eliminate this advantage; but it would ensure that these gifts were taxed to the newly independent individual at the same rates as other gains.

In summary then, our approach to the taxation of gifts and bequests would have two major effects. First, it would completely remove the tax burden from gifts and bequests flowing from the taxpayer to his spouse and dependent children. Second, our proposals would in general increase the tax burden on other gifts and bequests that exceed the exemption level. Thus, a widow would be free of tax on transfers from a deceased spouse, while large transfers between generations would usually be subject to substantially higher tax, although not higher than the recipient would pay on any other kind of income.

B. Municipal Bond Interest

Code Section 103 provides a general exemption for interest on obligations of states and territories and their political subdivisions, as has every federal income tax law since 1913. Certain "industrial development" and "arbitrage" bonds are excepted. The exemption thus is one of the oldest methods by which federal financial assistance is provided for other governmental units. Whether the Supreme Court would decide today that such assistance is the involuntary consequence of a constitutional requirement is uncertain.

The exemption also provides a way for taxpayers to avoid the federal income tax, but only if they are willing to assume the risk of loss from inflation and rising interest rates that usually accompanies investing in fixed income securities. Certainly the present holders of tax-exempts who paid par for bonds with coupons of 2% or less in the mid-1940's have not enjoyed any fiscal bonanza as a result.

In considering whether the exemption is justified, it should be contrasted with other methods by which the federal government may directly or indirectly assist state and local governments. Such methods include revenue-sharing and other alternatives discussed in Chapter X of this book.

Professor Surrey's article which follows is the first in a series of four articles.[a] The other three are: Healy, The Assault on Tax-Exempt Bonds, 36 Tax Policy, July-August 1969; Surrey, The Tax Treatment of State and Local Government Obligations—Some Further Observations, 36 Tax Policy, Sept.-Oct. 1969; Healy, Further Comments on Proposed Capital Financing Alternatives, 37 Tax Policy, Jan.-Feb. 1970.

[a] The House-passed version of the Tax Reform Act of 1969 contained a provision authorizing state and local governments to issue taxable bonds of the type described by Professor Surrey, but the provision was eliminated in conference.

SURREY, FEDERAL INCOME TAXATION OF STATE AND LOCAL GOVERNMENT OBLIGATIONS *

36 Tax Policy, May-June 1969.

The subject of the federal income taxation of state and local government obligations is again under serious attention in the Congress. This attention is appropriate and desirable, for this perennial and previously intractable problem is urgently in need of a solution.

At present there are over $120 billion of outstanding state and local tax-exempt obligations, and about $15 billion in new obligations are being issued annually (for about a $10 billion net annual growth). The outstanding issues and the annual new crop of obligations present different problems. These remarks relate primarily to the enormous increase in new issues of these obligations that now looms up before us and the effects of adding this new huge volume of tax-exempt obligations to the present market. The concern and the proposals to meet it can be briefly summarized:

> The probable high level of new issues of tax-exempt state and local bonds over the next decade raises very serious problems for state and local governments and for the equity of our federal tax system. This high level can come about under the enormous financing requirements of the vast social programs so vitally necessary to meet our domestic needs.
>
> The basic problem is that piling more and more reliance on the tax-exempt privilege as a way of helping states and localities to meet these financing requirements creates a powerful buyer's market for tax exempts. The state and local governments pricing their bonds on the basis of this exemption as a consequence will get less and less for it—that is, they will have to pay closer to the market rates of interest on taxable bonds—and their financing costs must inexorably rise. At the same time, the buyers would still get the tax exemption with even greater tax savings.
>
> Those who are anxious to preserve the strength of state and local governments in the federal system should give serious thought to these problems.
>
> We should all consider whether *new financing techniques* are available and appropriate to avoid these problems—techniques which at the same time operate to preserve the independence of action on the part of state and local governments in our national system to which the principle of tax exemption has contributed.

Projections of State-Local Credit Demands

Let us first consider the rate of growth of new state and local issues that looms ahead. The congressional Joint Economic Committee in 1966 made a projection of the likely level of growth of capital needs and thus of state and

* Reproduced with permission of the Tax Institute of America.

local bond issues through 1975. The JEC figures themselves suggested that this growth would be in line with the likely growth in gross national product. Since the supply of savings should also grow at about the GNP rate, the general conclusion would be indicated that the marketability of state and local bonds should not change markedly relative to other bonds.

But the JEC report itself emphasized one reservation about this outlook, namely, the heavy reliance placed on commercial bank takings. They recognized that if commercial banks, for example, were attracted more heavily into mortgages (e.g., by the much touted housing boom of the 1970's) there would be problems for state and local governments in floating even a level of state and local issues that was growing in line with GNP.

Another set of qualifications should be added to this forecast of marketability of state and local bonds. The JEC projections basically assumed only the development of current programs. They did not make much allowance for new programs.

The expansion of federal programs that lies ahead is likely to induce even more substantial increases in state and local government borrowing than may have been anticipated in the study. The Congress has already considered a wide range of new federal programs in a variety of areas, such as pollution control and housing. In addition, pressures on the federal budget have recently caused attention to be focused on the potentialities of debt service grants to state and local governments, as are now used in the public housing area, rather than the lump-sum grants that have been more traditional. From a financial viewpoint, these debt service grants would shift the financing of the federal share of local project costs from the taxable market (i.e., away from the federal bonds that provide the funds for the lump-sum grants) to the tax-exempt market to absorb the local bonds that would be issued to finance the project (the debt service grants would help defray the interest and principal on these tax-exempt bonds).

Another factor that may well have been underestimated in the JEC work is the size of replacement needs. For example, much of the physical plant in our urban school system is aged and inadequate to the school needs of urban children. Replacement will be very expensive. These replacement needs alone could cause the annual net increase in state and local bonds to double in the next five to ten years.

In summary, the growth of new programs, especially federally aided ones, an increasing reliance on debt service grants to shift federal debt to state and local debt, and exploding replacement needs could increase the annual net growth in state and local debt from the present $10 billion to as high as $30 billion a year in ten years. *This would represent a rate of growth twice as high as the rate of growth of the savings supply.*

If state and local governments are to sell this enormous increase in tax-exempt bonds, then they will be commanding a larger share of the savings flow. To do so they will have to compete more sharply with other borrowers, such as homeowners and corporations. The question is whether tax exemption is an effective instrument with which to conduct this competition. The experts can readily demonstrate that this exemption is "inefficient" in the sense that state and local governments get less benefit from it in lower interest costs than the federal government gives up in lost tax revenues.[1] Some may say in reply, however, that even conceding this "inefficiency" it can be regarded as the price to be paid for the independence of decision-making that the interest exemption offers in general to state and local governments. But even if this were in turn conceded—and many would say that the price is already too high in terms of the effect on the federal tax system and the wastage involved—we must certainly give serious thought to the question of how this will work out if state and local governments suddenly try to become much heavier borrowers.

The Market for Tax-Exempt Bonds

To understand the significance of this enormous potential growth in tax-exempt bonds, it is necessary to remember that the institution of tax-exempt interest has an impact not only on federal tax returns but also on bond markets. It does save state and local governments money by reducing interest rates on their bonds, but it does so by narrowing the range of customers for those bonds. It narrows the range to groups that find tax exemption valuable. You do not find exempt pension trusts buying tax-exempt bonds.[2]

The rate on tax exempts is determined, like any other price, by demand and supply. If the supply of tax exempts is limited, they can be sold to the buyers who are most anxious to get them. If more tax exempts are to be sold, the price of those tax exempts will have to fall, i.e., their interest rate must increase. The price fall will be necessary to get existing buyers to take more tax exempts (and thus less of other investments) and to induce new buyers to enter the tax-exempt market.

It is significant that interest of all kinds—taxable and tax-exempt together—is a modest component of the income of upper-income individuals. That income consists mostly of dividends and capital gains, reflecting the fact that the wealth position of these individuals inclines them to the higher risk-higher return features of equity investment (which features are also associated with favorably taxed capital gains and untaxed unrealized appreciation). Inducing these investors into the relatively safe investment of state and local government bonds through tax exemption is in a sense swimming against the tide.

By and large, since the most distinctive feature of these state and local bonds is their tax exemption, the process of selling more bonds must involve widening the market by appealing to taxpayers with lower marginal tax rates than those now acquiring tax-exempt bonds. The appeal must involve the process of selling tax-exempt bonds at rates more closely comparable to those on taxable bonds, so as to make the exempt bonds attractive to those who get less tax advantage from the exemption.

---

[1] See generally David J. Ott and Allan H. Meltzer, *Federal Tax Treatment of State and Local Securities*, Washington: The Brookings Institution, 1963.

[2] Tax-exempt entities have purchased tax-exempt obligations in the past and still do because of legal limitations on their investment powers. These limitations, however, are rapidly being removed.

The Inevitable Increase in Interest Rates on Tax Exempts

Higher Costs to Local Governments

It is not possible to say exactly how much tax-exempt bond interest rates would rise with an increase in the relative share of tax exempts in the market. Obviously, it depends for one thing on the levels of general interest rates, which are subject to a great many forces. We can make some progress if we talk about the yield differential between high-grade municipals and high-grade corporate bonds. That differential has hovered around 70 per cent since 1954, i.e., high-grade municipals have in general sold at interest rates about 70 per cent of those on high-grade corporate bonds.

Table 1 presents some estimates of the possible response of the state and local bond rate to future developments. The table covers a range of possibilities respecting the size of state and local borrowing and the role of commercial banks in the market, since they are now the dominant institutional investor in municipal bonds. The future course of that role is of obvious importance—can the banks continue that role, keeping in mind that business loans are their primary function? What happens when they reach the limits of their taxable income, as some are now doing, so that the use of expenses, in fact allocable to tax-exempt issues, against taxable income as now permitted, no longer produces tax savings?[3]

TABLE 1

SOME PROJECTIONS OF SPREAD BETWEEN STATE AND LOCAL (S & L) BOND RATES AND CORPORATE RATES[a]

Rate of Growth of State and Local Bonds Outstanding	Rate on High-Grade S & L Bonds as Percentage of Corporate Rates		Difference in Points Between High-Grade S & L's and Corporates		Rate on High-Grade S & L Bonds	
	With S & L Market Favorable[b]	With S & L Market Unfavorable[b]	With S & L Market Favorable[b]	With S & L Market Unfavorable[b]	With S & L Market Favorable[b]	With S & L Market Unfavorable[b]
GNP rate (6%)[c]	70%	75%	1.8	1.5	4.4%	4.7%
Moderate rate (10%)	75	80	1.5	1.2	4.7	5.0
High rate (20%)	80	87	1.2	0.9	5.0	5.3

[a] Assumes corporate AAA rate at 6.2 per cent. The 70 per cent relationship used as a base point here reflects the typical relationship of recent years.

[b] The favorable-unfavorable distinction involves the role of commercial banks in this market. Rates will be favorable to state and locals if commercial banks remain a large holder. They will be unfavorable if commercial banks hold a smaller share.

[c] This would be a sharp slowdown for state and local government borrowing.

---

[3] For recent discussions that describe some pessimistic possibilities of the role of commercial banks, and hence increased difficulties in marketing state and local debt, see Edward F. Renshaw, "Improving the Market for Municipal Bonds," *Congressional Record*, February 17, 1969, at E1026; Edward F. Renshaw, "Some Alternative Ways to Improve the Market for Municipal Bonds," *Congressional Record*, February 17, 1969, at E1031.

Table 1 shows that the interest rate increase resulting from a high volume of tax-exempt securities could be put as likely to be about one-half point (keeping in mind that it might come to a full point). At current levels of state and local debt issuance ($15 billion gross) this would mean an increased annual interest cost of around $75 million on one year's issues. This annual cost would of course cumulate if the increase persisted for subsequent new issues. With new issues rising at 10 per cent a year, a persistent increase in the state and local bond interest rate of one-half point would increase the annual cost by about $500-$600 million in seven years. This increased cost, remember, does not include the increased debt service itself, which would be something in addition. The increased cost is just the cost of the interest *rate increase* caused by the increased debt. It is the increase in cost caused by going to the well too often.

This is a substantial burden to put on local property taxpayers.

It should be observed that this discussion is based largely on data as of the end of 1968. It does not reflect the high interest rates prevalent in 1969 under the fiscal and monetary efforts to curb the inflationary aspect of the economy. Municipal financing clearly suffered under those efforts. But the discussion is in terms of what "normally" can be expected in the bond markets and therefore does not draw upon the current difficulties.

Higher Tax Savings to Buyers

This is not the full story, however. This process of bidding up the interest rates on tax-exempt bonds means that their benefits will automatically become much larger to those upper-bracket taxpayers who are already buying them and would, of course, continue to do so under such higher interest rates. In addition, the higher interest rates will bring more and more taxpayers into a position where the exemption makes holding state and local bonds attractive even at their lower marginal rates.

Table 2 shows for taxpayers at various effective rate brackets the value of tax exemption for an investment in state and local bonds which yields $100 of exempt interest at current rates. The taxpayer in the 70 per cent tax bracket who earns $100 in exempt interest when the exempt interest rate is 70 per cent of the corporate rate is in effect initially sacrificing $43 of before-tax yield. But he is then rewarded by the larger after-tax benefits. Thus, if he had obtained a taxable bond paying $143 (of which 70 per cent is $100), he would have paid a tax of $100 and would net $43. The purchase of a tax-exempt bond instead thus already produces a saving of $57 for every $100 he receives in exempt interest.

We can now see the increased benefits for taxpayers when the state and local governments go to the well too often. The increased interest cost indicated in Table 1 is an increased payment on bonds that would have been sold anyway to the present buyers. The result, therefore, is an automatic increase in the tax savings enjoyed by the present group of buyers of tax-exempt bonds, which they enjoy because the market discount on the bonds is less than the tax savings the bonds provide. Thus, if the interest rate on exempt bonds rises

TABLE 2

VALUE OF TAX EXEMPTION FOR VARIOUS TAXPAYER SITUATIONS BEFORE AND AFTER RISE IN EXEMPT BOND RATE RELATIVE TO CORPORATE RATE

Marginal Tax Rate	Net Advantage of Tax Exemption on Investment Yielding $100 When Exempt Rate Relative to Corporate Rate Is		
	70%	80%	85%
70%	$57	$71	$78
60	43	57	64
48	26	40	47
30	0	14	21
20	–14	0	6
15	–22	–3	0

to 85 per cent of the corporate bond rate, the net saving of $57 for a taxpayer in the 70 per cent bracket will rise to $78—a gain of 37 per cent.

Looking down Table 2 one can see that as the relative interest rate on state and local bonds rises, taxpayers at lower marginal tax rates come into the position where they would be saving more in taxes from the exemption than they would lose on the interest differential; that is, their tax savings (which is the federal government's revenue loss) would be greater than the savings in interest to the state and local governments. If the state and local rate rises to 85 per cent of the corporate bond rate, even a taxpayer whose marginal tax rate is over 15 per cent would find these bonds a good investment.

In summary, the penalties for excessive reliance on the tax-exempt privilege to finance new programs are substantial. These penalties would be visited upon state and local governments through increasing the interest rate on all the bonds they sell, including the basic school and other bonds that they will have to sell anyway. The result occurs because the advantage of the present tax-exempt privilege of state and local bond interest works in a limited market that can be swamped by overuse of the tax exemption.

At the same time the tax savings to present buyers of bonds will rapidly pyramid and new groups of buyers will be drawn to these tax benefits. This expansion of the tax preference will be coming at a time when the patience of many with existing tax preferences is becoming exhausted—as is shown by the rapid and widespread rise in sentiment for tax reforms to counteract the effect of tax preferences that now permit many taxpayers with high annual incomes to pay little or no federal income taxes. While we observed earlier that interest of all kinds is only a modest component of the income of upper-bracket individuals, nevertheless tax-exempt interest ranks second after capital gains taxation—perhaps third if we knew more about the magnitude of accelerated depreciation on buildings—among the factors enabling high-income taxpayers to reduce their effective rates of tax.[4]

The present exemption for interest on state and local bonds has the general effect of a blanket, no strings attached, federal grant-in-aid to the issuing

[4] *Tax Reform Studies and Proposals, U.S. Treasury Department,* Joint Publication, Committee on Ways and Means, U.S. House of Representatives, and Committee on Finance, U.S. Senate, Washington: Government Printing Office, 1969, p. 83.

governments. It is achieved by giving tax favoritism to high-bracket individuals with conservative investment instincts, to commercial banks, and in lesser degree to some other financial institutions. The state and local governments clearly desire the general effect to continue. Those interested in the federal tax structure deplore the method of achieving this effect because of both the tax favoritism and the inefficiency or wastage involved in resorting to the technique of favoritism, in that more federal tax revenue is lost than the local governments obtain in aid.

The state and local governments carry no brief as such for the federal tax windfalls and the wastage. Up to now, however, they have not seen any other mechanism which can achieve for them the general effect that the tax exemption produces. But the future heavy financial demands on state and local governments will diminish for them the amount of the grant-in-aid that the tax exemption mechanism produces. The restraint on the scope of the market for their bonds that tax exemption involves will cause their interest rates to rise relative to taxable obligations and thus the amount of the grant-in-aid to lessen. At the same time, the tax favoritism perversely is increased.

The inefficiency inherent in the use of the tax exemption mechanism to achieve the grant-in-aid will thus hurt *all* the governments involved. They now have a common interest in finding a better path to the grant-in-aid. We should, therefore, turn to describing some of the alternatives proposed.

Possible New Financing Techniques

Local Taxable Bonds

In a talk on June 13, 1968, before the Municipal Forum of New York I described one possible new financing technique—that of local taxable bonds. I gave the example of a local project—it could be an anti-pollution project, an airport, an urban development project, and so on—as to which federal assistance would be provided not through the traditional initial capital grant but through a system of paying part of the debt service of a bond issue by the locality to meet the cost of the project. The federal share of the debt service—as respects both principal and interest—would be paid periodically over the life of that bond. I then indicated that instead of having the local bond a tax-exempt obligation, there could be used a *local taxable obligation* with two attributes: the federal government would fully guarantee the bond and, in addition, would use the tax revenue gained through the taxable status to pay to the local government an interest subsidy that would bring the interest cost to it down to a level lower than, or at least comparable to, the interest rate on a tax-exempt bond. This interest subsidy would be in addition to the share of the annual debt service provided by the federal government under the particular program.

This alternative of a *local taxable bond* could of course be used in connection with any state or local obligation, and need not be limited to a bond issued in connection with a federally aided project.[5] The federal guarantee for

[5] See remarks of Congressman John W. Byrnes on tax reform, *Congressional Record*, January 30, 1969, at E658-59.

the local bond would be relevant to the latter since the project itself would presumably have to conform to the contours of the particular substantive program under which federal aid was granted. Where such a federally aided project was not present, presumably there would be no federal guarantee of the local bond and no federal share of the debt service as such. But there would be a federal subsidy paid to the local government to cover part of the interest cost so as to make the issuance of the taxable bond worthwhile to the local government. The decision to issue a taxable bond would remain with the local government, and it could always if it preferred—which presumably would be a matter of financial calculation—issue a tax-exempt bond. The purpose for which the bond was issued would here be irrelevant, and the federal government would not be concerned with that aspect.

The mechanics of the local taxable issue and the payment of the federal subsidy would have to be explored. Thus, the federal government could pay annually a stipulated amount, agreed on when the bond was to be issued, such amount being a percentage of the interest. The basic authority for such arrangements would be a federal statute, and it could specify the amount of the interest subsidy or provide guidelines for the federal authorities to follow. Another possibility is a procedure under which the bond would carry two coupons, both taxable, but one for interest to be paid by the local government issuer and the other for interest to be paid by the federal government. Where necessary, steps would have to be taken to revise relevant state and local laws to permit the issuance of taxable obligations at market rates.

The marketing of this new kind of obligation—a local *taxable* issue—would of course involve a whole new dimension in state and local financing. I suppose analysts will differ as to the prospects for such a bond, the degree of time needed to gain wide market acceptance, the marketing patterns that would emerge, the effect of such issues on the market for presently taxable bonds, and so on. But it is difficult to see why the combined expertise of the federal government, state and local governments, and the investment banking profession could not evolve processes and procedures for the successful marketing of these issues.

Use of Centralized Borrowing Power

The interest rates that would obtain on local taxable bonds would probably be similar to those of comparable corporate obligations. While there would be no federal guarantee as such (except on bonds connected with federally aided projects where such a guarantee could be worked out), the promise of the federal government to pay part of the interest should help the issue along. But at any event, the interest rates on local taxable bonds—even those guaranteed by the federal government—would be expected to be higher than the rate at which the federal government can borrow. The smallness of some local issues, the novelty of local taxable bonds, and the other marketing problems involved would support this conclusion. Since the federal government would have to pay a part of the interest cost, perhaps on a percentage basis, it would be concerned in seeking paths to reduce that cost. The state and local governments would have an equal interest in that objective. This has led to the suggestion of alternatives under which the federal borrowing power, or some other form of centralized borrowing, could be utilized in ways that would reduce the interest cost for the funds to be obtained from the investing public with respect to these state and local borrowings.

One suggestion, which I discussed in a talk on September 27, 1968, at the Fifth Municipal Conference of the Investment Bankers Association in New Orleans, would utilize a new central institution called an Urban Development Bank. This approach was the subject of exploration in the latter part of 1968, and President Johnson submitted a proposal for such a bank in 1969. The bank would make long-term development loans and provide technical assistance to state and local governments and their agencies to help meet needs for essential public works and community facilities.[6] It would be governed by a board of directors representing federal, state, and local governments and private investors in the bank. Its funds essentially would be raised from taxable debt obligations sold to the public. While the obligations would not be guaranteed by the United States, the bank would be authorized to issue obligations to the Treasury to insure the financial integrity of the bank. Presumably its public obligations would bear a rate reasonably close to the going rate for federal obligations. In turn the bank would make loans to state and local governments to finance capital expenditures for public works and community facilities at an interest rate not less than two-thirds of the rate at which the bank itself was able to borrow funds. The outstanding obligations of the bank could reach over $20 billion in five years.

Thus, as respects its financing aspects, the bank in effect would be purchasing state and local obligations (while technically tax exempt this would be irrelevant since the obligations would be held by the bank, whose income would itself be exempt) and raising the funds to do so in the private market on a centralized taxable basis. The differential in interest rates, i.e., the subsidy to state and local governments, would be met by the federal government through authorized appropriations to the bank. The funds for this subsidy would come in effect from the income tax revenue derived from taxing the obligations issued by the bank. This process would permit a pooling of the various local government obligations, so that any disadvantages under the local taxable bond approach of issue size, of lack of a ready market in which local taxable bonds could be sold and bought, and of the novelty of such bonds, are all eliminated. The state and local governments would participate directly in the management and control of the bank. Use of the bank would be on a voluntary basis, however—any state or local government could still finance projects directly through its own tax-exempt obligations.

This type of bank is one method by which the efficiencies of centralized

---

[6] S. 409, 91st Cong., 1st Sess., introduced by Senator John Sparkman, *Congressional Record,* January 21, 1969, S583-84. See also testimony of Budget Director Charles J. Zwick, in *The 1969 Economic Report of the President,* Hearings Before the Joint Economic Committee, 91st Cong., 1st Sess., Washington: Government Printing Office, 1969, pp. 114-37.

borrowing and marketing could be achieved, so that the interest cost would be largely comparable to the rate on federal obligations. Another proposal to this end has been suggested by Professors Donald Reeb and Edward F. Renshaw of the State University of New York at Albany.[7] They suggest that the twelve Federal Reserve Banks be authorized to acquire state and local obligations directly, obtaining funds for this purpose by selling some of the federal bonds they now hold. They envisage the banks under this authority as operating in the secondary market and purchasing new issues on a broad basis. As an illustration, they consider a degree of purchase of state and local bonds that would produce a yield differential of 40 per cent in relation to the yield on federal bonds. Assuming the latter rates to be stabilized around 4.5 per cent, about the 1964-1967 average, this would give an average interest cost of 2.7 per cent for state and local bonds as compared with the 3.6 per cent average on high-grade municipals that characterized the 1964-1967 period. Since the Federal Reserve Banks are now paying their surplus earnings to the Treasury, the cost of this subsidy to the state and local governments would be met by the Treasury. But it would in effect be reimbursed by the tax revenues from the taxable federal bonds that would be held by the public in lieu of holding tax-exempt obligations.

Whatever may be the merits of these two approaches to achieving centralized borrowing through taxable issues, with an interest subsidy to the state and local governments, they need not be looked on as alternatives. The bank would be designed to be more than a mechanical financing intermediary, and presumably would also develop technical skills in many phases of community development that would be of assistance to localities. The state and local bond market is large enough to permit various centralized borrowing approaches to operate. Indeed, the widening realization that new financing techniques are needed may well produce further alternatives for consideration.

Remaining Tax-Exempt Obligations

The various financing techniques discussed above are all optional in the sense that they do not preclude the continued direct issuance to the public of local tax-exempt obligations. It could well be, therefore, that a significant volume of exempt obligations would continue to be issued. Since the interest rate would be held down under these financing techniques, the exempt obligations would be attractive only to higher-bracket investors and to banks, where the rate of tax would still make the lower exempt interest rates advantageous. There would also remain for a considerable period the large volume of presently outstanding obligations. Perhaps the use of subsidized local taxable bonds would make the refinancing of the presently outstanding bonds attractive to local governments where that opportunity was available under their terms.

The suggestion for a "minimum income tax" to lessen the tax reduction effect of tax-exempt interest and other tax preferences[8] is here useful in reduc-

---

[7] See various papers by Professors Reeb and Renshaw in *Congressional Record*, February 17, 1969, at E1025-32.

[8] See *Tax Reform Studies and Proposals*, *op. cit.*

ing the tax escape that the continued presence of the exemption would permit. The minimum tax would not, in view of the ability of the state and local governments to use the new financing techniques, affect their ability to obtain funds on new issues. In the case of already outstanding bonds, the reduction in tax benefit would cause some reshuffling of holdings.

Even the minimum tax, however, would leave an advantage to the large volume of outstanding bonds. As time passed those bonds would become relatively more valuable and present holders would receive a windfall gain. This has led in the past to various suggestions that would remove the tax-exempt status on these bonds and provide some compensation to existing holders, such as a credit against tax, to leave them in the same net position as if they had originally bought taxable bonds.[9] A recent suggestion would make the outstanding bonds taxable but with an offer by the federal government to exchange federal bonds at current interest rates for the outstanding local bonds. The holders of the latter while losing a future tax advantage would not suffer a loss of principal.[10] Such approaches as to outstanding bonds of course would also end for the future any option to issue tax-exempt obligations. Also, like the minimum tax, they would involve ultimately a decision by the Supreme Court on the constitutionality of federal income taxation of state and local bond interest. The Department of Justice in 1942[11] stated with confidence that the step would be constitutional, and certainly nothing has happened in the intervening years to cause lawyers to believe that such a prediction would, to say the least, be any less valid today.

At any event, the congressional focus now is on the large volume of new issues that lie ahead, and a solution for those issues plus the minimum tax approach for the remaining issues would, together with inevitable attrition as to outstanding issues, be a very major step forward in meeting the present problems.

Conclusion

In conclusion, we may return to the summary at the outset:

The possible high level of new issues of tax-exempt state and local bonds over the next decade—a level required to meet the huge financing requirements of the vast array of needed social programs—raises very serious problems for both state and local governments and the federal government. The price for the state and local governments in the use of tax-exempt bonds on such a greatly increased basis under those programs will be in very sizable increases in their interest costs. The price for the federal government will be in serious inroads on the equity of its tax system.

---

[9] E.g., Lyle C. Fitch, *Taxing Municipal Bond Income,* Berkeley and Los Angeles: University of California Press, 1950.

[10] Statement of George Meany, President, AFL-CIO, before Ways and Means Committee, on April 1, 1969, in Hearings on Tax Reform.

[11] *Revenue Revision of 1942,* Hearings Before House Ways and Means Committee, 77th Congress, 2d Session, Volume 3, pp. 3106-10 (1942). For a contrary argument, see Statement of Francis B. Burch, Attorney General of Maryland, before the Ways and Means Committee on March 1, 1969, in Hearings on Tax Reform.

Those anxious to preserve the strength of state and local governments and the integrity of the federal tax system should seek to develop new financing techniques that avoid such a high price.

New financing techniques have been offered for consideration. One is the use of local taxable bonds placed directly on the market. The second is a pooling of local obligations through centralized borrowing, either through a new financial institution which would raise its funds in the private market on a taxable basis or through Federal Reserve Bank purchases of local obligations. Both approaches permit the local governments to receive an interest subsidy to offset their departure from the use of the tax exemption privilege. Both approaches also permit that independence of state and local government which is now obtained through the tax exemption privilege, but do so without the tax favoritism, inefficiency, and consequent wastage of funds now associated with the historical solution to one of the problems of our federal system.

It is not enough, in thinking about these financing techniques, to say that they possess some rough edges or will take time to perfect. Such an outlook cannot end the inquiry or militate against moving forward with a new approach, for the present tax-exempt approach with its roots in history rather than logic clearly has serious known weaknesses. Nor can state and local governments seriously claim that tax exemption per se is the guarantor of their independence and vitality. That exemption is a way of supplying federal aid—presently amounting to about [$1.86] billion annually (at a revenue cost of [$2.63] billion)—to those governments through the lower interest rates. The removal of such aid would be a blow. But an even greater blow would be the removal of the $25 billion in grants from the federal government.[12]

The fact that this far greater aid depends on federal legislation has not meant the disappearance of local government. On the contrary, it is generally agreed that the future strength of state and local governments will depend on still larger voluntary grants in a variety of forms from the federal government. Moreover, no one is suggesting that the fiscal aid now obtained by state and local governments through tax exemption be eliminated, and all the new financing techniques seek to provide comparable aid through interest subsidies. Even here in recognition of the desire to maintain as much freedom of decision as possible at the local level—whether in this matter or in other matters where federal aid is involved—the new techniques suggested keep open the option to issue tax-exempt obligations.

Certainly state and local governments presenting claims—claims which are valid and compelling if we intend to solve our problems of urban existence—for generous federal assistance to meet their operating and capital needs should join in seeking modern financing techniques rather than rigidly cling to the inefficiences, wastages, and tax favoritism implicit in the historical technique of tax exemption.

---

[12] Estimate for fiscal 1970; see testimony of Budget Director Charles J. Zwick, *op. cit.*, p. 108.

In sum, there are paths to be explored by those who are willing to face this serious problem in a constructive way. That very exploration can in turn open up still other avenues for consideration. The proper federal role and the proper state and local government role in the necessary federal-state-local partnership required to meet the fast growing credit demand for new public facilities and social projects can thus be structured in the light of our pressing present needs.

For we are at a crucial crossroads. One way, a blind following of the past, could financially weaken state and local governments and thereby weaken the independence of these governments though outwardly preserving the trappings of independence. The other way, utilizing our knowledge of newly developed credit tools and the new financial institutions to operate them, can preserve and advance that independence.

C. Imputed Income

Whether imputed income, particularly from owner-occupied housing, should be taxed is one of the perennial classics of tax policy. As is pointed out by Richard Goode in the piece that follows, what is at issue is a basic question of equity as between owners and renters. The recommendation of Mr. Goode for taxing imputed income should be compared with that of the Canadian Royal Commission on Taxation, p. 89, supra. Consider also *Helvering* v. *Independent Life Ins. Co.*, 292 U.S. 371 (1934), which suggests that the rental value of an owner-occupied building is not "income" within the meaning of that term in the Sixteenth Amendment.

GOODE, THE INDIVIDUAL INCOME TAX 120–29 (1964) *

A person who resides in his own house or apartment obtains an income in the form of consumer services. This imputed return is classified as personal income in national income and product accounts, and individuals often recognize that homeownership is an alternative to other income-yielding investments.[25]

Homeowners are often puzzled by economists' assertions that they derive an income from their houses; these owners look on their houses as a source of expense rather than income. They are

[25] For a more detailed treatment, see my paper "Imputed Rent of Owner-Occupied Dwellings Under the Income Tax," *Journal of Finance*, Vol. 15 (December 1960), pp. 504-30 (Brookings Institution Reprint No. 50, 1961).

* © 1964 by The Brookings Institution. Reproduced with permission.

right in insisting that homeownership entails expenses, but they neglect that part of their shelter costs are covered by the imputed return on their equity. A homeowner is an investor who takes his return in the form of services. If he wishes to do so, he can convert his imputed return to a cash return by moving and letting his house.

Imputed rent of owner-occupied dwellings is taxable in a number of countries, but is not included in AGI in the United States. The United Kingdom taxed imputed rent from the beginning of the income tax early in the nineteenth century but allowed the provision to become rather ineffective after World War II, owing to obsolete assessments, and dropped it in 1963.[26]

Under a net income tax, the item to be included in income would be imputed net rent, defined as gross rental value minus necessary expenses of ownership. The expenses consist of interest on mortgage debt, property taxes, depreciation, repairs and maintenance, and casualty insurance. Homeowners may now deduct interest and taxes, even though imputed rent is not included in AGI. The taxation of imputed net rent, therefore, would involve an addition to taxable income equal to gross rent minus expenses other than interest and taxes. This increase in the tax base would equal the sum of imputed net rent and the personal deductions now allowed for mortgage interest and property taxes on owner-occupied dwellings. Merely to increase the tax base by the amount of net rent would imply double deductions for interest and property taxes, one set in the form of the personal deductions now granted and a second set in the computation of net rent.

Estimates of imputed net rent, mortgage interest, and property taxes in selected years appear in Table 6. These items have been growing rapidly. In the 1950's, the annual rate of increase of the total was 9.7 percent, while the growth rate for total personal consumption was 5.3 percent.

[26] In April 1962, the then Chancellor of the Exchequer, Selwyn Lloyd, had announced the intention of making the change, mentioning the great increase in tax that would occur when pending revaluations of properties were completed and terming imputed rent "notional income." *The Economist* (London) characterized Mr. Lloyd's statement as "near double talk" (April 14, 1962, p. 168). In 1955, the Royal Commission on the Taxation of Profits and Income had supported the continued taxation of imputed rent. See its *Final Report,* Cmd. 9474 (London, 1955), pp. 249-51.

TABLE 6. Net Rent, Mortgage Interest, and Property Taxes on Owner-Occupied Dwellings, 1929, 1940, 1950, and 1960[a]

(In billions of dollars)

Item	1929	1940	1950	1960
Net rent	2.7	1.5	3.8	6.8
Mortgage interest	1.0	0.7	1.7	6.6
Property taxes	1.0	0.9	2.3	5.9
Total	4.7	3.1	7.8	19.3

Sources: Net rent and property taxes, estimates of Office of Business Economics, U.S. Department of Commerce, *National Income* (1954), pp. 214-15; *U.S. National Income and Output* (1958), p. 229; *Survey of Current Business*, July 1963, p. 39. Mortgage interest, estimates based on H. D. Osborne, "Rental Income and Outlay in the United States, 1929-52," *Survey of Current Business*, June 1953, p. 22; materials in Department of Commerce files; and my supplementary estimates.

[a] Includes farm and nonfarm dwellings.

The omission of imputed net rent from AGI and the personal deductions for mortgage interest and property taxes discriminate in favor of homeowners compared with renters and with other investors. Homeowners obtain a tax-free return on their investment and at the same time are allowed to deduct important items of housing costs that tenants also pay as part of their contract rent but without obtaining a tax deduction.

The size of the discrimination is substantial. In recent years, net rent, mortgage interest, and property taxes have amounted to about two-thirds of the gross rental value of owner-occupied dwellings. Under the 1954-63 tax rates, the typical income tax payer who was a homeowner realized federal income tax savings which offset about 15 percent of his annual housing costs. Under the rates that will be effective in 1965, the saving will be about 12 percent. The saving rises with income and tax rates. At the $50,000 income level, it will equal almost one-third of housing costs in 1965.[27]

My estimates of the distribution of imputed net rent, mortgage interest, and property taxes among income classes in 1958 are

[27] The weighted average marginal rate under the 1954-63 schedule was approximately 23 percent on taxable income and is estimated at 18.5 percent under the 1965 schedule. For a married couple with $50,000 of AGI and the amount of personal deductions characteristic of that income level, the marginal rate will be about 48 percent under the 1965 schedule. The figures given in the text were obtained by multiplying 67 percent (the excluded and deducted portion of average shelter costs of owner-occupants) by the marginal tax rates.

TABLE 7. Net Rent, Mortgage Interest, and Property Taxes on Owner-Occupied Nonfarm Dwellings, by Income Classes, 1958[a]

Family Money Income	Percentage Distribution			Percent of Money Income[b]	
	Net Rent	Interest and Taxes	Net Rent, Interest, and Taxes	Net Rent	Interest and Taxes
Under $2,000	12	4	7	7	4
$2,000–$2,999	8	4	5	3	2
3,000– 3,999	9	5	7	3	3
4,000– 4,999	9	8	8	2	3
5,000– 5,999	11	14	13	2	4
6,000– 7,499	13	17	15	2	4
7,500– 9,999	16	24	21	2	4
10,000 and over	23	24	24	2	3
All classes	100	100	100	2	3

[a] Derived from data from 1959 Survey of Consumer Finances and national income estimates. For details see Richard Goode, "Imputed Rent of Owner-Occupied Dwellings Under the Income Tax," *Journal of Finance*, Vol. 15 (December 1960), pp. 526-30 (Brookings Institution Reprint No. 50, 1961).

[b] Percent of money income of all nonfarm families in income class.

summarized in Table 7. Data are not available for later years. These estimates indicate that for families with money incomes above $2,000, imputed net rent plus mortgage interest and property taxes equaled about 5 to 6 percent of money income in each income class. If a breakdown were available above the $10,000 income level, perhaps the impression of rough proportionality would not be confirmed. The estimates for the lowest income class may be unrepresentative, because this class probably includes a high proportion of persons whose income is temporarily low and of retired persons who bought their houses when their money income was higher.[28]

If imputed net rent had been taxable in 1958, I estimate that the federal income tax liability of owner-occupants of nonfarm dwellings would have been increased by roughly $3.2 billion, including $1.2 billion of tax on imputed net rent proper and $2.0 billion of tax from eliminating the personal deductions for mort-

[28] Margaret G. Reid finds statistical evidence that housing expenditures rise about 1.5 to 2.0 times as fast as normal income, which she defines as income exclusive of positive or negative transitory items. See *Housing and Income* (Chicago: University of Chicago Press, 1962), p. 376 *et passim*.

gage interest and property taxes on the dwellings. The corresponding estimates for 1960 are about $3.8 billion, $1.2 billion, and $2.6 billion.[29] With allowance for both the reduction in tax rates provided by the Revenue Act of 1964 and the continued growth of the exclusion and deductions, the effect on tax liability may be about the same in the mid-1960's as in 1960. (Information is not available on owner-occupied farm dwellings; however, these units account for only about 5 percent of total imputed rent and inclusion of them would not appreciably raise the estimates.)

The information on imputed net rent in Table 7 suggests that the ending of the exclusion and associated deductions would not greatly alter the progressivity of the income tax. This finding is at variance with the common opinion that the ratio of rental value to income diminishes as income rises. As noted above, the findings might be modified if the group with incomes above $10,000 could be subdivided.

The tax saving due to the exclusion and deductions may be viewed as a reduction in prices of housing services. The influence on consumption of housing services depends on the elasticity of demand with respect to price. The available evidence suggests that price elasticity is on the order of -1,[30] which means that a small reduction in price will be accompanied by an increase of consumption in the same proportion, leaving total expenditures for housing services unchanged. If this is correct, the income tax advantages enjoyed by homeowners were responsible for additional consumption of housing services of about $3.2 billion in 1958 and about $3.8 billion in 1960, or about 8½ to 9 percent of the total housing consumption of homeowners and tenants.[31]

The above estimates relate to aggregates or averages. Pre-

[29] For the derivation of the 1958 estimates, see my paper in the *Journal of Finance*, Vol. 15, pp. 527-30. The 1960 estimates were derived by applying the 1958 weighted average marginal rates for imputed net rent, for property taxes, and for mortgage interest separately to the 1960 totals for these items, which were obtained in the same manner as the 1958 totals. The estimates do not allow for the use of the standard deduction by some homeowners; however, the standard deduction presumably would be reduced if itemized deductions were curtailed.

[30] Richard F. Muth, "The Demand for Non-Farm Housing," in *The Demand for Durable Goods*, Arnold C. Harberger, ed. (Chicago: University of Chicago Press, 1960), pp. 29-96; Reid, *Housing and Income*, p. 381.

[31] Derived from *Survey of Current Business*, July 1963, p. 20.

sumably the effect would be greater for higher-priced units of the kind which are likely to be occupied by persons who gain most from the exclusion and personal deductions.

Although its influence cannot be isolated, the favorable income tax treatment accorded to homeowners has probably been one of the factors responsible for the rapid increase in consumer expenditures for housing in the postwar period. In current prices, housing expenditures (space rental value of tenant-occupied and owner-occupied dwellings) were still a smaller fraction of total personal consumption in 1960 than in 1929 and prior years, but, in constant prices, housing expenditures represent a much larger share of total consumption than in 1929. Estimates of housing expenditures as percentages of total private consumption are shown in the accompanying table.[32] The constant price estimates are suspect,

Year	*Current Prices*	*Constant (1954) Prices*
1909	19.3%	. . .
1919	13.3	. . .
1929	14.4	10.0%
1950	10.9	11.4
1960	12.8	12.7

in view of the surprisingly small increase shown by the implicit price deflator for housing expenditures from 1929 to 1960.[33]

The income tax probably has more influence on the choice between homeowning and renting than on the total amount of housing services consumed. The price differential that will induce a shift from renting to owning is doubtless much smaller than that required to divert expenditure from other goods and services to

[32] The estimates for 1909 and 1919 are from J. Frederick Dewhurst and Associates, *America's Needs and Resources* (New York: Twentieth Century Fund, 1955), p. 206; the figures for later years are derived from estimates of the Office of Business Economics, U.S. Department of Commerce: *U.S. Income and Output* (1958) and *Survey of Current Business*, July 1963. The constant-price estimate given for 1929 (*U.S. Income and Output*, p. 5) is in 1957 prices.

[33] The increase in the OBE implicit price deflator from 1929 to 1960 is only about 25 percent for housing expenditures but is 177 percent for residential nonfarm construction (*U.S. Income and Output*, pp. 5, 220-21, 228, and *Survey of Current Business*, July 1963).

housing. There has been a sharp increase in homeownership in the postwar years. In 1960, 62 percent of all dwelling units were owner-occupied, compared with 44 percent in 1940.[34] Although the 1940 ratio may have been abnormally low owing to the great depression, a trend toward homeownership appears.

The preferential treatment of investment in owner-occupied dwellings greatly increases the attractiveness of homeownership relative to other investment. In 1958, the estimated net rate of return on owners' equity in nonfarm owner-occupied dwellings was only about 2.7 percent but, with allowance for the federal income tax saving attributable to the exclusion of imputed net rent from taxable income and the personal deductions for mortgage interest and property taxes, the rate of return was equivalent to a taxable yield of 4.1 percent. The average yield on common stocks was 4.0 percent in 1958.[35]

Nontax factors must have been important in the postwar growth of homeownership. Among these are the movement of population to the suburbs, the rise in real income, and the gains realized by debtors in a period of inflation.

There is no evidence that the present income tax treatment of owner-occupied houses was deliberately devised to promote housing and homeownership. The personal deductions for interest and tax payments are general allowances. Nor does the omission of imputed rent indicate special concern for housing, since other imputed income is also omitted.

In retrospect, however, the present treatment has been sup-

[34] U.S. Bureau of the Census, *Statistical Abstract of the United States, 1962,* p. 758.

[35] Based on: (1) estimates of net rent of owner-occupied dwellings by Office of Business Economics, U.S. Department of Commerce, *Survey of Current Business,* July 1962, p. 34 (assuming that nonfarm units accounted for 95 percent of the total); (2) my estimates of federal income tax saving; (3) estimates of owners' equity in owner-occupied units in one-to-four-family nonfarm houses (average of beginning and end of year) derived from Raymond W. Goldsmith and Robert E. Lipsey, *Studies in the National Balance Sheet of the United States* (Princeton, N.J.: Princeton University Press for National Bureau of Economic Research, 1963), Vol. I, pp. 261, 400; and (4) dividend yield of common stocks included in Standard & Poor's index (*Economic Report of the President, January 1964,* p 288). In calculating item 3, I allocated mortgages on owner-occupied nonfarm houses between owner-occupied units and rental units in these structures in proportion to the respective values of the two kinds of unit.

ported as a means of fostering homeownership and the civic virtues associated with it. While homeownership does seem to enjoy wide public esteem, the nature of the social advantages claimed for it is somewhat vague. A possible disadvantage is that homeownership decreases mobility. Furthermore, if housing is like most other industries, landlords, being specialists, can provide services at lower cost than owner-occupants.

Like other special provisions, the treatment of imputed rent involves a conflict between the objective of encouraging a particular kind of behavior and the goal of equal taxation. And, as always, it is reasonable to ask whether the tax provision is more effective, relative to cost, than other governmental programs designed to accomplish the same social purpose. The present provisions afford assistance for housing and homeownership that varies directly with the family's income and marginal tax rate, whereas encouragement and assistance may be more needed in low-income and middle-income brackets than at the higher income levels. The loss of tax revenue due to the exclusion of imputed net rent and the personal deductions for mortgage interest and property taxes is large relative to the federal government's expenditures for housing and community development, including urban renewal, public housing, and the net cost of FHA mortgage insurance. For example, the revenue loss in the calendar year 1958 was approximately sixteen times the average annual federal expenditures for housing and community development in the fiscal years 1955 through 1959.[36] There seems to have been no systematic comparison of the merits of aiding housing and homeownership by the present tax provisions and by larger government expenditures.

When the federal, state, and local tax systems are considered simultaneously, it may seem that property tax payments outweigh the income tax advantages of housing. In 1960, for example, property taxes on owner-occupied dwellings amounted to $5.9 billion, compared with about $3.8 billion of federal income tax reduction attributable to the exclusion of imputed net rent and the associated personal deductions. Property taxes on owner-occupied dwellings would have amounted to only about $0.6 bil-

[36] *Budget of the United States Government for the Fiscal Year Ending June 30, 1964*, p. 427.

lion if they had been no higher in relation to gross rental value than the ratio of property taxes to gross national product originating in other industries.[37] The federal tax preference for owner-occupied dwellings can be defended on the ground that it merely offsets differential property taxation at the local level. A weakness of this argument is that it does not meet the point that the present treatment discriminates against renters compared with homeowners. Renters presumably have to bear much of the burden of the property tax on rental houses and apartments but obtain no federal income tax concession. The property tax, moreover, is partly a payment for services that specially benefit local residents and property owners; the criterion of neutrality derived by computing the ratio of tax to income originating is inappropriate.

The only method of eliminating the discrimination between homeowners and renters and of equalizing the return from owner-occupied dwellings and other investments would be to require that the net rental value of owner-occupied dwellings be included in adjusted gross income for tax purposes. Owing to the novelty of this solution in the United States and the undoubted difficulties of administration and compliance, the suggestion has been made that the discrimination between owners and tenants be attacked either by disallowing personal deductions for mortgage interest and property taxes or by allowing tenants to deduct rental payments. Inasmuch as the personal deductions for mortgage interest and property taxes on owner-occupied houses are considerably larger than the estimated net rent of these dwellings, the elimination of personal deductions associated with homeownership would accomplish a substantial part of the objective of taxation of imputed net rent. The disallowance, nevertheless, would be an incomplete solution. The elimination of the interest deduction, for

[37] In 1960, total property taxes other than those on owner-occupied dwellings were $10.5 billion, and GNP minus the $28.2 billion estimated rental value of owner-occupied farm and nonfarm dwellings was $474.4 billion. Applying the ratio 10.5/474.4 to the rental value of owner-occupied dwellings yields the figure of $0.6 billion. Estimates of GNP, rental value, and property tax accruals are from *Survey of Current Business,* July 1963. I assumed that the rental value of owner-occupied farmhouses equaled 74 percent of the rental value of all farm dwellings; according to Census data, 74 percent of the number of occupied farm housing units were owner-occupied in 1960 (*Statistical Abstract, 1962,* p. 758).

example, would have no effect on persons who own their dwellings free of mortgage debt and hence would do nothing to reduce the discrimination between this group and tenants. Among home-owners, denial of the interest deduction would remove a difference in the taxable income of those with and without mortgages which corresponds to a difference in economic income. From the stand-point of equity, the case for eliminating the property tax deduction is stronger (see Chapter VII).

Under the Civil War income tax in the United States, tenants were allowed to deduct rental payments on their residences in computing taxable income. If this precedent were followed, the present discrimination against renters would be replaced by a discrimination in their favor, since the sum of the deductions and exclusion now allowed owner-occupants is less than gross rent. In the aggregate, rough equality could be achieved by allowing a deduction equal to about two-thirds of rental payments. The deduction, however, would increase the favoritism for housing consumption over other goods and services and would further narrow the tax base.

The administrative problems in taxing imputed net rent, which would be substantial, would turn mainly on the establishment of rental value, by direct estimation or by taking a conventional percentage of capital value or owner's equity. The valuation difficulties would not be novel, since appraisals are frequently made for mortgage loans and property tax assessments. However, higher standards of accuracy have customarily been demanded in the measurement of taxable income than in the establishment of values for the other purposes. Property tax assessments have been poor in many areas but fairly good in other places. Federal administrators could derive assistance from assessment records of governmental units with good administrations, whereas in other areas the availability of federal income tax valuation data might help improve local property tax assessments.

The gains in tax equity, economic efficiency, and federal revenue seem to be great enough to justify the effort that would be required to take account of imputed net rent in the assessment of the individual income tax. This tax reform merits serious consideration.

D. Fellowships and Educational Expenses

The three excerpts that follow deal with various aspects of the tax consequences of educational expenses and receipts. How do they interrelate? Which represents the best solution to the subject? Section 917 of H.R. 13270 passed the Senate as part of the Tax Reform Act of 1969, but was rejected in conference. With these three proposals, compare the suggestion of a panel of the President's Science Advisory Committee that the government set up an "educational opportunity bank" from which any student could borrow sufficient funds to finance his college (and conceivably also his graduate) education. The loan would be repaid as a percentage of post-education income (e. g., 1% of gross income over a 30-year period for each $3000 borrowed); to protect students who attained an exceptionally high income, there would be an option to repay the full balance due, with 6% interest. See New York Times, Sept. 8, 1967, p. 1. Compare also the proposal of the Canadian Royal Commission on Taxation (Carter Commission), p. 422, n. 176, infra.

GOODE, THE INDIVIDUAL INCOME TAX 82–93 (1964) *

Educational Expenditures

Expenditures for education that increases earning capacity or that is intended to do so are a strategically important cost of earning income but are deductible to only a limited extent.[5] Those who invest in themselves are discriminated against compared with persons who have spent little in preparation for their occupations and investors in physical assets. The tax provisions are paradoxical at a time when the country is becoming increasingly conscious of the

[5] This section is based on my paper "Educational Expenditures and the Income Tax," in *Economics of Higher Education,* Selma J. Mushkin, ed. (U. S. Department of Health, Education, and Welfare, Office of Education, Bulletin 1962, No. 5; Brookings Institution Reprint No. 64, 1962). For a general treatment of economic aspects of education, see Theodore W. Schultz, *The Economic Value of Education* (New York: Columbia University Press, 1963).

* © 1964 by The Brookings Institution. Reproduced with permission.

need for highly trained persons and of the contribution of education to economic progress.[6]

Present Regulations

Treasury regulations[7] are highly restrictive. * * *

Unsatisfactory as the regulations may seem, the difficulties of devising better rules should not be underestimated. In many other countries, the tax treatment of educational expenses is less liberal than in the United States; however, university students often pay little or no tuition and, in certain European countries at least, may receive subsidies to cover living expenses. In Canada, students in full-time attendance at a university or other post-secondary educational institution are allowed to deduct tuition fees in computing taxable income; the deduction may be taken even when the fees are paid by parents or others.[9]

Possible Revisions

By analogy with the treatment of investment in physical capital, it seems that persons who make expenditures for education that increases their earning power, or that is intended to do so, should be permitted to capitalize these outlays and write them off against taxable income through depreciation or amortization allowances. Income-producing educational expenditures are investments with a limited life and, if it is feasible, they should be given the same tax treatment as other investments. Failure to allow tax-free recovery of educational outlays means that the income tax falls in part on the return of capital rather than on net income.

In order to bring out significant issues, I shall attempt to give the broad outlines of a suitable plan. The suggestions are intended

[6] Edward F. Denison estimates that increased education was responsible for 23 percent of the growth of real national income in 1929-57 and 42 percent of the growth of real national income per person employed in that period. See *The Sources of Economic Growth in the United States and the Alternatives Before Us,* Supplementary Paper No. 13 (New York: Committee for Economic Development, 1962), p. 73.

[7] Treasury Regulations, sec. 1.162–5.

[9] CCH Canadian, Ltd., *Canadian Master Tax Guide,* 18th ed. (Don Mills, Ont., 1963), para. 505a. In his budget speech in March 1964, the Minister of Finance proposed that the deduction be allowed also for part-time students and for tuition fees for secondary education. See *House of Commons Debates,* 26 Parliament 2 sess., Vol. 109 (1964), p. 981.

to serve as a basis for discussion rather than as recommendations for immediate legislation. The plan, in brief, is that part of the personal costs of college education and professional, technical, and vocational education should be capitalized and written off against the student's future earned income over a period of ten to twenty years or more. Minor costs of part-time study would be currently deducted. Provisions limiting deductions to expenses relating to the taxpayer's current position would be dropped.

If the amortization of educational expenditures is justified as a refinement in the definition of income, the deductions should be taken against the income attributable to the education. The deduction should be taken by the student, rather than his parents, even when the latter pay the educational expenses. Expenditures by parents, relatives, or friends may be considered as gifts to the student. He would be allowed to recover free of income tax the value of these gifts just as he can now write off against income the cost of a depreciable asset acquired as a gift. The privilege of writing off the value of gifts in the form of education probably should not extend to scholarships and other aid received from educational institutions, governments, corporations, or other organized bodies.

The personal costs of education are far less than total costs because of heavy expenditures by governments and nonprofit institutions. Personal costs are those met by students, parents, and other private individuals. They include (1) money outlays for tuition and fees, books and supplies, and travel; (2) any additional living expenses of the student; and (3) earnings forgone while studying. Forgone earnings are by far the largest component of the costs of college and graduate education, and they constitute an important part of high school costs. This part of costs is already excluded from the tax base, and no special deduction is necessary or appropriate. Although living expenses above those that would be incurred by a person who was not a student should be deductible, it would be difficult to distinguish these additional expenses from ordinary living costs; therefore, as a practical matter, no allowance is suggested for additional living expenses. The costs to be capitalized and amortized would be those listed under item 1 above.

In principle, expenditures for education should be classified as costs of earning income when incurred for that purpose, regardless of whether they could clearly be shown to result in additional income. The taxpayer's intention is the dominant factor governing the distinction between other "ordinary and necessary" business and professional expenses and personal expenses. Mixed motives are especially common, however, with respect to education, and there is no body of accounting and administrative rules to distinguish one kind of educational outlay from another.

As a practical possibility, the current deduction or amortization of educational expenditures might be allowed with respect to: (1) any courses creditable toward a degree at an accredited college or university, regardless of whether a degree is earned; (2) vocational training at a recognized trade school, business college, or similar institution; and (3) a supplementary, continuation, or refresher course of a predominantly professional or vocational nature taken at a recognized or accredited institution. Part-time studies and correspondence courses as well as full-time resident study should be eligible. Expenditures for ordinary high school studies and elementary school would be classified as personal expenses rather than costs of earning income.

As regards college and university studies, this plan would err on the side of liberality, because it would cover some educational expenditures that are predominantly consumption, as judged by presumed motivation or apparent influence on income. Most college and university education, however, seems to add to earning capacity, and it is difficult to rule out the possibility of economic motivation in connection with any part of it. The rate of private monetary return on total private costs of college education appears to be high—about 12½ percent net of income tax in 1940 and 10 percent in 1950, according to Becker's estimates.[10] If a large fraction of college costs were classified as consumption expenditures, the calculated rate of return on the remaining outlays would be high indeed. The imperfection due to a liberal allowance for college costs seems less objectionable than the present practice of permitting

[10] Gary S. Becker, "Underinvestment in College Education?" *American Economic Review,* Vol. 50, Papers and Proceedings (May 1960), pp. 346-54. Becker's estimates are for urban white males. His figures on costs include forgone earnings, and returns are adjusted for differential ability. The decline in the rate of return between 1940 and 1950 is due almost entirely to higher income tax rates.

virtually none of these expenditures to be charged against taxable income.

The diversity of trade schools, business colleges, and similar institutions and the absence of a comprehensive accrediting system for them would complicate the application of administrative checks to assure that the expenses of study at these institutions were legitimate educational expenditures. A difficulty in connection with supplementary training and continuation or refresher courses would be to identify vocational courses. Many extension courses, evening classes, and correspondence courses are almost entirely consumption, dealing with subjects such as hobbies, arts and crafts, current events, and music appreciation. Courses cannot always be distinguished on the basis of their content. A music course, for example, may be vocational training for one person but avocational for another. It seems that the best rule would be to allow current deductions or amortization charges only for expenses relating to education which the taxpayer represents as being primarily vocational or professional and which the authorities consider reasonably related to his occupation or occupational plans. This standard would be harder to apply than the present rule respecting education but little if any more difficult than the rules on a number of other deductions. The amounts involved may be smaller and many may feel that it is better public policy to be liberal with respect to educational expenses than with respect to some of the items now deductible.

The suggestion that no income tax allowance be made for ordinary high school education is debatable. There is considerable overlap between high school courses and the training offered by trade schools and business colleges, on the one hand, and by liberal arts colleges, on the other. For pupils in public high schools, however, the amount that could be written off would be small even if the plan were extended to them. Since most young people now go to high school, the principal effect of an income tax allowance for the personal costs of secondary education would be to encourage attendance at private schools.

It would seem reasonable to limit the deductions or amortization charges to taxable earned income, without insisting that a direct link be shown between the education and the taxpayer's occupation. Although education may make one a better investor, the relation between property income and education is tenuous. If educational expenditures could be written off against property income, persons with inherited wealth might gain an undue advantage. Even with the earned-income limitation, the applicable marginal tax rate, and hence the value of the deduction, would be influenced by the amount of property income received.

The requirement that deductions or amortization charges be taken only against taxable earned income would disqualify housewives when they were not working outside the home.[11] This would not be as unfair as it may seem. Although a housewife's services have economic value and her contribution to the family's economic welfare is enhanced by her education, the value of her services does not enter into taxable income. Hence denial of a writeoff for educational costs that qualify the housewife to perform her services at home more effectively cannot be regarded as discriminatory in the same way as failure to take account of costs of earning a taxable income.

By analogy with physical assets, educational expenditures should be capitalized and written off against taxable income over the period in which they contribute to earnings, ordinarily the whole working life of the person. This approach, however, might be cumbersome for major expenditures and ridiculous for small items. A practical procedure would be to allow persons incurring large educational expenses to capitalize them and amortize them over a fixed period of say ten or twenty years, or the period ending at age sixty-five if that is shorter. Students could be permitted to begin amortization immediately or to postpone it until they are established in their occupations. Taxpayers incurring minor educational expenses might be given the option of capitalizing their outlays or deducting them currently.

Persons who become totally and permanently disabled and the estates of those who die before completing the amortization of their educational expenses might appropriately be allowed to deduct the unamortized balance in the last taxable year and be granted a carryback of net loss and refund of prior-year taxes if the deduction reduced the last-year's income below zero. Similar treatment might

[11] The attribution to a wife of part of the earnings of her husband under a state community property law should be disregarded in determining qualification for the deduction.

be urged for women who withdraw from the labor force after marriage, but this would be questionable since many of these women later resume outside employment.

Consequences of Revised Treatment

Estimated expenditures by college and university students for tuition and fees, books and supplies, and travel amounted to $1.6 billion in 1959-60, almost twice the estimated total in 1953-54 (Table 2). Comparable information is not available concerning trade schools, correspondence schools, and other institutions offering courses that would give rise to amortizable or deductible expenditures.

TABLE 2. Selected Expenditures of College and University Students, 1953-54 to 1959-60[a]

(In millions of dollars)

Item	Academic Years			
	1953–54	1955–56	1957–58	1959–60
Tuition and fees	508	667	873	1,075
Books and supplies	129	152	179	214
Travel[b]	190	219	260	313
Total	827	1,038	1,312	1,602

[a] Estimates for academic years 1953-54, 1955-56, and 1957-58 from Richard Goode, "Educational Expenditures and the Income Tax," in *Economics of Higher Education*, Selma J. Mushkin, ed. (U.S. Department of Health, Education, and Welfare, Office of Education, Bulletin 1962, No. 5; Brookings Institution Reprint No. 64, 1962), p. 294, with the figure for 1957-58 slightly revised; 1959-60 estimate made in the same way as the estimates for earlier years.

[b] Travel between home and a college or university located in another place; excludes local travel between college address and campus and "other" travel.

On the basis of assumptions that seem to me to be reasonable,[12] I estimate that, if the 1959-60 expenditures shown in Table 2 had been currently deductible or amortizable, the ultimate revenue loss would have been about $320 million. This loss would occur only over a period of ten or twenty years if the suggestions made above concerning amortization were adopted. After introduction of the

[12] That 90 percent of eligible expenditures would be deducted and that the average marginal tax rate of those claiming the deductions would be 22 percent; see my paper in *Economics of Higher Education*, pp. 293-95 for an estimate for an earlier year and lower tax rates.

plan, the annual revenue loss would increase year by year as successive groups began to claim deductions or amortization allowances for expenditures made in later years. If students' expenditures remained constant at the 1959-60 level, the annual revenue loss would stabilize at approximately $320 million after ten or twenty years. Educational expenditures, however, can be expected to increase rapidly with the growth of enrollment and with probable increases in tuition charges. On the basis of projected increases in enrollment and tuition charges, but assuming no change in prices of other items, amortizable or deductible expenditures made in 1969-70 may be placed at $3.1 billion or more.[13] The ultimate revenue loss with respect to that year might amount to $0.6 billion, spread over one or two decades. These estimates make no allowance for an increase in taxable income due to a stimulus to education provided by tax revision.

Regardless of its merits as a refinement of income measurement, adoption of a plan for amortization of educational expenditures would not be likely to have a great influence on the total investment in education and on the choice between occupations requiring different amounts of such investment. The role of economic calculations in educational and occupational choices is uncertain, and the tax benefits of an amortization plan would equal only a small proportion of the total personal costs of college and university education. Forgone earnings of college and university students, which are a part of personal costs but which would not be amortizable, are much larger in the aggregate than expenditures for items which might properly be subject to amortization (tuition and fees, books and supplies, and travel). In academic years 1955-56, 1957-58, and 1959-60, the amortizable items accounted for only about 15 to 17 percent of estimated total personal costs of college and university education, exclusive of any additional living expenses of students; the remaining 83 to 85 percent of personal costs consisted of forgone earnings.[14]

[13] For the derivation of the projection, see *ibid.*, p. 294.

[14] See estimates of expenditures for tuition and fees, books and supplies, and travel, Table 2. Theodore W. Schultz estimates forgone earnings of college and university students at $5,821 million in 1955-56 ("Capital Formation by Education," *Journal of Political Economy*, Vol. 68 [December 1960], p. 580). Applying Schultz's method, I estimate forgone earnings at $6,328 million in 1957-58 and $7,939 million in 1959-60. My estimates, however, rely on the Department of

On the assumption of a marginal tax rate of 20 to 25 percent, it appears that the tax saving attributable to amortization of educational expenditures would have equaled only about 3 to 4 percent of total personal costs of college and university education under conditions prevailing recently. This figure should be discounted because of the distribution of the tax saving over a period of years. An item as small as this can hardly be a strong influence on the amount of educational expenditures or on occupational choice.

The tax benefits from amortization would not represent a major fraction of personal costs of even the most expensive kinds of education. Although students' outlays for tuition and fees and other expenses at certain prestige colleges and at professional schools of private universities are much larger than average expenditures for all colleges and university students, forgone earnings are still the largest item of personal education costs.[15]

The most important incentive effects of the amortization plan might be a contribution toward overcoming reluctance to lend and to borrow for educational purposes. With better credit facilities and the amortization plan, much could be said for tuition charges high enough to cover the full marginal costs of instruction in vocational or professional courses, especially in fields such as medicine, where educational costs and earnings are much above the average.[16]

Objections Considered

Two kinds of objection can be raised against the amortization plan—one relating to its claim to be a refinement of the income measure and the other to its efficiency as an aid to education. The first, and more weighty, objection is that part of the educational expenses that would be deductible or amortizable are really consumption rather than costs of earning income. Although this is undoubtedly true, it is also true that part of the expenses are costs.

Labor figure for unemployment rather than on the series compiled by Clarence D. Long, which Schultz uses for 1955-56.

[15] See, for example, my estimates of the cost of medical education, in *Economics of Higher Education,* p. 298.

[16] Milton Friedman, "The Role of Government in Education," in *Economics and the Public Interest,* Robert A. Solo, ed. (New Brunswick, N.J.: Rutgers University Press, 1955), pp. 123-44; William Vickrey, "A Proposal for Student Loans," in *Economics of Higher Education,* pp. 268-80.

I know of no evidence that the consumption component is greater than the cost element, and I believe that it is good social policy to resolve doubts in favor of more liberal writeoffs.

A different kind of objection is that the amortization plan would offer less effective help to education than an immediate deduction for parents of students, as provided in many bills that have been introduced in Congress. However, a deduction for parents would be quite different in principle from the proposed deduction for students and should be evaluated by different standards. A deduction for parents could not be justified as a refinement in the measurement of the parents' earnings. The general rule is that costs, including investment outlays, are properly chargeable against the gross income that they generate, and neither the Internal Revenue Code nor popular opinion treats parents and their adult sons and daughters as a single economic unit.

A deduction for parents of college students would be subject to the objection that it would give the greatest amount of assistance to families with the largest incomes and no assistance to those with very small incomes; it would resemble a federal scholarship that increased as the parents' means increased. The tax value of deductions for students would also increase with the size of their income, but this is not a valid criticism of deductions for genuine costs of earning taxable income.

Proposals to allow parents to deduct tuition payments and other educational expenses call for a subsidy or special encouragement of a socially desirable form of expenditure and should meet the exacting standards that are properly applicable to such subsidies. In particular, the efficiency and equity of the deduction should be compared with that of additional government expenditures to aid education. Although this kind of comparison is not wholly extraneous to the evaluation of the proposal for amortization of educational expenses against students' income, it is less significant. Under the net income tax, there is a presumption in favor of the deduction of costs against the gross income to which they relate, but other deductions require special justification. Few would argue that depreciation allowances for each kind of physical capital should be allowed or denied on the basis of a judgment whether the government could do more to promote capital formation by denying the deduction and spending more for direct government investment or by allowing the deduction and relying on private investors.

Conclusions Regarding Educational Expenditures

Current and deferred deductions for students pursuing education that increases their earning capacity are consistent with income tax principles. A suitable plan would allow a refinement of the income definition, would improve equity, and would have incidental consequences of a desirable character. The particular scheme outlined here is intended only as a basis for discussion; further consideration might indicate that provisions different from those mentioned in the preceding pages should be adopted with respect to eligible expenditures and the amortization period. The essential point, in my opinion, is that the deductions should be limited to actual expenditures and should be available to students rather than parents. Although the adoption of the amortization plan would stimulate educational investment to some extent, this effect probably would not be great because forgone earnings, which would not be amortizable, are the major component of costs of education beyond high school. Nevertheless, the recognition for tax purposes that certain educational expenditures are investments would help establish an important principle that may be overlooked in personal and public decisions.

91st Cong., 1st Sess. (Dec. 11, 1969).

SEC. 917. TAX CREDIT FOR CERTAIN EXPENSES OF HIGHER EDUCATION.

(a) **In General.**—Subpart A of part IV of subchapter A of chapter 1 (relating to credits allowable) is amended by renumbering section 40 as 41, and by inserting after section 39 the following new section:

"SEC. 40. EXPENSES OF HIGHER EDUCATION.

"(a) **General Rule.**—There shall be allowed to an individual, as a credit against the tax imposed by this chapter for the taxable year, an amount, determined under subsection (b), of the expenses of higher education paid by him during the taxable year to one or more institutions of higher education in providing an education above the twelfth grade for himself or for any other individual.

"(b) **Limitations.**—

"(1) Amount Per Individual.—The credit under subsection (a) for expenses of higher education of any individual paid during the taxable year shall be an amount equal to the sum of—

"(A) 100 percent of so much of such expenses as does not exceed $200,

"(B) 25 percent of so much of such expenses as exceeds $200 but does not exceed $500, and

"(C) 5 percent of so much of such expenses as exceeds $500 but does not exceed $1,500.

"(2) Proration of Credit Where More Than One Taxpayer Pays Expenses.—If expenses of higher education of an individual are paid by more than one taxpayer during the taxable year, the credit allowable to each such taxpayer under subsection (a) shall be the same portion of the credit determined under paragraph (1) which the amount of expenses of higher education of such individual paid by the taxpayer during the taxable year is of the total amount of expenses of higher education of such individual paid by all taxpayers during the taxable year.

"(3) Reduction of Credit.—The credit under subsection (a) for expenses of higher education of any individual paid during the taxable year, as determined under paragraphs (1) and (2) of this subsection, shall be reduced by an amount equal to 2 percent of the amount by which the adjusted gross income of the taxpayer for the taxable year exceeds $15,000.

"(c) **Definitions.**—For purposes of this section—

"(1) Expenses of Higher Education.—The term 'expenses of higher education' means—

"(A) tuition and fees required for the enrollment or attendance of a student at a level above the twelfth grade at an institution of higher education, and

"(B) fees, books, supplies, and equipment required for courses of instruction above the twelfth grade at an institution of higher education.

Such term does not include any amount paid, directly or indirectly, for meals, lodging, or similar personal, living, or family expenses. In the event an amount paid for tuition or fees includes an amount for meals, lodging, or similar expenses which is not separately stated, the portion of such amount which is attributable to meals, lodging, or similar expenses shall be determined under regulations prescribed by the Secretary or his delegate.

"(2) Institution of Higher Education.—The term 'institution of higher education' means—

"(A) an educational institution (as defined in section 151(E) (4))—

"(i) which regularly offers education at a level above the twelfth grade; and

"(ii) contributions to or for the use of which constitute charitable contributions within the meaning of section 170(c); or

"(B) a business or trade school, or technical institution or other technical or vocational school in any State, which (i) is legally authorized to provide, and provides within that State, a program of postsecondary vocational or technical education designed to fit individuals for useful employment in recognized occupations;

and (ii) is accredited by a nationally recognized accrediting agency or association listed by the United States Commissioner of Education; and (iii) has been in existence for 2 years or has been specially accredited by the Commissioner as an institution meeting the other requirements of this subparagraph.

"(3) State.—The term 'State' includes, in addition to the several States of the Union, the Commonwealth of Puerto Rico, the District of Columbia, Guam, American Samoa, the Virgin Islands, and the Trust Territory of the Pacific Islands.

"(d) **Special Rules.**—

"(1) Adjustment for Certain Scholarships and Veterans' Benefits.—The amounts otherwise taken into account under subsection (a) as expenses of higher education of any individual during any period shall be reduced (before the application of subsection (b)) by any amounts received by such individual during such period as—

"(A) a scholarship or fellowship grant (within the meaning of section 117(a) (1)) which under section 117 is not includible in gross income, and

"(B) education and training allowance under chapter 33 of title 38 of the United States Code or educational assistance allowance under chapter 35 of such title.

"(2) Noncredit and Recreational, etc., Courses.—Amounts paid for expenses of higher education of any individual shall be taken into account under subsection (a)—

"(A) in the case of an individual who is a candidate for a baccalaureate or higher degree, only to the extent such expenses are attributable to courses of instruction necessary to fulfill requirements for the attainment of a predetermined and identified educational, professional, or vocational objective.

"(3) Application with Other Credits.—The credit allowed by subsection (a) to the taxpayer shall not exceed the amount of the tax imposed on the taxpayer for the taxable year by this chapter reduced by the sum of the credits allowable under this subpart (other than under this section and section 31).

"(e) **Disallowance of Expenses as Deduction.**—No deduction shall be allowed under section 162 (relating to trade or business expenses) for any expense of higher education which (after the application of subsection (b)) is taken into account in determining the amount of any credit allowed under subsection (a). The preceding sentence shall not apply to the expenses of higher education of any taxpayer who, under regulations prescribed by the Secretary or his delegate, elects not to apply the provisions of this section with respect to such expenses for the taxable year.

"(f) **Regulations.**—The Secretary or his delegate shall prescribe such regulations as may be necessary to carry out the provisions of this section."

(b) **Clerical Amendment.**—The table of sections for such subpart A is amended by striking out the last item and inserting in lieu thereof the following:

"Sec. 40. Expenses of higher education.
"Sec. 41. Overpayments of tax."

(c) **Effective Date.**—The amendments made by this section shall apply to taxable years beginning after December 31, 1971.

BENSON, PROPOSALS FOR TAX REFORM (CANADA) § 2.24 (1969) *

Until now most fellowships, scholarships, bursaries and research grants not related to services have been treated as exempt from tax. There seems no valid reason for continuing such exemption. Post-graduate students and research workers are, in effect, professional workers and should pay tax as others, after allowances for tuition fees and for research expenses properly deductible from research grants. Payments to undergraduates normally fall well within the personal exemptions, after deducting tuition fees. Where they exceed exemptions or where the student has other income, he should pay tax just as other Canadians do.

* Reproduced with the permission of the Queen's Printer for Canada.

*

Chapter III

DEDUCTIONS

A. Depreciation

Although the Tax Reform Act of 1969 has substantially curtailed the availability of accelerated depreciation for real estate, the controversy over the role and purpose of the deduction continues. Some of its intensity has been muted by the recapture provisions of Code Section 1245 for tangible personal property and Section 1250 for real estate, which limit the extent to which the deduction may have the effect of converting ordinary income into capital gains.

Particularly troublesome has been the determination of depreciation for mortgaged property. The real estate "tax shelters" of recent years have built largely on the inclusion of mortgages in the taxpayer's basis for purposes of depreciation. The second selection which follows examines the implications of the leading Supreme Court decision dealing with the tax consequences of a transfer of depreciable property subject to a mortgage: *Crane* v. *Commissioner*, 331 U.S. 1 (1947).

EISNER, EFFECTS OF DEPRECIATION ALLOWANCES FOR TAX PURPOSES

House Committee on Ways and Means,
2 Tax Revision Compendium 793 (1959).

There are a few basic but widely ignored or misunderstood facts about the role of depreciation in our tax structure.

1. Higher depreciation allowances in themselves mean lower taxpayments.

2. Acceleration of depreciation—whether by 5-year amortization, double rate-declining balance, sum-of-the-years-digits, or extra initial writeoffs—means higher depreciation allowances.

3. The effects of any change in depreciation policy upon the economy, considering reasonable concomitant effects such as associated changes in tax rates, are different from the effects upon an individual firm or an industry on the assumption that all other things in the economy remain unchanged.

As to the first of the facts indicated above there can be no direct challenge. It is common to argue for higher depreciation allowances on the grounds that they encourage investment, promote growth, meet the problem of inflation or accomplish some other presumably worthy social purpose. But all of these alleged results are usually doubtful and variable, as we shall note. The simple fact is that when a taxpayer (corporate or individual) is allowed to make greater charges for depreciation against his income he saves taxes. Without meaning to be cynical, one might ask how many of the pleaders for liberalization of depreciation provisions would change their tune if they were told that the liberalization would be accompanied by an increase in, say, corporate profits tax rates such that there would be no change in tax incidence.

Four years ago, in testimony before the Joint Economic Committee, I made a number of predictions about the increase in depreciation charges, and consequent loss in tax revenues, which would result from adoption of the new, relatively accelerated methods of depreciation authorized by the Internal Revenue Act of 1954. Examination of the estimates and reports of actual corporate depreciation charges made by the Treasury and Commerce Departments and the staff of the Joint Economic Committee confirms the soundness and conservatism of those predictions. The facts as thus far available from the Treasury Department[2] indicate, for example, that total depreciation and accelerated amortization deductions of corporations rose from $12 billion in 1953 to $17.6 billion in 1956. Estimates of the Department of Commerce show corporate depreciation and amortization rising from $11.8 billion in 1953 to $19.7 billion in 1957, and the staff of the Joint Economic Committee has estimated for 1958 a further rise to $21.3 billion.[3] When depreciation deductions of noncorporate taxpayers are added it becomes clear that the rise in depreciation deductions between 1953 and 1958 accounts by the latter year for an annual loss to the Treasury of over $5 billion in tax revenues. In 1955, on the basis of a 4 percent assumed rate of growth in the rate of gross capital additions, I projected that by 1958 the excess in annual depreciation charges accountable to the new depreciation methods would be in the neighborhood of $5 billion.[4] This in itself would have amounted to a 1958 tax loss to the Treasury of some $2.5 billion, due merely to the change in depreciation methods. The greater loss of $5 billion now reported includes the direct effects of the rate of growth of gross capital additions, aside from the results of changes in depreciation methods. However, because the increase in capital additions was equivalent to more than the average 4 percent growth which I conservatively assumed, the part of that $5 billion loss which can be ascribed specifically to the change in depreciation methods is undoubtedly more than the $2.5 billion I predicted. And, it is important to emphasize, not only will the total loss to the Treasury accumulate, year after year, but the rate of annual loss will increase rapidly beyond the $5 billion figure already attained.

While these ideas are by now no longer new, it may be well to review briefly the essential analytical relation that made it possible to predict this sharply increased upward trend in depreciation. For, all too widely, a failure to appreciate the analytical relation results in erroneous statements and decisions by business leaders, accountants, and public policymaking bodies. In particular, it has been argued in reference to all forms of acceleration of depreciation, that it involves merely the postponement of taxes and saves the taxpayer nothing "in the end." This compounds a number of confusions:

1. The typical American company has no "end"; it just goes on and on, generally growing. (In fact, were it to "end" it would no longer pay profits taxes anyway.)
2. Individual pieces of equipment (which do have finite lives or "end") do not present the same issue as a going firm which repeatedly makes capital additions, and accrues new depreciation charges from the new capital additions.
3. A firm shifting to relatively accelerated depreciation, and still charging normal depreciation on old capital while charging extra depreciation on new capital, is not in the same situation as a firm that is fully adjusted to accelerated depreciation.
4. A firm that is growing, that is, on the average making more capital expenditures each year than the year before, is not in the same situation as one that is not growing.

---

[2] See "Statistics of Income, 1956–57, Corporation Income Tax Returns," p. 19 (also prior years), and Joint Economic Committee, "The Federal Revenue System: Facts and Problems, 1959" (U.S. Government Printing Office, No. 38184), p. 204.

[3] Joint Economic Committee, op. cit., p. 209.

[4] "Federal Tax Policy for Economic Growth and Stability," table 4, p. 520.

When these confusions are stripped away we learn that—

1. Any form of accelerated depreciation results in initially higher depreciation charges for a substantial period, even without growth. These higher initial charges, which take place for a great many years, will generally not be matched by later lower charges.

2. Accelerated depreciation in a growing firm, as we have defined it above, will raise depreciation charges not just for an initial period, however long, but permanently. In effect, with accelerated depreciation the firm is always charging depreciation in greater proportion on its "younger" assets. But the younger assets are the ones that were acquired more recently and, if the firm is growing, these are greater in amount than older assets. Hence, by always charging depreciation on assets which are greater in value, the firm employing accelerated depreciation is actually charging more depreciation.

It has been argued that higher depreciation allowances will encourage investment and growth. This is ultimately a difficult and subtle issue to settle. We can, however, easily point out that most of the arguments that have been advanced in this regard in support of accelerated depreciation are irrelevant and incorrect.

Essentially it has been argued:

1. "Higher depreciation charges make more funds available for capital expenditures."

But except to the extent capital markets are significantly imperfect there is little ground for arguing that the availability of funds determines their expenditure. Where profitable investment opportunities exist, modern corporations can raise the funds. If profitable opportunities do not exist, business will not squander its money. (Nor, might we add, should the Congress want it to.)

2. "Higher anticipated depreciation charges make prospective capital expenditures more attractive by increasing the aftertax return or bringing expected aftertax returns nearer in time."

This argument has a small, but only a small germ of truth. The fallacy looming large relates again to the naive assumption that everything else can remain unchanged when depreciation rates are increased or accelerated. If all else does remain unchanged it is true that capital expenditures should increase. And so, indeed, should consumption increase. For the phenomenon involved is simply a decrease in taxes. With a decrease in taxes business has more aftertax earnings. If the decrease in taxes is expected to continue business can expect to continue to have increased earnings.

But first, if increased demand and expenditures are the object—as they should be in a situation of unemployment and resultant inadequate growth—any decrease in taxes would accomplish essentially the same objective. There is no particular argument for an increase in depreciation charges. Indeed there is good reason to believe that variation in depreciation charges is relatively poor as a countercyclical tool. For in a period of bad times, when profit and profit expectations are poor, increased depreciation allowances would have a reduced effect upon taxes and an even lesser effect upon capital expenditures, which are not likely to be undertaken anyway. And in good times, expectations of profit on investment are usually so great that low depreciation rates are not likely to be a serious deterrent. (This is probably less likely to be true of the kinds of taxes which cut heavily into consumption expenditures.)

Second, if we assume that the Congress will continue to strive for a balanced budget, we must reckon with either an increase in other taxes or a reduction in Government expenditures to make up for the loss in revenue resulting from higher depreciation allowances. When this is taken into account there is little reason or possibility left for increased capital expenditures. Except for the chance that the new incidence of taxes implies greater expenditures—and it might just as well imply lesser expenditures—we should be left with no increase in aggregate demand. (If the loss in tax revenues as a result of higher depreciation allowances were met by a reduction in Government expenditures we would in fact expect a decrease in aggregate demand.) But with no increase in aggregate demand what justification would there be for more investment, which would still further increase capacity? If businessmen did increase expenditures and thus make capacity higher than it would otherwise have been, one might expect them to reap the resultant whirlwind. In time the excess capacity would become too insistent to permit further expansion. Capital expenditures would then drop and we would have the makings of a general economic downturn. Such a development is perhaps more than faintly suggestive of the pattern of the 1955–58 period of recent history.

However, we did concede a germ of truth to the argument that more rapid depreciation might increase capital expenditures. This stems from the tendency of accelerated depreciation to induce a somewhat more capital intensive method of production. In choosing allocations of funds a profit-maximizing company must compare the discounted values of expected future aftertax returns. The effect of accelerated depreciation, if balanced by an increase in the corporate profits tax rates sufficient to prevent any loss in revenue, should be to increase the relative attractiveness of long-lived capital. It might pay, figuratively speaking, to build the more expensive, long-lasting house of wood rather than the one of straw. It might pay even better to build the still longer lasting and even more expensive house of brick. To the extent that the economy adopts such longer lived capital the capital-output ratio is likely to be higher and capital expenditures, for purposes of replacement and expansion and to meet changes in product demand and factor supply, are likely to be greater.

In evaluating both the magnitude and significance of this depreciation-induced increase in capital expenditures one must remember again that other things cannot be assumed to be unchanged. Capital expenditures are thus likely to be substituted for other kinds of expenditures, such as those for research and development, which do not benefit from the liberalized depreciation allowances. We should generally find ourselves encouraging expenditure on brick, mortar, and machines, discouraging expenditures on brains, know-how, public relations, and advertising. Some of us may prefer such a shift in the allocation of resources. But some of us may find this quite undesirable. There is certainly no prima facie case for it by objective standards.

Let us now consider the implications of our analysis in terms of the "major objectives and guides for tax reform" set forth in the outline of study of Federal income tax revision by this committee.

1. *Equity and fairness.*—The depreciation deduction is of direct benefit to the business firm and its owners. Its chief justification in terms of equity is that the income tax purportedly relates to income and it would be inconsistent to apply an "income" tax to expenses which should be charged against income. This justification is in large part vitiated, however, by the failure to apply either the law generally or a definition of depreciation itself in a manner consistent with the economic concept of income. In particular, if we were concerned with income we should allow as a charge against income only the loss in the value of property. But once we come to subtract losses in the value of property in arriving at income we should, to be consistent, add increases in the value of property. We should then find, partly as a result of the price inflation of the last few decades, that the complaints about the inadequacy of depreciation allowances and the arguments that taxes are being paid out of capital are turned on their heads. For the value of business assets has tended to increase rather than decrease. The house built for $10,000, 25 years ago, is worth not less but more, perhaps $30,000 today; yet mortgage (or business) debt is dependent upon original cost. Business has in fact failed to declare the tremendous amounts of income embodied in increased value of its plant. The correctness of this observation may be readily confirmed by examination of the balance sheets of almost all American corporations, certainly the large ones. In how many cases is the book value of the firm as great as its market value?

This would not matter, of course, if capital gains were treated as income in our tax laws. But in fact capital gains as a rule are not taxed at all. Where for some reason investors are constrained to "realize" their gains—which is not the dominant case—the tax rate is of course considerably less than the income tax rate. Depreciation charges which are greater than the loss in value of capital (and since capital has frequently appreciated, depreciated charges in the main have been greater than the loss in value) will generally constitute undistributed earnings, which are, however, reflected only in gains in the value of the firm and hence are not taxed or are taxed at relatively low rates. By this relevant value criterion, depreciation charges are already higher than consideration of equity would dictate. Any further increase in the allowances for depreciation would be unjust.

However, aside from this questionable goal of limiting taxes to income, it is even more difficult to set up widely acceptable criteria of equity. As suggested above, allowances for depreciation tend to favor those who acquire goods on capital account; correspondingly they tend to injure those who do not. Society may tend to accept what is. In these terms changes may be considered as inequitable and, if they are recognized for what they are, the changes with regard to depreciation in the Internal Revenue Act of 1954, stripped of other arguments to justify them, are inequitable insofar as they disturbed the balance existing under prior law.

2. *Progression in the distribution of tax burdens.*—Taken in conjunction with current easy treatment of capital gains, depreciation charges reduce the degree of progressiveness in our tax structure;

owners of equity gain; and ownership of equity in American business is unevenly distributed and highly correlated with income. It may also be observed that depreciation charges are most beneficial to existing corporations that own large amounts of physical capital and these tend to be the large, frequently giant-sized firms. Thus depreciation charges tend to benefit large, older firms as opposed to small and new businesses.

3. *Allowing free play of the market in allocating resources.*—Depreciation allowances for tax purposes reduce the free play in the capital market and thus restrict long run competitive forces. In an ideal competitive situation each firm would have to compete fully with existing firms and potential new firms in all industries. Firms with better profit expectations (as viewed by the market) will attract more capital. If an existing firm has such poor profit expectations that owners want to withdraw their capital from it and invest elsewhere they should do so. Capital should thus flow out of that firm—the firm should "depreciate"—until it is down to such a size that its low profit expectations represent a fair rate of return on still invested capital. (It is of course conceivable that by this standard capital will flow out of such a firm indefinitely until it is out of business.)

However, the effect of depreciation allowances for tax purposes is to "put an umbrella" over existing firms. The Government says, in effect, "If you already have a lot of capital we will not tax you until you have recouped the capital you are using up in production. Even though you are using all of the services of Government (for which taxes are levied) we will levy the taxes on someone else—your potential competitor or the customers of your potential competitor—so that you can stay in business (keep your capital intact) and thus (implicitly) so that more efficient and profitable firms are prevented by the burden of these taxes from squeezing you out."

4. *Providing a climate for economic growth.*—This is a broad question, not susceptible of a unique, universal answer.

One critical point at issue, for stable economic growth, is the need for adequate and steadily growing demand. From this standpoint, the combination of high profit and income tax rates and high depreciation allowances is likely to be stabilizing. This is because the relative constancy of depreciation charges over the business cycle implies a greater relative fluctuation of profits net of depreciation than of gross profits without the depreciation deduction, and consequently a greater countercyclical variation of taxes. However, it must then be noted that acceleration of depreciation, such as was accomplished in the 1954 tax revisions and is still being recommended, and the linking of depreciation to "replacement cost," would both tend to make depreciation charges themselves fluctuate more with the cycle and thus reduce the built-in counter cyclical action in our tax structure.

Partial answers may be given in terms of various of the issues urged earlier in this paper. Thus, if depreciation allowances tend to encourage the acquisition of plant and equipment at the expense of "investment" in research and development our growth is encouraged or discouraged as expenditures for plant and equipment have a greater or lesser "payoff" at this time than expenditures for knowledge. If depreciation allowances favor large existing firms at the expense of small firms and potential new firms, growth is encouraged or discouraged as growth stems more from large existing firms or from small and potential new firms (or from these latter and the increased efforts on the part of existing firms forced to meet their competition). My personal leanings tend to be against depreciation allowances as a positive factor in economic growth but I cannot say either that professional opinion on the matter is agreed or that the issue is clearcut.

5. *Ease of taxpayer compliance and administration of the law.*—This is a matter on which tax experts and administrators would be better qualified to testify. I may briefly venture the view, however, that a substantial amount of cost is incurred by taxpayers in finding means of maximizing depreciation deductions and in keeping records to support such deductions. These costs are increased by the increasing variety in depreciation provisions as the law is amended in an effort to benefit certain taxpayers. The changes and varieties in accounting for depreciation which result from changes for tax purposes have also resulted in substantial confusions and costs both for investors and other interested parties trying to understand business financial statements and for public commissions in regulated industries.

I should like to conclude on what may appear to be a provocative note. I believe that in pursuance of the objectives and guides indicated by this committee, and in the interest of "Federal individual and corporation income taxes with broader, more uniform bases and lower rates than at present," serious consideration should be given to outright elimination of the allowance for depreciation for tax purposes. In order to avoid confusing this issue with the broader question of the desirability of business as opposed to individual income taxes, such a change in the tax system might be coupled with reductions in the corporate income tax rates (and some adjustments in taxes on noncorporate business) such that the total tax liability of business would not be affected. There would be a number of problems of changes in incidence to be worked out but it is in the direction of elimination of deductions from taxable income rather than their increase, as self-interested individuals and groups tend to push, that I believe this committee and the Congress should move.

ADAMS, EXPLORING THE OUTER BOUNDARIES OF THE CRANE DOCTRINE: AN IMAGINARY SUPREME COURT OPINION *

21 Tax L.Rev. 159 (1966).

THE *Crane* case was decided by the Supreme Court almost 20 years ago. It is generally regarded as having established two principles which are close companions: one, that the basis of property subject to a mortgage includes the amount of the mortgage even though the owner of the property assumes no liability on the mortgage debt; two, that when such property is sold the amount "realized" includes the amount of the unassumed mortgage.

It is by no means clear, however, that the doctrine can be stated so broadly. In *Crane* the property was acquired not by purchase but by inheritance; the appraised value of the property was stipulated to be equal to the amount of the mortgage at the time of the decedent's death; and the Court considered that the value of the property exceeded the principal amount of the mortgage at the time of sale.

Visibility in this area has not substantially improved during the years which have passed since the decision in the *Crane* case. It is still not entirely clear whether the rule of the *Crane* case is applicable when property is acquired by purchase rather than by inheritance. Athough it has been generally assumed by taxpayers, and perhaps also by the Commissioner,[1] that *Crane* applies to a

---

1 Compare, however, the advice which the Commissioner has given "average" taxpayers with regard to determining "cost" with what he has said with regard to determining "gain or loss":

"Cost or Other Basis of Assets
Assumption of a Mortgage. When you acquire property subject to an existing debt, the basis is the amount paid for the property plus the unpaid amount of the debt *assumed* by you.
Example. If you acquire for $20,000 cash a building that is subject to a debt of $80,000 which you assume, your basis is $100,000." COMMISSSONER OF INTERNAL REVENUE, TAX GUIDE FOR SMALL BUSINESS 99 (1966).

* Copyright 1966, by New York University School of Law. Reproduced with permission.

purchase, the Tax Court recently reserved this issue for subsequent determination.[2] It is also not yet clear whether the principle of the *Crane* case is applicable if the mortgage exceeds the value of the property at the time of acquisition, nor whether when property subject to an unassumed mortgage is sold or otherwise disposed of the amount "realized" includes the mortgage if it exceeds the value of the property. And, finally, it is not clear whether in such a case a taxpayer can avoid the realization of gain by abandoning the property or donating it to a charitable institution, subject to the mortgage.

It seems inevitable that at some future date the Supreme Court may be called upon to resolve some of these open questions. Perhaps the following imaginary opinion will serve to indicate, if not the solution, at least some of the difficulties the Court may encounter in dealing with these issues.

BLANK v. COMMISSIONER OF INTERNAL REVENUE
CERTIORARI TO THE CIRCUIT COURT OF APPEALS
FOR THE TWENTY-SECOND CIRCUIT

No. 100. Argued December 7, 1964.—Decided 1966.

THE CHIEF JUSTICE delivered the opinion of the Court.

The facts of this case raise several interesting questions: first, how a taxpayer computes depreciation on property acquired by purchase subject to an unassumed mortgage; second, whether any gain is realized on the donation of such property to an exempt organization, and if so; third, whether the gain is ordinary income or capital gain.

The property involved is a small office building which was erected in 1940 at a cost of $3,000,000. A mortgage of $2,000,000 was placed on the property through the device of a professional dummy who after assuming personal liability on the note transferred the property to the true owner subject to the mortgage. For the first fifteen years of its life the building had difficulty weathering the adverse economic climate prevailing in the area.

"How to Determine Gain or Loss
You should also include in the amount you realize any of your liabilities which were assumed by the purchaser and liabilities to which the property you traded is subject, such as real estate taxes or a mortgage." COMMISSIONER OF INTERNAL REVENUE, TAX GUIDE FOR SMALL BUSINESS 70 (1964).
"If an indebtedness is attached to the property transferred such indebtedness must be included at face value in the amount realized even though neither you nor the purchaser were personally liable for the debt." COMMISSIONER OF INTERNAL REVENUE, YOUR FEDERAL INCOME TAX 73 (1966).

2 Columbus & Greenville Ry. v. Comm'r, 42 T.C. 834 (1964).

The owner was unable to meet the amortization payments but managed to pay all interest as it accrued. The mortgagee was content to allow the owner to continue to operate the property, since all of the rents were applied to maintenance, taxes and interest.

In 1952 the petitioner purchased the office building for $100,000, subject to the $2,000,000 mortgage. He engaged the previous owner to manage the property and regarded himself as a passive investor.

The petitioner held the property for five years. Conditions improved somewhat but from a business standpoint the investment was not particularly successful. Total rental income over the period was $300,000, against which there were out-of-pocket expenses of $200,000, consisting of interest $50,000, taxes $50,000, insurance, maintenance and repairs $80,000, and management fee $20,000. The net cash profit of $100,000 was applied to the reduction of the principal of the mortgage.

The petitioner maintains, however, that by virtue of our decision in *Crane v. Commissioner,* 331 U.S. 1, he was entitled to depreciation deductions of $525,000 over the five-year period. This he arrives at by including the $2,000,000 mortgage in his basis for the property, assuming a remaining life of 20 years, and applying straight-line depreciation of $105,000 each year. If the petitioner is right his investment of $100,000 did not return him any profit in a business sense but afforded him deductions of $425,000 in excess of income from the building. These deductions he claims to be entitled to apply against his taxable income from other sources, which over the period exceeded $1,000,000.

In 1957 the holder of the mortgage threatened foreclosure. Confronted with this possibility the petitioner offered to make a further payment of $25,000 on the mortgage on the condition that no steps would be taken to foreclose the mortgage for at least a year. This proposition was accepted. Shortly thereafter the petitioner donated the property to the Bide-A-Wee Animal Home, an exempt organization. The property was taken by the Home subject to the mortgage which by that time had been reduced to $1,875,000. The petitioner reported no income from the gift but claimed a charitable deduction of $100,000 on the ground that this was the value of the equity. The Commissioner disallowed the charitable deduction and was sustained by the Tax Court, which held that the value of the property was not in excess of the mortgage. No appeal was taken on this issue and the Tax Court's finding stands.

In addition to disallowing the charitable deduction the Commissioner also contended that the petitioner was not entitled to include the mortgage in the basis of the property or, in the alternative, that he realized income at the time of the gift on the difference between the amount of the mortgage and his adjusted basis. The Tax Court, however, held that the petitioner was entitled to the depreciation deductions claimed and that he realized no income from the gift. The Court of Appeals affirmed, and we granted certiorari because the question is an important one in the administration of the tax law and has not been settled by this Court.

Both parties rely upon our decision in the *Crane* case, the pertinent facts of which may be briefly stated. The taxpayer's husband died in 1932, devising to her an apartment building and lot subject to a mortgage in the amount of $262,042.50. The property was appraised for estate tax purposes at this value. The taxpayer held the property for seven years, during which time she collected the rents, paid the operating expenses and taxes and remitted the net rentals to the mortgagee. Not only were the net rentals insufficient to effect any reduction in the principal of the mortgage but, in fact, interest arrearages increased. With the mortgagee threatening foreclosure the taxpayer sold to a third party subject to the mortgage for a net cash payment of $2,500 after deducting expenses.

The taxpayer reported a taxable gain of $1,250. Her theory was that the property she had received from her husband was worth zero at the date of his death. She reasoned that all she received when she sold it was $2,500, only half of which was taxable under the capital gain provisions.

The Commissioner had a different idea. His theory was that the "property" acquired and sold was not the equity but the physical property undiminished by the mortgage. He therefore started with an original basis of $262,042.50, allowed depreciation thereon of $28,045.10 over the seven-year period, and arrived at an adjusted basis at the time of sale of $178,997.40. By including as part of the amount realized the principal amount of the mortgage (but not the interest due since this was "a deductible item") the Commissioner determined that the taxpayer sustained a capital loss on the land and an ordinary gain of $24,031.45 on the building.

We agreed with the Commissioner. In reaching this conclusion we approached the matter first from the standpoint of original basis at the time of acquisition. We noted that the basis of property acquired from a decedent is "the fair market value of such property at the time of such acquisition". The crux of the matter was thus the meaning of the word "property," and we held that this meant the physical thing, the land and buildings, or the owner's legal rights in them.

Our reasons were several in number and persuasive in nature. First, we observed that the words of statutes—even revenue acts—should be interpreted where possible in their ordinary, everyday sense. We consulted the dictionary and it confirmed our view. "Equity" was not included as a synonym for "property."

Second, the administrative construction was in accord. Thus, the regulations required that the full value of property, undiminished by liens, be reported as part of the gross estate and that mortgages be deducted separately in computing the net estate.[3]

Third, we examined the entire Code and found no confusion on the part of Congress as to the difference between the words "property" and "equity." Each had been used throughout in its proper sense.

We were also acutely aware of the problems that would arise with regard to depreciation deductions should a contrary view be adopted. The Code permits deduction of "a reasonable allowance for exhaustion, wear and tear,"[4] but if the basis of the property is limited to the mortgagor's equity the depreciation deductions will represent only a fraction of the cost of the corresponding physical exhaustion. Finally, we were concerned with the accounting burden that would be imposed on both the taxpayer and the Commissioner were the basis required to be adjusted as each payment was made on the mortgage.

This brought us to the ultimate issue, *i.e.,* in determining the "amount realized" on the sale of the property, was the principal amount of the mortgage required to be included? Having already decided for the purpose of basis that the "property" was the land and the building, this last question was not as difficult as it might otherwise have been. We had only to ask ourselves whether the taxpayer would have accepted a mere $2,500 for the land and the building. Such an absurdity could be avoided only by holding that the taxpayer must have received and thus "realized" the amount of the mortgage even though not personally liable on the debt. We were careful to point out, however, that our decision was limited to a case in which the property was not worth less than the amount of the lien. We stated in footnote thirty-seven:

"Obviously, if the value of the property is less than the amount of the mortgage, a mortgagor who is not personally liable cannot realize a benefit

3 Reg. Sec. 20.2053-7 (1958).

4 I.R.C. § 167(a) (1954).

equal to the mortgage. Consequently, a different problem might be encountered where a mortgagor abandoned the property or transferred it subject to the mortgage without receiving boot. That is not this case.''

We have only to apply these princples to the case at bar. The first issue is whether our holding in *Crane* is applicable when the acquisition is by purchase rather than by inheritance. The Commissioner contends that we are controlled by entirely different statutory language, that ''the cost of such property''[5] is not the same as ''the fair market value of the property.''[6] He reasons that the only payment which petitioner made in order to acquire the property was the $100,000 he paid in cash. Not having assumed any liability on the mortgage, his cost must be limited to what he actually paid. He reminds us that the words of the statute should be interpreted where possible in their ordinary, everyday sense, and insists that no layman would ever think that the property had cost him more than the $100,000 which he had paid. He cites Webster's New Collegiate Dictionary defining ''cost'' as the ''amount or equivalent paid, given, or charged, or engaged to be paid or given, for anything; charge; price; hence, whatever, as labor, self-denial, etc., is requisite to secure benefit.''

While we recognize some merit in the Commissioner's argument, we think it incompatible with the conclusion we reached in the *Crane* case in including the mortgage in the amount ''realized.'' Everyday meanings are of only secondary importance when construing the words of a tax statute and are very seldom given any weight when a more abstruse and technical meaning is available. If a taxpayer can ''realize'' the amount of a mortgage for which he is not personally liable when he transfers property, then surely it must follow that one who buys the property has the right to include the amount of the mortgage as part of his cost. The Tax Court so held in a case involving the purchase of property on which there were outstanding tax liens.[7]

---

[5] I.R.C. § 1012 (1954).

[6] I.R.C. § 1014(a) (1954).

[7] In Blackstone Theatre Co., 12 T.C. 801 (1949), the taxpayer acquired property in 1941 subject to tax liens and penalities outstanding against the property; the basis for depreciation included the amount of those liens and penalties. The court echoed our dictum in *Crane* to the effect that depreciation might not be computed upon basis including unassumed liens if the property were worth less than the liens. *Id.* at 805. Subsequent satisfaction of the liens at a figure less than face amount did not retroactively affect the depreciation basis for prior years. *Ibid.* The court did not pass upon the effect on basis for the future, but earlier cases indicate that there should be a reduction in basis by the difference between the indebtedness and the actual cost of its extinguishment. See Fulton Gold Corp., 31 B.T.A. 519, 521 (1934); P. J. Hiatt, 35 B.T.A. 292, 296 (1937); Hotel Astoria, Inc., 42 B.T.A. 759, 763 (1940).

The Commissioner's next line of defense is more worthy of his craft. Even granting that our decision in *Crane* can be applicable to a purchase, it is not applicable, he insists, where the mortgage exceeds the value of the property at the time of acquisition. All that we held in *Crane* was that the basis of the property was its value undiminished by the mortgage. Thus, if the mortgage had exceeded the value of the property, the basis would not have included such excess.

The petitioner counters with the argument that the property for which we must determine the cost is the office building and not merely the equity, and that it is "cost" and not "value" that is involved. He contends that once we concede that an unassumed mortgage can be part of the cost there is no reason to limit the inclusion of the mortgage to a case in which the value of the property is at least equal to the amount of the mortgage.

We think that the petitioner has failed to grasp the unexpressed but none the less underlying rationale of our *Crane* decision. The reason why it is proper not to deduct the mortgage from the value of the property is because the taxpayer can be expected in the normal case to satisfy the mortgage rather than lose the property, but—and this is the heart of the matter—this is only true where the value of the property is at least equal to the amount of the mortgage.[8]

Where property is acquired by purchase, therefore, we hold that an unassumed mortgage is includible in the purchaser's basis if, and only if, it is not in excess of the value of the property. We recognize that in the application of the rule a relatively small difference in value may have a drastic effect on the purchaser's depreciation deductions. If this appears to impose a somewhat arbitrary result when the purchaser is not liable on the mortgage in either event, we can only say that we must take the law as we find it and leave it to Congress to correct the inequities or absurdities which follow in our wake.[9]

Unfortunately, in the present case neither party undertook to

---

[8] Compare Albany Car Wheel Co., 40 T.C. 831 (1963), *aff'd per curiam*, 333 F.2d 653 (2d Cir. 1964); Lloyd H. Redford, 28 T.C. 773 (1957), *appeal dismissed per stipulation*, 4th Cir. 1957, and Rev. Rul. 55-675, 1955-2 CUM. BULL. 567, excluding an amount from basis which is contingent, *i.e.*, unlikely to be paid.

[9] Consideration was given by the Mills Subcommittee, in 1956, to the addition of a new provision to the Code which would have limited basis to cash investment when there was no personal liability and liens exceeded value. STAFF SUBCOMM. ON INTERNAL REVENUE TAXATION, COMM. ON WAYS AND MEANS, *List of Substantive Unintended Benefits and Hardships*, part 1, item 12, (Comm. Print 1956). No such provision was enacted.

establish the value of the property at the time of purchase. The petitioner points to the fact that he paid $100,000 in cash as clear evidence that the property was worth more than the mortgage. It must be acknowledged that there is some support for his position in the significance we attached to the payment of a small amount of cash by the purchaser from Mrs. Crane. Evidently we were more confident at that time than we are today of our ability to pass upon the value of property in the absence of any finding by the trial court.

Be that as it may, there was no evidence in the *Crane* case that the purchaser was motivated by tax considerations. We therefore chose to presume that the sum of $3,000 represented the amount of the equity. We cannot say the same of the petitioner.[10] The record raises a strong inference that the $100,000 was paid not for an equity in the property but in order to obtain the benefit of large tax deductions. Under these circumstances we have no alternative except to send the case back so that evidence may be introduced as to the fair market value of the property at the time of purchase. Our views expressed herein should enable the trial court to determine the basis of the property and the allowable deductions for depreciation, if any, once the value has been established.

For the same reason we believe it is proper to express our views on the remaining issues, dependent though they may be in part on the outcome of the preceding issue.

The Commissioner contends that, if the petitioner was entitled to depreciation deductions on a basis which included the amount

---

[10] The Commissioner surprisingly has failed to make his usual argument for disallowance on the grounds that the purchase of the office building in question was motivated solely by tax avoidance, and that nothing of substance could have been realized by the petitioner. See Knetsch et ux. United States, 364 U.S. 361 (1960), where interest deductions were denied because the indebtedness arose in a transaction which could "not appreciably affect his beneficial interest except to reduce his tax". *Id.* at 366. Similarly, interest deductions were denied in a parade of cases resulting from broker-inspired deals in which taxpayers using borrowed funds acquired U. S. Government bonds without any risk or benefit in view other than a tax deduction, Sonnabend v. Comm'r, 267 F.2d 319 (1st Cir. 1959); Lynch v. Comm'r, 273 F.2d 867 (2d Cir. 1959); MacRae v. Comm'r, 294 F.2d 56 (9th Cir. 1961); Bridges v. Comm'r, 325 F.2d 180 (4th Cir. 1963), and in other instances where commercial reality was lacking because there was *no* chance for gain, Hart v. Comm'r, 338 F.2d 410 (2d Cir. 1964); Kapel Goldstein, 44 T.C. 284 (1965).

Counsel for the Commissioner wisely refrained from making this argument. The facts in this case do not indicate a sham transaction, *i.e.*, mere paper-shuffling, or transactions offsetting each other within an extremely brief period of time. On the contrary there was some reasonable hope of an appreciable effect upon the petitioner's beneficial interest—either a gain or loss—and we would not deny a deduction merely because the transaction proved to be unprofitable.

of the mortgage, he must necessarily be treated as realizing income to the extent of such depreciation when he donated the property to the Bide-A-Wee Animal Home. The Commissioner's argument rests on the proposition that a sale is not a prerequisite to the realization of income on the transfer of property.[11] Thus, he points to the fact that section 1001 provides that "gain from the sale *or other disposition* of property shall be the excess of the amount realized therefrom over the adjusted basis" (emphasis supplied). The only question, he contends, is whether the mortgage can be regarded as the "amount realized," and this, he says, has been settled in his favor by our decision in *Crane*.[12]

He also relies on the decision of the First Circuit in *Parker v. Delaney,* 186 F.2d 455. In that case the taxpayer purchased real property subject to a mortgage. When he later surrendered the property to the mortgagee the question arose as to whether he had "realized" the amount of the mortgage. The First Circuit held that the mortgage had been realized on the authority of our decision in *Crane* but left open the question of whether it would have reached the same conclusion if the property had been worth less than the lien. The court reasoned that the taxpayer had derived the same benefit from the mortgage when he surrendered the property as Mrs. Crane had when she sold the property. Whether the gain was ordinary or capital was not before the court, but it inferred that had it been required to decide this question it might have held the gain to be ordinary.

The petitioner strenuously opposes the application of this rule to a charitable donation. He maintains that from time immemorial it has been the rule that income is not realized from a gift to charity of property which has a value in excess of its adjusted basis.[13] Whether he was entitled to depreciation deductions has nothing whatever to do in his view of the matter with whether he realized income from the gift.

---

[11] Compare Reg. Sec. 1.306–1(b)(1) (1955) which indicates that a pledge of section 306 stock is a disposition if the pledgee can look only to the stock itself as security; *but see* Woodsam Associates v. Comm'r, 198 F.2d 357 (2d Cir. 1952), in which it was not argued that transfer of title in a tax-free exchange resulted in realization of income to the extent that a "subject to" mortgage placed on the property by the transferor through a dummy exceeded basis.

[12] See also Clinton H. Mitchell, 42 T.C. 953 (1964) ["subject to" mortgage included in selling price for purposes of computing eligibility to elect installment sale treatment].

[13] L.O. 1118, II–2 CUM. BULL. 148 (1923); Rev. Rul. 55–410, 1955–1, CUM. BULL. 297; White v. Brodrick, 104 F. Supp. 213 (D. Kan. 1952), *appeal dismissed* 198 F.2d 751 (10th Cir. 1952); Campbell v. Prothro, 209 F.2d 331 (5th Cir. 1954); Rev. Rul. 57–328, 1957–2 CUM. BULL. 229 [donation of section 306 preferred stock].

We do not quarrel with the petitioner's statement of the law in regard to charitable contributions, but we do not think the petitioner has brought himself within the principle on which he relies. The Tax Court found that the value of the property was not in excess of the mortgage at the time of the gift, and the petitioner has not appealed on this issue. Therefore, there was no equity to be transferred and without an equity there could be no charitable contribution. It appears to us that the petitioner has not made a gift to charity at all. He has simply made use of a charitable organization to relieve himself of property which might give rise to income were he to dispose of it in any other way.[14]

This does not necessarily dispose of the matter. Our decision in *Crane* was carefully circumscribed. We stated that "a different problem might be encountered where a mortgagor abandoned the property without receiving boot." When the value of the property is in excess of the lien one may reason that a purchaser would be willing to pay more for the property than the amount of the mortgage and that it should make no difference whether he pays the full consideration to the mortgagor who discharges the mortgage and pockets the balance or pays only the value of the equity to the mortgagor and takes subject to the mortgage. Thus, we observed (at p. 14):

"If a purchaser pays boot, it is immaterial as to our problem whether the mortgagor is also to receive money from the purchaser to discharge the mortgage prior to sale, or whether he is merely to transfer subject to the mortgage—it may make a difference to the purchaser and to the mortgagee, but not to the mortgagor. Or put it another way, we are no more concerned with whether the mortgagor is, strictly speaking, a debtor on the mortgage, than we are with whether the benefit to him is, strictly speaking, a receipt of money or property. We are rather concerned with the reality that an owner of property, mortgaged at a figure less than that at which the property will sell, must and will treat the conditions of the mortgage exactly as if they were his personal obligations."

In the present case the Tax Court found that the value of the property was not in excess of the mortgage at the time of the gift, but this does not preclude the possibility that the value of the property may at that time have been exactly equal to the mortgage. If it was, we think the petitioner would have difficulty escaping from the logic of our decision in *Crane*. There appears to us to be

[14] Mendham Corp. 9 T.C. 320 (1947) [foreclosure]; Woodsam Associate v. Comm'r, 198 F. 2d 357 (2d Cir. 1952) [foreclosure]; Parker v. Delaney, 186 F.2d 455 (1st Cir. 1950) [surrender to mortgagee]; I.R.C. §§ 351 & 357 (1954) [transfer to controlled corporation].

just as much reason to believe that a person desirous of acquiring the property would have been as willing to discharge the mortgage by payment to the petitioner as was the purchaser in the *Crane* case who paid only $3,000 to acquire the property subject to the mortgage. If this was the case we think *Crane* requires us to hold that the petitioner realized the amount of the mortgage at the time he transferred title to the charity.

On the other hand, if the property was worth less than the amount of the mortgage we clearly have, as we said in our *Crane* opinion, "a different case." Even under the strongest lens of our judicial microscope the benefit to the mortgagor becomes exceedingly difficult to observe.

The issue perches us squarely on the horns of a dilemma: either we must adhere to the reasoning of the *Crane* case and hold that if the property is worth less than the amount of the mortgage no income is "realized," in which case the petitioner may have obtained the benefit of large depreciation deductions for a relatively small out-of-pocket cost without incurring any tax liability when the property is disposed of; or we must depart from the reasoning behind our decision in *Crane* and hold that the concept of "realized" income does not necessarily depend on the receipt of a benefit in the usual sense of the word.

We are, however, not entirely helpless. Our judicial license permits us to look beyond our reasoning in *Crane* and search for a more significant rationale. If we were correct in allowing the mortgage to become a part of the taxpayer's basis in the first place when he is not personally liable, are we not equally warranted in saying that he should be charged with the gain attributable to the use of this basis when the property is disposed of and the transaction is closed? [15]

This question must be answered in the affirmative. By doing so we rid ourselves with one clean stroke of the unfortunate shackles which the reasoning in *Crane* imposed upon us. No longer are we required to say that the taxpayer has realized an economic benefit when the mortgage on which he was not liable follows the property into the hands of its new owner. We find ourselves on firmer ground when we say that the taxpayer's economic benefit stems

[15] The Seventh Circuit apparently came to this conclusion in a very recent case involving a sale of property held subject to a mortgage where the payment made by the purchaser was subsequently treated by the parties as an "overcharge" and required to be repaid. The court applied *Crane* in sweeping terms: "Relief from an outstanding mortgage constitutes an economic benefit to the seller when the property is sold subject to the mortgage". Teitelbaum v. Comm'r, 346 F.2d 266 (1965).

from the deductions which we have allowed him to take on the unassumed mortgage. These deductions arose by reason of the tax law and not because of what the taxpayer paid for the property. Hence, when the property is disposed of—whether by sale, abandonment, charitable gift, or otherwise—the tax law must be interpreted as requiring the taxpayer to account for these deductions.[16]

When the disposition is by gift and not by way of sale or exchange the gain must, of course, be ordinary.

This approach brings us squarely up against the problem of the Sixteenth Amendment to which the petitioner has devoted considerable attention in his brief. He points out that we gave this matter very short shrift in our *Crane* opinion, and in this he is surely right. On the other hand, our reasoning in *Crane*—which we now feel compelled to depart from—had the advantage of avoiding this problem, since we concluded that in effect the taxpayer should be treated as having received the amount of the mortgage along with the boot. Without this mooring to anchor our craft to we must face the question of whether the reasoning which now appeals to us as more realistic has constitutional infirmities. Does a taxpayer realize income in a constitutional sense when he disposes of property without receiving anything of economic value in return?

A profound student of our tax law many years ago succinctly described income as:

> "(1) any item of money, and (2) any interests in property having a money value, and differing in kind or in extent from those previously held by the recipient, which he has actually received, which he may obtain upon demand, or which have accrued during the period according to a recognized method of accounting employed in keeping his books, (3) any increase in economic worth resulting from the discharge of his obligations."[17]

Concededly this definition is not broad enough to encompass the case at bar. The Government suggests that we rely on the fact that deductions are a matter of legislative grace, and in permitting a taxpayer to deduct depreciation on a cost which includes an unassumed mortgage the legislature could condition the deduction on the taxpayer's inclusion of the amount of the deductions in his

[16] The First Circuit virtually so held in Parker v. Delaney, *supra* note 14, when it imposed a tax upon the mere surrender of property to the mortgagee, although L. Hand, J. was of a different mind when he wrote the opinion for the Second Circuit in the *Crane* case. See 153 F.2d 504, 506 (1945).

[17] Magill, TAXABLE INCOME, 398, 399 (1st. ed. 1936).

taxable income in the year in which he disposes of the property and the transaction is closed out.[18]

This has a superficial plausibility about it which is quite tempting. We reject it on two counts. First, Congress did not so condition the deduction. Despite a recent decision of the Second Circuit to the contrary,[19] deductions are not elective but mandatory. Second, Congress may allow deductions or not as it sees fit, but the problem we are faced with is whether the taxpayer has realized *income*. Congress cannot create income by means of its power over deductions.

We prefer to rest our constitutional base on a more modern conception of the Sixteenth Amendment. The definition which appeals to us has been advanced by two scholars of the present day. They suggest that "the concept of income is a flexible one, with the result in a particular case determined by the interplay of common usage, accounting concepts, administrative goals, and judicial reaction to these forces." [20]

With this definition the constitutional problems of the present case can be resolved without difficulty. "Accounting concepts" and "administrative goals" both argue strongly for treating deductions as income when the property is disposed of Our "judicial reaction to these forces" is favorable. The requirements of the Sixteenth Amendment are thus met in full, and the case is *Reversed and remanded.*

---

[18] In support of this proposition, the Government cites cases holding that the balance in a bad debt reserve constitutes taxable income at the time accounts receivable are transferred pursuant to a section 337 liquidation [West Seattle National Bank, 33 T.C. 341 (1959), *aff'd,* 288 F.2d 47 (9th Cir. 1961); J. E. Hawes Corp. v. Comm'r, 44 T.C. 705 (1965)] or a section 334(b)(2) merger of a subsidiary into its parent, Argus Inc. v. Comm'r, 45 T.C. 63 (1965).

We are not convinced that these cases are relevant, because the value of the receivables transferred was apparently in excess of adjusted basis [See 33 T.C. at 344 and 44 T.C. at 709] and further, as was so ably stated by the Ninth Circuit, bad debt reserves are distinguishable from depreciation reserves:

"A depreciation or depletion reserve is founded not upon the expectation of loss but upon facts. It recognizes that through depletion, wear and tear or obsolescence, the asset has to a certain extent actually been used up and that what is recovered by sale is recovered only from the unused portion of the asset. It recognizes that to the extent that the asset has been used up the owner has already realized or spent the asset's value and that his remaining investment is limited to the unrealized portion. The adjustment reflects the extent to which the asset has actually been exhausted by depletion, wear and tear or obsolescence. The question is whether a gain or loss has been realized on that which remains." 288 F.2d at 49.

[19] Standard Oil Company (New Jersey) v. United States, 338 F.2d 4 (1964).

[20] Surrey and Warren, *The Income Tax Project of the American Law Institute,* 66 Harv. L. Rev. 761, 771 (1953).

MR. JUSTICE INDIGNATION, dissenting

In its eagerness to frustrate the aim of a taxpayer who sought to take advantage of the revenue laws the Court has once more demonstrated its propensity for judicial legislation.

The dilemma in which the Court finds itself stems from the *Crane* case. The case at bar has offered us the opportunity to re-examine the reasoning of the *Crane* opinion, and if we now regard it as erroneous we should not hesitate to overrule it or at least confine it to its own facts.

In the *Crane* case the taxpayer argued that because all she received on the sale was $2,500 the "property" which she sold must have been only the equity, and if the equity was all she sold it must also have been all she inherited. Since the equity had no value when she acquired it, she was entitled to no depreciation and her gain was limited to her actual profit. Such a simple solution did not appeal to us, and the reason we rejected it, I venture to suggest, was not so much our concern over the technical meaning of the word "property" as it was our mistaken conception that depreciable property must give rise to allowable deductions. Obviously, the mortgagee could not take the deduction as he was not the owner; any loss that he sustained would be on the mortgage debt, not on the property. Therefore, if anyone was to have the benefit of the deduction it must be the mortgagor.

It was apparent, however, that the mortgagor could not take the deductions unless we held that his basis was the value of the property undiminished by the mortgage. Our concern with this aspect of the problem is manifest from the following excerpt from the opinion (at pp. 9, 10):

> "Under these provisions, if the mortgagor's equity were the § 113(a) basis, it would also be the original basis from which depreciation allowances are deducted. If it is, and if the amount of the annual allowances were to be computed on that value, as would then seem to be required, they will represent only a fraction of the cost of the corresponding physical exhaustion, and any recoupment by the mortgagor of the remainder of that cost can be effected only by the reduction of his taxable gain in the year of sale. If, however, the amount of the annual allowances were to be computed on the value of the property, and then deducted from an equity basis, we would in some instances have to accept deductions from a minus basis or deny deductions altogether."

Granting all this, it still does not seem to me sufficient reason for allowing the mortgagor to take deductions in excess of his actual cost.[21] The tax law does not proceed on the theory that a taxpayer is entitled to recover the *value* of depreciable property through depreciation deductions. Depreciation must be computed on the taxpayer's "basis," and "basis" for this purpose is the same as "basis" for determining gain or loss upon sale, *i.e.,* the "cost" of the property.

It is true that in the case of property acquired by inheritance the law allows the taxpayer to treat the value of the property as his cost, but this only means that the statute permits him to use as his basis what he would have paid for the property had he purchased it at its fair value instead of acquiring it by inheritance. All that Mrs. Crane inherited from her husband was an apartment house subject to a mortgage, the net value of which was stipulated to be zero. This therefore became her cost just as if she had purchased the property, and no depreciation deductions were necessary to make her whole.

The Court's failure to recognize the true function of depreciation under the Code led it disastrously astray. Having mistakenly concluded that depreciation deductions must be taken by Mrs. Crane, the Court set out to justify this result under the language of the statute. The answer hinged on the meaning of the word "property." Did it mean just the apartment house and the land on which it stood, or did it mean the physical property together with any liabilities inherent in its ownership, *i.e.,* the equity? Without undue violence to the English language it appears to me that either interpretation could have been adopted. Seeking as we were to find the necessary basis for depreciation, however, we had little difficulty satisfying ourselves that the reasons which favored disregarding the mortgage were "overwhelming."

We applied the "everyday sense" test, admittedly a welcome relief to readers of our tax opinions. If we are to look at the matter through the eyes of a layman, however, would it not be as reasonable to say that Mrs. Crane did not think she had inherited an apartment house in view of the mortgage which was in default and subject to foreclosure at any time? More likely, what she thought she inherited was merely the opportunity to operate the property with the consent of the mortgagee in the hope of salvaging what had been an unsuccessful venture up to that time.

The most that can be said about this game of words is that it

[21] As we stated in Detroit Edison Co. v. Comm'r., 319 U.S. 98, 101 (1943): ". . . the purpose of it all is to . . . reflect the financial consequences to the taxpayer . . .".

has about it an air of unreality. We were on a more practical level when we pointed out that if the taxpayer's basis was limited to the mortgagor's equity the basis would have to be changed with each payment on the mortgage, "and that the attendant problem of repeatedly recomputing basis and annual allowances would be a tremendous accounting burden on both the Commissioner and the taxpayer." We also noted that the mortgagor would acquire control over the timing of his depreciation allowances. The latter point hardly seems of much weight; a taxpayer can always affect his deductions by buying property, and each payment on an unassumed mortgage in effect increases the taxpayer's investment in the property. A basis which changes with each mortgage payment will undoubtedly involve some practical problems, but this would be no startling innovation to anyone who has to deal with our revenue laws.[22]

Of possibly more serious concern, though not referred to in our opinion, is the fact that if deductions depend on actual payments on the mortgage they will be low at the outset and increase as the property ages, contrary to the usual rate of physical exhaustion. However, as I have noted, depreciation deductions are intended to recoup the taxpayer's cost and if he has chosen to make his investment in the property in this way it is not unreasonable to require that his depreciation deductions correspond with his investment.

The final question before us in the *Crane* case was the determination of the amount "realized" upon the sale. Viewed strictly from the standpoint of "everyday sense" it is not easy to see how a taxpayer can be said to have "realized" the amount of a mortgage for which he is not personally liable when he merely transfers the property subject to the mortgage. Had the Court been as diligent in consulting the dictionary as it was when interpreting the word "property," it would have found that the word means "to gain; as, to *realize* large profits." Mrs. Crane gained nothing from the mortgage, at least in the everyday sense of the word, when she transferred her property.[23] We did not, however, choose to engage

---

22 One possible procedure for accomplishing the desired result would be to (1) tentatively compute depreciation by dividing useful life into the total of basis [equity] plus the unassumed encumbrance, but (2) limit the annual deduction and adjustment of basis to an amount not in excess of the remaining adjusted basis [equity, *i.e.,* (cash and property expended plus assumed debt) less accumulated depreciation allowed to date].

23 An entirely different problem would be encountered if the petitioner had placed the mortgage on the property himself without incurring personal liability. In such a case he would have had the use of the proceeds. Since he would not have been taxed at the time of the borrowing, on the theory that no closed transaction had occurred, it would be proper to tax him on the excess of the mortgage liability over the adjusted

in any such debate. Having established the proposition that for purposes of basis the "property" was the physical thing unaffected by the mortgage, we had only to point to what an absurdity it would be if the amount "realized" from the "property," *i.e.,* the apartment house, was only $2,500 when the "property" was worth at least $250,000. Obviously, on the sale of *the* "property" the taxpayer must have "realized" the amount of the mortgage in addition to the $2,500.

It would have been better had we stopped there. We attempted to reinforce our position, however, by arguing that Mrs. Crane had actually received a benefit "in the amount of the mortgage as well as the boot". Our theory was that the payment of boot was conclusive proof that the property was worth more than the boot, and that where this is so the mortgagor has no alternative other than to protect his equity by treating the conditions of the mortgage as if they were his personal obligations.

On both counts we were sadly misled. A purchaser may pay something for property even though he thinks it is not worth more than the mortgage, provided he does not have to assume the liability. This is because all he has to lose is his cash investment, whereas if the property increases in value the leverage will work in his favor and he will have the possibility of a large profit. The mortgagee's funds, which have already been invested in the property, provide the leverage and assume the major share of the risk. Merely because the purchaser paid Mrs. Crane $3,000 in cash

basis of the property when the property is disposed of and the transaction can be considered closed. Lutz & Schramm Co. v. Comm'r, 1 T.C. 682 (1943), *nonacq.* 1943 Cum. Bull. 35 [surrender to mortgagee]; Magnolia Development Corp. v. Comm'r, 19 CCH T.C.Mem. 934 (1960) [mortgage followed immediately by charitable gift and sale]; J. B. Simon v. Comm'r, 285 F.2d 422 (3d Cir. 1961) [contribution to capital but treated by court as taxable sale]; letter ruling from National Office, November 26, 1954, and letter ruling from St. Paul District Director, December 1955 (RIA Fed. Tax Coordinator ¶ K-3110) [apparently owner placed encumbrance on property before donating it to charity].

Whether the taxpayer should be considered to realize income, to the extent of the proceeds of the mortgage which he has enjoyed, when he disposes of such property in a transaction which would normally not be taxable poses an interesting question. In principle it would seem that the transaction by which the taxpayer obtained the proceeds of the mortgage without personal liability should be treated as closed and a tax imposed whenever the property subject to the mortgage passes out of the taxpayer's hands, for example, by gift, by death, by a contribution to capital or a tax-free exchange (subject to section 357 where applicable). However, in two cases where the Commissioner failed to impose a tax at the time of disposition he was later permitted to tax the corporate successor in interest when the mortgage was foreclosed. Mendham Corp. v. Comm'r, 9 T.C. 320 (1947) [foreclosure after tax-free exchange from predecessor corporation in 1932]; Woodsam Associates, Inc. v. Comm'r, 198 F.2d 357 (2d Cir. 1952) [foreclosure after transfer to controlled corporation in 1934].

does not mean that he would have paid $250,000 for the property without the mortgage. By the same token it also does not mean that Mrs. Crane would have been able to make a profit if she had satisfied the mortgage out of her own funds before selling the property. This would undoubtedly have been a pleasant surprise to the mortgagee who was threatening foreclosure in the face of rising interest arrearages, but it would have been a disastrous step for Mrs. Crane to take.

The fundamental error which the majority have made in the present case is to accept the original proposition on which *Crane* was predicated. There is neither rhyme nor reason in allowing a taxpayer to have the benefit of depreciation deductions attributable to another taxpayer's investment merely because the other taxpayer has made his investment in the form of a loan and will not himself be entitled to take depreciation. If personal liability is assumed on the mortgage, then of course it is proper to consider the mortgage debt as part of the taxpayer's cost. "Cost" does not require an immediate payment, but it does contemplate at least a firm commitment. The folly of departing from this principle is graphically illustrated by the scheme to which we have given our blessing today.

We have permitted the petitioner for an initial investment of $100,000 and a total investment of $225,000 to obtain depreciation deductions of $525,000. In five short years the taxpayer has not only been allowed to recover his cost but a part of someone else's investment as well. I do not believe Congress ever contemplated such an absurd and fictitious result. Having made this misstep at the threshold, the majority apparently feel compelled, in order to avoid the windfall which they have sanctioned, to rectify the matter by recapturing the mortgage for the Commissioner at the time of disposition regardless of what the value of the property may be at that time.

But even if the statute gave us no choice except to adopt the *Crane* basis rule I cannot subscribe to the proposition that we should manhandle the "realization" provision in order to set things straight. I find no provision in the law which authorizes us to hold that a taxpayer realizes income when he gives property away or abandons it, merely because he has had the benefit of depreciation deductions. This is a dangerous journey on which the Court has embarked. If the view of the majority is correct, how far does it extend? Is it applicable when the taxpayer's interest is transferred by death? I would have thought it was beyond debate that taxable gain is not "realized" by a taxpayer unless he receives or is entitled to receive something of material benefit. In departing from the ordinary meaning of the word the Court has opened Pandora's Box and invited the Commissioner to help himself.

To sum up: 1) I think the *Crane* case was wrongly decided and should be overruled now. 2) The only depreciation which the taxpayer should be allowed is on the $100,000 which he paid for the property and the $125,000 which he paid in reduction of the mortgage. 3) I agree with the majority that in view of the Tax Court's finding the taxpayer did not make a charitable gift—he in effect abandoned the property. 4) On the abandonment he is entitled to an ordinary loss equal to the amount of his adjusted basis at that time.

Mr. Justice Exasperation, dissenting.

I hesitate to express still another view, but when neither the majority or any of my dissenting brethren have adopted what to my mind is so clearly the correct rule I cannot remain silent. To allow a taxpayer to take deductions on a mortgage in excess of the value of the property appears to me to be absurd. I find nothing in the statute which requires such a result. No mortgage without personal liability will even be discharged for more than the value of the property.

At the same time any owner looking at the matter realistically must consider the mortgage as in substance his obligation up to the value of the property, and he should be entitled to take depreciation up to that amount. This will properly reflect the wear and tear over the useful life of the property. By the same token when the property is disposed of, the amount of the mortgage should be treated as realized to the extent that it does not exceed the value of the property.

This is a simple and wholly defensible rule to apply. We should not encourage the Commissioner to indulge in senseless refinements of a technical nature that the taxpayer will neither be able to understand or apply. While it is true that this rule requires that the value of the property be determined, this is no novel experience either to those who pay or those who collect taxes.

Mr. Justice Forthright, dissenting.

The Court has adopted what appears to me to be both an illogical and an impractical test. If an unassumed mortgage is to be taken into consideration in determining basis and the amount realized on sale, it should make no difference whether the morgtage is less than, equal to, or greater than the value of the property. In any case it must be paid off before the mortgagor can consider the property entirely his own. Furthermore, hinging the result on the value of the property injects troublesome problems of valuation and almost insuperable difficulties if the property fluctuates in value during the time it is held by the mortgagor.

I would include the full amount of the mortgage in determining both basis and the amount realized regardless of the value of the property.

MR. JUSTICE BEWILDERED, dissenting.

Were the issue before us, *de novo,* I would hold that the basis of property acquired subject to an unassumed mortgage is limited to the actual amount paid by the taxpayer if he purchased the property, and is limited to the value of the equity, if any, if he acquired the property by inheritance. But this issue was decided otherwise in *Crane,* and I do not think the decisions of this Court will enjoy the respect to which they are entitled if we feel free to overrule them merely because the membership of the Court has changed and the membership as presently constituted might reach a different conclusion.

Almost twenty years have passed since our decision in *Crane.* During this time it has been discussed by learned writers[24] and relied upon not only by taxpayers but by the Commissioner of Internal Revenue and even the Congress.[25] It is too late in the day to change our minds.

Nor do I think that it would be proper to say, much as I might wish to, that the decision in *Crane* should be limited to property acquired by devise. True, the question there was what the "value of the property" means whereas here the statutory language is the "cost of the property." If, however, the "property" is *the property* unreduced by the mortgage, it seems to me that we must

---

[24] See, *e.g.*, Silverstone, *Charitable Giving: The Need for a Logically Closed System,* Taxes (July 1964) pp. 432–435; Rusoff, *The Federal Income Tax Consequences of Transactions Relating to Mortgages on Land,* 4 Buffalo L. Rev. 181 (1954); Spears, *Mortgages in Excess of Basis,* 11 U. So. Cal. L. S. Institute 883 (1959); Rubin, *Tax Problems on Real Estate Mortgages Transactions,* 9 Tul. Tax Institute 524 (1960); Berl, *Disposition of Property Mortgaged in Excess of Basis,* 19 N.Y.U. Institute 1033 (1961).

[25] Provisions enacted after our decision in *Crane* reflect Congressional acceptance of a view which would generally equate liabilities assumed with those to which property is subject [§§ 108(a), 334(b)(2), 955(b)(5), 956(a)(3) and 970(c)(1)] and with appropriate modifications when the liability exceeds the fair market value of the property [§§ 311(c) and 752(c)].

also say that the "cost" of *such* property is not limited to the amount paid for the equity.

It is in the determination of what the "cost" should be in such a case, however, that I find myself beset by the greatest doubt. If the mortgage is in excess of the value of the property, I agree with the majority that the "cost" should be limited to the actual amount paid by the purchaser. In such a case, to permit the purchaser to include either the amount of the mortgage or the amount of the mortgage up to the value of the property would be inconsistent with the reasoning underlying our *Crane* decision, *i.e.,* that where property is mortgaged at less than its value the owner "must and will treat the conditions of the mortgage exactly as if they were his personal obligation," inferring that he will have no reason to do so where the mortgage exceeds the value of the property. Admittedly, this result substitutes the equity test for the word "property." However, in view of my doubts with regard to the wisdom of our *Crane* decision, I would not be disposed to extend its boundaries beyond those limits which I think have with justification been relied upon.

If, on the other hand, the mortgage does not exceed the value of the property, I agree with the majority that we should include the mortgage in determining the purchaser's "cost." It seems to me important, however, that we state the reasons for the position we are taking and recognize its ramifications.

In the first place, where the mortgage exceeds the value of the property it will not work any undue hardship on taxpayers to limit their "cost" to the amount which they have paid in cash. Their cash investment will be less than the value of the property and they will have the right to take depreciation on their cash investment in any event. Furthermore, should they choose to increase their investment and reduce the mortgage to the value of the property they should then in my judgment be entitled to include the mortgage in their basis. The rule, however, should deter taxpayers from taking advantage of the law by acquiring heavily mortgaged property for a nominal sum in order to enjoy the benefit of large tax deductions.

Nor will the rule cause any difficulty when property subject to a mortgage is sold and we are faced with determining the amount realized. If the value of the property continues to be less than the mortgage while held by the taxpayer, he will not be charged with having realized the amount of the mortgage when he sells it. On the other hand, if at any time the property increases in value, or the mortgage is reduced to a point where the mortgage no longer exceeds the value of the property, the taxpayer's basis should be considered to be the amount of the mortgage and he should in that event be charged under the *Crane* decision with realizing the amount of the mortgage on sale.

It would of course pose a troublesome problem if we should be confronted with a case in which property, which had at one time been worth as much as the mortgage while held by the taxpayer, should be sold after it had declined in value to less than the amount of the mortgage. *Crane* left this open, and while perhaps it is premature to venture an opinion at this time, I would prefer, again, not to extend *Crane* and to say therefore that the amount of the mortgage was not realized in this case even though it had at one time been a part of the taxpayer's basis for depreciation.

My basic disagreement is with that part of our decision which determines that any amount is "realized" when property in which there is no equity is abandoned.

I recognize that the *Crane* decision, although it dealt with a sale, took a step in this direction. If income can be realized from a mortgage on which there is no personal liability when the property is sold, there is at least some logical justification in holding that income can be realized when such property is abandoned.

But, as we have seen, *Crane* proceeded on the assumption that the property was worth more than the mortgage. Perhaps we were too quick to jump to this conclusion merely because the purchaser was willing to pay a small sum in cash. Yet, that is what we said, and we made it quite clear that we would not necessarily reach the same conclusion if this were not so.

I would not go an inch further. Obviously, no one would be anxious to buy the property for the amount of the mortgage when the owner is willing to abandon it. I would therefore confine the *Crane* doctrine to taxable sales or exchanges where some consideration is paid. It is true that the First Circuit felt compelled by our reasoning to apply *Crane* to an abandonment. Unlike the lower courts, however, we are always free to re-examine the reasoning of an earlier case and refuse to apply it when the facts are different.

I am also deeply disturbed at what the Court has said about the Sixteenth Amendment. The definition of "income" which it has approved is so all inclusive that virtually no constitutional safeguard remains.[26] Our Constitution was not founded upon "ac-

---

[26] Congress itself has shown more concern for the Constitution than the majority. In

counting concepts" or "administrative goals." I do not believe "income" is "realized" unless something of value is received.[27] The transaction does not make available any assets previously offset by an obligation. *United States v. Kirby Lumber Co.,* 284 U.S. 1. There has been no accession to wealth, or receipt of funds or valuable property over which the taxpayer has complete dominion. *General Am. Investors Co. v. Comm'r.,* 348 U.S. 434; *Commissioner v. Glenshaw Glass Co.,* 348 U.S. 426; *Commissioner v. Lobue,* 351 U.S. 243. There has been no enhancement in value of any asset of the taxpayer which becomes subject to tax upon the occurrence of an event, *i.e.,* transfer of title. *Helvering v. Brunn,* 309 U.S. 461, 469.

I have enough difficulty reconciling our treatment of an unassumed mortgage as realized when the property is sold or exchanged and the mortgage does not exceed the value of the property, without extending the principle to cover a wide range of other cases.

The Court has also unnecessarily extended itself, it seems to me, in holding that the petitioner's gift was the equivalent of abandoning the property. It is true that the Tax Court found that the petitioner had no equity in the property at the time of the gift and was not entitled therefore to a deduction for a charitable contribution. The fact remains, however, that the charity became entitled to receive net income of some $20,000 annually until the mortgagee exercised its right of foreclosure, and this could not take place for at least a year by reason of the agreement which the petitioner made immediately before the transfer.

In my judgment this case is an excellent example of why we should confine our attention to more pressing matters of a broad constitutional nature and leave the technical aspects of the Internal Revenue Code to the lower courts except where a clear conflict between the Circuit Courts must be resolved. We should have let *Crane* stumble along on the guiding arm of the lower courts and never have granted certiorari in the first place. I am authorized to state that all of the Justices concur in the preceding sentence.

---

enacting the depreciation recapture provisions, it did not see fit to require that a taxpayer take into income the entire balance of accumulated post-1962 depreciation merely because he transferred the related asset to a charity. Instead, recapture operates only to the extent that the property contributed has a fair market value in excess of adjusted basis. § 170(e) I.R.C.

27 The Ninth Circuit recently refused to "disregard the economic realities" and rejected the Commissioner's attempt to "create fictitious income, never received in fact". It reversed the Tax Court's decision that the bad debt reserve must be taken into income upon a section 351 incorporation. *Estate of Heinz Schmidt v. Comm'r,* 66–2 U.S. Tax Cas. 9202 (1966); 17 Am. Fed. Tax Rep. 2d 242 (1966), rev'g 42 T.C. 1130 (1964).

B. Depletion

As in many other areas, the Tax Reform Act of 1969 made some changes in the treatment of the extractive industries—most notably, by reducing the percentage depletion rate for oil and gas from 27½% to 22% of gross income—but the changes did not eliminate the basic controversies reflected in the following selections. The potential effects of tax changes on the oil and gas industry are explored in depth in a report by CONSAD Research Corporation, "The Economic Factors Affecting the Level of Domestic Reserves," prepared for the Treasury's Office of Tax Analysis and published as Part 4 of the Treasury's Tax Reform Studies and Proposals (91st Cong., 1st Sess. 1969).

Of at least comparable financial importance to the domestic oil industry are restrictions on oil imports. The policy aspects of such restrictions are analyzed intensively by a Presidential Task Force in its report, "The Oil Import Question" (1970). It estimates the cost of such restrictions to consumers at about $5 billion in 1969 (p. 22). Thus in appraising the total cost of public assistance to the industry, the impact on consumers of import restrictions should be added to the loss of potential revenues from special tax incentives.

MENGE, THE ROLE OF TAXATION IN PROVIDING FOR DEPLETION OF MINERAL RESERVES

House Committee on Ways and Means,
2 Tax Revision Compendium 967 (1959).

DIFFERENTIAL TAX TREATMENT OF EQUALS

Despite the fact that all productive assets are economically similar, we find that certain types of these assets are accorded preferential treatment under our present tax laws. Specifically, in the extractive industries assets, in the form of mineral deposits, can be written off against revenue for tax purposes, not only once, as is true of assets in other industries, but two, three, or even four or more times over. All assets, however, are used up in production only once, regardless of the fact that they may have different forms and last for varying periods of time. Furthermore, all are replaceable. Hammers, machine tools, dies, jigs, lathes, buildings, oil and gas wells, and copper mines have a common characteristic of replaceability. The mode of replacement varies but slightly with the asset. Money or dollars are used to purchase the wood, steel, and labor necessary for a new hammer or the steel, bricks, and labor for a new building. Similarly, dollars are used to purchase the steel, labor, and drilling equipment used in discovering new reserves of ore, gas, or oil.

The productive factors used up within the current period present no particular economic or tax accounting problem. If any firm incurs an expense for productive factors which will be used up within a year, such expense is uniformly charged against current revenues to determine annual net income. Fuel consumed during the year, the salaries of sales clerks, and the amount of stationery supplies used are examples of this type of direct current cost or expense. However, there are productive factors that are not totally used up within the year, e.g., the machine tool, the stamping press, the forge, the mine, the oil well, the sand pit. For these longer lived productive factors, or assets, the annual decrement of value, the amount ostensibly used up in current production, is an estimate, and this annual expense is designated as either depreciation, amortization, or depletion.

For a representative business, therefore, we have two types of charges against current revenues, direct current costs and the estimated current costs of either depreciation, amortization, or depletion. By way of illustration, assume that you own a small plant producing stamped metal hood ornaments for trucks. You gross $200,000 in revenues during the year and you incur direct current costs or expenses for labor, fuel, and other materials of $100,000. In addition, your general purpose assets such as the plant building itself and your lathes and larger stamping presses depreciate by $20,000 per year. Your special fixtures, i.e., your dies, which have to be charged off over a 3-year period to take account of the regularly recurring model changes in truck ornamentation, are amortized at the rate of $30,000 per year over 3 years and selling and miscellaneous expenses are $20,000. At the end of the year your profit position can be summarized as follows:

Current revenues	$200,000
Direct current costs	100,000
Depreciation	20,000
Amortization	30,000
Miscellaneous expense	20,000
Total expense	170,000
Total taxable income	30,000

Note that although your stamping firm takes depreciation and also amortization it does not—and cannot—take the two on the same asset. For any one asset at any given instant you are allowed depreciation or amortization, but never both. To allow a firm to depreciate and amortize the same asset at an instant of time would allow the deduction of the same cost twice, once as depreciation and once as amortization. A good trick if you can do it—and you can do it.

You can do it if you happen to own mineral deposits, an oil well, for example. Let us say that the Acme Oil Co. spends $500,000 in exploratory drilling. Of the approximately 20 holes that it drills, suppose that one proves to be productive. The Acme Oil Co. has thus far spent $500,000 to create a new asset, a producing well. Of this amount $300,000 is of a general nature resulting from expenses directly connected with drilling dry holes or unsuccessful wells. This amount is a current cost, exactly analogous to the labor, fuel, and materials in the stamping plant, and is written off against current revenue. The remaining $200,000 incurred in creating the one succesful well represents money, and, therefore, labor and materials, directly associated with this particular well. This sum is capitalized and an estimated charge against current revenue is made in ensuing years, until the entire $200,000 has been written off against such revenues. If the Acme Oil Co. charges off $20,000 of depreciation and has sales and other expenses of $100,000 per year and receives $500,000 of current revenue from the successful well, its total income will be $80,000.

Current revenue	$500,000
Current drilling costs	$300,000
Depreciation	20,000
Sales and miscellaneous expense	100,000
Total expense	420,000
Total income	80,000

As with our metal stamping concern, so with our oil firm, we have written off all of our expenses against our total revenues. Both companies have been treated equally with relation to the determination of net profit.

But the firm with the oil well does even better. This is possible only as a result of deducting the same expenses more than once. It will be noted that all expenses were accounted for in both firms prior to determining the profits shown above. Nevertheless, the Acme Oil Co. is subsequently allowed to deduct a depletion allowance on its oil well—in addition to the current expense and depreciation it has already taken on the full cost of the well. This is similar to allowing your metal stamping firm to take depreciation on its general purpose lathes and then allowing it also to amortize this same cost against current revenue. A lathe that cost $4,000 would on this basis be charged off against revenue to the extent of $8,000. An oil well that cost the Acme Oil Co. $200,000 in capitalized costs could be written off as approximately five or six hundred thousand dollars or even more.

The case of duplicative cost deductions involved in the determination of Acme Oil's profit can be illustrated by referring again to our numerical example:

Current revenues	$500, 000
Current drilling costs	$300, 000
Depreciation	20, 000
Sales and miscellaneous expense	100, 000
Total expense	420, 000
Total income	80, 000

From total income, to secure total taxable income, 27½ percent of the current revenue of the well is subtracted, i.e., $137,500. However, because this amount is in excess of 50 percent of the net income we use the 50 percent figure, or $40,000. Taxable income is thereby reduced by $40,000. Thus:

Total income	$80, 000
Less depletion allowance	—40, 000
Total taxable income	40, 000

Now, the average oil well has a life of approximately 20 years and if a fairly constant rate of exhaustion is assumed, so that this particular well is worth zero in 20 years, the average annual total income over its productive life will be about $40,000 per year. Determining the depletion allowance on the basis of 50 percent of total income, the average annual depletion allowance would amount to $20,000. Multiplied by 20 years this is $400,000. Therefore, an asset, an oil well, that cost $200,000 is written off against revenue to the extent of $600,000, $200,000 as depreciation and an additional $400,000 as depletion. There is the possibility that firms can do even better than this, especially where the net profit is sufficiently great to allow the full 27½ percent of gross revenue to be deducted from profit. Some firms, of course, would not do quite as well. However, the ordinary manufacturer or retailer, the flour mill, the electrical appliance firm, the drugstore and the corner grocer are not granted this privilege. The oil industry, natural gas, coal mining, metals mining, sulfur and sand and gravel are.

A BRIEF HISTORY OF THE DEPLETION ALLOWANCE

The history of the present depletion allowance most properly begins in 1913 when Congress authorized cost depletion. Under these early provisions owners of oil and gas wells and mines were allowed to deduct annually from taxable income a percentage of the costs of the property. This particular provision was complicated in 1916 when market value was made the basis for the depletion allowance for properties discovered prior to 1913. This greatly favored the owners of properties discovered before 1913 because the market values of producing properties usually exceed their development costs by a considerable margin—this being generally true of all types of assets; mines, wells, factories, and service and trade establishments. This discrimination in the treatment of depletable properties led to the enactment of legislation in 1918 which provided that where the market value of the property was not adequately reflected by the cost of the property, the depletion allowance would be based upon the "fair market value of the property at the date of discovery, or within thirty days, thereafter." This allowance, commonly known as discovery depletion, was subsequently limited in 1924 to 50 percent of the annual net income from the property.

In 1926 percentage depletion was substituted for discovery depletion. Discovery depletion foundered upon the difficulty involved in determining, for tax purposes, the fair market value of the property. In place of market value the oil or gas well owner was to deduct from taxable income 27½ percent of the gross income from the oil or gas well, provided that such allowance did not exceed 50 percent of the net income from the well. The choice of a 27½-percent rate for gas and oil properties was the result of an attempt to duplicate the allowances actually allowed under the earlier discovery depletion concept. Properties other than gas and oil, having had a different experience under discovery depletion, could, therefore, be expected to have, and did have, different rates of percentage depletion. Subsequently, by 1932, sulfur was allowed a 23 percent rate, metals 15 percent, and coal 5 percent. Cost depletion was still required in many instances, if it exceeded the percentage depletion allowance. In 1954 eligibility for the depletion allowance was broadened to include basically all minerals. Considered as minerals, and eligible for a depletion allowance, were those ubiquitous elements, sand, gravel, and clay, ingredients that must comprise at least 99 percent of the farmland in my home State of New Hampshire. There were a small number of specific exclusions.

ECONOMIC EFFECTS OF DUPLICATIVE DEDUCTIONS OF COST

Introduction.—For most minerals there is now an extra or duplicative cost deduction from taxable income ranging in extent from 27½ to 5 percent of gross revenue. This is an extremely lucrative privilege to be granted to so select a group of American firms. There can be little wonder that the minerals industry as a whole campaigned so vigorously for a blanket inclusion of all minerals under the depletion provisions. The real wonder is why other industries do not similarly push just as strongly their own claims for a slice of this pie. There is, after all, no inherent difference between the Chrysler Corp. and the Gulf Corp. in respect to possession of assets, the real value of which is not adequately measured by means of depreciation alone.

Nonetheless, it is frequently claimed that mineral assets somehow are essentially different from other assets because normal depreciation or amortization do not fully reflect their true value or worth. In other words, even after the costs of the asset are written off against revenue, through the use of the device of depreciation, not all of the realizable market value of the asset will have been accounted for. Two comments are in order. The first is that successful firms in all industries find that depreciation and amortization allowances fall far short of reflecting the actual market value of their assets. This is only in part the result of price changes. This surplus market value is frequently the result of the successful, imaginative, or lucky management of a given component of assets. If certain new types of facilities were acquired at extremely favorable prices by an able purchasing staff, should an extra cost deduction be allowed to fully account for the greater real value of these assets? Or should a corporation be allowed an extra cost deduction against taxable income merely because it is profitable and the going market value of the firm is, therefore, in excess of the cost of its assets? Any subsequent gains in the market value of assets, over their original cost, cannot be written off against taxable income in any but the minerals industry.

Overinvestment in certain mineral industries.—In some quarters, especially in the oil industry, many spokesmen contend that the depletion allowance is necessary to encourage further exploration for mineral reserves. In the preceding sections it was pointed out that the depletion allowance leads to serious inequities as among firms by allowing certain ones to deduct the same costs several times over. The problem here is a slightly different one, i.e., the overall economic effects of allowing a double counting of costs. It is possible that some beneficial effects could ensue from this policy for the economy as a whole, or, on the other hand, it is also possible that such policies could lead to unsound economic effects. To anticipate the conclusion of this paper, it is that the depletion allowance is decidedly unsound from an overall economic point of view. The end result is a misallocation of the country's productive resources. It can be expected that where the return on investment in an industry is artificially enhanced, as by allowing duplicative cost deductions, more capital will flow into that industry until the rate of return is the same as in any alternative source of investment. This is only a tendency which never completely works itself out because of imperfections in the capital market and in the competitive structure of the economy itself, but given this tendency any change in relative industry returns will distort the normal flow of capital.

It is interesting to note that Prof. Arnold C. Harberger in testimony before the Joint Committee on the Economic Report, "Federal Tax Policy for Economic Growth and Stability, Papers," pages 439–449, emphasized this same distortion of investment flows, as do most economists, and made certain interesting calculations concerning the extremes to which certain types of investment might be misallocated. Professor Harberger calculated, for instance, that because of capital gains taxation, and because of duplicative cost deductions in the oil industry an oil firm would be willing to spend up to $1.95 to discover $1 worth of oil. The figures for other mineral industries were even more surprising. In sulfur the ratio of expense to potential discovery was $2.12 for $1, in iron $2.13 for $1, in copper $1.96 for $1, in lead and zinc $2.27 for $1, and in coal $2.30 for $1 (p. 449). These figures should not be interpreted to mean that firms in these respective fields are presently spending approximately $2, on the average, for every $1 of newly discovered resources. They merely indicate the extent to which it is profitable, under our present tax laws, to push exploration given certain demand and potential supply relationships. Where potential supply, or potential reserves, are relatively large compared to demand there will be little pressure to push exploration to the point of spending more in finding reserves than the reserves themselves are worth. Sand and gravel is a prosaic illustration. Little effort or investment is required to unearth new sources of this material.

Oil, on the other hand, is an altogether different proposition. There is at present relatively greater pressure on reserves in this industry for two reasons. One is the natural relative scarcity of oil reserves compared to sand and gravel, and the other is an artificial scarcity created by import restrictions, i.e., quotas on foreign crude and refined petroleum products. Some indication of the effect of the imposition of these latter controls can be seen by referring to import statistics for the first and second quarters of 1958, and the first quarter of 1959 before controls, and the second quarter of 1959 after controls:

[In barrels]

	1958	1959
Crude oil imports: [1]		
1st quarter	[1] 959,000	985,000
2d quarter	919,000	[2] 874,000
Imports of refined products: [1]		
1st quarter	721,000	1,259,000
2d quarter	675,000	[2] 573,000

[1] All figures are in terms of average daily imports in barrels.
[2] After controls.

Source: The Oil and Gas Journal, vol. 57, No. 31.

The import controls hit refined products especially hard, and it is these which have shown the most steeply rising import trend over the past several years. In part, this trend reflects a rather general oversupply of oil in the world today, which, if allowed to enter the domestic market, could have profound effects on the price level, and which would also enhance the relative adequacy of existing United States reserves.

Measurement of overinvestment.—Because of the allowable extra cost deductions under the depletion allowance, and the differential treatment between ordinary profits or gains and capital gains—a point that is more appropriately discussed at another time, there is the aforementioned tendency for oil exploration to be pushed beyond the point at which society obtains optimum economic benefits. The question of what constitutes excess reserves or uneconomic capacity has been hotly—and frequently—debated. There is little to be gained, and little has been gained, by attempting to measure excess reserves in terms of so many barrels or so many years' supply of oil, given existing or projected demand. Honest and intelligent students of the industry can hold various views based upon varying assumptions as to demand, substitute energy sources, etc. However, it is not necessary to rely upon assumptions, hunches, or guesses in this instance. If tax policies alone increase the profit return in one industry relative to the returns in other industries, there will be a tendency for investment to be shifted to the industry receiving preferential tax treatment. If a dollar earns less than can be earned elsewhere, after allowing for differences in risk, the investor will shift his funds out of the industry; if it earns more, the investors in other industries will transfer their funds to the more profitable industry. If industry A, therefore, has a lower profit per dollar invested before tax than industry B, under normal circumstances resources would flow out of A and into B. But this corrective flow of resources will not occur if the investor in A is able to collect just as much or more on his dollar invested in industry A as in industry B, as is possible in the extractive industries. Because of duplicative counting of costs, taxes on income in A are less than in B, thus artificially increasing returns in A.

Take as an example, firm 1 in industry A earning $20 profit on every $100 invested and firm 2 in industry B earning $25 profit on every $100 invested. Investors would normally put their money in firm 2 rather than in firm 1. However, suppose that firm 1 is allowed a duplicative deduction of costs through a depletion allowance, for purposes of computing taxable income. If this cost deduction brings taxable income down to the level of $10 per $100 invested, than the return to the investor in 1, assuming a 50-percent corporate tax rate, will be $15 for every $100 he has invested; i.e., the $10 excluded from taxation plus $5 remaining after deducting taxes from taxable income. How fares the investor in firm 2? Industry B has no depletion allowance, and, therefore, the whole $25 profit is subject to the 50-percent tax rate or a tax of $12.50. The investor in 2, therefore, finds that his return is only $12.50 for every $100 he has invested, $2.50 less than the return in 1. Now, the investor in no way cares a fig about the fact that firm 2 is actually more profitable than firm 1; he is simply interested in getting greatest return on his dollar investment. In this instance then, he would transfer investment funds from firm 2 to firm 1, leading to a misallocation of resources and overinvestment in industry A merely as a result of a particular tax policy of the Federal Government. The Government takes a greater proportion of industry B's profits than of A's, and the usual corrective flow of resources is prevented.

John Doe, the average U.S. consumer, ultimately must bear the costs of this inefficiency. He pays more for his gasoline and home heating fuels as a result of import quotas and he pays more in taxes. Estimates are that he pays between $750 million and $1 billion more, to make up for the tax loss resulting from the beneficial treatment of the extractive industries. The consumer is the oddman out. In real terms, because of overinvestment in the extractive industries, there are fewer resources left to be invested in steel, automobiles, highways, national parks, or candy bars. The overinvestment in oil is not just dollars, it is part of the standard of living of every many, woman, and child in the United States.

Ramifications of overinvestment.—Oil industry spokesmen have usually advanced two arguments to justify the inequity of this maldistribution of resources. The first is that in the future the U.S. economy will need more oil reserves than we have today and that, at our present and projected rate of oil consumption, we shall have to step up the pace of our current discovery and development programs.

This hypothesis rests upon two rather tenuous assumptions. The first is that oil will continue to be as important an energy source in the future as it is today. The second assumption is more fundamental, and, if true, of greater significance than generally realized. According to this hypothesis, the free market price system cannot be relied upon to adjust future oil reserves to future demand conditions. In other words, the price mechanism does not work in the oil industry and, therefore, exceptions should be granted to the industry such as the privilege of the depletion allowance. Traditionally, where the price system has not worked satisfactorily the Government has stepped in either to regulate the industry in question, as is true of public utilities, or to take over the actual operation of the industry itself, such as has happened with the postal service. It may be true that the oil industry cannot, of course, cover its average costs in the long run under a free market price system and, therefore, will have to be subject to increasing governmental assistance and regulation, such as the present Oil Import Administration. But, despite many industry spokesmen to the contrary, I doubt that this is a true picture of the competitive strength of the industry.[1]

There is every indication that the oil industry, without duplicative cost deductions in the guise of the depletion allowance, can compete successfully and contribute its rightful share to future productivity in the United States. In 1958 the industry added to its reserves despite a drop in drilling, and reserves reached alltime highs. In part, of course, this was the result of a temporary drop in the demand for oil, but, even disregarding this factor, the further extension of existing oilfields and the continuing development of more efficient secondary recovery methods gives promise of more than doubling our existing reserves in the next two decades. Today our proved reserves are in the vicinity of some 30,500 million barrels and our 1958 production was 2,373 million barrels. In 20 years, according to Mr. Morgan Davis, president of Humble Oil & Refining Co., in a speech before the American Association of Petroleum Geologists this spring, our domestic reserves will be increased by 20 to 25 billion barrels as a result of developing more fully existing fields, and by 20 billion barrels as the result of better secondary recovery methods. He termed these estimates conservative. Thus, without encouraging new drilling leading to the finding of any other new domestic fields, we could bring into being additional reserves greater than those reserves existing at present. In fact, in the past 5 years the industry has been adding, on the average, 2.4 billion barrels to reserves annually merely through extension and revision of known fields according to Davis—a rate approximately equal to the rate of U.S. production in 1958.

Where, then, is the need for the extra spur or stimulus to the discovery of additional domestic reserves through further exploration? Even without more domestic exploration the industry is doing very well indeed, creating new reserves at a rate equal to production. Nevertheless, it would be folly to suggest that no further domestic exploration is needed. It is necessary, and Davis again

---

[1] Senator Paul F. Douglas of Illinois observed in the 1955 "Hearings on Federal Tax Policy for Economic Growth and Stability," p. 376, that the three witnesses who were industry spokesmen all believed that it was necessary to modify the results of the free price mechanism's actions in the extractive industries. The three academic economists who testified did not believe that such modification was required.

presents an optimistic view of the industry's strength and vigor. He maintains that at least 35 billion barrels will be added to reserves in the next 20 years through the discovery of new fields. He also disagrees with those numerous industry spokesmen who have declared that major oilfields are becoming increasingly scarce. Newly discovered fields, it is true, are apt to be small when discovered—but they frequently develop in time into large ones.

There is some interesting evidence on the need for or usefulness of the depletion allowance in developing these new fields Davis mentions. In 1958 most of the 40 largest oil firms, ranging in asset size from $7.9 billion to $42 million, reported data on the number of wells drilled, broken down as between productive and dry. It is worth noting that the worst experience of any of the 40 was by one firm that drilled 105 productive wells and 96 dry wells. This is a far cry from the 1-to-10 figure of productive to dry wells so often indiscriminately cited by some industry spokesmen. Furthermore, the largest five reporting firms had the following experience:

Wells drilled [1]

Firm	Productive	Dry
1	387	100
2	1,301	239
3	489	201
4	537	109
5	733	217

[1] Source: Oil and Gas Journal, vol. 57, No. 16.

Of the 47,800 domestic wells of all types drilled by all firms in 1958, only 60 percent were productive and 40 percent were dry. All wildcatting operations resulted in 2,567 productive wells and 10,632 dry holes.

These statistics summarize an important fact in the case against the depletion allowance. The large firms do not need it. Their drilling experience is good, they discover more productive than dry wells. The risk in these instances can truly be said to be minimal and there can be no doubt that the depletion allowance is not necessary to compensate for added risk and to encourage exploration. Independents, however, present a rather different picture. Their activities are fairly risky and many fail, relative to large firms, to contribute to reserves in proportion to their drilling activity. Nevertheless, the U.S. taxpayer is asked to grant substantial tax privileges to the industry as a whole, so that many marginal operators can continue to use up scarce economic resources. It is asking a great deal to insist that the public give an extra bonus to the successful firms and then turn around and reward failure as well.

The second argument frequently advanced in favor of the depletion allowance is the necessity of maintaining excess capacity, or overinvestment, in the event of war. Again, several assumptions of doubtful validity underlie this thesis. One proposition is that oil will be necessary in a possible future war, if such an event should come to pass. There are certainly several reasons to suppose that other energy sources may be more important in the future than oil. As we all know there are now in existence atomic-powered submarines and atomic-powered icebreakers, and there will soon be atomic merchant ships and electrical power generating stations, to mention a few. We are firmly launched into the atomic age. Closely related to this point is the presumption that any such war would be long enough to enable us to utilize the excess reserves still in the ground. The reserves in the local gas station's fuel pumps might well be all that we would have time to make use of in these days of guided missiles and atomic warheads.

This argument also presumes that oil has a particular priority over all other industries as far as national defense is concerned. Is oil more important to national defense than steel, automobiles, electrical machinery, and chemicals? Who is to make this decision? Certainly not the industry concerned. And if it is difficult to choose between industries vital to national defense, then should not a privilege extended to one be extended to all? Why not give tax advantages to steel to maintain surplus facilities manned and ready to go on an instant's notice, rather than having to wait upon a conversion period? There is about as much logic one way as the other.

It is possible, of course, that after a thorough inventory of our resource needs, a competent governmental body might decide that a certain level of oil reserves was necessary for defense purposes—and it might also decide that it would be proper to consume foreign oil in peacetime to conserve our own resources. The present depletion allowance, however, is totally unsuited to the task of maintaining a proper level of standby reserves. In the first place, the present allowance covers many industries that could qualify as necessary to the national defense only by the sheerest stretch of the imagination, e.g., clay, sand, and gravel. Further, it has created an ephemeral type of excess capacity, which is here today and gone tomorrow. The more capacity that is created the more that is needed. The explanation of this paradox is not difficult. As more capacity is created, induced by the depletion allowance, greater pressure is put on the domestic market by the greater supply of oil thereby available. The capacity created is used up in domestic consumption, even if it is necessary to drastically limit foreign imports to do so. It is then supposedly essential to discover even greater reserves to balance against the resultant increased usage of domestic supplies. Eventually, commonsense should dictate that there will have to be a halt in this cycle. Newly discovered reserves should be kept as reserves, not made available for current consumption—that is, if it is felt desirable to subsidize directly any additional reserves above what the free market would dictate. Even if it should be determined that we need increased reserves for defense we cannot continue to finance them in such a manner that they slip away like sand in a sieve.

Also, it is somewhat bewildering, after being told so repeatedly that national defense requirements make provisions for the depletion allowance necessary in order to insure adequate domestic reserves of oil in the event of war, to find that the depletion allowance applies to foreign wells of U.S. firms as well. Clearly, this is a non sequitur. If one espouses the national defense argument as the reason for having the depletion allowance, then there is no logical justification for its application to foreign wells. If its application to foreign wells is advocated, then one must in effect admit that the allowance is merely a privilege granted the industry with little regard for defense considerations.

Lastly and, in a sense, most importantly, regardless of the various claims of the extractive industries to government aid and sustenance, the Nation's tax system is a most inappropriate means of satisfying such claims. Our Federal tax system is designed to fulfill three different primary roles:

(1) The transfer of resources from the private sector of the economy to the public sector;

(2) The maintenance of a stable full employment level of national income; and

(3) Such redistribution of income as the society decides is appropriate.

Obviously, any hypothetical necessity for society to maintain excess reserves of oil and other minerals does not fall under any of the above headings. If efforts are made to stretch the tax code to cover other areas it begins to bulge at the seams. Our tax system is too encumbered with diverse attempts to manipulate consumption and production. As a result it contains regulations and provisions which offer a haven for various types of vested interest and privilege. It cannot be too strongly emphasized that the tax system should not and cannot be used in an attempt to cure all of the ills of mankind. More inequities arise as a result of this type of approach, as is evident with regard to the depletion allowance, than any tax exemptions, allowances, or deductions could possibly ameliorate.

If it should be determined that the oil industry, or any other industry, requires special assistance it is preferable to make use of such direct aid as subsidies rather than to go, as it were, around Robin Hood's barn. A subsidy is a clearly defined and known quantity given for a specific purpose and can be varied in amount with the needs of the recipient and the economy. It creates less continuing privilege and is easier to control and regulate than various tax privileges.[2]

There remains, of course, the problem of eliminating the depletion allowance provision from our tax system. It has been quite rightly pointed out by many observers that the withdrawal of this privilege would entail a capital loss on the part of present-day holders of oil and other minerals shares. The reason is that the value of the present depletion allowance has been capitalized and is, therefore, reflected in a higher market value for these shares than would be true if no depletion allowance were in effect. Conversely, then, the elimination of the depletion allowance could be expected to result in a drop in the value of such shares. Someone, to be sure, gained a windfall profit, because the value of his shares increased with the advent of percentage depletion. However, it is more than likely that these particular individuals no longer are living and holding these shares. The investors who have subsequently purchased the stock have merely paid a higher price based on the capitalization of present earnings.

The best reply to this justifiable argument is simply that every time the Congress changes the tax laws someone gains or loses. If we were to seek to avoid all economic privation resulting from tax

[2] The same remarks about using the tax system to aid in national defense apply also to arguments in favor of the depletion allowance as an aid to keeping small firms in the industry. If there is a problem here, there is antitrust legislation which is designed to deal with any alleged abuses of competition.

changes there would never be any changes in the tax laws and the Nation would have to live with the status quo. Obviously, this is unrealistic. Changes have to be made and whenever they are one can be assured that the economy will adjust to them. The process of adjustment is not always an easy one, and this is also a principal argument against trying to regulate all aspects of our economic and social structure through the tax system. Each time that a new set of tax regulations is put into effect the economy will have to make new adjustments. The more often and the more complicated our tax changes, the more frequent and complicated the adjustment process.[3]

There is perhaps no better time to correct structural defects in the tax system than at present. When our economy is near full employment and gross national product is steadily growing and most stock prices are at a high level, adjustments to a change in the depletion allowance are much easier and can be made with less financial trauma to the groups concerned than would be the case where the economy was in a downturn. The deletion of the depletion allowance would not completely eliminate the incentive to overinvest in the extractive industries. Part of this effect is the result of the capital gains provision of the present tax law. However, this particular tax regulation is not exclusively confined to the extractive industries and should be evaluated on the basis of experience with it in other industries as well. All that is argued here is the equity of the elimination of the depletion allowance, regardless of the merits or demerits of other provisions of our present tax code.

SUMMARY

In summary, five points deserve emphasis:

(1) The depletion allowance discriminates among individual firms, allowing duplicative cost deductions to a privileged few.

(2) The duplicative deductions of cost allowed under the depletion allowance provision result in a misallocation of the resources of the U.S. economy. Too many of our limited resources are in the extractive industries and too few are in industries satisfying our other consumption demands. This results in a lower standard of living for the average U.S. consumer.

(3) The free market price mechanism should and can be allowed to determine the extent to which the extractive industries utilize a given share of the total resources of our economy.

(4) The tax system should not be distorted by attempts to remedy any specific defects in our economic structure through special provisions in the tax laws. Special considerations with regard to certain industries are better handled through long or short term grants, subsidies, etc.

(5) The present is as propitious a time as any to eliminate the provision for the depletion allowance, given the present level of high employment, high level of gross national product, and the high level of the stock market, all of which make any necessary adjustments easier to bear.

---

[3] The economy, of course, also has to adjust to other types of policy changes, i.e., farm subsidies, changes in social security benefits, etc., but when put in these other forms the changes are easier to observe and supervise.

STATEMENT OF ROBERT G. DUNLOP (PRESIDENT, SUN OIL COMPANY)

Hearings on Tax Reform Act of 1969 Before The Senate Finance Committee, 91st Cong., 1st Sess., pt. 5, at 4455–65 (1969).

My colleagues and I appreciate this opportunity to present the petroleum industry's views on proposed tax changes for oil and natural gas. We feel strongly that this Committee's decisions on petroleum tax policies will significantly affect the Nation's future economic progress and its security. Accordingly, we feel that it is vitally important that the Committee's decisions be based on a comprehensive review of the effect of the proposed changes on our Nation and all of its citizens. It is our intent to contribute to this review by providing you with pertinent background information on the present petroleum situation and how it would be affected by the tax changes now under consideration.

In providing an over-view, I will attempt to define the role of tax incentives in the Nation's petroleum progress; to place the industry's tax payments, prices and profits into perspective; to discuss the relevance of petroleum tax policy to national security; to describe the present status of the industry; and to look at the impact of the tax proposals on the United States petroleum supply position.

First, however, I would like to state the industry's basic position on proposed changes in tax policy. It is this. Our experiences as oil men demonstrates that tax incentives provided by the Congress in present law have very effectively achieved the purpose for which they were created: to provide an incentive for development of our petroleum resources. That our resources have, in fact, been effectively developed is a matter of record—a record of which we in the industry are indeed proud.

We observe two kinds of pressure being applied for a reduction in petroleum tax incentives. One is the pressure of emotional argument for boosting taxes on oil companies, come what may. The second is a more reasoned approach, recognizing the need for incentives but questioning whether the present level is necessary.

The facts of the situation appear to be of little interest to those who have been advancing the emotional arguments. But we are hopeful that the facts will be of paramount importance to those who are sincerely interested in reaching tax policy decisions that will be in the long-run best interests of the people of the United States.

We seek to be open-minded. We are not blindly opposed to change. If petroleum tax policy changes can be demonstrated to be in the best interests of the American public, we will surely not oppose them. But we strongly oppose change based on emotion rather than reason—change which is inimical to the progress of this Nation and to its security.

PETROLEUM ENERGY IN THE UNITED STATES

Against that background, I want first to look with you at the role of petroleum energy in the United States today. I submit that it would not be overstating the case to say that petroleum is the virtual lifeblood of this country. The Department of the Interior has aptly summed up the Nation's heavy dependence upon oil and natural gas in these words:

"The importance of petroleum to the national life of the United States at this particular moment in history is abundantly in evidence. It supplies nearly three-fourths of all energy consumed. Virtually all movement of goods and people depend on it. The Armed Forces would be immobilized without it. Countless industrial processes employ it exclusively, and nine-tenths of all space-heating is provided by it. And quite apart from its use as a fuel, petroleum forms the base for 88 percent of all organic chemicals manufactured in the United States."

I have taken a moment to include that quotation because I feel that it points up sharply why we are here today. Petroleum is vital to our country—so vital that the Nation could not exist today as we know it without adequate supplies of oil and natural gas.

The industrial revolution which is at the base of our prosperity could just as accurately be characterized as an energy revolution. Our ability to substitute inanimate energy for muscle power has made possible the tremendous increase in per capita production which is the essential measure of economic development.

The correlation between energy consumption and income is one of the significant facts of modern life. (See Exhibit I.)

Petroleum is also essential to our defense capability, although in this age of nuclear weapons some observers seriously challenge this view. I would remind those challengers that, fortunately, the nations of the world have so far avoided nuclear war as a means of solving differences. And we all live in the hope that they will continue to do so. Conventional warfare, on the other hand, is likely to be with us for the foreseeable future. So petroleum is now, and will continue to be, vital to our national security.

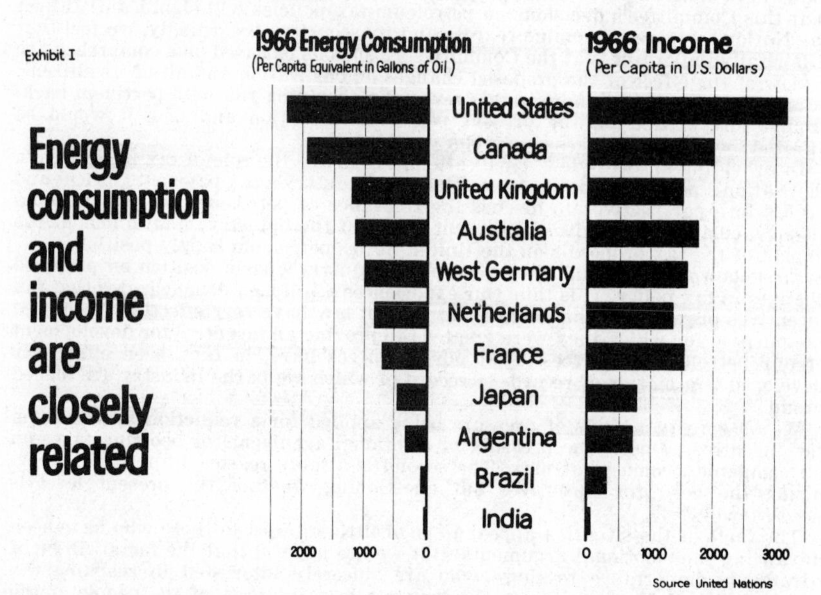

Although surprising to many, the truth is that petroleum is becoming increasingly important to our defense capability. In 1968, defense procurement of petroleum per man under arms *was twice the peak World War II level*—even though the fighting in progress last year was restricted to a very limited geographic area.

The Department of Defense has put it this way:

"The part that oil plays in the defense posture of the United States is vitally important. It is a strategic material and one of the few items that is absolutely essential and foremost in the minds of military commanders. Along with weapons and ammunition, the needs of petroleum get the most attention."

In my view, these facts add to an inescapable conclusion: The future of the United States as we know it is vitally dependent upon assured supplies of oil. Realistically, we have only two routes to travel in obtaining oil:

(1) maintaining a strong domestic industry capable of meeting our essential needs, or

(2) turning increasingly to foreign supplies and, ultimately, becoming dependent upon those less secure foreign sources.

PETROLEUM DEVELOPMENTS UNDER EXISTING TAX POLICIES

Up through the present day we have chosen to travel the first route, seeking to provide the incentives necessary to assure the continuance of a strong domestic petroleum industry capable of meeting the essential oil and gas needs of the Nation.

Was this a wise course of action?

Petroleum needs fully met

The record affirms that it was. For under past and present policies the United States petroleum industry has historically met the petroleum supply needs of this Nation and at the same time contributed immeasurably to the needs of our friends and allies. I need not recount to this Committee the major supply crises we have successfully met in the past.

It would perhaps be of interest and value, however, to show by example how petroleum tax incentives, working in conjunction with other incentives, have contributed to the development of our petroleum resources.

At the close of World War II, the heavy war-time drain on United States petroleum supplies had resulted in a situation where productive capacity was barely equal to demand.

The tax incentives, together with the thrust of rising prices during the late 1940's, enabled the industry steadily to improve the supply situation. By 1955, as shown in Exhibit II, we had reserve capacity of more than 2,000,000 barrels daily. In 1968, reserve capacity was 3,000,000 barrels daily.

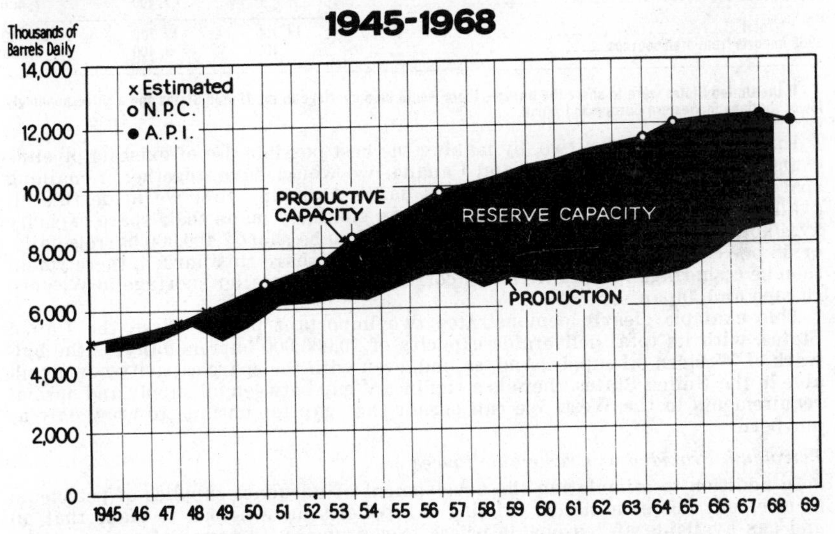

I suggest that this is a dramatic demonstration of the role played by the depletion provision and other incentives in helping to assure adequate supplies of petroleum for the United States.

To carry the discussion one step further, we might with profit examine our present available spare producing capacity in the light of potential requirements. I am referring now to deliverable capacity—that capacity which can be produced and transported with existing facilities.

I can best demonstrate this by posing a hypothetical situation. Assume for a moment a Middle East war in which the United States, Canada, Western Europe and Japan would be denied Arab bloc oil—that is, all oil from North Africa and the Middle East with the exception of Iran.

Assume also that the United States, Canada, Latin America and Iran choose to supply oil to the maximum of their ability to Western Europe and Japan, which are heavily dependent on Arab bloc oil.

First, what would be the oil supply position of the United States and Canada in this hypothetical situation? And, second, what would be the combined position of the United States, Canada, Western Europe and Japan?

A table demonstrating the supplies that could be made available in relation to requirements is attached as Exhibit III.

In response to question one, the figures show that the United States and Canada would lose 400,000 barrels daily of supply from the Arab Bloc. However, our country and Canada have a combined spare capacity of some 1,200,000 barrels daily, and could cover that loss.

EXHIBIT III.—EFFECT OF LOSS OF ARAB BLOC SOURCES OF CRUDE OIL FOR THE UNITED STATES, WESTERN EUROPE, AND JAPAN

[In thousands of barrels per day]

	United States and Canada	Western Europe and Japan	Combined
1968 requirements	14,700	12,700	27,400
Available from—			
Domestic production	11,700	400	12,100
Present production from non-Arab sources	2,600	3,000	5,600
Spare capacity:			
United States	200	800	1,000
Canada	200		200
Iran and Latin America		1,100	1,100
Total available sources	14,700	5,300	20,000
Shortage		[1] 7,400	7,400
Total	14,700	12,700	27,400
1968 imports from arab sources	400	9,300	9,700

[1] If the United States were to share the burden, there would be a shortage in the United States and a correspondingly lower shortage in Western Europe and Japan.

In regard to question two, by making the best possible use of existing pipeline connections between the U.S. and Canada, we would have, together, remaining spare capacity of only 800,000 barrels daily. Assuming that we made this oil available, and that Latin America and Iran similarly made their spare capacity available, Western Europe and Japan would then be short 7,400,000 barrels daily, or 58 per cent of their needs. If the U.S. were to share this burden, there would then be a shortage in the U.S. and a correspondingly smaller shortage in Western Europe and Japan.

This example clearly demonstrates two important points. First, the United States, with its total deliverable capacity of 10,000,000 barrels daily, is the bulwark of Western oil supply. And, second, even with the spare capacity now available in the United States, there is a significant gap between oil supply and normal requirements in the West. We can permit that gap to continue to grow only at our peril.

Petroleum Provided at Reasonable Prices

In addition to stimulating the development of adequate supplies of petroleum to meet our domestic needs, existing tax policies have helped to make that oil and gas available at reasonable prices to consumers. In terms of real purchasing power, the average price of crude oil has declined in the neighborhood of 20 per cent since 1926. Price comparisons over a more recent period show that since 1957–59 the wholesale price index for crude oil has risen just five per cent while the index for all commodities has increased by 13 per cent.

Gasoline prices, excluding direct taxes, are up only 10 per cent, or approximately two cents per gallon, since 1926. Over the same period, the consumer price index has doubled. Again, over a more recent period, the price of gasoline has advanced approximately 10 per cent since 1957–59 while consumer prices generally went up some 28 per cent. (See Exhibit IV.)

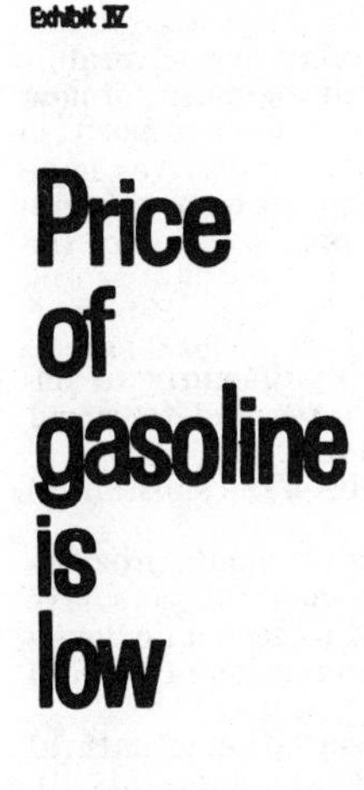

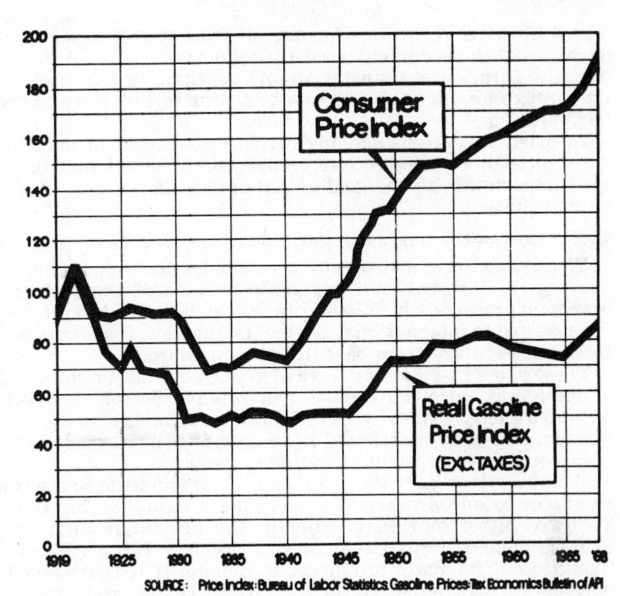

Technological Advances Benefit the Nation

I also want to point out that tax incentive have helped to create benefits for the Nation over and above the development of adequate supplies of petroleum at favorable prices.

The depletion provision, for example, through encouraging investment in the industry and helping to keep it strong, has spurred technological advances in finding and recovering America's oil and gas. The economic impact of these advances has been substantial.

It should be emphasized that percentage depletion is a particularly effective incentive for research leading to technological improvement, since it is based on production. A direct subsidy to exploratory drilling might stimulate that activity, but percentage depletion stimulates *both* exploration and technological advance after discovery. Percentage depletion rewards the successful explorer in proportion to the amount of oil he finds and produces—and hence in proportion to his contribution to the national interest. After successful exploration, it rewards successful research designed to increase producibility of the reserves discovered. It applies in neither case in the event of failure because it becomes effective only when oil is produced. In contrast, a subsidy applies regardless of failure or success.

In exploration technology, improved drilling capabilities have enabled the industry to recover oil and gas at depths that were formerly impossible to drill. In 1930, the deepest well yet drilled went down only slightly more than 9,200 feet. Today the industry is drilling below 25,000 feet.

On another front, offshore drilling in the United States was negligible until the latter half of the 1940's. Today, in contrast, offshore production accounts for some 10 per cent of oil output and 12 per cent of gas output, and the offshore search is one of our brightest prospects for the future. Again, improved technology was the key.

To cite one more example, improved exploratory and drilling know-how is playing an important role in tapping the tremendous reserves of the Alaskan Arctic.

Technological advance is also opening many new horizons in older fields once thought to be nearly-depleted. Before World War II, production was limited to primary recovery—pumping out the oil until the flow became so small as to be economic. This procedure left five or six times more oil in the ground than was recovered, with only 15 to 20 per cent of the oil in place actually produced.

The development of waterflood and other secondary stimulants changed this picture sharply. By upping recovery to 30 to 35 percent of the oil in place, the new techniques have esssentially doubled the Nation's recoverable reserves.

I repeat, technology has doubled recoverable reserves. It has increased the estimated ultimate recovery of crude oil from proved reservoirs by almost 60 billion barrels—20 times current annual production.

In the future, the industry should continue to increase cumulative recoverability through broader application of existing techniques and the development of new techniques.

In brief, invention and innovation encouraged in part by tax incentives have substantially augmented our recoverable reserves and in doing so have contributed importantly to the goal of strengthening the domestic supply position of the United States.

Other economic benefits attributable to tax incentives

Finally, existing petroleum tax policies have contributed significantly to improving the international payments balance of the United States and to world economic progress which has in turn been beneficial to this country.

In regard to international payments, the key plus factor has been the substantial inflow of earnings from past investments abroad.

These same investments have also played a major role in the economic progress of developing nations. Revenues generated by petroleum development projects have provided these nations with the foreign exchanges so essential to economic development, and have contrbuted to secondary benefits such as the creation of modern transportation and communication systems.

Tax incentives have likewise made a contribution to the conservation of natural resources by encouraging the use of marginal oil rather than abandoning this oil. To leave oil of marginal value in the ground is an inexcusable waste of an exhaustible, non-replaceable natural resource. If a marginal well is shut down, the likelihood of its again producing is remote. If it is reopened, it will only be at a considerably higher price for its output. If the production is lost, the country is the poorer.

Incentives provided are not excessive

All of these benefits—adequate oil supplies, favorable oil prices, technological progress—have been achieved with the aid of incentives which are not excessive.

If the percentage depletion rate were excessive, for example, this should be reflected in petroleum industry profit performance considerably better than that of other industries. This is not the case. Rather, figures compiled by the First National City Bank of New York demonstrate that the petroleum industry earns only average profits. In 1968, 99 petroleum producing and refining companies earned a 12.9 per cent return on net assets compared with an average return of 13.1 per cent for all manufacturing companies. In fact, the rate of return on net assets for the petroleum industry was higher than the average for all manufacturing companies in only two of the last 10 years. (See Exhibit V).

Exhibit V

Return on net assets Petroleum Industry and all manufacturing after Taxes

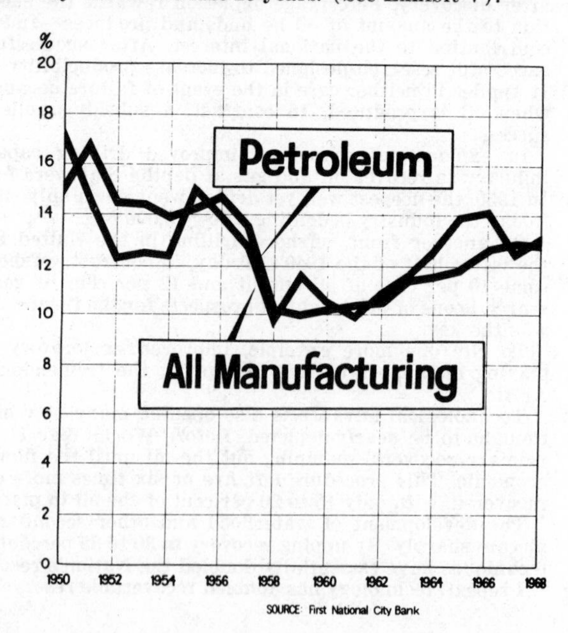

The May 15, 1969 issue of *Fortune* magazine published 1968 financial data of the 500 largest industrial companies in the United States. These data show that, of the 25 largest companies (determined on the basis of sales), seven were oil companies. From a profitability standpoint, however, the record is quite different. Only one of those seven oil companies that rank in the top 25 on the basis of sales was even in the top 100 when ranked on the basis of return on invested capital—and that company ranked only 99th. The companies in the *Fortune* study included 27 oil companies, whose weighted average rate of return on invested capital was 12.0 per cent compared to 12.3 per cent for the other companies.

Similarly, the petroleum industry carries an overall direct tax burden exceeding that borne by other industries, even though its federal income tax bill is reduced by the depletion provision. Lower income taxes are offset by the heavier burden of other direct taxes such as severance and property taxes. As a result, studies have shown that total taxes paid by the petroleum industry, exclusive of motor fuel and excise taxes, in 1966 were equivalent to 6.0 per cent of revenues. (See Exhibit VI). Mining and manufacturing corporations paid direct taxes equivalent to 5.8 per cent of revenues in that year, and all business corporations paid taxes equal to 4.8 per cent of revenues.

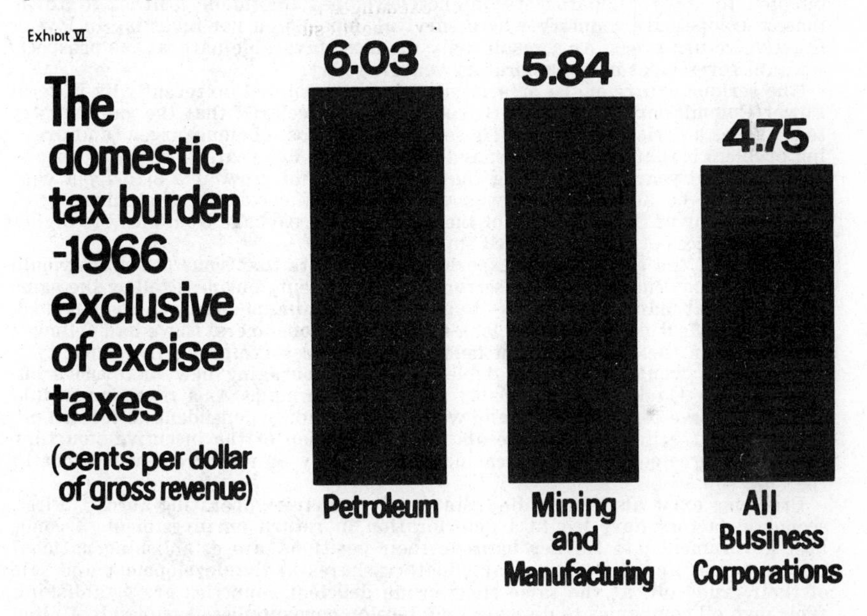

Current problems and future prospects

Against that background of past experience, I would like now to direct your attention to the petroleum industry's present situation and to its future prospects.

Very frankly, the industry today is eyeball to eyeball with some very serious problems. Steady and substantial increases in petroleum demand have collided head-on with sharply-rising oil finding and development costs, with the result that reserves relative to requirements have been declining. Last year the decline was not only relative, but absolute. Proved petroleum reserves dropped across-the-board during 1968, with the life index of crude oil reserves falling to under 10 years and that of natural gas reserves decreasing to less than 15 years. This does not include the new Alaska reserves which are still being evaluated.

The industry's capability to respond successfully to this challenge could well be determined by the decisions made by this Committee. For this reason I will take a few moments to delineate our major difficulties.

First, the domestic industry is caught squarely between sharply rising costs and moderately rising prices. As I noted earlier, the price of crude oil has risen considerably less than the wholesale price index over the past decade. On the other hand, inflation has boosted exploration costs sharply, and, more significantly, unit costs have been rising because fewer giant fields are being discovered. This upward trend in unit costs is likely to continue since the major new successes are occurring in offshore areas and in Alaska where per well costs are several times higher than onshore ventures in the "lower 48." Parenthetically, it should be recognized that in the long run the cost of crude from Alaska's North Slope will likely average substantially above the unit cost of the enormous field initially discovered.

While improvements in exploration technology have helped to offset rising unit costs a gap continues to exist, particularly in onshore areas where economic exploration ventures are becoming increasingly scarce. A similar problem exists in regard to recovery technology. The most attractive opportunities have already been developed, and further expansion will be dependent upon improved economics based on new technology and the continuance of effective tax incentives.

The natural gas problem differs somewhat from that of crude oil in that the federal government has provided incentives with one hand and taken them away with the other. In other words, the positive effect of tax incentives has been offset by Federal Power Commission regulation of well-head natural gas prices. Under regulation, natural gas sold in interstate commerce is priced below its free market value. In carrying out its gas regulatory responsibilities, the Commission has unfortunately focused its efforts on costs at the expense of supply. It has attempted to apply regulatory techniques developed for public utilities to an intensely competitive industry where survival depends on not investing in low or negative return areas. As a result, only the most favorable natural gas prospects warrant investment in an exploratory venture today.

The serious nature of the present situation was pointed up recently by Federal Power Commissioner Albert B. Brooke, Jr., who declared that the gas industry today faces a "crisis situation." He said that the most obvious, urgent and pressing problem is that of gas supply, and that the next five years "may well prove to be the crucial years." Estimating that demand would grow at a 5 to 7 per cent annual rate, he added that it was unquestionably certain that eliminating or modifying any of the provisions of the tax incentive package would lead to higher consumer prices or more restricted supplies.

In spite of the gas industry experience, it appears that some observers would like to see the crude producing sector of the petroleum business follow the same course as that mandated for gas—to produce at minimum short-run costs regardless of the effect on supply and long-run costs to consumers. If we had followed this advice in the past, the giant fields where our reserve productive capacity is concentrated would be largely depleted, and encouraging new discoveries offshore and in Alaska would probably not have been made. As a result, we would have no reserve capacity today and we would be unduly dependent on foreign oil. In contrast, I believe that proposals for modification of the incentive structure should be directed toward increasing the efficiency of resource development in the long run.

Problems exist also for United States oil companies operating abroad. First, economic factors have led to a deterioration in return on investment. Second, host governments, to further improve their positions, are establishing national oil companies and demanding participatory shares in the development and sale of their crude oil. At the same time, crude deficient countries are establishing their own oil companies to discover and develop new supplies. As a result, United States firms find the going increasingly difficult. They must compete with nationally supported companies to obtain the right to explore and develop new areas, and then, having done so, must compete with national producing companies in selling their crude in foreign markets.

In the financial area, sharply increased capital requirements pose additional problems for the industry. I will mention just two points for your consideration. First, there has been a substantial increase in the debt to equity ratio of the larger oil companies. Since this trend cannot, of course, continue indefinitely, any further reduction in internally generated funds must necessarily lead to reduced expenditures on petroleum exploration. And, second, present tax proposals that would reduce the availability of funds to independent operators will immediately and directly reduce their exploratory activities.

As I noted earlier, the petroleum industry is not excessively profitable. To the extent that tax change proposals are geared to the assumpton that it is, they are off base, indeed.

In brief, our present petroleum situation suggests that the industry today requires increased rather than reduced incentives.

THE IMPACT OF HIGHER TAXES ON PETROLEUM

Now, in the light of the current petroleum situation and the problems faced, what would be the impact of higher taxes on the industry?

Increased taxes, in the absence of any remedial action, must affect either profits and investment or prices. The alternative effects would be (1) reduced earnings and consequent reduction in capital invested in petroleum exploration and development; (2) increased product prices; or (3) some combination of the two.

Since the petroleum industry at present earns only average profits, a decline in profitability due to higher taxes would impair its earnings position relative to that of other industries. Since added tax costs cannot reasonably be expected to be absorbed, a tax increase would mean a reduction in the rate of investment by the industry. However, decreased investment in the face of a declining reserve trend and a steady increase in petroleum requirements is an unacceptable alternative if we are to continue our present policy of maintaining a strong domestic industry capable of meeting essential petroleum requirements.

The second alternative would be to shift the increased tax costs to consumers through product price increases. Because of the relative price of competitive fuels for other uses, price increases would probably be limited to fuels supplying transportation energy, such as jet fuel, diesel fuel and gasoline.

To the extent these products are used in business endeavors, the added cost would simply shift the deduction from one industry to another with no net gain to the Federal revenues, or shift the impact further along the line through succeeding price increases. The Federal Government, as the largest single consumer of petroleum products, would bear a significant portion of any price increase. Only to the extent such additional costs were borne by individuals in non-business pursuits can it be assumed that, in the short run, the federal revenues would benefit.

An examination of this phenomenon discloses the effect to be regressive. A recent study indicates expenditures for gasoline per dollar of income are greater for the low income group than for middle and high income groups. The lowest income group, with earnings of less than $3,000 annually, spends an average of 6.2 cents of every dollar of income on gasoline, compared to only 1.5 cents per dollar in the group earning $15,000 or more. Because much of the driving of the low income group is work-oriented, their demand is relatively fixed, according to this study. Hence, the impact of an increase in gasoline prices would be four times greater on the lowest income group than on the highest income group.

Thus, a price increase to offset a tax increase would bear most heavily on the federal government and on low income households. It is by no means clear to me that this would be a net social gain.

Before leaving this topic, I would like to present some background information indicating the effect on the industry of complete elimination of tax incentives. In my view, these data point up very sharply the importance of present petroleum tax provisions to our national security.

Elimination of all petroleum tax incentives would have approximately the same impact on the domestic industry as the elimination of import controls, which would reduce revenues per barrel by about one-third. In the view of most industry respondents to the questionnaire issued by the Cabinet Task Force on Oil Import Control, the key effect of a one-third drop in revenue per barrel would be the "virtual cessation" of exploratory drilling. According to one company, elimination of the import control program or an equivalent decrease in revenue would result in an 85 per cent drop in the volume of exploratory drilling. According to another, the resulting reduction in industry cash flow would mean a "sharply curtailed" exploration program with a resultant permanent loss of "supporting industries, technology and trained people."

What this reduction in exploratory drilling might mean for future reserves was examined by another respondent. According to this estimate, "the amount of oil not discovered—which otherwise would be discovered—might approximate 1 to 2 billion barrels *each year* in the established older exploration provinces." This would amount to some 10 to 20 billion barrels lost over the next decade, *not* including the unknown amount which "otherwise would be discovered" in newer or future geologic provinces. The same respondent estimated the loss in reserves in existing developed fields at 6 to 10 billion barrels. The loss in reserves in fields which have been discovered but not developed was estimated at 5 billion barrels.

Six companies estimated that by 1980 the United States would be dependent on foreign sources for one-half to two-thirds of its petroleum supplies if oil import controls were eliminated. (See Exhibit VII). The average of these forecasts was 57 per cent dependency on foreign oil. And this allows for remaining production from reserves already discovered today, including the prolific discovery on the

North Slope of Alaska, which has not yet been produced. The estimates made by these companies are in close agreement with projections made by the United States Department of the Interior, which predicted 48 per cent (optimistic) to 58 per cent (pessimistic) dependency on foreign oil by 1980 if oil import controls were eliminated.

EXHIBIT VII

1980 percentage dependency on foreign oil in the absence of oil import controls during the 1970's

Respondent:	Percent
Cities Service	68
Gulf	54
Humble	49
Marathon	61
Phillips	57
Sohio	54
Average	57
Department of the Interior	48–58

Source: Computed from data in submissions in July 1969 to the Cabinet Task Force on Oil Import Control.

Earlier, I indicated that the only alternative to maintaining a strong domestic industry was increased reliance on foreign oil. The above data clearly indicate how heavy that reliance would be if all petroleum tax incentives were eliminated.

In respect to the security aspect of these foreign supplies, I would like to quote from the summary of a recent API statement on this subject:

"Interference with foreign petroleum supplies can come from any of three sources: (1) military action during war; (2) shutdown (or sabotage) for political reasons; or (3) shutdown for economic reasons. The first of these is most important in general wars. Even in the absence of general war, however, there can be serious petroleum security problems in all three categories. Since World War II, there have been *eight* noteworthy interruptions of overseas petroleum supply—all in the prolific Middle East and African producing areas.

"None of these interruptions has succeeded in obtaining economic or political concessions from the United States or its allies—primarily because there has been a large, viable North American oil industry on which to rely in the event of emergency.

"If the United States were to adopt public policies which would make further exploration in North America generally unattractive, the United States would then have to turn to the Middle East-North Africa region for the bulk of its petroleum supplies because 86 per cent of overseas reserves are concentrated in this area (Venezuela currently accounts for 17 per cent of production but has only 4 per cent of reserves—See Exhibit VIII.) While no single overseas producing country has a sufficiently large share of reserves to be able to dominate the international oil market, *groups* of countries having common interests do have large shares.

EXHIBIT VIII

Share of 1968 free world crude oil reserves outside North America

Areas:	Percent
Persian Gulf countries	75
North African countries	11
Subtotal	86
Venezuela	4
Indonesia	3
All other	7
Total	100
Groups:	
OPEC [1]	85
Arab nations	71

[1] Organization of Petroleum Exporting Countries.

> "Certain groups have, in fact, demonstrated an intent to operate as economic units for certain objectives. In the absence of a viable North American industry to counter the potential market power of these groups, there is every reason to anticipate that they would act as monopolistic entities for economic and political gains at the expense of consuming countries. The potential danger of this situation to the security of Free World energy supplies is compounded by increasing Russian adventures in the Middle East and North Africa, the principal overseas producing areas."

While we would gain a short-run benefit from foreign oil in temporarily lower prices, we would bear a long-run cost that cannot be measured in monetary terms. If we became dependent upon that oil, we might well be drawn into any conflict that occurred in the Middle East in order to insure stability. This position would be analogous to our present role in Southeast Asia, execept that here the the military and economic reasons for intervention would be compelling.

Furthermore, given the Soviet Union's support of the Arab world, any increased United States role in the Middle East could lead to a direct confrontation between the two nuclear superpowers. In any event, our options in international affairs would be severely limited and our military commitments would be increased at a time when we seek to limit them.

In summary, I would like to leave these five salient points with you.

(1) Present petroleum tax incentives have served the national interest by providing *adequate*, *secure* supplies of oil and gas, efficiently produced.

(2) Petroleum industry profits have been *less* than average.

(3) Petroleum industry total taxes have been *more* than average.

(4) Petroleum industry prices have risen *less* than average.

(5) Petroleum industry supply problems over the next decade will be enormous, since we *must produce 40 per cent more oil than in the 1960's*.

Before closing, I should like to dispel two contradictory notions which are prevalent today. The first is that the United States is running out of oil. The second is that we have found enough oil in Alaska to meet our needs forever. Neither of these notions is true. In my view, recent experience indicates that it is reasonable to expect a substantial uptrend in new oil found in the United States during the next decade. Crude oil reserves in Alaska could very well be as large as the present total in the continental United States—31 billion barrels. However, that would only be 55 per cent of estimated required additions to reserves during the 1970's (and all of the Alaskan oil will probably not be found and developed during that period). We need, therefore, more discoveries in the "lower 48" states. I am convinced that a realistic national petroleum policy continuing to provide reasonable tax incentives for investment will enable us to find and develop the oil we need, to the benefit of this Nation and all of its people.

In conclusion, I urge the Committee to give careful consideration to the future outlook for the United States petroleum situation in reaching its decision about petroleum tax policy. The continued existence of the United States as we know it could well rest on the decisions you reach.

C. Contributions

The selections which follow deal both with the nature and purpose of an income tax deduction for charitable contributions and with the structure of the deduction. It is not feasible to summarize here the many changes in the deduction which resulted from the Tax Reform Act of 1969. One structural change that was in accordance with the Treasury's recommendation, as reflected in the second selection here, was an increase in the percentage limitation on the deduction from 30% to 50% of the taxpayer's adjusted gross income. There was, however, much more than this to the Treasury's proposed structural revisions. They merit careful consideration in the light of the purpose of the deduction and its apparent effects on the level of contributions.

RABIN, CHARITABLE TRUSTS AND CHARITABLE DEDUCTIONS *

41 N.Y.U.L.Rev. 912–25 (1966).

I

INTRODUCTION

AMONG statutes affecting charitable trusts the Revenue Act of 1917[1] should rank in importance with the Statute of Charitable Uses, 1601.[2] The Statute of Charitable Uses provided a firm legal basis for charitable trusts;[3] the Revenue Act of 1917, which made charitable contributions by individuals deductible for income tax purposes, provided a firm economic basis for them. The existence of the deduction created by the 1917 act may help to explain why almost 5,000 trusts and foundations were created between 1920 and 1959, while only 112 were created before 1920.[4] Despite the charitable deduction's importance to

1. Ch. 63, 40 Stat. 300.

2. 43 Eliz. 1, c. 4.

3. Of course, charitable trusts existed long before the Statute of Charitable Uses. See Miller, The Legal Foundations of American Philanthropy: 1776-1844 (1961).

4. See Andrews, Analytical Introduction to Foundation Library, The Foundation Directory 9, 13 (2d ed. 1964). As used in this article, a charitable trust or foundation is a trust or corporation "having a principal fund of its own, managed by its own trustees or directors, and established to maintain or aid social, educational, charitable, religious, or other activities serving the common welfare." Id. at 9. The figure of 5,000 trusts and foundations includes only American trusts or foundations that have capital assets of over $100,000 or that make grants of at least $10,000. Id. at 10.

Although there were a number of income tax acts prior to 1917, none of them included an income tax deduction for charitable contributions. Among these were the Revenue Act of 1916, ch. 463, 39 Stat. 756; the Revenue Act of 1913, ch. 16, 38 Stat. 114; the Revenue Act of 1909, ch. 6, 36 Stat. 11; the Revenue Act of 1894, ch. 349, 28 Stat. 509; the Revenue Act of 1870, ch. 255, 16 Stat. 256; the Revenue Act of 1864, ch. 173, 13 Stat. 223; the Revenue Act of 1862, ch. 119, 12 Stat. 432; and the Revenue Act of 1861, ch. 45, 12 Stat. 292. An attempted introduction of an income tax deduction in 1913 was rejected by the House. See 50 Cong. Rec. 1259 (1913). Yet, charitable trusts or foundations were not unknown before 1917. Thirteen per cent of all foundation assets (counting only foundations with assets of over $1 million) are owned by foundations created before 1920. Andrews, supra at 19. Among some of the more noted foundations established be-

* © Copyright, 1966, by New York University. Reproduced with permission.

the law of charitable trusts, the basic policy considerations justifying it have received scant comment in legal literature.[5] In addition, charitable and tax motives have become so intertwined that some seem to equate tax subsidies to charity with charity itself and confuse the right to a deduction with the right to give.[6] In view of the continuing importance of the deduction, it deserves a reexamination.

Charitable institutions enjoy different kinds of tax subsidies. On the state and local levels, the exemption from real estate taxes is probably the most important, although advantages pertaining to other state taxes such as income and death taxes can hardly be ignored.[7] On the federal level, charitable organizations enjoy major tax subsidies in the form of (1) an "exemption" from federal income tax for charitable institutions[8] and (2) a "deduction" that tax-paying entities can take for charitable contributions.[9]

Only the federal tax deduction will be discussed here. Prior attempts to deal with the deduction as it affects charitable trusts or foundations (especially "private" trusts or foundations) have

---

fore contributions were deductible are the Rockefeller Institute for Medical Research (1901), General Education Board (1902), Carnegie Corporation for the Advancement of Teaching (1905), Milbank Memorial Fund (1905), Russell Sage Foundation (1907), Carnegie Corporation of New York (1911), and the Rockefeller Foundation (1913). Bremner, American Philanthropy 117 (1960).

5. A number of economists, cited throughout this article, have studied the question. Most legal commentators, however, merely discuss the technical requirements of the law and avoid any moral judgments. See, e.g., Lowndes, Tax Advantages of Charitable Gifts, 46 Va. L. Rev. 394, 395 (1960) ("beyond the depth of this article"). Attention is usually focused on "abuses" of tax subsidies for charities rather than on the subsidies themselves. See, e.g., Hellerstein, Taxes, Loopholes and Morals 194-99 (1963); Stern, The Great Treasury Raid 238-50 (1964). A notable exception is a thoughtful piece by Professor Wolfman. Wolfman, Federal Tax Policy and the Support of Science, 114 U. Pa. L. Rev. 171 (1965). See also Forer, Book Review, 66 Colum. L. Rev. 988 (1966). In 1934 Senator LaFollette urged outright repeal of the deduction. 78 Cong. Rec. 5959 (1934).

The constitutionality of tax benefits to religious organizations has frequently been questioned. See, e.g., Murray v. Comptroller of the Treasury, 241 Md. 383, 216 A.2d 897, cert. denied, 87 Sup. Ct. 36 (1966) (rejecting constitutional objection); Paulsen, Preferment of Religious Institutions in Tax and Labor Legislation, 14 Law & Contemp. Prob. 144 (1949); Comment, Constitutionality of Tax Exemptions Accorded American Church Property, 30 Albany L. Rev. 58 (1966).

6. See, e.g., Case, Philanthropy as a Social Investment, Foundation News, March 1964, p. 1.

7. See generally Fisher, Charities and the Ohio Tax Laws, 18 Ohio St. L.J. 228 (1957); Lynn & Oster, Economic Aspects of Tax Benefits Accorded Ohio Charitable Trusts, 18 Ohio St. L.J. 248 (1957); Paulsen, supra note 5.

8. See Int. Rev. Code of 1954, §§ 501-04.

9. See Int. Rev. Code of 1954, §§ 170, 545(b)(2), 642(c), 702(a)(4), 873(c), 882(c)(3), 2055, 2106(a)(2), 2522.

for the most part not questioned that the deduction in general is justifiable, and have assumed that it is only the unique nature of private trusts or foundations that makes some limitations on the deduction necessary as to them.[10] The opposite approach will be taken here. It will be assumed that a deduction for contributions to charitable trusts or foundations is at least as justifiable as is a deduction for other types of charitable contributions. What will be questioned is the desirability of the deduction itself.[11]

To urge repeal of all charitable deductions would be an exercise in futility. This article is not meant to be that. It is believed, however, that an unhurried look at the deduction may place in perspective proposals for changes that are less radical than outright repeal.

II

The Principle of the Deduction

A. Some Perspective

A tax deduction for contributions to charitable trusts is not an inevitable or "natural" incident of a high tax structure and a high national regard for charitable activities. Great Britain, whose 110,000 charitable trusts own substantial amounts of securities and money in addition to vast amounts of land, has officially recognized that voluntary charitable organizations are of "indispensable service" to that country.[12] Nevertheless, Great Britain gives no income or estate tax deduction for charitable contributions. Other types of tax subsidies, however, do exist. Charities are exempt from paying income taxes, and, if a taxpayer "assigns" a portion of his income to a charity for a period of seven or more years, the income will be treated as the charity's for tax purposes.[13] Although, unlike the British system, the analogous American provision, which permits the assignment of income via a trust for ten years, and in some cases for as little

10. See, e.g., Treasury Dep't Report to the Senate Comm. on Finance, 89th Cong., 1st Sess., Private Foundations (Comm. Print 1965); Chairman's Report to the House Select Comm. on Small Business, 87th Cong., 2d Sess., Tax-Exempt Foundations and Charitable Trusts: Their Impact on Our Economy, First Installment (Comm. Print 1962) ("Patman Report").

11. The constitutional issues raised by tax deductions for contributions to religious organizations are beyond the scope of this paper.

12. Committee on the Law and Practice Relating to Charitable Trusts, Report, Cmd. No. 8710, at 3, 27 (1952).

13. See generally Royal Commission on the Taxation of Profits and Income, Final Report, Cmd. No. 9474, at 54-60 (1955); Owen, English Philanthropy: 1660-1960, at 336-38 (1964).

as two years,[14] requires a formal trust of income-producing property, it seems clear that the American tax subsidy to charities is considerably greater than that of the British.[15]

The charitable deduction is unique among deductions. Deductions applicable to individuals may be classified as: (1) expenses for the production of income (including those items that might ordinarily require capitalization but that by special provision may be treated as current expenses),[16] and (2) "relief" provisions, which recognize that income sometimes is not freely spendable, but may be subject to strong legal or moral claims that are in a sense involuntary. Examples of the latter would include the personal exemption, and the deductions for interest, taxes, medical expenses, care of certain dependents, and alimony.[17]

The charitable deduction obviously fits within neither the business expense nor the relief provision category. Most relief provisions are designed primarily to mitigate hardship, not to encourage expenditures. For example, the personal exemption provision recognizes that a taxpayer with a large family may be unable to pay as much as one with a small family. Few would contend that it is designed to encourage large families. The same is true of the medical expense deduction. Although the deductions for taxes and interest encourage home ownership, they also relieve taxpayers who have expenses that are not easily avoidable. In contrast, the charitable deduction exists almost solely to encourage charitable giving, not to relieve hardship caused by "involuntary" expenses.[18]

The first charitable deduction was introduced from the floor of the Senate as an amendment to the Revenue Act of 1917. As originally introduced it would have permitted deductions of up to twenty per cent of the taxpayer's taxable net income.[19] After the limitation was reduced to fifteen per cent the provision was unanimously approved by the Senate.[20] There was virtually no debate. Probably many of the Senators considered the deduction a temporary wartime measure that would last only while high wartime tax rates were in effect.[21]

---

14. Int. Rev. Code of 1954, § 673.
15. Owen, supra note 13, at 330, 345.
16. Int. Rev. Code of 1954, §§ 162, 168-80, 182, 212.
17. Int. Rev. Code of 1954, §§ 151, 163-64, 213-15.
18. White, Deductions for Nonbusiness Expenses and an Economic Concept of Net Income, in Joint Comm. on the Economic Report, 84th Cong., 1st Sess., Federal Tax Policy for Economic Growth and Stability 353, 364 (Joint Comm. Print 1955).
19. See 55 Cong. Rec. 6728 (1917).
20. See id. at 6741 (1917).
21. The charitable deduction was proposed by Senator Hollis as an amend-

From 1917 to the present the trend has been toward increasing the deductible amounts that donors may contribute to charity. For example, although the 1917 provision limited the deduction to income taxes for individuals, the 1918 act widened it to permit estates and trusts to take an income tax deduction, and individuals to take an estate tax deduction.[22] In 1935 the statute explicitly gave corporations the privilege of taking an income tax deduction for charitable contributions but limited it to five per cent of their net income.[23]

In 1924 individuals who contributed over ninety per cent of their taxable net income to charity in each of the ten preceding taxable years were allowed to deduct all charitable contributions.[24] Subsequently this privilege of unlimited deduction was considerably broadened. The 1954 act provided that a taxpayer qualified for the unlimited deduction if the sum of his federal income taxes and his charitable contributions exceeded ninety per cent of his taxable income in eight of the ten preceding taxable years.[25] In 1958 it became even easier to qualify since taxes paid with respect to one year qualified even if paid in another year.[26] In 1964, however, the types of organizations qualified for the unlimited deduction and the manner by which a taxpayer qualified for it were somewhat restricted.[27] The main effect of the 1964 changes was to encourage gifts to operating or publicly supported charities as opposed to private trusts or foundations.

In 1944 adjusted gross income was substituted for net income in computing the fifteen per cent limitation, thus significantly increasing the allowance.[28] In 1950 certain improper practices

---

ment to the Revenue Act of 1917, the so-called War-Revenue Act, and most of the newspaper editorials in support of the deduction inserted in the Congressional Record by Senator Hollis considered the deduction only in connection with wartime needs. Senator Hollis also stressed the significance of the war. "I believe that the Senate will see the necessity for voting that exemption in war times." 55 Cong. Rec. 6728 (1917). See also Surrey, The Federal Income Tax Base for Individuals, 58 Colum. L. Rev. 815, 825 (1958).

22. Revenue Act of 1918, ch. 18, §§ 219(b), 403(a)(3), 40 Stat. 1071, 1098.

23. Revenue Act of 1935, ch. 829, § 102(c), 49 Stat. 1016. The statute was in response to the case of Old Mission Portland Cement Co. v. Helvering, 293 U.S. 289 (1934). The background of the legislation is well told in Cutlip, Fund Raising in the United States: Its Role in America's Philanthropy 318-30 (1965).

24. Revenue Act of 1924, ch. 234, § 214(a)(10), 43 Stat. 271. "This provision is designed substantially to free from income taxation one who is habitually contributing to benevolent organizations amounts equaling virtually his entire income." S. Rep. No. 398, 68th Cong., 1st Sess. 24 (1924).

25. Int. Rev. Code of 1954, ch. 736, § 170(b)(1)(C), 68A Stat. 58.

26. Int. Rev. Code of 1954, § 170(b)(1)(C).

27. Int. Rev. Code of 1954, § 170(g), added by 78 Stat. 43 (1964).

28. Individual Income Tax Act of 1944, ch. 210, § 8(b), 58 Stat. 236. See also H.R. Rep. No. 1365, 78th Cong., 2d Sess. 23 (1944); S. Rep. No. 885, 78th Cong., 2d Sess. 2-3 (1944).

relating to charitable trusts and foundations were curtailed, but the amounts deductible for contributions to bona fide charities remained unaffected.[29] In 1952 the fifteen per cent limitation was increased to twenty per cent.[30]

Today, contributions to certain qualified organizations are deductible to the extent of thirty per cent of adjusted gross income.[31] A five-year carryover provision applicable to thirty per cent organizations in effect permits contributions made in one year to be treated as if made in a subsequent year for purposes of avoiding the thirty per cent limitation.[32]

At the same time that the percentage limitations on deductible charitable contributions were being relaxed, the general trend (despite occasional tax rate reductions) was for tax rates to increase.[33] The result of these two movements, extending over some fifty years, has been to increase very gradually, but very substantially, the Government's "share" of a charitable contribution. In 1919 an unmarried taxpayer earning $50,000 per year could receive a maximum income tax benefit of $2,295 for charitable contributions. Today's maximum for the same taxpayer is $8,730.[34] If he qualified for the unlimited deduction it would be even higher. Thus, from its modest beginnings, the extent of governmental "encouragement" for charitable giving has increased substantially. Professor C. Harry Kahn has estimated that, because of the deductible aspect of charitable contributions, the Government's "share" of all charitable contributions rose from 12.2 per cent of the contributions in 1924 to 31.5 per cent in 1956.[35] The percentage in the intervening years has varied but the trend is very clearly upward.

---

29. Revenue Act of 1950, ch. 994, §§ 301-41, 64 Stat. 947.

30. Int. Rev. Code of 1939, § 23(*o*), as amended, ch. 588, § 4(a), 66 Stat. 443 (1952).

31. Int. Rev. Code of 1954, §§ 170(b)(1)(A)-(B). Private charitable trusts or foundations are excluded from the list of qualified organizations. Int. Rev. Code of 1954, § 170(b)(1)(A).

32. Int. Rev. Code of 1954, § 170(b)(5).

33. For a helpful presentation of changes in individual tax rates from 1936 through 1965 for all tax brackets see Goode, The Individual Income Tax 325 (1964).

34. Under the Revenue Act of 1918, ch. 18, §§ 210-11, 40 Stat. 1062, if the taxpayer contributed the maximum amount then deductible, $7,500 (fifteen per cent of a taxable net income of $50,000), he would save $2,295 in taxes. Under the present statute a single taxpayer with an adjusted gross income of $50,000 who takes full advantage of the thirty per cent provision would reduce his taxes by $8,730. Int. Rev. Code of 1954, § 1(a)(2). When one considers that adjusted gross income is usually considerably greater than taxable net income the difference is even more striking. Of course, the disparity would be less if we were dealing with a married man using a joint return, since the joint privilege was not available in 1918.

35. Kahn, Personal Deductions in the Federal Income Tax 56-57 (1960).

B. A Quantitative Analysis

The charitable deduction was originally based on the assumption that any loss in tax revenues would be amply outweighed by increased giving. It was viewed as a method by which the Government could obtain a full dollar's worth of public services in return for a tax concession costing it only thirty or forty cents. Senator Hollis, the sponsor of the deduction when it was first passed, argued:

> For every dollar that a man contributes for these public charities, educational, scientific, or otherwise, the public gets 100 per cent; it is all devoted to that purpose. If it were undertaken to support such institutions through the Federal Government or local governments and the taxes were imposed for the amount they would only get the percentage, 5 per cent, 10 per cent, 20 per cent, or 40 per cent, as the case might be.[36]

The Senator also requested that a statement of the *Washington Post* be incorporated in the record:

> If a man with a $2,000,000 income wished to give 20 per cent of it to charity, the Government under the proposed exemption might lose a little revenue, but it would be infinitesimal compared with the amount that would be given to the public.[37]

Recent statistical studies of tax returns, however, have shown such arguments to be fallacious. In practice it appears that the revenue loss attributable to the income tax charitable deduction is substantially greater than the amount of contributions induced by the deduction.

The Treasury Department estimates that in 1963 all charitable deductions taken under the estate, gift, and income tax laws diminished federal revenues by about $2,800 million.[38] Economist Michael K. Taussig, Research Associate at the Brookings Institution, estimates that charitable deductions under the individual income tax diminished total revenues by about $2,195 million in 1962.[39] The annual loss of revenue has been increasing. In 1953 deductions claimed on individual income tax returns totaled $3,552 million and by 1962 they had grown to $7,516 million.[40]

---

36. 55 Cong. Rec. 6728 (1917).

37. Id. at 6729.

38. Treasury Dep't Report to the Senate Comm. on Finance, supra note 10, at 11.

39. Taussig, The Charitable Contributions Deduction in the Federal Personal Income Tax 152 (1965) (unpublished doctoral dissertation on file at Massachusetts Institute of Technology Library and at New York University Law Library) [hereinafter Taussig]. Taussig's work is by far the best analysis of the available statistics.

40. IRS, U.S. Treasury Dep't, Statistics of Income 1962: Individual Income Tax Returns 160 (1965).

Dr. Taussig's estimate that the individual income tax deduction on itemized returns reduced federal revenues by $2,195 million is probably quite accurate. To arrive at this figure one need only ascertain the taxes due from all itemizing individual taxpayers, and calculate what would be due if charitable contributions were not deductible. The difference is the cost of the deduction. Taussig used 103,386 individual income tax returns for the year 1962 as a sample, and concentrated on a subsample of 47,678 itemized taxable returns.[41] The returns were made available to Dr. Taussig by the United States Treasury Department.[42] Using standard statistical and computer techniques, he obtained the $2,195 million figure. If anything, the figure is too low. He was able to measure only individual tax savings appearing on returns as charitable deductions.[43] Thus the $2,195 million figure omits tax savings flowing from the avoidance of income realization. These latter savings are probably considerable.[44]

The $2,195 million loss due to individuals' deductions should be compared with Taussig's estimate that in 1962 only $57 million in contributions by individuals was induced by the deductibility of contributions.[45] Thus, if one looks at the charitable deduction as a method by which the Government "purchases" increased charitable contributions, and if Taussig's estimates are accurate, it cost the Government $2,195 million to purchase $57 million in charitable contributions. This hardly seems a bargain.

Dr. Taussig's estimate that the individual income tax charitable deduction induced only $57 million of extra contributions has all of the indicia of reliability and scholarship. Moreover, other economists, working from less complete data, have reached roughly similar conclusions. For example, Professor Vickrey found that the "tax exemption, particularly the deduction under the income tax, seems to be much more an expression of the general predilection in this country for privately organized and controlled philanthropy rather than a significant stimulus to *net* giving."[46]

If the charitable deduction were a significant stimulus to giving, one would expect a significant drop in contributions by persons who adopted the standard deduction, when in 1944

---

41. Taussig 95.
42. Taussig 95.
43. Taussig 152.
44. See text accompanying notes 67-73 infra.
45. Taussig 142.
46. Vickrey, One Economist's View of Philanthropy, in Philanthropy and Public Policy 31, 56 (1962).

it was extended to incomes over $3,000. There was no such drop. Professor Kahn cautiously concludes:

> There is no evidence that the institution of the standard deduction had a repressive effect on the share of income devoted to philanthropy. A large segment of the public, subject to marginal rates ranging from 20 to 30 per cent, may not be influenced by tax incentives in making such gifts.[47]

To the extent that taxpayers overstate their charitable contributions, the deduction is a tax on honesty, burdening the Government and the honest taxpayer, not benefiting charity, and enriching the tax cheat. On the basis of various statistical studies, Professor Kahn estimates that in 1954 contributions claimed for tax purposes may have been as much as 150 per cent of actual contributions.[48]

C. A Qualitative Analysis

As shown above, under our present system most of the tax benefit from the charitable deduction serves merely to reduce taxes rather than to stimulate giving. Therefore, charities would be helped far more effectively, at no additional cost to the Government, if contributions were not deductible and the Government were to pay directly to the charity the amount of tax benefit that would have accrued to the taxpayer had the contribution been deductible. Undoubtedly, if such a procedure were instituted, many would protest direct governmental contributions to such disparate organizations as the "Vegetarian Brotherhood of America, the Degree of Honor Protective Association, and the Recreation Home of the Salesmanship Club of Houston."[49]

If, however, such protests are appropriate in the case of direct contributions, they are equally appropriate under the present system, which costs the Government just as much and benefits charities far less. In essence, the present system is a type of matching program under which the Government agrees to spend a certain amount (depending on the taxpayer's top tax bracket) for each dollar contributed to charity. With few exceptions,[50] the Government treats all charities as equally worthy

---

47. Kahn, supra note 35, at 72. See 109 Cong. Rec. 3879 (1963) (remarks of Assistant Secretary of the Treasury Surrey).

48. Kahn, supra note 35, at 67 (listing four other possible reasons for this discrepancy).

49. Stern, The Great Treasury Raid 227 (1964).

That direct government handling of areas formerly believed to be the province of private donations is not so politically unfeasible as might have been assumed is illustrated by the recent law permitting taxpayers to channel political contributions of $1 each through the federal government. See N.Y. Times, Oct. 30, 1966, § 4, col. 5.

50. See text accompanying note 120 infra.

and thus the Government's "expenditures" are determined by the individual choice of each taxpayer rather than by some overall government plan.

What are the reasons for preferring this method of distributing government funds over the more usual method? Charities are aided through the income tax exemption and through the various state and local tax exemptions. Why is it necessary to add income, estate, and gift tax deductions and to permit, under certain circumstances, the avoidance of taxable income as well as the deduction? If the answer is that the federal government wants to benefit charities more, why does it stop with tax deductions? Why does it not add a program of matching private gifts with government funds to its present disguised matching program?

If there were no special tax privileges afforded charitable trusts and other charitable organizations, most statutes designed to check "charitable abuses" would be unnecessary. Undoubtedly fraudulent or misleading solicitations would have to be curbed,[51] and statutes establishing registries of charitable trusts would be useful in facilitating the exposure of indolent or dishonest trustees.[52] Most difficulties, however, would merely be aspects of the comparatively simple problem of seeing to it that the manager or trustee of a charitable fund was honest, diligent, effective, and loyal to the contributors to that fund. Apart from tax reasons, the creator of a charitable trust would have little reason to make an illusory gift that really benefited himself since he could more easily benefit himself by not making a gift at all. To the extent that anyone did make an illusory gift he would be cheating no one.

So far as religious institutions are concerned, there is obviously a good reason for using the tax deduction method of governmental subsidy rather than a more direct method. The deduction method largely avoids the constitutional and practical problems surrounding direct aid to religion. As for other kinds of charitable organizations, the reason for using the deduction method is less obvious. The deduction may be viewed primarily as a device for

---

51. See, e.g., Solicitation of Charitable Funds Act, Conn. Gen. Stat. Rev. §§ 17-21e to -21r (Supp. 1965); Solicitation of Funds for Charitable Purposes Act, Ill. Rev. Stat. ch. 23, §§ 5101-14 (1965); Solicitation and Collection of Funds for Charitable Purposes Act, N.Y. Soc. Welfare Law §§ 481-83a. See generally National Health Council, Viewpoints on State and Local Legislation Regulating Solicitation of Funds From the Public (1965).

52. See, e.g., Uniform Supervision of Trustees for Charitable Purposes Act § 4. A complete discussion of the various state enactments and the uniform act may be found in Fremont-Smith, Foundations and Government: State and Federal Law and Supervision 272-351 (1965). See also Taylor, Public Accountability of Foundations and Charitable Trusts (1953).

decentralizing decisions concerning government expenditures.[53] A decentralized system, however, if it is to be better than a centralized system, should result in (1) a better allocation of government funds, and (2) a more efficient collection and administration of such funds.

1. *Allocation*

It has been argued that the system of allocating funds via the deduction is undemocratic because it subsidizes "much more heavily the charities favored by the wealthy as distinct from those appealing primarily to the poorer contributors."[54] Charities appealing to the wealthy are favored by the present system in several ways. First, progressive taxation makes the Government's "share" of a contribution larger for high-income taxpayers. Second, even ignoring the effects of progressive taxation, under the present system a wealthy taxpayer who contributes a large amount attracts a greater government "contribution" to his charity than a poor man who contributes a small amount. Finally, lower-income taxpayers are more likely to give ordinary cash gifts, whereas higher-income taxpayers are more likely to use the additional tax advantages of noncash gifts or gifts of interests in trusts.[55] In contrast, many believe that the tax deduction system is more democratic than a system of direct government payments since it places decisions concerning the allocation of government resources directly in the hands of the taxpayers rather than in those of government officials.[56] Notwithstanding these arguments, the existing system should probably be judged not by how closely it approaches an ideological ideal, but rather on pragmatic grounds: Does it promote the most rational allocation of government resources?

---

53. For a well reasoned defense of decentralization see Broughton, The Economic Functions of Foundations, Foundation News, Sept. 1964, p. 1. See also White, Proper Income Tax Treatment of Deductions for Personal Expenses, in House Comm. on Ways and Means, 86th Cong., 1st Sess., Tax Revision Compendium 371 (Comm. Print 1959).

54. Vickrey, supra note 46, at 54; White, Deductions for Nonbusiness Expenses and an Economic Concept of Net Income, in Joint Comm. on the Economic Report, 84th Cong., 1st Sess., Federal Tax Policy for Economic Growth and Stability 353, 364-65 (Joint Comm. Print 1955).

55. Persons with adjusted gross incomes in excess of $100,000 accounted for more than half of all itemized contributions of property but less than 7% of all contributions. IRS, supra note 40, at 6, 8. See text accompanying notes 67-73 infra.

56. See, e.g., Case, Philanthropy as a Social Investment, Foundation News, March 1964, p. 1:

> [T]here is virtue in the diffusion rather than the concentration of the decision-making power. This is in notable and obvious contrast to the organization of Soviet society, where the social surplus, if any, is allocated by governmental fiat.

It has been argued that free enterprise in philanthropy, as free enterprise in commerce, is conducive to creative innovation, productivity, and change while government supervision of the disbursement of its own funds is likely to be characterized as routine and unimaginative.[57] The analogy is misleading. Private business is spurred to innovation by the inexorable demands of the market place. Unless a good service or product is provided at a reasonable cost a private business cannot long survive. Those who pay for the product or service use it, and therefore are in a good position to judge its worth. The same does not apply to philanthropy. Except for contributions to churches—a subject outside the scope of this paper—the average donor can hardly be compared with the purchaser of a product. He does not use the "product" and is rarely in a position rationally to weigh the importance of one charity over that of another. In fact, as the National Health Council has observed, the flow of contributions "is not determined by need but by effectiveness of . . . fund-raising techniques."[58]

The National Foundation for Infantile Paralysis, admittedly a worthy charity, is an example of the extreme misallocation of resources that may result when allocation depends on private decisions. In 1958 Americans contributed some $325 million to national voluntary health organizations, and of this sum, nearly $40 million went to the National Foundation.[59] It is inconceivable that there could be any rational reason for allocating almost twelve per cent of the total to polio when there were so many other more serious and widespread diseases to be combatted.

Professor Cutlip contrasts the public support given to combat polio in the years before the Salk vaccine with that given to combat multiple sclerosis. The incidence of both diseases, and the fatalities attributable to each, were roughly equal:

> These diseases were, before polio's cure, roughly comparable in the way they strike, in their role as crippler, and in their effects. . . . In 1954 . . . the National Foundation for Infantile Paralysis had an income of more than $42 million, more than $40 million of which came from public contributions. In the same year the Multiple Sclerosis Society was floundering in its effort to raise a mere $1.1 million. . . . In 1958 [after the Salk Vaccine] . . . the National Foundation was raising nearly $35 million to provide research in the areas of arthritis and birth defects, and care for polio sufferers. In the same year the National Multiple Sclerosis Society

57. Broughton, supra note 53, at 5.

58. Quoted in Cutlip, Fund Raising in the United States: Its Role in America's Philanthropy 531 (1965).

59. Id. at 351.

received $1,136,400 in contributions to carry on its work in a demonstrably greater cause.[60]

It is not suggested that private charities such as the National Foundation are not worthwhile objects of voluntary private benevolence; rather, it is likely that the Government could achieve a more rational allocation of its own funds.

2. *Administration*

It does not follow that, because the Government should be happy to have charities performing certain governmental functions at private expense, it should also prefer to have charities perform those functions at the Government's expense. Yet only if the latter proposition is true can the charitable deduction be defended. In support of this latter proposition it might be argued that charities can spend the Government's money (*i.e.*, the contributions induced by the tax deduction) more efficiently than can the Government.[61] The charity, with limited resources, perhaps is likely to administer its funds more frugally than the government bureaucrat who may eagerly spend all the money available in order to justify a bigger request next year. In addition, the charity is likely to be able to stretch its dollars by relying on unpaid volunteer help.

There are areas, however, in which charities may administer government-induced funds less efficiently than can the Government. Collection costs may be one such area. The large, reputable, honest charities have fund-raising costs ranging from a low of 5 per cent of revenues to a high of around 15 per cent. For example, according to spokesmen for the respective charities (who would be inclined, if anything, to give a low estimate), in the early 1950's CARE expended 7.6 per cent of its revenues for fund raising, the United Hospital Fund spent between 8.5 and 15 per cent, and the Greater New York Fund spent about 9 per cent.[62] In contrast, the total cost of operating the Internal Revenue Service is about .5 per cent of federal revenues.[63] While fund-

60. Id. at 491-92.

61. See Quiggle & Myers, Tax Aspects of Charitable Contributions and Bequests by Individuals, 28 Fordham L. Rev. 579, 580 (1960) ("the federal tax dollar, in its somewhat tortuous course from taxpayer to college, is so worn down that for each dollar received by a college, the taxpayer must provide two or three").

62. N.Y. Joint Legislative Comm. on Charitable and Philanthropic Agencies and Organizations, Report 34 (N.Y. Legis. Doc. No. 26, 1954).

63. See 1964 Comm'r of Internal Revenue Ann. Rep. 73, 99.

In comparing the fund-raising to the collection costs, it is necessary to recognize that any funds that charitable organizations might spend to attract federal contributions under a centralized system are equally a "cost" of collecting the

raising expenses and the cost of the Internal Revenue Service may be of very different natures, each represents the "cost" of raising the revenues in question. Of course it could be argued that voluntary contributions are less "painful" than taxes, but since collection costs seem to run from ten to thirty times higher for voluntary giving than for taxes this argument assumes that it is "better" to spend between $10 and $30 for carrots than $1 for sticks to induce contributions for worthwhile causes. Perhaps it is.

Obviously, the organizations mentioned above do not represent the fund-raising costs of all types of charitable organizations. Most churches probably spend a far smaller proportion on fund raising. At the other extreme, however, there are the frauds, contributions to which merely line the pockets of the promoters. Presumably many such contributions are deducted for tax purposes, thereby making the Government an unwilling contributor. It has been estimated that approximately three per cent of all contributions go to rackets.[64] An unknown amount is paid to charities that, although not frauds, are poorly administered and have excessive fund-raising and other costs.[65] Presumably "excessive" fund-raising costs would be those above seventeen per cent, the highest figure reported by the American Association of Fund-Raising Counsel for ethical, professional fund raisers.[66]

No doubt charity rackets and high overhead costs would continue were the charitable deduction abolished. The figures presented are not intended to suggest the contrary. They are offered to indicate that the position that charities can collect and spend the Government's money (the money induced by the tax deduction) more efficiently than the Government is debatable.

charitable monies. Such expenses, however, would certainly be far less than fund-raising costs under the present system.

64. N.Y. Joint Legislative Comm. on Charitable and Philanthropic Agencies and Organizations, Report 16 (N.Y. Legis. Doc. No. 26, 1954).

65. Ibid.

66. See id. at 34.

PROPOSED STRUCTURAL REVISION OF THE CHARITABLE CONTRIBUTION DEDUCTION

U. S. Treasury Dept., Tax Reform Studies and Proposals, 91st Cong., 1st Sess. pt. 2, at 194–200 (1969).

Under existing law taxable income is computed by subtracting a taxpayer's allowable deductions and personal exemptions from adjusted gross income. As an alternative to itemizing his deductions separately, a taxpayer may elect to use the standard deduction. The standard deduction permits a taxpayer to deduct a specified percentage of his income (or a minimum dollar amount) subject to a maximum dollar limitation without separately listing each deductible item. A taxpayer who finds it advantageous to use the standard deduction may not separately deduct his charitable contributions. A taxpayer who itemizes his deductions may deduct all charitable gifts subject to a general limitation that the allowable deduction may not exceed 30 percent of adjusted gross income, (20 percent in the case of gifts to certain types of charitable institutions).

PROPOSAL

Under the proposal all taxpayers—even those who elect to claim the increased standard deduction that is recommended in a separate proposal—would be entitled to separately deduct their charitable contributions. However, as a necessary corollary to increasing the standard deduction and making charitable contributions deductible independent of the standard deduction, the charitable deduction would be restricted to the amount by which contributions exceed 3 percent of taxpayer's adjusted gross income. In addition, the 30-percent limitation on deductible contributions would be increased to 50 percent of an amount equal to his adjusted gross income plus the exempt income items (in excess of $5,000) which are taken into account under the allocation of deductions and minimum tax proposals.

REASONS FOR THE PROPOSAL

The vital role that charitable organizations fulfill in our society is recognized by the provisions of existing law which exempt such organizations from Federal income tax. The provisions allowing private persons to deduct contributions to certain tax-exempt organizations also reflect the Federal Government's commitment to private charity and are principally justified as an incentive for charitable giving.

Under existing law persons who find it advantageous to use the standard deduction may not deduct their charitable contributions. The standard deduction is one of the most important and desirable features of our tax system combining both tax simplification and tax equity. Most taxpayers now use the standard deduction. (In the absence of any tax reform proposals approximately 57 percent of the total returns to be filed in 1969 will claim the standard deduction.) Since persons in this category are not entitled to separately deduct charitable contributions, the charitable deduction provisions of existing law do not function as an incentive for charitable giving for this group. In addition, because of the importance of the standard deduction to our tax system, a substantial increase in the standard deduction has been proposed. It is estimated that as a consequence of this and other reform proposals approximately 80 percent of all persons filing tax returns in 1969 will use the standard deduction. Accordingly, in order to preserve and strengthen the charitable contribution deduction as an incentive for donations among a broadly based segment of taxpayers, it is recommended that the charitable contribution deduction be allowed independently of the standard deduction.

In order to achieve the objectives of the proposals relating to the increased standard deduction and the charitable contribution deduction outside of the standard deduction (COSD), the charitable contribution deduction must be made inapplicable to routine gifts. Only in this manner can the simplification and tax equity objectives of the increased standard deduction be harmonized with the preservation of the charitable contribution deduction as an incentive for charitable giving. Moreover, since persons making only routine contributions each year are generally uninfluenced by tax considerations, the recommendation that the charitable contribution deduction be limited to amounts in excess of 3 percent of a taxpayer's adjusted gross income is unlikely to have any significant effect on the total flow of contributions to charitable organizations. In addition, if such a limitation were not imposed, the revenue loss that would result from allowing the deduction of routine contributions would make it impractical to permit charitable deductions independent of the increased standard deduction.

The increased standard deduction proposal in conjunction with the proposal allowing all taxpayers to deduct charitable contributions subject to a 3-percent threshold would vastly simplify our tax system. The need for maintaining detailed records to substantiate deductions for routine contributions would be eliminated. The 3-percent threshold also is necessary to avoid the intolerable administrative burden that would otherwise be imposed upon the Internal Revenue Service if all charitable contributions were deductible, regardless of amount, and subject to examination.

Allowing all persons to deduct contributions subject to a general 3-percent threshold will also do much to alleviate the structural inequities in the charitable contribution area which presently prevent the deduction from functioning efficiently as an incentive for charitable giving. Present law provides no incentive for above average gifts in the case of persons who have few noncharitable deductions and, therefore, use the standard deduction; and, of course, this will become more marked when the recommended increases in the standard deduction become effective. At the same time, present law permits persons who have large noncharitable deductions to deduct nominal gifts which would have been made under any circumstances. The proposal would correct this situation by limiting the tax benefit to persons making routine gifts and providing an incentive that does not presently exist for persons using the standard deduction—including those persons who will use the proposed increased standard deduction—to make above average contributions.

The remaining structural proposal would increase the ceiling on deductible contributions from 30 percent of adjusted gross income to 50 percent of an amount equal to adjusted gross income plus excluded items (in excess of $5,000) which are taken into account in the allocation of deductions and minimum tax proposals. This will permit larger deductions for contributions by taxpayers in the upper income ranges where the incentive effect of the charitable deduction is strongest.

EFFECT OF THE PROPOSAL

In the absence of these reform proposals, approximately 57 percent of all persons filing returns use the standard deduction and could not separately deduct their charitable contributions. Under this program it is estimated that 80 percent of all persons filing returns will use the new, increased standard deduction, as follows:

(1) Taxpayers who presently use the standard deduction, but nevertheless contribute more than routine amounts to charity. The effect of allowing charitable deductions in excess of 3 percent in addition to the standard deduction will constitute a benefit. This group will involve about 11 million returns which will receive a tax saving of about $118 million.

(2) Taxpayers who presently itemize their deductions but (including charitable deductions in excess of 3 percent of AGI) will shift to the standard deduction as a result of the recommended increase in the rate and ceiling of the standard deduction. This group will involve about 6 million taxpayers who will have a tax saving of $206 million.

(3) Taxpayers with large charitable contributions and modest noncharitable deductions who will switch to the standard deduction because the increased standard deduction is greater than their noncharitable deduction. This group which will be composed of 2 million taxpayers who will save $116 million since the effect of a 3-percent threshold will be partially or totally offset by their ability to use the proposed new standard deduction.

Table 1 indicates the revenue effects of both the 3 percent threshold and the COSD proposal by income level, after taking into account the proposed changes in the standard deduction, the minimum standard deduction, and after the disallowance of the gasoline tax deduction. The former provision increases revenue about $1.5 billion; the latter produces a loss in revenue of about $440 million. The effect of increasing the ceiling to 50 percent of the expanded income base is a revenue loss of approximately $20 million. Thus, the combined effect of all three provisions is a revenue increase of about $1 billion.

NUMBER OF RETURNS WITH CHARITABLE DEDUCTIONS

Under the overall reform program the number of returns claiming itemized deductions would be cut approximately in half (from 34 million to 16 million). Accordingly, of the present law itemizers taking the contribution deduction, about one-fourth should continue to itemize and to deduct contributions over the 3 percent threshold. Another fourth will continue to deduct contributions over 3 percent of AGI, but will no longer itemize other deductions. In addition, 11 million claiming the standard deduction under present law will also deduct charitable contributions in excess of the 3 percent floor under the program. Thus, the overall number of returns with a contribution deduction would not materially change; in 1969 it would be close to 26 million returns—including 18 million returns under COSD—compared to about 32 million estimated for that year under present law.

THE 3-PERCENT DEDUCTION THRESHOLD

Among 27 million persons who claimed itemized deductions including a charitable deduction in 1966, 78 percent of the total contributions were made by approximately 13 million people whose contributions were over 3 percent of their AGI. It is important to recognize that for these contributors the marginal contribution will be as valuable in terms of tax savings as it is now, despite the threshold provision. If a taxpayer has already contributed 3 percent of his AGI, the tax savings involved in an additional $100 contribution is unchanged whether or not the first part of his contribution is deductible. In other words, the price of giving at the margin (which is relevant to taxpayers' decisions to increase or decrease contributions) is unaffected by the imposition of a deduction threshold. Table 2 provides some detail material on the patterns of contributions in relation to AGI.

THE EFFECT OF THE PROGRAM ON CHARITABLE CONTRIBUTIONS

THE 50-PERCENT DEDUCTION LIMIT

The increase in the upper limitation on the charitable contribution deduction from 30 percent of adjusted gross income to 50 percent of the expanded income base will benefit those who presently donate substantial portions of their income to charity. These are principally upper-middle and upper income taxpayers for whom the deduction incentive is strong.

The history of special benefits in the income tax law has been dominated by considerations of the sort: "This incentive may do some good; we don't know for sure. Let's put it in the law anyway." A provision of this sort is thereafter strongly defended on the grounds that taking it out may eliminate the hypothetical benefit.

A serious effort to improve the tax law requires a hard look at evidence to reach some judgment on just what the effect is and whether it is worth the burden that this imposes on the rest of society.

This discussion undertakes to provide some analysis of how much difference might be made in contributions to charity as a result of the reform program. It will be convenient here to put the various parts together in one place by including a discussion of the effects of other provisions besides the 3 percent threshold, COSD, and the 50 percent upper limit. Table 3 provides some summary estimates of the possible impact of the complete program on charitable contributions.

A preliminary explanation is called for: A particular tax provision can affect the contributions of an individual in two ways.

1. *Income effect.*—If a tax provision increases or decreases income after tax, the provision should bring about a corresponding change in the individual's various uses of disposal income, including charitable contributions. What we need to know to estimate this effect is the portion of after-tax income which is allocated to contributions. In general, we can estimate this to average 4 percent for all itemizers, 3 percent for nonitemizers, and 7 percent for all high incomes. Further, we can estimate that these relationships tend to remain constant for moderate changes in after-tax income.

2. *Price effect.*—Some tax changes affect not only the after-tax income of an individual but also the cost to him of putting a dollar at the disposal of charity. The individual may respond to this in various ways. He could incur more cost and give the charity just as much; he could decide to incur the same cost as he did before and let the charity get along with a smaller contribution; or he could assume some compromise position between these two extremes. Several economists who have addressed this problem have found little evidence that changing the tax value of contributions has a noticeable effect on contributions. Fund raisers, on the other hand, persist in giving considerable emphasis to deductibility in their fund appeals.

For the present discussion we can suggest a range of possible effects. At the one end it seems too extreme to assert that when the tax advantage of a contribution is reduced contributors will maintain the same net cost of the contribution. Logically this is equivalent to asserting that every dollar of tax saving from the contribution deduction goes to increasing the contribution, and this is not consistent with the evidence.

NONECONOMIC INFLUENCES ON CHARITABLE GIVING

In addition to the economic motivations for charitable giving, the American Association of Fund-Raising Counsel recognizes many noneconomic incentives for giving. These include responses to social awareness, generosity, social pressure, pity, and habit. To the extent that the noneconomic factors influence charitable giving patterns, changes in the tax treatment of charitable donations have little repercussion on the level of contributions.

Since these noneconomic motivations are largely nonquantifiable, the importance of the economic incentive is difficult to distinguish from that of the noneconomic incentive. There is reason to believe, however, that noneconomic motivations have considerable influence on the level of giving. This is substantiated by the fact that studies relating variations in charitable contributions to changes in both the tax treatment and the incomes of contributors have been successful in explaining scarcely half of the observed variation in contributions.

The estimated $20 million income effect shown on table 3 is relatively small because in the aggregate the program is balanced and will leave income after tax unchanged. Some small net effect is possible because there is some shift in burden from low incomes to high incomes.

It is likely that the price effect will appear principally among people who now contribute less than 3 percent because, for larger contributors, the price of putting an additional dollar at the disposal of charity is not changed. About 40 percent of the revenue comes from this former group, and if they reduce their contribution by half of the increased tax their contributions would fall by $300 million. In this income area, contributions are most often associated with noneconomic incentives, for example, social pressures of community chest campaigns at the place of work, so this rate of decline would appear unrealistically high. The high estimate figure is only plausible if some price effect is attributed to people whose contributions are now a little over 3 percent.

Under the allocation of deductions proposal, about 40 percent of the allocated deductions will be contributions. Half of the contribution share of the revenue effect of allocation would be $80 million, which is increased in the high estimate to take account of the fact that some contributions of appreciated property will have the effect of causing more loss of deduction through allocation.

The price effect on foundations is a calculation of the additional contributions that some foundations would have to make to comply with the minimum distribution rule.

The COSD effect is related to the deduction allowed present standard deductors. (The remainder of the COSD offsets the effect of the increased standard deduction.)

The increase in the contributions limit from 30 percent of adjusted gross income to 50 percent of an expanded income base has an effect on giving of about the same magnitude as does the removal of the unlimited contribution deduction. They roughly balance each other.

The other effects will be small. The minimum tax will tend to provide a stimulus to contributions, especially for taxpayers who presently pay only the alternative capital gains tax and, thus, have no advantage from charitable contributions at this time. There will be some deterrent working through the contribution of appreciated property. The maximum tax should slightly increase the net cost of contributions by lowering the marginal tax rates for some taxpayers.

This implication of table 3 is that the program could on balance reduce contributions by an amount ranging between $100 and $300 million. To put this in context, it is important to recognize that the aggregate of contributions is in the neighborhood of $15 billion, and increasing from growth in the income of contributors by about $1 billion a year. The tax reform program might reduce this annual rate of growth in 1 year from about 6 to 5⅓ or to 4 percent. (By comparison, this growth rate would be affected more drastically by 1 year of recession.) After the year in which the tax law was changed, the normal growth should resume.

TABLE 1.—REVENUE EFFECT OF 3 PERCENT THRESHOLD IN CONTRIBUTIONS DEDUCTION AND COSD

AGI class (in thousands of dollars)	Revenue change			
	3 percent floor		COSD	
	Dollar in millions	Percent of total tax	Dollar in millions	Percent of total tax
0 to 3	2	0.2	−15	−1.3
3 to 5	15	0.5	−35	−1.1
5 to 7	65	1.2	−55	−1.0
7 to 10	205	1.5	−105	−0.8
10 to 15	270	1.9	−135	−0.7
15 to 20	155	2.1	−50	−0.7
20 to 50	370	2.9	−40	−0.3
50 to 100	205	3.2	−5	−0.1
100 to 500	142	3.0	(1)	(1)
500 to 1,000	20	3.1	(1)	(1)
1,000 and over	23	2.6	(1)	(1)
Total	+1,470	+1.9	−440	−0.

TABLE 2.—CHARITABLE CONTRIBUTION DEDUCTIONS (BASED ON STATISTICS OF INCOME FOR 1966)

AGI class (in thousands of dollars)	Returns with contribution deductions	Returns with contributions in relation to AGI			
		0 to 1 percent	1 to 2 percent	2 to 3 percent	Over 3 percent
Total	27,005,815	2,251,425	6,086,863	5,822,502	12,845,025
Below 5	5,000,953	224,396	691,586	747,446	3,337,525
5 to 10	12,047,691	1,089,259	2,772,195	2,629,404	5,556,833
10 to 20	8,238,297	770,687	2,145,664	2,046,664	3,275,282
20 to 50	1,458,717	133,523	404,542	349,269	571,383
50 to 100	208,511	25,000	60,682	42,458	80,371
100 to 500	49,468	7,978	11,915	7,131	22,444
500 to 1,000	1,550	398	210	105	837
1,000 and up	628	184	69	25	350

AGI class (in thousands of dollars)	Amount of contribution deductions	Contributions on returns with contributions as percent of AGI (in thousands)				Contributions over 3 percent as percent of all contributions
		0 to 1 percent	1 to 2 percent	2 to 3 percent	Over 3 percent	
Total	$9,122,491	$75,033	$700,521	$1,260,398	$7,086,539	77.7
Below 5	861,497	2,371	25,519	54,988	778,619	90.4
5 to 10	2,835,668	23,206	212,622	399,993	2,199,847	77.6
10 to 20	2,947,265	29,167	285,544	533,528	2,099,026	71.2
20 to 50	1,195,977	11,112	117,706	194,422	872,737	73.0
50 to 100	473,411	4,653	39,255	54,352	375,151	79.2
100 to 500	489,646	3,438	17,357	20,767	448,084	91.5
500 to 1,000	106,955	524	1,278	1,363	103,790	97.0
1,000 and up	212,074	562	1,240	985	209,287	98.7

TABLE 3.—ESTIMATES OF THE EFFECT OF THE PROGRAM ON CONTRIBUTIONS

[Millions of dollars]

	High estimate	Low estimate
1. Income effects	−20	−20
2. Price effects:		
3 percent threshold	−300	−100
COSD	+60	+20
Minimum tax	−20	−20
Maximum tax	−15	−10
Allocation of deductions	−100	−40
30 percent limit increase to 50 percent and repeal of ULCD	0	0
Foundations	+100	+100
3. Total (rounded)	−300	−100

*

Chapter IV

INDIVIDUALS AND FAMILIES

A fundamental question that must be answered in any tax system is how to treat families vis à vis individuals. As is made clear in the first excerpt that follows, that question in turn devolves into two separate, albeit related, issues—whether the system should recognize some tax unit larger than the individual (e. g., husband and wife, or husband, wife and minor children), and if so, what should be the relation between the tax burdens borne by such larger units and by individuals receiving similar income. Consider, for example, a single man earning $10,000. Suppose he marries a girl without income. How should that fact affect their previous tax liabilities? Is it any different if each previously earned $5000 and continues to earn the same amount after marriage? Should the answers vary as one moves up and down the income scale? These questions obviously involve not only a consideration of marginal tax rates but also of applicable personal exemptions. Hence it is important to note some changes in these areas that were introduced by the Tax Reform Act of 1969.[a] To what extent do the new rates for single persons and heads of household (beginning in 1971) cure the problem described at p. 411, infra? And what is the effect of the "low income allowance" introduced by the 1969 Act, and the gradual increase in the personal exemption to $750 by 1973? Should Congress have adopted instead the credit approach recommended by the Canadian Royal Commission on Taxation, p. 403, infra? [b]

The second excerpt deals with one of those typical corners of the law where present doctrines can only be explained in terms of a patchwork evolution, and where some comprehensive reform is therefore very much in order.

Chapters VB. and VIII of this book should also be considered in connection with the piece that immediately follows.

[a] Of lesser relevance is the increase in the maximum standard deduction (Section 143 of the Code), which may also halt the recent trend toward itemization of personal deductions.

[b] In a letter to the New York Times endorsing such a change, Professor James Tobin of Yale also added: "Finally, any liberalization of exemptions should be accompanied by the following reforms: no person should be claimed as an exemption or tax credit on more than one tax return, and a tax return must include all the income of every person claimed." New York Times, Dec. 8, 1969, p. 46, col. 3.

NOTE, TAX TREATMENT OF THE FAMILY: THE CANADIAN ROYAL COMMISSION ON TAXATION AND THE INTERNAL REVENUE CODE *

117 U.Pa.L.Rev. 98–132 (1968).

* * *

In September, 1962, the Canadian government appointed a Royal Commission on Taxation vested with a broad mandate to

> inquire into and report upon the incidence and effects of taxation imposed by Parliament . . . upon the operation of the national economy, the conduct of business, the organization of industry and the positions of individuals; and to make recommendations for improvements in the tax laws and their administration that may be consistent with the maintenance of a sufficient flow of revenue.[2]

More than seven hundred witnesses and three hundred briefs later,[3] the Commission in December, 1966, submitted its *Report*: six volumes (nearly 2700 pages) of proposals for sweeping revision of the Canadian federal tax system.[4]

The *Report* appears destined for considerable controversy as well as acclaim. One commentator observes:

---

[2] Order in Council P.C. 1962-1334. Named to the Commission were Kenneth LeM. Carter, chairman, J. Harvey Perry, A. Emile Beauvais, Donald G. Grant, Eleanor Milne and Charles E. S. Walls.

[3] 1 REPORT OF THE ROYAL COMMISSION ON TAXATION xiii (limited ed. 1966) [hereinafter cited as REPORT].

[4] Volume 1 includes an introduction, acknowledgments and minority reports; volume 2 treats the use of the tax system to achieve economic and social objectives; volumes 3 and 4 are devoted to the taxation of income; volume 5 covers sales taxes and tax administration; and volume 6 encompasses implications of the various proposals made in the other volumes.

In regard to the current status of the Commission's proposals, Canadian Finance Minister Sharp is reported to have stated that no legislation embodying the major proposals would be presented to Parliament "for some time." *Report of the Canadian Royal Commission on Taxation,* 16 OIL & GAS Q. 179, 180 (1967).

For the rather sketchy commentary appearing to date on the REPORT, see *id.;* CANADIAN TAX FOUNDATION, REPORT OF PROCEEDINGS OF THE 19TH TAX CONFERENCE (1967) [hereinafter cited as CANADIAN TAX FOUNDATION]; Barbeau, *The Report: "The Premise Dictates the Conclusion,"* 10 CAN. B.J. 153 (1967); Goodman, *Royal Commission Would Tax as Income Gifts and Inheritance of Canadians,* 26 J. TAXATION 370 (1967); Vineberg, *Royal Commission Proposals Would Revolutionize Canadian Tax System,* 26 J. TAXATION 258 (1967).

* © Copyright 1968 By The University of Pennsylvania. Reproduced with permission.

> The *Report* is likely to evoke awe and admiration for its imaginative scope and depth and, at the same time, intensive criticism and debate on some of its omnivorous accounting and taxing proclivities.[5]

Another has called the *Report* "stern, uncompromising, ungenerous, tight-fisted and mean."[6] More broadly, the *Report* has been deemed "an ideological manifesto designed to promote a new social order in Canada . . . as much a political as a fiscal compendium."[7]

While the *Report* is a unified document, many of its features can be closely examined on their own. Among its more notable proposals are the following: a "comprehensive tax base"[8] to include gifts and bequests, *inter alia*, as ordinary income; elimination of estate and gift taxation of donors; taxation of capital gains at ordinary income tax rates; reduction of progressive income tax rates to a maximum of fifty per cent; and integration of personal and corporate income taxes, entailing a fifty per cent tax at the corporate level, coupled, upon distribution of income by the corporation, with a tax refund to the shareholder based on the difference, if any, between his tax rate and the corporate rate.

One of the Commission's most provocative and timely recommendations is for adoption of a "family unit" (together with an individual unit) for purposes of (1) measuring income and reporting and paying income taxes, (2) allocating the income tax burden and (3) attaching tax consequences to transfers of property (including cash) within and between tax units. The proposed family unit has been heralded as a "much-needed step in the development of the equitable income tax."[9]

This Comment consists of three parts. The Commission's family unit is discussed first.[10] Next, the Internal Revenue Code's treatment of the family is outlined. Finally, the Commission's family unit is evaluated with reference to the goals of a tax system and in light of the shortcomings in the Internal Revenue Code.

---

5 Vineberg, *supra* note 4, at 261.

6 Remarks of F. D. Gibson, in CANADIAN TAX FOUNDATION 271.

7 Barbeau, *supra* note 4, at 153.

8 For recent treatment of the notion of a "comprehensive tax base," see the series of articles, Bittker, *A "Comprehensive Tax Base" as a Goal of Income Tax Reform*, 80 HARV. L. REV. 925 (1967); Musgrave, *In Defense of an Income Concept*, 81 HARV. L. REV. 44 (1967); Pechman, *Comprehensive Income Taxation: A Comment*, *id.* at 63; Bittker, *Comprehensive Income Taxation: A Response*, *id.* at 1032 (1968); Galvin, *More on Boris Bittker and the Comprehensive Tax Base: The Practicalities of Tax Reform and the ABA's CSTR*, *id.* at 1016.

9 Remarks of Joseph A. Pechman, in CANADIAN TAX FOUNDATION 443.

10 It should be stressed that the Commission's family unit, like most of the Commission's proposals, cannot be fully understood except in the context of the entire *Report*. Limitations of space prevent full discussion here.

I. The Royal Commission's Family Unit

Structure

The proposed family unit encompasses five groupings: [11]

(1) a husband and wife, and any dependent children; [12]

(2) a surviving spouse, and any dependent children; [13]

(3) a divorced or separated parent and one or more dependent children;

(4) one or more dependent children who have been in a family unit but who are separated from both parents by reason of the parents' death or residence outside Canada; and

(5) an individual and one or more dependent children, in the cases of adoption and unwed mothers.[14]

Dependent children are defined as unmarried children, resident in Canada, natural-born or adopted, and under 22 years of age.[15] In addition, two options are available. To account for self-sufficiency at an early age, a child under 22 employed full-time and not living with his parents can withdraw from the family unit at his or his parents' option. To account for the full-time university student, a student 22 to 25 years of age can remain a member of the family unit if both he and his parents so desire.[16] Actual support is irrelevant for purposes of inclusion or exclusion.[17]

Although other persons, such as an elderly parent, are sometimes dependent in fact upon, and may be an integral part of, the proposed family unit, they are excluded from that unit [18] and comprise an

---

[11] 3 Report 132-33.

[12] Common-law marriages qualify so long as the couple have cohabited for one year and file a joint declaration that they wish to be treated as husband and wife for tax purposes. *Id.* at 142. For the definition of dependent children, see text accompanying note 15 *infra.*

[13] For rate purposes a surviving spouse without dependent children is treated as an individual; however, he or she is deemed to still be in the original family unit so that transfers of property by the deceased spouse's estate to the surviving spouse constitute intrafamily transfers and hence entail no tax consequences. *Id.* at 151 n.16. Intrafamily transfers are discussed in text accompanying notes 49-60 *infra.*

[14] Possible tax units other than the Commission's family unit include the individual unit (which the Commission recommends for taxpayers not in a family unit), the marital unit (husband and wife only), the broad family unit (all relatives living together) and the household unit (all persons living together).

[15] 3 Report 133. *Id.* at 151 n.17, suggests that arguably the age should be 18. Mentally or physically "infirm" children of any age are also considered dependent. *Id.* at 133.

[16] *Id.* at 133.

[17] *Id.* at 134.

[18] *Id.* at 141.

individual unit. The supporting unit is allowed a tax credit of ten per cent of all expenditures (up to $1000) made in support of a "close relative," defined as children who are no longer members of the family unit, a parent of either spouse, aunts, and uncles.[19]

In the usual case, the family unit commences at marriage; it also commences when an unwed mother retains custody of her child, when a single person adopts a child, or when a divorced or separated spouse retains custody of one or more dependents. In the last situation, the original family unit in effect continues without the other spouse, who is in yet another family unit if he or she also retains a dependent. The first tax year for the family unit is the calendar year of its creation.[20]

The income of all the unit's members is aggregated. Income is broadly defined by the Commission to include almost all flows of property into the unit—gifts, bequests, and earnings[21]—as well as previously unrecognized appreciation on property transferred outside the unit, whether by sale, gift or bequest.[22] Transfers of property within a unit give rise to no tax consequences.[23] Joint and several liability of husband and wife, in the usual case, is computed with the family rate schedule.[24] Husband and wife can at their option file separately, in which case any income of their children must be aggregated with that of a parent.[25] However, separate returns almost invariably entail a higher total tax liability for the family since each spouse's individual liability is computed by doubling his taxable income, applying the family unit's rate schedule, and halving the amount due on that income.[26]

The family unit terminates upon:[27]

(1) the death of the last of the unit's members;

---

19 *Id.* at 228-29. Complete dependency is not a condition for the credit. Provision of room and board in the donor's home is deemed to be worth $1000. The recipient, meanwhile, is required to report the support assistance as income to the extent it exceeds his $250 annual and $5000 lifetime gift exemption. In view of these exemptions and relatively low tax rates, the Commission foresees little or no income tax liability for the recipient of such support gifts.

20 *Id.* at 126, 134.

21 Transfers for value and loans, *inter alia,* do not in themselves give rise to income. For the Commission's discussion of its "comprehensive tax base," see *id.* at 39-116.

22 *Id.* at 51.

23 For a discussion of transfers within the unit, see notes 49-60 *infra* and accompanying text.

24 3 Report 134-35. A dependent child is liable for the tax attributable to any amount of the total reported income for which he is responsible. *Id.* Only his earned income in excess of $500 and his gifts in excess of a $100 annual exemption must be reported by the family. *Id.* at 135, 138.

25 *Id.* at 126, 134, 189. Presumably the parents can divide the children between them as they wish.

26 *Id.* at 189. The higher total liability is attributable to the progressivity of tax rates and results unless husband and wife separately report equal taxable incomes. See recommended rates, *id.* at 179, table 11-9.

27 *Id.* at 128-30, 139-40.

(2) the non-residence of the last of the unit's members;

(3) the remarriage of a surviving spouse, with or without dependent children;

(4) divorce or legal separation; or

(5) the coming of age of the last dependent child in a family where the parents are no longer in the family unit.

Allocation of the Income Tax Burden

In its proposed allocation of the income tax burden among various tax units, the Commission relies on the standard of "ability to pay." Taxation in accord with "ability to pay" is "achieved when taxes [are] allocated in proportion to the discretionary economic power of tax units."[28] "Discretionary economic power" is the product of the tax unit's total economic power (defined as the unit's power to command goods and services for personal use) and the fraction of that power available for "discretionary use" by the unit, that is, which does not have to be exercised to maintain the members of the unit ("maintenance" is defined as "the appropriate standard of living . . . relative to others").[29] The Commission provides this illustration. Assume tax units *A* and *B*. *A* has an income of $10,000, one-tenth of which can be spent at *A*'s discretion. *B* has an income of $20,000, two-tenths of which is available for the discretionary use of *B*. Then, in accord with the "ability to pay" principle, the relative taxes on units *A* and *B* should be:

$$\frac{\text{Tax on } A}{\text{Tax on } B} = \frac{\text{Income of } A \times \begin{array}{c}\text{Fraction available for}\\ A\text{'s discretionary use}\end{array}}{\text{Income of } B \times \begin{array}{c}\text{Fraction available for}\\ B\text{'s discretionary use}\end{array}}$$

$$= \frac{10{,}000 \times .10}{20{,}000 \times .20} = \frac{1000}{4000} = \tfrac{1}{4}$$

To raise $1000 in tax revenues, for instance, a uniform rate of 20 per cent would be imposed on the discretionary income of each unit. *A* would pay $200, or 20 per cent of its "discretionary economic power" of $1000, and *B* would pay $800, or 20 per cent of its $4000.[30] The Commission does recognize, however, that "discretionary economic

---

28 *Id.* at 5.

29 *Id.* No specific explication is given of the "appropriate standard" except to indicate that it is more than "bare subsistence." The "others" are not defined.

30 *Id.* at 6-7.

power" is not an "objective phenomenon," and proceeds to set forth three central factors to be considered in ascertaining fractions of a unit's income available for discretionary use: family responsibilities, income, and certain non-discretionary expenditures.[31]

To recognize differing family responsibilities, the Commission distinguishes unattached individuals, married couples without dependent children, and couples with varying numbers of dependent children. An individual has fewer non-discretionary maintenance expenses than a married couple with the same total income and thus should pay higher taxes. And while "two cannot live as cheaply as one," there are economies to marriage and thus as a rule when two people with the same income marry they should pay more tax than the sum of their taxes before marriage.[32] Dependent children reduce "discretionary economic power," though in smaller amounts for each successive child.[33]

The Commission argues that "[a]t the bottom of the income scale there are often diseconomies to marriage," [34] notably because after marrying the parties generally can no longer share living accommodations with more than one person and, in order to establish a household, must make expenditures that are greater than the possible savings on other expenses. Consequently, there should not be an increase in total taxes at low income levels after marriage takes place. Conversely, at very high income levels

> marital status has relatively little effect on discretionary economic power. When two wealthy individuals marry, their total tax should be greater than the sum of the taxes they paid as single individuals to take into account the economies of living together, but these economies are small when compared to their income. The increase in tax upon marriage for such people should consequently be relatively smaller than for individuals with less income who marry.[35]

Finally, the Commission argues that account should be taken of "non-discretionary" gifts to close relatives to provide them with support,[36] special expenses of working mothers with young children, and extraordinary medical expenses.[37]

To implement these goals the Commission recommends separate rate schedules for individuals and married couples. Use of a single

---

31 *Id.* at 7-8.
32 *Id.* at 14, 142-43.
33 *Id.* at 17.
34 *Id.* at 15.
35 *Id.* at 15-16.
36 See note 19 *supra* and accompanying text.
37 3 REPORT 19.

schedule with either an exemption or a credit to differentiate individuals from couples is rejected. The exemption is rejected because

> To use one schedule for both kinds of units and a fixed [dollar] exemption for the couple would be tantamount to the acceptance of the assumption that the extra non-discretionary expenses of a couple not only increase with income but increase at the same rate as the marginal rates of tax increase with income. This we cannot accept. We believe that when the level of income is substantial, the fraction of additional income for discretionary use is the same for the couple as for the unattached individual. *Adoption of an exemption would give an unwarranted tax reduction to upper income couples and would not be sufficiently generous for low income couples.*[38]

As to credits,

> The adoption of a credit to differentiate the tax on couples and unattached individuals would pose exactly the opposite problem. This would be tantamount to the acceptance of the assumption that the extra non-discretionary expenses of the couple do not increase with income. *If a substantial credit were provided, this would be too generous for low income couples and not sufficiently generous for middle and upper income couples.*[39]

Thus the Commission recommends as a middle ground between exemptions and credits the use of separate rate schedules to allow for a more precise and equitable adjustment.[40]

The Commission does, however, reject the extension of separate rate schedules to distinguish among various kinds of family units, specifically those with different numbers of dependent children. The Commission argues that because of the various combinations that would be needed such schedules are not administratively feasible and that, their "refined technique" notwithstanding, such schedules "would introduce complexities for taxpayers that would not be justified by the relatively small amounts involved."[41] The Commission rejects use of exemptions

---

[38] *Id.* at 16 (emphasis supplied). The Commission refers to a fixed dollar exemption, not to a percentage exemption. The former is exemplified by the $600 personal exemption deduction allowed by INT. REV. CODE OF 1954, § 151. The tax savings attendant upon the exemption are basically a function of the taxpayer's marginal rate of tax. A fixed percentage exemption, meanwhile, is exemplified by a constant percentage of income. Its value also rises with the taxpayer's marginal rate, but is sharply accelerated by the fact that its amount as well as the marginal rate on that amount increase with income.

[39] *Id.* at 16-17 (emphasis added). A credit, it will be remembered, is a fixed reduction of the tax liability, and by the Commission's definition does not vary with the taxpayer's income.

[40] *Id.* at 17.

[41] *Id.*

on the ground that actual expenses for children, while probably increasing with income, do not rise as rapidly as the marginal rates of tax increase with income. Instead, credits are recommended:

> Credits against tax are simpler than separate rate schedules and the inherent bias of fixed credits would be in favour of low income families as we think it should be.[42]

The credits are $100 for the first child and $60 for each additional child.[43] The Commission acknowledges that these credits

> are low in relation to the non-discretionary expenses of raising children. However, to adopt larger credits would reduce revenues and necessitate higher marginal rates with their unfavourable effects on incentives.[44]

In recognition of the additional non-discretionary expenses incurred when both parents work, a family unit in which both husband and wife work for more than 120 days a year is entitled to an $80 credit if there is also a child in the unit; an additional $120 credit is granted if the child is under seven.[45] As discussed above, expenditures to support a "close relative" give rise to a credit of up to $100, based on 10 per cent of the support expenditures.[46] Finally, a credit "equal to a substantial proportion (preferably 50 per cent—the top marginal rate) of the medical expenses in excess of a percentage of income" is available to the family unit, as well as to the individual unit.[47] Again, credits were chosen to make these adjustments because they are less complicated than schedules, less costly than exemptions, and provide a disproportionately greater reduction of "the tax burden on low income families whose ability to pay is most affected by the additional non-discretionary expenses . . . ."[48]

Tax Consequences of Transfers Within and Without the Family Unit

Property held by members of a newly formed family unit is usually not included in the income of the new unit.[49] Only where commence-

---

42 *Id.*

43 *Id.* at 181. This means the following average credits per child for various families: one child—$100; two children—$80; three—$73; four—$70; five—$68; six—$67. *Id.*

44 *Id.* at 18.

45 *Id.* at 193.

46 See note 19 *supra* and accompanying text.

47 3 REPORT 214. The Commission suggests that the expenses be required to exceed an unspecified minimum percentage of income before the credit becomes available. Medical credits in general are apparently considered by the Commission an "interim solution" pending some form of complete medical insurance coverage. *Id.*

48 *Id.* at 179-80.

49 *Id.* at 126, 134. This rule applies to family units formed by marriage of two non-dependent children, by an unwed mother retaining custody of her child, by a single person adopting a child, and by a divorced or separated spouse retaining custody of one or more dependents.

ment of the family unit coincides with a dependent child leaving his original family unit is such property income to the new unit.[50] This exception is designed to preclude circumvention of the proposed treatment of withdrawal by a child from his family unit, which requires that property taken by the child constitute income to his new unit.[51] Thus, dependent children do not avoid the tax consequences of withdrawal by marriage.

Transfers of property within a family unit involve no tax consequences:

> It is not that [such] transfers . . . would be exempt from tax; it is simply that these transfers would be removed from the purview of the tax system.[52]

Title can thus be transferred within the unit, be it by sale, gift or bequest, with no tax consequences; there is no income or gain to be reported and the property's basis remains unchanged.[53] One exception is made to this rule. Until a couple has a natural-born child or until the marriage lasts for five years, tax-free transfers to the other spouse can be made only in an amount up to one-half of the income reported by the unit. Any transfers (other than for fair consideration) in excess of this amount constitute income to the family unit. The Commission believes this exception necessary "to reduce tax avoidance through artificially arranged marriages" designed to take advantage of the tax immunity of transfers.[54]

With two exceptions here relevant, flows of income (broadly defined by the "comprehensive tax base" [55]) into and between tax units are recognized.[56] The relevant exceptions are for gifts to and earnings of a dependent child, which are eligible for deposit in a government-administered, interest-bearing "Income Adjustment Account" in the year of receipt. Amounts so deposited are deducted from income. Income is recognized when the deposit is withdrawn, which may be no later than the child's withdrawal from the unit. These

---

[50] *Id.* at 138. This rule applies as well, of course, to an individual unit so commenced.

[51] *See* text accompanying note 58 *infra*.

[52] 3 REPORT 125.

[53] Trusts qualify for this treatment where the beneficiary is a member of the settlor's family unit. *See* 4 REPORT 160.

[54] 3 REPORT 127.

[55] *See id.* at 39-116.

[56] Two non-recognition provisions not directly relevant here are for gifts in kind (the tax on which can be spread over a period of 5 to 10 years) and for amounts deposited in a government-administered, non-interest bearing "Income Adjustment Account." (Amounts so deposited do not give rise to taxable income until withdrawn by the depositor; this Account provision must be distinguished from the dependent child's Account, treated immediately following in the text above.) 3 REPORT 269, 503-04.

exceptions are defended on the ground that such amounts do not increase the "discretionary economic power" of the unit. The gift exemption is thought necessary to avoid a double tax on large gifts to a dependent child from outside the unit, which would otherwise be taxed first to the family and then to the child upon his withdrawal from the unit. For a similar reason the child's employment or business income in excess of a proposed $500 exemption is eligible for deposit.[57]

A member is deemed to have withdrawn from the family unit in a number of circumstances, notably when a child ceases to qualify as a dependent (by coming of age, marrying or opting out) and when a member dies or becomes a non-resident. Two tax consequences follow: first, previously unrecognized appreciation of property taken by the withdrawing member constitutes income to the family unit in the year of withdrawal; and second, the withdrawing member includes in the income of his new unit the fair market value of the property taken in excess of his $5000 lifetime and $250 annual gift and bequest exemptions.[58] The exemptions are thought sufficient to ensure that most new units commenced by the child's withdrawal are free of tax upon formation.[59]

A family unit terminates in one of two basically different ways. First, if the unit ends by the death or non-residence of the last of the unit's members or by the remaining member(s) coming of age, there is (1) income to the unit in the amount of previously unrecognized appreciation of property which thereby passes from the unit and (2) income to the recipient unit (be it another family unit or an individual one), if any. In other circumstances, no tax consequences attend termination. This results on the remarriage of a surviving spouse (with or without children), on divorce or legal separation, and on the marriage of an unwed person with a dependent child.[60]

Policy Objectives

As outlined above, the family unit constitutes a single tax unit for three purposes: measuring income and paying income tax, allocating the income tax burden among various units, and attaching tax consequences to transfers of property within and between units.

---

[57] *Id.* at 135-36.

[58] *Id.* at 137-38. The $5000 lifetime exemption does not accrue until an individual ceases to be a dependent. *Id.* In the case of withdrawal by death, property taken from the unit is that property bequeathed to persons outside the decedent's family unit. In the cases of death and non-residence, the withdrawing member does not form or become part of a new unit.

[59] *Id.* at 137-38. A dependent child is thus free of income tax on account of property taken into his new unit upon withdrawal (*i.e.*, property he receives from his earlier deposits, if any, in the Account, plus any other property he may possess on leaving the family) to the extent the fair market value of such property does not exceed $5250. Amounts in trusts created by a member of the family and of which he is beneficiary are included in the property deemed taken. 4 REPORT 175. The general income averaging provisions are also available. *See* 3 REPORT 138, 276-80.

[60] 3 REPORT 128-30, 139-41.

For these purposes, the Commission's choice of the family unit [61] proceeds from its assertion that a tax system should reflect "the basic economic and financial entity" in society.[62] The Commission argues that upon marriage a couple "adopts the economic concept of the family as the income unit" and that it is "the continued income and financial position of the family which is ordinarily of primary concern, not the income and financial position of the individual members." [63] Husband and wife thus act as a unit. As the family grows by the addition of children, the family continues to pool its resources and make decisions and expenditures on a group basis.[64] As a corollary of this unity, the Commission regards taxation of transfers of property between members of a family as "wrong in principle" and gift and death taxes on these transfers as anachronistic.[65]

Then as children come of age, marry, opt out or leave Canada, they are viewed as forming their own economic units and ceasing to be members of their original families. Any other person, even if in fact a full, functioning member of the family in social and economic terms, is excluded from the family unit. The Commission argues that it would "unduly complicate the family unit concept" to allow such persons to become members of the family unit for tax purposes "because it would require elaborate provisions to prevent tax-free transfers between generations." [66]

Intertwined with the social and economic justification for the family unit is the overriding objective of the entire *Report*: equity, both horizontal and vertical. The Commission defines horizontal equity as individuals and families in similar circumstances bearing the same taxes, vertical equity as those in different circumstances bearing appropriately different taxes.[67]

On the horizontal level, the individual unit is depicted by the Commission as inequitable in two respects. First, the total tax liability of a family whose members are taxed as individuals can vary between two families with the same total income depending on the distribution of income among the members of the respective families: due to the progressivity of income tax rates, the more even the distribution of income within a family the less its tax liability.[68] Second,

---

[61] Canada presently employs only the individual unit for income tax purposes, with no aggregation except indirectly through a $1000 deduction allowed a husband for his wife (reduced by the amount of her income in excess of $250) and a deduction ($300 or $550) for a dependent child whose income does not exceed $950. *Id.* at 117, 180. Gift and death taxes are presently applicable, *inter alia,* to transfers between members of a family. 1 REPORT 18-19.

[62] 3 REPORT 124.

[63] *Id.* at 123.

[64] *Id.* at 123-24. The Commission acknowledges that a child's income may have only an indirect bearing on the family income. *Id.*

[65] 1 REPORT 18-19.

[66] 3 REPORT 228.

[67] 1 REPORT 4-5.

[68] 3 REPORT 118, 143.

the individual unit allows for income splitting (here meaning the deflection of income, whether or not the transaction giving rise to the deflection is motivated by tax minimization) between members of the family,[69] as by the transfer of income-producing property, by family trusts and partnerships, and so forth.[70] For the Commission, different distributions of income and income splitting within families should not give rise to different tax liabilities.[71]

In vertical as well as horizontal terms, the Commission believes that only by treating families as entities can their "discretionary economic power" be satisfactorily measured. In turn, it is only through proper income measurement that family units can be equitably compared with individual units and with one another for purposes of equitable allocation of the tax burden.

A third major concern of the Commission is that of enforcement and administration, principally with respect to income tax. At present the Canadian federal tax system contains complex, stringent provisions designed to nullify the income tax effects of family income splitting.[72] Witnesses before the Commission termed these provisions "inconsistent and discriminatory as between taxpayers" (thereby a departure from horizontal equity) and "too rigid and restrictive in dealing with relationships between spouses." [73] For example, a salary paid to a wife by her husband may be deductible to the husband's business if the business is incorporated, but not otherwise.[74] Implementation of the family unit would, the Commission hopes, allow for the repeal of the provisions against family income splitting and thus eliminate attendant administrative and enforcement problems.[75]

---

[69] *Id.* at 120.

[70] Literature on income splitting techniques is voluminous. See, *e.g.*, Alter, *The Family Business*, N.Y.U. 16TH INST. ON FED. TAX. 755 (1958); Davies, *Shifting of Family Income for Tax Purposes*, 6 ST. LOUIS U.L.J. 281 (1961); Yohlin, *Assignment and Deflection of Income*, N.Y.U. 20TH INST. ON FED. TAX. 147 (1962); Note, *Family Partnerships and the Federal Income Tax*, 41 IND. L.J. 684 (1966).

[71] A similar rationale supports the Commission's provision of tax immunity for intrafamily property transfers. Transfer tax burdens can differ between various families, depending upon the legal ownership of family assets, the *inter vivos* gifts made, and the circumstance of which spouse dies first. The Commission provides this illustration. Families *A, B* and *C* have each accumulated $200,000. Presumably, both husband and wife have contributed to this amount in one way or another. In *A* all the assets are owned by the husband and in *B* by the husband and wife, one-half each (as a result of gifts or otherwise). If the husbands in *A* and *B* die before their wives, the estate tax will be much greater for family *A* than *B*. If in each family the wife dies first, family *B* will pay much heavier estate taxes. Meanwhile, family *C* might avoid estate taxes on the deaths of both spouses by having part of its assets accumulated in trust for the children. And if the husband in *A* makes a substantial gift before death to his wife or children, a gift tax might result that families *B* and *C* would have avoided. These inequalities are eliminated by removing intrafamily transfers of property from the purview of the system. *See* 3 REPORT 119-20.

[72] For a discussion of these provisions, see E. Mockler, J. Smith & C. Frenette, STUDIES OF THE ROYAL COMMISSION ON TAXATION, TAXATION OF THE FAMILY 3-38 (the Studies were prepared for the Commission and not by it).

[73] 3 REPORT 121.

[74] 1 REPORT 18; 3 REPORT 122; for additional anomalies see *id.* at 121.

[75] 1 REPORT 18.

II. The Internal Revenue Code's Treatment of the Family

The Internal Revenue Code's treatment of the family is often and intensely maligned.[76] The Code's patchwork treatment stands in marked contrast to the comprehensive family unit of the Commission.

Recognition of the Family

The Code does not formally recognize the family as an entity; however, a taxpayer's marital and family relationships are taken into account for some purposes. Separate rate schedules are maintained for married couples, surviving spouses with dependent children,[77] and heads of households;[78] dependency exemptions are provided;[79] deductions are allowed for certain alimony payments,[80] medical expenses for dependents,[81] and expenses for care of certain dependents;[82] no deduction is allowed for certain losses, expenses and interest with respect to transactions between brothers, sisters, spouses, ancestors and lineal descendants;[83] constructive ownership through spouses, children, grandchildren, and parents is employed in the treatment of certain corporate distributions and adjustments;[84] a deduction of up to one-half of the adjusted gross estate is allowed for bequests to the surviving spouse;[85] gifts by one spouse to a person other than his spouse may, with consent, be treated as if given one-half by each spouse;[86] and a gift to a donor's spouse entitles the donor to exclude one-half of the gift in computing his taxable gifts for the year.[87]

On the other hand, individual family members often are—or, at their discretion, can be—treated as isolated units: husband and wife can file individual income tax returns[88] and unmarried persons, including dependent children, must;[89] gains on sales to spouses, children and certain other relatives are recognized as income,[90] as are gifts[91] and bequests[92] to spouses, children and other relatives.

---

[76] *See, e.g.*, Groves, *supra* note 1, at 3: "A considerable number of [tax] critics . . . are firmly convinced that our present tax treatment of the family is irrational and inexpedient."

[77] Int. Rev. Code of 1954, § 2.

[78] *Id.* § 1(b).

[79] *Id.* § 151.

[80] *Id.* § 215.

[81] *Id.* § 213.

[82] *Id.* § 214.

[83] *Id.* § 267.

[84] *Id.* § 318.

[85] *Id.* § 2056.

[86] *Id.* § 2513.

[87] *Id.* § 2523.

[88] *Id.* § 1.

[89] In certain circumstances, a surviving spouse who has not remarried can file jointly with the deceased spouse. *Id.* §§ 2, 6013.

[90] *Id.* §§ 267, 1002.

[91] *Id.* § 2501.

[92] *Id.* § 2001.

Dependent children are not, for purposes of income measurement and income tax assessment, included in their parents' unit.[93] Prior to 1948 there were a few suggestions that the income of minor children be reported with that of the parents.[94] Apparently, the question of children's income was not considered by Congress at the time of the 1948 tax reforms.[95] Since then some attention has been given to the question and reportedly "many tax scholars" now favor inclusion of minor children in the parents' unit.[96] Some would limit the inclusion to a child's property income or, more narrowly, to a child's income deriving from property received initially from a parent.[97]

Criticism of independent income taxation of children is based largely on equitable grounds. In terms of horizontal equity, families with the same total income are unequally treated depending upon how the income is distributed among the members. The distributions of income within a family can often be affected by various income splitting devices.[98] In terms of vertical equity, there are two flaws in exclusion of children. One is that the income of children in high income families is taxed at the lowest marginal rates, if at all, when in fact the children's income is available, at least beneficially and indirectly, to the parents.[99] The other involves the double $600 exemption possible in the case of a child who is a student, under 19 years of age, or earns less than $600 annually. The double exemption arises when a child takes the exemption on his return[100] and the parents, if qualifying, claim him as a dependent and take a similar exemption in their return.[101] This means discrimination against lower income families because the parents are less likely to qualify for the dependency exemption (which requires provision of one half the child's support), lower income families being able to contribute less to the child's support while the child is more likely to be making a substantial contribution

---

93 Two other areas of criticism—treatment of heads of households and working wives—arguably functions of structured recognition, are treated under burden allocation *infra* at notes 127-35 and accompanying text.

94 D. THORSON, THE SELECTION OF A TAX UNIT UNDER THE INCOME TAX: THE INDIVIDUAL UNIT VERSUS THE FAMILY UNIT 75 (1962) (unpublished doctoral thesis submitted to the University of Wisconsin) [hereinafter cited as THORSON, SELECTION OF A TAX UNIT]. For several such suggestions, see DIVISION OF TAX RESEARCH, U.S. TREASURY DEP'T, THE TAX TREATMENT OF FAMILY INCOME, reprinted in *Hearings on Proposed Revisions of the Internal Code Before the House Comm. on Ways and Means,* 80th Cong., 1st Sess. 846, 861-63, 865-66 (1947); Ervin, *Federal Taxes and the Family,* 20 S. CAL. L. REV. 243, 247-48 (1947).

95 THORSON, SELECTION OF A TAX UNIT 242.

96 Thorson, *An Analysis of the Sources of Continued Controversy over the Tax Treatment of Family Income,* 18 NAT'L TAX J. 113, 130 (1965) [hereinafter cited as Thorson, *Tax Treatment of Family Income*].

97 *See* GROVES, *supra* note 1, at 42, 100.

98 The inequity is facilitated by the fact that earned income cannot be split, or dispersed, within the family while unearned income can be.

99 A child's income is taxed to him even if payments for his services are made to his parents. INT. REV. CODE OF 1954, § 73.

100 *Id.* § 151(b).

101 *Id.* §§ 151(e), 152.

on his own.[102] It also means that qualifying families receive a $1200 exemption for the child, with a limiting effect on the progressivity of the tax rate applied to the total family income.

Allocation of the Income Tax Burden to Families

The least reasonable and most criticized aspect of the Code's treatment of the family is the allocation of income taxes among single persons and families. The Code's treatment appears to be more accidental than coherent. Joseph A. Pechman has observed that it is indeed "time to clean up the messy and arbitrary differences in the tax burdens of single and married people." [103]

The central feature of allocation between single persons and couples under the Code is the split-income rates allowed couples.[104] Under this provision, a couple halves its taxable income and pays a tax of twice the tax liability on the half.[105] Heads of households, meanwhile, receive one half the split-income advantage.[106] The following table illustrates the impact of split-income rates.[107]

Taxable Income	*Rate on Single Return*	*Rate on Joint Return*[108]	*Tax on Single Return*	*Tax Reduction on Joint Return*	*Percentage Reduction on Tax on Joint Return*
$ 500	14.0%	14.0%	$ 70	$ 0	0%
1,000	14.5%	14.0%	145	5	3%
2,000	15.5%	14.5%	310	20	6%
3,000	16.7%	15.0%	500	50	10%
6,000	18.7%	16.7%	1,130	130	10%
10,000	21.9%	17.2%	2,190	470	22%
14,000	25.4%	19.7%	3,550	790	22%
20,000	30.4%	21.9%	6,070	1,690	28%
26,000	34.8%	24.6%	9,030	2,650	29%
32,000	38.2%	26.9%	12,210	3,550	29%
40,000	41.7%	30.3%	16,670	4,530	28%
50,000	46.4%	34.1%	22,590	5,530	24%
100,000	55.5%	45.2%	55,490	10,310	19%
200,000	62.7%	55.5%	125,490	14,510	13%
400,000	66.4%	62.7%	265,490	14,510	5%

Split-income rates are subject to sharp criticism not only with respect to differentiation between single persons and couples but for

---

[102] *Cf.* GROVES *supra* note 1, at 39-41. The inequity is compounded by the greater worth, in taxes saved, of exemptions to higher tax bracket families.

[103] Pechman, *Income Splitting,* 1 TAX REVISION COMPENDIUM 473, 486 (1959) (paper submitted to House Comm. on Ways and Means).

[104] Split-income rates are to be distinguished from income splitting, *see* text accompanying notes 69-70 *supra,* which is income deflection or dispersion through devices such as trusts or gifts of income-producing property.

[105] INT. REV. CODE OF 1954, § 2.

[106] J. PECHMAN, FEDERAL TAX POLICY 83-84 (1966). INT. REV. CODE OF 1954, § 1(b)(1), provides the rate schedule for heads of households, as defined by § 1(b)(2) & (3).

[107] Figures are based on INT. REV. CODE OF 1954, § 1(a)(2).

[108] The rate is arrived at by dividing the tax by the taxable income.

their effect on progressivity as well.[109] As the table indicates, middle and upper income couples receive a substantial tax reduction, a maximum of 29 per cent at the $26,000-$32,000 level. Approximately 66.5 per cent of all returns either cannot claim the benefits of splitting or receive little benefit from it and only about 17 per cent of all returns receive significantly more than a $40 benefit.[110] The revenue lost by the use of split-income rates instead of individual reporting was estimated in 1959 to be over $4 billion a year.[111]

The net result of split-income rates, therefore, is a disproportionate reduction to middle and upper income couples (especially the latter) at the ultimate expense of single persons and lower income couples.[112] Even without recalling the Royal Commission's goal of sensitive adjustments in relation to the economies of marriage at various income levels,[113] split-income rates are clearly haphazard and inequitable.

Split-income rates originated in 1948. Their adoption has been attributed to "historical developments rather than design" and to "political compromise dictated by a high-pressure historical situation." [114] Split-income rates resolved two problems: the discrimination in favor of couples in community property states who could split their income in separate returns while couples in other states could not, and the unequal treatment of couples with like incomes in non-community property states based on the distribution of income between husband and wife, with the least tax liability arising from an equal distribution.[115] Aggregation of the incomes of husband and wife was a logical step in the resolution of these problems; split-income rates as a means of burden allocation was not.

Split-income rates have been popular, despite their flaws, and Congress has not seriously considered alternatives.[116] Nonetheless, justifications for their disparities are few. One is that the benefits accruing to middle and upper income families are appropriate in view of the alleged failure of personal exemptions to provide adequate relief for the costs of raising children. However, lower income couples may also have children; and split-income rates at any event do not distinguish between childless and childbearing couples.[117] It is also argued

---

[109] *See, e.g.*, J. DUE, GOVERNMENT FINANCE 155-56 (1959); Musgrave, *How Progressive is the Income Tax?* 3 TAX REVISION COMPENDIUM 2223 (split-income treatment "punctures the pattern of progression . . . in an arbitrary and inequitable fashion"); Pechman, *supra* note 103, at 473-86.

[110] GROVES, *supra* note 1, at 72-73.

[111] Pechman, *supra* note 103, at 474.

[112] Professor Groves terms the treatment of singles "unconscionable." GROVES, *supra* note 1, at 106.

[113] See notes 35-39 *supra* and accompanying text.

[114] GROVES, *supra* note 1, at 17, 59. *Accord,* Oldman & Temple, *Comparative Analysis of the Taxation of Married Persons,* 12 STAN. L. REV. 585, 593-94 (1960) [hereinafter cited as Oldman & Temple].

[115] Pechman, *supra* note 103, at 473.

[116] J. PECHMAN, FEDERAL TAX POLICY 84 (1966).

[117] *Id.*

that splitting eliminates the disincentive to a wife's working inherent in income aggregation.[118] A third defense is that it is "a necessary incentive for advancement to executives and professional people."[119]

The Code further differentiates on the basis of marital status and family responsibility through the personal and dependency exemptions, allowing $600 deductions for the taxpayer, his spouse, and each of his qualifying dependents.[120] It is helpful to consider at the same time the standard deduction of up to $1,000, computed as the larger of 10 per cent of adjusted gross income or $200 plus $100 for each exemption claimed under section 151.[121] The standard deduction is, in a sense, simply an additional exemption,[122] and is claimed on about 65 per cent of all returns.[123]

The following table indicates the extent to which the $600 exemptions and standard deduction insulate income from taxation among various family groupings. Included in the table are comparative figures based on data contained in a Study by the Survey Research Center, Institute for Social Research, at the University of Michigan with respect to costs of living and the percentages of these covered by the minimum amounts of income insulated by the exemptions.[124]

---

[118] *See* GROVES, *supra* note 1, at 76.

[119] *See* GROVES, *supra* note 1, at 76-77. A related defense is that increasing the tax burden on upper income taxpayers would only lead to higher professional charges to offset the increase, which in turn would pose the prospect of inflation. Brenner, *An Inquiry into the Possibility of Lowering the Tax Rates by Increasing the Tax Base through Elimination of Income Splitting,* 1 TAX REVISION COMPENDIUM 487, 492 (1959).

[120] INT. REV. CODE OF 1954, §§ 151, 152. For a discussion of various rationales of exemptions, see GROVES, *supra* note 1, at 23-26; Bittker, *A "Comprehensive Tax Base" as a Goal of Income Tax Reform,* 80 HARV. L. REV. 925, 940-43 (1967); Kassalow, *To Restore Balance and Equity in Family Income Taxation,* 1 TAX REVISION COMPENDIUM 515 (1959); Pechman, *What Would a Comprehensive Individual Income Tax Yield?, id.* at 251, 266, 267. For consideration of the alleged inadequacies of the exemptions in view of the various rationales, see GROVES, *supra* note 1, at 29, 45; J. PECHMAN, FEDERAL TAX POLICY 69-70 (1966). For the revenue costs of the exemption and of increasing the $600 amount, see *id.* at 71; Bittker, *A "Comprehensive Tax Base" as a Goal of Income Tax Reform,* 80 HARV. L. REV. 925, 940 (1967); Magill, *Federal Income Tax Revision,* 1 TAX REVISION COMPENDIUM 87, 92 (1959). For alternative forms of exemptions, see GROVES, *supra* note 1, at 34-38; Note, *A Proposed Flexible Personal Exemption for the Federal Income Tax,* 18 STAN. L. REV. 1162 (1966).

[121] INT. REV. CODE OF 1954, § 141. Where husband and wife file separately, the deduction is reduced. *Id.* § 141(c), (d).

[122] GROVES, *supra* note 1, at 43. The standard deduction is an additional exemption in that it is an automatic deduction in computing taxable income. However, it is taken in lieu of itemizing specific deductions and thus is not a free, automatic deduction for all taxpayers.

[123] Seltzer, *The Place of the Personal Exemption in the Present-Day Income Tax,* 1 TAX REVISION COMPENDIUM 505 (1959).

[124] J. MORGAN, M. DAVID, M. COHEN & H. BRAZER, INCOME AND WELFARE IN THE UNITED STATES 189 (1962) [hereinafter cited as MORGAN]. The figures are provided for the purposes of comparison and not to point up the adequacies or inadequacies of the exemptions with respect to a minimum cost of living, subsistence, etc.

It is assumed that the husband is employed, the wife not employed; costs for children are averaged for different aged children.

Taxpayer	*Exemptions and Minimum Standard Deductions*	*Cost of Living*	*Per cent of Coverage*
Individual	$ 900	$2,284	39
Husband and Wife	1,600	3,038	52
Husband and Wife plus			
1 child	2,300	3,688	62
2 children	3,000	4,278	70
3 children	3,700	4,926	75
4 children	4,400	5,682	78
5 children	5,100	6,332	81

The ratio between the above exemptions is .6 (single) : 1.0 (couple) : 1.4 (couple with child) : 1.9 (couple with two children). In marked contrast, the cost of living ratio from the above table is: .7 (single) : 1.0 (couple) : 1.2 (couple with child) : 1.4 (couple with two children). Professor Groves and Joseph A. Pechman report similar ratios on the basis of other cost of living studies.[125] In relative terms, therefore, couples and their children receive exemptions considerably out of proportion, from a cost of living standpoint, to those allowed single persons.[126]

The Code is also criticized for its failure to take direct account of a wife's employment. Split-income rates, it will be remembered, do not distinguish between income-earning and non-income-earning wives. The appropriateness of such a distinction is clear.[127] Apparently, the matter received no consideration by Congress in 1948 and only slight consideration in 1954.[128] The Code indirectly accounts for a working wife's expenses (or imputed income lost) by conceding a working mother a deduction up to $900 for expenses of caring for children infirm or under 13 years of age, if incurred "for the purpose of enabling the taxpayer [a woman or widower, or husband whose wife is incapacitated or institutionalized] to be gainfully employed." [129] The

---

125 GROVES, *supra* note 1, at 28 n.15; J. PECHMAN, FEDERAL TAX POLICY 67-69 (1966).

126 See notes 100-01 *supra* and accompanying text.

127 *See, e.g.,* GROVES, *supra* note 1, at 17 ("Differentiation between married couples with two jobs and those with one is at least as compelling as that between married couples and single persons"); Atlas, *Personal Exemptions,* 1 TAX REVISION COMPENDIUM 525, 530 (1959); Oldman & Temple 603; Thorson, *Tax Treatment of Family Income* 116.

128 THORSON, SELECTION OF THE TAX UNIT 243.

129 INT. REV. CODE OF 1954, § 214.

deduction has been castigated as inadequate and less than one half what it should be.[130]

Finally, the Code is criticized for its treatment of heads of households.[131] Section 1(b) provides one half the split-income benefit [132] to an unmarried taxpayer who maintains a household which is the principal place of abode of his child or a section 151 dependent, including a parent. Section 2 allows a surviving spouse with a section 151 dependent child living at the spouse's place of abode full split-income benefit for two years after the death of his spouse. The provisions are faulted on a number of grounds. One is that, in the case of section 1(b), one half the split-income benefit is insufficient. It is argued that heads of households may have no greater taxpaying ability than some married couples with the same taxable income. Another is the requirement that the dependent live with the taxpayer, when in fact the cost of supporting the dependent elsewhere may be more costly.[133] A House proposal in 1954 to liberalize the head-of-household provision to allow full splitting (irrespective of whether the dependent lived with the taxpayer) was rejected by the Senate.[134] Professor Groves states that "[p]robably most critics would agree that the rationale of all these classifications is tenuous." [135]

Taxation of Intrafamily Property Transfers

As a general rule, transfers of property between members of a family are within the purview of the Code and are subject to transfer taxation, in the case of gifts and bequests, and to income tax in the case of transfers for value. Several Code provisions qualify this rule. Section 267 provides that losses on certain sales between related taxpayers are not recognized. For estate tax purposes, section 2056 allows as a deduction from a decedent's gross estate "an amount equal to the value of any interest in property which passes or has passed from the decedent to his surviving spouse . . . to the extent that such interest is included in determining the value of the gross estate," up to one half the value of the adjusted gross estate. For gift tax purposes, section 2523 allows a donor a deduction (in computing taxable gifts) of one half the value of his gifts to a spouse. No provisions expressly immunize intrafamily gifts and bequests to children, although children may of course benefit indirectly from the limited immunity

---

130 GROVES, *supra* note 1, at 82. For interesting statistics on the frequency and costs of child care, see MORGAN 111-12 (indicating, *inter alia,* that of two-job families with children under six years of age—presumably the age of entry into school—one half do not pay anything for child care).

131 *See, e.g.,* GROVES, *supra* note 1, at 17, 69; J. PECHMAN, FEDERAL TAX POLICY 84 (1966); Pechman, *supra* note 103, at 481-85.

132 J. PECHMAN, FEDERAL TAX POLICY 83 (1966).

133 Pechman, *supra* note 103, at 482.

134 GROVES, *supra* note 1, at 69; Pechman, *supra* note 103, at 482-83.

135 GROVES, *supra* note 1, at 69.

granted interspousal transfers. Also, spouses and children may benefit from the $60,000 estate tax exemption of section 2052 and $3,000 annual and $30,000 lifetime gift tax exemption of sections 2503(b) and 2521, respectively.

Sections 2056 and 2523 were new to the Code in 1948, and, like the split-income rates of that year, were the result of "a political compromise dictated by a high-pressure historical situation and . . . were hardly a deliberate choice made after all the equities and other consequences were weighed." [136] In purpose the sections represent an attempt to equalize federal estate and gift tax treatment of spouses in common law states with those in community property states. Their failure to fully achieve this objective is often decried.[137]

Critics of transfer taxes on interspousal transfers are legion. After a conference of experts on federal estate and gift taxation sponsored by the Brookings Institution, Carl Shoup reported that a majority of the conferees favored complete interspousal immunity.[138] Professors Casner and Andrews, in their recent work on the American Law Institute Federal Estate and Gift Tax Project, have recommended complete interspousal immunity from transfer taxation.[139] Professor Casner states the case for the critics:

> [Immunity] is designed to simplify the handling of property dispositions between husband and wife; to lessen the economic adjustment that may now be required, when the earning power of a spouse ceases on death, by making it possible to avoid any transfer tax payment at such time; to make the impact of the transfer tax felt in the same degree regardless of the state in which the transferor resides; and to carry out the philosophy of the average husband and wife who regard the property they own as "our" property.[140]

There is likewise considerable criticism of the Code's failure to provide immunity to certain parent-child transfers. The criticism has focused on bequests, stressing the inequity of taxing bequests to dependent children and students for their support and education. Had the parent lived, there would have been no transfer tax on such amounts. As already mentioned, some such amounts can be transferred to the child indirectly and free of taxation by bequest to a surviving spouse who can in turn provide the child with support and

---

[136] *Id.* at 59-60.

[137] *See, e.g.,* J. Pechman, Federal Tax Policy 186 (1966); C. Shoup, Federal Estate and Gift Taxes 51-52 (1966) [hereinafter cited as Shoup]. *See generally* 38 Calif. L. Rev. 1-182 (1950); 22 Tax L. Rev. 515-684 (1967).

[138] Shoup 122; *cf.* DeWind, *The Approaching Crisis in Federal Estate and Gift Taxation,* 38 Calif. L. Rev. 79, 110 (1950).

[139] Andrews, *The Accessions Tax Proposal,* 22 Tax. L. Rev. 589, 592 (1967); Casner, *American Law Institute Federal Estate and Gift Tax Project, id.* at 515.

[140] Casner, *supra* note 139, at 549.

education. The participants in the Brookings conference referred to above agreed that some allowance should be made for bequests made to children.[141] One proposed set of mechanics would allow an estate with no surviving spouse a $3,000 deduction for each year by which each recipient child is under 21 years of age.[142] Bills have been introduced in Congress to ease the tax on transfers to dependent children.[143]

III. An Evaluation

Complete and accurate evaluation of the Commission's family unit will be possible, if ever, only after implementation of statutory provisions which evolve from the proposal. Even then the evaluation will depend upon other components of the tax system into which the family unit is introduced. What follows is an examination of the Commission's family unit on three interrelated levels. The principle level is theoretical, apart from either the full context of the *Report* or that of the Internal Revenue Code, and confronts the question how the family *should* be treated by a tax system. The second level consists of evaluation of the family unit in the context of the *Report*, including the Income Adjustment Account and treatment of gifts and bequests as income. Third, and least emphasized, is analysis in the context of the Internal Revenue Code, notably with respect to its transfer taxation.

Structure

An income tax system must initially define the appropriate tax unit or units. Income must be measured and reported, assessments and payments made. While the tax unit is a necessary first step, the focal point of an income tax system is, of course, its allocation of the tax burden.[144] In turn, the choice of units is one focal point of the controversy over allocation of the burden among various family and individual groupings at various income levels.[145] Given a philosophy of progressive taxation—whatever, exactly, it may be[146]—that takes

---

141 Shoup 122-23, 132.

142 *Id.* at 59.

143 *E.g.,* H.R. 1845, 88th Cong., 1st Sess. (1963). See also *Children's Estate Tax Deduction, Hearings on H.R. 7924 Before the House Comm. on Ways and Means,* 86th Cong., 1st Sess. (1959).

It will be recognized that the support and education argument for an allowance on bequests to minor children is inapplicable to *inter vivos* gifts and to bequests in excess of the child's support and education needs during minority.

144 *See, e.g.,* Groves, *supra* note 1, at 105, British Royal Commission on the Taxation of Profits and Income, Second Report, ¶ 116, at 35 (1954).

145 *See, e.g.,* Oldman & Temple 585.

146 A precise philosophy of progressive taxation is of course basic to tax treatment of the family. As Professor Groves has noted, "Underlying all of the specific problems of family taxation are conflicting philosophies of equity in taxation." Groves, *supra* note 1, at 3. Full discussion of these issues is beyond the scope of this Comment; however, they are confronted briefly in the discussion of allocation of the income tax burden at text accompanying notes 190-92 *infra.*

account of personal circumstances,[147] the tax unit should then be structured to facilitate this philosophy, as well as such other goals of taxation as enforcement and administration.

The Commission appears quite correct in recommending a supplement to Canada's present individual unit. To be sure, the individual unit has been defended from time to time. A. P. Herbert once declared that combining the incomes of husband and wife "is in effect a tax upon marriage and a tax upon virtue." [148] Further, it has been argued that, conceptually,

> the family as a unit has no combined taxpaying ability per se; that its taxpaying ability is composed of the separate taxpaying abilities of its individual members; and that the taxpaying ability of each of these is determined by the amount of income of which he or she is the owner without reference to the income of other members of the family.[149]

Japan, Australia and many of the states in this country use only the individual as an income tax unit.

Nonetheless, the case for inclusion of husband and wife as a single unit is compelling. The Commission's analysis of the economic and social utility of husband and wife, and the equitable, administrative and enforcement advantages of the family unit [150] amply explain the broad consensus among tax critics.[151] Equally well entrenched—at least since the 1948 congressional tax revisions—are the notions that state-determined property rights [152] and a wife's citizenship or legal equality [153] are not barriers to the inclusion of husband and wife in one unit.

---

147 The secondary and related question of the *propriety* of taking account of various family responsibilities in burden allocation is considered at text accompanying notes 185-89 *infra*.

148 A. HERBERT, THE UNCOMMON LAW 237 (1936).

149 DIVISION OF TAX RESEARCH, U.S. TREASURY DEP'T., THE TAX TREATMENT OF FAMILY INCOME, reprinted in *Hearings on Proposed Revisions of the Internal Revenue Code Before the House Comm. on Ways and Means,* 80th Cong., 1st Sess., 846, 851 (1947). Oldman & Temple, at 603, argue that the individual unit can be justified only if it is impossible to establish a family unit entailing fewer inequities.

150 See notes 61-75 *supra* and accompanying text.

151 On the financial, economic and decision-making unity of husband and wife, see E. LEMASTERS, MODERN COURTSHIP AND MARRIAGE 466-68 (1957); MORGAN 23; J. PECHMAN, FEDERAL TAX POLICY 83 (1966) (noting that there is less economic unity at high income levels); Oldman & Temple 596-98; Thorson, *Tax Treatment of Family Income* 115-16.

152 *See, e.g.,* Thorson, *id.* at 115. The spirit of the state property rights approach is apparent in Justice Roberts' opinion in Poe v. Seaborn, 282 U.S. 101 (1930):

> We are of opinion that under the law of Washington the entire property and income of the community can no more be said to be that of the husband, than it could rightly be termed that of the wife.
>
> The District Court was right in holding that the husband and wife were entitled to file separate returns, each treating one-half of the community income as his or her respective income . . . .

Id. at 113, 118.

153 *See, e.g.,* GROVES, *supra* note 1, at 70; Oldman & Temple 602.

However, a significant problem raised by inclusion of the wife in the tax unit is that she may be discouraged from working. Aggregation of the wife's income with that of her husband means that her income is taxed at least at her husband's marginal rate, and most likely at a higher rate due to the likelihood that the combined incomes will fall into a higher bracket.[154] But because a wife's income probably gives the couple greater "discretionary economic power," a greater tax burden is appropriate.

The Commission, however, unnecessarily discourages wives from working by failing to make proper adjustment for a working wife's additional expenses and the imputed income lost to the family.[155] Failure to take account of these items, which in itself departs from the concept of "discretionary economic power," compounds the inevitable disincentive resulting from aggregation. The Commission's view is that while working wives may incur "some additional family housekeeping expenses," "[m]any of these expenses are nothing more than a purchase of increased leisure time and freedom from unpleasant housekeeping tasks." [156] The Commission would grant a family unit with a working *mother* an $80 tax credit (a reduction of the total tax the unit would otherwise have to pay) if there are children in the unit, or $120 if there is a child under seven.[157] The family rate schedule itself does not differentiate between one- and two-worker families.

Arrayed against the Commission's view of the working wife is a consensus among economists and tax commentators that a married couple with a working wife should be treated differently from a couple in which the wife is not working. This need to differentiate has been termed as great as the need to differentiate couples from single persons.[158] One study of family budget costs concluded that the annual cost of goods and services for an employed wife was $1,092, compared with $546 for a nonworking wife.[159] Arguably the credits for working mothers compensate in part for the failure to provide a working wife's allowance, assuming that many working wives are mothers as well. However, at least some wives would be discouraged from working; this, it has been suggested, could have considerable

---

[154] For the changes in tax liability resulting from the aggregation of income of husbands and wives who would otherwise be taxed as individuals, see 3 REPORT 191 (table 11-15).

[155] *See* text accompanying note 159 *infra*.

[156] 3 REPORT 193, 210 n.22.

[157] See note 45 *supra* and accompanying text.

[158] See note 127 *supra* and accompanying text.

[159] MORGAN 189 (figures from the Community Council of Greater New York, Budget Standard Service, Annual Price Survey and Family Budget Costs, October, 1959).

impact on middle class two-job families.[160]

One of the most debatable aspects of the Commission's family unit is its inclusion of dependent children. On the theoretical level, it is clear that the conceptual neatness of including husband and wife in a unit does not appear in the case of dependent children. A child is only a temporary member of the family. While it may be true that "[w]e think in terms of dad, mom, and the kids,"[161] pooling and sharing income with a child does not occur to the same degree as between husband and wife.[162] A child's income is frequently regarded as his spending money and outside the family budget, especially in higher income families; and he is not as directly a part of the decision-making process within the family as are the husband and wife. On the other hand, even if there is not *always* pooling and sharing with children, there generally is some, and the income of the child is at least indirectly available to the family as a whole, relieving the family of some of the child's expenses.[163]

It is of course possible that inclusion of dependent children within the family unit might discourage some children from working.[164] A proposal in the state of New York to aggregate a child's income with that of his parents led some parents to assert that they would ask their children to stop working.[165] Putting aside the psychological aspects of inclusion, the incentive argument is not persuasive. A survey conducted in the United States found that only 6 per cent of "spending units" (defined as a group of relatives living together and pooling their incomes for major items of expense) contained children under 18 earning money, only 1 per cent contained children earning $500-999 annually and only 1 per cent contained children earning over $1,000.[166] Such small amounts, especially if an exemption is provided, would not be likely to raise the family's marginal rate. And, in the United States at least, the marginal rate for the "vast majority"

---

[160] *See* Remarks of Frank E. A. Sander, CANADIAN TAX FOUNDATION 17, 21. Presumably, wives in lower income families are in sufficiently great need of income for consumption purposes that the disincentive is not crucial; upper income wives inclined to work (of whom there are likely fewer than in lower income families), meanwhile, arguably are not greatly influenced by the relatively slight amounts represented by the disincentive.

[161] E. MOCKLER, *supra* note 72, at 75.

[162] D. THORSON, SELECTION OF A TAX UNIT 189.

[163] *Id.; see* GROVES, *supra* note 1, at 34, 70; Surrey, *Federal Taxation of the Family—The Revenue Act of 1948,* 61 HARV. L. REV. 1097, 1114 (1948).

[164] As with the working wife, the child's income will be taxed at least at the family's marginal rate. *See* text accompanying note 154 *supra.*

[165] N.Y. Times, March 1, 1960, at 1, col. 6.

[166] *See* MORGAN, *supra* note 124, at 140. These figures are not comprehensive for purposes of the Commission's family unit because children 19, 20 and 21 are not included, nor are students 22-25 who could remain in the family unit. Nonetheless, they are indicative of the slight amounts of earned income that would generally be aggregated with parental income.

of children will be among the lowest irrespective of inclusion.[167] Furthermore, lower and middle income children of working age often must work to help to pay for their support and education in any event. There is little doubt, however, that there will be some disincentive in high income families.[168]

A third point, related to the incentive issue, is the impact of inclusion of dependent children's gifts and bequests from persons outside the family unit. Inclusion means that any income produced by such property (be it in trust, securities or whatever) is taxed at the family's marginal rate. This could well discourage the making of gifts that would increase the family's marginal rate and the amount of tax directly attributable to the income produced by the donated property. In turn, increasing the family rate can be said to constitute a disincentive for the child to work.

Fourth, it might be argued that a sound tax policy would be to provide low rates for children in order both to encourage them to work and to subsidize their education. However, as indicated above, it is unlikely that children would be significantly deterred from working by inclusion. While inclusion might thwart a policy designed to subsidize education, it is questionable that encouraging children to work is the best, or even an appropriate, method of providing for the expenses of education.

Fifth, it may be argued that inclusion would result in enforcement problems, principally because increased rates would provide greater incentive for avoidance.[169] However, an exemption (such as the Commission's $500 one) will mitigate the impact of any increase in rate and such an exemption, combined with the reporting of income by employers, should solve any problems that do arise.

Finally, aggregation may appear harsh for large, low-income families in which there may be several working children, each of whom may receive little support from his parents. An annual exemption, such as the Commission's $500 for earned income, alleviates this problem to a considerable degree. As a practical matter, there are few families with more than one or two working children and their earnings, in themselves or at least in excess of an exemption, are no doubt generally small.[170] Further, older children with significant annual earnings could and presumably would leave the family unit.

In summary, the Commission's case for inclusion of dependent children is strong if not compelling.[171] On a financial and social

---

[167] Harriss, *Parent and Child—And Taxes: Some Problems in Dependency*, 1 TAX REVISION COMPENDIUM 531, 532 (1959).

[168] *Cf. id.*

[169] GROVES, *supra* note 1, at 70.

[170] See note 166 *supra* and accompanying text.

[171] It should be noted that other aspects of a tax system can militate against any single recommendation, including that of inclusion. For example, if adequate tax relief is not allowed a family for the expenses of raising children then indirect relief through separate taxation of children may seem more appropriate.

analysis, they belong in the family unit. As a practical matter, inclusion should not amount to a significant disincentive for working children or donors outside the family unit. Inclusion would mean, quite reasonably, the application of the parents' tax rate to the child's income in excess of the exemption. It would also be equitable in ending the advantages of most income splitting within the family. Moreover, inclusion would end many of the administrative problems of enforcement of statutory provisions [172] and judicial doctrines [173] against family income splitting.

An analysis of the Commission's specific proposals for the inclusion of dependent children within the context of the full *Report* is now in order. First, the proposal that gifts and bequests from a person outside the tax unit constitute income to the recipient unit may mean that such gifts will be discouraged. Unless the gift is deposited in the Income Adjustment Account by the child,[174] it comprises income to the family, and will likely raise the family's rate and then be taxed at that rate. This disincentive is in addition to the inevitable disincentive to any giving caused by treating gifts and bequests as income.[175] Treating gifts as income also means potential difficulty for the child leaving the unit. Any property received from his parents subsequent to leaving constitutes income to him. Thus, so long as he is young enough to remain in his parents' unit, he must weigh the tax benefits of avoiding inclusion of his income with the family's against the detriment of having to pay taxes (after he leaves) on property received from his parents either while he was a member of the unit or at the time he leaves.

---

172 *E.g.*, INT. REV. CODE OF 1954, §§ 641-83 (trusts), 704(e) (family partnerships).

173 *E.g.*, the rubrics "anticipatory assignment," "beneficial enjoyment," "control," and "fruit and tree" where used in a family setting.

A possible constitutional problem should be mentioned. The Supreme Court in 1931 held that a Wisconsin statute aggregating the income of husband, wife and dependent children under 18 years of age and applying a progressive income tax rate schedule to the total violated due process. Justice Roberts, speaking for the Court, said that "any attempt . . . to measure the tax on one person's property or income by reference to the property or income of another is contrary to due process . . . ." Hoeper v. Tax Comm'n of Wis., 284 U.S. 206, 215 (1931). Justices Holmes, Brandeis and Stone dissented. Since that time, however, courts in the United States have moved away from the "technical tests of local property laws," GROVES, *supra* note 1, at 62, and have sustained other joint-return statutes. *See, e.g.*, Ballester v. Court of Tax Appeals, 61 P.R.R. 460 (1943), *aff'd sub nom.* Ballester-Ripoll v. Court of Tax Appeals, 142 F.2d 11 (1st Cir. 1944), *cert. denied*, 323 U.S. 723 (1944); Albanese D'Imperio v. Secretary of the Treasury, 76 P.R.R. 302 (1954), *aff'd* 223 F.2d 413 (1st Cir.), *cert. denied*, 350 U.S. 874 (1955). It is to be expected that federal legislation taxing families as a unit would be held constitutional. *See generally* R. MAGILL, TAXABLE INCOME 329-34 (Rev. ed. 1945) (qualifying this conclusion as being "likely" where the tax liability is apportioned to family members); D. THORSON, SELECTION OF A TAX UNIT 82-108.

174 The child's Account is different from the Account available to adult taxpayers, the latter being designed as an income-averaging provision which does not earn interest. *See* 3 REPORT 259-60, 269-73, 278-79.

175 Of course, increasing the family's rate in turn increases the possibility of disincentives to work.

Second, the Commission proposes a number of provisions to ameliorate the harsher effects of inclusion. One is a $500 exemption for a child's earned income. This is a strong counter to disincentive. Another provision is for an education credit, which counters the argument that inclusion will discourage education.[176]

Finally, the Commission proposes an Account into which income earned by a child in excess of $500 and gifts from outside the family can be deposited. Amounts so deposited constitute income only upon their withdrawal from the Account, which can occur no later than the child's withdrawal from the unit.[177] The child's Account is a qualification on inclusion of children and an acknowledgment of their transient membership in the family unit. The Commission believes that without the Account these sums would be taxed first to the family and later to the child upon leaving the family unit. The Account thus acts to preserve incentive for a child to work and for donors outside the family to make gifts to children by effectuating a pass-through which avoids the double tax. The Account is treated below in detail.[178]

The Commission's standards for termination of a child's membership in the family unit are reasonable. With the exception of the provision for opting out, the termination events are automatic, and none are necessarily coincidental with the child's actual departure. However, most of them will be coincidental, and when combined with the administrative ease of automatic cutoffs, the Commission's choice of termination events seems appropriate.

A problem does exist, however, with married students. Treating gifts and bequests as income means that parental gifts for support and education made subsequent to the child's marriage[179] are taxed to the child.[180] Married students often continue—financially, at least—as members of their original families. One solution would be to permit bona fide, full time students to postpone formation of their own unit until they complete their full time education. A problem still would remain, however—how to treat the couple vis-à-vis their original families. The couple could be placed in the husband's (or wife's)

---

176 3 REPORT 229-33. The proposed credit for expenses incurred for post-secondary education is an amount equal to one fourth of the "fees" paid, allowed to the unit of which the student is a member, plus an annual credit to the student's unit of up to $300 for living costs if he is not a dependent child. Unused credits could be carried forward.

177 *Id.* at 136.

178 *See* text accompanying notes 243-63 *infra.*

179 The education credit, note 172 *supra,* is not relevant at this juncture because (1) it is designed to encourage education, not to mitigate the harshness and conceptual inappropriateness of the deemed withdrawal, and (2) it does not change the result of income flows between two separate units but constitutes relief only for the paying unit. Similarly, the credit for support payments for once-dependent children provides relief only to the paying unit. *See* note 19 *supra.*

180 Such additional taxation would presumably create strong pressure on young students to avoid marriage, as those who could count on continued parental support would be able to avoid taxes on these payments until they reached the age of 25.

original family or each spouse could remain in his original unit. Optional filing with the respective original family units seems the more appropriate of the two solutions. Such a provision would, however, pose several problems. First, it would be necessary for both sets of parents to consent to the election. Where the student husband's family, for example, is supplying a portion of his wife's expenses, her family may be unwilling or unable to assume responsibility for taxes attributable to the inclusion in their income of these payments to their daughter. Also, it would not be easy to apportion payments to the student couple between husband and wife. Moreover, it is by no means clear how long a student couple should be permitted to put off forming a new unit. While a requirement that both husband and wife be full-time students seems reasonable, it is also arguable that a couple should continue to qualify if the wife leaves school to raise a family.

A simpler approach for married students would be to provide their unit with an exemption for financial assistance received from either parental unit for educational and support purposes. While tuition will vary from school to school, a maximum support allowance could be fixed, and the exemption limited to the amount by which the couple's tuition and support expenses exceed their income from sources other than their parents. Husband and wife would still be deemed to have withdrawn from their original family units, thus preserving the conceptual integrity of withdrawal, and thereby eliminating the problem of determining when to deem withdrawal to have taken place if marriage is not to be the measuring event. Additionally, the exemption would alleviate the administrative difficulties of apportioning to husband and wife sums received by the couple from their parents. Despite its departure from the neatness of the Commission's "comprehensive tax base," the exemption seems the more appropriate means of accommodating the economic realities of married students.

The Commission's recommendation that the family unit not extend beyond husband, wife and dependent children is sensible. From some statistics gathered for the University of Michigan, it appears that the number of relatives [181] living with the immediate family has decreased as living standards in the United States have risen, so that only 17 per cent of family heads provide housing for relatives. These 17 per cent average 1.4 relatives each. The average cost to each family is a net of $492 a year for food and housing.[182] Almost no one with an income of $5,000 or more lives in a relative's house. Families with annual incomes of less than $1,000 or over $15,000 seldom take in relatives.[183]

---

181 "Relative," as here used, excludes spouses and children.

182 MORGAN 173-79.

183 *Id.* at 163, 170.

On the "entity" analysis, a close relative (for example, an elderly parent) living with a family may in fact share whatever income he has, but he is often more of a boarder than an integral part of the family. Inclusion in the context of the Commission's intrafamily transfer tax immunity would be most attractive to persons, relatives or not, who intended to make gifts or bequests to members of another unit.[184] On the other hand, neither a close relative nor the family would want to incur the potentially greater tax burden attendant upon income aggregation. It would be administratively impossible to make distinctions on the basis of whether the close relative, or perhaps a friendly stranger, is in fact sufficiently a member of the family to justify inclusion.

Allocation of the Income Tax Burden

A threshold question in allocating the income tax burden among various units is the relevance of family responsibilities.[185] The *Report* is bottomed on taxation in accord with "ability to pay," and it might be anticipated that this standard makes family responsibilities relevant. It is arguable, however, that the choices people make respecting marriage and family size are irrelevant to "ability to pay" and that the general expenses of family responsibilities represent the exercise of "discretionary economic power," rendering them consumption choices.[186] Thus a bachelor and a married man have merely chosen to spend their money in different ways, and, such being the case, their choices are irrelevant to tax burdens.

The Commission appropriately rejects this "strange" [187] argument and treats expenses arising from family responsibilities—as well as savings attributable to family groupings—as relevant to tax allocation. A wife and children are not easily regarded as mere consumption choices. And as a matter of social policy, the notion is well-entrenched that taxation should be neutral respecting marriage and children.[188]

---

[184] The adequacy of the credit for support of a close relative would also affect the attitude of the relative and family. *See* note 46 *supra* and accompanying text.

[185] The idea of making allowance for the fact that persons of equal income may have different responsibilities was of later origin than the income tax itself and is said to have been an "outgrowth of the rising sense of social responsibility and concern for the individual member of the state." P. STRAYER, THE TAXATION OF SMALL INCOMES 44 (1930).

[186] Professor Bittker suggests that a "comprehensive tax base" implies that family expenses are indeed irrelevant. Bittker, *A "Comprehensive Tax Base" as a Goal of Income Tax Reform,* 80 HARV. L. REV. 925, 941 (1967).

[187] Thorson, *Tax Treatment of Family Income* 122; *cf.* J. PECHMAN, FEDERAL TAX POLICY 50 (1966).

[188] Oldman & Temple 602:

> There may be social policies which should be implemented by a government through its tax system, or other quasi-compulsory devices, but decisions as to marriage and children should be left to the widest range of individual choice

Unless allowances are made for necessary costs arising from marriage and having children, the system cannot be neutral, *i.e.*, there will be a tax cost, a disincentive.[189]

The second question preliminary to allocation is one of general goals. It has been noted that

> The formulation of universally applicable principles to guide in the allocation of tax burdens will be a difficult task until a rational theory of progressive taxation is developed and demonstrated. Even then, it is likely that the basic decisions in the application of progressive taxation will continue to involve value judgments of a character that only the electorate can make.[190]

The Commission subscribes to the central objective of equity, vertical and horizontal, as expressed in the standards of "ability to pay" and "discretionary economic power." The Internal Revenue Code's rate structure, meanwhile, is said to reflect a public policy choice made during the depression to redistribute income in order to increase aggregate spending and to attack the economic power of high income groups.[191] Thus equity, while a principal objective of allocation, is by no means the only possible one. Further, equity is not simply defined. The Commission certainly does an impressive job of solving the definitional problems, with its standard of "discretionary economic power," but it is finally compelled to conclude that, "In a democracy, equity questions ultimately must be resolved in terms of the shared values of the people." [192]

> that is consistent with the morés and with the economic and sociological needs of a given society.

See Atlas, *supra* note 127, at 530; Pechman, *supra* note 103, at 481; Thorson, *Tax Treatment of Family Income* 129-30.

189 Apart from the consensus for neutrality, it is widely believed that, within limits, the tax treatment of the family cannot have any actual effect on decisions people make about marriage and having children. Oldman & Temple 602; *cf.* GROVES, *supra* note 1, at 76; P. TAYLOR, THE ECONOMICS OF PUBLIC FINANCE 402 (1948). *See also* BRITISH ROYAL COMMISSION OF THE TAXATION OF PROFITS AND INCOME, Second Report, ¶ 118, at 36 (1954):

> [T]he reasons that impel men and women to prefer marriage to more casual associations are many and powerful and . . . the present treatment of the income of married couples for the purpose of tax is not more likely to lead people away from matrimony than tempt them into it.

But cf. SHOUP 53 (suggesting that complete exemption of interspousal transfers might stimulate more marriages between persons in different generations); Thorson, *Tax Treatment of Family Income* 129 (noting that economic factors may be crucial in "family planning" and are of "secondary importance" in other marriage decisions such as those concerning "marital adjustment and divorce").

190 Oldman & Temple 603.

191 Magill, *Federal Income Tax Revision,* 1 TAX REVISION COMPENDIUM 87-88 (1959).

192 3 REPORT 5.

The Commission's specific yardsticks for allocation, for the most part, seem to be quite reasonable and in accord with the views of economists and tax critics.[193] One problem, discussed above in the context of undue disincentive to a wife's working,[194] is the failure to distinguish between one- and two-job families. Failure to draw such a distinction penalizes the working wife and constitutes a departure from the discretionary economic power standard, from equity as defined by the Commission, and from neutral treatment of marriage.

A second problem exists in *measuring* the degrees of various distinctions. The Commission admits that "judgments" are necessary,[195] primarily because of the lack of sufficient statistical, comparative data and because of the unreliability of such data as is available. Unquestionably, there is a shortage of information on, for example, the expenses and economies of marriage.[196] What is available is often met with skepticism.[197] Complete and reliable data are prerequisites to making the subtle differentiations proposed by the Commission.

Turning to implementation of goals, the Commission proposes separate rate schedules for single persons and married couples. Separate rate schedules are "an especially flexible instrument," and permit "an almost infinite number of compromises." [198] Even though difficult to construct,[199] their theoretical capacity to differentiate married couples from singles is clear.[200] A secondary advantage of their use is that by eliminating exemptions, rates can be reduced, with attendant psychological benefits.[201] Two criticisms can be made of their use. One is that it is difficult to change them later relative to one another,[202] since, presumably, the basic data would have to be reevaluated. For this reason, Joseph A. Pechman recommends use of a single schedule coupled with adjustments through credits or, prefer-

---

193 *See, e.g.*, Oldman & Temple 603-04; Sander, *supra* note 160, at 20.

194 See text accompanying notes 156-60 *supra*.

195 3 REPORT 7, 167.

196 *See, e.g.*, GROVES, *supra* note 1, at 105-06; E. MOCKLER, *supra* note 72 at 110; Pechman, *supra* note 103, at 479.

197 *See, e.g.*, Fortune, Dec., 1967, at 98 (a section entitled "Shadowy Statistics" ridicules the recent "City Worker's Family Budget" published by the Bureau of Labor Statistics of the United States Department of Labor).

198 GROVES, *supra* note 1, at 77. *Accord*, Oldman & Temple 604.

199 Pechman, *supra* note 103, at 479-80.

200 The idea of separate rate schedules is not new. See GROVES, *supra* note 1, at 22 (respecting their use internationally); W. VICKREY, AGENDA FOR PROGRESSIVE TAXATION 274-87 (1947); Pechman, *supra* note 103, at 473-86.

201 Seltzer, *supra* note 120, at 510.

202 Remarks of Joseph A. Pechman, in CANADIAN TAX FOUNDATION 443.

ably, varying deductions. The deductions would vary with family income and the number of family members. The adjustments would be designed to accommodate the needed differentiation.[203] It is also arguable that separate schedules are vulnerable to political forces seeking to make disproportionate adjustments, quite likely to the disadvantage of singles (as happened in the United States with the split-income rates granted married couples in 1948). While these criticisms may have some validity, it is not clear that a single schedule, or any solution, can solve the problems. The Commission recommends as a means of making short-term adjustments that the tax liability of each individual be multiplied by a factor chosen to increase or decrease each taxpayer's liability by the same percentage amount,[204] *e.g.*, a ten per cent surcharge on tax liability computed under the rate structure existing at the time.

In addition to dual rate schedules, the Commission recommends use of credits rather than exemptions. The value of a fixed credit does not rise with income; the value of a fixed exemption does, in proportion to the taxpayer's marginal rate. The Commission acknowledges that the expenses of raising children—and by implication other "non-discretionary expenses"—increase with income, though not as rapidly as the marginal rates of tax increase with income.[205] The Commission also admits that the proposed credits are not adequate, at least in the case of dependent children.[206]

Thus the Commission moves away from the subtle, precise adjustments it recommends through the dual rate schedules for differentiation of singles and couples. The proposed credits also constitute a departure from the "discretionary economic power" and "equity" goals: in absolute terms the credits are inadequate at all levels, and in relative terms they discriminate in favor of low income families. The impact is hardest on large, low-to-moderate income families for whom the inadequacies of the credits would be compounded (by the number of children) and would be most disruptive to meeting non-discretionary expenses.

To consider alternatives to credits is to raise a whole spectrum of questions relating to the philosophy of progressive taxation, forms and rationales of exemptions, administrability, revenue needs, and so forth. However, given the Commission's goal of taxing on the basis of "discretionary economic power" as measured by sophisticated statistical data, one proposition is particularly worthy of consideration:

---

203 *Id.* An extensive study of the forms and rationales of the various credits and exemptions is beyond the scope of this Comment.

204 3 REPORT 197.

205 *Id.* at 17.

206 *Id.* at 181.

use of more sophisticated rate schedules based on comprehensive data as to the "discretionary economic power" of various tax units. Size of families, ages of members, total income, various non-discretionary expenses (as those of a working wife), and cost of living differences between geographical regions and types of communities could theoretically be built into the schedules.[207] If the data could be collected—and admittedly this might be difficult and costly—the Commission's "discretionary economic power" standard could be fully effectuated. To administer the application of such complex criteria, publication of complicated schedules might be possible. Or, in this computerized era, it would seem possible for the government, at reasonable cost, to figure the taxpayer's liability on the basis of specified information reported by the taxpayer at the end of his tax year. However, this technique, in its lack of openness, could well prove unpopular, and thus the degree of sophistication of rate schedules could appropriately be limited to a level found manageable by the average taxpayer. The Commission's view is that more sophisticated rate schedules are not administratively feasible.[208] This is debatable.[209]

Before considering the resultant burdens under the proposed rate schedules, two warnings are in order. First, the Commission is careful to stress that its allocation is made with a view to other taxes in Canada. For example, it believes that, due to the regressivity of other forms of taxation, the income tax must be progressive merely to achieve a proportional tax system and markedly progressive to obtain a progressive tax system.[210] Therefore, the schedules cannot be fully evaluated without the context of the entire Canadian system. Second, the Commission has not attempted "to present an 'ideal' set of rates, but rather to achieve a suitable progression within the rate schedules." [211] For this reason, the schedules can be considered only in terms of relative, not absolute, burdens.

The table below indicates the proposed burdens of single persons vis-à-vis married couples with the same total income. It should be noted that, due to the use of credits rather than deductions, "taxable income" is very nearly equal to total income received.[212]

---

[207] Data as a basis for adjustments for the latter two factors can be acquired by studies similar to the recent U.S. BUREAU OF LABOR STATISTICS, DEP'T OF LABOR, CITY WORKER'S FAMILY BUDGET FOR A MODERATE LIVING STANDARD (1966).

[208] 3 REPORT 179.

[209] The Commission merely makes the assertion of infeasibility, without explanation or, apparently, examination.

[210] 3 REPORT 153.

[211] 3 REPORT 197.

[212] However, taxable income would not include (for example) amounts paid into qualifying "retirement income plans," *id.* at 301, or into the child's Account, *supra* note 53 and accompanying text, or certain gifts in kind, *supra* note 56.

PROPOSED RATES[213]

Taxable Income	*Tax Liability* *Single*	*Tax Liability* *Couple*	*Reductions of Tax for Single Man Upon Marriage to Woman With No Income* *Amount*	*Reductions of Tax for Single Man Upon Marriage to Woman With No Income* *Percentage*
Less than $1,000	0	0	—	—
1,500	60	0	$60	100%
2,100	152	0	152	100%
3,500	405	197	208	51%
5,000	725	457	268	37%
7,000	1,195	847	348	29%
10,000	1,955	1,467	488	25%
12,000	2,515	1,907	608	24%
15,000	3,415	2,627	788	23%
20,000	5,015	3,977	1,038	21%
25,000	6,765	5,527	1,238	18%
40,000	12,515	11,077	1,438	11%
70,000	25,715	24,277	1,438	6%
100,000	40,315	38,677	1,638	4%
200,000	90,315	88,677	1,638	2%

These rates seem to follow the Commission's belief that at low incomes there are diseconomies to marriage and that at high incomes economies are insubstantial. Hence, little account is taken of marriage at the $25,000 level and almost none at $70,000 and up.[214]

One criticism potentially to be levelled at the schedules is Pechman's contention that, despite their availability to couples with and without children, they take account of expenses for dependent children.[215] If the schedules are so constructed—and it is unclear whether or not they are—then childless couples receive undue relief.[216] Also, it should be noticed that the family schedule is quite generous to certain persons who qualify for it, notably surviving, divorced or separated parents with a dependent child, unwed persons with an adopted child, and a unit consisting of two "dependent" children whose parents are deceased or resident outside the country.

---

213 Adapted from 3 REPORT 170 (table 11-4), 174 (table 11-6), 175 (table 11-7).

214 A $25,000 "cut-off" point for economies of marriage was suggested by Professor John W. Ervin in 1947. Ervin, *Federal Taxes and the Family,* 20 S. CAL. L. REV. 243, 256 (1947).

215 Pechman, *supra* note 202, at 443.

216 The Commission may assume (a) that most couples have dependent children for many of their married years and (b) that it is more advantageous, perhaps for welfare policy purposes, to provide additional relief for children through manipulation of the rates in favor of lower income families than through increasing the dependent child credit, the benefit of which could not be limited to low income families.

Tax Consequences of Property Transfers Within and Without the Family Unit

Placing intrafamily property transfers outside the purview of a tax system is a logical, albeit not a compelled, corollary of the choice of the family unit for income tax purposes. For if the family is a social and financial entity, sharing and acting as one, it is logical that transfers of what is, in effect, common property do not rise to the level of taxable events.[217] Beyond this simple logic, however, one must confront the philosophy of transfer taxes, the Commission's recommendation that all transfers by gift or bequest recognized under its proposals be treated as income to the recipient, and the policy of recognizing gains and losses on sales.

There is no clear consensus as to the precise goals of transfer taxation. Certainly one is taxing property once a generation.[218] Another is reducing the concentration of wealth.[219] A third is taxing windfalls as a special type of "ability to pay" attendant upon a gift or bequest.[220] And a fourth, sometimes cited, is encouraging *inter vivos*, gifts, especially to younger generations, by diminishing any incentive to hold property until death.[221]

The Commission proposes that, as a rule, permanent, gratuitous transfers of property be treated as income to the recipient.[222] Such transfers are depicted as increasing the recipient's economic power in the same way as wages, dividends, interest and property gains and thus as appropriately included in the "comprehensive tax base."[223]

As a rule, gains on the exchange of property are recognized as income under both the Internal Revenue Code[224] and the *Report.*[225] Losses are also recognized under the Commission's proposed "comprehensive tax base."[226]

---

217 Conversely, it is arguable that the appropriateness of intrafamily transfer immunity suggests that the family should be the basic unit for tax purposes.

218 *See, e.g.*, SHOUP 100, 119; G. WHEATCROFT, ESTATE AND GIFT TAXATION—A COMPARATIVE STUDY 121 (1965); DeWind, *The Approaching Crisis in Federal Estate and Gift Taxation*, 38 CALIF. L. REV. 79, 110 (1950).

219 *See, e.g.*, SHOUP 100-19; Lowndes, *A Practical Program for Reforming the Federal Estate Tax*, 5 VILL. L. REV. 1, 3 (1959); Rudick, *What Alternative to the Estate and Gift Taxes?*, 38 CALIF. L. REV. 150, 158 (1950).

220 *See, e.g.*, SHOUP 110, 119.

221 *See, e.g.*, SHOUP 120.

222 The merits of treating gifts and bequests as income are beyond the scope of this Comment. It has been suggested that this proposal will engender more controversy than any other aspect of the *Report*. Goodman, *supra* note 4, at 373.

223 3 REPORT 465. Gifts are exempt, however, to the extent of a $250 annual and $5000 lifetime exclusion. *Id.* at 478.

224 *See* INT. REV. CODE OF 1954, § 1002.

225 *See* 3 REPORT 39-42.

226 3 REPORT 39-42.

REVISED TAX TREATMENT OF THE ELDERLY

U. S. Treasury Dept., Tax Reform Studies and Proposals,
91st Cong., 1st Sess., pt. 2, at 223–27 (1969).

BACKGROUND

There are about 20 million people over the age of 65 in the United States. Of these, about 4.8 million pay Federal income tax. The recommendations for revising the income tax relief of the elderly basically concern only the taxpaying group. Within that group, these recommendations would result in reduced taxes for about 3.6 million individuals, including 600,000 persons who would become completely exempt from tax.

NEED FOR REVISION

In addition to social security, medicare, and other direct programs, significant assistance is afforded the elderly through special income tax relief granted to those over the age of 65. This tax relief reduces Federal income tax revenues by approximately $2.5 billion each year.

The major tax relief extended to the elderly consists of a complete tax exclusion for social security and basic railroad retirement benefits, a corresponding retirement income credit for those who are not eligible to participate in full under either of these two programs, and an extra $600 personal exemption and related extra $100 addition to the minimum standard deduction. This program of tax relief for the elderly has been developed in a piecemeal fashion over the years and, despite the very large amount of revenue which is devoted to it, has never been subject to a careful review to see whether it is accomplishing its objectives. In fact, when these provisions are subjected to careful review, it becomes apparent that they fail to meet the tests of fairness and efficiency on three grounds:

First, they afford little relief to one who continues working after age 65, although his financial needs may be no different from those of his retired neighbor. This arises because wage income operates to reduce or eliminate an individual's social security benefits and, in addition, to reduce or eliminate the amount of any retirement income credit otherwise available to him. Under the present formula an elderly person who, for example, earns $4,200 per year from employment will not be eligible to receive social security benefits or to utilize the retirement income credit. His tax liability would be $420. On the other hand, the elderly individual who is no longer working and whose $4,200 annual income consists of maximum social security benefits plus dividends, interests, and so forth, will have a tax liability of only $96. This is because his social security income is completely free of tax. Table 1 demonstrates the inequitable tax burdens as between elderly workers and elderly retirees.

TABLE 1.—COMPARISON OF TAX LIABILITY UNDER PRESENT LAW OF ELDERLY WORKER AND ELDERLY SOCIAL SECURITY RETIREE[1]

Present money income	Elderly worker with wage income only	Elderly retiree: With maximum social security benefits and other income[2]	Elderly retiree: With average social security benefits and other income[3]
Single, over 65:			
$3,000	$209	0	$35
$5,000	557	$221	358
$6,500	833	484	617
Married, both over 65:			
$6,000	450	16	138
$7,500	686	232	368
$10,000	1,114	620	770

[1] Taxpayers are not eligible for retirement income credit.
[2] Maximum social security benefits in 1969 are: Single—$1,926; married—$2,889.
[3] Average social security benefits in 1969 are: Single—$1,150; married—$2,015.

Second, in addition to this discrimination against elderly persons who continue working, the present system of benefits gives the greatest advantage to those in the highest income brackets. For example, the extra $600 exemption is of increasing benefit as the individual's tax bracket increases; it reduces the taxes of those in the highest bracket by $420 a year but is worth only $84 to a married taxpayer in the lowest bracket. Similarly, for those elderly persons eligible for the social security and railroad retirement exclusions, the value of each dollar of exclusion rises as the recipient's income and tax bracket rise.

Third, the income tax system applicable to the elderly is made exceedingly complex by the detailed and complicated rules involved in computing the retirement income credit. This computation requires an extra page on the tax return, and experience indicates that it is so complicated that many of the elderly do not understand it and, therefore, lose the benefits to which they are entitled.

It would seem abundantly clear, therefore, that the present tax program for the elderly falls far short of meeting the objective of giving financial aid to the elderly in an equitable, uniform, and efficient manner.

PREVIOUS PROPOSAL

In early 1967 the President, in his "Message on Older Americans", recommended a complete revision of the income tax treatment of the elderly to meet the problems outlined above. Legislation to implement this recommendation was introduced in Congress as part of H.R. 5710, the forerunner of the administration's 1967 social security bill. However, Congress decided not to consider this important income tax revision in the context of social security legislation. Therefore, the proposal is being resubmitted, but with modifications to meet certain problems which were raised with respect to the original proposal.

CURRENT PROPOSAL

The current proposal retains the basic framework of the original program. It would eliminate the inequitable and complex features of existing law applicable to elderly taxpayers and would provide, instead, a flat exemption applicable to all middle and lower income elderly alike. The proposal would provide overall net tax reduction for the elderly as a group, and substantial tax reductions for those at lower and middle income levels. Those in the higher income brackets would pay additional tax. Elderly taxpayers, in addition to benefiting from the changes directed specifically at the elderly, will also benefit substantially from the proposed increase in the standard deduction (from 10 to 14 percent), and the proposed increase in the minimum standard deduction (from $200 plus $100 for each exemption to $600 plus $100 for each exemption) which are being recommended for all taxpayers in another proposal.

The following is a more detailed description of the proposals for revising the tax treatment of the elderly:

PERSONS WHO HAVE ATTAINED THE AGE OF 65

The present patchwork of benefits available to persons over 65 would be replaced by a single special exemption. Thus, the retirement income credit and the extra, but not the basic, $600 personal exemption and related extra $100 increase in the minimum standard deduction would be eliminated. Social security and railroad retirement annuities paid as retirement benefits would be included in the gross income computation. On the other hand, disability benefits, death benefits, and children's benefits under these programs would remain exempt.

These existing tax benefits would be replaced by a new special exemption of $2,500 for single taxpayers 65 or over (and for married couples when only one spouse is 65 or over) and a special exemption of $4,200 for a married couple where both are over 65. These special exemptions would be available regardless of the composition of the taxpayer's income. Thus, they could be claimed by an elderly individual who is still working as well as by one who is retired. Tables 2 and 3 demonstrate that the tax liabilities of elderly workers and retirees with the same income would be equal under the proposal.

TABLE 2.—THE AMOUNT OF TAX DECREASE UNDER THE AGED PROPOSAL, SINGLE TAXPAYER AGE 65

Present money income	Present tax [1]	Tax under proposal	Tax decrease
Maximum social security benefits ($1,926):			
$3,000	0	0	0
$5,000	$221	$209	$12
$6,500	484	452	32
$6,667	513	513	0
Average social security benefits ($1,150):			
$3,000	35	0	35
$5,000	358	209	149
$6,500	617	452	165
$7,000	704	633	71
$7,365	776	776	0
Wage income only:			
$3,000	209	0	200
$5,000	557	209	349
$6,500	833	452	388
$7,500	1,031	833	191
$8,000	1,130	1,042	88
$8,400	1,220	1,220	8

[1] No retirement income credit.

TABLE 3.—THE AMOUNT OF TAX DECREASE UNDER THE AGED PROPOSAL, MARRIED, BOTH OVER 65

Present money income	Present tax [1]	Tax under proposal	Tax decrease
Maximum social security benefits ($2,889):			
$6,000	$16	0	$16
$7,500	232	$192	40
$10,000	620	552	68
$11,727	915	915	0
Average social security benefits ($2,015):			
$6,000	138	0	138
$7,500	368	192	176
$10,000	770	552	218
$12,485	1,203	1,203	0
Wage income only:			
$6,000	450	0	450
$7,500	686	192	494
$10,000	1,114	552	562
$14,500	2,062	2,062	0

[1] No retirement income credit.

On the other hand, the special exemptions would not be available to elderly individuals in the upper income brackets where there is no financial need to justify tax relief because of age. Withholding of the new benefit from these individuals would be accomplished by reducing the exemption dollar for dollar for all income (including social security and railroad retirement benefits) received during the taxable year in excess of $6,500 in the case of a single individual and $11,500 in the case of a married couple.[1] However, in order to reflect the retiree's own contributions to the social security or basic railroad retirement system, the amount of his special exemption would, in no case, be reduced below an amount equal to one-third of the amount of those benefits included in income for tax purposes.

The amount of the special exemption is higher than under the original proposal by $200 both for single individuals and for married couples. These increases will bring the special exemption to a level where it takes account of the recent increase in social security benefits.[2] The level at which the special exemption begins to phase out have also been raised: from $5,600 to $6,500 for a single person and from $11,200 to $11,500 for a married couple. Thus, as so modified, the new special exemption could not be phased out completely below an income level of $9,000 for a single taxpayer (as compared to $7,900 under the original proposal) and $15,700 for a married couple (compared to $15,200 under the original proposal). Besides raising the income levels below which tax reduction will be realized, this modification recognizes, by raising the phaseout level for single people to over half that for a married couple, that the cost of living for single elderly people is, in general, appreciably more than one-half that of elderly married couples.

PERSONS UNDER THE AGE OF 65

Under existing law, persons under age 65 need not include their social security or railroad retirement benefits in income and, in addi-

[1] Tables 2 and 3 demonstrate the income level *at which* tax liability under present law and under the proposal would be the same and *above which* tax under the proposal would be higher than under present law.

[2] The new $2,500 special exemption is roughly equivalent to the sum of the 1968 maximum primary social security benefit ($1,800 rounded) and the existing extra $600 personal exemption and its related $100 minimum standard deduction. To arrive at the $4,200 married couple's exemption, there is added $900 representing the wife's social security benefit and $700 representing her extra $600 personal exemption and related $100 minimum standard deduction, with the total rounded to $4,200.

tion, those individuals receiving a pension under a public retirement system are eligible for the retirement income credit. The proposal would eliminate these preferences and substitute instead, for the individuals involved, a special deduction equal to the lesser of (1) the actual amount of pension, social security or railroad retirement benefits received or (2) $1,600. The $1,600 limitation would be reduced at the upper income levels in the same manner as the special exemption is phased out for those over age 65.

SPECIAL PROVISIONS FOR RAILROAD RETIREMENT ANNUITANTS

In addition to his special exemption of $2,500, a railroad retiree over age 65 would be allowed a supplemental exemption for any railroad retirement benefits he receives in excess of $1,800, but with an overall limit on this extra exemption of $600. For a married couple, the extra exemption would relate to their railroad retirement benefits in excess of $2,600, but with an overall limit on the additional exemption of $600. In each case, the supplemental exemption plus the special exemption would be subject to the phaseout provisions for higher income individuals.

These special provisions were not a part of the original proposal. They have been added to assure that people now receiving a railroad retirement annuity at or near the current maximum level (which is considerably greater than the maximum social security annuity) will not realize a significant tax increase merely as a result of the inclusion of their benefits in gross income if they are not affected by the phaseout provision.

*

Chapter V

ENTITIES

A. Corporations

A basic issue in the taxation of corporations and shareholders is the extent to which corporate earnings should be taxed both to the corporation and the shareholder. A threshold question in that connection—as is made clear in the initial two excerpts that follow—is the incidence of the corporate tax, a subject on which there is no general agreement.[a] If at least some part of the corporate tax is in fact borne by the shareholders rather than being passed on to the corporation's customers, employees, or suppliers, the issue of "double taxation" arises.

A variety of alternatives to deal with such "double taxation" are discussed in the first paper by Professor Smith.[b] The problem is closely related to the treatment of gains or losses on corporate stock. See generally Chapter VI, and in particular Professor Slawson's article.

The second excerpt, drawn from the report of the Canadian Royal Commission on Taxation (Carter Commission), spells out the reasons why that body opted for full integration of the corporate and shareholder taxes through adoption of the "withholding" approach referred to at the end of Professor Smith's piece. The Commission also recommended the optional use of a "partnership" approach for smaller corporations along the lines of Subchapter S in the United States tax law.[c] The rationale for such a policy is that such corporations are in fact more akin to partnerships; moreover, if full integration is de-

[a] Various views are discussed in Pechman, Federal Tax Policy 103–08 (1966).

[b] In an omitted portion of Professor Smith's paper, he discusses another integrative device at the shareholder level—the dividend credit and exclusion. During the years 1954–63, there was a $50 dividend exclusion and a 4% credit against the tax for dividends received in excess of the exclusion. The Revenue Act of 1964 increased the exclusion to $100 and reduced the credit to 2% for 1964; for subsequent years the credit was repealed altogether.

[c] See 4 Report of the Royal Commission on Taxation 68–70 (1966). Compare Sections 1371 et seq. of the U.S. Code. In order for a corporation to qualify for Subchapter S treatment, there may not be more than 10 shareholders and not over 20% of the corporation's gross receipts may be passive investment income. In direct contrast are the criteria for taxation of a corporation, trust or association as a regulated investment company or real estate investment trust under Subchapter M, with the right to deduct dividends paid and thus

sired, this is a relatively simple and feasible method for such entities.

The Canadian Government, in its implementation of the Carter Commission report, adopted the "partnership" proposal for closely held corporations but, in part because it doubted that the full brunt of the corporate tax fell on the shareholders, recommended that only one-half of the corporate tax be creditable by the shareholder. See Benson, Proposals for Tax Reform 50–52 (1969).

In his canvass of integrative devices Professor Smith refers to the differential tax treatment of dividends and interest payments. This issue, as well as others, turns on whether a security is "debt" or "stock." A major new development in this area is Code Section 385, added by the Tax Reform Act of 1969, specifically authorizing regulations to deal with the matter. The new provision is analyzed critically in a Note, Toward New Modes of Tax Decisionmaking—The Debt-Equity Imbroglio and Dislocations in Tax Lawmaking Responsibility, 83 Harvard Law Review 1695 (1970).

The final two selections are of major importance because they seek to bring some order to the proliferating complexities of corporate distributions, liquidations, and reorganizations.

avoid corporate taxes. Here disqualification results if ownership is insufficiently dispersed or if excessive amounts are received from other than passive investment sources. From rules such as these it is not easy to determine whether the basis for imposing a corporate tax is business activity or its absence, or concentration or dispersion of ownership of the enterprise.

SMITH, TAX TREATMENT OF DIVIDENDS

House Committee on Ways and Means,
3 Tax Revision Compendium 1543–46 (1959).

* * *

The need for relief from double taxation clearly depends on the extent to which there is in fact double taxation, and this in turn depends on the incidence of the corporation income tax. Traditional economic theory has consistently held that a corporate income tax rests on the corporation and is not shifted either forward to consumers or backwards to employees or suppliers. This conclusion is based on a theory which gives critical importance to marginal costs in determining price, and by definition there is no net profit, and hence no income tax element, at the margin. This position has been questioned on both pragmatic and theoretical grounds and a rather extensive literature has developed on the subject. At present there seems to be a fairly widespread uncertainty on the incidence of the corporation income tax, with no very great confidence by anyone on sweeping generalizations or categorical statements that the tax is wholly shifted or wholly borne by the corporation.

* * *

For purposes of this discussion, it is both correct and adequate to say that the corporation income tax does to some extent rest on corporations which pay it. This means that dividends paid to individual stockholders are doubly taxed, both to the corporation and to the individual recipient. Furthermore the double taxation is unique, since all other payments by the corporation to recipients of other forms of income—be they wages, or interest, or royalties—are deductible by the corporation and thus taxable only to the final recipient. The issue of fairness is complicated by the fact that the extra tax burden may be reflected in the price of corporate stock by the process referred to as the capitalization of a tax. With a lower net return available because of the tax, stocks will sell at lower prices than they otherwise would to give yields which are competitive with other investments not subject to double taxation. Lower stock prices, though they permit new purchasers of stock to secure reasonable net returns after allowing for the burden of the tax, discourage new stock issues because they make it more likely that new stock will dilute the interests of existing stockholders.

Direct relief for specific discrimnatory burdens of the double taxation of dividend income is not possible. A long-range and comprehensive point of view is necessary to restore as close an approach to the neutrality that would exist in the absence of any income tax as may be feasible. No perfect solution is available. We must select the best among the imperfect alternatives. Among the most obvious methods of relief are (1) elimination of the corporate tax, (2) elimination of any tax on dividends, (3) some adjustment in the corporate for dividends distributed, in recognition of the individual tax to be paid on them, or (4) some adjustment in the individual tax for dividends received, in recognition of the corporate tax previously paid.

The first alternative is not acceptable because it would mean that retained earnings would be completely untaxed, as well as all corporate income distributed to tax-exempt organization or individuals whose income is below the taxable level. In this country, at least, corporations are regarded as separate taxable entities; historically, the corporation income tax was in effect for 4 years from 1909 before the individual income tax was first enacted. Though there are many bad results from a too high income tax, the tax has come to have a place in our revenue system and any proposal for its elimination should be considered on its merits and not simply as a device for alleviation of double taxation.

The second alternative, the elimination of the individual income tax on dividends, is also unacceptable as long as individual tax rates go above the corporate rate. If dividends were not taxed to individuals, they would escape the full effects of those surtax rates which exceed the corporate rate. This might be useful to induce risk investment, and help to counteract the pernicious effect of tax-exempt bonds, but it cannot be advanced under the guise of relief from double taxation.

From some points of view there is much to be said for the third alternative, some adjustment in the corporate tax for dividends distributed, in view of the fact that they will be taxed in the hands of the individuals receiving them. A full deduction in computing corporate taxable income for dividends paid would seem at first sight to give complete relief. Retained earnings would be taxed to the corporation at a flat rate and distributed earnings would be taxed to individuals at their respective personal tax rates. From this point of view, the solution appears perfect. A deduction for dividends paid might also be thought of as balancing the deductibility of interest, and hence securing tax neutrality between debt and stock financing. But from other, and more significant, points of view this approach to a solution is not good and does not achieve its intended objectives.

If dividends are deductible, the corporate tax becomes a tax on retained earnings, and retained earnings are by far the most important source of equity capital for industry in this country. What is intended as relief for dividends paid becomes a penalty on earnings retained. For those companies which have to retain all or virtually all of their earnings there is no relief—to be sure, there is by definition no double taxation and hence perhaps no need for relief in this case. Nonetheless, a corporate tax solely on retained earnings would surely be regarded as a penalty on growth.

More significantly, the deductibility of dividends would not really equalize the tax status of debt and equity financing unless all earnings were distributed. Dividends paid are only superficially a measure of the cost of equity financing; the dilution of prospective earnings per share is the more significant measure of cost of new capital. When funds are secured by debt, the interest payable is a proper measure of the cost, and the deductibility of the interest keeps the corporation income tax from influencing the cost. But, when funds are raised by stock, there must be sufficient earnings on the new capital to maintain total earnings per share on all the stock if dilution of the existing stockholders' interests is to be avoided. To the extent that earnings are not distributed, the corporate tax would not be made neutral as between debt and stock financing. The relief would be greatest in mature companies and least in growing companies which typically retain a higher proportion of their income. The deductibility of dividends accordingly falls short of being the ideal method of relief. It does not produce neutrality between debt and stock financing, except in rare cases, and it makes the corporate tax subject to the criticism that it is a penalty on retained earnings.

In one respect, however, the deductibility of dividends is logical and theoretically preferable to any other method of relief, including the method now in effect. Dividends on preferred stock are much more similar to interest than to dividends on common stock. The corporate income tax does not rest on preferred stock, even if the tax rests fully on the corporation. So long as there is enough income after tax to pay the preferred dividends, the burden falls entirely on the common stockholders. The existence of preferred stock merely constitutes an element of leverage on the common stock. The tax makes preferred-stock financing very expensive; the 52-percent rate makes it so expensive that it is hard to see why preferred stock is ever issued. Preferred-stock dividends should be deductible, like interest on funds raised by debt obligations. If one were designing a tax system anew, one would certainly want to allow such a deduction. At the time the relief provision was adopted in 1954, a differentiation in treatment between preferred and common stock would have been unduly complicating, especially in view of the limited relief possible. A minor deduction for a small part of preferred dividends would have seemed peculiar and hardly worthwhile. If the time ever comes for a general overhaul of the tax law, with a margin of funds available for drastic changes, preferred dividends should be made fully deductible.

At the stockholder level, relief may be given in several ways. The method favored in much theoretical analysis is that of treating the corporation income tax as a withholding tax on behalf of the stockholders. The latter "gross up" their dividends to report as individual income their proportionate shares of the corporate income before tax from which the dividend is paid; that is, they add back the corporate tax to the dividend. They then compute their individual taxes on this grossed-up dividend and offset the corporate tax as a credit against it. If the individual and corporate rates are the same, there will be no further tax due; to the extent that the individual rate is higher than the corporate rate, the individual will pay the difference in rate, applicable to the grossed-up dividend; to the extent that his rate is lower, he will be entitled to a refund.

4 REPORT OF THE ROYAL COMMISSION ON TAXATION (CANADA) 3–9, 19–28 (1966) *

Because income tax is collected from corporations, trusts, and cooperatives, it does not mean that these organizations bear the burden of the tax. Ultimately, the burden of the tax on the organization is the relative reduction in the power of people to consume. This reduction can take the form of reduced payments to people who sell goods and services to the organization, increased prices for those who buy goods and services from the organization, reduced incomes to those who hold interests in the organization or reduced sale prices received for these interests by those who dispose of them. We recognize that it has been extremely useful to treat corporations as persons "in contemplation of law", and we agree that the shareholders of a large, widely held corporation usually do not have a major voice in the decisions of the corporation. But the rights and obligations of the corporation or the decision-making powers of those who control the corporation are irrelevant considerations from the viewpoint of deciding who bears the corporation income tax. The fact that an individual shareholder or a manager may be able to make the major decisions of the corporation does not mean that he bears any particular proportion of the burden of the tax on the corporation. His power to consume goods and services for personal use may be completely unaffected by the corporation income tax.

Taxing the income of organizations is an inexpensive method of collecting taxes, but unless the tax is integrated with the taxation of the incomes of the individuals or families who hold interests in these organizations, the tax system cannot be either equitable or neutral. When the income of organizations is taxed differently from other kinds of income, and the income of different kinds of organization is not taxed in a similar manner, avenues for tax minimization are created that are more readily available to some individuals than to others. As we explain later, to the extent that such taxes are not avoided they may be quickly shifted on to consumers and suppliers through prices and cost changes and thus become crude sales and cost-factor

* Reproduced with the permission of the Queen's Printer for Canada. Footnotes have been omitted.

taxes. When these taxes on organizations are neither avoided nor shifted in this sense, they become capricious taxes on some kinds of wealth at the time they are imposed. Unless they are completely avoided, they distort the allocation of resources and reduce the value of our national output.

Equity and neutrality would best be achieved under a tax system in which there were no taxes on organizations as such, and all individuals and families holding interests in organizations were taxed on the accrued net gains from such interests on the same basis as all other net gains. Under such a system, shareholders of corporate organizations would be required to bring the following into their annual tax bases:

1. Dividends received during the year.
2. The gains or losses on shares disposed of during the year, that is, realized gains and losses.
3. The change in the value of the shares held over the year end, that is, accrued gains and losses.

The net gains from holding interests in other organizations would be treated in the same way.

Although we can see no grounds in principle for taxing corporations and other organizations, we have reluctantly reached the conclusion that there are good and sufficient reasons for continuing to collect a tax from them. The main reason is the practical difficulty of taxing accrued share gains as required under the ideal approach we have just described. Another reason is the loss in economic benefit to Canada that would result if nonresidents holding shares in Canadian corporations were not taxed by Canada on their share of corporate income at approximately the rates that now prevail.

Valuation problems preclude the annual taxation of share gains on an accrual basis, while to tax shareholders only on dividends received and gains realized without any tax on corporations, would permit massive and unwarranted postponement of personal income tax. In the absence of a tax on the undistributed earnings of corporations, those individuals who could arrange to receive income through corporations could retain their savings untaxed in the corporation. These untaxed savings would earn a return that would also escape taxation if the return was also retained and reinvested by the corporation. The result would be an inordinate tax advantage to those who could channel income through a corporation.

* * *

After an exhaustive examination of the alternative methods of taxing corporate income, we have come to the conclusion that the method we recommend for the full integration of personal and corporation income taxes is without doubt the best system. It would achieve the greatest equity and neutrality consistent with the inescapable facts that accrued share gains cannot be brought initially into income each year and that Canada should tax the Canadian corporate income of non-residents at a rate of about 50 per cent.

* * * The following are the basic features of the full-integration system we recommend:

1. The income of Canadian corporations should be subject to a flat rate of tax of approximately 50 per cent.
2. Individuals and families should be subject to progressive rates of tax with a top marginal rate of 50 per cent.
3. The tax base of the resident shareholder should include the corporate income paid or allocated to him, "grossed-up" for the corporation tax paid.
4. The resident shareholder should receive credit against his personal income tax liabilities for the full amount of the corporation tax paid in respect of the after-tax corporate income paid or allocated to him, with a refund if the credit exceeded the liability.
5. Realized gains or losses on corporate shares should be included in income and taxed at full progressive rates.
6. The corporation should be allowed to allocate after-tax corporate income to shareholders without having to pay cash dividends.
7. The cost basis of shares should be increased when the corporation allocated retained corporate earnings to shareholders, so that share gains resulting from the retention of earnings that had been taxed to the shareholder would not be taxed again to the shareholder when realized.

Under the system we propose, the receipt by a resident shareholder of a $50 cash dividend from a corporation which had been taxed at 50 per cent would be treated as shown in Table 19–1 which follows. As this table illustrates, each shareholder would ultimately pay only his personal tax on an original income of $100 at the corporate level.

TABLE 19-1

ILLUSTRATION OF THE
FULL-INTEGRATION SYSTEM

		Tax Bracket of the Shareholder		
		15 per cent	35 per cent	50 per cent
1.	Income (grossed-up dividend)	$100	$100	$100
2.	Personal tax	$ 15	$ 35	$ 50
3.	Minus: tax already paid by corporation	($50)	($50)	($50)
4.	Tax (refund)	($35)	($15)	(-)
5.	Plus: cash dividend	$ 50	$ 50	$ 50
6.	Total cash received by the shareholder	$ 85	$ 65	$ 50

* * *

We have already described the general equity and neutrality advantages of the full-integration system; we also draw attention to the following specific advantages it possesses:

1. The tax system would neither encourage nor discourage the retention of earnings by corporations, because the shareholder would be entitled to the same tax credit on an allocation by the corporation of its income as on the payment of a dividend.
2. Corporate cash retentions could be increased without worsening the cash position of most shareholders.
3. Corporations raising capital in Canada would be less affected by tax considerations in the choice between debt and equity financing.
4. To the extent that the reduction in the tax on corporate source income was not passed on in the form of lower prices or higher costs, the after-tax income from Canadian equities would be increased to most Canadians with the result that share prices would rise, the cost of equity capital would fall and the rate of capital formation by corporations would increase.
5. The increase in Canadian share prices should encourage non-residents holding shares in Canadian corporations to sell

them to Canadians, and Canadian corporations wholly owned by non-residents would be encouraged to raise capital by issuing equities in Canada.

6. The advantages of, and facility for, tax avoidance by means of "surplus-stripping" that are inherent in the present tax structure would be removed.
7. Tax avoidance through the creation of associated companies to take advantage of the dual rate would be eliminated.
8. The tax treatment of corporations, trusts and mutual organizations would be put on substantially the same basis.
9. The allocation of resources would be improved with a resulting increase in the output of the goods and services that Canadians want.
10. All corporate source income (other than the income accruing for nonresident shareholders) would be taxed at the progressive rates applicable to the individual shareholder.

* * *

THE DOUBLE TAXATION ARGUMENT

Under a neutral tax system all kinds of net gains, both realized and accrued, would be brought into the base and all would be taxed in the same way. There would be no distinction between the net gains from employment, from operating a business, from membership in a co-operative, from holding shares, bonds or other property, or from being a beneficiary under a trust. To the extent that the net gains from different types of activities and from holding different kinds of property are subject to differences in tax treatment, the tax system distorts the allocation of resources.

As we have shown, the present tax system lacks neutrality in a multitude of respects. Nowhere is the lack of neutrality greater, however, than in the tax treatment of income from the corporate form of organization. Only corporate source income is subject to so-called "double" income taxes, under which income is taxed to the corporation and that part of corporate income distributed to shareholders is taxed again to them at personal rates without full credit for the corporation income tax. Examples of the effect of this double taxation are set out in Appendix E to this Volume. Other forms of organization, such as partnerships, proprietorships, co-operatives and trusts, are not faced with this double taxation (or can readily avoid it in the case of co-operatives).

The corporate form of organization offers some unique advantages. In particular, the corporate form has been found to be best suited for marshalling capital. Those economic activities that are dependent upon large pools of assets are unable to avoid double taxation by organizing as a partnership, proprietorship, trust or co-operative, except at the cost of paying a higher price for their capital.

To the extent that corporations pass on the corporation tax through higher prices for the goods and services they provide, or through lower prices for the goods and services they buy, consumers and suppliers buy fewer other things than they would otherwise be able to buy. This distorts the allocation of resources. To the extent that corporations do not pass on the tax through these price changes, their rate of return on investment is reduced and the allocation of resources to their economic activity is reduced (assuming that the shareholders could not avoid the extra tax by carrying out the activity through a non-corporate form). Thus, the tax on corporate income distorts the allocation of resources whether or not the tax is passed on. Because of the corporation income tax, Canadians, as a group, are less well off than they would be in its absence, assuming total government revenue is unchanged, because fewer of the goods and services they want are produced. Removal of the distortions created by the corporation income tax would mean that output would be greater so that some Canadians could be made better off without causing others to be worse off.

This question of double taxation and the "passing on" of the corporation income tax is so important and so controversial that we think it is essential to make our point of view abundantly clear. While we focus attention on the corporation income tax, it must be borne in mind that virtually all taxes can be passed on under some circumstances.

Three terms have to be carefully distinguished:

1. Tax avoidance, that is, changing the form of an activity, of an organization or of an asset to escape the tax that otherwise would apply.
2. Tax shifting, that is, maintaining after-tax income from a fixed (tangible) asset in the face of a change in the tax on

that income, either by changing the selling price of the goods and services produced by the asset or by changing the prices paid for goods and services used in conjunction with the asset to produce the goods sold.

3. Tax-induced changes in the supply and allocation of fixed (tangible) assets among alternative uses, that is, maintaining the expected after-tax rate of return on fixed assets used for certain purposes or held by certain organizations by an adjustment of the relative quantity of the assets available.

The extent to which taxes can be avoided depends upon the structure and language of the statutes, the interpretation of the statutes by the courts and the knowledge of the taxpayer and his advisors. The extent to which taxes can be shifted depends, among other things, upon the competitive position of the taxpayer and the state of the economy. The greater the degree of competition, whether from imported goods and services, from existing firms or from the possible entry of new firms, the more difficult it will be to shift tax increases forward through higher prices (or lower costs), or resist shifting tax reductions backward through lower prices (or higher costs).

The extent to which tax-induced changes occur in the amount of capital invested in a particular kind of fixed asset depends upon the nature of the asset and the speed with which the amount invested in the asset can be adjusted to changes in the expected rate of return. The supply of nonreproducible assets (such as a developed mineral deposit) obviously cannot readily be adjusted; on the other hand, the supply of some short-lived assets can quickly be adjusted simply by not replacing them. The adjustment can be rapid and complete or slow and incomplete, depending on the speed with which the total amount invested in an asset can be changed by changing the allocation of new savings among alternative investments.

When taxes are avoided by changing form without changing substance, tax shifting and tax-induced changes in the composition and amount of fixed assets do not occur. Similarly, when tax changes are not avoided, but after-tax income is maintained through shifting the tax, induced changes in the stock of fixed assets do not occur. However, when tax changes are not avoided and not shifted, the change in after-tax income from a particular kind of asset changes the expected after-tax rate of return on such assets. The search for the highest expected after-tax rate of return may induce a contraction or expansion in the amount invested in the particular kind of asset. Tax increases that lower expected after-tax rates of return on particular assets induce reductions in the amount invested in them. With the reduction in the amount of a particular kind of asset over what it would otherwise be, the supply of the goods or services produced by such assets is also reduced. This will usually increase the prices of the goods and services produced by such assets (we ignore here the international aspect of the problem). With higher prices for the goods and services produced by such assets, the after-tax income and expected rate of return on the assets rises, and thus eliminates part of the initial impact of the tax change on rates of return. Conversely, tax reductions that increase expected after-tax rates of return on a particular kind of asset induce increases in the supply of such assets that in turn tend to reduce the amount by which the expected rate of return is increased.

While the present method of taxing corporate source income involves double taxation in the sense that the same dollars of income are taxed twice without full credit to the shareholder for the tax levied at the corporate level, the before-tax income of the corporation may have adjusted to the tax in one of several ways. The corporation income tax may have been shifted forward when it was imposed or increased. In that event shareholders would have been unaffected by the tax change, but consumers would have been subjected to a crude sales tax on goods and services. This sales tax would have reduced consumption or saving or both, and probably would have changed the pattern of consumption and hence the allocation of resources in a deleterious way. Because low income individuals and families consume a larger proportion of their income than others, a corporation tax, to the extent that it is shifted forward, is a regressive tax.

To the extent that the corporation tax or an increase in the corporation tax was not shifted, it must have changed expected after-tax rates of return to shareholders. The market value of the shares in corporations that were unable to shift the tax must have fallen. Those who held such shares at the time the tax was imposed, or increased, and sold them after they fell in price, would have suffered a capital loss at that time, and so in effect would have been subjected to a tax on their wealth. Those who purchased the shares subsequent to the tax change would have bought them at a price that capitalized the tax on the anticipated earnings of the corporation. Those who held shares at the time the tax was imposed, or increased, and held them since that time, would also have suffered a capital loss because the after-tax income from their shares would have been reduced following the imposition or increase of the tax.

When a corporation income tax is imposed or increased, the cost of equity capital to corporations that are unable to shift the tax is raised (because of the decline in share prices) and the rate of investment by such corporations is lowered relative to what it otherwise would have been. With less investment and less output, the prices charged by non-shifting corporations tend to rise more rapidly, thus, over a period of time, bringing about a relatively greater increase in after-tax income and a corresponding recovery in the prices of the shares. Other things being equal, when the adjustment to the corporation tax was complete, the relationship between the rates of return on all corporate shares and other assets, such as bonds, would be approximately what it was prior to the imposition of the corporation income tax. The original equilibrium would thus be restored. If the adjustment was complete but the imposition of the tax changed rates of saving, risk preferences and other fundamental features of the economy, a different equilibrium would be reached, in which asset prices would bear a new, but stable, relationship to one another.

The main point, and it is an extremely important point, is that if the corporation income tax was not shifted, it was inequitable to those who held shares at the time the tax was imposed or increased, whether or not they subsequently held their shares or sold them. Those who bought shares following the imposition or increase of the tax did so at prices that capitalized the tax. The recovery in after-tax income that would generally follow the imposition of the tax would in many cases generate capital gains for those who accepted the uncertainty of the extent and timing of the adjustment and purchased shares at low prices soon after the tax was imposed. However, Canadians generally have lost through the taxation of corporate income at higher average rates than other income, even if the tax was not immediately shifted, for the reduced investment in corporations that could not shift the tax distorted the allocation of resources. The stock of assets of the non-shifting corporations is less than it otherwise would have been. As a result, fewer goods and services of the kinds that Canadians want are being produced than would have been produced had there been no "double" taxation of corporate source income.

It is, of course, utterly impossible to rectify the inequitable consequences flowing from the "double" taxation of corporate income. The tax was first imposed in 1917, and the rates have been substantial for 25 years. No one knows who held particular shares at the time each increase in the tax took place, much less the extent to which particular shareholders in the past suffered capital losses because the tax was not shifted. Certainly it is impossible to compensate all consumers and suppliers for the corporation income taxes that were shifted at the time, and to compensate all Canadians for the reduction in the value of national output that has resulted from the lower rates of investment that subsequently have ensued. What we wish to emphasize is first, that the double taxation of corporate source income does not mean that present shareholders are being unfairly treated, and secondly, that the only relevance of the shifting question is in deciding to what extent the corporation income tax has been a crude sales tax and to what extent a crude tax on wealth.

This leads to the question of what would happen if the present system of taxing corporate source income was changed and the double tax effect removed. The converse of the previous analysis applies. To the extent that the reduction in the tax on corporate source income was shifted, consumers would be better off because the prices of some goods and services would decline, and suppliers (including employees) would be better off because the prices paid for some goods and services would increase. To the extent that the tax reduction was not shifted, some shareholders at the time of the reduction would obtain capital gains. Shareholders in corporations that did not shift the tax reduction but which were not expected to be able to maintain prices for many years because of the entry of new firms, or because of the more rapid expansion of existing firms attracted by the higher after-tax rate of return, would have small capital gains. Shareholders in corporations that did not shift the tax reduction and were not expected to face strong competition from other corporations would have larger capital gains. These capital gains would be "unfair" in the same way that the capital losses created by the imposition or increase of the tax were "unfair". It is in this sense that the adage "an old tax is a good tax" is valid:

even though it has had effects on the allocation of resources, the market has capitalized these effects, and removing the tax would give rise to unfair gains for existing shareholders.

Under our proposals the taxation of capital gains would to some extent offset the tax reduction and would mitigate the amount of the net gains after tax which the integration proposal in itself would produce.

Where increases in share prices occurred, however, the cost of capital to the corporation would be reduced and an expansion in the rate of capital formation for those corporations would be encouraged. This in turn would increase the future output of the goods and services produced by the affected corporations, would tend to reduce the prices of these goods and services and, over time, would bring about a relative reduction in expected after-tax corporate income toward its original levels, with a consequent reduction in the prices of the shares of these corporations relative to what they otherwise would have been. (It is not suggested that an absolute reduction in share prices would occur.) This reduction in share prices is the converse of the situation described above of the decline in price of a premium bond as it approaches maturity. The expansion in the output of these corporations would benefit all Canadians.

We recommend the abolition of the double taxation of corporate income, not to help existing shareholders, but primarily to obtain this additional output and to eliminate differences in tax treatment between different kinds of organizations that inevitably provide opportunities for tax avoidance. The capital gains that some shareholders would obtain on the abolition of the double taxation of corporate income would be an undesirable, but inescapable, consequence of the proposal. In equity, these capital gains should be taxed at 100 per cent. In practice, it is not possible to distinguish these capital gains from other capital gains. However, it would be grossly unfair to allow the gains resulting from the integration proposal to escape being taxed at anything less than full rates.

Even with the taxation of capital gains at full rates, implementation of our integration proposal would probably give rise to gains to some shareholders. Since the overall net reduction in taxation of corporate source income would be offset by increases in taxation of income from other sources, these gains would in effect be financed by those whose taxes would be increased under our proposals. We believe that the financing of such gains to shareholders as may occur should be regarded as an investment by other sectors of the economy which would more than pay for itself as a result of the gains in future output that the implementation of our integration proposal should produce.

If the tax system is to be neutral, persons who carry on an activity through one form of organization should be subject to tax on the same basis and at the same rates as persons who carry on the same activity through another form of organization As we have indicated, the corporation tax is probably shifted to an undetermined extent to consumers and suppliers. By the same token the tax imposed on an individual proprietor or on members of a partnership or syndicate may be shifted. The income taxes imposed on employees may be shifted, to some degree, to employers, and possibly by the employers to consumers and suppliers. There is no certainty that taxes are borne by the persons on whom they are imposed or that they are borne to the same degree by all persons on whom they are imposed. It is obviously impossible to measure the ultimate impact of a tax on all members of the community.

INTEGRATION AND CAPITAL GAINS

Although we do not wish to dwell upon the matter here, the relationship between the taxation of corporate income and the taxation of the gains or losses on corporate shares is very important. The failure to tax share gains in the past has undoubtedly reduced the adverse impact of the double taxation of corporate income. Without a tax on share gains, it frequently has been possible to arrange the form of transactions to avoid the full impact of the double tax. The earnings of the corporation generally could not escape the tax net, but by retaining the earnings in the corporation and selling the shares of the corporation at a price that reflected the additional assets of the corporation, the personal tax on retained corporate income could be avoided. To this extent the pressure to shift the tax was reduced, or the capital losses imposed on shareholders at the time the tax was imposed on the corporation were less. By the same token, removing the double taxation of corporate income would result in less reverse shifting or smaller capital gains to those who held shares at the time, if share gains were subject to full personal income tax. This is one of the reasons why we advocate both the full taxation of property gains and the full integration of personal and corporation income taxes. We could not countenance the unwarranted benefits that some shareholders would obtain from full integration if share gains were not taxed in full; similarly, we could not accept the adverse effects of taxing share gains in full without removing the double taxation of corporate source income. The two proposals are part of a package. Neither can be recommended in isolation.

LEWIS, A PROPOSED NEW TREATMENT FOR CORPORATE DISTRIBUTIONS AND SALES IN LIQUIDATION

House Committee on Ways and Means,
3 Tax Revision Compendium 1643, 1644–51 (1959).

There are two kinds of corporate liquidations. One kind is the distribution by a corporation of its properties and business in liquidation to its shareholder or shareholders, who thereafter own and operate them as sole proprietor or as partners. The corporation itself realizes no gain or loss on assets distributed to the shareholders but it must pick up any unreported income from installment sales or long-term contracts and any other earned but unreported income. The shareholders are taxed under any of four methods: (1) generally, their gain or loss is reported as capital gain or loss; (2) if the corporation is a collapsible corporation, gains of some or all of the shareholders may be taxable as ordinary income; (3) if a sufficient number of shareholders so elect, they may treat as a dividend their shares of the corporation's accumulated earnings and profits and pay no further tax unless the cash distributed to them exceeds their shares of the accumulated earnings and profits; (4) if a corporation is at least an 80 percent shareholder, it pays no tax.

In the second kind of liquidation the corporation sells its properties and business to outsiders and distributes the proceeds to its shareholders. There are several ways in which sales of corporate assets are taxed: (1) if the plan of complete liquidation is adopted before the sale, the corporation's gain or loss is not recognized and the shareholders have capital gain or loss; (2) however, if in such case the corporation is collapsible, the corporation may be taxed on its gain and the shareholders are also taxed on their capital gains; (3) if the sale is made before the plan of liquidation is adopted, the corporation's gain or loss is recognized and the shareholders have capital gain or loss; (4) if the corporation, after selling its assets, operates as an investment company instead of liquidating, the corporation's gain or loss is recognized but there is no shareholder tax.

Several conclusions are readily apparent from analysis of these provisions:

(1) In providing so many possibilities, the statute is almost unbelievably complex.

(2) The choices are largely elective and thus are used to defeat the revenue. If the corporation's assets have appreciated in value, it can either distribute them to its shareholders or sell them in liquidation to outsiders without having the gain taxed; but if they have depreciated in value, it can sell them and obtain the loss. If the corporation has a high basis for its assets, it can utilize it by selling assets and operating as an investment company; if the shareholder has a high basis for his stock, he can utilize it by selling stock or by

having the corporation sell assets in liquidation. Frequently, the shareholders can postpone taxation of most of their gain by electing to pay a dividend tax on accumulated earnings; but they can take losses immediately. Corporate shareholders at about the 80 percent level can escape tax on gains or take losses by buying or selling a few shares of stock.

(3) The provisions hardly pay lip service to the "double tax" system. Congress has sawed off the tailgate of the corporate tax wagon. In so doing, it has weighted the tax system in favor of business liquidators and traders and against continuing owners. The latter are exposed to the double tax; the former (provided they escape that erratic policeman, the "collapsible corporation" provision) are not.

On three grounds—simplicity, revenue protection, and equity—the present system fails. Yet its development, upon reflection, seems almost (but not quite) inevitable. To review the story at the corporate end we may begin with the Supreme Court's 1936 decision, in the *General Utilities* case, that a corporation derives no taxable gain from the distribution of appreciated property to its shareholders. The *Court Holding* and *Cumberland Public Service* cases, decided by the Supreme Court in 1945 and 1950, dealt with sales of corporate assets to outsiders coincident with liquidation. The corporation was taxable if it sold the property before liquidation, but not if the shareholders sold the property after its distribution in liquidation. This rule was not easy to apply, particularly where the shareholders were also corporate officers and where sales negotiations commenced before liquidation; it thus led to substantial uncertainty and dispute. Also, it was not always feasible to distribute the property in kind to the shareholders, particularly where they were numerous. To introduce a greater degree of certainty, and to open the corporate tax escape hatch to larger corporations, Congress, in 1954, waived the corporate tax on sales and exchanges made after adoption of a plan of complete liquidation carried out within 12 months (Internal Revenue Code, sec. 337).

The new owner of the assets, instead of purchasing them directly from the corporation, might have purchased the corporation's stock and liquidated it. The selling shareholders paid a capital gains tax, the corporation was not taxed, and the new owner held the assets at a new basis reflecting his investment. The only difficulty was that under the principle of the *Kimbell-Diamond* decision, the new owner, if a corporation, obtained a new basis for the assets only if it could prove that it intended to liquidate the purchased corporation when it purchased the stock. Congress eliminated this problem of proof in 1954 by giving the corporate purchaser of stock a new basis for the underlying assets if it began liquidation of the purchased corporation within 2 years following the purchase (Internal Revenue Code, sec. 334(b)(2)).

Congress has recognized since 1924 that if a stockholder could obtain a capital gain by selling his stock to another person who could liquidate the corporation without further tax, he might as well be given capital gain treatment on liquidation (now Internal Revenue Code, sec. 331). Continuously, since the Revenue Act of 1924, gains and losses upon liquidation have been capital gains and losses, although the gains were short-term between 1934 and 1936, and gains from partial liquidations were short-term between 1934 and 1942. In 1936 and 1938 Congress adopted two exceptions from the shareholder capital gains tax on liquidation. Since 1936 the law has excused parent corporations from the tax upon liquidation of controlled—i.e., 80 percent or more owned—subsidiaries (now Internal Revenue Code, sec. 332). The reasoning was that the capital gains tax should not be paid upon the shift of the assets from one corporate owner to another, but only upon their final removal from corporate solution. In 1938 Congress accompanied the enactment of the present stringent personal holding company provisions with a special provision to encourage liquidation of such companies. This provision, which has several times been extended or reenacted, limits the taxable income or gain to the larger of the corporation's accumulated earnings and profits or the cash distributed (now Internal Revenue Code, sec. 333).

In combination, the *General Utilities* principle that a corporation is not taxed upon the distribution of property to its shareholders and the availability of capital gain treatment to shareholders upon sale of stock or liquidation permitted the most elementary tax avoidance. Corporations were formed for single projects—e.g., the production of a motion picture or the construction of an apartment house by stockholders who were frequently dealers in the kind of property involved. Upon completion, when the value of the property could be established, often by reference to contracts for its exploitation, but before the actual receipt of income, the corporation would be liquidated, or its stock would be sold and the purchaser would liquidate it. In either case, there was no corporate tax, the shareholders paid a capital gains tax, and the resulting increased basis of the property could be written off against ordinary income from its exploitation. Congress enacted the collapsible corporation provision in 1950 to forestall this practice (now Internal Revenue Code, sec. 341). This statute, despite repeated amendment, is still one of the most unsatisfactory provisions of its income tax law, almost unreadable, erratic and uncertain in its impact, and insufficiently provided with guides for administration.

When we consider the haphazard growth of liquidation provisions, we should perhaps be surprised that they are not worse. Congress has never undertaken the hard task of analyzing them as a whole to see whether a simpler, fairer, and more coherent liquidation statute might be fashioned. The Advisory Group on Subchapter C and the American Law Institute project would make only limited and piecemeal changes which would further complicate the statute. No one has undertaken the difficult search for a possible unifying principle.

The root of the complexity lies in two features of the present system: (1) The forgiveness of the corporate tax upon liquidations and other distributions in kind, and upon sales in liquidation; and (2) the imposition of a shareholder tax upon liquidations in kind. The following system might be substituted under a broader base, lower rate income tax:

(1) Recognition to the corporation of (*a*) all gains and losses accrued on property distributed in kind to its shareholders, in liquida-

tion or otherwise; and (*b*) all gains and losses realized on sales or exchanges of property, in liquidation or otherwise.

(2) Nonrecognition of gain or loss to shareholders upon corporate liquidations in kind. Cash received in liquidation would be first applied in recoupment of the shareholder's basis for his stock; any excess of cash over basis would be taxed as capital gain.

(3) The shareholder's basis for his stock would become the basis of the assets received by him in kind in the liquidation. Such basis would be increased by any gain taxed on liquidation and decreased by the amount of cash received. The basis, as thus adjusted, would be allocated among the assets in proportion to their fair market values.

(4) Distributions in kind to shareholders which are corporations would not be subject to the above rules. Such distributions, whether in liquidation or otherwise, would be tax free to both the distributor and the distributee; the distributee would inherit the distributor's basis (even though the stock of the distributor was recently purchased).

Several criticisms of this set of proposals may be anticipated and answered.

Criticism: The shareholder may escape with a single capital-gains tax by selling stock; therefore, the proposal would be so easily avoided that it would be largely ineffective. Answer: The purchaser of corporate stock would be unable under the proposal to obtain a new basis for the corporation's assets without payment of tax by the corporation. Liquidation by an individual purchaser would result in a corporate tax upon gain accrued to the corporation; liquidation by a corporate purchaser would not step up the basis of the assets. Purchasers could be expected to take the prospective corporate tax or lack of new basis into account in negotiating the purchase price.

Criticism: The double tax is inherently objectionable, and, therefore, should not be strengthened. Answer: The present system singles out for favored treatment one kind of income (accrued gains on certain kinds of property) for relief against the double tax, and then only in two types of transactions (distributions in kind to shareholders and sales during liquidation). As to other types of income, and as to realized gains in other circumstances, the double tax system operates. Students of taxation are not in agreement as to the impact of the corporate tax upon shareholders, consumers, suppliers, or wage earners. Under any theory as to the impact of the corporate tax, the reasons for relief restricted to one kind of income in two situations have not been articulated.

Criticism: The provisions under discussion are utilized mostly by small business, which the tax laws should be designed to encourage. Most small corporations do not pay dividends and thus are not subject to the double tax prior to their liquidation; therefore, it is logical to relieve them from double tax at liquidation. Answer: These provisions have frequently been utilized by large and publicly held corporations to escape the corporate tax on sales of assets during liquidation. As regards small corporations, not all of them are able to avoid paying dividends. Those which do not pay dividends are postponing rather than eliminating the shareholder tax.[1] Postponement of the shareholder tax during the corporation's life does not justify elimination of the corporate tax at its death. If the tax laws are to foster small business, they should foster its formation and growth, not its liquidation and sale.

Criticism: The double tax could easily discourage the liquidation or sale of corporate business enterprises because such transactions are usually voluntary. Moreover, its timing is severer upon gain from liquidation or sale than upon operating profits, which can be at least partially retained by the corporation. Answer: Under the proposal, a liquidation in kind would not incur a simultaneous double tax; the shareholder tax would be postponed until he disposes of the assets received. Nor would a sale by the corporation of its assets incur a simultaneous double tax if, instead of liquidating, it invests the proceeds in another business or operates as an investment company; the second tax is postponed until the proceeds are ultimately distributed to the shareholders. If sale and liquidation both take place, the tax will usually be a double capital gains tax having a combined effective rate of 43¾ percent. This is, of course, a lower effective rate than that of the combined tax upon corporate operating profits. It is questionable whether the tax laws should go further than this in favoring liquidations and sales over continuing business ownership and operation.

Criticism: The proposals would tax, and therefore require the valuation of, business good will in liquidations in kind. Answer: The present statute does the same in taxing shareholders on gain upon such liquidations. Moreover, this is necessary to equate the tax at the corporate level on sales and liquidations.

A further criticism of the proposal might be its taxation of gains accrued prior to incorporation. If an individual incorporates property which cost him $50,000 and is worth $500,000, the accrued gain of $450,000 is not taxed upon incorporation. If the value of the property remains at $500,000, it may be urged that the tax law should permit a liquidation in kind without a corporate tax; and if the property increases further in value after incorporation, that the corporate tax should fall only upon that further increase. If this right is granted, then it would be realistic also to permit the corporation to sell the property during liquidation without being taxed on the gain accrued prior to incorporation. Such rules, combined with the proposed deferment of the shareholder tax until the property was sold to outsiders, would give persons who incorporate appreciated property rashly and without an understanding of the tax laws an opportunity to repent. Present law does not completely offer that opportunity; however, the proposal, in closing the escape hatch from the double tax, may accentuate the need for such relief. Shielding of the pre-incorporation accrued gain from tax would interfere to some extent

---

[1] The shareholder tax is ultimately eliminated to the extent that stock receives a new and higher basis at the death of its holder, provided the stock is thereafter sold or the corporation liquidated. However, the stock is subject in that event to the estate tax. Whether or not provision for a new basis on death is appropriate, in any event its existence should not militate against an appropriate structure for the corporate income tax.

with the statutory simplification outlined below. Nevertheless, and although no tax system can completely protect those who act ignorantly, the better course might be to grant some limited protection of preincorporation accruals from corporate tax upon distribution in kind or sale during liquidation. Possibly the protection should be limited to the original shareholders who incorporated the property, and possibly it should also be available for only a limited time following incorporation of the appreciated property.

The proposals would result in substantial statutory simplification, as the following review of Internal Revenue Code provisions shows:

Section 311.—Present law: Gain or loss is not recognized to the corporation upon a nonliquidating distribution of property in kind as a dividend or in redemption of stock (subsec. (a)). There are three exceptions: The corporation recognizes gain upon distribution of LIFO inventories (subsec. (b)), property subject to liabilities in excess of its basis (subsec. (c)), or installment obligations (sec. 453 (d)). Proposal: The corporation would recognize gain or loss on such distributions. No exceptions.

Section 312.—Present law: Accrued but unrealized gains and losses on corporate property are not reflected in the corporation's earnings and profits either as they accrue or when the property is distributed in kind; upon distribution of the property, earnings and profits are reduced by its adjusted basis (subsec. (a)). As an exception, unrealized gain on "inventory assets" and "unrealized receivables and fees" are added to earnings and profits when such assets are distributed (subsec. (b)). Proposal: Accrued gains and losses, being recognized to the corporation upon distribution of the property in kind, would be reflected in its earnings and profits. No exceptions.

Section 331.—Present law: Amounts distributed in corporate liquidations are treated by the shareholder as in payment in exchange for the stock. Proposal: Same, except that the shareholder's gain or loss would not be recognized as to distributions in kind.

Section 332(a).—Present law: No gain or loss is recognized to a corporate parent on the liquidation of a controlled—i.e., 80 percent or more owned—subsidiary. Proposal: Nonrecognition for all shareholders, individuals or corporate, regardless of level of stock ownership, except for distributions of cash to individuals.

Section 332(c).—Present law: No gain or loss recognized to corporate subsidiary upon transfer of property in satisfaction of indebtedness to controlling—i.e., 80 percent or more owning—parent. Proposal: Same with percentage limitation on stock ownership removed; but gain or loss upon distributions in kind in satisfaction of indebtedness to individual shareholders would be taxed.

Section 333.—Present law: Limited recognition of gain (and partial taxation as a dividend) in certain 1-month liquidations. Proposal: Repeal.

Section 334(a).—Present law: Basis of property received in ordinary liquidation is fair market value at time of receipt. Proposal: As to individual distributees, such property would succeed to the basis of the distributee's stock, with appropriate adjustment for any gain taxed on liquidation and any cash received. As to distributees which are corporations, see the next two paragraphs.

Section 334(b)(1).—Present law: Basis of property received in liquidation by controlling—i.e., 80 percent or more owning—parent is inherited from subsidiary unless subsidiary's stock was purchased within 2 years before liquidation. Proposal: Same to any distributee which is a corporation, regardless of level of stock ownership and regardless of when subsidiary's stock was purchased.

Section 334(b)(2).—Present law: Property received in liquidation by controlling parent from subsidiary the stock of which was purchased within 2 years before liquidation succeeds to basis of subsidiary's stock with adjustments. Proposal: Repeal.

Section 334(c).—Present law: Prescribes basis of property received in 1-month liquidations under section 333. Proposal: Repeal.

Section 336.—Present law: Prevents recognition of gain or loss to the corporation upon a liquidating distribution in kind. Exception for installment obligations (sec. 453(d)). Proposal: Recognize such gain or loss to the corporation. No exceptions.

Section 337.—Present law: Prevents recognition of gain or loss to the corporation upon sales or exchanges of property during 12-month liquidating period. Exceptions for inventory not sold in bulk, installment obligations, collapsible corporations, and controlled subsidiaries. Proposal: Repeal.

Section 341.—Present law: Treats as ordinary income gain from sale or exchange of stock of a collapsible corporation, liquidating distributions from such a corporation, and certain nonliquidating distributions from such a corporation. Several complex exceptions relating to size of shareholding, source of gain, holding period and nature of porperty, and business history of stockholders. Proposal: Repeal.

The varied and cumulatively numerous exceptions under sections 311, 312, 336, and 337 reflect congressional concern over abuse of the present system. The elimination of those exceptions would be one of the chief simplifications inherent in the proposal. The other, and more important, principal simplification would be the elimination of the fantastically complicated and uncertain collapsible corporation provision. The two features of the present system which made such a provision necessary—the nontaxability to the corporation of accrued gains on property distributed to shareholders and the obtaining by the shareholders of a new and higher basis for the property on liquidation—would both be eliminated under the proposal. As explained earlier, sale of corporate stock would not be a vehicle for abuse because the corporate tax would ultimately be payable and the purchaser of the stock could be expected to take this into account in negotiating the purchase price.

Under the proposal, dealers in various kinds of property might, by incorporating projects involving such kinds of property, still obtain too great a tax advantage in the form of a double capital-gains tax. This problem could be dealt with by provisions far simpler than the present collapsible corporation section. The shareholder-dealer's business history would simply be taken into account in determining whether ordinary income or capital gain should result to the corporation from its sale of the property or distribution of the property in kind or to the shareholder from his sale of stock.

The proposed revision of section 331 to provide nonrecognition of gain to shareholders upon liquidations in kind differs from the revision of that section proposed by the Advisory Group on Subchapter C. The Advisory Group would provide for recognition of gain to the extent that the corporation's basis for the property distributed in kind exceeded the shareholder's basis for his stock, and for recognition of loss in all cases. The present proposal is simpler, more uniform, and easier to administer.

The proposed repeal of section 333 is based on two grounds. The general postponement of gain to shareholders on liquidations in kind would make any such special provision unnecessary. Moreover, the lapse of more than 20 years since the enactment of the personal holding company provisions that gave rise to this section should now permit its elimination.

With the proposed repeal of the basis provisions of section 334(b), it should be made clear that a purchaser of stock cannot shift his basis for the stock to the assets upon liquidation, even if he bought the stock with the intention to liquidate. The principle of the *Kimbell-Diamond* decision would thus be legislated out of existence.

Under the proposed repeal of section 337 there would be no revival of the uncertainty posed by the *Court Holding* and *Cumberland Public Service* cases, for the tax to the corporation upon liquidations in kind would make irrelevant the question of whether property sales coincident with liquidation were made by the corporation or by its shareholders.

BROWN, AN APPROACH TO SUBCHAPTER C

House Committee on Ways and Means,
3 Tax Revision Compendium 1619, 1621–25 (1959).

II. REORGANIZATION AND RELATED EXCHANGES

Presumably every exchange of property could constitutionally be taken as an occasion on which gain or loss cognizable for income tax purposes could be computed. Indeed, it is more than possible that without delaying until sale or exchange of assets, periodic computations of changes in worth could be required and made significant in the computation of income subject to tax. But to state the constitutional possibility of such programs is not to suggest their legislative or administrative wisdom. At least since 1918, though the general rule has been that gain or loss was to be recognized upon the sale or exchange of property, there have been statutory provisions for nonrecognition upon certain exchanges. Indeed, if it were necessary to choose between extremes, it would seem preferable for the economy and no great loss for the Treasury to choose the opposite general rule and, assuming provision for continuity of basis, to recognize gain or loss on an exchange only as the taxpayer received cash or consumable goods, the consumption of which gave rise to no deduction for tax purposes. Obviously in the latter instances it would be appropriate to treat receipt as a taxable transaction, though even there we have in recent years provided for nonrecognition in certain instances.

But we have not had to choose extreme positions, and we have not done so. We have, in the reorganization and related sections, provided for nonrecognition of gain or loss on exchanges where the exchange resulted in a continuity of investment, as that concept has been set forth in the statute. That there should be some such provision—broad or narrow in scope as one may choose—has seemed wise, and almost necessary, if, in Chairman Mills' phrase, we are to have "a tax system which interferes as little as possible with the operation of the free market mechanism in directing resources into their most productive uses." The prospect of tax liability resulting from a possible or projected exchange is undoubtedly to some perhaps immeasurable extent a deterrent to the taxpayer who is considering the exchange, particularly where it is to produce no cash to him, and money to pay the tax will have to be raised from some other source or transaction. Very roughly speaking, our provisions for tax-free exchanges, as we have called them, have served something of the same economic purpose that exemption of capital gains does in other taxing systems, while preserving to the Treasury the potentiality of revenue upon the ultimate liquidation of the investment.

We are, however, faced with the continuing legislative choice whether the provisions for tax-free exchanges should be broad or narrow in scope. It is possible to argue that they should be narrow, and narrower than they have been. See Hellerstein, "*Mergers, Taxes and Realism,*" 71 Harvard Law Review 254 (1957). One of the arguments tending to this conclusion is that the provisions for nonrecognition of gain encourage mergers and other reorganizations which result in an unfortunate trend toward monopoly. If all, or even the predominant majority, of reorganizations had economic consequences which were accepted as unfortunate, there would be little reason to lower tax barriers to such transactions generally. But few would contend that all reorganizations have unfortunate economic implications, and about many such transactions there is obvious room for difference of economic opinion. Certainly some reorganizations do direct resources into channels productive of economic growth. If this is so, it seems unlikely that a revenue act can be adequately selective by its terms to encourage the reorganizations which will result in growth, and to discourage those which will have monopolistic or other economically unfortunate tendencies. Rather than narrowing the scope of the nonrecognition sections in the revenue acts for the purpose of applying nonselective collateral sanctions upon mergers, it would seem better to obtain enforcement of the antitrust and related statutes by reliance upon those agencies of Government which are responsible in that area and which presumably can make intelligent differentiation between transactions according to standards relevant to the statutes they are charged with administering and enforcing.

Starting with a unitary concept of the unifying reorganization, and similar treatment of the control, or divisive reorganization, the revenue acts during the past 25 years have undergone the imposition of a series of differentiations and limitations. In 1934, the terms permissible in a statutory merger were differentiated from those allowed in the so-called practical mergers, the (B) and (C) reorganizations. No reason was suggested for this differentiation then, and none has been advanced to carry conviction since then. The 1954 code perpetuates this difference, makes new and inexplicable differentiations between the (B) and the (C) reorganization, and creates a highly intricate system of controls over the (D), or divisive, reorganization and related transactions. Certainly, the Advisory Group is correct in proposing to simplify this structure, and at least to the extent of that simplification broadening the concept of the tax-free exchange. The (A), (B), and (C) reorganizations represent in the end only different corporate procedures to produce substantially similar results. The Advisory Group would make uniform the permissible nature of the property to be received in the three types of reorganization, and would further produce similar end results by requiring the transferor corporation to liquidate in a (C) reorganization. As far as they go, these proposals seem eminently sound.

I would propose to the committee that it go measurably further in broadening the scope of the tax-free exchange in reorganization but that at the same time it give greater protection to the Treasury against converting ordinary income into capital gain and adopt more carefully conceived basis provisions which would make of the tax-free exchange a real continuum and not the fortuitous occasion for untaxed gain or nondeductible loss by reason of inappropriate basis provisions. This could be done, I believe, without loss to the Treasury, and with gain in simplicity of statutory structure and ease of administration. As long as there is a marked difference between the rates applicable to ordinary income and those applicable to capital gain, the threat to the revenues resulting from broadened reorganization provisions comes principally from one or another variation on the bailout: the apportionment of basis and the subsequent realization of capital gain. This is true in the situations which gave rise to the *Gregory* and *Bazley* cases as well as in the more recent *Chamberlin* situation arising from a stock dividend in preferred stock. The elaborate structure of sections 355 and 356 comes largely as a result of the attempt to prevent the conversion of potential dividend income into capital gain. To reduce this hazard with at least equal effectiveness but greater simplicity of method, we can borrow an idea from section 306 but simplify it so that it does not produce the anomalously variant results which now accompany that section; in doing so we can and should apply the simplified version to section 306 itself.

The first step in the proposed revision is to divide, or classify, stock and securities into two classes, the equity and the nonequity, or fixed. Ordinary common stock is, of course, the prime example of the equity security. A debt is, of course, characteristically the nonequity, or fixed, security, but a fixed, nonparticipating preferred stock is equally so. Preference alone would not necessarily make a stock nonparticipating, as it would have under section 312(b) of the House bill in 1954; a stock participating equally, or even substantially, in earnings along with common stock would be regarded as an equity security. In this connection, we should not be concerned whether stock was voting or nonvoting. As the advisory group has pointed out, this differentiation, which was originated in the 1934 act and carried forward since then, appears to have been ill conceived even for the purposes of the 1934 statute.

Having thus classified securities into equity and nonequity groupings, we could adopt a definition of reorganization at least as broad as that employed prior to 1934 and provide that an exchange of stock or securities of one corporation, a party to a reorganization for stock or securities of the same, or another corporation, a party to the reorganization, could be made without recognition of gain or loss. Gain, of course, would be recognized to the extent of cash or other property received, and it might be received without limitation of percentage or amount; nor would there be any limitation on debt obligations such as is now contained in section 354(a)(2).

Accompanying this broadening of the reorganization concept and the scope of the permissible exchange would be provisions which it is believed would guard it from abuse. They would be to the effect that if a stockholder gave up an equity security and received in exchange an equity security and one or more nonequity securities, or if he retained an equity security but received with respect to it one or more nonequity securities, there would be no apportionment of basis to the nonequity securities. The nonequity securities received in such instance would take a basis of zero. Moreover, they would be noncapital assets. And since they would thus be recognized as the potentiality of income, a provision somewhat analogous to section 691 would require that such a security retain its zero basis and non-capital-asset character in the hands of donees or legatees, or others in equivalent positions.

As will be recognized, this would facilitate reorganization transactions by imposing no tax (if there were no boot) at the time of the exchange. On the other hand, it would prevent the conversion of potential ordinary income to capital gain by any variety of the bailout device. The recipient of nonequity securities would have ordinary income to the extent of the amount received when they were disposed of, or otherwise realized upon, but bunching of this income into 1 year, and brackets unusually high for the taxpayer, could be avoided by spreading disposition over 2 or more years. As long as there is a proper continuity of basis with respect to the equity securities exchanged, the revenues suffer little loss by virtue of making the exchange tax free. It may be objected that the more the scope of the tax-free exchange is broadened, the greater the chance that death will overtake the taxpayer before he engages in a taxable realization of his investment, and a new basis will be substituted by virtue of section 1014. This argument is not entirely without force. But the answer is that defense of section 1014 is difficult in any circumstances. If any provision of the statute should yield, it should seem that it would be 1014. In any event, a rational statute cannot be constructed if 1014 is used as a fixed point of reference and all other considerations of legislative policy are required to yield to it.

The special treatment of nonequity securities would not be followed if the taxpayer gave up equity securities and received only nonequity securities. Having liquidated his equity position, he would not be in the bailout position and his basis in the equity securities given up would be transferred to the nonequity securities received, and they presumably would be capital assets in his hands. Similarly, securities received in exchange for nonequity securities would be received without recognition of gain and would take the basis of the securities surrendered.

Analogous provisions would apply to what are now section 355 transactions without the limitations of that section. If a stockholder held stock in one corporation and then, as a result of distribution or exchange of stock or securities of controlled corporations, became the owner of stock or securities of two or more corporations (the old and a new; or two new; etc., etc.), the stock of only one of them—and, of course, only the equity stock of that corporation, if the original holding had been an equity—would take the basis of the stock originally held. Probably the basis should continue with, or be applied to, the equity stock of greatest value in the case of a division giving the stockholder a plurality of corporations in which he held stock. All stock of other corporations which was received or held through the section 355 transaction, equity and nonequity alike, would take a zero basis and a non-capital-asset characterization. If the stockholder wished to retain his investment now divided into two or more corporations, he would be able to do so without tax burden and without particular limitation upon the occasion for the division. If, on the other hand, he wished to realize upon any part of his investment other than that in the one corporation in which his stock would retain basis and capital-asset character, he would do so at ordinary income rates.

B. Trusts

Code amendments have changed the taxation of trust income in several respects since the following selections were published. For example, the Tax Reform Act of 1969 eliminated the five-year limitation and other exceptions to the throwback rule, thus greatly reducing the potential tax advantage in many situations for future accumulations of trust income. The new rules are highly unpopular with many attorneys and fiduciaries and may not represent a final solution to the problem. Similarly, Section 677 of the Code was amended to treat income from property transferred in trust for the grantor's spouse after October 9, 1969, in the same manner as income from such transfers for the grantor himself, eliminating one tax avoidance technique. Finally, trusts are now subject to the rate schedule which applies to married persons filing separate returns, rather than that for single individuals (Code § 1(d)).

But the underlying problem of how to tax trust income persists today. In the first selection which follows, Professor Smith would deal with the problem by eliminating trusts altogether as a separate taxable entity and taxing trust income in all cases either to the grantor (or his estate, if he is dead) or to the beneficiaries. This approach would give increased importance to the question of when the grantor should remain taxable, which is the subject of the second selection, by one of the editors.

Professor Smith also proposes major changes in the treatment of trusts for estate and gift tax purposes. This topic is examined further in Chapter VIII.

SMITH, FEDERAL TAX REFORM 291–294 (1961) *

Trusts should be ignored for income tax purposes. Trust income should continue to be taxed to the person establishing the trust unless the transfer is sufficiently permanent and complete to make it taxable to another individual or charity. This is the first major change proposed. A transfer to be sufficiently complete to shift the liability for income taxation would be subject to either the gift or estate tax on the principal amount. When one has a sufficient interest in the income from property to be taxable on it, that is, when someone else has made a sufficiently firm transfer of property to be *not* taxable on the income from it, the property would then become subject to estate or gift tax when it or the right to receive income from it was permanently transferred on to still another person. This is the second major change. To permit discretion and flexibility in handling property for a surviving spouse or minor children, an estate might be permitted to continue as a single taxable entity for some period of time, perhaps up to twenty-one years or for the life of a surviving spouse, whichever is longer, with income from any property not definitely transferred to heirs taxable to the estate.

The results of this proposal would be to wipe out completely the tax advantages of multiple trusts or even single trusts which accumulate income, as well as the multiple-generation trusts. It would not in any way destroy the usefulness of trusts for purposes other than taxation. They could continue to be used as they have been, but they would no longer receive major tax benefits which are so great as to force their creation even where trusts are not desired for other reasons.

In its simplest terms, this set of rules would provide that a person is taxable on the income from his own property and would continue to be taxable on it until he made a complete and final transfer of the property to another person. He could not get out of his tax liability by a temporary transfer to anyone else whether the other person is an individual or a trustee. To shift liability for income taxation, he would have to make a transfer of the property to another individual, with the transfer subject to the estate or gift tax if applicable. An irrevocable transfer to a trustee would qualify if a definite beneficiary were established. If the income were to go to any one of

* Copyright © 1961 by McGraw-Hill, Inc. Reproduced with permission of McGraw-Hill Book Company.

several beneficiaries at the discretion of the trustee, the transfer would not be complete and the income would still be taxable to the person establishing the trust or to his estate.

This does not seem an unduly stringent rule for tax liability. Certainly if a person left his bonds in several safe-deposit boxes with instructions to his surviving children to go to the boxes once a year to clip the coupons and divide them up in whatever way they chose for tax purposes, with the additional right to leave some of the coupons in the boxes, each of which thereby became a separate taxable entity to be taxed on any unclipped coupons, there would be a general outcry against tax avoidance. But that is exactly the result achieved by trusts, with a trustee taking the place of the safe-deposit boxes and making them legal taxable entities.

Property could still be left in trust for as many generations as the trust law permits, but when each life interest or other definite interest was terminated, the principal amount from which the income was paid would be subject to gift or estate tax. This would not curtail the usefulness of trusts for nontax purposes; they could and would still be established to prevent a squandering of capital and to assure continued income to several generations in the future, but there would be no tax advantages over normal outright bequests. We may revert again to the analogy of the safe-deposit box. If a person could leave bonds in his boxes with instructions to his children to clip the coupons but never take out the bonds except to exchange them for other bonds to be placed in the boxes, with further instructions to leave the keys to the boxes to their children who would continue the process for their lifetimes and then turn the keys over to their children who would be the great-grandchildren of the person who rented the safe-deposit boxes in the first place—if all this could be done with only an original transfer tax when the bonds were put in the safe deposit box, there would be objection to avoidance of intervening gift or estate taxes. But that is just what can be done now if one thinks of each safe-deposit box as a trustee. Trustees have all the tax advantage of the hypothetical safe-deposit box and many other advantages, because a trustee can exercise his judgment and change investments and even pay out some of the principal to maintain a customary standard of living or meet some other specified objective.

Drastic though it may seem from some standpoints, the inclusion in one's estate of the principal sum from which one receives income seems fair and reasonable if one has not been brought up to think of trusts as separate legal entities. If a person unfamiliar with them were to hear them proposed as a new device to conserve property and permit an original owner's desires to be carried out after his death, he would probably react sympathetically and regard the proposal as a good one as long as it did not create an area for tax avoidance. What is proposed here is to unravel and wipe out the entire fabric of tax maneuver that has developed around trusts and in many instances has been the sole reason for their creation.

The new rules as a matter of fairness should be applied only to trusts created in the future. As a practical means of handling property left at death for varying uses, an estate might be permitted to be continued for a considerable period as a taxable entity. A person, in a sense, would be permitted to project himself in time as a taxable entity but not to proliferate himself into a group of new nonpersonal taxable entities. Income would be taxable to the estate until the property from which it came was transferred to an heir or to a trust with sufficiently definite terms to make the income from it and the capital sum attributable to a specific individual. Estates would not be given deductions as they now are for income distributed here and there on an interim basis to various heirs, any more than a living person can shift the liability for tax on his income by distributing the income year by year to his children and prospective heirs. The law would be no more strict on an estate than on the person whose property went into the estate. It would, to repeat, permit an individual to continue himself, through his estate, as a single taxable entity but deny the possibility of creating other new nonpersonal entities.

There would doubtless be many administrative problems in working out this new concept. It is proposed here as an objective for major reform. If the concept is accepted, exceptions should be made only to avoid impossibly complicated provisions covering special situations. The approach should be to bring all aspects of the tax law into conformity with the general objective, not to make minimum changes in the tax law to give recognition to the objective while maintaining as much of the present substance as possible.

WESTFALL, TRUST GRANTORS AND SECTION 674: ADVENTURES IN INCOME TAX AVOIDANCE *

60 Colum.L.Rev. 326 (1960).

In few other areas is a lawyer's work as tax-dominated as it is in the creation of irrevocable inter vivos trusts.[1] The articles on the subject mention only in passing, if at all, the possibility that such a trust will enable a grantor to do something with his property that he could not do as readily in other ways. Emphasis is placed almost exclusively on opportunities to use the trust device to make, at a lower tax cost, the same disposition that the grantor would have made if he had created no trust.[2] The conclusion is inescapable that irrevocable inter vivos trusts usually are created primarily to save taxes and in forms dictated by tax considerations. They are part of a nationwide adventure in tax avoidance.

The consequences of this artificially induced activity in the creation of irrevocable inter vivos trusts in general, and in particular in the creation of those most favored from a tax standpoint, are matters for public concern. The time and talent of lawyers and others have been absorbed in mastering and applying some of the most complex and intricate provisions of the Internal Revenue Code. If a trust may last a long time, the draftsman of the trust instrument must seek to anticipate such a variety of hypothetical but possible eventualities that a severe strain is placed upon human ingenuity in foreseeing and dealing clearly with the problems. And the availability of trust funds for the most attractive investment at a given time often is restricted, either by legal impediments that may be imposed by the trust instrument or by trust doctrine, or by practical limitations that may result from the conservatism of

---

1. An irrevocable trust, as the term is used in this article, is a trust that is not currently subject to revocation by the grantor, either alone or in conjunction with anyone else who is not an "adverse party" within the meaning of INT. REV. CODE OF 1954, § 672(a) [hereinafter cited CODE]. Such a trust may provide for return of the trust property to the grantor at the expiration of a stated period or may be revocable by him at that time.

Trusts revocable by the grantor alone will not be discussed in this article, as such trusts are not created to save federal income taxes during the grantor's life or federal estate taxes at his death. Reasons for their creation are discussed in CASNER, ESTATE PLANNING 87-106 (2d ed. 1956). Trusts revocable by the grantor in conjunction with another person are likewise includible in the grantor's estate, CODE § 2038, although the existence of the power to revoke will not cause the income to be taxed to him if the other person is an adverse party with respect to the exercise of such power within the meaning of CODE § 672(a). The practical significance of the "adverse party" exception is, however, somewhat limited. See note 21 *infra*. A reason for the creation of a trust revocable by the grantor in conjunction with another person may be to protect the grantor from his own indiscretions. See CASNER, *op. cit. supra* at 108-09.

2. See, *e.g.*, Drew, *Paying Family Expenses and Saving Taxes*, 37 TAXES 689 (1959); Johnson, *Trusts and the Grantor*, 36 TAXES 869 (1958); Mansfield, *Short-Term Trusts and the Clifford Rules*, N.Y.U. 15TH INST. ON FED. TAX 837 (1957); Yohlin, *The Short-Term Trust—A Respectable Tax-Saving Device*, 14 TAX L. REV. 109 (1958).

*** Copyright 1960 by Directors of the Columbia Law Review Association, Inc. Reproduced with permission.**

the trustee or the smallness of the investing units. Of course some of these objections can be minimized, at least, by adequate drafting, common trust funds, and progressive trustees; but a basic question remains: from a public standpoint, is the game worth the candle—or would we rather play another one instead?

An equally serious objection to the contemporary stress on the use of irrevocable inter vivos trusts to save taxes is that it is a game that not all taxpayers in the same income tax bracket are equally able to play. In the first place, it is open only to players who own or can borrow property to transfer in trust. Although such borrowing may permit an individual whose income is derived from personal services to get into the game, his ability to do so is likely to be relatively limited because he may be disqualified if the trust property is security for the loan.[3] Secondly, there are wide variations in the abilities of property owners to play the game successfully, or indeed to play it at all. The least sophisticated may be psychologically hobbled by a lingering linking that persists, despite the promotional zeal of corporate fiduciaries, between trusts and combinations in restraint of trade.[4] Others on a more advanced level of sophistication may be handicapped by a lack of competent counsel and cooperative trustees. And still others may be unable to bring themselves to make commitments on the basis of predictions and projections extending for a substantial period into the future.

If the device is not truly available to all, it nevertheless achieves impressive results for a few. The size of the potential income and estate tax savings is well known, and often the gift tax cost of the transfer may be kept comparatively low. What is less widely recognized is that tax reduction may often be achieved by sophisticated taxpayers without any real loss of control over the trust property. Although this is true of the estate tax as well as the income tax, the Code sections that deal with inclusion of inter vivos transfers in the gross estate are written in sufficiently general terms to leave some scope for judicial and administrative interpretation in their application to tax-minimizing arrangements.[5] There is much less room, however, for similar

3. CODE § 677(a) would seem clearly to require this result, but the cases to date have based taxability of the grantor in this situation upon actual use of trust income for repayment of his debt, rather than upon the mere possibility of such use that arises from the fact that the trust property is security. See, *e.g.*, Helvering v. Blumenthal, 296 U.S. 552, *reversing per curiam* 76 F.2d 507 (2d Cir. 1935); Rev. Rul. 54-516, 1954-2 CUM. BULL. 54. *But see* Hays' Estate v. Commissioner, 181 F.2d 169 (5th Cir. 1950).

4. At least one corporate trust officer seeks to allay such suspicions by avoiding use of the term "trust" and referring to the institution's services as an "arrangement."

5. The Commissioner's contention that the "substantial ownership" concept of Helvering v. Clifford, 309 U.S. 331 (1940) is applicable to inclusion of property in the gross estate was rejected in Helvering v. Safe Deposit & Trust Co., 316 U.S. 56 (1942). But a related contention seems to have found acceptance in State Street Trust Co. v. United States, 263 F.2d 635 (1st Cir. 1959). And Lober v. United States, 346 U.S. 335 (1953) interpreted the predecessor to § 2038 in a manner that makes it extremely difficult

flexibility in the taxation of trust income to the grantor.[6] The Code provisions are detailed and specific. If the grantor has complied with the express statutory requirements for shifting taxability, the Commissioner is expressly denied use of the general definition of gross income to require inclusion of trust income in a grantor's return on the ground of his dominion and control.[7]

Congress and the Treasury have recognized the need for revision of the Code provisions dealing with taxation of trust income.[8] An Advisory Group has recommended extensive and detailed amendments, many of which have been included in a bill recently passed by the House of Representatives.[9] However, neither the bill nor the recommendations of the Advisory Group, which in this area the bill generally follows, would make any basic change in the present rules governing taxation of trust income to the grantor. The Advisory Group did not feel authorized to propose completely new approaches,[10] and the tenor of its proposals in this area suggests acceptance and endorsement of the *status quo*. The recommendations are concerned with matters of detail and seek to make the current mode of taxing grantors work more smoothly. Changes of a more fundamental nature are needed if the present tax-motivated use of irrevocable inter vivos trusts is to be checked.

This article will be chiefly concerned with only one section of the Code: section 674, which determines the effect of a power in the grantor or a nonadverse party to control beneficial enjoyment. This section appears to have

---

for a grantor to have significant discretionary powers as trustee if the trust is not to be includible in his gross estate.

It should also be noted that although §§ 2036 and 2038 refer to a right or power of the decedent, the Regulations treat powers of a trustee as powers of the decedent if the decedent had the unrestricted right to remove the trustee and appoint himself. See Treas. Reg. §§ 20.2036-1(b)(3), 20.2038-1(a)(3) (1958). And it has been intimated that an unrestricted right of removal may cause powers nominally given to the trustee to be deemed powers of the decedent even if he could not have appointed himself as trustee. See Van Beuren v. McLoughlin, 262 F.2d 315, 318 (1st Cir. 1958), *cert. denied*, 359 U. S. 991 (1959).

6. The Code refers to treating the grantor as the "owner" of a given portion of a trust. The result of such treatment is to require inclusion of the income therefrom in his taxable income, CODE § 671; hence, that term will be used herein. "Income" will refer to the ordinary income of the trust, exclusive of capital gains.

7. CODE § 671. Justification for thus disarming the Commissioner has been found in an assumed "need for tax certainty in the area of family property planning." See Holland, Kennedy, Surrey & Warren, *A Proposed Revision of the Federal Income Tax Treatment of Trusts and Estates—American Law Institute Draft*, 53 COLUM. L. REV. 316, 361 (1953). Such certainty is not desirable if the rules themselves fail to prevent the use of tax avoidance arrangements. See *ibid.*

8. See STAFFS OF JOINT COMM. ON INTERNAL REVENUE TAXATION AND THE TREASURY DEPARTMENT, LIST OF SUBSTANTIVE UNINTENDED BENEFITS AND HARDSHIPS AND ADDITIONAL PROBLEMS FOR THE TECHNICAL AMENDMENTS BILL OF 1957, at 8 (1956); *Hearings Before the House Committee on Ways and Means on General Revenue Revision*, 85th Cong., 2d Sess., pt. 3, at 2761 (1958).

9. See ADVISORY GROUP ON SUBCHAPTER J OF THE INTERNAL REVENUE CODE OF 1954, FINAL REPORT ON ESTATES, TRUSTS, BENEFICIARIES, AND DECEDENTS, in *Hearings Before the House Committee on Ways and Means on Advisory Group Recommendations on Subchapters C, J, and K of the Internal Revenue Code*, 86th Cong., 1st Sess. 257 (1959) [hereinafter cited REPORT OF ADVISORY GROUP ON SUBCHAPTER J]; H.R. 9662, 86th Cong., 2d Sess. (1960) (proposed Trust and Partnership Income Tax Revision Act of 1960).

10. See *Hearings*, *supra* note 8, at 2759.

played the most important role in permitting the use of irrevocable trusts to achieve tax savings without any real loss of control by the grantor. But if this abuse of an ancient and honored institution is to be fully curbed, revisions may be needed in other Code sections dealing with taxation of trust income to the grantor: section 673, which allows one type of trust to shift taxability of income from the grantor even though its duration is as short as two years; section 675, which allows a grantor to have the opportunity to borrow back that which he purportedly has given away, without loss of income tax benefits when he does so; and section 677, which allows him to retain the power to use income for the support of his legal dependents without incurring tax liability for income not thus used.

Finally, revisions may also be needed in the present rules governing taxation of trust income to persons other than the grantor. Under section 678, a non-grantor often may exercise a substantial degree of effective control over the beneficial enjoyment of trust income or principal, or both, without being taxed on income not actually distributed to him or used for the support of his legal dependents.[11] In this situation, however, the problems are quite different from those that arise with respect to taxation of the grantor. There may be a sound basis for not treating a power exercisable by someone other than the grantor as having the same tax consequences to such other person as the same power would have for the grantor if possessed by him.[12] The grantor could, if he wished, have retained complete control over the property, so that any restrictions upon his control are of his own making. A person other than the grantor, on the other hand, had no similar choice unless the grantor or testator allowed him to determine the trust provisions in this respect.[13]

Moreover, any revision of the rules governing taxation of trust income to persons other than the grantor should give due consideration to the importance of flexibility in post-death property dispositions. Creation of a discretionary inter vivos trust provides no amount of flexibility in the disposition of property during the grantor's life that he would not have enjoyed as owner if he had created no trust, so long as the property remained free from claims. Thus, an assumed need for "flexibility" in property dispositions should not

11. See Casner, *Responsibilities of the Corporate Trustee as to Discretionary Trusts*, 32 TRUST BULL., March 1953, p. 21, at 24-25; Pedrick, *Familial Obligations and Federal Taxation: A Modest Suggestion*, 51 NW. U.L. REV. 53 (1956); Winton, *Taxation of Nongrantors Under Trusts for Support of Their Dependents*, 33 TAXES 804 (1955).

Minor revisions of § 678 are contained in § 109 of the proposed Trust and Partnership Income Tax Revision Act of 1960, H.R. 9662, 86th Cong., 2d Sess. (1960).

12. Of course, if a person other than the grantor partially releases a power exercisable by him alone to vest corpus or income in himself, the income tax consequences of the partial release are determined, in effect, as if he were the grantor. CODE § 678(a) (2).

13. It is not uncommon for a grantor or testator to find out before making a gift or testamentary disposition whether the prospective recipient wishes to avoid the adverse tax consequences of the possession of unrestricted rights over the property in question.

be the controlling consideration in the tax treatment of inter vivos trusts during the life of the grantor. The situation changes, however, with the grantor's death. At that time, it may be desirable, for non-tax reasons, for a grantor or testator to be able to delegate to a trustee (who may also be a beneficiary) the power that he had as owner to dispose of his property or periodically to dispose of the income from that property in the light of the changing needs of different members of his family.[14] Thus, the discussion in this article of tax-minimizing motives in the creation of discretionary trusts during the life of the grantor is not equally applicable to the use of a discretionary trust to control the post-death devolution of property of a grantor or testator. On the other hand, such post-death use may also be tax-motivated and may accordingly create problems comparable to those dealt with herein.

I. Factors That Should Be Relevant in Determining Whether a Power To Control Beneficial Enjoyment Should Cause Trust Income To Be Taxed to the Grantor

In *Helvering v. Clifford*,[15] the Supreme Court sustained the taxation of trust income to a grantor on the ground that "the bundle of rights which he retained was so substantial that [he] . . . cannot be heard to complain that he is the 'victim of despotic power when for the purpose of taxation he is treated as owner altogether.'" The grantor's retention of such substantial rights is generally accepted today as a sound basis for taxing trust income to him, but there are differences of opinion as to what rights are to be deemed "substantial" for this purpose.[16] In any event, substantiality should not be an exclusive test, either with respect to powers to control beneficial enjoyment or with respect to the other types of rights that presently may cause trust income to be taxable to the grantor.[17] If the definition of "substantial" remains liberal from the taxpayer's standpoint, as it appears to be today, the tax-motivated creation of trusts can be expected to continue unchecked. If, on the other hand, the definition were made so strict as to cause such arrangements to be ignored for tax purposes in all cases, a serious problem would be presented. It would be almost impossible to establish for any trust that the grantor could not exercise some amount of control over the enjoyment of the trust property, either because he reserved a power or because of his

14. *Cf.* Casner, Estate Planning 566 (2d ed. 1956).
15. 309 U.S. 331, 337 (1940).
16. When the Treasury Regulations based on the *Clifford* case were promulgated, there was no unanimity as to whether they interpreted the decision correctly. *Compare* Pavenstedt, *The Treasury Legislates: The Distortion of the Clifford Rule*, 2 Tax L. Rev. 7 (1946), *with* Eisenstein, *The Clifford Regulations and the Heavenly City of Legislative Intention*, 2 Tax L. Rev. 327 (1947).
17. See Rice, *Judicial Trends in Gratuitous Assignments to Avoid Federal Income Taxes*, 64 Yale L.J. 991 (1955).

ability to influence the action of a trustee or beneficiary. Rather than seek to satisfy such a rigorous requirement, prospective transferors would turn to non-trust gifts if they wished to achieve the tax savings now available from the creation of trusts. And the result would be to inhibit the use of types of trusts that may serve significant non-tax purposes and that may have only a limited potential impact upon the relative burdens of different taxpayers in similar income brackets if deemed effective to shift the taxability of income from the trust property.

All three factors, it is submitted, should be considered in determining whether a power to control beneficial enjoyment should cause trust income to be taxed to the grantor: (1) whether the grantor has retained substantial rights with respect to beneficial enjoyment of the trust property; (2) whether the type of trust he created is likely to serve significant non-tax purposes; and (3) whether the potential impact upon the relative burdens of different taxpayers in similar income brackets is likely to be serious in comparison with the impact of comparable non-trust gifts.

If *A* gives property that he owns absolutely to *B*, almost all would agree that fairness requires that *A* not be taxed upon income that is properly deemed to be realized from the property after the gift is made. The historically and constitutionally protected rights of property generally have been assumed to include the right to rid oneself of all incidents of ownership, even though the necessary result is that the taxability of income derived from property ownership may be shifted much more easily than that of income derived from personal services.[18]

Apart from questions of fairness, there are sound reasons for believing that most donors do not make widespread use of absolute gifts solely to save taxes on income properly deemed to have been realized after the gift is made. It is true that *A* may have made the gift because he wanted the income taxed in *B*'s lower bracket and because *A* thought that at the same time he could control, in one way or another, what *B* did with the property. But the potential tax savings are counterbalanced and made less significant by two factors that could even cause these savings to be nullified if *A* gives very much property to *B*: (1) The amount of taxable income that is shifted is likely to be small in relation to the value of the gift for gift tax purposes—and even if *A* thinks of the gift tax as a bargain-basement substitute for the estate tax (a concept accepted by only the more sophisticated donors), it is due shortly after the gift is made and can be large enough to be burdensome; (2) No new taxpayer is brought into the world by the gift; *B* merely has been substituted for *A*, and if *B* acquires enough income-producing property he will have tax problems of his own, if he does not already. Moreover, many donors

18. *Cf. id.* at 1001.

in *A*'s position have been disappointed in their expectations of keeping indirect control of property given away absolutely. Legally, *B* has the same control over property *A* gave him that he has over any of his other property: he can use it for his own purposes, or he can follow *A*'s directions. Over the years a large number of donees have found the first alternative irresistably attractive.

If *A* gives *B* not absolute ownership but rather some limited interest in property, without creating a trust, there is no similar uniformity of opinion that *A* should never be taxed upon the income that *B* derives from that limited interest. If *B*'s interest is merely income for a term of a few years, for instance, the income that *B* receives during the term is taxable to *A*.[19] And there are sound reasons, it is submitted, for making a distinction between gifts of absolute ownership and of limited interests of substantial duration, on one hand, and gifts of short-term interests, on the other. In each case, to be sure, *A* assumes the risk that *B* will prefer to use his interest for his own purposes, so that *A* will no longer be able to control that which he has given away unless *B* chooses to let him do so. Thus, there is reason to believe that in many instances the transfer, whether of absolute ownership or of a limited interest, is not made solely for tax reasons. But if *B*'s interest is limited and of short duration, *A*'s rights may be regarded as so substantial, because of his reversionary interest, that the first of the three factors referred to previously requires that *A* remain taxable on the income that *B* receives. Furthermore, a contrary rule would create a far more serious risk that the relative burdens of different taxpayers in similar income brackets would be distorted than in the case of absolute gifts or of gifts of limited interests of substantial duration. The shorter the limited interest given to *B*, the weaker is the deterrent effect of the gift tax, because the amount of annual income shifted to *B* becomes larger in relation to the value of the transfer for gift tax purposes.

II. The Present Statutory Scheme

Section 674, as it now stands, appears to reflect a congressional belief that property owners should be accorded a large measure of flexibility in choosing the kinds of interests they may create by transfers in trust, without loss of the income tax benefits otherwise obtainable by immediate, absolute gifts.[20] All should not be forced to pour their assets into receptacles fashioned from a common mold, to fit their varying dispositive desires into a Procrustean bed, even though such preferences may be shaped primarily by a desire to

19. *Cf.* United States v. Shafto, 246 F.2d 338 (4th Cir. 1957); Rev. Rul. 58-337, 1958-2 Cum. Bull. 13.
20. See Holland, Kennedy, Surrey & Warren, *supra* note 7, at 359.

secure a lower effective income tax rate. Accordingly a grantor is given several alternatives.

The basic choice that the grantor faces is whether he wants freedom in choosing the trustee or freedom in postponing the choice (by someone other than himself) of the beneficiaries who will actually enjoy income or principal. The Code also provides an intermediate alternative for grantors who would like a measure of each variety of freedom at the same time.

If the grantor decides he is more interested in latitude in selecting the trustee or trustees, he can name anyone, including himself, without adverse income tax consequences to him by reason of the trustee's powers to control beneficial enjoyment, so long as those powers are limited in the manner prescribed by section 674(b).[21] If, on the other hand, the grantor decides that what he wants is not so much a free hand in choosing the trustee as it is to postpone the determination of who will actually benefit from his gift, he may confer upon the trustees, if they are selected within the limitations of either section 674(c) or section 674(d), the broader discretionary powers authorized in those sections. Thus, the choice is essentially between giving the trustee the grantor really prefers limited discretionary powers and giving a trustee selected from a restricted list broader discretionary powers.

A. *Limited Discretion in the Trustee: Section 674(b)*

If the grantor is most interested in being able to select anyone, including himself, as sole trustee, without incurring adverse tax consequences for himself, the trustee's powers must be limited in the manner prescribed by section 674(b). Before considering the extent to which that section permits the trustee to be given explicit powers to affect beneficial enjoyment, it is appropriate to examine the extent to which a trustee, notwithstanding the absence of provisions in the instrument dealing explicitly with control of beneficial enjoyment, is nevertheless likely to be able to affect such enjoyment by the manner in which he exercises his usual powers as fiduciary.

1. *Usual fiduciary powers.* Although a trustee may be denied the power to change the manner in which the trust property is invested, such

21. In the following discussion it is assumed that the grantor does not hold the power in question with someone who is, with respect to the exercise or nonexercise thereof, an "adverse party" within the meaning of CODE § 672(a). A grantor may, as trustee, have broader powers than those described in the text if the powers are exercisable only with the consent of an adverse party. But the practical significance of the Code's recognition of adverse parties is limited by the tax consequences to such parties from the exercise of these powers. For example, if the grantor and *B*, as trustees, jointly hold powers affecting the beneficial enjoyment of the trust property, the mere existence of such a power has no adverse tax consequence to *B*; from an income tax standpoint, it is not exercisable "solely" by *B*, CODE § 678(a)(1), and from a gift and estate tax standpoint, it is exercisable only in conjunction with the creator of the power. CODE §§ 2041(b)(1)(C)(i), 2514(c)(3)(A). But its exercise in favor of someone other than *B* may constitute a transfer of *B*'s interest as a beneficiary and thus be taxable as a gift. See Treas. Reg. § 25.2514-1(b)(2) (1958). *But see* Self v. United States, 142 F. Supp. 939 (Ct. Cl. 1956).

power is customarily given, subject to whatever restrictions on its exercise may be imposed by the terms of the instrument or by local law. And the power to change investments may necessarily affect the beneficial enjoyment of the trust property. Assume that *A* transfers property to *T* as trustee to pay the ordinary income to *B* for ten years or until *B* dies, whichever event first occurs, and then to return the principal, including capital gains, to *A*. On its face the trust instrument gives *A* no right to control beneficial enjoyment, even if he himself is sole trustee; and the ordinary income of the trust is not taxable to *A* under either section 673[22] or section 674, although he will, of course, be taxed on capital gains realized by the trust.[23] But, as a practical matter, *A* may have retained, as a result of *T*'s power to change investments, an important element of control over the ordinary income that is payable to *B*, and, accordingly, if such a trust is treated as shifting taxability of the ordinary income from *A* to *B*, the potential impact upon the relative burdens of different taxpayers in similar income brackets may be serious in comparison to the impact of comparable non-trust gifts.

a. *Grantor's control.* The amount of income payable to *B* will depend on how the trust principal is invested. The trustee may benefit *B* by buying securities with a high yield, or he may prefer low-yield growth stocks, which may produce an increase in the value of the principal to be returned to *A* on the termination of the trust. If the trustee is *A* himself, or someone whom *A* can influence, the choice of investments may be made in a manner that allows *A* to determine, in effect, whether income is to be paid to *B* or not. But in this situation the law of trusts provides substantial protection for *B*'s interest by imposing upon the trustee a duty to dispose of unproductive property.[24] If such protection is expressly excluded by the instrument, a court should be able to find that the trust income is taxable to *A* on the ground that it could, in effect, be accumulated for *A* in the discretion of the trustee.[25] It is difficult, however, to find authority that expressly supports this conclusion.[26]

b. *Non-tax purposes.* An important non-tax motive for the creation of irrevocable inter vivos trusts may be a grantor's desire to make his depend-

22. See Treas. Reg. § 1.673(a)-1(b) (1958); Johnson, *Trusts and the Grantor*, 36 TAXES 869, 871 n.11 (1958).
23. CODE § 677(a).
24. See RESTATEMENT (SECOND), TRUSTS § 240 (1959); 3 SCOTT, TRUSTS § 240 (1956).
25. CODE § 677(a).
26. *Cf.* Treas. Reg. § 1.674(b)-1(b)(5)(i) (1956) (power to distribute corpus not limited by a "reasonably definite standard" if trust instrument provides that trustee's determination is conclusive). In the case of the federal estate tax marital deduction, the Code merely provides that a gift of income for life coupled with a general power of appointment would avoid the disqualification of an interest as a terminable one. See CODE § 2056(b)(5). But the Regulations have read into the statute a requirement that the property be income producing. See Treas. Reg. § 20.2056(b)-5(f)(5) (1958); Casner, *Estate Planning Under the Revenue Act of 1948—The Regulations*, 63 HARV. L. REV. 99, 101 (1949).

ents financially independent.[27] Undoubtedly there are grantors who have such desires, although it is the common experience of lawyers that many are only reluctantly induced to confer such independence in order to secure tax benefits.[28] Therefore, if the trust term is long enough to indicate that the grantor genuinely wished to confer independence upon the beneficiaries, the existence of such motives may be a factor that supports according recognition for income tax purposes to the creation of trusts with limited discretion in the trustee.

c. *Potential impact on relative tax burdens.* The most serious consideration opposed to recognition of trusts with limited discretion in the trustee as shifting taxability of the trust income from the grantor to the beneficiary is the potential discrimination between those taxpayers in a given income bracket who are able to create such trusts and those who, for one reason or another, are not. The amount of income that is shifted is no larger in relation to the value of the gift for gift tax purposes than in the case of a comparable non-trust gift of income from property for a term of similar duration, and in each case the beneficiary is legally free to ignore the grantor's desires as to the disposition of income that he receives. But the making of such non-trust gifts is deterred, it seems probable, by the difficulty in changing the form of investment once the gift has been made, as the beneficiary must concur in any such change. Therefore, if trusts with limited discretion in the trustee were deemed ineffective to shift taxability of the trust income, it appears probable that some would-be grantors would choose to make no transfer, rather than to make a non-trust gift of income that would make more difficult any subsequent changes in the form of investment that might appear to be desirable. On balance, however, the factor of potential discrimination between taxpayers does not appear to be sufficiently serious to warrant the denial of tax recognition to trusts with limited discretion in the trustee, if the trust term is long enough to be deemed "substantial" in a realistic sense.

2. *Variations permitted by section 674(b).* Section 674(b) does not stop with the basic type of trust with limited discretion in the trustee, which has just been described. It also uncritically places its seal of approval, for

---

27. See CASNER, ESTATE PLANNING 109 (2d ed. 1956).

28. Of course, to the extent that the trust income is used to discharge the grantor's legal obligation to support a dependent such a trust will not reduce his income tax liabilities. See CODE § 677(b). But the Regulations, in dealing with the taxation of trust beneficiaries, state that such an obligation exists "if, and only if, the obligation is not affected by the adequacy of the dependent's own resources." Treas. Reg. § 1.662(a)-4 (1956). Presumably, the reference in Treas. Reg. § 1.677(b)-1(b) (1956) to Code sections dealing with the taxation of trust beneficiaries incorporates as well the quoted definition of legal dependency, which is, of course, far more restrictive than that generally provided by state law. It is still more limited in comparison to the extent of the moral obligation that many parents feel to provide adult children with a professional education.

federal income tax purposes, upon types of trusts in which the discretionary power of the trustee is considerably greater.

a. *Permissible variations that reduce the need for court proceedings.* One category of permissible variations that appears to be unobjectionable consists of those that reduce the need for court proceedings as a result of the creation of the trust. In this category is the power to allocate receipts and disbursements between principal and income.[29] This necessarily increases the trustee's control over the amount the income beneficiary will actually receive,[30] but at the same time it performs an important function by reducing the need for recourse to the uncertain and unsatisfactory rules that have been developed in some states as to what falls into one category or the other.[31] Similarly, a power to apply income for or withhold it from a beneficiary under a legal disability may permit the use of income for the beneficiary and investment of that which is in excess of his current needs without the necessity for appointment of a guardian, or if a guardian has already been appointed, without subjecting such investment to the limitations imposed upon guardians.[32]

b. *Permissible variations that permit the alienation of the trust principal.* A second category of permissible variations consists of powers that are not very susceptible of being used primarily for the minimization of current income taxes but that do serve to allow principal to be alienated during the term of the trust. Thus a discretionary power in the trustee to distribute principal to or for a current income beneficiary with such distribution required to be charged against the proportionate share of principal held in trust to pay income to that beneficiary does not shift taxability of income if the beneficiary is currently entitled to all the income produced by his share.[33] Similarly, a power exercisable only by will has no effect on current income taxes prior to the

29. CODE § 674(b)(8).

30. This power should not, in any event, be construed to permit the trustee to diminish substantially the beneficiary's right to income. See note 24 *supra.*

31. See 3 Scott, TRUSTS § 233 (1956); Dunham, *A Trustee's Dilemma as to Principal and Income*, 26 U. CHI. L. REV. 405 (1959).

32. CODE § 674(b)(7). The Code provision goes considerably beyond what has been suggested in the text, as it does not require that the income withheld be distributed to the beneficiary if his disability terminates during his lifetime. Such a requirement would, however, introduce the complicating necessity of accounting separately for such income.

33. CODE § 674(b)(5)(B). This section does not state whether it is applicable to a discretionary power to distribute principal to a current income beneficiary if the beneficiary is not entitled, as a matter of right, to all of the income from the share held in trust for the payment of income to him. If he is not thus entitled, income may be withheld from him in one year, so that it is taxable as income of the trust. In a later year the accumulated income may be distributed to the beneficiary as "principal," and the distribution is not taxable as income to him if it falls within one of the exceptions to the five-year throwback rule contained in CODE § 665(b). Even if the throwback rule applies, the beneficiary has the benefit of a choice between different taxable years. See CODE § 668(a).

death of the holder of the power,[34] although the manner of its eventual exercise may, of course, be influenced by tax considerations.[35]

c. *Other permissible variations.* Aside from the two categories of powers just referred to and the usual power to change the form of investment of the trust property, it is submitted that the other powers that a trustee may be given under section 674(b) without adverse income tax consequences to the grantor are inconsistent with any substantial surrender of rights by the grantor if he is trustee or can dominate the trustee, are unlikely to serve significant non-tax purposes, and may have a serious impact upon relative burdens of different taxpayers in similar income brackets.[36] In the first place, the trustee (or the grantor, if he is trustee) may be given discretion to use trust income to satisfy the grantor's obligation to support his legal dependents,[37] although there is some uncertainty as to the precise effect of this provision.[38] Second, he can be authorized to withhold income from beneficiaries who are under no legal disability. Such withholding may be wholly tax motivated and not

34. See Code § 674(b)(3). It has been proposed that the provision be broadened to include powers exercisable by deed if the exercise will not confer enjoyment upon anyone until after the death of the donee. See H.R. 9662, 86th Cong., 2d Sess. § 115(a) (1960) (proposed Trust and Partnership Income Tax Revision Act of 1960); Report of Advisory Group on Subchapter J 311-14.

35. If the holder of the power predeceases the grantor, his exercise of the power may create a problem that neither the Code nor the Regulations deal with explicitly. He may exercise the power to create interests that, if created by the grantor, would have resulted in taxation of the trust income to the grantor. For example, the holder of the power may direct the grantor as trustee to pay income and principal to one or more members of a group, in the grantor's uncontrolled discretion. If the grantor had created such a trust himself, the income would have been taxable to him under Code § 674, so the critical question is whether the holder of the power is to be deemed the grantor of interests created by his exercise thereof. Under Code § 678(a), a holder of a power is, in effect, deemed to be a grantor for other purposes if he had a power exercisable solely by himself to vest income or principal in himself. But if he did not have such a power, it would seem that the original grantor should also be deemed grantor with respect to interests created by the exercise of a testamentary power by someone else. Otherwise, a grantor could create such a power in a person who had no beneficial interest and who, therefore, might have no reason to refuse to exercise the power in the manner desired by the grantor to create the type of trust that the grantor could not himself create without continuing to be taxable on the trust income.

36. Code § 674(b)(2) merely correlates the section with Code § 673, relating to reversionary interests.

37. Code § 674(b)(1).

38. The uncertainty arises from the fact that income of a trust that may be used, in the discretion of the grantor as trustee, to discharge the grantor's support obligations, could be taxable to the grantor for either of two reasons: (1) under Code § 677, on the ground that such use of income would be, in effect, a distribution to the grantor; or (2) under Code § 674, on the ground that the discretion to make such a distribution is a power of disposition. Taxability on the first ground is expressly limited by § 677(b) to amounts actually used for support. Taxability on the second ground is dealt with by § 674(b)(1), but that section does not indicate clearly whether the grantor may, as trustee, be authorized to divert income from any other use to the support of his legal dependents without becoming taxable on such income, whether or not such diversion in fact occurs. If the ability to use income for support obligations is the only discretionary power that the grantor possesses with respect to income, such power would appear to fall within § 674(b)(1). But if the grantor already possesses discretion to withhold income from a beneficiary under the type of power authorized by § 674(b)(6) or § 674(b)(7), may he, in addition, be given discretion to use income for support of dependents? The Regulations provide no clear answer.

justified as a means of avoiding the expense and formalities of guardianship,[39] and there need be no assurance that withheld income will ever be payable to the beneficiaries from whom it was withheld.[40] Third, the trustee may be authorized to distribute principal to one beneficiary, if his discretion to do so is limited by an appropriate standard,[41] even though the effect is to reduce the income payable to another beneficiary.[42] Finally, he may be given power to spray income among certain charitable beneficiaries,[43] thus permitting circum-

---

39. See p. 336 *supra*. It may be contended that a similar purpose is in fact served even though the beneficiary is not under a legal disability if his ability to handle his affairs is impaired because of age and it is desired to avoid the publicity that would result from proceedings for an adjudication of incompetency. However, this factor is unlikely to be present with the great majority of beneficiaries of trust income, and it is submitted that avoidance of such publicity in a minority of cases does not justify permitting the general use of a power with such great tax-minimizing possibilities.

40. Code § 674(b)(6). * * *

41. Code § 674(b)(5)(A). It seems to be assumed that so long as the standard is observed, the grantor lacks real power to shift enjoyment from one beneficiary to another, and that fear of suit for breach of trust will deter the grantor as trustee from straying from such observance. Both assumptions may be quite unrealistic. See p. 341 *infra*.

42. For example, assume that the current trust income is payable to beneficiary *A*, but that the principal may, in the trustee's discretion (limited by an appropriate standard), be distributed to *B*, who is not an income beneficiary. Any distribution to *B* inevitably reduces the amount of income taxable to *A*, to the extent that the principal distributed to *B* would have produced income after the date of its distribution.

If the trustee could be authorized to withhold income from *A* and at the same time to distribute principal to *B*, taxability of the withheld income could be shifted from *A* to *B*. See Code § 662(a)(2). However, the Regulations state that Code § 674(b)(6), which authorizes the creation of discretionary powers to withhold income from beneficiaries who are not under a disability, is inapplicable "if the power is in substance one to shift ordinary income from one beneficiary to another." See Treas. Reg. § 1.674(b)-1(b)(6)(i) (1956).

43. Code § 674(b)(4).

vention of the percentage limit on charitable deductions[44] without the requirement of an advance decision by the grantor as to who will benefit from the circumvention.

B. *Broad Discretion in the Trustee: Sections 674(c) and 674(d)*

If the grantor decides that what he wants is not so much a free hand in choosing the trustee as it is postponement of the determination as to who will actually benefit from his gift, he can have a spray trust in the fullest sense of the word. If the trustee is properly selected, he can be given all the powers the grantor could have had and, in addition, uncontrolled discretion either to make distributions and to decide, from time to time, which of the described beneficiaries will actually receive income or principal, or, on the other hand, to accumulate income so that for the time being no one receives any.[45] It is in this situation that the Code provisions appear to reflect a remarkably naïve set of assumptions with respect to the effective exercise of control by a grantor.

1. *Grantor's control.* The statute first recognizes that a grantor may be able to dominate a trustee who is his wife, close relative, or employee.[46] This is sound, as far as it goes, but the converse is not equally true. Because a trustee does not occupy one of these relationships it does not follow that the grantor will be unable to dominate the trustee's decisions. Nor does it follow, as the Code seems to assume, that even if one or more trustees may be dominated by the grantor because of such a relationship to him, he can not dominate the trustees as a body if an equal number are not thus related.[47]

The statute then authorizes an intermediate arrangement for grantors who are unwilling to have outsiders as trustees, but who can not quite decide whom the trust should benefit. The grantor's close relatives and employees can be made the only trustees, and they can be given discretionary power to spray income among the described beneficiaries or to accumulate it, if the power is limited by a standard.[48] It apparently is assumed that the presence of the standard will stiffen the trustees' backbones so that they will not succumb to domination by the grantor in the exercise of their discretionary power. In this respect, however, the Code sounds two refreshing notes of realism: (1) If all the trustees are close relatives or employees of the grantor,

44. See Johnson, *Trusts and the Grantor*, 36 TAXES 869, 871 (1958).
45. CODE § 674(c).
46. See CODE § 672(c).
47. See CODE § 674(c). REPORT OF ADVISORY GROUP ON SUBCHAPTER J 317-18, and H.R. 9662, 86th Cong., 2d Sess. § 115(e) (1960) (proposed Trust and Partnership Income Tax Revision Act of 1960), would change the present requirement that one-half of the trustees be "independent" to a still milder version. Only one such trustee would be needed, if concurrence of that trustee were required for exercise of the power.
48. CODE § 674(d).

they can not be given greater powers over principal than the grantor could have been given if he himself were trustee; and (2) not even the presence of a standard will be assumed to stiffen the spine of the grantor's spouse so long as the couple is living together.

If the approach of the Code is naïve, the writers on the subject have not been. The Code would confine the assumption of trustee domination by the grantor arising out of a business relationship to the situation in which the trustee is an employee,[49] and this is commonly believed not to include professional people who perform services for the grantor.[50] But it has been pointed out that the grantor's lawyer or accountant can be named as trustee and may be expected to "exercise discretion in these matters comparable to his own."[51] Even a corporate fiduciary may be susceptible to pressure from the grantor in its exercise of discretionary powers as trustee.[52] The grantor may be a customer of the commercial department as well as the trust department, or the corporate fiduciary may anticipate serving as executor of the grantor's estate and as trustee under his will if no untoward development should mar the relationship. Quite apart from such specific pressures is the more general one that arises from the nature of a fiduciary's business. As the name implies, it is engaged in the administration of trusts. A reputation in the community for being hard to get along with is unlikely to assist the work of the new business department. Finally, the grantor may have a relative who is not on the forbidden trustee list, such as a niece or nephew or an in-law, who can be counted upon in the particular family situation to be responsive to his wishes.

Of course there are, no doubt, trustees who refuse to be influenced at all by a grantor. But the position of a trustee (if he is not also a beneficiary, and normally he can not be one without complicating his own tax position[53]) is quite different from that of the donee of an absolute gift or the beneficiary

49. See CODE § 672(c)(2).

50. The Regulations contain no definition of "employee" as used in CODE § 672(c)(2).

51. Yohlin, *The Short-Term Trust—A Respectable Tax-Saving Device*, 14 TAX L. REV. 109, 130 (1958).

52. See Baer, *Keeping Control of the Spray Trust in the Family: Income Tax Problems*, 34 TAXES 734, 736 (1956); *cf.* Casner, *Responsibilities of the Corporate Trustee as to Discretionary Trusts*, 32 Trust Bull., March 1953, p. 21, at 24-25.

53. A trustee who is also a beneficiary may suffer adverse tax consequences either from (1) possession of a power to vest income or principal in himself, or (2) exercise of a power to distribute income or principal to persons other than himself. Possession of a power exercisable in his own favor solely by himself makes him taxable on trust income (unless such income is taxable to the grantor) under CODE § 678; its exercise or release may be taxable as a gift under CODE § 2514(b) and may require inclusion of all or part of the trust in his taxable estate under CODE § 2041(a)(2). Exercise of a power in favor of someone other than himself may constitute such a release of a power exercisable in his own favor, with the tax consequences just mentioned. See Treas. Reg. §§ 25.2514-3(c)(4), 20.2041-3(d)(1) (1958). Similarly, exercise of a power in favor of someone other than himself may constitute a transfer of the trustee's beneficial interest, taxable as a gift. See Treas. Reg. § 25.2514-1(b)(2) (1958). *But see* Self v. United States, 142 F. Supp. 939 (Ct. Cl. 1956).

of a non-discretionary trust. A donee or beneficiary can follow the grantor's wishes, and thus permit him to continue to exercise control over that which he purportedly has given away, but the donee or beneficiary will do so only if he is able to resist the temptation to use what he has received for his own purposes. No similar temptation confronts one who is merely the trustee of a discretionary trust, unless he wishes to commit the most flagrant form of breach of trust. Thus, such a trustee may have many reasons for doing the grantor's bidding and no compelling reason for doing otherwise.

Finally, there is the matter of the assumed spine-stiffening effect of a "reasonably definite external standard" upon trustees who are in relationships that the Code recognizes as creating susceptibility to domination by the grantor.[54] The assumption is presumably based upon a belief that so long as such trustees observe the standard they lack real power to shift enjoyment from one beneficiary to another, and that fear of suit for breach of trust will deter them from being led astray as a result of pressure from the grantor. This view is more easily stated than sustained. Even a "reasonably definite" standard is far from being so precise that a given exercise or non-exercise of the discretionary power is likely to fall clearly within or without its scope.[55] And even if the trustee recognizes that following the grantor's wishes may give a beneficiary grounds for suit, he may assume that suit will not be brought, either because of the beneficiary's relationship to the grantor or his relationship to the trustee himself.[56]

2. *Non-tax purposes.* The creation of a trust in which the trustee has limited discretion, may be motivated by a desire to give a dependent of the grantor the feeling of financial independence.[57] But if the trustee has broad discretionary powers, creation of the trust will not give the beneficiaries any justified feeling of financial independence; there will be merely a substitution of dependence upon the trustee for dependence upon the grantor. Therefore, we must look elsewhere to find a non-tax reason for the creation of such discretionary trusts.

---

54. See CODE § 674(d) (power over income). Such trustees may also be given powers over principal identical to those that a grantor may himself have as trustee without causing adverse tax consequences to the grantor. CODE § 674(b)(5).

55. The Regulations state that the entire context of a provision of a trust instrument must be considered to determine whether the required standard is present, and that if the trustee's determination is conclusive, the power is not limited by a reasonably definite standard. See Treas. Reg. § 1.674(d)-1 (1956), referring to Treas. Reg. § 1.674(b)-1(b)(5) (1956).

56. The trustee may also be immunized from suit in greater or lesser degree by an exculpatory clause or by a provision in the instrument for binding approval of his accounts by the grantor or someone else. See Westfall, *Nonjudicial Settlement of Trustees' Accounts*, 71 HARV. L. REV. 40 (1957). It is uncertain whether such a clause or provision would result in a conclusion that the trustee's discretionary power is not limited by a reasonably definite standard. See note 55 *supra*. A power in the grantor to make a binding approval of the trustee's accounts, however, may itself have adverse tax consequences to the grantor. See Westfall, *supra* at 58-59.

57. See pp. 334-35 *supra*.

It has been suggested that one such reason, applicable to irrevocable inter vivos trusts generally, is to protect the grantor's family from his creditors when the grantor is about to undertake a hazardous business venture.[58] Of course a non-discretionary trust would provide the same protection from creditors, but it may be that the grantor has funds that he wants to keep available for the benefit of the persons in his family who, from time to time, will most need assistance. A trust in which the trustee has broad discretion is ideally suited to such a purpose, but it does not follow that the grantor should be freed from taxability upon the income from the trust property.

If the anticipated threat to family financial security is from business creditors, other devices, such as broad insurance protection and non-recourse loans, may provide limited liability as well as a trust.[59] Moreover, if it is deemed unduly harsh to tax a grantor upon trust income that no longer is legally his, provision could be made by the Code for placing a prorata part of the tax upon the trust.[60]

The fundamental need that is fulfilled by irrevocable inter vivos trusts with broad discretion in the trustee is that of grantors who want to make gifts but are uncertain about to whom they want to make them.[61] This paradoxical dilemma can logically be attributed to a desire to minimize taxes and at the same time to retain effective control over the disposition of the trust property by dominating the trustee. If the grantor's real desire were for flexibility in disposing of the property, he would not create a trust at all during his lifetime. He would retain ownership himself, thereby enjoying, up to the moment of his death, the maximum flexibility of disposition known to American law.

Assume, for example, that *A* transfers property to *T* as trustee. For ten years the income is to be disposed of in *T*'s uncontrolled discretion either (a) by paying such income to *A*'s wife or to anyone who is a descendant of *A*; or (b) by accumulating income for distribution after expiration of the ten-year period to *A*'s descendants who are then living, per stirpes, or if none are then living, to *A*'s wife if she is then living or to the *X* Charity if she is then dead. When ten years have elapsed, the principal (including capital gains) is to be returned to *A*. Although the law of property has succeeded in assigning names to the interests of *A*'s wife and to those of each of *A*'s

58. See Casner, Estate Planning 110 (2d ed. 1956).

59. See Anthoine, *Federal Tax Legislation of 1958: The Corporate Election and Collapsible Amendment*, 58 Colum. L. Rev. 1146, 1175 (1958).

The corporate form may also be used in conjunction with an election under subchapter S, which may eliminate federal corporate income taxes.

60. See U.S. Treasury Department, Federal Estate and Gift Taxes—A Proposal for Integration and for Correlation With the Income Tax 50-54 (1947); *cf.* Code §§ 2206-07 (recovery of portion of estate tax from beneficiaries of life insurance and recipients of appointive property included in decedent's gross estate).

61. Another possible motive is to minimize the claims of a surviving spouse. *Cf.* Westfall, *Estate Planning and the Widow's Election*, 71 Harv. L. Rev. 1269, 1286 n.62 (1958).

descendants, merely giving names to the interests does not impart real substance to them as well. Each person is, in effect, the object of a special power of appointment and also has an interest in default of the exercise of the power,[62] but the plain fact of the matter is that no member of the group can count on getting anything until the trustee decides who is to get what. Although in form *A* may have surrendered substantial rights of ownership for the term of the trust, in fact he has not done so if he is able to exert enough influence upon the trustee to control his decisions. Of course, even a discretionary power that is in terms uncontrolled may be subject to some judicially enforced limitations, but such restrictions are unlikely to be invoked except in extreme situations.[63]

3. *Potential impact on relative tax burdens.* It must be borne in mind that recognition for income tax purposes of trusts in which the trustee has broad discretionary powers poses a far more serious threat of discrimination between different taxpayers in a given income bracket than does tax recognition of non-discretionary trusts or trusts in which the trustee's powers are relatively limited. The gift tax, to be sure, may be a greater deterrent with respect to discretionary trusts; thus, no present interest exclusion would be available for the trust described in the previous paragraph.[64] But the deterrent effect of the gift tax tends to be diminished before the greater advantages that can be gained by the use of discretionary trusts. First, income can be shifted not merely from *A* to *B*, but to *B*, *C*, *D*, *E*, or *F*—or to any one or more of as many beneficiaries as are described in the instrument—and the award of income can be made annually or more often upon the basis of projections as to the respective tax brackets of the beneficiaries for a single taxable year. Second, creation of the trust brings a new taxpayer into the world, almost as if the grantor had become a parent, but without incurring comparable liabilities for the support of a child.

The new taxpayer is granted a smaller personal exemption,[65] but in other respects it is taxed at the rates applicable to a single individual without dependents. In concrete terms, this means that a trust that accumulates $4,000 from a given year's income pays a federal income tax of $818, the same amount that is demanded of an individual if he has an income of $5,000 and claims the standard deduction. It matters not that the trust incurs none of the nondeductible personal expenses that usually absorb a large part of the income of an individual; that the accumulations may ultimately be paid

---

62. Technically, it is not the existence of the power, but rather the requirement of survival, that makes the interests in default contingent interests. See 5 AMERICAN LAW OF PROPERTY § 21.31a (Casner ed. 1952).

63. See 2 SCOTT, TRUSTS § 187 (1956).

64. See CODE § 2503(b).

65. CODE § 642(b).

to a beneficiary who was in an eighty-eight per cent bracket both in the year of accumulation and in the year distribution is made to him; or that the trust may be but one member of a large family of trusts created by a single grantor solely to secure a reduction in his income tax.[66]

If the present Code provisions were revised to restrict the number of instances in which accumulated trust income is not taxable to the grantor, the tax-minimizing use during a grantor's lifetime of trusts permitting accumulations would necessarily be reduced. Such use, however, may also continue after his death or in testamentary trusts, and thus the problem presented here is but part of a much larger problem. A partial attempt to deal with it was made in the 1954 Code, with the enactment of the five-year throwback provisions,[67] but there are such broad exceptions to the application of the throwback rule that for all practical purposes the tax advantages are as readily available today as they were under prior law.[68] Current proposals dealing with the taxation of accumulated trust income would leave unaffected the important tax advantages now available in a discretionary trust under which income can be shifted among beneficiaries from year to year as variations occur in their respective tax brackets.[69]

III. Conclusion

To date, the use of irrevocable inter vivos trusts for saving income taxes during the grantor's life has apparently been comparatively limited. In 1956, the latest year for which complete figures are available, returns were filed for approximately 360,000 trusts, reporting a total income of less than four billion dollars; and income taxable to trusts was less than seven hundred million dollars.[70] The trusts' income tax was almost two hundred and fifty million dollars,[71] indicating that much of the accumulated income is not kept in the bottom twenty per cent bracket. Probably the great majority for which returns were filed were either testamentary trusts or inter vivos trusts created by a deceased grantor, so that the amounts of taxable income actually shifted each year from living grantors to trusts or to beneficiaries may, as yet, be relatively small.

66. Both the Advisory Group's recommendations and the proposed Trust and Partnership Income Tax Revision Act of 1960 include provisions dealing with multiple trusts. See H.R. 9662, 86th Cong., 2d Sess. § 113 (1960); Report of Advisory Group on Subchapter J 263-71. A comparison of these proposals is outside the scope of this article.

67. See Code §§ 665-68.

68. See Casner, Estate Planning 599 (2d ed. 1956).

69. See note 9 *supra*.

70. See U.S. Internal Revenue Service, Dep't of the Treasury, Statistics of Income—Fiduciary Income Tax Returns—1956, at 4-5 (1959).

71. *Ibid.* See Johnson & Vernon, *Income of Estates and Trusts*, House Committee on Ways and Means, 3 Tax Revision Compendium 1759-60 (1959).

But the historical experience is alarming. Legislative attempts to curb the use of trusts to minimize taxes, from the Statute of Uses in 1536[72] to the Internal Revenue Code of 1954, have tended merely to hamper the uninformed. The statement of the Secretary of the Treasury when Congress was considering abuses of the trust device in 1937 is still pertinent today: "Vested interests grow up in tax-avoidance devices in the course of time, so that it becomes very difficult to change them after they receive a semirespectable standing."[73]

If tax-motivated transfers in trust are to be discouraged, revision of section 674 is necessary. Repeal of sections 674(c) and 674(d) would bring realism to bear upon the legislative assumptions concerning the ability of grantors to influence "independent" and "related and subordinate" trustees and would greatly restrict the opportunities that now exist to secure income tax benefits by making a gift in trust without deciding who is to receive the income from the trust property. It would also encourage the selection of trustees upon the basis of ability to render fiduciary service, rather than because of a trustee's formal qualifications to exercise discretionary powers without causing adverse tax consequences to the grantor. In addition, if income tax benefits are to be denied for the creation of trusts unless the grantor has determined, at the time of creation, who shall receive the income, sections 674(b)(4), 674(b)(5)(A) and 674(b)(6) should also be repealed.

The suggested revisions of section 674 would, of course, leave many problems still unsolved. Inadequacies in the present versions of sections 673, 675, and 677 would, no doubt, continue to lead to tax-motivated transfers in trust with the retention of substantial rights by grantors. And there would remain the problem of the taxation of non-grantors who may exercise a substantial degree of effective control over the beneficial enjoyment of trust income or principal, or both.[74] Of course, any such piecemeal approach as that proposed here inevitably encounters the initial objection that it deals with but part of a still larger problem: tax-motivated property dispositions generally.[75] But if revision of the trust provisions must await a solution of the larger problem, the wait is likely to be a long one. In the meantime, a piecemeal solution, it is submitted, is better than no solution at all.

Almost every proposal for changing Code provisions to the detriment of some taxpayers encounters the fundamental objection that there has been reliance upon the old law and that such reliance has taken the form of irrevocable arrangements.[76] Congress has, in a number of situations involving

---

72. 27 Hen. 8, c. 10 (1536).
73. See *Hearings Before the Joint Committee on Tax Evasion and Avoidance*, 75th Cong., 1st Sess., pt. 1, at 16 (1937).
74. See text accompanying note 11 *supra*.
75. See, *e.g.*, Johnson & Vernon, *supra* note 71, at 1760.
76. See, *e.g.*, Novick & Petersberger, *Retroactivity in Federal Taxation*, 37 TAXES 499 (1959).

other areas of the Code,[77] and in a few involving the taxation of trust income,[78] accorded recognition to such reliance by making new provisions inapplicable to completed transfers. It would seem, however, that no exemption of existing trusts from Code changes is appropriate here.

In the first place, it is questionable whether a majority, or even a significant minority, of the living grantors of irrevocable inter vivos trusts may properly be regarded as having "relied," at the time such trusts were created, upon an indefinite continuance of the present mode of taxation of trust income. The present scheme was first enacted with the adoption of the Internal Revenue Code of 1954, and although its provisions dealing with taxation of grantors were copied in large part from the predecessor *Clifford* Regulations,[79] reliance upon such administrative regulations is not usually thought to preclude legislative change of the underlying statute. Accordingly, the allegation of reliance would appear to be limited to grantors of trusts created after August 16, 1954, the date of enactment of the Code.

Did the post-August 16, 1954 grantors indeed rely upon indefinite continuance of the Code provisions? To assume that they did so is to credit them (and their tax advisers) with a remarketable naïveté, as the Code itself made significant changes in the pre-existing mode of taxation of trust income in respects other than the taxation of grantors. Certainly no well-advised draftsman of a long term discretionary trust would neglect to include an appropriate avenue of relief in case of an adverse change in the tax law.[80]

Second, even if some of the post-August 16, 1954 grantors were indeed sufficiently naïve to rely upon an indefinite continuance of the new provisions, a revision of section 674 along the lines just described need produce no undue hardship. A grantor who is required to include trust income in his taxable income may be given the right to recover from the trust a part of his tax.[81]

77. See, *e.g.*, CODE §§ 269, 1551.

78. The present sections dealing with taxation of trust income to the grantor, CODE §§ 671-78, are applicable to all trusts, without regard to the date of their creation. The same may be said of the tier system and the five-year throwback rule, with two minor exceptions: § 663(b) and § 665(b)(3). In view of this statutory pattern, it is difficult to find support for the statement by one member of the Advisory Group that "Congress has always been careful to prevent a statute from operating retroactively where it is too late to change what the taxpayer has already done." *Hearings Before the House Committee on Ways and Means on General Revenue Revision*, 85th Cong., 2d Sess., pt. 3, at 2792-93 (1958).

79. See Treas. Reg. 118, § 39.22(a)-21 (1953).

80. See, *e.g.*, CASNER, ESTATE PLANNING 970-71 (2d ed. 1956) (provision for release by trustee of discretionary powers).

81. Such right of recovery should, it is submitted, be created by the Code itself, rather than by state legislation, since the problem is national in its scope. In the analogous situation of inclusion of inter vivos transfers in the gross estate for federal estate tax purposes, the scope of the federal tax apportionment provisions is quite limited. See note 60 *supra*. A large number of states have enacted state apportionment legislation. See, *e.g.*, MASS. ANN. LAWS c. 65A, § 5 (1953); N.Y. DEC. EST. LAW § 124. Variations in the state statutes have created problems, see Scoles, *Apportionment of Federal Estate Taxes and Conflict of Laws*, 55 COLUM. L. REV. 261 (1955), and

Although such a recovery would, no doubt, create problems of computation and payment, it is difficult to believe that they are insurmountable.[82] Thus, the effect would be merely to change the tax rates applicable to the income of the trust, with the increase borne, in effect, by the grantor, by means of an increase in his marginal tax bracket, or by the trust, or by both the grantor and the trust, depending upon the mode of computing the amount recoverable. It has not been seriously contended that a taxpayer is entitled to a lifetime of taxation at the rates prevailing in the year of his birth.[83] Likewise, it is submitted, fairness does not require that trust income be taxed throughout the existence of the trust under the law in effect when it was created.

---

have led to proposals for enactment of more comprehensive federal provisions, see Note, 30 IND. L.J. 217 (1955), or for uniformity in state legislation, see Scoles & Stephens, *The Proposed Uniform Estate Tax Apportionment Act*, 43 MINN. L. REV. 907 (1959).

82. At least three methods for determining the amount of tax recoverable by the grantor from the trust deserve consideration. Assume that *G*, an unmarried grantor, has a taxable income of $16,000 without inclusion of $2,000 of trust income taxable to him under the proposed revision of CODE § 674. For simplicity, assume further that no part of *G*'s or the trust's income consists of capital gains. Ignoring the dividends received, retirement income, and other credits, *G*'s tax is $5,200 without inclusion of the trust income and $6,200 if it is included. *G* could be given the right to recover from the trust either (a) $1,000, the amount his tax was increased as a result of inclusion of the trust income in his taxable income; (b) $688.89, representing two-eighteenths of $6,200, or the same proportion of *G*'s total tax as his trust income bears to his total taxable income; or (c) $380, representing the tax the trust would have paid on the $2,000 if all of its income had been accumulated.

Clearly the last is the easiest method for the trustee, as the grantor's recovery is based upon the amount of trust income alone, a figure that the trustee may be expected to anticipate and to be guided by in making distributions to beneficiaries. See U.S. TREASURY DEP'T, FEDERAL ESTATE AND GIFT TAXES—A PROPOSAL FOR INTEGRATION AND FOR CORRELATION WITH THE INCOME TAX 51-52 (1947). But, in the example given, there would be a $1,000 increase in *G*'s tax, only $380 of which would be recoverable from the trust. On the other hand, under either the first or the second method it would be more difficult for the trustee to anticipate, in making distributions to beneficiaries, the amount that should be withheld to meet the liability for a prorata or marginal part of the grantor's tax. A compromise solution would allow such prorata or marginal recovery only to the extent of income received by the trustee after a demand therefor from the grantor. *Cf. ibid.*

83. *Cf. Hearings Before the House Committee on Ways and Means on General Revenue Revision*, 85th Cong., 2d Sess., pt. 3, at 2792 (1958).

Chapter VI

CAPITAL GAINS

The tax treatment of capital gains continues to be as controversial as any topic in income taxation. The first three selections here reflect a variety of proposals for change—two toward increasing the burden and one toward reducing it. Professor Slawson's article is an appropriate point of departure because of its comprehensive treatment of the problem of unrealized appreciation, even though it is confined in terms to publicly held stock. After the stock market decline of 1969 and 1970, which has, as these materials go to press, reduced the total value of listed securities by at least $250 billion from the December, 1968, level, the assumption that appreciation can be projected on a regularly recurring basis clearly is unwarranted. But the problem of how it should be treated for tax purposes when it does occur is a persistent one.

That Professor Slawson's proposal is not confined to academic discussion is indicated by the recent proposals of the Canadian Government to deal with the problem. In 1969, it proposed to its Parliament a tax reform program which included taxing certain unrealized gains. See Benson, Proposals for Tax Reform 41–42 (1969). In their treatment of shares of widely-held Canadian corporations, the proposals have many similarities to Professor Slawson's, except that only one-half the appreciation would be taxed every fifth year under the Canadian proposals instead of a tax on the full amount, computed annually, under Professor Slawson's. The proposals were based on the Report of the Canadian Royal Commission on Taxation (Carter Commission).

The Benson report also recommended taxing appreciation of property transferred by gift, but that for transfers at death there should be a carryover of the transferor's basis instead. This approach differs from that set forth in the fourth selection, in which the United States Treasury proposed that appreciation be taxed on transfers either by gift or at death, with enumerated exceptions.

With the Tax Reform Act of 1969, the United States tax system moved in the direction of treating capital gains more like other kinds of income. The Act increased the maximum tax rate for gains for both individuals and corporations, so that the application of the 25% alternative tax is limited. The total effect of the Act, however, is still to leave long-term capital gains in a much more favorable tax position than other types of income. So long as that continues to be true, there will continue to be substantial pressure on the line which separates the two. This problem is explored by Professor Surrey in the last selection in this chapter.

SLAWSON, TAXING AS ORDINARY INCOME THE APPRECIATION OF PUBLICLY HELD STOCK *

76 Yale L.J. 623–37, 644–47, 651–55, 664–76 (1967).

This nation is committed to the individual income tax as its principal source of revenue. Since 1958, the federal government has collected more money from the individual income tax than from all other taxes combined,[1] and the proportion is rising. Congress enacted legislation in 1965 that will more than double the per capita burden of the Social Security system[2]—another form of individual income tax—and repealed or reduced several important taxes not based on income.[3] Thirty-seven states levy a tax on individual incomes,[4] along with many municipalities,[5] including New York.[6] All proposals for increased public spending in the cities[7] rely heavily upon an individual income tax.[8]

1. U.S. Bureau of the Census, Historical Statistics of the United States, Colonial Times to 1957, Ser. 259-77 [hereinafter cited as Historical Statistics]. *See also* a companion volume to the above publication, Continuation to 1962 and Revisions [hereinafter cited as Continuation and Revisions].
2. Social Security Amendments of 1965, Pub. L. No. 89-97, 79 Stat. 286.
3. Excise Tax Reduction Act of 1965, Pub. L. No. 89-44, 79 Stat. 136.
4. U.S. Advisory Comm'n on Intergovernmental Relations, Tax Overlapping in the United States 25, 141 (1964).
5. *Id.* at 140-42 (29 cities with population of 50,000 or more had an individual income tax as of January 1, 1964).
6. Laws of the City of New York, 1966, chs. 773, 774 (July 1, 1966).
7. *See* Heller, *Deductions and Credits for State Income Taxes*, 51 Ky. L.J. 260, 264-67 (1962); R. Martin, The Cities and the Federal System 13-19 (1965); J. Alsop, The Washington Post, March 30, 1966, at A-25, cols. 1-3.
8. *See, e.g.*, Heller, *supra* note 7 *passim* (proposal to permit a portion of state or local income taxes to be credited against the federal income tax); Alsop, *supra* note 7 (proposal to refund part of federal income tax collected in a metropolitan area to the core city).

* Copyright © 1967 by The Yale Law Journal Co., Inc. Reprinted by permission of The Yale Law Journal Company and Fred B. Rothman & Company from *The Yale Law Journal*, Vol. 76, pp. 623–37, 644–47, 651–55, 664–76.

This method of taxation has become so important that any fault in the individual income tax is now, *ipso facto*, a fault in the American tax system as a whole.

Yet income tax laws barely touch what has become one of the most important and highly concentrated kinds of individual income: the annual increment in value of publicly traded corporate stock. Such holdings now constitute about a fourth of the nation's wealth; more than 70 per cent of it is held by or for the wealthiest one per cent of the population. The corporations that issued it typically have thousands of shareholders, few of whom exercise significant control over corporate operations. These companies obtain most of their funds for reinvestment from their earnings and almost all the rest from borrowing, and once established, they seldom issue more stock. Their self-sustained growth proceeds rapidly, at a faster pace than the rest of the economy. Their stock prices grow apace.

Shareholders with other sufficient sources of income can allow this stock appreciation to continue indefinitely; if they should need to sell, their assets are as liquid as a bank deposit. Their relationship to the process that produces their wealth is as passive as that of a depositor to his bank. But unlike depositors, shareholders enjoy substantial tax immunities. They realize only a small part of their profits as taxable dividends. Most corporate profits are reinvested in the company and reflected as appreciation in the value of its stock. Under present law less than a sixth of such appreciation is ever reported, and then usually not until years after it has accrued. Even then it is taxed at only a fraction of the rate applicable to other income. The consequent loss of revenue is immense, amounting to thirty to fifty per cent of total federal individual income tax receipts. An equally important result is that income tax liability does not even roughly correspond to ability to pay, because corporate stock is so intensely concentrated among the wealthy.

It is the thesis of this article that publicly held corporations, having grown independent of their scattered shareholders and the equity capital market, no longer require the tax incentives which encourage investment in their outstanding stock. These tax privileges, by unnecessarily favoring wealthy investors and passive accumulation, unjustly burden the talented and the energetic as well as the poor. If appreciation of publicly-traded stock were taxed annually as ordinary income, whether or not the stock was sold, the tax system would become genuinely progressive without impairing industry's accumulation of capital.

A conceptual difficulty with this proposal is its frank treatment of what has not been sold—what is "unrealized"—as "income." To date, such treatment has been used only as a marginal device to prevent tax avoidance by premature gifts of about-to-be realized assets, transfer of high-income property to private trusts, failure to call callable obligations, and the like.[9] It does not yet occupy a prominent place in income tax law[10] or, especially, in the layman's financial thinking. The typical homeowner, for example, does not consider an upward fluctuation in the value of his house as income. But even conventional thinking treats unrealized appreciation as income in some situations. For example, a depositor probably considers the rising value of his savings account as income whether or not the account is withdrawn. The Internal Revenue Service certainly takes that view.[11]

Liquidity and measurability characterize the kind of appreciation that can also be regarded as "income." Liquidity is here used in its broadest sense, taking into account any reasonable obstacle to converting property to cash—factual, legal or subjective. When all the barriers to conversion are low, the increased value of appreciated property is indistinguishable from cash in its effect on the owner's ability to pay, and ability to pay is the touchstone of liability for an income tax.

Measurability is necessary simply because if appreciation is taxed before property is sold, there must be some convenient measure of its amount other than the price realized on an actual sale. Measurability thus operates as a practical limit on how close the individual income tax can approach its own ideal of matching tax liability to ability to pay.

A few illustrations may clarify the use of the terms. Unimproved real estate held as an investment and located in or near a populated

9. *See, e.g.*, Treas. Reg. § 1.451-2 (1957) (constructive receipt of income); Rev. Rul. 66-44 and Rev. Rul. 66-45, 1966 INT. REV. BULL. no. 9 (interest accrued in respect to bank savings certificates, even though not payable until certificate for both principal and interest is surrendered, is "income" even to a cash basis taxpayer); Corliss v. Bowers, 281 U.S. 376, 378 (1930) ("The income that is subject to a man's unfettered command and that he is free to enjoy at his own option may be taxed to him as his income, whether he sees fit to enjoy it or not."—income of a revocable trust); Hedrick v. Commissioner, 154 F.2d 90 (2d Cir. 1946), *cert. denied*, 329 U.S. 719 (1946) (uncashed check); Thomas Watson, 12 P-H TAX CT. REP. & MEM. DEC. 1411 (1943) (interest accrued to account); Doyle v. Commissioner, 147 F.2d 769 (4th Cir. 1945) (right to proceeds from law suit which seemed certain to be won but on which judgment had not yet been entered). *See also* 2 MERTENS, LAW OF FEDERAL INCOME TAXATION § 12.39, at 129-30 ("A taxpayer may not turn his back upon income and postpone the year of its recognition for tax purposes by choosing not to actually receive income which is available to him. [Such income] . . . is taxable when the amount is ascertained and available to the taxpayer without restriction or is subject to his control.").

10. *Cf.* BROWNLEE & ALLEN, ECONOMICS OF PUBLIC FINANCE 242-47 (2d ed. 1954); SIMON, PERSONAL INCOME TAXATION 50-51 (1938).

11. Thomas Watson, 12 P-H TAX CT. REP. & MEM. DEC. 1141 (1943).

area is usually highly liquid, because buyers are not hard to find and because a sale of the property, by hypothesis, will deprive the seller of nothing except its investment value. But since every parcel of real estate is to an extent different from every other, smoothly functioning markets or "exchanges" in which they can be bought and sold at predictable prices do not exist. On the other hand, real estate which the owner occupies as a residence or operates for a profit, for example, a farm or a restaurant, is normally neither readily measurable in value nor readily liquidable, because a sale would materially inconvenience the seller.

But publicly traded stocks amply meet both the test of liquidity and of measurability. They can be sold quickly, easily and at a known price. For reasons that will be shown, their sale has no detrimental effect on the corporation or the economy and imposes no extraordinary hardship on the selling shareholder. Appreciation of publicly held stock therefore must be regarded as income if the income tax is to remain true to its own basic rationale, ability to pay, within the limits of measurability. How such stock could be fitted into the scheme of the individual income tax, and why that is both possible and desirable, remain to be discussed.

I. The Present System of Taxing, and Not Taxing, Capital Appreciation

Capital appreciation generally receives three tax privileges that in the case of corporate stock render its appreciation nearly taxfree. First, it is taxed only when property is sold or exchanged,[12] thus allowing the owner who retains his property to continue earning a return on the money he would otherwise have had to pay in taxes. For example, a thousand dollars of stock appreciating ten per cent per year would be worth $47,500 in fifty years if the shareholder had to reduce each year's appreciation by one-fourth in order to pay the maximum income tax applicable to such gains. The same amount of stock appreciating at the same rate for the same period without offset for an annual tax is worth $135,500. The advantage of not having to pay an annual tax is thus equal to $88,000—almost two-thirds the entire appreciation. Holding periods of this magnitude are not unusual for corporate stock. About 85 per cent of it is apparently not sold or otherwise exchanged in a taxable transaction from one generation to the next.[13]

12. INT. REV. CODE of 1954, §§ 1001, 1002 [hereinafter cited as IRC].
13. *See* text accompanying note 16 *infra*.

The second privilege eliminates all taxes on appreciation if the owner of property dies while holding it. His heir, if he sells the property, is taxed only on appreciation subsequent to his benefactor's death.[14] Finally, when (if ever) appreciation is taxed, it is at a singularly low rate: either at half what would have been paid had the same amount been earned as wages or other ordinary income, or at a rate of 25 per cent, whichever is less.[15]

The result is to reduce the effective tax rate on corporate stock appreciation to less than 4 per cent. The first two privileges permit individuals holding appreciated securities to reap the benefits of better than 85 per cent of their appreciation without ever reporting it,[16] and on the fraction reported the third privilege insures that the tax liability is never more than 25 per cent.[17] The average effective rate on ordinary income, most of which, unlike stock appreciation, is received by individuals in the lower income brackets, is about 12 per cent.[18]

14. IRC § 1014.
15. IRC §§ 1201(b), 1202.
16. In 1961 the net capital gain less loss from sales of capital assets reported as adjusted gross income was $6.0 billion. U.S. TREASURY DEPT.-INTERNAL REVENUE SERVICE, STATISTICS OF INCOME, 1961, INDIVIDUAL INCOME TAX 7, Table H. In 1960, the closest year for which data is available, the comparable figure on taxable estate and fiduciary income tax returns was $1.0 billion. U.S. TREASURY DEPT.-INTERNAL REVENUE SERVICE, STATISTICS OF INCOME, 1960, FIDUCIARY AND ESTATE TAX RETURNS 3, Table A, 25, Table 8. About 60 per cent of the income reported by fiduciaries on taxable returns was rendered nontaxable by the "distribution to beneficiaries deduction," so to avoid duplication the $1.0 billion should be reduced to $0.4 billion. *Id.* at 10-12, Table 2. Only half of capital gains reported on individual returns are includable in adjusted gross income (IRC § 1202) so the total is $6.0 times 2 plus $0.4, or $12.4 billion. About half or less of this derives from sales of corporate stock. U.S. TREASURY DEPT.-INTERNAL REVENUE SERVICE, STATISTICS OF INCOME, 1959, SALES OF CAPITAL ASSETS 10, Table 2 [hereinafter cited as STATISTICS OF INCOME, 1959, SALES OF CAPITAL ASSETS] (including a portion of the item "share of gain or loss from partnerships or fiduciaries"). So the stock-derived capital gains reported was probably about $6.2 billion. Stocks in the hands of individuals and nonprofit institutions in 1961 appreciated about $100 billion. See SEC Release No. 2042 (April 7, 1965). But because 1961 was an atypically high year, the average yearly appreciation from 1950 to 1964 will be used instead. It was $42.5 billion. (The value of such stock at the end of 1960 was $379.3 billion. *Id.* The average yearly appreciation was 11.2 per cent. Standard and Poor's Index, cited in U.S. BUREAU OF THE CENSUS, 1965 STATISTICAL ABSTRACT OF THE UNITED STATES 473, Table 647 [hereinafter cited as STATISTICAL ABSTRACT]). Nonprofit institutions hold about 5 per cent as many stocks as do individuals. NEW YORK STOCK EXCHANGE FACT BOOK 1965 [hereinafter cited as NYSE FACT BOOK 1965]. $42.5 billion less 5 per cent is about $40 billion. The fraction reported in 1961 was therefore about 15.5 per cent, that is, $6.2 billion out of $40 billion. This method of computation yields approximately the same result no matter what year is chosen.

See M. Bailey, Capital Gains and Income Taxation, 1963, pp. 8-11 (unpublished, available at the Brookings Institution, Washington, D.C.). Bailey concluded that from 1926 to 1961 the ratio of reported capital gains on corporate stock to capital gains actually accruing was about 10 per cent. His method is essentially the same as mine, but much more statistically precise.
17. IRC §§ 1201(b), 1202.
18. Total adjusted gross income from all sources in 1962 was $348.7 billion. U.S. TREASURY DEPT.-INTERNAL REVENUE SERVICE, STATISTICS OF INCOME, 1962, INDIVIDUAL INCOME TAX RETURNS 33 & Table 1 [hereinafter cited as 1962 INDIVIDUAL INCOME TAX RETURNS]. $5.8 billion of that was from sales of capital assets. *Id.* at 38 & Table 4. Total tax liability was $44.9 billion. *Id.* at 33 & Table 1. The $5.8 billion of sales of capital assets

The concern of this article, however, is only with the appreciation of the stock of large corporations with widely held stock—so-called "public corporations." To determine the revenue loss represented by the failure to tax this appreciation as ordinary income, we shall first estimate the average annual amount of such appreciation; second, estimate the distribution of the appreciating stock among taxpayers in various ordinary-income rate brackets; third, calculate the tax which that amount of annual appreciation would pay if it were realized as ordinary income; and fourth, subtract the amount of tax that it is already paying.

Annual Appreciation

The value of all individually held corporate stocks at the close of 1964 was slightly less than $600 billion.[19] They account for about a third of all individually owned wealth[20] and about half of the capital gains reported on individual and fiduciary income tax returns.[21] The value of the stock of public corporations alone at the close of 1964 was about $478 billion.[22] From 1950 through 1964 prices of publicly held stocks rose an average of 11 per cent per year, compounded.[23]

could not have accounted for more than $2.9 billion of the tax. IRC §§ 1201(b), 1202. The effective rate on ordinary income is thus at least $44.9 billion less $2.9 billion divided by $348.7 billion less $5.8 billion, or 12 per cent.

19. SEC Release No. 2042 (April 7, 1965), Table 2 (total of corporate stocks plus 81 per cent of investment company shares). Investment company portfolios contain about 81 per cent common stocks. A STUDY OF MUTUAL FUNDS, H.R. REP. NO. 2274, 87th Cong., 2d Sess. 119, 129 (1962). About 5 per cent has been subtracted for securities held by nonprofit institutions. *See* NYSE FACT BOOK 1965 at 25.

20. First National City Bank of New York, Monthly Economic Letter, July 1964, at 78.

21. STATISTICS OF INCOME, 1959, SALES OF CAPITAL ASSETS 10 & Table 2 (including an indeterminate portion of the item, "share of gain or loss from partnerships and fiduciaries").

22. (i) At the end of 1964 individuals held about $400.2 billion of the common stocks of American companies listed in the New York Stock Exchange. NYSE FACT BOOK 1965, at 25, 36 (including holdings of common trust funds and investment companies).

(ii) Institutions other than common trust funds and investment companies held about 13.9 per cent of the stocks listed on the NYSE. *Id.* The stocks listed on the NYSE as of 1962 constitute about 92.5 per cent (in value) of all listed stocks. REPORT OF SPECIAL STUDY OF SECURITIES MARKETS OF THE SECURITIES AND EXCHANGE COMMISSION, H.R. DOC. 95, 88th Cong., 1st Sess., pt. 1, at 27 (1963) [hereinafter cited as SPECIAL STUDY]. Assuming that the same per cent of all listed stocks are held by individuals as are those listed on the NYSE, this gives another $33 billion of listed stocks not on the NYSE that are held by individuals.

(iii) The value of over-the-counter stocks is something "less than one-third" of those listed. SPECIAL STUDY pt. I, at 14. We will use the figure 25 per cent to be conservative. About 41 per cent of such stocks represent companies with assets of at least $3 million and with 500 or more shareholders. *Id.* at 27. We will assume that such companies, at least, are "public." *See* text accompanying note 120. Again assuming that the per cent held by institutions on the NYSE holds approximately true throughout, we have ($400.2 plus $33) times 25 per cent times 41 per cent or about $45 billion of unlisted public-corporation stocks held by individuals. The grand total is then $478 billion.

23. During that period the average value of an NYSE-listed common stock increased 379.2 per cent. *See* STATISTICAL ABSTRACT 473 & Table 647 (stock prices, 1950 to 1964); STANDARD AND POOR'S CORPORATION, TRADE AND SECURITIES, STATISTICS: CURRENT STATISTICS COMBINED WITH BASIC STATISTICS 69 (January 1966) (stock prices, 1965). On a compounded-

However, during that period stocks underwent a revaluation, being valued substantially higher relative to earnings and book value at the end of the period than at its beginning, so 11 per cent represents somewhat too high a figure for predicting future growth. From 1950 through 1964 (data for 1965 is not yet available) the average book value per share of publicly traded stocks increased about 6½ per cent per year.[24] That rate, on the other hand, probably represents too low a figure for predicting future growth. The argument over the intentional use of federal deficits to promote full employment and rapid growth was not resolved in the affirmative until about 1964. The amount of stimulus which the economy can safely tolerate is still under dispute, but the principle of federal fiscal intervention now seems too solidly established ever to permit a recurrence of the long periods of recession and sluggish advance that characterized the fifties and early sixties. So it can reasonably be predicted that the long range rate of growth of publicly traded stocks will be better than 6½ per cent, less than 11 per cent, and probably closer to the lower figure. Applying these long range averages to 1965 stock values yields an amount of public stock appreciation for that year of from $31 billion to $53 billion.[25]

Distribution Among Taxpayers

Five years ago, Robert J. Lampman, working under the sponsorship of the National Bureau of Economic Research, published his study of

annually basis, that equals 11 per cent per year. Stocks listed on the New York Stock Exchange account for about 80 per cent of all publicly traded stocks. See note 22 *supra*. However, the other 35 per cent probably appreciated more rapidly than those listed on the New York Stock Exchange and so using the 11 per cent figure is conservative.

Values for all stocks are not available back to 1950, so a more recent period must be used for comparing the rates of growth. From 1960 to 1964 the Standard and Poor's "Standard 500" Index increased from 55.85 to 81.37, or about 46 per cent. STATISTICAL ABSTRACT 473 & Table 647. That index covers about 85 per cent in value of all stocks listed on the New York Stock Exchange, so it is fully representative of them. Letter to author from Research Department, Standard and Poor's Corporation, July 23, 1965. During the same four-year period individually held common and preferred stocks, listed and unlisted, appreciated about 58 per cent. SEC Release No. 2042, Tables 1, 2 (April 7, 1965). Thus, since the total of all stocks appreciated more than those listed on the New York Stock Exchange, those not listed on the Exchange must have appreciated much more than those that were.

24. STANDARD AND POOR'S CORPORATION, TRADE AND SECURITIES, STATISTICS, CURRENT STATISTICS 31 (August 1966) (industrials). Data for industrials had to be used because the more comprehensive "Standard 500" data is available only through 1962. But the rates of growth shown by the two sets of data are almost identical, so the use of industrials introduces no significant error. *Compare* STANDARD AND POOR'S CORPORATION, TRADE AND SECURITIES, STATISTICS, 1964 SECURITY PRICE INDEX RECORD 124 ("Standard 500" book values through 1962).

25. Eleven per cent of $478 billion is $52.58 billion, and 6½ per cent of $478 billion is $31.07 billion. The actual appreciation of public stocks during 1965 was about $40 billion. STANDARD AND POOR'S CORPORATION, TRADE AND SECURITIES, STATISTICS, CURRENT STATISTICS 31 (August 1966).

the distribution of national wealth as revealed in estate-tax data from 1928 to 1953.[26] He concluded that 82 per cent of the individually owned corporate stock was held by or for the richest one per cent of the families in the population, and counting only adults, by or for the richest 1.6 per cent,[27] and that this distribution had held steady over a twenty-five year period.[28]

Professors Butters, Thompson and Bollinger of the Harvard School of Business Administration in a 1952 survey using a confidential interview technique, found a concentration that in some ways was even more striking:[29] 65 to 70 per cent of all individually owned marketable[30] stock was held by "spending units" with a net worth of more than $250,000.[31] The authors concluded that at the time of their survey, only a "small fraction of one per cent" of the population had this net worth.[32] They concluded further that 35 per cent of such stock was held by spending units with income in excess of $50,000 (then about one tenth of one per cent of the population) and 75 per cent by spending units with incomes over $10,000 (then about 3 per cent of the population).[33] And in their opinion this data substantially understated the true concentration.[34]

There is good evidence that a larger proportion of all corporate stocks are held by institutions such as charitable foundations and pension trusts today than in the early 1950's.[35] But there is no evidence that the proportion that still remains in the hands of individuals is any less concentrated in the hands of the wealthiest. Certainly, in the light of Lampman's conclusion that the concentration did not change materially from 1922 to 1953[36]—a period spanning a series of major economic disruptions and the imposition of very high corporate and individual income taxes—it is reasonable to conclude, in the absence

26. R. LAMPMAN, THE SHARE OF TOP WEALTH-HOLDERS IN NATIONAL WEALTH, 1922-56 (1962).
27. *Id.* at 191, 195.
28. *Id.* at 208.
29. BUTTERS, THOMPSON & BOLLINGER, EFFECTS OF TAXATION, INVESTMENTS BY INDIVIDUALS (1953).
30. That is, stock that can be purchased by the public. *Id.* at 373.
31. *Id.* at 396, 399.
32. *Id.* at 399.
33. *Id.* at 440.
34. *Id.* at 393-96.
35. *See* NYSE FACT BOOK 1965 25. The portion of NYSE-listed stocks held by institutions has grown from 12.7 per cent in 1949 to 20.4 per cent in 1964. If investment companies are eliminated from the category of institutions, on the grounds that they are purely holding companies for their own shareholders, the respective portions are 8.7 per cent and 14.4 per cent. The percentage of stocks held by institutions fell slightly in 1965, however. Wall Street Journal, Feb. 3, 1966, at 13, col. 2.
36. LAMPMAN, *supra* note 26, at 209; BUTTERS, THOMPSON & BOLLINGER, *supra* note 29, at 397 ("no great change" apparent during three-year course of their study).

of any evidence to the contrary, that the distribution remains approximately the same.

The comprehensive statistical analysis of individual income tax returns published by the Internal Revenue Service for the year 1962[37] discloses that tax returns reporting adjusted gross income of $20,000 or more comprise 1.7 per cent of the total.[38] Since Lampman found that the 1.6 per cent of the adult population holding 82 per cent of the stock was also the wealthiest 1.6 per cent in other respects[39] and since personal wealth is by far the most important source of income of individuals in the highest brackets,[40] it is a fair approximation to conclude that this 1.6 per cent coincides with the 1.7 per cent of the taxpaying public reporting $20,000 or more income.[41] The accuracy of the approximation is further confirmed by the Butters, Thomson and Bollinger data,[42] and a study made in 1959 by the Internal Revenue Service.[43] An estimate of how the 82 per cent of the stock is distributed among the income levels above $20,000 can be obtained from the same Internal Revenue Service study, which also shows the distribution among various income levels of the amount of capital gains reported.[44]

Estimate of the Tax Loss

On these assumptions the $31 to $53 billion of public stock appreciation[45] would have incurred a tax liability between $16 and $27 billion

37. 1962 INDIVIDUAL INCOME TAX RETURNS was the most recent available data when this article was written.
38. *Id.*, pt. I at 38, Table 4.
39. LAMPMAN, *supra* note 26, at 191, 195.
40. 1962 INDIVIDUAL INCOME TAX RETURNS pt. I, at 38-40, Table 4.
41. In any event the accuracy of the approximation is not critical. If it is assumed even that the 82 per cent of the stock held by or for the richest 1.6 per cent of the adult population is spread out among the 11 per cent of individuals reporting the highest incomes (those reporting incomes of $10,000 or more), the estimated revenue loss from the failure to report appreciation of public stock as ordinary income amounts to only about a fifth less than if the approximation stated in the text is used.
42. BUTTERS, THOMPSON & BOLLINGER, *supra* note 29, at 393-97. Their data shows a very high concentration of corporate stock among those with the highest incomes—though because their computations were carried out in "spending units" rather than individuals and because they admitted that their results substantially understated the true concentration, their data cannot be used directly for our purposes.
43. *See* STATISTICS OF INCOME, 1959, SALES OF CAPITAL ASSETS 33, Table 3. This study showed a strikingly high concentration of reported capital gains from sales of corporate stock by members of the highest income brackets.
44. *Id.* at 36, Table 3, col. 10. No breakdown for capital gains from corporate stock alone for adjusted gross income levels of $20,000 and above is available, but the distribution of all capital gains probably does not differ materially from the distribution of such gains from corporate stock alone in the highest brackets. The distribution of the two quantities can be compared in STATISTICS OF INCOME, 1959, SALES OF CAPITAL ASSETS 11, Table 3. The distributions are seen to be very similar in the brackets above $50,000, but corporate-stock capital gain is much less common than other kinds below the $50,000 bracket.
45. *See* text accompanying note 25 *supra*.

if it had been taxed as ordinary income at the 1965 rates applicable to married couples filing joint returns. The rate tables applicable to married couples filing joint returns are the lowest of the several provided by the Internal Revenue Code.[46] Since this same appreciation in fact incurred a tax liability of only about $1 billion,[47] the revenue loss was approximately $15 to $26 billion. In 1965 the total revenue from the entire individual income tax was about $48.8 billion.[48]

The estimated revenue loss thus obtained is almost certainly too low. Approximations were intentionally conservative.[49] But even a

46. See IRC, § 1.

47. The total reported adjusted gross income derived from sales of capital assets was $5.8 billion. 1962 INDIVIDUAL INCOME TAX RETURNS 36, Table 3. Less than half of that derived from corporate stock. See note 21 *supra*. Only about 80% of that half derived from publicly traded corporate stock. See text accompanying notes 19-23, *supra*. So only $2.3 billion of reported adjusted gross income derived from sales of publicly traded stock. That means that $4.6 billion of appreciation of such stock was reported, because only half of that which is reported is includible in adjusted gross income. IRC § 1202. The maximum tax rate on that reported is 25 per cent. IRC § 1201(b), § 1202. Twenty-five per cent of $4.6 billion is $1.15 billion.

48. THE BUDGET OF THE UNITED STATES GOVERNMENT FOR THE FISCAL YEAR ENDING JUNE 30, 1967, at 55.

49. The "exclusion plus deduction" effect of charitable gifts of appreciated property was ignored. Such gifts not only fail to count as a realization for tax purposes of accrued appreciation, but are deductible to the full extent of their appreciated value against other income. Elsie Sorelle, 22 T.C. 459 (1954); Rev. Rul. 55-531, 1955-2 CUM. BULL. 520 (gift of appreciated property is not income to the donor); IRC § 170, Treas. Reg. § 1.170-1(c) (1966) (amount of deduction for gift of property to charity is market value of property at time of gift). The estimate took account of the exclusion of accrued appreciation on such gifts but not its deductibility. Certain underlying assumptions in the computation also tended to understate the amount of revenue loss. First, it was assumed that the corporate-stock appreciation received by taxpayers in different tax brackets is proportionate to the value of the stock they hold. In fact, wealthier people are probably motivated to purchase stocks that have high potential for growth but relatively low dividends in order to escape the high ordinary-income tax rates that apply to dividends. Individuals in the higher tax brackets therefore benefit from proportionately more appreciation than the value of their stock holdings indicates.

Second, the distribution of the 82 per cent of the stock held by those with adjusted gross incomes of $20,000 or more ("the wealthiest 1.6 per cent") was assumed to be proportionate to the amount of capital gains from sales of corporate stock reported on individual income tax returns. Yet most capital appreciation from corporate stock—more than four-fifths of it (see text accompanying note 16 *supra*)—goes unreported. The principal reason must be that stock is either not sold at all or sold only after its tax basis was raised by the death of the person holding the shares. The very rich must account for much more than their proportionate share of such unreported appreciation because only they can commonly afford to live on dividends or other income alone and to pass on their stock to their descendants instead of selling it. The 1959 study on capital gains, STATISTICS OF INCOME, 1959, SALES OF CAPITAL ASSETS, contains an item supporting this conclusion. The average price at which a share of stock was sold by the wealthiest category that reported capital gains income (those with adjusted gross income of $1 million or more) was almost five times the price at which it was purchased, or the value at which it was inherited, whichever initial value applied. STATISTICS OF INCOME, 1959, SALES OF CAPITAL ASSETS 11, Table 3. For those with incomes of about $10,000, on the other hand, the average share of stock had appreciated only by 1/3 its initial value before it was sold. *Id.* Stock that had appreciated by a factor of five is likely to have been held much longer than stock that appreciated only by a factor of 1/3. It seems clear that families in which stock is characteristically held for much longer periods without being sold are also families in which stock is much more likely to have been held until the owner dies.

The necessity of resorting so frequently to conservative approximations and assumptions

revenue loss of from $15 to $26 billion is serious enough. Since the loss occurs almost entirely in the highest brackets, it also contributes a severe regressive factor that eliminates most progression at all levels and introduces a sharp regression above $25,000. Counting as income the average annual stock appreciation since 1950, the effective tax rate in 1962 was 8 per cent on incomes over $1,000,000; 12½ per cent on incomes between $100,000 and $1,000,000; and 15½ per cent on incomes between $20,000 and $25,000.[50] These calculations take into account only the effect of failing to tax public stock appreciation. An even more strongly regressive pattern would reveal itself if other factors were taken into account, for example, depletion allowances.

If the available data permitted an accurate separation of investors from earned-income recipients at the same income level, it would undoubtedly show the wealthy corporate investors virtually riding free when compared to other taxpayers. The regression above $25,000 is apparent even from data that fails to differentiate the incomes of large investors from those of doctors, engineers, executives and others whose earnings over $25,000 are subject to the full progressive rates. Al-

points up the difficulty of making reliable estimates of the distribution of capital appreciation when the only accessible data are income-tax data. The fact is, wealth in the United States is immensely more concentrated than income. Some indication of how much more is that in 1959 the four one-hundredths of one per cent of the tax returns reporting the highest incomes accounted for 1.6 per cent of the total income, U.S. TREASURY DEPT.-INTERNAL REVENUE SERVICE, STATISTICS OF INCOME, 1959, INDIVIDUAL INCOME TAX RETURNS 24, Table 1 [hereinafter cited as 1959 INDIVIDUAL INCOME TAX RETURNS] whereas the same small fraction reporting the most capital gains from sales of corporate stock accounted for over 50 per cent of the total of such gains.

50. Individuals held directly or through investment companies and common trust funds about $478 billion of public-corporation stocks at the end of 1964. *See* note 22 *supra.* The average rate of appreciation of such stocks from 1950 to that time was 11.2 per cent. Authorities cited note 24 *supra.* Their appreciation during 1962 can therefore be taken as about $39 billion. At least 82 per cent of such appreciation was probably accounted for by stocks held by individuals reporting adjusted gross incomes of $20,000 or more. *See* text accompanying notes 37-44 *supra.* Eighty-two per cent of $39 billion is $32 billion. No more than 20 per cent of the $32 billion was reported. *See* text accompanying note 16 *supra.* Only half of that which is reported is includible in adjusted gross income. IRC § 1202. So the adjusted gross incomes of those with adjusted gross incomes of $20,000 or more fail to show about $28.8 billion (90 per cent of $32 billion) of appreciation on public-corporation stocks held by the individuals reporting such incomes. The percentages in the text are obtained by assuming that the $28.8 billion is distributed among the brackets above $20,000 in proportion to the amount of net gain less net loss from sales of capital assets reported by each such bracket as shown in 1962 INDIVIDUAL INCOME TAX RETURNS 36, Table 3, and that the actual tax paid by each bracket and the adjusted gross income reported by each bracket are as shown in *id.* at 33-34, Table 1. The rate for the $5000-$6000 bracket is taken directly from *id.* at 33-34, Table 1, without regard for the negligible amount of unreported public-corporation stock appreciation accruing to that bracket.

Since the foregoing computation used *averages* of public-stock appreciation taken from a 14-year period and since the *relative* amounts of gains and losses from sales of capital assets and of adjusted gross income among different brackets do vary widely from year to year, the results of the computation are not dependent upon the use of the year 1962. They would have been approximately the same no matter what year was used.

though the tax liability on $22,500 of ordinary income in 1962 was 39 per cent for a separate return and 28 per cent for a joint return, the average rate actually paid on this income was 15 per cent. The gap in tax receipts is largely accounted for by the favored treatment of investment income which begins to become a prominent income source in this bracket. The effective tax rate for higher income levels is even smaller.[51] The fact that the investor is fully taxed on his dividends changes the picture very little. From 1960 to 1964, New York Stock Exchange common stocks appreciated more than $140 billion[52] while paying dividends of only $47 billion,[53] and the wealthy investor with his "growth stocks" probably obtains an even higher appreciation-to-dividends ratio than the average.

Both the loss of revenue and the injustice to earned-income recipients will probably grow worse, because the relative importance of stock appreciation to other forms of income is increasing. The wealth represented by publicly held stocks has grown about a third more than the economy as a whole since 1950. From 1950 to 1964 the total book value of common stocks listed on the New York Stock Exchange increased about 168 per cent.[54] The sample is representative: New York Stock Exchange stocks account for about 70 per cent of the value of all marketable stocks in the country, both listed and over-the-counter,[55] and their rate of growth is probably slightly *less* than that of the other 30 per cent.[56] Over the same fourteen years the gross national product increased only 119 per cent.[57] And since the wealth represented by gross

51. 1962 INDIVIDUAL INCOME TAX RETURNS 188.

52. The figure is obtained by multiplying the average value of such stocks during 1960, *see* NYSE FACT BOOK 1965, by the Standard and Poor's price-index change from 1960 to 1964, *see* STATISTICAL ABSTRACT 473, Table 647. The figure is conservative because it ignores the appreciation attributable to shares that obtained listing privileges after 1960 whereas it includes their dividends.

53. NYSE FACT BOOK 1965, at 47.

54. Average book value increased 144 per cent. *See* note 24 *supra*. The approximate growth of total book value is derived by assuming that it bore the same relation to growth of average book value as the growth of total market value bore to the growth of average market value. The ratio of the latter two growth rates for 1950 to 1964 was 1.17. *Compare* the growth of average market prices, Standard and Poor's Stock Price Index, summarized, STATISTICAL ABSTRACT 473, Table 647, *with* the growth in total market price of all NYSE-listed stocks, NYSE FACT BOOK 1965, at 36. One and seventeen-hundredths times the growth of average book value, which was 144 per cent, is 168 per cent.

55. The stocks listed on the NYSE constitute about 92.5 per cent (in value) of all listed stocks. SPECIAL STUDY pt. I, at 27. Over-the-counter stocks equal something "less than one-third" of listed stocks. *Id.*, pt. I, at 14.

56. From 1960 to 1964 all corporate stocks held by individuals and nonprofit institutions appreciated at the rate of 12.08 per cent per year. SEC Release No. 2042 (April 7, 1965). During the same period the Standard and Poor's representative index of stocks listed on the NYSE rose at the average rate of 9.9 per cent per year. STATISTICAL ABSTRACT 473, Table 647.

57. STATISTICAL ABSTRACT 324, Table 444.

national product includes the wealth represented by publicly held stock, it can be estimated that the wealth represented by such stock has grown about twice as much as other forms of individual and institutional wealth since 1950.[58] The value of New York Stock Exchange stocks is substantially higher relative to the gross national product and the national income now than at any other time in our history, including the peak of the stock market boom in 1929.[59]

Those who write the federal tax laws have shown little enthusiasm for closing the gap between the shareholders' burden and the wage and salary-earners'. President Kennedy's 1963 Special Message to Congress on Tax Reduction and Reform proposed that the tax rates applicable to capital gain be reduced even further but also that capital assets be valued as of the date of the owner's death and appreciation up to that time be deemed "realized" and taxed.[60] The proposal would have substantially increased the revenue from capital gains tax on corporate stock,[61] but it never came close to enactment. The only significant new tax-connected proposal that has become law in recent years, the Medicare[62]-Old Age and Survivor's Insurance[63] package, will be financed in part by an increase in the Social Security tax and in part by funds from the general revenues. The increase in the Social Security tax will be sharply regressive, burdening all earned income from $0 up to $6600, taxing no income at all in excess of that amount, and applying only to wages and salaries. Not only will all profits of capital appreciation escape the tax, but so will the dividends, interest, and rents that are derived from investments.[64] A tax better fashioned to aggravate existing inequities is hard to imagine.[65]

58. The figures on gross national product and national income do not include a category for stock appreciation, so the comparison suggested in the text can only be rough. *Id.*

59. At the end of 1964, the value of stocks listed in the NYSE stood at $622.6, $509.8 (STATISTICAL ABSTRACT 324, Table 444) and $474.3 billion (NYSE FACT BOOK 1965, at 36) respectively, compared to $104.4, $87.8 (STATISTICAL ABSTRACT 324, Table 444) and $64.7 billion (NYSE FACT BOOK 1965, at 36) in 1929. The total value of all stocks, listed or not listed, is now more than $600 billion (see note 19 *supra*).

60. PUBLIC PAPERS OF THE PRESIDENTS OF THE UNITED STATES, JOHN F. KENNEDY 1963, *Special Message to Congress on Tax Reduction and Reform, Jan. 24, 1963*, at 73, 89-90.

61. See text accompanying notes 16 and 45-48 *supra*.

62. Health Insurance for the Aged Act, 42 U.S.C. § 1395 (1964).

63. Social Security Amendments of 1965, 79 Stat. 286.

64. 42 U.S.C. §§ 411(2)-11(3) (1964).

65. Its founders did not intend the Social Security tax to be as egregiously regressive as postwar Administrations and Congresses have allowed it to become. When enacted in 1937 the tax applied to wages and salaries up to $3,000 per year. STATISTICAL ABSTRACT 294, Table 403. The median wage or salary income for white employees in 1939 (the closest year for which this figure is available) was $1,112. HISTORICAL STATISTICS 168, Ser. G 169-190. In 1962 it was $5,462. *Id.*; CONTINUATION AND REVISIONS 25, Ser. G 169. A combined white-nonwhite figure is not given. The data for nonwhite shows that if it were, the propor-

Yet it is difficult to blame the Johnson Administration for choosing it. Current thinking on tax policy practically compels such a choice. Investments are considered sacrosanct, and what non-investment income remains to be taxed is almost all in the lower brackets. Ordinary earned income among the prosperous is already subject to very high rates—taxable income above $20,000 enters the 48 per cent bracket with the rate rising eventually to 70 per cent.[66] High salaries cannot be milked much further without making the tax virtually confiscatory and even a confiscatory tax would not materially increase revenues. If all taxable income above $26,000 had been taken away in taxes in 1963, for example, the additional revenue would have amounted only to $717 million,[67] less than one per cent of federal spending for that year.[68] Medicare alone will cost about four times that amount.[69] Since their preconceptions impelled them to look only to earned income, President Johnson's advisers were forced to look primarily to those whose earned incomes are small.

The prognosis is therefore that if government spending rises to meet growing needs, the wage and salary earner will have to carry the burden. Increasingly the acquisition or inheritance of investment property will become the only road to substantial personal wealth. The effect can only be to turn wealth-motivated talent away from executive, technical and professional occupations and toward positions that offer an opportunity to acquire and manipulate investments for personal gain.

Conversely, if government expenditures fail to rise to meet public needs, it may well be because wage and salary earners will balk at the sacrifice. Their resistance can be expected to stiffen as the comparative affluence of the propertied classes becomes more obvious. If taxes are to meet the growing needs of the nation without becoming a grossly disproportionate burden on wage and salary earners, they must bear more heavily on incomes derived from investments.

tionate growth would be even greater than that shown by the white-only data. *Id.* If the maximum salary or wage to which the tax was applicable bore the same relation to the median salary or wage now as it did in the late 1930's, the tax would now apply to wages and salaries up to $14,740. In fact, it was only recently raised to $6,600. *See* authorities cited notes 62-63 *supra.*

66. IRC § 1.

67. TAX FOUNDATION, INC., FACTS AND FIGURES ON GOVERNMENT FINANCE 108, Table 84 (13th ed. 1964-65).

68. Federal expenditures in 1963 were $92.6 billion. STATISTICAL ABSTRACT 392, Table 526.

69. 1965 U.S. CODE CONGRESSIONAL AND ADMINISTRATIVE NEWS 2227.

II. Adapting the Income Tax to the Situation of the Public Shareholder

* * *

C. *A Proposed System for Taxing Appreciation*

Public stock appreciation could be taxed annually. The shareholder would be taxed on the amount, if any, by which his stock increased in value during the year, each year, for as long as he had it. If he sold it, he would be taxed on the amount by which the sale price exceeded its value for the previous year. A large amount of untaxed appreciation thus would never be permitted to accrue, and there would be no tax-imposed obstacle to selling the shares whenever a more attractive use for the invested funds appeared.

The common argument against imposing a tax on the increased value of an asset before it has been sold is the difficulty of assessing the extent of the increase. The exchanges, however, eliminate this difficulty for public stocks. A shareholder could not justly complain if in his opinion the market was too low a measure of the value of his shares for tax purposes, because the tax difference would be in his favor. He could not justly complain that it was too high either, because (unless he were a control shareholder, whose special problems will be discussed below) he could sell the shares and, with no tax penalty for liquidating his investment, make an extra profit on the market's apparent miscalculation.

Only those relatively few individuals or, more often, institutions, that hold such large blocks of a single stock that they cannot sell any large portion of it in a short time without depressing the market, might reasonably complain that the market price was an unfairly high measure of real value. Such unfairness should be minor. Every day brokers and large-portfolio administrators manage the problem of disposing of large blocks of stock at a price that is not very far below the market.[100] Even if it is assumed that the market would always exceed by a few points the realizable value of a large block of stock, the over-estimate of appreciation during the first year the shares were held would be cancelled out when they were sold. Full freedom to average gains and losses over successive tax years would insure this. The problem might also be attacked directly. The same factors making it diffi-

100. The average turnover of mutual fund portfolios in 1965 was 19 per cent, compared to only 16 per cent for all NYSE-listed stocks. Many funds were substantially higher than even 19 per cent. Wall Street Journal, March 8, 1966, at 1, col. 6, and 28, col. 1.

cult to dispose of a large block except at a few points below the market might have been in operation when the block, or chunks of it, were acquired. The holder who could show that he acquired a block at less than the market price might be permitted to value it thereafter at the amount below the market at which it was purchased, to avoid paying tax on an artificially high measure of income the first year after the purchase. Such an exception to the otherwise uniform valuation rules should be manageable if limited to very large blocks.

The relatively minor fluctuations of day-to-day trading could be adjusted for tax purposes with an appropriate formula for defining "official tax value." The average of the daily closing prices for the calendar year or perhaps for the last few months of the year might be used, for example. Exact figures could readily be computed and published by the Internal Revenue Service itself, or by the principal exchange on which the particular stock was traded. The officially computed values could be published shortly after the close of the year in leading newspapers, and supplied to brokers and banks.

For those public corporation stocks that are not listed on an exchange (in terms of dollar value, something less than 14 per cent of the total)[101] the "bid" and "asked" quotations on the over-the-counter markets—an informal collection of brokers and dealers throughout the nation who buy and sell stocks not listed on an exchange[102]—could serve the same function as the daily closing prices on the exchanges. Much of the uncertainty and roughness presently existing in the quotations could be ironed out by computerizing the operation of the market as an SEC special study recently recommended.[103] But the principal guarantee of a fair tax valuation for over-the-counter as well as listed stocks would be the use of a long-term average rather than any given daily quote; the value for tax purposes would thus never be higher than a price at which the stock could actually have been sold for substantial periods during the year.

Under some circumstances taxing stock appreciation annually would force a shareholder to sell a part of his portfolio to pay the tax on the whole. For example, in a good year during which the value of his shares rose an average of 15 per cent and paid dividends of 3 per cent, a shareholder in the 50 per cent bracket who was unwilling to borrow and had

101. The value of over-the-counter stocks is something "less than one-third" of those listed. SPECIAL STUDY pt. I, at 14. About half in value of over-the-counter stocks are stocks of corporations with 500 or more shareholders. *Id.* at 27.

102. SPECIAL STUDY pt. II, at 541.

103. *Id.* at 657, 669-70.

no other source of cash would have to sell shares equal in value to 5.2 per cent of his holdings. He would be left with a portfolio equal to 109 per cent of its pre-rise value, free of all future tax claims. It is immaterial that he might have preferred not to sell, even at an appreciated price. Tax assessments limit everyone's ability to invest, and there is nothing in the situation of the public shareholder to justify giving him any special consideraton. And any supposed loss from having to sell a part of his holdings to pay the tax on the rest in a market that supposedly failed to reflect the shares' "true" worth, as will be shown below, would have been offset, or more than offset, by his not having to pay tax on the appreciation of their full value.

To permit those public corporations which needed equity financing to raise capital by issuing more shares,[104] new shares might be granted the privilege of taxation at the present low capital-gains rates and only if they were sold or exchanged, for a substantial period after their issuance. Capital-gains treatment for about fifteen years would seem long enough to maintain the individual's (or financial institution's) incentive to make such an investment. Favorable tax treatment for new issues would mean that they would temporarily command a higher price than a corporation's previously outstanding stock of the same class. But the additional complication thus injected into the market would still be less than already exists with respect to bonds. Several issues, or "series," of bonds are frequently outstanding from a single issuer at one time, and the market has long since shown that it can adapt to them. The certainty that the favorable capital gains treatment would terminate in a set number of years would, of course, still represent a slight deterrent to investors, compared to the present promise of endless tax freedom. But the period of exemption from the appreciation tax could be made long enough to minimize any deterrence. Moreover, when the great bulk of outstanding public stock was being taxed annually at ordinary rates, newly issued shares carrying a fifteen-year immunity would look very attractive by comparison and probably would be more saleable than they are now. The proposed tax on appreciation, therefore, if the government chose to couple it with a sufficiently liberal exemption for newly issued shares, could even serve to stimulate the issuance of new stock.

* * *

104. Whether shares issued under executive stock option plans should be deemed "new issues" for this purpose is a question beyond the scope of this article. Such shares are issued in order to compensate executives to an extent that the tax laws would otherwise not permit rather than to raise capital.

E. *Defining "Public Corporation Stock"*

Public corporations ought to be distinguished from other corporations for tax purposes simply by the number of shareholders: 500 would seem ample to assure the public character of the corporation. This is the number set by the Securities Act Amendments of 1964 for deciding which corporations must meet the proxy and reporting requirements of the Act.[120] The rationale of the "500 rule" is that the stock is certain to be publicly traded when it has so many stockholders, and the relationship between management and actual and potential shareholders has become so distant that regulatory safeguards are necessary to assure access to information about the company.[121] (The Securities and Exchange Commission found 300 to be the appropriate number of shareholders[122] but Congress chose the higher number.) Similar reasoning supports use of the same number for defining a public corporation in our sense. Taxation of stock appreciation also rests on the existence of a market for public trading; and the dispersal of ownership, which prevents easy access to information, also diminishes shareholder control, a significant factor in our analysis of the public corporation.

The only other test which the Securities Act Amendments impose for a "public corporation" is gross assets equal to or in excess of $1 million.[123] Such a test would be convenient for weeding out companies whose total appreciation probably would not produce enough revenue to make it worthwhile to tax them. However, nothing in the logic of taxing public corporation stock requires an assets test.[124]

A second problem would be to avoid discouraging normal corporate financial activity through the application of the tax. A closely held corporation and its controlling shareholders might hesitate to make a public offering either of newly issued shares or of the controlling shareholders' stock. Shareholders of a closely held corporation might hesitate to sell out to, or merge with, a larger corporation if the bargain required them to receive publicly traded shares in exchange. Or two or more closely held corporations might hesitate to combine if the combined number of their shareholders was sufficient to constitute a public corporation. Of course, shares with a public market are substantially

120. § 3, 78 Stat. 567 (1964).
121. SPECIAL STUDY pt. V, at 150-51; H.R. REP. No. 1418, 88th Cong., 2d Sess. 3013, 3018 (1964).
122. *Id.*
123. § 3(c), 78 Stat. 567 (1964).
124. In the opinion of the SEC, nothing in the logic of the securities laws required it either. *See* SPECIAL STUDY pt. V, at 150-51.

more valuable—all other things being equal—because they have a higher degree of liquidity. But in most cases, the advantages of high liquidity would probably not be enough to offset the unfavorable tax consequences of going public.

In order not to discourage the transition, shares might be exempted from the appreciation tax for a substantial period, say fifteen or twenty years, after they enter the category of publicly traded stock. The length of the delay period would determine the impact of the tax on the decision to go public: the longer the period, the smaller the effect on price of the impending tax liability. A sufficiently long delay period would reduce the impending tax's effect on price to the point where it was outweighed by the increased value attributable to going public. Fifteen or twenty years ought to suffice for such a result, since the liability of virtually all other publicly traded shares to the appreciation tax would render those with a temporary tax immunity especially desirable. The deterrent to going public could also be reduced by leaving sales of the shares during the grace period entirely free from taxation, even at the capital gains rates that currently apply.

Transactions in the other direction would also have to be taken into account. A relatively small number of persons might seek to buy up all the outstanding stock of a public corporation, or the corporation itself might seek to redeem its shares from a number of shareholders. A public corporation might "spin off" a smaller corporation to a small group of its shareholders. Or a large publicly held concern could conceivably divide itself into two or more parts, each with a smaller number of shareholders. But each of these possible courses of action would seem distinctly less likely than its opposite. The second and third would require the corporation to divide its business into two or more parts, a difficult maneuver,[125] made especially troublesome by the need to assign shareholders to different parts of the company while maintaining the relative value of their holdings. All three courses would threaten management's power and therefore usually incur its opposition. The first would create or enlarge concentrated centers of shareholder power capable of challenging management's exclusive control, the second would reduce the scope of management's power by splitting off a portion of the business and the third would have the same effect by dividing the company. Finally, the second and third courses would normally threaten the profitability of the business itself, to the detriment of both management and shareholders. The component

125. *E.g.*, First Security Nat'l Bank & Trust Co. v. United States, 382 U.S. 45 (1965).

corporations would have less monopoly power than the single large company of which they once formed the parts, and if the spin-off or division cut across related product lines, they might also have fewer economies of scale.

Nevertheless, the tax rewards of ceasing to be public might overweigh all other considerations unless some provision were made to reduce them. Again, it would seem sufficient to delay the new units' relief from the appreciation tax for a substantial period beyond the status-changing event. Under the circumstances something like ten years should suffice. The period need not be as long as the period chosen for changes in the other direction because of the nontax considerations mentioned and because when the contemplated changes are in the nonpublic direction, delaying their tax consequences would have an especially powerful effect. First, it would reduce the present value of escaping from the appreciation tax by delaying the change of tax status. Second, it would subject the shares involved to very heavy taxation during the period of the delay, because their price would rise in anticipation of their freedom from the appreciation tax at the end of the period, and price rises during the period would continue to incur annual taxation at ordinary-income rates. Third, since the shareholders could not sell sizeable portions of their holdings in order to pay taxes on the remainder without dispersing ownership and thereby defeating the whole tax avoidance scheme, their high tax liabilities would have to be paid out of other assets. And finally, the third effect would reinforce the second. The necessity of limiting sales would drive the price of the shares higher and so impose even greater tax liabilities.

There might be an exception to the ten year delay for companies whose stockholders could show that there was no longer a readily available market for their shares and that the disappearance of the market was not a result of their own tax-motivated actions. The appreciation tax would be a real hardship for such investors since they could not conveniently sell shares in the company to meet the tax assessments. These corporations are also likely to be the ones which lack a sufficient volume of recent trading to measure their appreciation during the year. For the sake of avoiding the evaluation problem the Internal Revenue Service might be just as happy to forego the tax proceeds they would generate if covered by the appreciation tax.

Once established, delay periods could be used for a variety of regulatory purposes. For example, since current tax law strongly favors corporate mergers,[126] overall tax neutrality might be achieved by choosing a somewhat shorter delay period for corporate acquisition or combinations than for other methods of going public. If an acquisition or combination involving a sufficient number of shareholders to render the combined corporation public would result in the shares becoming subject to the appreciation tax in, say, only ten years instead of fifteen or twenty, shareholders' reluctance to incur the appreciation tax might just offset their eagerness to receive the more traditional tax benefits of combining corporate units, and would leave their decision, as it probably should be, unaffected by the totality of tax factors.

The difficulties that might arise from a too frequent or too easily manipulated change of status could also be alleviated by establishing not one but two changeover lines: the higher one to operate to change a company's status from nonpublic to public and the lower to change it from public to nonpublic. A corporation that became public by virtue of an increase in the number of its shareholders could then lose the status only if the number was quite substantially reduced, and a similar result would follow from a change in the other direction.

* * *

126. Hellerstein, *Mergers, Taxes and Realism*, 71 HARV. L. REV. 254 (1957). There are also powerful nontax pro-consolidation forces at work in the economy, *see* McCarthy, ACQUISITIONS AND MERGERS 11-13 (1963); Houghton, *Mergers, Superconcentration and the Public Interest*, in SUBCOMM. ON ANTITRUST & MONOPOLY OF THE SENATE COMM. ON THE JUDICIARY, ADMINISTERED PRICES: A COMPENDIUM ON PUBLIC POLICY, 88th Cong., 1st Sess. (1963) [hereinafter cited as ADMINISTERED PRICES].

IV. The Chimera of Double Taxation

A. *Taxes and Profits*

The proposed tax would radically redistribute the burden of the federal income tax and ultimately bring about a wider dissemination of the profits of big business. Hence, it will be vigorously opposed. One certain objection[151] is "double taxation"—the alleged unfairness of taxing stock appreciation as individual income when it is already subject to the 48 per cent levy on corporate income. Supposedly, corporate profits are reduced by about half before the shareholders benefit from them. According to this argument, even the present application of the individual income tax to dividends constitutes "double taxation." Applying it also to appreciation would complete the injustice. But in fact, the 48 per cent corporation income tax is not reducing corporate profits by anything close to that amount, because the corporate economy has long since shifted all, or at least substantially all, the tax forward to the consumer in the form of higher prices.[152]

For many years, it was economic orthodoxy that the burden of the

151. *See, e.g.*, Humphrey, *How the New Tax Bill Can Promote Prosperity*, LIFE, Mar. 15, 1954, at 37-43; D. HOLLAND, THE INCOME TAX BURDEN ON STOCKHOLDERS xi and *passim* (1958) (entire book written on assumption that shareholders bear at least half of the corporation income tax); D. SMITH, FEDERAL TAX REFORM, THE ISSUES AND A PROGRAM 189-203 (1961).

152. The discussion that follows assumes for simplicity that the principal method of shifting the corporation income tax, by raising prices, is the only method. There are others. As will be argued below, a long-range failure to shift the tax to consumers may result in not just an impairment of shareholders' profits but also of labor's; *i.e.*, a failure to shift the tax to consumers may result in a partial shift to labor. To an indeterminate but probably substantial extent there is also shifting back to the government—a shift that operates as a reduction of the effective tax rate. The laws permitting the value of an asset to be depreciated for tax purposes more rapidly than it actually declines, *e.g.*, IRC § 167-70, operate to defer taxes and so give a corporation the use of money that it would otherwise have to pay currently to the government. Such money, since the obligation to repay it at the deferred day of tax reckoning is dependent upon there then being sufficient profits to permit repayment, is essentially that most valuable kind of money—equity money, available for high-risk investments. Estimating its value conservatively at 10 per cent per year, the value to a corporation of being able to defer the first 5 years' tax on the profits of an asset with a useful life of 10 years until the last 5 years of its life is about one-fourth the amount of the entire tax. The effective rate on the asset is thus reduced from 48 per cent to 36 per cent, 12 per cent being "passed back" to the government. *Cf.* Alabama-Tennessee Natural Gas Co. v. FPC, 359 F.2d 318 (5th Cir. 1966) (FPC may require natural-gas company to pass on to consumers savings from accelerated depreciation permitted by IRC § 167). Because this and other methods of shifting also exist, the method of raising prices does not have to bear the whole burden of keeping profits at their pre-tax level.

corporation income tax fell on the corporation and its stockholders.[153] If the firm were assumed to be maximizing profits, supposedly the normal behavior in both competitive and monopolistic markets, it followed that the tax could not be shifted. The profit-maximizing output of the firm is determined by its marginal revenue and marginal cost for additional units of production, which in turn are dependent upon the demand for the firm's output and the cost of inputs. Because neither demand levels nor input costs seemed to be affected by a "mere" profits tax, economists traditionally thought that the profit-maximizing level of output would be unchanged by the imposition of the tax. The hapless entrepreneur could do no better than to continue at his pre-tax level of output, turning over part of his profits to the government.

Modern economic theory, however, is more optimistic about the ability of corporate business to shift the corporation income tax forward to consumers. Obviously, if businesses are not in fact maximizing profits—in the sense of equating marginal revenue and marginal costs—they may be able by raising prices to shift forward part of the tax,[154] and there is increasing agreement that businessmen work for

153. To avoid misunderstanding, I want to emphasize that my concern is *only* with the shifting that occurs *from shareholders* (which is to say, from corporate equity capital), not from capital generally or even from corporate capital generally. Thus, the conclusion drawn by Harberger, *The Incidence of the Corporation Income Tax*, 70 J. POL. ECON. 215 (1962), that the corporate income tax is in substantial part not shifted from capital (generally) is not directly pertinent here.

But it can be made pertinent. Professor Harberger's conclusion rests on the premise that the market for capital throughout the United States is sufficiently fluid, or "perfect," that the return net of risk and tax on *all* kinds of capital tends toward uniformity in the long run. *Id.* at 215-17. So his conclusion that capital generally bears the burden of the tax is tantamount to saying that the tax is "spread out" over all the capital in the economy, uniformly reducing returns everywhere. Since the total amount of capital is approximately four times the amount of corporate equity capital (*see* STATISTICAL ABSTRACT 407, Table 549 (debt capital); 490, Table 671 (relative amounts of corporate and noncorporate business); 495, Table 679 (corporate equity capital)), even if his conclusion that none of the burden of the corporate income tax is shifted from capital generally is correct, corporate equity capital itself will bear only a fourth of it. That is, about 75 per cent shifting *from shareholders* does occur.

However, Professor Harberger's reliance on the premise undermines even his own initial conclusion. It follows from the premise that if the return on any kind of capital has been reduced by the corporation income tax, so has the return on debt capital, and by the same amount. But if interest rates are lower than they would be absent the tax, it must be because the tax has influenced the thinking of the Board of Governors of the Federal Reserve System, which controls the level of interest rates. However, Professor Harberger's demonstration contained no reference to government monetary policy.

154. An oligopolistic industry might not be producing at a profit-maximizing level either because the members fear that antitrust eyebrows will be raised if they make a concerted effort to find the profit-maximizing level of output and prices, or because side-payments among firms would be required to obtain agreement upon the price which would maximize industry-wide profits. *Cf.* W. FELLNER, COMPETITION AMONG THE FEW (1949).

goals other than profit maximization.[155] But even in an economy of profit-maximizers, the corporate income tax is passed on if the proceeds of the tax finance additional government spending which, in turn, causes sufficient inflation to restore the old level of net corporate profits.[156] This result is consistent with profit-maximizing, because the rise in total spending has changed the companies' demand functions. The result is no different than if a general sales tax had been imposed instead.

But one need not resort to economic theory to get a rough picture of how taxes are commonly shifted in two sectors of the economy which together include most of the public corporations. The government commissions that set prices for the regulated industries[157] are required by law or custom to set them high enough for companies under their jurisdiction to earn profits equal to some fixed proportion, usually about 6 per cent, of their invested capital. An income tax on profits is regarded as an additional cost, which the regulated companies are allowed to cover by raising prices. Where the regulated company has a complete, or nearly complete, local monopoly on whatever it sells, it faces no effective restraint on its power to raise prices and so will do so to the full amount allowed. Even where regulated competition exists (for example, between railroads and trucks), the result is ultimately the same, because the commissions will, if necessary, force both competitors' prices up to prevent either from making "uncompensatory" marginal profits at the other's expense.[158] Regulated industries

155. *See, e.g.*, E. PENROSE, THEORY OF THE GROWTH OF THE FIRM (1959).

156. In a time of rapidly rising aggregate demand, the ability of the corporation to shift the burden of the corporation income tax will be enhanced by the fact that wages and salaries are likely to rise less quickly than commodity prices. If all prices were completely flexible, input costs would move up as rapidly as output costs, and shifting could not occur so readily.

157. *E.g.*, COLO. REV. STAT. § 115-3-1(1). *See generally* NICHOLS, RULING PRINCIPLES OF UTILITY REGULATIONS, RATE OF RETURN ch. 1, §§ 1 and 2, at 1-7 (1955).

158. NICHOLS, *supra* note 157, ch. 1, § 1, at 1, and ch. 24, § 4, at 435; Cook & Cohn, *Capital Structures for Public Utilities Under the Public Utility Holding Company Act*, 45 VA. L. REV. 981, 997-98 (1959). The actual process of rate setting is more complicated than the text indicates, but the result is the same. Rates are set with reference to a "base" that normally equals, or is closely related to, gross investment. For example, a utility with assets of $100 million, debt of $60 million and shareholder equity of $40 million, might have its rates set so as to guarantee a return of 6 per cent on $100 million, not $40 million. Utility managements therefore commonly try to borrow as much as they safely can at interest rates below the rate of return on their "base," in order to increase profits on shareholders' equity. Cook & Cohn, *supra* note 158, at 981, 998-1001. However, it can easily be demonstrated that an increase in rates sufficient to keep the return on the "base" at 6 per cent despite an increase in taxes will also keep the return on shareholders' equity at the same level as before the tax increase. *See, e.g.*, All Freight from Eastern Ports to the South, 251 I.C.C. 361 (1942); All Commodities, L.C.L., between Maine, Massachusetts, and New Hampshire, 255 I.C.C. 85 (1942) (regulated competition).

account for 12 to 16 per cent of the corporate business in the country.[159] Most of the prices set by large corporations outside of the regulated industries are "administered," that is, set by deliberate private decision.[160] One company announces a price, which the others then parallel or lower. The process ends when all prices reach the level of those of the lowest-priced company having significant market power. But since every company wants to keep its profits as high as possible without inviting new competition or serious public disapproval, prices normally end up high enough to provide what the industry consensus regards as a reasonable return on capital for most companies in the industry.[161] And since here too taxes are regarded as costs, the "reasonable" return is net of taxes and thus the same whatever the tax rate.[162]

The evidence points to the conclusion that the shifting forward of the corporation income tax has been substantially complete. Although the necessary data are not available for earlier periods,[163] in which there was no corporation income tax, the double taxation argument is seriously damaged if it can be shown that, between the nineteen-twenties and the present, corporations have been successful in shifting the great increase in corporation taxes.

During the late twenties, the federal corporation income tax ranged from 11 to 13½ per cent;[164] from 1951 to 1965, the tax was between 48 and 52 per cent.[165] In addition, state corporation income taxes were rare in the twenties but had become common in the fifties.[166] The

159. In 1962, assets of utilities accounted for about 12 per cent of all corporate assets, and profits of utilities accounted for about 16 per cent of all corporate profits. STATISTICAL ABSTRACT 498, Table 684, and 499, Table 687.

160. KAPLAN, DIRLAM, & LANZILLOTE, PRICING IN BIG BUSINESS 130 (1958). *See* ANN. REP. OF THE COUNCIL OF ECONOMIC ADVISORS 88 (1958), printed as part of the 1966 ECONOMIC REPORT OF THE PRESIDENT ("The exact diagnosis [of inflation not caused by excessive demand] remains a matter of some disagreement among economists. But almost all agree that an important part of the explanation lies in the fact that, in many industries, unions or managements or both possess considerable discretionary power to set wages and prices, . . .").

161. *See* Means, *Pricing Power and the Public Interest,* and Means, *The Reality of Administered Prices,* in THE CORPORATE REVOLUTION IN AMERICA 77-96, 213-22, 226 (1962). *See also* KAPLAN, DIRLAM & LANZILLOTE, *supra* note 160, at 130.

162. Means, *Pricing Power, supra* note 161, at 221-22.

163. *See* HISTORICAL STATISTICS 581, 582-85, for other relevant data.

164. CCH 1966 STAND. FED. TAX REP. ¶ 153.

165. TAX FOUNDATION, INC., *supra* note 67, at 110-11, Table 86.

166. UNITED STATES ADVISORY COMMISSION ON INTERGOVERNMENTAL RELATIONS, TAX OVERLAPPING IN THE UNITED STATES 25-26 (1964). Thirteen states had a corporation income tax before 1929. Thirty-seven plus the District of Columbia now do. From 1959 to 1963 one state enacted a corporation income tax, 12 raised their rates, two raised their rates twice and one repealed its tax. *See also* TAX FOUNDATION, INC., *supra* note 67, at 174-75. The combined effect of federal and state corporate income taxes is compared for 1929, 1939, 1949, 1959, 1962, and 1963 in *id.* at 43, Table 26. See rows entitled "Corporate profits before tax" and "Corporate profits tax liability."

depression of the thirties was a period of abnormally low corporate profits. If depression rates of return were used as a base, the postwar corporation income tax would seem to be the handmaiden of a great increase in profits on equity capital.[167] The late twenties, on the other hand, provide a conservative comparison. If the after-tax rate of profits on equity capital is as high today as it was then, surely the much higher corporate income tax today cannot be having an appreciable effect.

The First National City Bank of New York has kept records which reveal the average ratio of corporate profits to net assets every year since 1925 for manufacturing corporations and every year since 1928 for all corporations.[168] The records are accurate;[169] they cover about 90 per cent of the corporate economy,[170] and the firms they represent are almost all publicly held corporations.[171] They are, therefore, ideal for our purposes.

These records disclose that corporate profits after taxes relative to investment today are slightly *higher* than they were when the corporation income tax took a much smaller portion of before-tax profits. According to First National City, the average after-tax rate of return was 10.4 per cent from 1950 through 1964, and 10.3 per cent from the years 1928 and 1929.[172] *Thus, despite a near quadrupling in the level of the federal corporation income tax and the imposition of numerous state corporation income taxes, the after-tax return on shareholder investment is at least as high today as it was in the twenties.*[173]

But historical comparisons are unnecessary to refute the assertion that the current corporation income tax rates of about 50 per cent are

167. *See* HISTORICAL STATISTICS 580-81. Profits as a percentage of shareholders' equity can be computed by dividing the amounts shown in Ser. 95 by the sum of the amounts shown in Ser. 81-85.

168. ECONOMICS DEPARTMENT, FIRST NATIONAL CITY BANK, NEW YORK, AVERAGE ANNUAL RATES OF RETURN.

169. Lewis, *Corporate Profits*, FINANCIAL ANALYSTS' J. 40-41 (July-August 1964).

170. *Id.*

171. *Id.*; ECONOMICS DEPARTMENT, FIRST NATIONAL CITY BANK, *supra* note 168. The First National City Bank records are made up from published reports of corporations to their stockholders, which strongly weights them toward publicly held corporations.

172. ECONOMICS DEPARTMENT, FIRST NATIONAL CITY BANK, *supra* note 168. And as this is being written, unofficial estimates place 1965 profits at a level 16 per cent higher than 1964 profits. Wall Street Journal, Feb. 17, 1966, at 1, col. 6, and 8, col. 2. *See also* Hall, *Direct Shifting of the Corporation Income Tax in Manufacturing*, 54 AM. ECON. REV. SUPP. 258, 271 n.9 (1964) (average rate of profit after taxes on gross investment in 1919-30 and 1936-40 was 5.94 per cent and in 1941-59, 5.97 per cent).

173. The recent empirical study of Krzyzaniak and Musgrave supports this conclusion. The authors developed an econometric model of the corporate economy of the United States and, on the basis of this model, determined that the corporation income tax had in fact been slightly over-shifted. M. KRZYZANIAK & R. MUSGRAVE, THE SHIFTING OF THE CORPORATION INCOME TAX (1963).

reducing corporate income by anything close to 50 per cent. The double taxation argument involves an assumption that "normal" corporate profits are twice those actually being earned. Under that assumption, the rate of profits on shareholders' equity in manufacturing corporations during the first half of 1965 would have been 26 per cent, instead of its actual 13.0 per cent,[174] the average rate for the four largest automobile manufactures in 1963 would have been 39.8 per cent,[175] and for General Motors alone in 1963, 46 per cent[176]—nearly enough profits to buy another General Motors every two years! Rates of return as high as these would be an absurdity in a mature industrial economy. Yet the "double taxation" argument forces its proponents to predicate them as the norm.

The "double taxation" argument also assumes a revolution in federal monetary and debt-management policies that, to say the least, would be unlikely. Corporate profits do not exist in a vacuum. The market for capital in the United States (and, increasingly, in the entire western world) is sufficiently fluid that abnormally high returns in one sector ultimately bring higher, or are reduced by lower, returns in other sectors.[177] Witness, for example, the strikingly quick and forceful manner in which higher interest rates drew money away from stocks and thereby lowered stock prices during the spring and summer of 1966.[178] So sustained corporate profits at twice their present levels would operate to draw interest rates, too, up to commensurately higher levels. If the Treasury and the Federal Reserve failed to take remedial measures to increase the availability of credit, to keep interest rates down,[179] rates would rise to levels never before seen in the United States in modern times. Among other results, the cost of carrying the national debt would be multiplied and the ability of state and local governments to borrow would be seriously impaired. But if, as seems more likely, the Treasury and the Federal Reserve did take remedial measures, the resulting increased supply of money and lower interest rates would in time bring down corporate profits too.

One other quantitative measurement indicates that the corporation

174. FTC News Release S-2076 (Sept. 13, 1965).

175. FTC, Report on Rates of Return for Identical Companies in Selected Manufacturing Industries, 1954-63, at 47, Table 9-3711.

176. *Id.*

177. Harberger, *supra* note 153, at 215-17.

178. N.Y. Times, Sept. 4, 1966, at E-1, cols. 1-2; Tobin, *Check the Boom*, The New Republic, Sept. 3, 1966, at 10.

179. *See* Robinson, Boehmler, Gane & Farwell, Financial Institutions 673-75 (3d ed. 1960).

tax has not reduced profits. Data compiled by Professor Simon Kuznets of the National Bureau of Economic Research show that from about the turn of the century to 1930, the share of equity (as opposed to debt) in long-term corporate external financing averaged 35 per cent, that in the twenties it reached a relatively high average of 43 per cent and that almost immediately after the Second World War, it dropped to a 1946-1953 average of 21 per cent.[180] The decline has not reversed itself since the period covered by the study. Except for the atypical AT&T offering in 1964,[181] the share of equity in corporate financing has been decreasing almost yearly since 1953.[182] Indeed, if midyear prognostications held true, net corporate bond issues for 1965 totaled $8 billion and net equity issues $800 million—a mere 10 per cent portion for equity, even disregarding the additional diluting effect of institutional borrowing other than through bonds.[183]

The drop in equity financing is too enduring to be merely a chance deviation.[184] Nor does it seem chance that the history of the corporation income tax almost exactly parallels that of the debt-equity ratio. The tax was first enacted in 1909, remained at a modest level until the Second World War, then shot up sharply, and has remained high since.[185] The increases in state income taxes since the war have reinforced the impact of the federal tax.

A simple example illustrates how the passing-on of the corporation tax could account for the parallel development of the tax and the debt-equity ratio. The Jones Corporation, operating in a tax-free business world, contemplates a one-million-dollar expansion program upon which it expects to realize a return in excess of costs of $100,000 per year. In determining how much of the investment it should borrow and how much it should finance by selling stock (we are ignoring the

180. S. KUZNETS, CAPITAL IN THE AMERICAN ECONOMY 278, 381-86, 417-19 (1961).

181. AT&T is atypical because as one of the wealthiest natural monopolies in the world it has a strong political incentive to have as many shareholders as possible. For an indication of how the support of its shareholders can serve its interest against the FCC, the agency that regulates it, *see* Wall Street Journal, Feb. 8, 1966, at 1, col. 1. *See also* THE NEW YORKER, Feb. 5, 1966, at 33.

182. Gorman & Shea, *Capital Formation, Saving and Credit*, SURVEY OF CURRENT BUSINESS, May 1965, at 14-15; Wall Street Journal, August 20, 1965, at 1, 11; STATISTICAL ABSTRACT 502, Table 693. The figures given in the cited authorities include the "Comsat" offering, which should be ignored because it was not for the purpose of raising capital for an existing company.

183. Wall Street Journal, August 20, 1965, at 1, col. 6 and 12, col. 6.

184. Professor Kuznets explores several possible explanations and remains unsatisfied that they are sufficient to account for the trend. KUZNETS, *supra* note 180, at 276-82, 418-19.

185. TAX FOUNDATION, INC., *supra* note 67, at 110-11, Table 86.

possibility of using internally generated equity funds), Jones will take into account three basic factors: the cost of borrowing, that is, the interest rate it must pay; the risk of borrowing; and the "cost" of equity money. The last factor is determined for externally obtained equity money by comparing the price at which the company can sell shares of its stock to the return it is already earning on its invested equity funds; the object is not to dilute the earning power of existing shares by selling new shares too cheaply, and, if possible, to increase their earning power.

Suppose that Jones can borrow up to $500,000 from its bankers at 6 per cent and decides to do so to the limit, leaving the remaining $500,000 to be financed from equity. It can then expect an interest cost of $30,000 per year and a return on equity of $70,000, or since $500,000 of equity funds are involved, a rate of return on equity of 14 per cent. If that rate of return is materially better than the price-earnings ratio of Jones' outstanding stock, the chances are that it can raise the additional $500,000 by selling new shares, without diluting its established earning power per share. If it is less, the investment will not give existing shareholders a profit and should probably not be undertaken. A measure of the risk of borrowing half the million dollars needed is that the expected return in excess of costs of $100,000 per year will exceed interest charges by $70,000; if actual earnings fall short of expected earnings by more than that amount, the company will be forced to meet its obligations by dipping into receipts from other operations. The $70,000 is sometimes called the "earnings coverage."

If a 50 per cent corporate income tax were imposed and generally not passed on in the form of higher prices, the three factors would remain the same. The expected after-tax rate of return on the equity portion of the investment would drop to 7 per cent, but since, by hypothesis, the rate of return on *all* corporate equity investment throughout the economy would have dropped by a like amount, stock buyers would be just as eager to buy Jones' shares now at its lower expected rate of return as they were prior to the imposition of the tax, and the number of shares that would have to be sold to raise the $500,000 would be no greater than it was before.

But if we assume that the corporate economy generally has been able to pass on the tax in the form of higher prices, the second of the three factors—the risk of borrowing—undergoes a striking change. The generally higher prices prevailing would have increased the total expected return of Jones' investment from $100,000 to $170,000.[186] That amount less $30,000 interest, less 50 per cent (for tax) of the balance, leaves $70,000 after taxes as the return on equity—the same as before. Thus, actual earnings could now fall short of expected earnings by $140,000—twice as much as the previous "earnings coverage"—without Jones Corporation having to meet its obligations out of receipts from other operations. The first and third factors again remain the same. In such a situation, the company and its bankers would be foolish not to re-assess the risks involved and substantially increase the amount of the loan. By doubling "earnings coverage," the corporation income tax has enabled a given amount of equity to carry with it a much larger amount of debt, at no greater risk. It is no wonder that the 50 per cent corporate levy in effect since about the Second World War has profoundly influenced the course of corporate finance. The SEC has even given official recognition to the tax's impact in this respect by allowing public utilities to carry higher debt ratios.[187]

B. *The Effects of Reduced Profits*

The "double taxation" argument has a second weak point, independent of any alleged reduction in corporate profits. The conclusion that the application of the individual income tax to the shareholder would be unfair presupposes that stockholders are uniquely disadvantaged by any reduction in corporate income resulting from the corporation income tax. But if the corporate tax were repealed, the additional after-tax income would ultimately have to be shared with other income recipients and/or reduced by lowering the prices of corporate products. Sustained extraordinary profits would almost certainly bring on irresistible union demands for wage increases. White-collar employees would participate in the increase too, in part because management would want to maintain what it considered a proper ratio between white-collar salaries and wages in the plant, and in part because when profits are high, management can take some of the credit and reward itself accordingly. About 44 per cent of the national

186. This is an approximation for the sake of simplicity. Actually, expected earnings would not have had to rise quite so much in order to bring the after-tax rate of return on equity up to what it was before the imposition of the tax, because the tax's effect of reducing the risk of borrowing would have encouraged corporations to borrow more heavily, which in turn would have increased equity's "leverage" and, consequently, its rate of return.

187. *Cf.* Cook & Cohn, *Capital Structures of Public Utilities Under the Public Utility Holding Company Act*, 45 VA. L. REV. 981, 1001-06 (1959); Cook, *We've Got the Most Enterprising Utility in This Country*, FORTUNE, May 1964, at 138, 182.

income is received as corporate wages or salaries.[188] Thus, if the corporation income tax is really reducing corporation income, about half the working taxpayers in the country have grounds for joining shareholders in the cry of "double taxation." But in the important industries at least—those whose prices figure prominently enough in the statistical price indices for the government to take notice when they rise—it is academic to talk of the possibility of much higher profits than now exist anyway. The recently institutionalized federal surveillance of all important price changes[189] would ultimately require that widespread extraordinary profits be shared with consumers through a price reduction or, more likely, through the slower process of holding prices steady while wages increased.

Finally, even if the corporation income tax has reduced corporate profits and the reduction has in turn reduced shareholder income more, proportionately, than other kinds of income, it still does not follow that every shareholder has a just cause for complaint if he is also subjected to an individual income tax. The corporate tax rates have been at their present level since about 1940. Shares that have been bought and sold since 1940 have therefore changed hands at a price that reflected their presumably lower after-tax earnings. The individual who has purchased his shares since 1940 is therefore earning as much on *his* investment as he would had the tax not existed.[190]

On the other hand, the individual who has owned his shares since before 1940 has probably been unhurt by the present tax structure even if the corporation income tax has not been completely passed on. If it is conceded that half of the burden of the corporation income tax has been passed on to consumers or others—and the comparative profit figures leave no reasonable doubt that at least that much must have been shifted—it can be shown that a shareholder who has held shares since before 1940 and has been in at least the 50 per cent tax bracket during most of the intervening years has by now benefited more from the present tax structure than he would lose from the enactment of a tax on appreciation.

A 52 per cent corporation income tax that is about half passed on

188. In 1962 national income was $453.7 billion, of which $198.7 billion was compensation of corporate employees. NATIONAL INDUSTRIAL CONFERENCE BOARD, THE ECONOMIC ALMANAC, 1964, 115, 131.

189. *See Guideposts for Noninflationary Price and Wage Behavior*, 1966 ANN. REP. OF THE COUNCIL OF ECONOMIC ADVISORS 88-93. See also *Government Considers Cut in Structural Steel Buying as Part of Effort to Push Back Bethlehem Price Rise*, Wall Street Journal, Jan. 3, 1966, at 3, col. 1-3.

190. GOODE, THE CORPORATION INCOME TAX 26 (1951).

would, by definition, reduce $100 of corporate profits to $74. Corporations generally distribute about two-thirds of their after-tax profits as dividends.[191] About $49 to $50 out of the $74 would therefore be paid as a dividend, and a shareholder in a 50 percent bracket would be taxed another $24 to $25 upon its receipt. The $24 to $25 retained by the corporation and reinvested would not be further taxed. The total reduction brought about by the combined effect of the corporation and individual income taxes on the shareholder's $100 of corporate profits would thus be about $50—exactly the same as he would have paid in taxes had there been no corporation income tax and he had instead been taxed directly on his full share of the company's profits. A similar computation would show that if the shareholder's topmost tax bracket had exceeded 50 per cent he would have had *more* left after taxes under the present system than if he had paid only his individual rate on his entire share of the company's profits. Prior to 1963, all taxable income above $16,000 for a single person and above $32,000 for a married couple was taxable at 50 per cent.[192] Since corporate stock is very highly concentrated among the wealthy[193] and since that stock which has been held for long periods is even more highly concentrated than stock generally,[194] it is reasonable to conclude that almost all stock that has been held continuously since 1940 has been held by taxpayers with incomes that usually placed them in brackets of 50 per cent or higher. Such stock, therefore, has contributed more after-tax income to its owners during the past twenty-five years than it would have if their share of corporate profits had been taxed directly as individual income—that is, *more* than if there had been no "double taxation." And a simple calculation shows that the extent of the benefit in nearly all instances has been enough to overweigh any detriment that would now occur if a tax on stock appreciation were enacted.[195]

191. From 1958 through 1964 corporations earned $170.7 billion and paid $110.0 billion in dividends. STATISTICAL ABSTRACT 496, Table 682.

192. 1962 INDIVIDUAL INCOME TAX RETURNS 188.

193. *See* text accompanying notes 26-40 *supra*.

194. *See* note 49 *supra*.

195. Pre-1963 rates went as high as 91 per cent, *see* 1962 INDIVIDUAL INCOME TAX RETURNS 188, but the calculation will be carried out for a taxpayer in only a 60 per cent bracket. Assuming a half-passed-on corporation income tax, $100 of corporate profits is reduced to $74, and $50 paid out as dividends is subject to a 60 per cent individual income tax and so reduced to $20. The shareholder's after-tax income is thus the sum of the $24 retained by the corporation after its taxes plus the $20 left in the shareholder's pocket after he has paid his own taxes on his dividends, or $44. Taxed directly and only once on all his profits at a 60 per cent rate, the shareholder would have had $40 left. So he benefited

V. Conclusion

The principal justification for favorable tax treatment of corporate stock appreciation is that an investment in stock constitutes an investment in production facilities. But once a share is issued, the investment in production facilities is complete and can hardly justify a tax immunity for as long as the share is outstanding. It is said, however, that a market for new stock must be continuously maintained by promising it the same tax freedom as is accorded the old. Even this secondary argument is weak when applied to public stock. The value of outstanding public shares is immense, and public corporations have demonstrated not only that they can, but that they prefer to obtain capital without issuing new stock. It is at least questionable that the preservation of an insignificant and disdained market is worth the loss of about $15 to $25 billion in annual revenue to the government and the destruction of virtually all correspondence between tax liability and ability to pay. In any event, the choice is unnecessary. Fixed-term immunities on new issues would maintain the market in spite of a tax on outstanding shares. Such a system would, in fact, increase the attractiveness of new shares in the total market.

The other possible justification for favorable tax treatment of stock is that it represents an effective instrument of corporate control. But no shred of operational control remains in the public shareholder, and the little, largely formal, power he still has over the election of directors and the disposition of facilities on a sale or merger would be unaffected by the removal of his tax privileges. What the public shareholder actually has is only a bare claim on corporate income—no more than an "uncashed check" payable to bearer in the amount of the latest market quote. On established principles, in the absence of the mystique of "investment," the shareholder's claim would clearly be taxable as current income.

$4 per year. Using a discount rate of only 6 per cent, $4 per year from 1940 through 1965 would amount to $300 today.

Now assume that the individual income tax is made applicable to appreciation as well as dividends. $100 of corporate profits would be reduced to $74 by the unpassed-on portion of the corporation income tax, just as before. The entire $74 would now be taxed to the shareholder at the rate of 60 per cent, however, rather than only that portion distributed as dividends. The retained portion would be manifested as an increase in the value of his stock, and be taxed as appreciation. So his individual income tax would be 60 per cent of $74, or $44.40. His $100 of corporate profits would suffer a total reduction of $74.40: $26 from the corporation income tax plus $44.40 from the individual income tax. That is $10.40 more than he would have had to pay had there been no corporation income tax and he had instead been taxed directly and only once on all of his portion of the corporation's profits. The present value of $10.40 per year from now to eternity discounted at 6 per cent is $173. The loss is thus only slightly more than half the gain already realized.

The results of the present tax treatment of corporate stock ownership are easy to see: the prices of public stocks are inflated and the great majority of shares are held by the very rich, who benefit most from their favorable tax treatment. The wealthy have been allowed to bypass the "progressive" individual income tax, because they are able to cast a large portion of their income in the form of stock appreciation. Those with earned incomes are virtually left to bear the burden of the tax alone, at a time when the earned-income occupations of administrator, scientist and professional are needed more than ever before and when the public corporation and its related financial institutions are rendering the individual holder of accumulated wealth almost economically superfluous. Whatever concentration of individual wealth is considered desirable could be more fairly maintained by taxing public stock and high earned income alike and, if necessary, lowering the rates on both.

The administrative difficulties of taxing public stock appreciation seem surprisingly few. The national exchanges already supply both the price information that would make annual taxation feasible and the ready market that is one of the principal justifications for it. Computers could hold and marshal the needed market data and produce it at year end for public use. The necessary exceptions for new issues and corporate reorganizations are relatively simple and seem workable.

Perhaps most significantly, the recognition that public stock appreciation is taxable income would effect an unprecedented redistribution of large-company stock. For the first time, those with moderate incomes would hold large numbers of public shares. Purchases by institutional trusts and funds that confer their benefits on a broad section of the population would be further stimulated. The nation as a whole, which through government grants and the money spent on corporate products, has for decades paid for nearly all corporate research and expansion, would finally begin to receive a fair share of the profits.

GOODE, THE INDIVIDUAL INCOME TAX 199–207 (1964) *

A New Method of Taxing Capital Gains and Losses

The arguments so far examined point to the conclusion that capital gains should be taxed like other income, except for a provision to alleviate the effect of the application in one year of graduated tax rates to gains that have accrued over several years. Equity also seems to call for full deductibility of capital losses from taxable income, again with a provision for correcting the effect of bunching.[23]

Even the case for relief from discrimination due to bunching of realized gains and losses is weaker than is sometimes implied. The discrimination is partly or wholly offset by the advantages of postponing tax until the gain is realized. Tax postponement allows the investor to earn a return on the amount that will later be paid in tax. Bunching, moreover, increases the tax only when the investor is raised into a higher tax bracket than he would occupy if the gains were distributed over the years during which they accrued. Movements between brackets may not occur when the gain is small relative to taxable income. If gains on different assets are realized in more or less equal amounts each year no discrimination occurs even if gains are bunched on each asset and are large relative to total income.

Some form of spreading of gains and losses, nevertheless, would be desirable to avoid harsh treatment of recipients of large and irregular capital gains or losses. The objective would be to approximate the tax result that would have occurred if the gain or loss had been realized in equal installments over the period during which the investor held the asset. Since it would be impracticable to reopen past-year returns, the adjustment would have to be made on the

[23] The bunching under consideration occurs because losses are taken into account only when realized; its alleviation is in principle distinguishable from general averaging of income for tax purposes (see Chapter IX). Capital gains and losses would be irregularly distributed among years even if taken into account as accrued; indeed the year-to-year fluctuations might be accentuated. The term "allocation" or "proration" will be used to refer specifically to the correction of bunching due to adherence to the realization requirement, whereas "averaging" will be reserved for the broader problem of smoothing out all kinds of irregularities in taxable income.

* © 1964 by The Brookings Institution. Reproduced with permission.

basis of the tax return of the year in which realization takes place (as in the limited general averaging plan adopted in 1964; see Chapter IX). Basically, the method would be to allocate or prorate the gain or loss and to determine the tax rate applicable to the whole gain or loss by regarding the pro rata amount as a marginal addition to, or deduction from, current-year income.[24]

Where only a few transactions were involved, it might be feasible to prorate gains or losses separately for each transaction by dividing by the number of years the asset was held; but this would not be practicable for large portfolios. It would be much simpler and almost equally effective to prorate by dividing the aggregate net long-term gain or loss by an arbitrary factor of say 3 or 5. To illustrate, suppose that the proration factor is 5 and consider the case of a married couple with taxable income from ordinary sources of $20,000 and a long-term capital gain of $20,000. The pro rata capital gain would be $4,000, and the marginal tax rate on an increment of income of this size would be 32 percent (under the schedule for 1965 and later years). Applying this marginal rate to the whole gain would yield a $6,400 tax on the gain; the total tax liability would be $10,780 ($4,380 of tax on $20,000 of ordinary income plus $6,400 of tax on the $20,000 long-term capital gain). If capital gains were taxed at ordinary rates without proration, the couple's total tax would be $12,140; under present law it is $7,880.

A more complete and formal statement of the proposal illustrated above is as follows: A taxpayer would first determine his net long-term capital gain or loss by combining gains and losses realized on assets held longer than 12 months. If he had a net long-term gain he would proceed as follows: (1) prorate the net capital gain by dividing it by 5, 3, or some other arbitrary figure; (2) compute a tentative tax at regular rates on his ordinary income plus the pro rata net capital gain; (3) compute tax on his ordinary income; (4) compute the tax on his net capital gain by (a) subtracting the tax on ordinary income, as computed in step 3, from the tentative tax computed in step 2 and (b) multiplying by the proration factor; and (5) determine final tax liability as the sum of the tax on or-

[24] For an early discussion of the idea, see U. S. Treasury Department, Tax Advisory Staff, *Federal Income Tax Treatment of Capital Gains and Losses* (1951), pp. 89-90.

dinary income, as computed in step 3, and the tax on the net capital gain, as computed in step 4. If a net capital loss was realized, the procedure would be analogous but would be directed toward determination of the tax reduction (or negative tax) attributable to the loss. Loss carrybacks and carryforwards would be granted when the pro rata loss exceeded ordinary income. Even when this did not occur, the tax reduction due to a capital loss could exceed the tax on ordinary income; in these cases, the excess could be set off against tax of prior or future years.

Proration would minimize the tax consequences of bunching by, in effect, widening the tax brackets for long-term capital gains or losses by a multiple equal to the proration factor. A proration factor of 5, for example. would be equivalent to setting up brackets for capital gains or losses 5 times as wide as the brackets for ordinary income. For persons realizing gains in roughly equal amounts each year, the tax on capital gains would continue to be less progressive than that on ordinary income. For those with widely fluctuating gains or losses, the timing of realization would affect tax liability because of variations in marginal tax rates due to fluctuations in ordinary income and changes in statutory tax rates. This kind of variation, though not peculiar to capital gains or losses, is especially important for them owing to the irregularity of accrual of gains and losses and the great flexibility that investors have in timing their realization. It could not be avoided, however, without a complex plan of cumulative income averaging.

Table 16 gives estimates of the tax on net capital gains in 1960 under the provisions then in effect and with full taxation at regular rates under a proration plan with a divisor of 5. The actual tax on capital gains was about half the amount that would have been payable under the proration plan. (With a proration factor of 3, the tax on capital gains would have been about 8 percent larger than that with a factor of 5; with a proration factor of 10, about 8 percent smaller.) In making the estimates, net capital gains were treated as marginal increments to income.[25]

[25] The estimated tax on net capital gains is the algebraic sum of the tax on gains and the negative tax, or tax reduction, attributable to net capital losses. The proration computations were made by electronic computer separately for each return in the 1960 Tax File (see footnote 2, Chapter VII) that reported capital gain or loss, and the aggregates were estimated by applying sample

TABLE 16. Total Income Tax and Estimated Tax on Net Capital Gains by Adjusted Gross Income Classes, Taxable Individual Returns, 1960[a]

(Money amounts in millions of dollars)

AGI Class ($000)	Total Tax	Estimated Tax on Capital Gains		Additional Tax on Capital Gains under Proration Plan	
		Actual	Under Proration Plan	Amount	Percent of Actual Total Tax
Under 5	$ 6,332	$ 34	$ 19	$ −15	−0.2
5–10	15,404	111	167	56	0.4
10–15	6,140	94	135	41	0.7
15–20	2,355	87	131	44	1.9
20–25	1,452	63	86	23	1.6
25–50	3,676	251	374	123	3.3
50–100	2,198	283	516	233	10.6
100 and over	2,123	696	1,900	1,204	56.7
All classes	$39,680	$1,620	$3,326	$1,706	4.3

[a] Derived from 1960 Tax File, a sample of individual income tax returns (see footnote 2, Chapter VII) and U. S. Treasury Department, *Statistics of Income, Individual Income Tax Returns, 1960*, p. 76. Total tax is actual tax after credits, including actual tax on net capital gains; it differs slightly from the amounts shown in *Statistics of Income* owing to sampling errors. The proration plan provides for ordinary 1960 tax rates with a proration factor of 5; for explanation see text. The estimates reflect the deduction of net capital losses; under the proration plan an allowance is made for full current deductibility of capital losses, but net losses in excess of the statutory limitation that was applicable in 1960 were not prorated.

For taxpayers with incomes below $5,000, the estimated aggregate tax is slightly smaller under the proration plan than under the 1960 law. In this income group, the limitation on the deductibility of losses increased tax liability more than the preferential treatment of gains reduced it. Of course, the persons who suffered from the limitation on loss deductibility were not the same ones who benefited from the capital gains provisions. Table 16 also shows that, if the tax under the proration plan is taken as the norm, the capital gains provisions had only a trivial influence on aggregate tax liability of persons with AGI below $15,000 but a

weights. Since the Tax File tapes showed the amount of net capital losses that was currently deductible, rather than total net losses before the statutory limitation, I estimated the effect of full deductibility of capital losses on the basis of *Statistics of Income* data, by applying marginal tax rates to reported losses. The result is an estimate reflecting full deductibility of losses, but with proration only of the part of losses that was currently deductible in 1960. The aggregate net tax under the proration plan is overstated but not greatly.

major influence on aggregate liability of those with AGI above $100,000.

In 1960, the adoption of full taxation of capital gains, under the proration plan, would have allowed statutory tax rates to be cut by 4 percent on the average without loss of revenue. If the rate cut had been evenly distributed over all brackets, the revision would have considerably increased the progressivity of the income tax. On the other hand, if the rate cut had been devised so as to maintain over-all progressivity unchanged, deep reductions in top bracket rates would have been possible. Under the latter approach, the average statutory rates applicable to persons with AGI above $100,000 could have been slashed by 36 percent (57/157). No doubt, some compromise between the two extremes would be accepted if the revision were enacted. Even with compensatory rate adjustments, taxpayers who received more than the average amounts of capital gains would find their liabilities increased, while those with less than average amounts of capital gains would have the opposite experience.

Admittedly, a proration plan like that described above would be complex. Although the computations would be similar to those required for the general averaging plan introduced in 1964 and for the proration schemes that had previously applied to certain kinds of income, the capital gains plan would affect far more taxpayers. In 1960, capital gains or losses were reported on about one-twelfth of all individual returns, taxable and nontaxable. However, the tax liabilities of many of those with gains or losses would not be affected by proration, because the amounts would be too small to cause the taxpayer's income to pass across the boundaries of a tax rate bracket. In 1960, 26 percent of the persons with gains or losses reported amounts of less than $200 and another 22 percent reported more than $200 but less than $1,000.[26] For these persons, the tax payable under the proration plan would not differ greatly in absolute amount from that payable if gains were made fully taxable and losses fully deductible without proration (though in some cases proration would effect a large percentage change in

[26] *Statistics of Income, 1960,* pp. 36-37, 59. The figures given in the text were obtained by doubling the amounts included in AGI, on the assumption that all net gains and losses were long term, which is not true but which yields figures that are accurate enough for present purposes.

tax). Moreover, for many persons with gains or losses greater than $1,000, proration would have little or no significance. It should be possible to devise a return form that would allow these taxpayers to omit the proration computations.

The effect of proration cannot be approximated by exclusion from taxable income of a fraction of realized gains or losses, as under present law or the more elaborate system in use in 1934-37 which scaled down the proportion of gain or loss taken into account for tax purposes according to the length of time the asset was held. Exclusion of a certain fraction of gains from taxable income gives a tax benefit that varies directly with the investor's marginal tax rate, whereas the benefit of proration depends on the width of the ordinary tax bracket and the difference in tax rates between brackets. To take an extreme example, partial exclusion would be most beneficial to those whose gains would fall entirely in the top rate bracket, whereas proration would not affect the liabilities of these persons.

A provision for constructive realization of capital gain or loss when assets are transferred by gift or at the death of the owner would be a desirable feature of any revision that increased tax rates on realized gains. Otherwise, the tax incentive for postponing the realization of gains would be unduly increased. (See the discussion of "locking-in" below.)

Effects on Investment

However strong the case in equity for taxing capital gains at the same rates as other income, this will not be acceptable if there is reason to believe that the economic consequences would be highly detrimental. It has been argued that preferential taxation of capital gains is a necessary means of shielding investment from the effects of high tax rates, that the lure of lightly taxed capital gains is needed to entice investors into risky ventures.

Since the favorable treatment of capital gains applies to only one form of investment return, it does not offer general tax relief for investment. Indeed, on the assumption that total revenue is to be maintained, it requires taxes to be higher on other income, including investment income. As shown above, a small general reduction in income tax rates or a substantial reduction in top-bracket rates would be possible without sacrifice of revenue or over-all progressivity if the differential in favor of capital gains were eliminated. Or consideration might be given to a more selective measure such as the further liberalization of depreciation allowances or loss offsets. On the other hand, the preferential taxation of capital gains may be supported on the grounds that the kinds of investment that benefit are especially likely to be discouraged by the income tax or have special social importance.

The preferential tax rate on capital gains offers an inducement to seek out investments that promise a return in the form of capital appreciation in preference to those that offer dividends, interest, rent, or other annual yield. A Harvard Business School study, based on extensive interviews in 1949 with a sample of 746 investors, confirmed that those with large incomes were greatly attracted by the differentially low tax rate on capital gains. According to the authors, "inherently venturesome" or "appreciation minded" investors had been induced "to shift funds out of relatively conservative investments, offering little or no opportunity for capital appreciation, and into more venturesome types of investments such as relatively speculative marketable common stocks, closely held companies, new ventures, real estate, and oil properties."[27] Although the study concluded that, for equity-type investors as a whole, the net influence of taxation was to induce a shift to less risky investments, the authors thought that the flow of funds to certain investments offering unusually large capital gains potentialities, such as new ventures, might actually be increased.[28]

The limitation on the deductibility of capital losses must partly offset the attractions of the low tax rate on capital gains. The limitation, however, applies mainly to the deduction of capital losses from ordinary income; capital losses may be deducted in full from capital gains in the current year and within an unlimited carryover period. For investors with diversified portfolios, the restriction on loss deductibility may not seem severe. Among the investors inter-

[27] J. Keith Butters, Lawrence E. Thompson, and Lynn L. Bollinger, *Effects of Taxation, Investments by Individuals* (Boston: Harvard University Graduate School of Business Administration, 1953), pp. 41-42.

[28] *Ibid.*, pp. 50-51.

viewed by the Harvard Business School group, a large proportion of whom were high-income persons, many more were attracted by the favorable tax rate differential than were repelled by the restrictions on loss deductibility.[29]

Although investments promising capital gains usually may be more risky than others, they are not always so. As already mentioned, a high-grade bond selling at a discount is virtually certain to produce a capital gain if held to maturity, but there is no economic difference between this security and another of the same quality and maturity that is selling at par because its coupon rate equals the market rate.

On the whole, it seems likely that the tax differential in favor of capital gains causes individual investors to allocate a larger fraction of their resources to risky items than they would if capital gains and losses were taxed as ordinary income and losses. The differential almost certainly encourages the retention of corporate profits and thus favors investment that can be financed from this source.

Although risk-taking is commonly regarded as wholesome, it may waste capital when carried too far. A prudent policy, therefore, might aim at neutrality toward risk assumption rather than its stimulation or discouragement. According to this standard, a tax preference for capital gains could be supported to the extent that it counterbalanced discrimination against risk-taking due to other provisions but would be undesirable if it did more. The standard is not very helpful because its application would require more precise knowledge about investors' reactions to taxation than is now available. A further difficulty is the lack of selectivity in capital gains tax treatment, which extends to gains from land speculation and other activities that contribute little to innovation and growth as well as to gains from highly productive investments.

The consequences of a tax incentive for retaining corporate profits, instead of paying dividends, are debatable. Many economists argue that capital will be most efficiently allocated if profits are distributed and individual shareholders are allowed to decide whether they should be reinvested where earned or placed else-

[29] *Ibid.*, p. 42. The capital loss provisions in 1949 were similar to the current ones but the carryforward of losses was limited to five years.

where. This attitude seems to be based on general confidence in the market mechanism rather than a systematic comparison of the investment decisions of shareholders and the executives of profitable corporations. The dividend-payout ratio, moreover, may affect shareholders' consumption and thus the total amount of resources available to corporations as well as the allocation of capital among firms.

The conclusion with respect to investment allocation must remain somewhat indefinite. On balance, the allocative effects of a tax differential in favor of capital gains may be economically desirable, but they are not unambiguously so. The capital gains potential of financial and real investments is not a reliable indicator of their social contribution, and there is much waste motion in turning investment income into capital gains.

SMITH, FEDERAL TAX REFORM 151–55 (1961) *

A Proposal for a Major Reform—Tax-free Roll-over of Investments with Withdrawals of Gains Taxed as Ordinary Income

The tax law permits an owner to sell his residence at a profit without paying any tax on the gain if the proceeds are reinvested in another residence. This is widely regarded as a desirable relief provision in the law. Less well known is the fact that all taxpayers may exchange investment property and property used in a trade or business for other property of like kind without incurring a tax.

* Copyright © 1961 by McGraw-Hill, Inc. Reproduced with permission of McGraw-Hill Book Company.

The exchange must be a direct one; a sale and purchase do not qualify. In both cases, tax is not waived; it is merely postponed by requiring the cost or tax basis of the old property to be carried over and used as the tax basis of the new property. The courts have been very liberal in interpreting "property of a like kind." Virtually all real estate, for example, is regarded as homogeneous, and a retiring farmer can exchange his farm for a city apartment house with no tax on the gain. Securities are specifically excluded from this tax-free exchange of investment property.

These precedents in the law are the basis for many suggestions to extend the tax-free exchange or roll-over to securities. This is advocated to reduce tax barriers to risky investment and more particularly to remove tax barriers to changes in investment portfolios. It would doubtless be effective in both respects. The question is whether it would be unfair to other taxpayers to permit gains to be accumulated in this way without interim taxes. Here, as is so often the case, a reform package seems possible which will tighten the law where it needs to be tightened and liberalize it where it needs to be made less onerous.

It would seem desirable to permit the tax on gains from sales of securities by individuals to be postponed if the entire proceeds are reinvested in other securities but to tax any net withdrawals of gains as ordinary income. This would improve the fairness of the law by applying full taxation to gains which are not embodied in capital. It would reduce or eliminate the adverse economic effects of taxing gains which continue to be part of one's capital. It would, however, make the law more complicated; perhaps it would not be administratively feasible. The proposal appears to have sufficient merit to justify a careful examination.

Much of the disagreement about the fairness of a lower rate of tax on capital gains comes from a difference of opinion as to what they actually are. The point of view advanced in this book is that appreciation in value is typically thought of as constituting part of capital and continues to be embodied in capital even when one investment is sold and another purchased. From this standpoint, a capital gains tax is a form of capital levy. From this point of view it also follows that a capital gain which is not continued as a part of one's capital should not receive a favorable tax treatment except in so far as it may be necessary to offset the effects of a bunching of income. When a profit on the sale of securities is used for consumption along with ordinary income, it should in fairness be taxed as regular income, regardless of the length of time the securities have been held. It is only because long-term gains are ordinarily not regarded or used as income that a lower rate of tax is theoretically justified. The lower rate may produce a rough equity by taxing on the average the part of gains which are consumed. But if it is possible to distinguish the uses of gains and tax them on the basis of use, greater equity could be achieved. This is what is proposed here.

Those who believe that even unrealized gains should ideally be taxed on the ground that appreciation in value is as much a part of income as salary or interest will, of course, not accept this proposal as improving the fairness of the tax law. The reasons for rejecting this very broad concept of income have already been given.

It is also true that if one were to permit gains to be free of tax when they are kept in a capital fund, one should also consider letting ordinary income be free of tax when it is put into a capital fund. There is much to be said for such a law. The concept of a tax on spending, on consumption rather than on income, has strong support from distinguished economists. It is not considered in this book because it would be such a drastic change that it is not within the range of possible tax reform in the immediately foreseeable future. It is enough to recognize that the more limited proposal made here concerning capital gains would be logically consistent with this much broader possible change. The fact that it would not go all the way to the new concept is no reason to reject it if it is sound within its own frame of reference.

Adoption of tax-free roll-overs for investments, though desirable on grounds of equity and economic policy, would raise two difficult administrative problems which require further examination. The first problem is one of identification. When a person sells one residence and buys another, there is no problem of identification, since one can bring only one residence at a time under the provision of the law. Likewise the direct exchange of investment properties involves no problem. But the sale and purchase of securities would involve a problem because an investor usually has many securities. Should there be an attempt to trace the proceeds from a particular sale into a particular new investment, or should there be a lumping together of all investments with a presumption that any withdrawal would be regarded as a withdrawal of a gain to the extent of any existing realized gain?

The second problem involves indirect withdrawals of gain. If gains are to be taxed as ordinary income unless they are reinvested, it is important to prevent avoidance of the tax by indirect withdrawals. One might, for example, develop a large fortune from a single investment, sell it and buy a diversified portfolio, and then borrow indefinitely against securities for living expenses. Deductible interest would be less burdensome than the income tax on a withdrawal of gain. The problem of indirect realization exists under the present law in that one may borrow against appreciated property and, in effect, consume the appreciation without even being subject to a capital gains tax. The elimination of the deduction for interest on personal loans, previously proposed, would discourage loans of long duration.

An indirect withdrawal also might be made by selling property which has not appreciated, perhaps bonds, and using that sum for consumption while some appreciated stock is sold and the proceeds used to purchase bonds and restore a balanced portfolio. To a lesser extent this problem also exists now in that an investor may sell and live on the proceeds of sale of nonappreciated property while continuously building up his net worth in other property. In an extreme case, one might be able to combine a high standard of living financed by the sale of nonappreciated assets with a large increase in net worth through appreciation on other assets and pay neither an income nor a capital gains tax. Such a possibility suggests, in passing, one advantage of a tax based on consumption.

If a tax-free roll-over were to be adopted, it would probably be desirable to give wide latitude to the forms of reinvestment. It has sometimes been proposed that fairly strict limits be established with funds from common stock having to be reinvested in common stock. This would be undesirable because, while removing one tax force which accentuates market fluctuations, it would substitute another artificial tax influence. Though one would be more willing to sell stock which he thought was overvalued, he would be forced to buy another stock which he considered less vulnerable, thus accentuating the price movements in the "defensive" stocks. It has also been proposed that a roll-over might be permitted only if the funds received were reinvested in government bonds. No such artificial support for government securities should be needed or accepted.

A change in the law to permit tax-free roll-overs of investments, with full taxation at regular rates of any withdrawals of gains, would make the tax law fairer and reduce its adverse economic effects. Its adoption would be a major reform. The administrative problems should not be insuperable; it is to be hoped that others may join in seeking a solution to them.

TAXATION OF APPRECIATION OF ASSETS TRANSFERRED AT DEATH OR BY GIFT

U. S. Treasury Dept., Tax Reform Studies and Proposals, 91st Cong., 1st Sess., pt. 3, at 331–40 (1969).

GENERAL EXPLANATION AND DESCRIPTION

Under present law, a person whose income consists of salaries, wages, dividends, or business profits is taxed at ordinary income rates on an annual basis. Special treatment is afforded to income from the sale of capital assets in that such income is taxed at a lower rate when the assets are sold. In both these situations, the estate which the taxpayer passes on to his wife and children at his death is accumulated after income taxes have been paid.

However, a person who holds capital assets which have appreciated in value until death can avoid taxation of this income altogether. Moreover, the recipient of the property takes as his cost or basis the fair market value at date of death, so that the capital gain income represented by the appreciation in value is never taxed under the income tax. This means that a person who can afford to accumulate income in the form or unrealized capital gains can then pass on that accumulated wealth free of income tax—in contrast to the wage earner, salaried individual, or taxpayer who has sold capital assets, all of whom transfer their accumulated wealth after it is reduced by income taxes.

As a result of this situation:

> There is inequality in the income tax treatment of people who accumulate their estates out of currently taxable income as compared to those who accumulate estates by means of unrealized capital gains.
>
> At least $15 billion a year of capital gains fall completely outside the income tax system.
>
> There are undesirable economic effects because of the resulting "lock-in" effect.

These problems—taxpayer inequity, revenue loss, and lock-in effect—must be analyzed in some detail to appreciate their significance.

TAXPAYER INEQUITY

A great deal of income after tax from wages, dividends, and the like is saved; that is, it serves to increase the wealth of the taxpayer. Another taxpayer may find that his wealth has increased because the assets he owns have increased in value.

A simple example will clarify the point that these two paths to wealth accumulation are at present given dissimilar tax treatment.

Assume Taxpayer A earns $200,000 and pays tax of 50 percent or $100,000. For simplicity, it is assumed that he intends to save half of his income and to consume half. This means that he will have $50,000 for consumption and $50,000 that he can invest in, say, common stock.

Taxpayer B earns $100,000 on which we will say he pays 50 percent in tax and he uses this entirely for consumption. Taxpayer B, however, differs from A in that when the year started he already owned common stock worth $200,000; and during this period it rose in value by 50 percent or by $100,000.

Clearly Taxpayer A tried to increase his wealth by $100,000. He wanted to save half of his income, but the tax cut it down. He only increased his wealth $50,000 after tax. B finds that his wealth has increased; and since our present tax law does not count unrealized appreciation in value as taxable income, he is able to add the whole increase in value to his wealth.

The fact is that the two taxpayers have paid quite different rates. A has paid $100,000 of tax, and B has paid only $50,000. But it cannot be said that A really has more ability to pay than B. They both paid the same tax on the $100,000 of the before-tax income that they used for consumption. They both spend the same on consumption, so it could even be assumed that they lived in the same kind of houses, ate the same food, and took the same vacations. The extra ability to pay that A has is really the extra income that he used to increase the value of his holdings in securities. But B increased the value of his holding in securities by twice as much as A did.

For administrative reasons the tax system does not every year make B calculate how much his holdings have appreciated in value. The law permits B to postpone including this appreciation until he sells his assets. But more often than not appreciation is not sold; it is used for estate building and at the time of death the gain is not subject to income tax. The heir treats as his "cost" the value of the property at the time of death.

The estate tax will fall on both A and B so it is not relevant to say that B ought not to pay any income tax on his accumulation of wealth "because he pays an estate tax." A has paid income tax on the money that he earned to build an estate *and* an estate tax. B avoided income tax on his wealth increase and *only* an estate tax was paid on it.

The substance of the present proposal is to reduce the estate tax rate by about the amount raised by capital gains tax at death. Thus the combined tax will be reduced on A and increased on B. The increase on B will be equivalent to what would have happened if B had sold his appreciated property just before death. B would then pay the capital gains tax, but the amount of the capital gains tax would be out of the estate making the estate tax somewhat lower. The proposal would tax the capital gain at death and then allow the capital gains tax as a deduction from the estate.

B. will still be taxed more favorably if he holds his appreciation until death than if he sold it during lifetime. This occurs because the postponement means that during his life B will have had more money invested and thus more income (or appreciation) than he would if he had sold before death. B is also benefited since a gain at death does not come into the proposed minimum tax base. B has an even greater advantage compared to an individual who accumulates his wealth out of ordinary income like salary or dividends. Not only does B get to postpone the tax on his wealth increase but he also pays tax on it at capital gains rates, not ordinary income rates.

Finally the transition proposal allows B to avoid tax on all appreciation up to the date of enactment.

To explain fully the case for this proposal, it is useful to address three issues that are often raised.

(1) *Question.* Is it sound to call the increase in value of B's property income at his death when the property has not yet been sold and may go down in value?

Answer. Assets that have not appreciated are valued under present rules for estate tax purposes and that value is the basis for an estate tax that goes up to 77 percent. These assets also might go down in value, and both kinds of assets might go up even more. These subsequent value changes can properly be treated as gains or losses to the heir.

(2) *Question.* Is it fair to tax B on an appreciation of value which just matches the general rise in consumer prices?

Answer. One answer is that A is taxed on the same thing. The entire tax system is based on money income. Inflation gains are not excluded, nor are deductions allowed for inflation losses. An obvious reason for taxing inflation gains is that to the extent of inflation gains an individual benefits by escaping from the reduction of purchasing power that inflation imposes on holders of fixed dollar claims. The burden can be shared more equally if some tax is imposed on the benefit from escaping inflation.

Further, over the long run the principal assets involved in appreciation, land and stocks, have increased in price over twice as fast as consumer prices. This is important when one recognizes that the capital gains rate is a maximum 25 percent.

(3) *Question.* Won't a tax on the appreciation transferred at death hurt families that have wealth in illiquid form?

Answer. To some extent the appreciation can be in relatively illiquid form, but the far greater portion of it will be in highly liquid common stocks. If there is reason to regard illiquidity as a problem, it makes far more sense to provide some appropriate means of paying death taxes in the illiquid cases than to favor a large group of estates with appreciation in liquid form. The present proposals deal with the illiquidity problem directly, both as to the proposed capital gains tax at death and the estate tax itself.

REVENUE LOSS

On estate tax returns filed in 1966, the total value of property of a type that might show appreciation (stock, real estate, trust interests and noncorporate business assets) was about $15 billion. The portion of this that represented appreciation was probably in the range of 40 to 50 percent.[1]

[1] B. Okun ("The Taxation of Decedents' Unrealized Capital Gains," *National Tax Journal,* December 1967, pp. 368–385.) Estimates the ratio of appreciation to value as 45 percent for real estate and 54 percent for stock. Brannon, McClung and Copeland ("Unrealized Appreciation Passing at Death," *American Statistical Association Proceedings,* 1967, pp. 147–167) derive minimum estimates of 37 percent for stock and 33 percent for real estate. These are minimum in the sense that they are derived from an assumption that assets sold by a taxpayer are randomly drawn from his holdings. A rational investment strategy would be to prefer to sell the assets with less appreciation and thus less current tax. This would imply a higher ratio of appreciation for assets left in the portfolio. Barlow, Brazer and Morgan (*The Economic Behavior of the Affluent,* Brookings, 1966) report the result of their interview survey that among the very high-income group capital appreciation was the source of 51 percent of their wealth.

This suggests that the appreciation passing through the estates of estate tax filers in 1966 must have been in the general magnitude of $6 to $8 billion, or about $7 billion. An additional amount of appreciation about 65 percent as large, or about $4.5 billion, passed from decedents for whom an estate tax return was not required.[2]

Table 1 following indicates some aspects of taxing appreciation at death by income level. The data indicate the situation 10 years after the new basis date (date of enactment), when it is assumed that the average property of a type subject to appreciation (principally stock, real estate, trust interests and noncorporate business assets) will reflect an average appreciation of about 25 percent.

TABLE 1.—DATA ON THE OPERATION OF THE PROPOSAL FOR TAXING GAINS AT DEATH 1981 [1]

Economic estate class (in thousands of dollars)	Percent of estate of appreciable assets [2]	Percent of appreciation [3]	Appreciation as percent of economic estate	Net capital gains tax as percent of economic estate [4]	Net capital gains tax as percent of present law estate tax after credits
60 to 100	62	20	12.3	0.7	84.0
100 to 200	67	22	14.5	1.4	30.0
200 to 400	75	23	17.4	1.6	15.2
400 to 600	78	25	19.7	1.9	12.9
600 to 1,000	80	27	21.4	2.2	13.3
1,000 to 2,000	83	30	24.5	2.6	13.5
2,000 to 3,000	82	32	26.2	2.7	12.4
3,000 to 5,000	83	35	29.1	2.9	12.0
5,000 and up	86	37	32.2	2.8	11.7

[1] An effective date of Jan. 1, 1970, is assumed.

[2] Includes stock, real estate, trust interests, and noncorporate business assets. The economic estate is gross estate less debts.

[3] This takes into account the observed patterns that appreciation rates and holding period are higher at the upper wealth levels plus some shifting asset composition. (E.g., the personal residence with a low appreciation rate is more important at low wealth levels.)

[4] This takes into account 4 factors: (a) the tendency for applicable capital gain rates to be higher at upper wealth levels, (b) the deduction for contributions which is higher at upper wealth levels, (c) the deduction of marital bequests which is greater at lower wealth levels, and (d) the deduction of the capital gains tax against the estate tax (at 1980 rates) which is more valuable at higher wealth levels.

UNDESIRABLE ECONOMIC EFFECTS

When tax liability is allowed to depend on whether an appreciated asset is sold or kept until death, the tax law operates to produce undesirable economic effects, particularly in cases of older people. Assets become immobilized; investors become "locked-in" by the prospect of avoiding income tax completely if they hold appreciated assets until death rather than selling them. This freezing of investment positions deprives the economy of the fruits of an unencumbered flow of capital toward areas of enterprise promising larger rewards.

PROPOSAL

To remedy these problems, under the proposal persons holding appreciated capital assets at death would be treated as if they had sold such assets just before death, and such gains would be taxed in the final income tax return of the decedent. The tax rate would be that now applicable to capital gains on assets sold during life. The tax on these gains at death would be due under the income tax, but the amount

[2] Okun, *op. cit.*, p. 385.

of the tax would be deducted in determining the amount of property subject to estate tax. The taxable estate would thus be net of the income tax paid, as is the case for those who accumulate their estates out of ordinary income or out of capital assets sold prior to death. The assets taxed at death would take as their cost or basis the fair market value at death, as is true today.

The transition to the new system will be smoothed for those who are now holding appreciated assets in anticipation of tax-free transfers at death, by a provision that only appreciation occurring after the date of enactment would be subject to tax at death.

The following measures insure the equitable operation of the new law:

Only appreciation occurring after the date of enactment would be subject to tax;

Taxpayers would be allowed a minimum basis of $60,000, with the result that no tax at all would be imposed on the appreciation when the total value of assets transferred is $60,000 or less;

Complete exemption would be allowed for gain on property transferred to a spouse or to charity;

Limited exemption would be allowed for gain on transfers of property to orphans and transfers of ordinary personal and household effects;

Present rules for payment of taxes due at death for those estates that have liquidity problems will be liberalized, and the new rules will apply to capital gains taxes as well as transfer taxes.

The tax on appreciation on transferred assets would be allowed as a deduction for estate tax purposes;

Net unrealized losses on business or investment property would be allowed as an offset against capital gain and, subject to appropriate limitations, against ordinary income for the 3 taxable years preceding the decedent's final income tax return;

Gains on assets giving rise to ordinary income transferred at death would be eligible for averaging.

OPERATION OF PROPOSAL

Under present law, property that has appreciated in value can be transferred at death without any income tax being imposed on the increase in value that accrued during the decedent's lifetime. At the same time these assets receive a new basis equal to their fair market value at the death of the decedent, so that the predeath appreciation escapes income taxation forever.

Under the proposal the appreciation in assets held at death will be subject to income taxation at that time. The tax will be reported in the decedent's final income tax return (prepared by the executor) and will be due at the same time as the estate tax return of the decedent, that is, 15 months after the date of death.

As under the present estate tax, the fair market value [3] of the decedent's property for income tax purposes would be determined as of the date of death or the alternate valuation date (generally 1 year

[3] The "fair market value" is the price at which the property would change hands between a willing buyer and a willing seller, neither being under any compulsion to buy or to sell and both having knowledge of all relevant facts.

after the date of death except with respect to property disposed of during the year following death). The 50-percent exclusion and the alternative 25-percent maximum rate applicable to long-term capital gain will be available regardless of the length of time the decedent has actually held the property. The transferee of the decedent's property would take as his basis the fair market value of the property on the date of death of the decedent, as under present rules.

LOSSES

Where an individual holds capital assets whose fair market value is less than their adjusted tax bases (ordinarily, cost) at the date of his death, the resulting losses will be allowed for tax purposes in the year of death. These losses, as well as losses sustained on sales during the last year of the decedent's life, and any capital loss carryforward from prior years, will be deductible as under the regular rules applicable to capital losses, by first offsetting capital gains of the last taxable year, with any excess allowed, to the extent of $1,000, as a deduction against ordinary income of that year. If there are still additional unused capital losses remaining, a special rule will permit an offset against capital gains of the decedent in his 3 prior taxable years. If there still remain unused capital losses, an offset against ordinary income in the last taxable year of a decedent will be permitted and then in his 3 prior taxable years.

This special offset of additional amounts of losses against ordinary income will, however, be limited so that capital losses will be deductible only to the same extent that capital gains are included in ordinary income. Thus, generally, 50 percent of capital losses will be deductible, but in no event will the tax benefit resulting from the offset against ordinary income be greater than the tax benefit that would have resulted had the income to be offset been capital gain rather than ordinary income. In other words, the tax saving resulting from the offset of a loss will not be permitted to exceed 25 percent of the amount of the ordinary income offset by the offset. The basis of the loss property in the hands of the decendent's transferee would be fair market value at death as under present law.

RELATION OF INCOME TAX TO ESTATE TAX

The income tax on the gain at death will constitute a debt of the estate and will be deductible for transfer tax purposes, so as to reduce transfer tax liability. The treatment here follows present estate tax rules dealing with debts of an estate and, coupled with the reduction in rates under the unified transfer tax proposal, means that on the average the total taxes paid on death under these proposals will be substantially the same as is paid for estate taxes under present law.

EXCEPTIONS

(A) Basic exemption

For purposes of computing gain, every taxpayer would be deemed to have a minimum basis in property owned at death of $60,000 or fair market value, whichever is lower. If the actual basis exceeds $60,000, then gain (or loss) is computed from actual basis. Thus, if a taxpayer has property the total basis of which was $80,000, gain would be computed from this figure; but if a taxpayer's property had a total basis of $20,000 and a fair market value of $35,000 at date of death, no gain would be taxed. In each case, a stepped-up basis equal to the fair market value will be acquired by the transferee.

In addition to the basic exemption, the following exemptions will also be available:

(B) Personal and household effects exemption

The proposal will permanently exempt all gain on ordinary personal and household items of the decedent of a value of less than $1,000 each. This includes the clothing of the decendent, furniture, appliances, cars, jewelry, furs, works of art, and so forth. Assets of this type that have a value in excess of $1,000 will not be exempt and will be treated like any other assets of the decedent.

Losses due to depreciation in value of personal and household items will be disallowed following the usual rules relating to losses of a personal nature.

The basis to the decedent's transferee of the personal and household effects passing under the exception will be their fair market value at the decedent's death.

(C) Marital exclusion

As part of the unified transfer tax proposal, a 100-percent marital deduction will apply to transfers between spouses by gift or at death. The marital exclusion under the gain proposal will correspond to the unified transfer tax provisions. No gain will be recognized on the appreciation in value of property passing to the surviving spouse at death which qualifies for the transfer tax marital exclusion.[4] Where the transferee spouse receives all the property of the decedent, the property will not receive a new basis but will carry over the basis of the decedent. Where the transferee spouse receives less than all the property of the decedent, the basis in such property will be allocated under the rules outlined in (F) below.

(D) Orphan exclusion

Gain on property passing to orphans, which is excluded from the transfer tax under the unified transfer tax proposal, will also be excluded from the gain proposal. The property will have a basis in the hands of the transferees computed under the rules set forth in (F) below, and gain will be subject to taxation upon disposition by them.

(E) Charitable bequests exemption

Gain on assets transferred to charity will be permanently exempt from tax if the amount of the interest given to charity can be measured with certainty. Thus, no tax would be imposed on the appreciation in property given outright to a qualified charity. Where a transfer creates split interests (e.g., a trust to pay the income to the transferor's son for life, with the remainder to the *x* charity or vice versa), the same rules will apply as apply to gifts or bequests to charity.

[4] This provision, the orphan exclusion, and the basic $60,000 exemption make it unnecessary to establish a separate rule for personal residences. Gain on intrafamily transfers will generally be exempted under these provisions. There is no reason to exempt gain on transfers of residences to persons other than spouses or orphans.

(F) *Allocation of basis*

The exemption of gain on property passing at death to a surviving spouse, to orphans, or to charity requires a special rule relating to basis, so that, in the case of the spouse or orphans, the gain that escapes tax at the death of the decedent will be taxed when the property is later transferred by such spouse or orphan. The basic objective of using allocated, rather than actual, basis is to eliminate any tax incentive for the decedent or his executor to transfer any particular piece of property to any particular person or entity, where such a disposition might be undesirable from a nontax standpoint. For example, if an estate consists of low-basis stock in a family corporation that the decedent would, in the absence of tax considerations, want to go to his son, and of high-basis property of equal value that he would want to go to his wife, it seems improper to create a significant tax incentive for achieving precisely the opposite disposition. A rule that taxed or exempted gain on the basis of the particular property going to each would have such an effect, since under such a rule the gain on the shares of stock in the family business could escape taxation at the decedent's death only if that property were left to the wife. To avoid this effect the proposed basis rule would require allocation of total basis among all property (other than cash) before computing the taxable gain, with a carryover of such allocated basis in the case of property on which gain is exempt. (This rule need not, and will not, apply where all the decedent's property passes to one person.) The same considerations that require allocation in the case of an estate passing in part to a spouse also require allocation in the case of property passing in part to orphans or charities.

ITEMS GIVING RISE TO ORDINARY INCOME

Under present law, special treatment is given to items of income which are earned by a decedent prior to his death, but which are not reportable in the decedent's final income tax return. Example of this type of income are wage claims of the decedent, receivables, certain deferred compensation payments, and interest on U.S. savings bonds. Such income must be reported by the person to whom the asset is given by the decedent at the time it is received by that person. Although the recipient of the income does not receive any step up in basis on the decedent's death, a deduction is allowed to the receipient for the estate tax attributable to the inclusion of the item in the decedent's estate for Federal estate tax purposes.

Present rules were designed to avoid bunching of ordinary income in the decedent's final return. However, complexities of present law have produced troublesome problems. Therefore, this proposal substitutes a new rule for decedents dying after December 31, 1969.

The new rule would be that gain on an asset, the sale or exchange of which would produce ordinary income or capital gain, or a combination of both, will be taxed at death with ordinary income to the required extent and capital gain as to the remainder. Thus, for example, in the case of a wage claim of a decedent, the entire amount of the wage claim will be includible in the decedent's final return and taxed at ordinary income rates.

To avoid the bunching problems for which the present rules were developed, the usual averaging rules will apply to ordinary income that is taxed at death by virtue of this proposal. In addition, the 100-percent marital exclusion, the orphans exclusion, the deduction for income taxes as a debt of the estate, and the basic $60,000 exemption [5] will all be applicable to such items of income, thereby further ameliorating the bunching problem.

Special rules for assets that give rise both to ordinary income and to capital gains will be provided. Deductions attributable to income taxed at death will be allowed, but no double deductions will be permitted as is sometimes the case under present rules.

Recipients of items giving rise to the taxation of ordinary income under this proposal will receive a market value basis as to such items.

TRANSFER OF LIFETIME GIFTS

In order that the proposed imposition of the tax on gain will neither encourage nor discourage lifetime transfers as opposed to death transfers, the gain on appreciated property transferred by gift by a taxpayer will be subject to income taxation at the time of transfer. A gift will not be treated as "completed," that is, subject to tax, unless the transfer is of a type on which the transfer tax is imposed under the unified transfer tax proposal. Generally, the rules applicable to death transfers will apply to lifetime transfers.

The following exceptions, corresponding to the exceptions for death transfers, will be applicable to lifetime gifts:

There will be an exclusion for ordinary personal household effects;

There will be an exclusion for charitable gifts;

There will be a marital exclusion on gifts between husband and wife so as to produce a result comparable to that produced by the marital exclusion on transfers at death.

Losses will be allowed on lifetime gifts under the same rules as apply at death. However, no losses will be allowed on transfers between related parties.

FUTURE INTERESTS

Under the unified transfer tax, a substitute tax, in addition to the basic tax, would be imposed on certain complex arrangements designed to avoid tax by passing property through several generations without subjecting the property to tax in each generation. A similar problem exists in the case of capital gains tax imposed on the appreciation in the value of property transferred at death or by gift. The tax could be avoided by transferring property in such a form that the appreciation would go untaxed through several generations.

To foreclose such a possibility, thereby assuring that all taxpayers will be treated equally, a special rule would tax the appreciation when distribution following an initial transfer is made to persons who are more than one degree lower than the transferor, for example, a grandchild.

---

[5] On death, the basic $60,000 exemption must be allocated first to capital assets. To the extent if it is not used up, the balance can be allocated to ordinary income items. The basic exemption will not be available for lifetime transfers of ordinary income items.

EFFECTIVE DATE

The new rule would apply to transfers by gift or by death after December 31, 1969.

For purposes of computing gain on property acquired before the date of enactment the taxpayer, or his personal representative, will have the option of using as his basis, either—

(1) Adjusted basis as computed under existing rules; or

(2) The value on the date of enactment as adjusted under present rules for any changes occurring after that date, including the depreciation or depletion (cost or percentage) actually taken after such date.

For purposes of computing losses on property acquired before the date of enactment, the basis is the lower of (1) or (2) above.

SURREY, DEFINITIONAL PROBLEMS IN CAPITAL GAINS TAXATION

House Committee on Ways and Means,
2 Tax Revision Compendium 1203, 1204–25 (1959).

The term "capital gain" has been used in the tax law for so long a period of time and with such wide publicity that it has acquired a very familiar ring. We are led to believe that it has readily ascertainable content and as respects its comprehensibility and application stands on no different a footing from other items of income such as salary, interest, rent, and the like. But we must remember that a fully developed concept of "capital gain" has not been offered to the tax law by either the economist or the accountant, so that its content cannot readily be supplied by reference to those branches of discourse. Many economists see "income" as a "gain"—the result obtained by adding to the wealth on hand at the end of a period of time the consumption during that period and then subtracting the wealth existing at the beginning of the period. But once having defined income as "gain," they do not offer—nor have they really any occasion to offer—any workable concept of a "capital gain" as a component of the "gain." The accountant in turn knows of "net income," and while he has occasion sometimes to seek a capital gain component so as to allocate a profit on the sale of certain fixed assets to surplus rather than to current operations, his concept of capital gain is a much narrower concept than, and one essentially different from, that sought in the tax law. And even the only definition of "income" seriously essayed by the Supreme Court before it abandoned the attempt—the *Eisner* v. *Macomber* [2] definition of "income" as "the gain derived from capital, from labor, or from both combined"—spoke of "gain derived from capital" and not "capital gain." Consequently, when Congress in the Revenue Act of 1921 introduced the term "capital gain" into our technical tax law [3] and was therefore faced with the problem of defining that term, it was embarking upon a journey through areas previously unexplored in this country.[4] When we turn from the beginning of that journey in 1921 and pass over 38 years to arrive at the present definition in the Revenue Code of 1954 we see that while Congress has added many maps and charts and much elaborate equipment, it still has not uncovered a clear and useful trail.

---

[2] 252 U.S. 189, 207 (1920).

[3] Sec. 206 42 Stat. 232 (1921).

[4] This article does not purport to provide detailed coverage of the case law or other materials in this field. See generally as to (1) history: Paul, "Taxation in the United States" (1954); Wells, "Legislative History of Treatment of Capital Gains Under the Federal Income Tax, 1913–48." 2 Nat'l Tax J. 12 (1949); (2) policy: Butters, Thompson, and Bollinger, "Effects of Taxation: Investments by Individuals" (1953); "Federal Tax Policy for Economic Growth and Stability," op. cit. supra note *; National Tax Association 46th annual proceedings, "Roundtable on Capital Gains Taxation 138" (1953; Seltzer, "The Nature and Tax Treatment of Capital Gains and Losses" (1951); Tax Institute, Inc., "Capital Gains Taxation" (1946); U.S. Treasury Tax Advisory Committee, "Federal Income Tax Treatment of Capital Gains and Losses" (1951); Blum, "A Handy Summary of the Capital Gains Argument," 35 Taxes 247 (1957); (3) case law: Surrey and Warren, "Federal Income Taxation" (1955): Miller, "Capital Gains Taxation of the Fruits of Personal Effort: Before and Under the 1954 Code" 64 Yale L.J. 1 (1954); Miller, "The 'Capital Asset' Concept: A Critique of Capital Gains Taxation," 59 Yale L.J. 837, 1057 (1950); (4) humor: Blum, "The Decline and Fall of Capital Gains: 1921–57," 28 Taxes 838 (1950).

I. THE DEFINITION OF "CAPITAL ASSET"

The code defines "capital gain" in terms of "the sale or exchange of a capital asset",[5] which for the most part merely passes us along to the question of what is a "capital asset." It is here, in the definition of "capital asset," that the code itself discloses the enormity of the problem. For it commences by defining "capital asset" as "property held by the taxpayer (whether or not connected with his trade or business)."[6] Since in one sense everything that the taxpayer holds is property and hence will be a capital asset, at this point it would seem to follow that all income could well be "capital gain"—for any moneys received by a taxpayer could readily be regarded as the result of the surrender by him of "property" in the form of either tangible assets or intangible property such as claims to moneys.[7] Hence, unless the definition is to be useless, exclusions must be found. But in seeking to give content to the definition through the development of appropriate exclusions, it must be recognized that one facet, and perhaps the basic facet, of the present difficulty thereby emerges. For unless a particular item of property is covered by an exclusion it will remain in the residual category of capital asset and the income arising on its disposition will be capital gain. Given a maximum capital gain rate of 25 percent when the starting rate for ordinary income is 20 percent and the top rate 91 percent, so that the taxpayer has a terrific stimulus to seek to classify his income as capital gain, this method of definition works directly to his advantage. In fact, as will be discussed later, the advantage is so great that the courts have in some cases attempted to produce a more reasonable situation by refusing to consider the term "property" as being here used by Congress in the normal, all-inclusive sense in which it is used elsewhere in the code. This judicial construction, however, in essence amounts in these situations to forgetting about the statutory definition and substituting instead a judicial concept.[8]

The generality of the definition of "capital asset," when placed in the chain of definitions involved in giving content to "capital gain," also involves another important decision. It is clear that an increase in the value of an asset can result from many causes. Thus, in the case of shares of stock an increase in value may come from accumulated corporate earnings, from innovations or discoveries, such as the development of a new product or market, from the seasoning of the business organization or the efforts of the shareholder-managers, from the weaknesses of competitors, from an improvement in the general level of economic activity, from inflation, and so on. An increase in the value of land may result from the discovery of new resources in the land, from the development of new uses for its resources, from the growth of population, from the growth of crops on the land, such

---

[5] Sec. 1222.

[6] Sec. 1221.

[7] Thus, since a claim to salary is certainly "property" in one sense of the term, the claim to salary would in that sense be a capital asset. While payment of the salary would not produce a capital gain because of the "sale or exchange" requirement under the existing interpretation of "exchange," a sale of the claim would produce a capital gain under this interpretation of property. And, if this interpretation were adopted, we might well find a national brokerage business developing overnight through which employees sold their salary claims. In effect, the "sale or exchange" requirement would not suffice to stem the capital gain flood waters if "capital asset" were all-inclusive. See infra.

[8] See the discussion of *Corn Products Refining Co.* v. *Commissioner*, 350 U.S. 46 (1955), infra.

as timber, over the passage of time. The value of a bond may increase through a change in general interest rates. And so it goes, through the effects of the expected and planned or the unexpected and erratic, through the effects of inflation, war, depression, invention, the vagaries of public taste. Are all of the resulting gains to be regarded as "capital gains"? Congress answered in the affirmative when it commenced its phrasing of the definition of "capital asset" to include all "property" and then did not embark on the search for exclusions essentially related to the causes of the increase in value. Consequently, the additional value imparted to a taxpayer's stock through factors within his control, such as the accumulation of corporate earnings or his personal efforts as corporate president, was regarded in the definition used as no different from increases in value caused by forces beyond his control. Taxpayers were quick to perceive the enormous range of possibilities in planning for capital gain under such a definitional approach. Here again, the pattern of definition was all in their favor.

II. THE PROBLEM OF DISTINGUISHING INVESTMENT AND BUSINESS

Let us turn to the all-important exclusions from "capital assets." The first is that, in section 1221(1), of—

> stock in trade of the taxpayer or other property of a kind which would properly be included in the inventory of the taxpayer if on hand at the close of the taxable year, or property held by the taxpayer primarily for sale to customers in the ordinary course of his trade or business. * * *[9]

The main objective of this exclusion is reasonably clear, but the scope of the problem is not so evident. For in these deceptively few words Congress is attempting to exclude from "capital gain" all of those profits which it regards as the everyday profits of the business and commercial world. Here is the first important concept to give content to capital gain—the division between "business" and "investment."

A. Property held for sale to customers

The intent of this exclusion and its application to the obvious situations are relatively clear—the daily receipts of the corner grocery store, of the big city department store, and of the large manufacturing concern are ordinary income even though they arise from the sale of "property." But a sale of stock on a stock exchange by the average investor, a sale of a parcel of undeveloped land purchased as an investment, or a sale of a residence are to give rise to capital gain.

But beyond the obvious are great areas of uncertainty. The investor to realize his increase in value must sell his investment, and at that point he will often be engaging in an activity that has many of the characteristics found in the activity of some of the everyday businessmen whose profits from sales are regarded as excluded from capital gains. William White is an attorney who from time to time buys unimproved land with the purpose of resale. The purchases and sales are not regular, but over the years the number is not minor. Is William White a "trader" in real estate; i.e., do his real estate activities both place him in a "business" and in one involving the requisite

[9] Property which falls within sec. 1221(1) is also excluded from the capital gain-ordinary loss treatment which sec. 1231 accords to real property and depreciable property used in business.

holding of the property for sale? At what point do "investment activities" become "trading activities"? [10] John Jones has bought a tract of land many years ago as an investment and now he desires to sell. He must find buyers and to do so he may have to add improvements, advertise, hire an agent, subdivide, and so on. John Jones is a college professor of the classics and would be shocked to think of himself as a real estate dealer. Yet he may have more land or choicer land to sell than the everyday real estate dealers in town, so that for the moment John Jones, classics professor, is in reality the biggest real estate operator in the area. Is the land which John Jones bought years ago as an investment now "property held by the taxpayer primarily for sale to customers in the ordinary course of his trade or business"? Suppose that the land is not even initially acquired as a nonbusiness investment. Thus Tom Brown acquires a million acres of land to use in a cattle-raising business. The cattle business is unsuccessful and Tom Brown must now dispose of a million acres. He does so by selling some land every year for 20 years, with a large sales force and making every effort to attract buyers. Is Tom Brown now holding the land primarily for sale in his business?

Two main issues emerge in these "liquidation" situations: (1) Are the nature and volume of the development activities and the sales activities such as to place the taxpayer in the business of developing and subdividing land, so that the property can be regarded as held primarily for sale in the ordinary course of that business (thus providing the taxpayer with a "business holding" for the property if it did not have one before, as in the case of John Jones, and in such a case as well as in the situation where it had a business use, as in the case of Tom Brown, establishing the new purpose for the holding of the property); (2) despite the nature and volume of activities, since the transactions are consequent upon the liquidation of an investment, will the original investment character of the holding still persist so that the properties cannot be regarded as held primarily for sale in the ordinary course of the taxpayer's business? The courts have struggled for years with these problems, and the results are inconclusive.[11] Congress in 1954 added a section covering a page and a half which resolves only a few situations and in doing so manages to create

---

[10] The courts use the terms "trader" and "dealer" interchangeably. However, a "dealer" is a person standing ready to buy and sell property as a middleman, whereas a "trader" would be a person who engages in purchases and sales with sufficient frequency and volume and with the objective of realizing profits from that activity. *Gamble* v. *Commissioner*, 242 F. 2d 586 (5th Cir., 1957) and *Saltzman* v. *Commissioner*, 14 T.C.M. 89 (1955), affirmed per curiam 232 F. 2d 167 (3d Cir., 1955) found ordinary income, whereas *Austin* v. *Commissioner* 263 F. 2d 460 (9th Cir., 1959), found capital gain—all are "trader" type cases.

[11] See, for example, *Chandler* v. *United States*, 226 F. 2d 403 (7th Cir. 1955), and *Consolidated Naval Stores Co.* v. *Fahs*, 227 F. 2d 923 (5th Cir. 1955), both the *Tom Brown* case of the text, but involving corporations, in which the courts, reversing lower courts, found capital gain. On the other hand, *Palos Verdes Corp.* v. *United States*, 201 F. 2d 256 (9th Cir. 1952), is on the ordinary income side, and the arguments used in cases such as *Rollingwood Corp.* v. *Commissioner*, 190 F. 2d 263 (9th Cir. 1951), would produce ordinary income in the text case. The recent trend appears to favor the taxpayer in the *Tom Brown* case.

In the subdivision situation, the "John Jones" aspect, ordinary income was found in *Brown* v. *Commissioner*, 143 F. 2d 468 (65th Cir., 1944); *Kaltreider* v. *Commissioner*, 255 F. 2d 833 (3d Cir., 1958); *Mauldin* v. *Commissioner*, 255 F. 2d 714 (10th Cir., 1952). Capital gain was found in *Fahs* v. *Crawford*, 101 F. 2d 315 (5th Cir. 1947) and *Smith* v. *Dunn*, 224 F. 2d 353 (5th Cir. 1955).

a great many problems.[12] Moreover, the section is essentially limited to unimproved land. What about Harold Smith, who decides to invest his money in rental housing and builds 200 houses? He had at first sought a return on his capital in the form of rent, but after several years he now desires to sell those houses and retire. He now has more houses for sale than many a real estate broker. Is Harold Smith holding the houses primarily for sale in his business? [13]

These issues are not restricted to land—the estate of Richard is disposing of an inventory of $1 million in furs left by the decendent in his fur shop;[14] Robert is selling a large quantity of antiques previously collected by him; the estate of Mary is selling a large amount of valuable jewelry which she had accumulated during her life;[15] Henry conducts a truck or automobile rental business and sells the cars after a period of use in the rental activities.[16] Consider, on the other side, the businessman whose inventory greatly appreciates because of unforeseen conditions, such as war, shortages due to strikes or other factors, and the like. Has the inventory become an investment? In all of this, what is "investment" and what is "business" and how can we describe the differences with the precision desirable in tax law?

In the subdivision cases, and often other areas, the court is faced with a situation in which an asset held for investment purposes has appreciated over the years. Then, when the taxpayer decides to realize on his investment, he is often required to engage in businesslike activities of subdivision and development. These activities in themselves may return additional profit. The court is forced by the code, however, to treat the entire profit as either capital or ordinary. If it finds that the taxpayer did not change the character of his holding of the property, then both the appreciation in the investment years and the profits from the subdivision and development activities are capital gain. If it finds that these activities did change the character of the holding, then both the investment appreciation and the later profits are ordinary. This last result probably seems harsh to many a court, especially where there has been a long period of investment holding and the major share of the overall profit is attributable to that period.

---

[12] Sec. 1237. The congressional goal in sec. 1237 appears to be that of treating the appreciation in value of the land between its acquisition and the time when selling activities commenced as capital gain but treating the business income from the selling activities (after the fifth lot was sold) as ordinary income. Congress used 5 percent of the sales price as the rule of thumb to determine the business income, by analogy to what it took to be the usual broker's sales commission. Any appreciation in value subsequent to the commencement of selling activities was left capital gain, though logically it would seem ordinary income under the approach of the section.

[13] The cases here also divide. E.g., capital gain: *Dillon* v. *Commissioner*, 213 F. 2d 218 (8th Cir. 1954); *Victory Housing No. 2, Inc.* v. *Commissioner*, 205 F. 2d 371 (10th Cir. 1953); *Delsing* v. *United States*, 186 F. 2d 59 (5th Cir. 1951); *Curtis Company* v. *Commissioner*, 232 F. 2d 167 (3d Cir. 1956); ordinary income: *Winnick* v. *Commissioner*, 199 F. 2d 374 (6th Cir. 1952), on retrial, 21 T.C. 1029 (1954), aff'd. 223 F. 2. 266 (6th Cir. 1955); *Rollingwood Corp.* v. *Commissioner*, 190 F. 2d 263 (9th Cir. 1951); *King* v. *Commissioner*, 189 F. 2d 122 (5th Cir. 1951).

[14] Compare *Estate of Jacques Ferber*, 22 T.C. 261 (1954) (capital gain), with *Commissioner v. Linde*, 213 F. 2d I (9th Cir. 1954) (ordinary income).

[15] Cf. *Reynolds* v. *Commissioner*, 155 F. 2d 620 (1st Cir. 1946) (capital gain). But see *Hollis* v. *United States*, 121 F. Supp. 191 (N.D. Ohio 1954) (ordinary income on a "one venture proposition" involving the importation and sale of 25 art objects).

[16] *Philber Equipment Corporation* v. *Commissioner*, 237 F. 2d 129 (3d Cir. 1956), reversing the Tax Court, 25 T.C. 88 (1956), found capital gain: *S.E.C. Corporation* v. *United States*, 140 F. Supp. 717 (S.D.N.Y. 1956), aff'd per curiam in 241 F. 2d 416 (2d. Cir. 1957), involving sales of previously leased water coolers, found ordinary income.

Would it be proper to develop in the statute a fragmentation approach under which the overall profit could be divided between investment gain on the one hand and development and selling profits on the other? Clearly, this approach would have its difficulties, such as determining the point of time at which the period of investment gain is to terminate and then to ascertain the value of the property at that time. But the results under a fragmentation approach would appear fairer and more appropriate than under the present system.[17]

B. Property used in business but not held for sale to customers

The aspect of "investment" as distinguished from "business" has another important facet—what about those assets of an admitted business activity which are other than inventory, such as the building and land on which the business is conducted or the machinery used in the business operations? If these are sold, is the profit ordinary income because we are dealing with an admitted business? Or may the businessman be regarded as "investing" in these business assets? Congress on this question has been deluged with advice, but unfortunately the advice has been conflicting. Thus, the farmers holding livestock for breeding or dairy purposes and then selling the livestock desired classification of the property as capital assets. This was only natural, after one considered that the sale of the livestock would invariably produce a tax profit, since the expense of raising it had been previously deducted and its tax cost was zero. On the other hand, railroads and other users of machinery and equipment which was sold after its utility had declined desired classification of that property as noncapital assets. This was only natural, after one considered that the equipment was usually sold at a loss which could have been deducted as an ordinary item through depreciation if the property had been retained until the end of its useful life or scrapped. But both livestock and machinery were "property"—and "property used in the trade or business." Faced with this dilemma, Congress resolved it in an intensely practical fashion—such depreciable property would in effect be a capital asset for gain purposes but not a capital asset for loss purposes.[18] A similar rule is applied to real property to avoid problems of allocation of sales proceeds between the land and the buildings and machinery on it, so that the loss on the sale of business real property is likewise ordinary while the gain is capital. Farmers and railroads could both depart pleased, but one searching for a concept of capital gain was left only with an added appreciation of both the theoretical difficulty of the task and the congressional flexibility in finding an escape from dilemmas.

Section 1221(2), the second exclusion, together with section 1231 thus excludes from the taxpayer's capital assets on the loss side, but not the gain side—

---

[17] There are elements of a fragmentation approach in various statutory sections of present law. Sec. 1237, note 12, supra, is an example. Secs. 631(b) and 1231 in dealing with cut timber, infra note 49, treat the appreciation in value of the standing timber as capital gain, to be realized when the timber is cut, and the profits made in selling the cut timber as ordinary income. The *Heiner* v. *Tindle* rule, 276 U.S. 582 (1928), measuring the loss on the sale of rental residential property by reference to the value at the time of conversion to rental use if that value is less than basis, is in effect a fragmentation approach.

[18] Secs. 1221(2) and 1231.

property, used in his trade or business, of a character which is subject to the allowance for depreciation provided in section 167, or real property used in his trade or business * * *

except—

property of a kind which would properly be includible in the inventory of the taxpayer if on hand at the close of the taxable year * * * [and] property held by the taxpayer primarily for sale to customers in the ordinary course of his trade or business * * *

The scope of this exception has been considered above in the discussion of property held for sale to customers.[19]

There are interesting ramifications of these congressional solutions in the business area. The value of standing timber before it is cut by a taxpayer in the timber business is specifically listed as a capital asset [20] and the value of unharvested crops sold with the land is also classified as a capital asset,[21] although in each case the distinction from everyday profits is debatable. Without such specific classification, these items were treated on sale as falling within the exception of property held for sale to customers.[22] And even within the specific treatment of these classes of business assets, Congress has solemnly adopted further refinements. Thus, is has expressly provided that the term "timber" includes "evergreen trees which are more than 6 years old at the time severed from the roots and are sold for ornamental purposes." [23] And in specifically treating livestock held for draft, breeding, or dairy purposes as a capital asset, Congress excluded "poultry." [24] Also, in another section, Congress has partially ventured into the area of exclusive dealing arrangements, sales agencies, profitable leases, favorable purchase contracts, and the like by in effect classifying the profits on the sale of certain but not all of these arrangements as capital gains.[25] The point here is that, lacking an adequate definition of capital gain, Congress is gradually moving to dealing with particular assets one by one. In such an endeavor any possible concept is likely to be lost in the welter of lobbyists.

* * *

The Supreme Court recently grappled with another variation of the division between investment and business, which neatly illustrates the essential dilemma involved in the statutory definition of "capital asset." [29] The Corn Products Refining Co. manufactured from corn various products such as starch and sugar. It entered into contracts with the buyers of its products calling for delivery at fixed prices.

[19] As far as the code sections go, nondepreciable personal property used in a business is a capital asset unless the property fall within the sec. 1221(1) category of property held for sale to customers. Also, sec. 1221(4) excepts from capital asset classification accounts or notes receivable acquired in the ordinary course of business for services rendered or from the sale of inventory or other property under sec. 1221(1).

[20] Sec. 1231(b)(2).

[21] Sec. 1231(b)(4).

[22] E.g., *Watson* v. *Commissioner,* 345 U.S. 544 (1953), treated the growing crops as ordinary assets prior to the specific classification.

[23] Sec. 631(a).

[24] Sec. 1231(b)(3).

[25] Sec. 1241. The case law is here also in confusion. See, e.g. *Hort* v. *Commissioner,* 313 U.S. 28 (1941) (ordinary income to lessor on cancellation of lease); *Commissioner* v. *McCue Bros. & Drummond, Inc.,* 210 F. 2d 752 (2d Cir. 1954) (capital gain to lessee on cancellation of lease); *Commissioner* v. *Ray,* 210 F. 2d 390 (5th Cir. 1954) (capital gain to lessee on cancellation of clause in lease prohibiting lessor from leasing other parts of building to lessee's competitors); *Commissioner* v. *Starr Bros., Inc.,* 204 F. 2d 673 (2d Cir. 1953) (ordinary income on termination of exclusive agency contract to distribute certain drugs at retail); *Jones* v. *Corby,* 186 F. 2d 450 (10th Cir. 1950) (capital gain on cancellation of exclusive general insurance agency); *Commissioner* v. *Pittston Company,* 252 F. 2d 344 (2d Cir, 1958) (ordinary gain on cancellation of an exclusive purchase contract); *Leh* v. *Commissioner,* 260 F. 2d 489 (9th Cir. 1958) (ordinary gain on cancellation of supply contract).

[29] *Corn Products Refining Co.* v. *Commissioner,* 350 U.S. 46 (1955).

Since the company did not maintain large inventories of corn, it was subject to a price squeeze if corn prices rose. As protection it purchased corn futures at harvest time, and then took delivery on these contracts when necessary to maintain a supply of corn for manufacturing operations. It sold the remainder of the futures in early summer if no shortage was imminent. If shortages appeared, it sold futures only as it bought spot corn for grinding. In this fashion it obtained protection against an increase in spot corn prices.

Were the gains on the sales of the corn futures capital gains? The taxpayer said yes: the futures were "property" and, not falling within any of the statutory exclusions, were therefore capital assets. The Court said no:

> We find nothing in this record to support the contention that Corn Products' futures activity was separate and apart from its manufacturing operation. On the contrary, it appears that the transactions were vitally important to the company's business as a form of insurance against increases in the price of raw corn. Not only were the purchases initiated for just this reason, but the petitioner's sales policy, selling in the future at a fixed price or less, continued to leave it exceedingly vulnerable to rises in the price of corn. Further, the purchase of corn futures assured the company a source of supply which was admittedly cheaper than constructing additional storage facilities for raw corn. Under these facts it is difficult to imagine a program more closely geared to a company's manufacturing enterprise or more important to its successful operation.
>
> * * * * * * *
>
> * * * Admittedly, petitioner's corn futures do not come within the literal language of the exclusions set out in that section. They were not stock in trade, actual inventory, property held for sale to customers or depreciable property used in a trade or business. But the capital-asset provision of [sec. 1221] must not be so broadly applied as to defeat rather than further the purpose of Congress. *Burnet* v. *Harmel*, 287 U.S. 103, 108. Congress intended that profits and losses arising from the everyday operation of a business be considered as ordinary income or loss rather than capital gain or loss. The preferential treatment provided by [sec. 1221] applies to transactions in property which are not the normal source of business income. It was intended "to relieve the taxpayer from * * * excessive tax burdens on gains resulting from a conversion of capital investments, and to remove the deterrent effect of those burdens on such conversions." *Burnet* v. *Harmel*, 287 U.S. at 106. Since this section is an exception from the normal tax requirements of the Internal Revenue Code, the definition of a capital asset must be narrowly applied and its exclusions interpreted broadly. This is necessary to effectuate the basic congressional purpose. This Court has always contrued narrowly the term "capital assets" in [sec. 1221]. See *Hort* v. *Commissioner*, 313 U.S. 28, 31; *Kieselbach* v. *Commissioner*, 317 U.S. 399, 403.
>
> * * * * * * *
>
> We believe that the statute clearly refutes the contention of Corn Products. Moreover, it is significant to note that practical considerations lead to the same conclusion. To hold otherwise would permit those engaged in hedging transactions to transmute ordinary income into capital gain at will. The hedger may either sell the future and purchase in the spot market or take delivery under the future contract itself. But if a sale of the future created a capital transaction while delivery of the commodity under the same future did not, a loophole in the statute would be created and the purpose of Congress frustrated.[30]

The Court thus resolved the dilemma posed by the use of the term "property" in section 1221 by placing the congressional definition of section 1221 gently to one side and then deciding the case on its own concept of the capital gain-ordinary income division between investment and business. This approach has not always meant a success for the Government. Suppose a manufacturer has a contract with a foreign government to deliver machines, and during the life of the contract is required to deposit U.S. Government bonds as security for performance. The manufacturer purchases bonds for this purpose

[30] Id. at 50, 51–52, 53–54.

and then sells them at a slight loss immediately after completition of the contract. Is the loss capital or ordinary? Or suppose a wholesale lumber dealer in need of sources of supply purchases some of the debentures of a newly formed lumber company and as a consequence receives a portion of the latter's production. The lumber company later fails and the debentures are sold at a loss. In these cases the Government bonds and the debentures are certainly "property" in the general sense, and moreover, being securities, are a type of property normally thought of as falling within the capital asset category. They are not "property" closely related to the statutory exclusion of "stock in trade," as was the case in *Corn Products*.[31] Yet in both situations the courts found an ordinary loss. As to the Government bonds:

The taxpayer's contention is to the effect that the whole transaction is merely an incident required and made necessary in the performance of a contract undertaken in the regular course of the taxpayer's business and is deductible from gross income in its entirety by reason of the provision of [sec. 162, permitting a deduction for ordinary and necessary business expenses].

* * * * * * *

In brief, it is urged [by the Government] that the all-inclusive language of [sec. 1221] requires that, since the bonds are property, they must be treated as capital assets unless exempted by the specific language of the section. The argument carries with it the necessary conclusion that the circumstances of the transaction, its factual background, the necessities of the business involved, and the intentions of taxpayer are of no importance except in determining whether the bonds are exempted under the section. We are not persuaded that [sec. 162] is so completely subordinate to [sec. 1221] and we find no authority which goes so far.

* * * * * * *

* * * Here there is a clear finding that no investment was intended. The taxpayer's lack of surplus capital, the interest return of the bonds, the interest obligation of the loan, and the almost immediate sale of the bonds when available make such a finding imperative * * *.[32]

As to the debentures, the court quoted the following from the first case:

[B]usiness expense [sec. 162], has been many times determined by business necessity without a specific consideration of [sec. 1221].

and continued—

So considered, the present problem becomes relatively simple. Petitioner's action in purchasing the debenture was a reasonable and necessary act in the conduct of its business. The loss of the purchase price was proximately related to that acquisition. Hence, under [sec. 162] the amount was a deductible business expense, or business loss, properly taken in the instant year since that was the first time the reason for holding the debenture disappeared and the extent of the loss could be accurately measured.[33]

Under these decisions[34] is there any escape from wild uncertainty? If the courts are to embark on a search for the reasons why individuals

[31] 350 U.S. 46 (1955).

[32] *Commissioner* v. *Bagley & Sewall Co.*, 221 F. 2d 944, 946 (2d Cir. 1955).

[33] *Tulane Hardwood Lumber Co.*, 24 T.C. No. 129 (Sept. 30, 1955). The court overruled an earlier case, *Logan and Kanawha Coal Co.*, 5 T.C. 1298 (1945), and indicated its inability to distinguish an earlier second circuit case, *Exposition Souvenir Corp.* v. *Commissioner*, 163 F. 2d 283 (2d Cir. 1947), in which a concessionnaire at a world's fair had to buy debentures issued by the fair.

[34] Another example is *Mansfield Journal Co.* v. *Commissioner*, 31 T.C. —— (1959), finding ordinary income when a newspaper, for a price, permitted other newspapers to buy paper under supply contracts which the taxpayer had entered into to assure itself of an adequate supply and which obligated it to buy a certain quantity.

The *Corn Products* case has had two principal effects. One is that considered in the text, whereby certain assets which on a literal reading of the statute would be "property" and thus secure capital asset treatment are nevertheless held under the particular transactions involved to yield ordinary income. The second is the admonition in the *Corn Products* opinion that the capital asset provision "must not be so broadly applied as to

or corporations buy stocks or securities and to weigh whether an "investment" motive is overbalanced by some other motive, many a stock or security can become an ordinary asset but no one will be able to predict when the transformation will take place. It must be realized that these are not the *Gregory* v. *Helvering* [35] type of situation, where judicial action is certainly proper to protect technical rules from distortion through tax-motivated transactions lacking a business purpose or other substantial economic reality. That situation is controlled by the business-purpose rule, which has a valid and important role in a tax system. The above situations, however—the corn futures, the Government bonds, and the debentures—are not tax-avoidance distortions. They involve everyday business-motivated transactions. But they forced the judicial action taken in reference to them because of the failure of Congress to face up realistically to the tremendous classification problem inherent in the attempted division between "investment" and "business." Put more narrowly, the decisions represent the courts' view that Congress has not realistically faced that problem and, therefore, did not desire to be taken literally when it used the broad term "property" in section 1221. The courts are willing to rescue Congress from its statutory straitjacket.

This approach simply turns property from an all-inclusive term into an elastic concept, contracting or expanding according to the courts' judgment of what a capital gain should be. But this is hardly a solution of the problem. What standards has Congress offered to guide the courts in separating investment from business? What standards can the courts discover when they explore the ground previously searched by Congress in its unsuccessful efforts to find solutions? The attempt to separate investment from business is no less difficult where the forum is judicial rather than legislative.

* * *

A more basic question would be why there should be any capital gain or loss treatment for business assets, whether or not held for sale to customers. As long as the asset is used in busines, it can be argued that any gain or loss associated with the asset simply be considered as a segment of the overall business income, which of necessity would be ordinary income rather than capital gain. Under this broad approach, the entire income of corporations would be ordinary, if the usual rule is followed, as it is under section 162, that corporations organized for profit are engaged in business. (An exception might be made for investment companies.) In the case of an individual, however, it would be necessary to define "business" and then to identify the assets used in the business. In contrast to this broad approach, it may be asserted that certain assets may represent investment in the business, and in this category would fall real property and depreciable property not held for sale. This approach would involve a classification of the assets between "permanent capital" (land, buildings, depreciable property with a fairly long life, long-term leaseholds, franchises) and "current capital" (inventory, raw materials, supplies, ac-

defeat rather than further the purpose of Congress." In the close questions of application that can arise under secs. 1221 and 1231—e.g., was particular property in fact held for sale to customers or as an investment; did the subdivision activities turn an investment into a business of selling to customers—the courts are using the *Corn Products* case to justify a decision against the taxpayer. See *Kaltreider* v. *Commissioner,* 225 F. 2d 833 (3d Cir. 1958) (subdivision case).

[35] 293 U.S. 465 (1935).

counts receivable). If this latter approach is taken, the problems respecting depreciable property considered above remain pertinent.

III. THE PROBLEM OF DISTINGUISHING INVESTMENT AND SPECULATION

Congress, in the few words earlier quoted from section 1221(1) which form the first important exclusion from capital assets, is also concerned with another set of distinctions which it regards as important. These involve the groups who make their profits in the stock market. Here Congress apparently saw three main groups: the dealer in securities, the speculator, and the investor. The dealer in securities was regarded as like the grocer except that his inventory consisted of securities and not groceries, and hence his assets, the securities, were not capital assets. The investor, who holds his securities for their annual return but whose securities appreciate in value, was the prime example for Congress of the capital gain taxpayer. Therefore, his securities were capital assets so that their appreciation in value would be a capital gain. Even here a problem presented itself when a taxpayer was both a dealer and an investor, and a section was adopted to aid in classifying his securities.[37] The profits of the speculator were not regarded as worthy of preferential treatment. However, Congress could see no way to distinguish the speculator from the investor by reference to the nature of the assets held, for both simply held securities and sold for their own account. So it resorted to another criterion and added a holding-period requirement under which a capital asset had to be held a certain length of time to obtain preferential treatment. That period is now 6 months.[38]

But the double test—capital asset and holding period—leaves some strange results. In the nonpreferential area are left most "traders," those speculators who are seeking an eighth or a quarter of a point and whose turnover of securities generally involves a period of hours or days rather than months. But the other market participants are all grouped together—the professional speculator whose purchases and sales are substantial and frequent but involve more than a 6-month holding period, the large investor who is constantly perfecting his portfolio through changes in its composition, the modest investor who occasionally changes his portfolio, and the amateur speculator who takes a chance now and then. The only differentiation possible under the statute is in the length of time that the securities have been held, and this factor cuts through these last four groups in indiscriminate fashion rather than between groups.[39] In fact, it is much more likely to put all of these groups safely on the capital gain side, in view of the short length of the holding period. In 1956, in the returns of individuals with gains or losses from capital assets, there were $9.7 billion in net long-term capital gains and only $319 million in net short-term capital gains; there were $636 million in net long-term capital losses and $962 million in net short-term capital losses.

---

[37] Sec. 1236.

[38] Sec. 1222.

[39] The professional speculator and even a large investor with frequent sales may be engaged in a "trade or business." Sol H. Morris, 38 B.T.A. 265 (1938); L. T. Alverson, 35 B.T.A. 482 (1937). But they do not hold their securities for sale "to customers." *Commissioner* v. *Burnett*, 118 F. 2d 659 (5th Cir. 1941); Thomas E. Wood, 16 T.C. 213 (1951). The "specialist" on the floor is treated as a dealer for tax purposes.

We are thus left with a congressional feeling that speculation and investment are different matters, but with no statutory differentiation between the two except as respects the in-and-out, daily traders. Also, we find that the person who makes his profits by sagacious buying and selling of securities is on the capital gain side but his counterpart in the real estate or other personal property area is on the noncapital side. Further, even this almost ineffective use of the holding-period requirement has brought with it considerable complexity, for Congress has found it necessary to adopt rather lengthy statutory provisions to protect that period from the manipulations possible through short sales, puts and calls, and then to protect certain arbitrage operations from the effect of the first set of provisions.[40]

So much for the first exclusion from capital assets in the words earlier quoted and its ramifying statutory provisions. Congress has in the most general way sought distinctions between "business" and "speculation" on the one hand and "investment" on the other. But its own concepts are unclear and it is beginning to appreciate that these terms do not have the settled significance in the world of economics or commerce necessary to support statutory differentiation. Hence, a piecemeal approach is developing and we are being led into a maze of complexity.[41]

IV. THE PROBLEM OF DISTINGUISHING INVESTMENT PROFITS FROM THE REWARDS FOR PERSONAL EFFORTS

The next principal exclusion of certain property from capital assets is that of—

> a copyright, a literary, musical, or artistic composition, or similar property, held by * * * a taxpayer whose personal efforts created such property * * *.[42]

Here Congress is pursuing another factor in its concept of capital gain. Apparently, profits attributable to creative "personal efforts" are not regarded as entitled to capital gain treatment. This is, presumably a result of the realization that salaries, wages, commissions, and professional fees are on the ordinary income side, along with the everyday profits of the businessman, and the feeling that profits coming from other personal efforts belong with these classes of income. One can readily understand such an attitude and accept the exclusion. Yet one becomes considerably nonplussed when he finds an entire section devoted to classifying the profits of an inventor as capital

---

[40] Sec. 1233.

[41] There are of course many other aspects that could be considered. For example, on the loss side, there are differences in the classification of (*a*) stocks and bonds, whether the taxpayer is an "investor" of "promoter," (*b*) debts represented by notes if he is an "investor," and (*c*) debts represented by notes if he is a "promoter." Secs. 165(g), 166. In addition, sec. 1244, allowing an ordinary loss on a stock investment in a small business corporation, draws a distinction between this stock investment and other equity investments, and also between a stock investment and a bond investment in the same corporation.

[42] Sec. 1221(3). Though personal efforts are obviously involved, the courts or the Service do not appear to have thought that a copyright on this ground could not be considered "property" for the purposes of the capital gain definition and thereby denied capital asset status. Consequently, prior to the adoption of sec. 1221(3) in 1950, the tax classification of a copyright, or other creative work, on its sale by the author depended on the status of the author. If he was an amateur, then his effort was not property held primarily for sale to customers in the ordinary course of business and the sale resulted in capital gain. But if he was regarded as being in the writing profession, then the sale resulted in ordinary income. See *Stern* v. *United States,* 164 F. Supp. 847 (E.D. La., 1958), aff'd per curiam 262 F. 2d 957 (5th Cir. 1959) involving receipts for years before and after 1950 from the sale of the character "Francis," a talking mule.

gain whether the inventor is an amateur or a professional.[43] Moreover, this capital gain treatment is extended even to one whose business is that of promoting inventions. And it applies whether the profits are received in a lump sum or through royalties. One's faith in the apparent conclusion regarding the congressional view of profits from personal efforts is further shaken when it is noted that several pages of the statute are devoted to classifying the rewards under employee stock option arrangements as capital gains [44] and to making the capital gain preferential status available to employees who on their retirement obtain lump-sum payments from pension plans.[45] The latter provisions of course lead into the intricacies of pension plans and profit-sharing arrangements, especially in the case of closely held corporations, since they become the rainbow leading to the capital gain pot of gold. One can only conclude that the exclusion regarding authors and other creative artists does evidence the basic congressional concept that the rewards for personal efforts should be outside the capital gain area, but that significant pressures can often turn aside the application of that concept.

These aberrations in the patent, stock option, and pension trust situations really involve a congressional tax bounty through the gift of a capital gain status and should not obscure the definitional problem.[46] Since all "property" unless excluded is a "capital asset" and since personal efforts result in creating "property"—be it a book, a patent, good will for an individual business, a trade name, a contract not to compete, a profitable employment contract, an exclusive agent's contract to represent an actor or a writer, or a promoter's corporate stock whose value rises because of his business sagacity—the magnitude of the problem is apparent. Where does the emphasis on the personal efforts cease so that the resulting "property" may become a "capital asset"? Congress has here given little guidance other than the ad hoc statutory decisions described above, and these are conflicting.[47] The problem of classification is largely left to the courts, which tend to find noncapital gain when the personal service element predominates or when the asset is of a character distinguishable from the traditional capital gain area. Hence the sale of an employment contract would probably produce ordinary income, but the promoter's stock would be a capital asset even if the promoter devoted all of his time to the promotion, organization, financing, and operation of

---

[43] Sec. 1235. Where sec. 1235 is not applicable, as in transfers of less than "all substantial rights to the patent," transfers to related persons, and transfers by corporations, the transaction is to be considered under the other code sections, since sec. 1235 is not regarded as itself requiring all noncomplying transactions to result in ordinary income.

[44] Sec. 421.

[45] Secs. 402, 403. In a sense, the "Mayer" amendment, sec. 1240, is traceable to the above pension plan provision. With respect to these provisions, see Surrey, "The Congress and the Tax Lobbyist—How Special Provisions Get Enacted," 70 Harv. L. Rev. 1145, 1161 (1957).

[46] The pension trust and other termination-of-employment situations are examples of the earlier prevalence of the quaint notion that the capital gain rate is an appropriate substitute for averaging. A more sophisticated view is evidenced in sec. 72(e)(3), which allows a 3-year spread of the income received on the maturity of an endowment contract instead of giving "relief" through bestowing a capital gain status on the transaction. The patent and stock option preferences are the result of congressional use of the capital gain device as an "incentive," in the one case to invention, in the other to the fuller application of executive talent spurred on by the acquisition of a stock interest in the corporations it serves.

[47] Pointing to an ordinary income status for personal efforts, sec. 1241 in treating the cancellation of a distributor's agreement as a capital gain transaction requires that the distributor have a "substantial capital investment" in the distributorship.

corporations.[48] But the fact that these problems are largely unanswered in the statute does not eliminate them. Again they illustrate that while Congress on the whole may be seeking to distinguish between "investment profits" and "the rewards of personal efforts," the world of affairs does not offer any neat division.

V. THE PROBLEM OF CLASSIFYING TRANSACTIONS INVOLVING RECURRING RECEIPTS

A consideration of the problems created by the all-inclusive scope of "property" in the statutory definition of capital asset leads to still another source of difficulty. Congress as respects capital gains presumably had in mind a distinction between recurring receipts such as salaries, wages, interest, rents, dividends, royalties, and the like on the one hand and the nonrecurrent realization of the appreciation in the value of property on the other. It is sometimes difficult to be clear about this, for here also there are aberrations; thus the capital gain status has been conferred by statute upon timber and coal royalties [49] and also on patent royalties.[50] But since Congress has so far refused to extend this treatment to oil and iron ore royalties, one may suppose the principle still stands, though in the end it may turn out to have little application in the natural resource area if the pressures for a capital gain status for oil royalties intensify. But the right to a salary earned, or to interest accrued, or a dividend due, is "property" in the legal sense. Does such a right when sold, therefore, transport the salary, interest, or dividend out of the ordinary income area and into the capital gain category via the term "property" in the definition of capital asset? Here again Congress has dealt piecemeal with parts of the problem. A cryptic clause added in 1954 appears to exclude from capital assets the sale of claims for salary earned as well as claims for goods sold,[51] but there is nothing as to other items. There is a lengthy section devoted to the allied problem of discount bonds, with the purpose of treating as ordinary income the interest element in the discount.[52] On the other hand, there is a section making the amounts received on the cancellation of a favorable busines lease or a favorable distributor's agreement involving a substantial capital investment capital gain,[53] though

---

[48] For examples on the ordinary income side, see *General Artists Corp.* v. *Commissioner*, 205 F. 2d 360 (2d Cir. 1953) (assignment of an exclusive agency contract by a theatrical booking agency); *Beals' Estate* v. *Commissioner*, 82 F. 2d 268 (2d Cir. 1936) (amounts received for a covenant not to compete); cases cited note 59 infra. For examples on the capital gain side, see *Jones* v. *Corbyn*, 186 F. 2d 450 (10th Cir. 1950) (cancellation of exclusive insurance agency); Jack Benny, 25 T.C. 197 (1955) (A) (sale of stock of theatrical corporation owned in part by Jack Benny to radio network where purchase set in motion transfer of Jack Benny's program and services to that network); *Marx* v. *Commissioner*, 29 T.C. 88 (1957) (A) (sale of interest in a radio quiz show) (these last two cases arose prior to the adoption of sec. 1221(3)).

Another illustration of the classification problems in this area is that involving the sale of a business in which the seller gives a covenant not to compete. Goodwill is a capital asset; amounts received for a personal covenant not to compete are ordinary income. Hence the allocation of the purchase price is highly important as respects these items, and yet the two are often so interwoven as to be incapable of proper separation.

[49] Secs. 631 (b), (c).

[50] Sec. 1235.

[51] Sec. 1221(4). This section excludes "accounts or notes receivable acquired in the ordinary course of trade or business for services rendered or from the sale of property described in paragraph (I) * * *."

While the purpose of this addition was to preserve ordinary losses on accounts receivable included in income and later sold at a loss, the words may have the effect, albeit presumably unintended, of providing a statutory classification of claims to salary as ordinary assets if the claims are regarded as "accounts receivable."

[52] Sec. 1232.

[53] Sec. 1241.

the continuation of the lease or agreement would have been reflected in larger profits for the business.[54] But aside from these stray pieces of legislation, the matter has been left to the courts, with varying results.

The problems presented to the courts in the area of recurring receipts are diverse and difficult to classify. The cases in general present these issues:

A. Sale of property versus division of interests in property

1. *Method of payment.*—If an owner of property sells it outright for a fixed price and the property is a capital asset, he secures capital gain. This is the "image" underlying the capital gain provisions. An investment risk has been concluded; the sale of the property has established the success or failure of the investment; and by the same token ended the investor's interest in that particular investment. This result remains, even though the purchase price is paid in installments, and the seller retains a security interest in the asset sold. This "security interest" is sufficiently removed from the former "investment interest" to permit the view that a final reckoning on the investment risk has been obtained. Any other view would seriously circumscribe the capital gain provisions. But suppose the sale of the property is on a royalty basis. Here the outcome of the investment risk has been partly determined, for the royalty contract establishes some measure of the worth of the investment. But that measure is based on estimates as to future events under the royalty contract, such as the quantity or value of production by the transferee, which in turn will be related to factors inherent in the investment property now subject to the royalty. Hence the investment risk is clearly not fully concluded. Moreover, the royalty payments involve recurring receipts, a characteristic which is closer to the ordinary income image. The Congress, however, as has been noted, has granted capital gain treatment to some royalty transactions—in coal, timber, and patents. The courts likewise have not been consistent.

In the case of oil and gas royalties, the decisions, influenced by depletion concepts, hold that the retained economic interest of the royalty holder prevents capital gain. These decisions are phrased in terms of the absence of a "sale or exchange"—one of the requirements under the capital gain rules.[55] But in cases involving patents and copyrights (before the statutory rules in these areas were adopted) the courts without much wrestling with the issues very early granted capital gain status to transfers on a royalty method; here the transaction was considered a sale despite the use of the royalty method.[56] And recently, in transactions involving the disposition of interests in sand or gravel, the courts have not followed the earlier oil and gas cases and have instead given capital gain treatment to royalty contracts.[57] Also, where the owner of mineral property divided the economic risks in the property in such a fashion as to fall between outright sale and outright royalty, by transferring the property for a

---

[54] See note 25 supra.

[55] *Burnet* v. *Harmel,* 287 U.S. 103 (1932).

[56] *Stern* v. *United States,* supra, note 42; *Meyer* v. *Commissioner,* 6 T.C. 258 (1946) (patent); *Commissioner* v. *Hopkinson,* 126 F. 2d 406 (2d Cir., 1942) (patent); Rev. Rul. 58-353. 1958-2 Cum. Bull 408.

[57] *Dann* v. *Commissioner,* 30 T.C. (1958), summarizing the cases.

large initial payment but also reserving an amount per unit of ore produced, the court found capital gain for both forms of receipt.[58] Hence, the relationship of the royalty method of payment to the capital gain concept remains an uncertain matter.

2. *Other divisions of interests in the property.*—In addition to the royalty situations and the outright sale there are many types of transactions in which the owner still retains some interest in the investment property and the receipts from it. Suppose a person transfers the right to 1 year's salary or a year's dividends or bond interest. Here the decisions require ordinary income treatment—a contrary conclusion would in effect have swept all such recurring receipts into the capital gain area.[59] More difficult situations arise when the interest sold becomes more important, so that the argument that the interest is "property" under local law concepts and hence is "property" within the meaning of the capital asset definition is more troublesome.

The recent litigation over oil payments reflects the perplexities inherent in any attempts at classification in this area. The continued receipt of current payments by one who has the right to oil royalties or an oil payment is ordinary income.[60] The sale of the entire right to the oil royalties or the oil payments is capital gain.[61] What, then, of the sale of the right to one-half the oil royalties or payments, where the part sold is to continue for the same length of time as the part retained. Presumably capital gain. But suppose a fixed amount in dollars or oil is carved out of the oil royalties or payment and only that part is sold. Thus, A, who owns oil royalties, or has the right to an oil payment of $1 million, sells an oil payment of $200,000 to B. Here B's interest will not continue throughout the life of A's interest. Is this difference sufficiently significant to make the proceeds received by A on the sale ordinary income? The fifth circuit said "No," the interest sold was "property" under local law and the Revenue Code and the sale should therefore receive capital gain treatment.[62] The Supreme Court, in the *Lake* case, accepted the local law characterization but found ordinary income:

> We do not see here any conversion of a capital investment. * * * The lump-sum consideration seems essentially a substitute for what would otherwise be received at a future time as ordinary income. The payout of these particular assigned oil payment rights could be ascertained with considerable accuracy. * * * The substance of what was received was the present value of income which the recipient would otherwise obtain in the future. In short, consideration was paid for the right to receive future income, not for an increase in the value of the income-producing property.[63]

---

[58] *Commissioner* v. *Remer,* 260 F. 2d 337 (8th Cir., 1958).

[59] In a sense, the exclusion of salaries, wages, commissions, and fees is the result of a gentlemen's agreement by the courts that they will not in this area take literally the use of the term "property" in the definition of capital asset, and will exclude from is scope claims to salaries and the like. Otherwise, these claims when sold would produce capital gains and thereby permit all earnings to escape ordinary income taxation. Sometimes the courts reach the desired result by not taking literally the "sale or exchange" terminology. In other instances they simply say "no" to the taxpayer's assertion of capital gain. For examples, see F. W. Jessop, 16 T.C. 491 (1951); Charles J. Williams, 5 T.C. 639 (1945); George K. Gann, 41 B.T.A. 388 (1940); Thurlow E. McFall, 34 B.T.A. 108 (1936). But the courts' willingness to rescue Congress from the ineptitude of the drafting does not eliminate the basic problem of classification.

See *Rhodes' Estate* v. *Commissioner,* 131 F. 2d 50 (6th Cir. 1942) (sale of dividend alone). But a sale of the stock just before it goes ex dividend will transform the dividend into capital gain.

[60] See *Lee* v. *Commissioner,* 126 F. 2d 825, 826 (5th Cir., 1942).

[61] Rev. Rul. 55–526, 1955 Int. Rev. Bull. 574.

[62] *Caldwell & Caldwell,* 218 F. 2d 567 (5th Cir. 1955); *Commissioner* v. *P. G. Lake, Inc.,* 241 F. 2d 716 (5th Cir., 1957) and companion cases.

[63] *Commissioner* v. *P. G. Lake, Inc.,* 356 U.S. 260 (1958).

The decision in one sense was almost inevitable. If the fifth circuit rule had stood and if the period of time necessary for the full amount of the carved-out payment to pay off, i.e., to be recovered by the purchaser, were short and without significant risk to the purchaser, it is hard to see what would have remained of the ordinary income status of oil royalties. Thus, the Tax Court had permitted the holder of an oil payment to obtain capital gain on his transfer of a carved-out payment to a contractor in return for the construction of a house.[64] Is there any real distinction between this situation and the use of the device to buy a fur coat, to pay a charge account at Neiman-Marcus, or the like? The reasoning of the court, however, is hardly more than the statement of the conclusion. (As respects the last sentence in the above quotation, what would the Court have said if the value of the basic oil royalty was a figure far in excess of expectations when the investment in the oil royalty had been made?) But one dissatisfied with the judicial analysis can hardly blame the courts, for the decisions simply underscore the inadequacy of the statutory definition of "capital asset."

Nor should dissatisfaction hide the real issue. In these situations we are concerned with property which has value because it is either yielding or is capable of yielding recurring receipts. Any sale of a capital asset reflects in this sense a transfer of those receipts. Suppose that a corporation decides to increase its dividend rate and this decision results in an increase in the value of its stock. If the stock is not sold, the recurring receipt of the increased dividends must remain ordinary income, for the contrary would mean a policy of giving capital gain treatment to investment income. But a sale of the stock at a profit because of that increase in value produces capital gain, for otherwise there could hardly be a capital gain concept. This is so even though the amount received represents, in the words of the *Lake* case, "the present value of income which the recipient would otherwise obtain in the future." Thus, since the capital gain concept covers an "investment profit" but not current "investment income," we must confine capital gain treatment to transactions which identify the investment profit obtained as a result of the investment risk. The extremes may be clear, but the area in between offers only gradations, as the oil cases indicate.[65] Will it be possible to devise workable statutory concepts and provisions to cover the myriad situations that lie in between?

B. Transfer of right to recurring receipts

In some of the cases above, as the *Lake* case, the owner of the property carved out an interest in time which resulted in someone else's receiving the recurring receipts while the owner retained the balance

[64] *Hawn* v. *Commissioner,* 23 T.C. 516 (1954), reversed in *Commissioner* v. *Hawn,* 231 F. 2d 340 (5th Cir., 1956), query if in effect repudiated in *Commissioner* v. *P. G. Lake, Inc.*, and companion cases, supra note 62.

[65] Other examples are: (1) a fee owner who sells a life estate carved out of the fee—*Estate of Johnson N. Camden,* 47 B.T.A. 926 (1942), affirmed per curiam, 139 F. 2d 697 (6th Cir., 1943), finding capital gain; is it consistent with the *Lake* case?; (2) a lessor who sells the lease and retains the fee interest—*Hort* v. *Commissioner,* 313 U.S. 28 (1941), finding ordinary gain, but not cited by the Supreme Court in the *Lake* case; (3) a copyright owner prior to the adoption of sec. 1221(3) who "divides" the property by transferring without limit of time one attribute of the property, such as a transfer of only the motion picture rights—Rev. Rul. 54-409, 1954-2 Cum. Bull. 174 found a "sale" and hence capital gain; but see *Cory* v. *Commissioner,* 230 F. 2d 941 (2d Cir., 1956) finding a "license" and hence ordinary income where the combination of (*a*) a transfer of part of the rights for (*b*) a royalty method of payment, was present.

of the property. Here the courts, on the whole, tend to an ordinary income characterization of the amount obtained for the carved-out interest. Suppose, however, that a person's entire interest consists of a right to receive recurring receipts, and that each receipt is ordinary income in its entirety to the person. If that person transfers the entire right to the recurring receipts, how is the transaction to be treated? Thus, suppose the income beneficiary of a trust transfers his life interest for a consideration? The courts here find capital gain.[66]

C. Merger of recurring receipts and principal in one asset

In some cases there is a merger of an item reflecting recurring receipts with the underlying principal. Thus, interest on a bond may have matured but not as yet been paid. Or the bond may be a non-interest-bearing bond issued at a discount such that at maturity the full amount is equal to the issue price plus interest, as in the case of a U.S. savings bond. Suppose such an asset is transferred or redeemed? The courts will usually protect the ordinary income character of the item, as in the case of matured interest, and "fragment" the property sold.[67] But this fragmentation approach does not always obtain. Thus, prior to the adoption of section 1232 preserving the interest aspect for discount bonds, the courts found capital gain on redemption of corporate discount bonds.[68]

D. The effect of the sale or exchange requirement

The definition of capital gain and capital loss also involves the sale or exchange of a capital asset.[69] This "sale or exchange" requirement in itself involves a host of problems, which add to the complexities of the capital gain definition. Yet its presence is an important factor in preventing many recurring receipts from being swept into the capital gain category. Since the payment of salary, interest, dividends, etc., is not a "sale or exchange," the receipt of these items cannot be capital gain even if we regard the claim to the item as "property." Moreover, even when such a claim is actually sold, the courts in keeping the transaction in the ordinary income area often do so by not regarding the disposition as a "sale" within the contemplation of the statute.[70] Hence, elimination of the "sale or exchange" requirement would in this area place the entire load on the term "property" and its application in the case of recurring receipts.[71] Further, as respects the method of payment, the "sale or exchange" requirement prevents some transfers for a royalty from being capital gain transactions, as in the oil and gas situations, though patent and copyright royalty transfers are regarded as "sales." The requirement has also been utilized in some

[66] *McAllister* v. *Commissioner*, 157 F. 2d 235 (2d Cir., 1956) (capital loss); *Evans* v. *Commissioner*, 30 T.C. — (1958) (A) (transfer of life estate for annuity).

[67] *Fisher* v. *Commissioner*, 209 F. 2d 573 (6th Cir., 1954) (note with matured interest).

[68] *Commissioner* v. *Caulkins*, 144 F. 2d 482 (6th Cir., 1944). The act authorizing the issuance of U.S. savings bonds expressly provides that the discount shall be treated as interest.

Compare *Phillips* v. *Commissioner*, 30 T.C. — (1958), finding capital gain on the sale of an insurance endowment policy just prior to maturity, with *Arnfeld* v. *United States*, 163 F. Supp. 865 (Ct. Cl. 1958) finding ordinary income, since the "gain" on the premium investment reflected essentially the interest earned on the premiums.

[69] Sec. 1222.

[70] See cases cited notes 48, 59 supra.

[71] See Surrey & Warren, supra, note 27, at 808.

cases to deny capital gain treatment in transactions involving the disposition of only some of the rights to property.[72]

On the other hand, the presence of the "sale or exchange" requirement produces incongruous results when an admitted capital asset is disposed of by methods other than sale or exchange, as in the cases of the redemption of a bond or a security's becoming worthless. Here capital gain or loss treatment, clearly proper if we are to have a capital transaction concept at all, would be denied because of the absence of a sale or exchange. Consequently, the statute contains a number of sections artificially qualifying these dispositions as "sales or exchanges" for this purpose.[73] But since these sections do not cover all possible forms of disposition, some investment profits do not have a capital gain status.[74] In sum, either the presence or the absence of a "sale or exchange" requirement is unsatisfactory, and another difficult dimension is thereby added to the definitional problem.

VI. THE TRANSFORMATION OF TANGIBLE ASSETS INTO INTANGIBLE PROPERTY RIGHTS TO THOSE ASSETS

A. Collapsible corporations

The problems considered so far have dealt with the attempts to classify the myriad types of "property" between capital and noncapital assets. Difficult as these problems are, their resolution unfortunately does not represent a successful end to the search for definition. Instead, the answer to these problems projects the capital gain definition into an entirely new set of problems which, in the structure of the income tax, raise difficulties even more complex than the previous issues. For when a particular piece of "property" has been neatly cataloged as a noncapital asset, the taxpayer may with relative ease change the legal cloak which covers his relationship to that property and substitute a new relationship from which a different piece of "property" emerges. Thus, suppose that an individual in business owns appreciated inventory which represents the major value of the business. Since "inventory" is in the property group classified as a noncapital asset, its sale will produce ordinary income. The

---

[72] See discussion above under "Sale of Property Versus Division of Interests in Property."

[73] Secs. 165(g), 1231, 1232(a), 1234.

[74] For example, the purchase and subsequent collection of a legacy, *Joseph A. Guthrie,* 42 B.T.A. 696 (1940), a judgment, *Ogilvie* v. *Commissioner,* 216 F. 2d 748 (6th Cir. 1954), or other debt, *Thomas* v. *Perkins,* 108 F. 2d 87 (5th Cir. 1939). Another problem area involves receipts or payments related to a prior capital transaction. See e.g., *Arrowsmith* v. *Commissioner,* 344 U.S. 6 (1952); *Dobson* v. *Commissioner,* 321 U.S. 231 (1944). On the loss side, the abandonment of property will produce only an ordinary loss, whereas a sale of the property would be a capital transaction.

Where an investment profit is involved and the normal method of receipt would be by way of payment, the courts appear sympathetic to the taxpayer's effort to secure a capital gain through a sale just prior to the time of payment. E.g., *Pacific Finance Corp.* 12 C.C.H. Tax Ct. Mem. 419 (1953) (purchase for $450,000 of right to receive first $550,000 of profits from distribution of a motion picture, then a sale when it was clear that the picture would be profitable); *Stanley D. Beard,* 4 T.C. 756 (1945) (sale of preferred stock just prior to its being called for redemption, when sale but not redemption resulted in long-term capital gain treatment under prior law). The approach of the courts here may be contrasted with that adopted when salary, dividends, and similar recurring receipts are involved. In the first group of cases, the issue is that of the obeisance to be paid to the statutory differentiation between "sale" and "payment" a differentiation hard to justify. In the second group, in addition to that issue there is also the question regarding the scope of "property" in the capital asset definition. However, unless the difference in issues is recognized, it may happen that the results in the first group of cases will—erroneously—be automatically carried over to the second group.

individual now incorporates his business, and then sells the stock of the corporation. "Stock," we have seen, is in the property group classified as a "capital asset." The obvious question is whether the individual has transformed the profit on the sale from ordinary income to capital gain by changing his legal cloak from that of individual proprietor to sole shareholder. Since stock is an accepted type of property, the courts could hardly come to any general conclusion, except possibly in the crudest of arrangements, other than that the individual in selling the stock was selling "property"—the stock itself—and the "property" so sold was a "capital asset." But this result obviously makes unimportant for this situation the classification of inventory as a noncapital asset. Nor is this result limited to the particular case of inventory. Whenever an individual could interpose a corporation between himself and a noncapital asset and then sell the stock in the corporation, the individual could thereby deal in a capital asset rather than in a noncapital asset although it was the noncapital asset which imparted value to the capital asset.

A wide area of the problem of defining capital gain thus became a shell game, with the taxpayer in control because he could determine under which legal shell to place the asset. Individuals formed corporations to produce a single motion picture, to construct a housing project, to develop a tract of real estate—all transactions which would if handled by the individuals themselves result in ordinary income—and then disposed of the corporate stock when the venture was ready for sale. The tax bar early gave the colorful name of "collapsible corporations" to these single-shot corporate ventures. Congress recognized that this procedure could make a shambles of the capital gain definition,[75] and in a complicated section attempted to meet the difficulty.[76] But the section, while highly intricate, is not generally regarded as a fully effective or even a theoretically proper solution.[77] More effective and more comprehensive solutions, however, would be even more intricate in their structure and operation.[78]

B. Collapsible partnerships

Congress, spurred on by the Treasury Department, in 1951 thus recognized the problem of the collapsible corporation and its threat to the capital asset definition. But both failed to comprehend how fluid and subtle was the capital gain shell game as conducted by resourceful tax practitioners. For soon the "property" was found under another shell, that of an "interest in a partnership." The individual simply adopted the partnership form of doing business and transferred his noncapital assets to the partnership. Then, when he was ready to sell, he was selling not the noncapital assets but a "partnership interest," and a "partnership interest" is "property" of the type classified as a capital asset. Again, the capital asset classifications could be turned into a shambles by this substitution of legal cloaks. The 1954

[75] For decisions sustaining capital gain classification in collapsible corporation situations, see *Herbert* v. *Riddell*, 103 F. Supp. 369 (S.D. Ca. 1952) (motion picture); *Pat O'Brien*, 25 T.C. 376 (1955) (motion picture); *Frank E. Gilman*, 14 T.C. 833 (1950) (real estate).

[76] Sec. 341.

[77] A complicated addition, sec. 341(e), was enacted in 1958 in an effort to meet some of the problems. See *Anthoine*, Federal Tax Legislation of 1958: The Corporate Election and Collapsible Amendments, 58 Colum. L. Rev. 1146 (1958).

[78] See Cohen, Surrey, Tarleau & Warren, "A Proposed Revision of the Federal Income Tax Treatment of the Sale of a Business Enterprise—American Law Institute Draft," 54 Colum. L. Rev. 157 (1954); American Law Institute, Income Tax Problems of Corporations and Shareholders, Report of Working Views (1958) 153.

code devotes a number of sections to this problem,[79] and they represent the most complicated portion of the partnership area. Whether they will be effective as presently written is questionable. Moreover, the solution here adopted for the collapsible partnership differs from that chosen for the collapsible corporation, although the problems are similar.[80]

In this general area of the sale of business assets the 1954 code presents three different solutions, depending on whether the business assets are owned by the individual as a proprietorship, a partnership, or a corporation.[81] This result concretely illustrates the tremendous difficulties inherent in the attempt to classify property between capital and noncapital assets under a complex legal structure which offers many patterns of property ownership. Such a legal structure, by permitting a tangible piece of property in effect to proliferate itself into various types of intangible assets, each in itself a form of "property," dooms any tax classification under the present definitional approach, if possible at all, to extremely intricate and detailed solutions.[82] Moreover, the fact that it has taken us over 30 years to perceive these structural problems underscores the difficulties of definition in the capital gain field.

[79] E.g., secs. 731, 732, 735, 741, 751.

[80] In general see Jackson, Johnson, Surrey, Tenen & Warren, "The Internal Revenue Code of 1954: Partnerships," 54 Colum. L. Rev. 1183 (1954); Little, "Partnership Distributions Under the Internal Revenue Code of 1954," 10 Tax L. Review 161,335 (1954–55); Phillips, "Some Aspects of the Taxation of Partners and Partnerships Under the New Internal Revenue Code," 34 Neb. L. Review, 25 (1954); Phillips, "The Collapsible Partnership Device and Partnership Distributions," N.Y.U. Tax Inst. (1956) 1007.

[81] In general, as to an individual the fragmentation of the business into its ordinary asset and capital asset components is required; as to a partnership there is fragmentation of the partner's interest to reflect accounts receivable and significantly appreciated inventory held by the partnership; as to a corporation there is ordinary asset treatment of the entire stock interest if there is an intention to utilize the corporation as a collapsible corporation under the intricate statutory definition of that term.

[82] See Cohen, Surrey, Tarleau, & Warren, supra note 78.

Chapter VII

PROFESSIONAL RESPONSIBILITY PROBLEMS

It is not surprising that a tax system as pervasive and intricate as ours—yet one relying so significantly on the taxpayer's honest self-assessment of his tax liability—should spawn troubling ethical questions for the taxpayer, as well as his professional advisers. Nor is it surprising that with the questions often so difficult, there is such a plethora of platitudes and such a shortage of sagacity in the literature on the subject.

In the piece that follows, the author, an experienced tax attorney, seeks to share with the reader his views on some very practical and commonplace problems. One such problem which he does not explicitly consider concerns the extent of disclosure required of a taxpayer in connection with a transaction of ambiguous tax effect. Suppose, for example, that a widow of a corporate executive concludes that a payment made to her by her husband's employer after his death is a gift. Is she justified in simply excluding the item without any rider disclosing the underlying facts? In support of an affirmative response, it has been urged that the government could always ask the taxpayer on the return whether she had received any tax-exempt items, and if so, to explain further.[a] Perhaps, too, the advent of the computer makes it theoretically possible for the government to unearth transactions that are likely to be reflected on other returns (as is true here if the corporation claims a deduction for the payment). But is there not considerable merit to the proposition that a taxpayer has a duty to furnish such information on his return as he believes is reasonably necessary for the government to make a fair judgment on the issue in question, even if such disclosure is likely to increase the chance of his return being audited? It is characteristic of most questions worth discussing in this area that there are few firm answers, and that sensitivity to the problems is often more important than their specific resolution.

[a] See Bittker, Professional Responsibility in Federal Tax Practice 250–56 (1970), for a fuller discussion of this and other professional responsibility issues.

DARRELL, THE TAX PRACTITIONER'S DUTY TO HIS CLIENT AND HIS GOVERNMENT *

7 Prac.Law., March 1961, p. 23, 24–39.

My subject today encompasses matters of conscience and propriety in relation to the professional tax practitioner's multiple responsibilities—his duty to his client, his duty to his conscience, and his duty to society, including his Government. These responsibilities, of course, include the duty to give wholehearted devotion and competent attention to the client's interests and to avoid representation of conflicting interests; the duty, subject to limited exceptions, to preserve the client's confidences in connection with legal consultations; and, of particular importance here, the duty to refrain from overzealous conduct on behalf of the client not in keeping with high professional standards and good conscience and to advise against and refuse to assist in wrongful or improper acts.

In addition, in my view certain social responsibilities should be added: the duty to help make our self-assessing income tax system work; and the duty—if I may be permitted to call it that—to lend under appropriate circumstances one's special talents and experiences to the never-ending search for means of improving that system in the public interest.

In attempting to deal with so broad an area, one can talk in a rather general way, or one can attempt to deal with a large part of the subject as I propose to do by taking up borderline questions in a practical fashion through a series of hypothetical illustrative cases.

However, this method has its problems since it is easier to generalize than to provide ready practical answers in concrete situations. Moreover, in attempting to deal specifically with practical problems in this area, one runs the risk of creating an unrealistic impression. I hope I shall be able to avoid these pitfalls. My purpose is more to direct thought and attention to difficult questions and to stimulate exchanges of views thereon than to provide positive answers; and such answers to unsettled questions as I may suggest are put forward tentatively and subject to change after further reflection and discussion.

Indeed, to speak too positively and precisely about what one should do on facts sketchily drawn might well be misleading, since a

* Reproduced with the permission of *The Practical Lawyer*, 4025 Chestnut Street, Philadelphia, Pa. 19104. Subscription rates: $10.00 a year, $2.00 a single issue. "The Tax Practitioner's Duty to His Client and His Government" by Norris Darrell, Esquire, appeared in the March, 1961 issue, Vol. 7, No. 3, pp. 23–40.

variance in a fact here and there might change the color and shape of the problem and justify a different conclusion. Moreover, in hypothetical cases the human element tends unrealistically to be ignored. In the last analysis, the lawyer must consider each situation as it arises, evaluate all the factors pertaining to it, and make his own decision; and what he may decide in good conscience in one situation may conceivably differ from the decision he may properly reach in another, though at first blush the two might superficially appear to be comparable. With this caveat, I turn first to general advisory problems.

General Advisory Problems

Perhaps the most important everyday ethical problems of the lawyer in tax practice, long antedating the tax return, have to do with general advisory matters. In principle we surely all agree on this: the lawyer's responsibilties include the obligation to make every reasonable effort to equip himself to advise and represent clients wisely, and he must have the stamina and sufficient detachment to tell them the truth.

Clients are for the most part reasonably honest innocents who must be guided not only away from transactions because unwise or merely colorable, but around tax pitfalls that abound in seemingly valid family and business affairs. Their fate rests in the hands of their tax advisers, perhaps to a greater degree than they themselves may realize. The tax adviser bears a heavy responsibility here, for his standards may become the guiding standards for his clients.

In ancient Rome, Coreolanus, in explaining to his mother why he would not modify his attitude to gain the support of the crowds in the market place, is made by Shakespeare to say: "Know, dear mother, I would rather be their servant in my way than sway with them in theirs." Such is the spirit I am talking about. Now for some cases.

I.

A corporate client consults you on the following proposal. Having learned that another corporation is about to pay $100 per share of dividend arrearages on its preferred stock, it proposes to purchase some of the preferred cum-dividend at $250 a share, receive the dividend of $100 per share, and then sell the preferred ex-dividend at $150 per share, a transaction expected to net zero results apart from the tax consequences but to produce a tax saving of between $17 and $44 per share through operation of the dividend received deduction and the short-term capital loss deduction provisions of the 1954 Code or, possibly, if it is a dealer, the ordinary loss deduction provisions.

The client points out that, even though the purchase price of the preferred cum-dividend is run up because of the tax saving opportunity so as to produce a net loss on the transaction, but for the tax consequences, the tax savings would still make the transaction worthwhile. He wants your advice as to how long he should hold before selling, as he does not wish to hold beyond the point necessary to obtain the desired tax results.

This case of course suggests problems relating to the familiar phrases "business purpose," "transaction entered into for profit," and "transaction entered into solely for tax purposes," upon which it is your duty to be well informed. It invites careful consideration in particular to the principles recently expounded by the Supreme Court and other courts with respect to transactions undertaken solely to acquire tax deductions.

Nevertheless, while one might have no stomach for promoting or encouraging tax schemes of this sort, or might question the long-range wisdom of burdening or abusing the dividend received deduction, and might be particularly concerned over the effectiveness of the plan where the only possible profit is through the tax differential, would it not be perfectly proper from an ethical standpoint for you to pass on the tax effectiveness of such a plan, as requested, and to advise to the best of your ability as to the tax risks involved, the importance of running a reasonable risk of stock ownership, and the advantages or disadvantages of holding the purchased preferred for periods of varying lengths? After all, the opportunity to utilize the dividends received deduction was created by Congress and, even after the recent legislation [section 246(c)] there may still be room for utilization of plans of this sort. Yet, conceding that you may so advise, may you not be charged with a public duty to try affirmatively to discourage the use of pure tax gimmicks that can produce no profit except one that flows from an unintended operation of the tax statute?

II.

You are consulted about a proposed family partnership between husband and wife, valid in form under the laws of the State, but to be operated on the unwritten understanding, which may never be discovered, that the husband will continue to control the property and manage the partnership, that the wife will pay family bills out of her share of the profits, and that the wife will hold her interest subject to his control, even to the point of returning it to him should he need it. What should your attitude be?

Schemes such as this often lead to harsh law and endless litigation, sometimes dragging valid arrangements into the mess. A question of ethics is clearly involved in furthering arrangements which, though superficially appearing to be valid, are factually colorable and artificial. Can we not go further and say that, apart from whether such a scheme would be legally or practically effective, there is an affirmative professional responsibility to discourage abortive tax plans of this sort in the interest of making the tax system work and of relieving the administration and the judiciary of undue burdens?

III.

You are consulted about a corporate reorganization or readjustment, the tax consequences of which may depend upon the existence of a good business purpose, or at least upon the existence of a purpose other than saving taxes. You know that the client is tax conscious and that a tax advantage is an important consideration. Is there any moral objection to your canvassing and seeking to develop with the client all possible nontax reasons that could fairly be given in support of the transaction? And can you properly suggest modifications of the plan to strengthen it from this standpoint?

The same sort of problem arises when clients are concerned over and seek aid in building up a current record that will enable them to put their best tax foot forward with respect to potential liability for accumulated earnings tax, or potential contemplation of death treatment of a gift, or the possible application of section 269 or, indeed, any situation where tax liability may depend upon motive or intent or upon existence of a business as distinct from a personal or purely tax purpose.

Obviously, it is improper to build a house of cards, to manufacture evidence; reasons given must be genuine, and the lawyer must search his conscience and be extremely careful to avoid misleading camouflage. But you would feel free, would you not, to advise on the law, the factual record, and possible amendments to the plan that would strengthen the tax position?

Purposes and motives are often by their nature elusive, and experience shows that clients often need help in thinking out and articulating their own real objectives. But, do you not agree that one must be very careful to avoid feeding motives into a tax-conscious client's mind? In the zeal of the undertaking, it is very easy to cross the dividing line without recognizing it, and we tax practitioners may not always tread carefully enough in these matters.

Tax Return Problems

Lawyers engaged in tax practice are often confronted with problems of another type—problems relating to tax returns. These may arise in a variety of situations, as illustrated by the following.

I.

A client confidentially asks you

for legal advice concerning a clearly taxable income item that he inadvertently omitted from his income tax return, filed six months previously, with the preparation and filing of which you had nothing to do.

Should not your advice be to file an amended return, or, if the client were a corporation or other taxpayer subject to annual audit and were not concerned over the running of interest, to put a note in the file to be submitted to the examining agent when he comes in to audit? If the client refuses to heed this advice, does not your responsibility cease?

The attorney-client relationship would appear to prevent you from turning informer, and Treasury Circular No. 230 does not require you to become one. Indeed, this would be true even if the omission had been deliberate and fraudulent, if it be concluded that at the time of the disclosure the fraud was a past and not a prospective or continuing one, disclosed to you in confidence.

II.

Assume the facts of the preceding case, except that in connection with your work as legal adviser to the client on tax matters, the income tax return had been prepared and certified by you or in your office, and the client refuses to authorize you to disclose the information he has given you.

The privileged communications doctrine does not apply to information received and advice given outside the scope of a lawyer's professional employment or to matters handled in other than a legal capacity. Communications with accountants are not privileged, except where the privilege is granted by statute.

Are services in connection with the preparation of a tax return within the scope of a lawyer's professional employment, or are they services of a ministerial or accounting nature rendered in a nonlegal capacity? In my view, if the preparation of the return is incidental to legal consultation and advice, communications in connection therewith should be deemed privileged.

Lawyers customarily prepare documents—contracts, deeds, trust instruments, etc.,—in connection with and incidental to their legal work; and the preparation of tax returns, though a proper function of the accountant, is also within the lawyer's field because of the legal questions normally involved in their preparation. However, if you were also a qualified accountant, the answer might be influenced, in states where the privilege is not extended to accountants, by whether you were retained in a legal capacity or simply to prepare tax returns and handle audits in the capacity of a qualified tax accountant.

But, even though confidential communications between attorney and client in such situations are privileged, it has been held that the privilege is inapplicable to information supplied for inclusion in a tax return intended to be filed with the tax authorities, since such information — unlike information furnished as the basis for legal advice—is not intended to be confidential.

Here, you received the information in your legal capacity subsequent to the filing of the return and the privilege applies. Accordingly, you are not free to disclose the information furnished against the client's wishes; and, if you cannot obtain his consent to disclosure, you would face the question whether you should refuse to represent him on audit of the return, or whether to do so would violate your duty under the canons of ethics not to withdraw to the client's detriment except for good cause. Your answer no doubt will be affected by the facts of the case in the light of past experiences with the client. In some cases it may not be an easy matter to decide unless, in keeping with your professional responsibilities as well as your self protection, you can succeed in obtaining his consent to the correction of the omission.

III.

On reviewing your client's income tax return for a prior year, you find he made two unrelated apparent mistakes, one favorable to him and the other favorable to the Government, both honestly made. He asks you to do what you think best in his interests. Would it be proper to raise the favorable item and remain silent on the unfavorable one?

It is of course difficult to be categorical where the balance of considerations depends so much upon the facts. But, broadly speaking, would you agree that the question should be resolved this way: would you have felt bound to disclose the unfavorable item if you had prepared the return in the first instance; if so, is there any justification for not pointing it out later when the favorable one is raised? If you should conclude that omission of the unfavorable item, although involving some risk, was not clearly a mistake and need not have been reported, would it be appropriate to postpone the filing of the refund claim until just before expiration of the statute of limitations, so that, if the Government discovered and raised the unfavorable point upon investigating the claim, it could do no more than offset the claim? The answer may depend upon the particular facts and the degree of doubt the unfavorable item involves. But, are there not situations where, as a precaution, this procedure would be appropriate? Yet, is there not common agreement that, where omission of the unfavorable item represented a clear error, to pursue this course would be too sharp a practice?

IV.

A client engaged in the manufacturing business submits to you for review and approval a federal income tax return reflecting the taxable income of the business, together with a letter from the client's regular auditors stating that in their opinion the return properly reflects taxable income, except that certain expenditures have been taken as current expense deductions which they consider should have been capitalized.

The client concedes that these items are clearly capital in nature but desires to claim them as expense deductions in the hope that, buried in a long list of items, they will not be discovered on audit or, if discovered, will be available to concede in order that the field agent might find an additional tax, which the client believes he would consider a mark to his credit and thereby reduce the likelihood of other unfavorable adjustments. What should you advise?

Is it not clear, there being no doubt as to the law, that you should not advise or encourage action on the basis of what the client may get away with—on the basis of what may slip by on audit, or be available at that time to concede? Indeed, should you not try to discourage the client from reporting on that basis? The practice of deducting items known to be nondeductible is one that I consider quite questionable and that, I regret to say, would be less appealing if the Service through its field agents could convince taxpayers that it does not pay.

V.

You represent the executor of an estate, the assets of which are situated in Michigan, where the decedent long lived, with the exception of a small bank account in California, where the decedent spent a substantial part of his declining years and died. Michigan is certain to regard the decedent as domiciled in Michigan, and there is some possibility that California might assert that his domicile was there, if the question were raised.

If proceedings were instituted to collect the California assets, the question might be raised, and the cost of the proceedings, even though successful, might well exceed the California assets. You are asked to advise whether it would be proper simply to abandon the California assets and do nothing about a possible California claim.

Assuming you are satisfied that any claim of domicile by California would be unfounded, would you not be justified under these facts in abandoning the California assets and making no report to the California tax authorities? If the facts were such that you believed the decedent's last domicile might reasonably be found to be California, would you not feel differently; would there not then be a duty, after pointing out the legal and practical situation as to enforcement and collection of any claim by California, to advise raising the question with California and getting it settled?

On the other hand, can you say you owe no duty to California; that collection of its taxes is its business; that, if it has a claim against assets beyond those in California, it must sally forth and assert it; and that your duty as a Michigan attorney is limited to meeting that claim fairly and truthfully only if raised?

Would your answer to the preceding questions be different if the decedent's California property had been such that California law required the filing of an inheritance tax return regardless of domicile? Should you not then advise the executor to file such a return even though the domicile question might be raised?

Finally, is there any rational basis for a different answer to any of these questions where the out-of-State assets are in Canada, or France, or some other foreign country?

The responsibility of lawyers in respect to taxes of foreign governments, and governments of domestic states other than their own, suggests questions in a seemingly uncharted field. Whether irrationally or not, there is no doubt a tendency to feel less sense of responsibility to such governments than toward one's own State and Nation.

Post Audit Problems

The most common contact lawyers in tax practice have with government officials is in connection with post audit problems, tax settlement negotiations, and litigation. In seeking the most favorable interpretation of the facts and the law applicable to his case, the lawyer can deliberately present the facts and legal precedents in the way calculated to appear most favorable to his client's position, but he must avoid trickery, misrepresentation of fact or law, and concealment of material matters relating to any issue under consideration. Sedulous though he must be in these latter respects, he need not lean over backward to help the Government's case. On this, all of you will no doubt agree.

I.

In preparing a protest for your client against an asserted additional income tax liability for an earlier year, you discover an unrelated weak point in your client's case that the Government has overlooked. He took a deduction for a legal fee for services in a gift tax case, whereas, though it was deductible under a federal District Court decision, an earlier Tax Court decision, affirmed on appeal but not yet reviewed by the Supreme Court, held it was not under the then existing statute. What should you do?

Of course, a weak spot such as this should be taken into account in appraising the desirability of filing the protest and the terms of any settlement, for the weakness may crop up later. But, if the Government overlooks it, and it could have been discovered from a careful examination of the record or by normal inquiry, do you not agree that there is no duty to call the matter to the Government's attention or to urge the client to do so? If the Tax Court decision had also been affirmed by the Supreme Court, would you not then hesitate to protest the disputed point without disclosing this item?

II.

You are retained to prepare a brief for submission to a court on an unsettled federal tax question. You find clearly pertinent federal tax decisions, some of which might be harmful to your case. You also find an obscure but well reasoned state court decision that might hurt you, and a British court decision of the same sort. Finally, you encounter a line of federal court cases, not pertinent to the Government's present theory in your case, but which might suggest to it a different approach that might prove harmful. Are you obliged to cite all cases you have found that might be harmful to your position?

Would you not say that all considerations dictate that federal tax decisions clearly pertinent should be cited? Would you not agree that as an ethical matter, citation is not required either of the state court and British decisions, even though other unrelated decisions from those jurisdictions are cited? Would not the answer be the same with respect to the potentially harmful federal tax decisions unrelated to the Government's theory of the case, particularly if you can conclude that these decisions are not clearly ones the court should consider in deciding the case? Would you not feel somewhat less responsibility with reference to this last proviso if the brief were for submission to the Internal Revenue Service and not to a court?

The opinion by Chief Justice Vanderbilt in the New Jersey case of *In re Greenburg,* 15 N.J. 132 (1954), a disciplinary proceeding, contains an interesting discussion of the lawyer's responsibilities to the courts in this regard. But, whether the lawyer's obligations to the Internal Revenue Service are as strict as those he owes a court has not been clearly established. But surely he owes no duty to inform it of its own rulings and other administrative decisions.

III.

You have a Tax Court case involving a large business expense deduction issue. A lazy examining agent accepted, without checking, your client's figures as to the amount of the expenses your client paid. The 90-day letter, accepting these figures, is based on the legal ground that the item was not a deductible business expense but a capital expenditure, though the amount of the expenditure is technically put in issue.

During your preparation for trial, you discover there is very real doubt as to the actual amount expended by your client, and you believe it would be extremely difficult to prove the amount claimed if you attempted to do so through witnesses at the trial. What should you do?

Government counsel frequently rely upon the findings of the revenue agents. May you properly ask Government counsel to stipulate the facts accepted by the examining agent, without calling attention to what you know? Do you not agree that this would be clearly improper? Would it not be preferable to arrange with your opponent for a joint investigation into the facts in the hope of arriving, by compromise if necessary, at an agreed statement of facts?

IV.

The executors of an estate of a relatively youthful but wealthy former client retain you to defend against an asserted additional estate tax liability based on a claim that certain inter vivos gifts to the decedent's daughter, slightly less than three years before his accidental death, were made in contemplation of death. You had advised the decedent in connection with the gift, and had explained to him the potential income and estate tax savings from the gift. The decedent then had told you privately and confidentially that, while he wanted to save income taxes and provide some income for his daughter, he did not expect to live very long in view of his family history and that he was primarily interested in the potential saving in estate taxes on his estate. The decedent had not discussed with you what you might say should a question later arise. What should you do?

Is it not clear that you cannot tell the whole story because you cannot disclose what you learned from the confidential communication with your deceased client? This being so, would it not be improper to present arguments in support of the nontestamentary motives while remaining silent as to the testamentary motives?

In these circumstances, since you cannot properly make full disclosure of pertinent facts within your knowledge, should you advise the executors to consult other counsel or should you advise them to concede liability? May you not properly explain the situation to the executors and, if in your opinion the gift was in fact clearly made in contemplation of death, recommend that liability be conceded, otherwise that other counsel be consulted?

Fraud Problems

Defrauders, repentant or otherwise, are entitled to counsel, and the lawyer in tax practice may properly represent them in their legitimate defense or in making full disclosure in an effort to arrive at the best possible settlement. Some lawyers are not experienced in this type of practice. Yet, even such lawyers may get into the periphery of it.

I.

The president and controlling stockholder of a corporation that he has caused to engage in deliberately fraudulent under-reporting of income in the past would now like to make a new start and comes to you for legal advice. If the past fraud is disclosed, the back taxes and penalties technically due are likely to ruin him and the corporation financially, so that the alternatives, as he sees it, are to disclose the past fraud and face practical financial ruin or to remain silent and in business, but be honest in the future. What should your advice be?

Does any one doubt that under the canons of ethics and Treasury Circular No. 230 you should advise him to disclose and pay up what is due, whatever the consequences? But may you not properly explain to him at the same time the current policy of the Internal Revenue Service with respect to voluntary disclosures and the treatment he may receive upon such disclosure, the possibility that the voluntary disclosure policy of the Service might some day be more lenient, and the probable consequences if before any voluntary disclosure the Service itself should discover the fraud?

This advice having been given, the president returns and informs you he really intends to turn over a new leaf but has decided not to have the corporation make disclosure. Seeking no further advice on the fraud question, he asks you to advise the corporation on a proposed corporate transaction and also to obtain a ruling on it from the Service. What is your duty here?

Is it not clear that you must remain silent as to the fraud? Since the fraud was a past and not a continuing one, knowledge of which was confidentially communicated to you in your professional capacity, its disclosure without the client's consent would seem clearly to violate your professional duty. But, knowing of the fraud, can you advise the corporation on the proposed corporate transaction?

A lawyer in a position to pick and choose clients might decide not to represent a client in the legal position of an unrepentant defrauder, but is there any ethical reason why you should not do so here? Believing that the corporation and its president will act properly in the future, would you not feel free to represent the corporation on these new matters if you wished to do so?

Suppose, however, that if you undertook to seek the Treasury ruling it would be pertinent and necessary to submit to the Service past corporate financial statements, the only statements available being known by you to be incorrect because of the fraud. Is it not clear under Code section 7206(2) and Treasury Circular No. 230 that you cannot undertake that assignment? After explaining to the client why you cannot do it, would you not hesitate to go so far as to suggest another lawyer innocent of your knowledge? And, if another lawyer were retained and were to ask you why you withdrew, must you not withhold your reason?

Lobbying and Influence Problems

I.

Your services are sought for the purpose of engineering tax legislation through Congress for the benefit of the client. May you properly undertake that assignment?

Apart from the question of personal taste or suitability for such matters, I am confident you will agree with this: acceptance of such a retainer is entirely proper under the canons of ethics if you comply with the lobbying law and do not conceal your relationship or use improper influence. But, if you accept the retainer, you should affirmatively disclose your status to those whom you seek to persuade.

II.

The client whom you are representing in a federal tax case proposes to pursue the influence route and wants to retain in the case an out-and-out politician-lawyer, clearly not qualified to help on a technical basis, in an effort to influence a favorable settlement through high level contacts. What should your position be?

Normally, should you not first endeavor to dissuade the client by pointing out to him the dangers of such associations and the probable futility of indulging in such things? If he persists, would you not, in the absence of special circumstances, normally feel obliged for your own protection to withdraw from the case? And would you not normally withdraw even though, in the then existing climate of things, you cannot be too sure that, however unlikely, the politician-lawyer would not somehow produce a better result than you might be able to obtain?

Fee Problems

I.

During the year you rendered legal services to an individual client the fees for which will be partly deductible by him (because they pertain to his investment or business affairs or tax advice) and partly not deductible (because they relate to the execution of a will or some other personal matter). How far can you go in loading the fee for the deductible items and lightening the fee for the others?

A lawyer does not work by the clock, and his fees are dependent on many factors, including the time spent, results accomplished, the importance, novelty and difficulty of the matter, custom, and the client's views. He may at times even work without fee. It seems clear that he need not automatically apportion his total charge according to the relative hours spent on all these matters and that he is fully entitled to differentiate on the basis of the above factors, including the factor of tax deductibility

But, would you not say that, whatever you may charge in respect of the nondeductible items, you should not be influenced by the tax consideration to the extent of charging more for services in respect of the deductible items than can fairly be justified therefor? The Government thus far usually accepts the lawyer's word as to the allocation of his fees; it would be most unfortunate if the time should ever come when his word will not be acceptable.

II.

Your client, suspecting that he might dislike any allocation you might make, requests that you simply bill him for services rendered, without description or itemization of any kind, thinking that this might serve him better. Would you see any objection to your doing this?

Your answer may be influenced by whether this would be a departure from your general custom, or your prior custom with the client, or by whether you knew or suspected what he had in mind. But, generally speaking, is not the ethical problem here simply one of avoiding any statement that would mislead the ordinary examining agent and deter him from inquiring into the facts? Or, have you an affirmative duty beyond that? This type of problem may be more acute where a large part of the services was rendered to a controlling corporate stockholder who desires the corporation to be billed.

Problems of Public Responsibility

I.

Your client informs you that, in connection with the audit of his income tax return, the examining agent has distinctly suggested that he would concede a disputed item and close the case if the client would hand him a round-trip ticket to Florida, and he asks you whether he should simply decline the suggestion or report to the authorities.

Is it your duty to advise the client to inform on the agent and to co-operate in efforts to trap him if requested to do so? Assuming you so advise in the belief that it is a public duty to do so, and that the client refuses to act himself, but waives any attorney-client privilege, is there then an affirmative duty on your part to report to the agent's superiors? Would the answer be the same in the unlikely event that the agent made the suggestion directly to you?

If your answers to these questions are in the affirmative, as I believe in crystal-clear cases they should be, do tax practitioners generally perform such duty? Is this essentially a matter of one's own sense of social responsibility, or is it more than that—a matter of professional responsibility as I am inclined to consider it? No rule or regulation apparently requires reporting of fraudulent or criminal suggestions, however clear, but without the co-operation of taxpayers or their advisers the policing of tax administration would be most difficult.

II.

A body of public spirited citizens asks you to join with them in signing a petition urging upon Congress a reform in the tax law that you believe to be much needed but that, if adopted, might seriously adversely affect some of your clients. What should you do?

Would you not consider yourself free to join in urging the reform, if you believe in it and it would not conflict with your duty to any client in any matter in which you have been retained? On the other hand, even though there were no such conflict, might you not properly conclude that you would be fully justified in remaining silent, if you believe you would get into difficulties with one or more clients by joining in the appeal; the importance of lending your name to the appeal might not outweigh the damage to your client relationships. I feel sure you will agree, however, that, generally speaking, a lawyer ought to try to participate in those things that he thinks are useful in the public interest; and ordinarily clients do not take offense at this.

Closing Observations

May I conclude with a few general observations. I question the notion that, where his adversary is the Treasury, the lawyer need give less than full devotion to his duty to his client because of a larger duty he owes to the Government or his fellow citizens. I believe the lawyer surely owes no less devotion to his duty to a taxpayer, who is his client, than he owes to a criminal whom he undertakes to defend. Both are entitled to full legal representation.

Yet, with respect to ordinary, everyday, administrative tax practice, especially where a crystallized controversy headed for the courts is not involved, there may be differences in shading or degree. The questions here are perplexing, and the area is one especially in need of further study and clarification.

It may be suggested, on the one hand, that the obligation of candor and fairness, involving the disclosure of distressing things, should be more strict and rigid when it runs to a court—a judicial umpire whom not even silence should be permitted to mislead—than when it runs to the Treasury which through its representatives of varying attitudes and qualifications is in the equivocal position of investigator, claimant, and administrative judge. On the other hand, it may be thought that this obligation of the lawyer should be at least as, if not more, strict and rigid when he is facing the Treasury, the thought here being that a tax matter is not simply a matter between taxpayer and Treasury but between taxpayer and the Treasury and other taxpayers.

To be broadly categorical about this, one way or the other, seems inappropriate because circumstances, settings, and opposition attitudes vary widely, and these may affect the extent of the lawyer's obligation.

But one thing I should like to emphasize. It may well be that some day persons performing so vital a function as those of the tax practitioner in the operation of our self-assessing, national, income tax system will more generally recognize, as I believe they should, and as many already do, that their work is affected with the public interest and, leaving aside responsibilities to clients with respect to issues joined in battle, will more freely accept a high level of responsibility for leadership in the co-operative effort necessary to the successful operation of the system. Such co-operation may be vital if the system, which is dependent for enforcement primarily upon voluntary compliance and not police state methods, is to survive as other than a deplorable muddle, destroying the moral stamina of our citizens by teaching or stimulating them to cheat.

If this be so, it means that the tax practitioner, while continuously struggling to keep his own tax house strictly in order, must try to develop qualities of leadership and help to educate and influence clients to conduct themselves in their tax affairs as honorably and ethically as the adviser would himself act under similar circumstances.

In most taxpayers, ourselves included, there is a tendency toward a little larceny when it comes to taxation, though none of us would think of stealing a cent from or deliberately hurting our friends. This natural tendency is nurtured whenever tax officials, also human, seem to act in an overzealous and partisan fashion, and it thrives in an atmosphere of distrust of the fairness of the tax law. For these if for no other reasons, may not the tax practitioner be charged with the further duty I mentioned at the outset, namely, a duty to do what he can to help make the tax law more fair, practical, and equitable, and to improve its administration?

I have the impression that during recent years there has been a considerable improvement in the tax practitioner's sense of public responsibility. The increased attention at tax practitioners' gatherings to ethical problems in tax practice indicates to me a growing interest in such problems. The increasing number of lawyers in tax practice who give time and energy toward helping improve the technical provisions of the tax law and its administration, and who try to do so dispassionately, indicates to me a growing sense of duty to society. It must be conceded, however, that in these respects there is much still to be desired, and further that with rare exceptions lawyers who specialize in taxation have not indidividually in their private capacities stepped forward to exercise notable leadership in informing or guiding the public on broad controversial questions of tax policy. It may be that this is largely because such lawyers have been so preoccupied with the ever increasing technical intricacies of modern taxation that they not only have become accustomed but feel compelled to devote themselves to tax techniques at the expense of broad tax policy. It may also be partly because the organized bar wisely tries to avoid taking sides on controversial tax policy questions not within the lawyer's special competence. But, perhaps the day will come when the individual lawyer in the tax field will find it possible, as a community leader, to render a more useful service in the larger area not unlike that of his professional brethren who in the past individually contributed so much to the development and understanding of our National Constitution and the intelligent solution of the political problems of their day.

*

Chapter VIII

ESTATE AND GIFT TAXES

WESTFALL, REVITALIZING THE FEDERAL ESTATE AND GIFT TAXES *

83 Harv.L.Rev. 986–89 (1970).

THE low yield of federal estate and gift taxes was attributed by President Truman in 1950 to "excessive exemptions, unduly low effective rates on most estates, and the fact that the law as written favors large estates over smaller ones, and leaves substantial amounts of wealth completely beyond the reach of the tax laws."[1] Commentators repeatedly have voiced similar concerns.[2] The immediacy of the problem is best illustrated by a comparison: before World War II seven percent of federal revenues came from estate and gift taxes; [3] today, at a time when federal fiscal needs are so intense that important programs are curtailed or deferred for lack of funds, their share is less than two percent (approximately $3.5 billion in fiscal 1969).[4]

[1] MESSAGE OF THE PRESIDENT ON REVISION OF THE TAX LAWS, H.R. DOC. NO. 451, 81st Cong., 2d Sess. 6–7 (1950).

[2] *See, e.g.*, DeWind, *The Approaching Crisis in Federal Estate and Gift Taxation,* 38 CALIF. L. REV. 79 (1950); Eisenstein, *The Rise and Decline of the Estate Tax*, 11 TAX L. REV. 223 (1956); Surrey, *An Introduction to Revision of the Federal Estate and Gift Taxes*, 38 CALIF. L. REV. 1 (1950).

[3] STAFF OF JOINT ECONOMIC COMM., 88TH CONG. 2D SESS., THE FEDERAL TAX SYSTEM: FACTS AND PROBLEMS 165 (Comm. Print 1964).

[4] TAX FOUNDATION, INC., FACTS AND FIGURES ON GOVERNMENT FINANCE 93 (15th ed. 1969). Even this figure overstates the real contribution of these taxes to total federal revenues because federal estate tax liability can be met by surrendering government bonds, now depressed in price, for redemption at face value.

Present law requires that bonds bearing interest in excess of four percent which have been held by the decedent for at least six months prior to his death be made redeemable. 31 U.S.C. § 765 (1964). The Secretary of the Treasury is authorized to make other issues similarly redeemable. 31 U.S.C. § 752 (1964). There are twenty-five eligible issues outstanding, 1 CCH FED. EST. & GIFT TAX REP. ¶ 4220.45 (1969), some with a gross discount of approximately thirty-five percent, for example, the three percent bonds due in 1995. *See* Wall St. J., Jan. 27, 1970, at 33. The net saving on estate taxes will be less than the gross discount, however, be-

* Copyright © 1970 by The Harvard Law Review Association. Reproduced with permission.

The recent surge of interest in tax reform offers Congress a rare opportunity to make the estate and gift taxes fairer and more productive in raising revenue. Restoration to the prewar share would require an increase of $10 billion in estate and gift tax revenues. However, the extensive reforms required for an increase of this magnitude are not an immediate prospect. A more realistic short term goal would be to double the present yield — an additional $3.5 billion in new federal revenues to meet pressing public problems.

* * *

From both a social and economic viewpoint the federal estate and gift taxes are a highly desirable vehicle for increasing federal revenues. First, these taxes now bear almost exclusively on families with incomes over $20,000 per year.[11] Thus, any increase in the rate of taxation will burden those who can afford additional taxes. Although the income tax could be revised to raise these needed revenues, the estate and gift taxes, unlike the income tax, have a minimal impact on risk-taking, entrepreneurial drive, and resource allocation.[12] Moreover, the estate and gift taxes are more efficient in raising revenue than the income tax because time and circumstances of payment are convenient for both the tax administrator [13] and the estate beneficiary (if he is not dependent on the decedent for support).

Reform of the estate tax is also desirable from the standpoint of equity. Today there is a striking contrast between the extent to which an individual's responsibilities in supporting others are considered in determining his income tax liabilities while he lives but are not considered in determining his estate tax liabilities when he dies. For income tax purposes additional exemptions are allowed in many instances for children and other members of the

cause a redeemable bond is valued in the estate at redemption price. Bankers Trust Co. v. United States, 284 F.2d 537 (2d Cir. 1960), *cert. denied*, 366 U.S. 903 (1961).

In 1966 twenty percent of reported estate tax revenues consisted not of cash but of such bonds. *See* Letter from D. A. Stacy, Chief, Division of Public Debt, Accounts and Audit, to David Westfall, Oct. 31, 1969 (redemptions for 1966 $487,061,600). Current federal fiscal needs are ill-served by the discharge of unmatured bonds, and it is not surprising that the Treasury proposes to stop issuing bonds redeemable in payment of the estate tax if Congress will authorize it to do so. U.S. TREAS. DEP'T, 91ST CONG., 1ST SESS., TAX REFORM STUDIES AND PROPOSALS, pt. 3, at 408–09 (Comm. Print 1969) [hereinafter cited as PROPOSALS].

[11] PROPOSALS, pt. 1, at 106.

[12] *See* C. SHOUP, FEDERAL ESTATE AND GIFT TAXES 104 (1966).

[13] *Id.*

taxpayer's family.[14] Even an unrelated individual may qualify the taxpayer for an additional exemption if the individual lives with the taxpayer and meets the gross income and support tests.[15] Married taxpayers and heads of households are assessed at different rates than single taxpayers without support responsibilities.[16] For estate tax purposes, on the other hand, a uniform $60,000 exemption [17] and rate schedule [18] apply to all decedents — the bachelor whose property goes to a third cousin and the husband whose savings must provide for a widow and six small children. Only the marital deduction recognizes any differing obligations, and even it operates without regard to the surviving spouse's needs and responsibilities. The deduction is limited to one-half the adjusted gross estate,[19] whether the estate is $200,000 or $20 million, despite the obvious differences in the potential impact of the estate tax on the widow's ability to maintain a comfortable standard of living.

If substantially larger revenues are to be sought from the estate tax, fairness requires that the distribution of tax burdens give greater recognition to decedents' obligations to dependents. If these responsibilities are appropriately recognized, higher rates and lower exemptions should not cause serious hardship.

[14] *See* INT. REV. CODE OF 1954, §§ 151(e), 152.

[15] *Id.* § 152(a)(9).

[16] *See id.* § 1.

[17] *Id.* § 2052.

[18] *Id.* § 2001.

[19] *Id.* § 2056(c).

STATEMENT OF JEROME KURTZ (FORMER TAX LEGISLATIVE COUNSEL TO THE TREASURY DEPARTMENT)

Hearings on Tax Reform Act of 1969 Before the House Committee on Ways and Means, 91st Cong., 1st Sess., pt. 11, at 3978–85 (1969).

The existing estate and gift tax system is a complete shambles. While the estate tax rates are steeply progressive, reaching 77 percent for estates over $10 million, it is only the uninformed, the ill-advised, or the altruistic individual who would subject an estate to these high rates as it passes from one generation to the next.

Highly skilled lawyers and other professionals devote vast amounts of time and energy to a discipline called "estate planning." In many law schools the courses which teach estate and gift taxes are no longer called "Estate and Gift Taxes." They are called "Estate Planning" because the course is devoted to teaching how the estate tax can largely be avoided by careful planning involving the use of particular dispositive arrangements. The drafting of wills and trusts is today a practice concerned primarily with taxes.

When a client with a large estate sees his estate planner he is advised generally that he cannot leave his property exactly as he had wished, but that changes, frequently minor, in his dispositive scheme are required for tax purposes, and that with such changes he can reduce the taxes which would otherwise be payable by a half or two-thirds or more.

And the changes that are made, that the tax laws compels a reasonable person to make, are not the type of changes that even the strongest advocates of tax incentives can justify.

Why, if a testator wants to leave his property outright to his children, should we be counseling him to provide only a life estate for his children with remainders to grandchildren, or to create successive life estates with ultimate remainders to great grandchildren? What interest can the Federal Government have in encouraging this pattern of disposition over others?

Why, if a testator wishes to leave all of his property to his wife, should we counsel him into a complex arrangement involving a division of his estate into two parts with limited powers in his wife over one of the parts and with the amount of his estate going into each of the two parts being arrived at by a formula beyond the comprehension of the testator?

Why, if a testator wishes to leave his property in trust with the income to his wife and the remainders to his children, should we say "no" and advise him to allow his wife to choose the remaindermen of half the property?

Why, if a testator is interested in retaining his property for his life, should we counsel him to make gifts during his lifetime, and frequently to make gifts in trust which tie up the property for several generations?

The Federal Government should have no interest in whether a husband or his wife decides who ultimately gets his property. It should have no interest in forcing property into trusts which last for generations and it should have no interest in forcing individuals to transfer property during their life rather than at death.

This latter seems particularly true where the lifetime transfers are not outright but frequently are in trusts which, rather than improving the mobility of capital, usually tie up property more than if the decedent had continued to own it.

Yet our existing tax system gives large rewards to those who follow these practices. And the magnitude of the benefits available to large estates by carefully following particular dispositive patterns, which frequently make little substantive difference in the interests of beneficiaries is enormous—permitting very large estates to reduce the aggregate transfer taxes which would be imposed over several generations to a quarter of what they would be if property were transferred directly from one generation to the next.

It is particularly troublesome that the opportunities for reduction of estate and gift taxes are available principally to those with large estates and, moreover, yield greater proportionate benefits as the size of the estate increases.

This is so for two reasons: First, individuals with anything less than large estates are financially unable to take significant advantage of tax saving opportunities involving transfers of significant amounts of property during lifetime or involving the creation of trusts which lasts several generations or extended periods of time.

Except as to those with quite large fortunes, the making of significant irrevocable gifts during lifetime is an impossibility. The individual himself may well need the property.

Second, the benefits granted by taxing transfers as gifts rather than as part of a decedent's estate are greater in the higher brackets.

The estate tax laws result in the creation of complex property arrangements which are not easily understood by the layman. Moreover, since the estate tax actually affects only a very small number of our taxpayers, it is not a tax in which, at least until this time, there has been any general interest.

And yet, when we look at the results of the application of the estate and gift tax, we can see clearly that it is operating badly. The idea that very large estates can go for generation after generation without the imposition of any estate tax is a symptom of the weakness of the system.

The fact that a wealthy individual, in a very real sense, can through the efforts of a knowledgeable estate planner and without seriously distorting his testamentary plans reduce his esatate taxes by a half, two-thirds or even more is a compelling indictment of the existing system.

There is no rhetoric that can justify a tax system under which the amount of tax paid is largely optional with the taxpayer. The existing estate and gift tax system could well be characterized as a government level on poor advice.

One can argue about whether the aggregate amount of taxes on gifts and at death is too large or too small. This argument, however, is wholly apart from the question of the way in which any given tax burden should be apportioned. Fairness and equity demand that it be apportioned so that equal amounts of wealth bear equal amounts of taxes regardless of the technicalities of dispositive arrangements.

This is a basic principle of the income tax; one that has been widely discussed and is becoming well understood. It should also be a basic principal of the estate tax.

There is, however, one requirement of achieving equity in the estate tax which is not present in the income tax. The income tax is levied annually and, therefore, we simply compare one individual's annual income with another's in making judgments about equity.

In order to achieve equity in the estate tax, however, it is essential over the long run that comparable fortunes be subjected to the tax at relatively comparable time intervals.

To put it another way, if there are two fortunes of the same size, we cannot achieve equity in allocating the tax burden between them if one is subjected to the estate tax every 30 years and the other only once every 90 years. While exact equity in this sense cannot be achieved in this instance, because the imposition of the tax depends on a person's lifespan to some extent it is essential that the fortune not escape tax for entire generations.

Relative equity can be achieved in the estate tax only if fortunes are subjected to tax at least as they move from generation to generation.

I have tried to describe the results of some of the deficiencies of our present estate and gift tax system. I believe these results show clearly that change is needed.

I would now like to discuss the specific features of the existing system which cause these problems and the solutions recommended in the Treasury's proposals.

There are basically three features of the present law requiring change if equity in estate and gift taxes is to be improved.

The first is the favoritism that our existing tax structure grants to gifts over testamentary dispositions; the second is the fact that certain dispositive arrangements result in transfer taxes being paid on property only once every several generations, rather than once each generation; and the third is the marital deduction.

Our present system greatly favors lifetime gifts over testamentary dispositions. There are three separate factors at work which result in this favoritism. And the different factors benefit different wealth classes differently.

The first and most obvious factor is that the gift tax rates are 25 percent lower than the estate tax rates. This factor applies equally to all sizes of estates and therefore grants the same degree of favoritism to gifts by all taxpayers.

The second factor is the existence of separate rate schedules for the estate and gift tax. This means that total transfers can be divided so that a portion is subject to the estate tax and a portion to the gift tax, thereby obtaining the advantage of two separate rate tables each starting at the lowest rate.

Because neither the brackets nor rate progressions of the estate and gift tax are equal, the extent of this advantage varies from bracket to bracket. It is of considerable advantage to estates of all sizes but of somewhat less proportionate advantage to the very large estates.

If we eliminate the effect of the 25-percent gift tax rate reduction and the effect of the failure to gross up the gift tax in order to focus solely on the tax saving attributable to splitting, we find the maximum saving possible in absolute dollar terms is about $1,700,000 for estates of $20 million or over.

Obviously, therefore, for estates over $20 million the same dollar saving is of less proportionate advantage. (For estates of less than that amount, the saving is roughly proportionate except in the lower brackets, but, of course, individuals with estates in the lower brackets are not usually in an economic position to make significant lifetime transfers.)

The third factor which favors gifts over testamentary dispositions is one the operation of which is somewhat more subtle and therefore frequently overlooked. But it is of the greatest importance of all to those with very large estates. That is the failure of the gift tax to gross up.

Let me illustrate this effect. If a decedent leaves an estate of $10 million to a child, the estate tax would be about $6 million and the child would take a net of about $4 million.

If, on the other hand, the same taxpayer decided to make the maximum gift he could make to the same beneficiary (and again I am using estate tax rates in order to focus solely on this feature during his lifetime) we find that he could make a gift of roughly $6½ million and incur a gift tax of about $3½ million, thereby consuming all of his assets.

By passing the property during his lifetime he would be able to increase the net amount given to the beneficiary from $4 million to $6,500,000 an increase of over 60 percent. This is because the estate tax is levied on the gross amount of the transfer including the tax, whereas the gift tax is levied only on the net amount of the transfer.

To put it another way, the estate tax is in a sense a tax withheld on the total amount transferred much as the income tax on wages is withheld. The gift tax, on the other hand, is paid only on the net amount of the transfer. Where the tax bracket of the transferor is very high, the fact that the tax itself is not included in the base makes an enormous difference.

To state this effect still another way, if the estate tax were expressed as a rate applied to the gift tax base, we would find that the rate on the $10 million estate is about 150 percent, that is, it imposes a tax of $6 million on a transfer of $4 million, which is the way the estate tax does apply.

The failure to gross up makes much less of a difference in more moderate estates. For example, a decedent leaving an estate of $500,000 pays a tax of $145,000 thereby transferring $355,000 to his heirs. By disposing of his entire wealth by gift he could increase the net amount passing to the transferee to about $375,000 or an increase of $20,000 over the net amount which would pass in the estate, or an increase of less than 7 percent.

On a $10 million transfer the increase, as I have said, would be about 62.5 percent. All of these figures again use estate tax rates. The actual amount that would pass by gift would be somewhat higher because the taxpayer would have the additional advantage of the lower gift tax rates.

These aspects of the favoritism accorded gifts raise two basic questions. The first is why the Federal Government should wish to encourage gifts at all through tax incentives. And more particularly, if gifts are to be favored because of some feeling that it is a good thing to put capital in the hands of younger people, should all forms of gifts be favored equally? Should the gift in trust be favored the same as an outright gift? And the second question is, if gifts are to be encouraged, at least certain types of gifts, why should we encourage gifts by the very wealthy to a much greater extent than gifts by the less wealth. I believe there is little to be said for favoring gifts at all.

To avoid favoring gifts would require the integration of the estate and gift taxes into a single transfer tax, and the "gross up" of gifts for purposes of computing the gift tax. These are the proposals of the Treasury Department.

Integration of the estate and gift taxes, togeher with gross up would have other incidental benefits. Without going into great detail, it would permit a considerable simplification of the tax structure because it would be much less important to determine whether a particular transfer constituted an inter vivos or testamentary transfer. Moreover, problems concening contemplation of death would vanish.

The second major structural defect has to do with the problem of generation skipping. Generation skipping can completely subvert the progressivity in the estate and gift tax, particularly because the ability to transfer property under generation skipping arrangements is available, as an economic matter, only to the very wealthy.

A simple example will illustrate the effect of progressivity on general skipping. This example assumes no growth of the assets transferred. The effect, of course, is even more severe when growth is assumed, because not only is there a saving in estate taxes but the amount which would otherwise have been paid in estate taxes appreciates in the hands of the donee.

The effective rate of tax on a taxable estate of $250,000 is about 26 percent and on a taxable estate of $8 million it is nominally 57 percent.

However, if the $250,000 is passed through generation to generation to great grandchildren, the result is that they will take a net of $106,000, again assuming no growth, which implies an average tax per generation of 19 percent of the original corpus.

If the man with the $8 million makes a disposition which avoids transfer taxes at the termination of his children's and grandchildren's estates, which is not uncommon, he converts his 57-percent rate to an effective 19-percent generation rate—exactly the same as that payable by a $250,000 estate.

The Treasury's proposal would impose a substitute tax on all transfers which skip a generation. This tax is intended to approximate the amount of tax which would paid on the net gift by the estate of the skipped generation.

That is, if property is transferred so that it ultimately vests in grandchildren without passing through a child's estate, the substitute tax would be imposed in an amount designed to approximate the tax which would have been paid on the transfer if it had been included in the child's estate.

This approximation is achieved by imposing an additional tax on the transfer at a rate equal to 60 percent of the decedent's marginal rate. Sixty percent represents the relationship between the overall effective rate on an estate and the marginal rate.

That is, at a marginal rate of, say, 50 percent, the effective rate overall is approximately 30 percent. It is recognized that this is only an approximately, but it is a vast improvement over the existing absence of any tax on these arrangements.

Moreover, a taxpayer, at his election, may achieve the exact result by agreeing with his child to treat the property as if it had passed to the child and then passed from the child to his child.

The third aspect of the estate and gift tax system leading to artificial patterns of disposition is the existing marital deduction. Consistent with the idea that transfer taxes ought to be paid once a generation is the idea that transfers to one's spouse should not be taxed at all.

The Treasury's proposal would allow a marital deduction for any amount of property transferred to a spouse, not only the 50 percent allowed under existing law. This means that one transferring all of his property to his spouse would pay no gift or estate tax.

It seems inappropriate to impose a transfer tax at the time a husband dies leaving his entire estate to his wife. The property has not moved down a generation and the wife may need it during her lifetime. There is ample time to impose the tax at her death.

Under present law, only certain forms of transfers or certain property interests qualify for the marital deduction—primarily outright transfers and life estates with general powers of appointments.

Once again, there would seem to be little reason for the Federal Government to be concerned in allowing a marital deduction whether, for example, it is the decedent or the decedent's spouse, who has the power to name the takers after the wife's life estate.

It would seem much more simple and equitable if the marital deduction were to be allowed if an income interest in property were given to a spouse. That is what the Treasury's proposals recommend. Moreover, since in not all cases would it be advantageous to claim 100 percent marital deduction, the donee of the executor would be able to elect how much of the property in which the surviving spouse has an interest is to qualify for the marital deduction.

As a corollary to these rules, gift splitting between spouses would be allowed without limit, that is, a particular transfer could be treated as having been made by the husband or by the wife in whatever proportions the parties decide on. While these rules mean that some care would have to be exercised by executors and estate advisers in making these various elections, it seems a much more appropriate time to impose the planning burden than at the time of preparation of wills, that is, at the time the tax computation is being made, rather than to impose the planning at the time the transfers are made and thereby forcing the transfers into certain patterns or imposing disproportionately large taxes if those patterns aren't followed.

Furthermore, the planning would not turn on the form of conveyance but rather on the relative tax computations.

The net result of an unlimited marital deduction would be to give substantial tax advantage in the aggregate to smaller and moderate estates. It would not be of great significance to very large estates because the total tax would still be minimized by splitting. It would, however, permit arrangements to be made wtihout the payment of taxes during lifetime which would permit the splitting of the estate tax regardless of which spouse died first.

* * *

Our existing estate and gift taxes apply unfairly and arbitrarily. Moreover, the complexities, pitfalls, and inequities in our transfer tax system are many and consume time, talent, and energy vastly out of proportion with the inherent needs of administering an equitable transfer tax system.

But for a natural resistance to change, I believe all would be happier under a system which was fairer, put less emphasis on form, and permitted testators to do what they want, not what we tax advisers tell them to do. I strongly recommend the Treasury's proposals for revision. Their adoption would constitute a major improvement in our tax structure.

Chapter IX

INTERNATIONAL ASPECTS

Although the passage of time has affected the accuracy of some of the illustrative examples cited by Mr. Norr, his outline of the general principles of international taxation, and of the operative trends, remains accurate and incisive. Owing to strong opposition from some of the United States companies having overseas subsidiaries, the 1961 Treasury proposal discussed at the end of his article was not adopted. Instead Congress once again opted for a complex compromise by enacting so-called Subpart F (Secs. 951 et seq.). The only other major change in the United States tax law affecting international transactions came in 1966 when Congress drastically overhauled the provisions for taxing foreign corporations and nonresident aliens.[a] Since 1967, both are taxable in the same manner as their United States counterparts on income "effectively connected with the conduct of a trade or business within the United States". A flat 30% rate is applied to United States source fixed or determinable periodic income (i. e., interest, rent, dividends, wages, etc.) which is not so connected. Capital gains which are likewise not so connected are taxable (at 30%) only if the taxpayer was present in the United States for 183 days or more during the taxable year. (Secs. 871, 881–82.)

[a] Resident aliens, as Mr. Norr points out, are essentially treated like U. S. citizens (i. e., taxable on their worldwide income).

NORR, JURISDICTION TO TAX AND INTERNATIONAL INCOME *

17 Tax L.Rev. 431 (1962).

No rules of international law exist to limit the extent of any country's tax jurisdiction.[1] Similarly, no rules exist to require a country to grant relief from international double taxation. Whether the world needs a modern Grotius to construct international rules of tax war and peace, rules of taxation and de-taxation, is a question better left for the end of this discussion. As of now there are no such rules, except to the extent they may be provided by treaty in any particular case.[2] Moreover, only in few countries are there any local constitutional limitations on jurisdiction to tax. The major thesis of this article is that within its own legal and fiscal framework a country is free to adopt whatever rules of tax jurisdiction it chooses. This is true no matter how broad may be the reach of the resulting tax net.[3]

The minor thesis of this article is a corollary of this freedom of choice. There is then nothing immutable about the rules of tax juris-

[1] CHRETIEN, A LA RECHERCHE DU DROIT INTERNATIONAL FISCAL COMMUN 208, 212 (1955) (There is no case in which any national court has condemned double taxation as a violation of international law.); I HYDE, INTERNATIONAL LAW 674 (2d rev. ed. 1945); III HACKWORTH, DIGEST OF INTERNATIONAL LAW 594 (1942).

[2] There is a comparable absence of international law limitations on jurisdiction in related fields of law. "Such limitations as there are seem to be self-imposed and not the consequence of any external limitations imposed by international law." BREWSTER, ANTITRUST AND AMERICAN BUSINESS ABROAD 327 n.50 (1958). *See* Skiriotes v. Florida, 313 U.S. 69 (1941); Blackmer v. United States, 284 U.S. 421 (1932).

[3] Not even diplomats are protected. "No rule of international law requires that a diplomatic person should be exempt from the payment of income tax on his personal income." Lyons, *Personal Immunities of Diplomatic Agents*, 31 BRIT. YB. INT'L L. 299, 338 (1954). It is international courtesy rather than law that provides relief. *See also* HARVARD LAW SCHOOL RESEARCH IN INTERNATIONAL LAW, DRAFT CONVENTION ON DIPLOMATIC PRIVILEGES AND IMMUNITIES 115 (1932).

* Copyright 1962 by New York University School of Law. Reproduced with permission.

diction, the extent of relief from international double taxation, or the methods of providing such relief which a particular country may apply at any particular time. These will be grounded in the country's economic, political, and fiscal status at home and abroad. As that status changes from generation to generation, change in these rules and methods may be necessary as well. With particular reference to this country, the conclusion is that the change in the world economic and political position of the United States since we adopted our present jurisdictional rules almost two generations ago suggests that change in those rules may at least be worth consideration.

Classification of Tax Systems

Both United States investment abroad and foreign investment in the United States have grown tremendously since World War II,[4] with the result that the rules of tax jurisdiction at home and abroad are matters of rapidly increasing importance to tax lawyers and accountants. The freedom of choice available to nations in their choice of jurisdictional rules, the different economic conditions with which these must deal, the resulting diversity in tax structures, all combine to make more difficult the task of the tax adviser. Nevertheless, there are guidelines which can be pricked out through the confusions of fiscal geography. Tax jurisdiction in practice is a different matter from tax jurisdiction in theory. However lawful an assertion of tax jurisdiction may be, power to make the assertion effective is nevertheless required. To be effective, in turn, jurisdiction requires some link, some nexus or minimum connection, between the country asserting the jurisdiction and the taxpayer or the income sought to be taxed. It is in the choice of the minimum connection necessary to permit the effective application of jurisdiction that the patterns begin to appear.

This choice of connection, in turn, depends largely on the basic nature of the tax system itself, so that it becomes necessary at the outset to analyze and classify the world's tax systems; here, as elsewhere in taxation, "classification is the beginning of wisdom."[5]

---

[4] Private United States investment abroad exceeds 50 billion dollars, 5 billion dollars in 1960 alone. Pizer and Cutler, *United States Assets and Investments Abroad,* 41 U.S. Dep't Commerce, Survey of Current Business 20 (Aug. 1961). Foreign investment in the United States exceeds 18 billion dollars. Pizer and Warner, *Foreign Business Investment in the United States, id.* at 11 (Oct. 1961).

[5] Seligman, Double Taxation and International Fiscal Cooperation 58 (1928).

The discussion in this article will pivot around the income tax as the great fiscal device of modern times, but first a caveat is essential.

Especially outside the Anglo-Saxon countries, taxes other than the income tax are important. Unless he is sophisticated in international tax matters, the United States tax adviser may overlook the impact of these indirect taxes. In France, for example, a country which at the moment seems to be attracting as much United States investment, at least non-petroleum investment, as any other,[6] the income tax, individual and corporate, will raise less than 30 per cent of the national tax revenues in 1961.[7] French tax advisers and tax officials emphasize the risk to American enterprises which may arise out of the failure of their United States tax advisers fully to take into account the other 70 per cent which, incidentally, is non-creditable.

But we must limit our concern here to the income tax. The world's income tax systems may be classified into two major groups or clusters. Each group has its own answers to the questions of jurisdiction to tax and treatment of foreign income. To put it another way, each has its own tests of what constitutes that minimum connection which will warrant the exercise of jurisdiction to tax.

Global or Unitary Systems

One type of income tax system is the global or unitary system. This is found primarily in the United States and in the advanced industrial countries of Northern Europe—the United Kingdom, Germany, Sweden, the Netherlands, for example. It is often referred to as the Anglo-Saxon system, although Japan has also adopted it. Such a system uses a broad concept of income, and within that concept every kind of income is taxed more or less the same way. The jurisdictional connection is the personal status of the taxpayer rather than the source of his income. If the taxpayer, whether an individual or a corporation, is a resident of the country, the country asserts jurisdiction to tax his entire income from all sources. Having jurisdiction over his person, the country is in a position to make the assertion effective. For present purposes, the significant result of such a system is that income from foreign sources is taxed along with domestic.

---

[6] In the years 1958 through 1961, more new American operations were set up in France than in any other single country. Chase Manhattan Bank, The New European Market 30; see also *Investissements Américains en Europe: La France au Premier Rang*, Fortune Francaise 3 (Aug. 5, 1960).

[7] Ministère des Finances, Le Budget de 1961, 15 (1961).

SCHEDULAR SYSTEMS

The other major category of income tax systems is the schedular system, often called the Continental system as distinguished from the Anglo-Saxon. The essence of this system is the concept that there are qualitative differences in different kinds of income. As a result, each different kind is taxed under different rules and at different rates—wages at one rate, business profits at another, dividends at a third, and so on. Whoever receives the income, and whatever his total income, each different kind of income or activity tends to be taxed differently. The jurisdictional connection is the source of the income, not the personal status of the taxpayer; only income from what are considered to be domestic sources is taxed. For present purposes, the significant result of such a "source-jurisdiction" pattern is that the country of residence does not assert jurisdiction to tax income from foreign sources.

France had this schedular kind of system until the recent modernization and reform of the French tax structure. It is still used in Belgium, Italy and other Mediterranean countries, and especially in Latin America.[8] Apart from their special jurisdictional rules, there are other characteristics of these schedular tax systems which may be important to the American lawyer or accountant concerned with overseas business. By contrast with the global or unitary systems of the advanced industrial countries, the schedular systems do not work well. They are "inadequate under modern conditions" and "have proved wholly inadequate as instruments of a modern tax policy."[9] The countries that use schedular systems find that the income tax does not work well enough to raise much revenue.[10] Since the governments of those countries need revenue as much as others, they are forced to seek alternative tax sources, that is, indirect taxes: sales taxes, turnover taxes, payroll taxes—the whole category of cost-increasing taxes. The French call this "fiscal anesthesia"; the total tax burden is as heavy as that in countries relying on a global or unitary income tax; indeed it is often heavier, but the taxpayer, hopefully, does not realize it.

---

8 Some countries, Brazil for example, apply a rule of world-wide jurisdiction to individuals, but do not tax corporations on income from foreign sources. WORLD TAX SERIES, TAXATION IN BRAZIL 11/2.1, 11/2.3 (1957). France now subjects the world-wide income of individuals to the global income tax adopted in the course of France's 1959 tax reform, but continues to exempt resident corporations from tax on income from permanent establishments located abroad. *See* WORLD TAX SERIES, TAXATION IN FRANCE c. 11 (in preparation).

9 ECONOMIC COMMISSION FOR EUROPE, *Changes in the Structure of Taxation*, 2 ECON. BULL. EUROPE NO. 3, 59, 62 (1950).

10 THE FISCAL SYSTEM OF VENEZUELA 15 (Shoup, ed. 1959).

In addition to having to supplement their schedular income taxes with indirect taxes, the schedular countries often seek to graft on top of their schedular systems another and supplemental tax which follows the global or unitary systems of such countries as the United States or Germany or Sweden. This double income tax pattern exists, for example, in Belgium, Italy, and in many Latin American countries, Venezuela being a good example. It follows that these Continental and Latin American systems tend to be more complicated than global systems. As a result of their complexity and their failure to work well, these schedular systems are often in process of reform. The history of income taxation in France during the past forty years, for example, is the history of reform designed to replace an archaic schedular system with a modern global system. Belgium has a similar reform pending. The efforts at tax improvement which the Alliance for Progress hopes to work out with our Latin American neighbors may also involve some movement away from schedular income taxation.

As a practical matter, few countries are purely global or purely schedular; even those countries which adhere most closely to the global system may provide special treatment—schedular treatment, in effect—for particular kinds of income. The special treatment of capital gains in the United States and the special treatment of earned income in the United Kingdom are examples. But most countries are predominantly one or the other, so that the classification serves as a useful guide to the country's jurisdictional rules.

Jurisdictional Connections

Schedular income tax systems tend to apply a territorial rule of source jurisdiction; they tax only income arising from domestic sources and not from foreign sources.[11] The schedular system apparently developed in continental Europe, notably in France, in the

[11] Venezuela is an excellent example of a country relying on the source principle. *See* THE FISCAL SYSTEM OF VENEZUELA 154 (Shoup, ed. 1959): "Venezuela follows the territorial principle in the application of its income tax. . . . The citizenship or the residence of the taxpayer are immaterial factors and do not have any effect, with a few minor exceptions, on the application of the tax. The statutory rule is that the tax is applicable to income obtained by virtue of economic activities in Venezuela, or to properties situated within the country. . . . As a result of this territorial base for the income tax, income received by Venezuelan citizens, residents or corporations from sources outside Venezuela is not subject to tax." According to United Nations sources, other countries using a source jurisdiction rule include Argentina, Costa Rica, El Salvador, Guatemala, Haiti, Nicaragua, Panama, and the Union of South Africa. For a more comprehensive list, *see* AVOIDANCE OF DOUBLE TAXATION, *Tax Treatment of Foreign Income in 64 Countries and Territories* (Int'l Chamber of Commerce Brochure No. 180, 1955).

17th, 18th, and 19th centuries, and then became a characteristic of other countries with a Latin background, including those in the Mediterranean basin and in Central and South America. It is fair to say that this limited concept of tax jurisdiction grew up in these countries at a time when the taxation of foreign income appeared to be neither important as a matter of revenue nor feasible as a matter of tax administration.[12]

In countries with a schedular background, the source-jurisdiction rule amounts to a unilateral solution to the problem of international double taxation: the country of residence does not assert jurisdiction to tax foreign income, whether or not the country of source chooses to do so.

The sweep of jurisdiction is different in the countries to which foreign source income has traditionally been more important—the great industrialized countries of the northern tier: the United States, the United Kingdom, the Netherlands, Sweden, for example. These are the major capital-exporting countries of the western world. As a general rule, these countries use a global or unitary tax system. In such a system, as is generally the case with the United States system, a taxpayer is taxed on his world-wide income, regardless of its geographical source. If there is no connection by way of geographical source, some other connection in the personal status of the taxpayer must be found if jurisdiction is effectively to be asserted. In the United States,[13] as in Mexico [14] and a few other countries (including France for some purposes),[15] citizenship alone is a sufficient connection.

Reliance on the factor of citizenship to determine jurisdiction, although not unique to the United States, is relatively rare. Most of the countries which tax foreign as well as domestic income rely on

---

12 Moreover, in France, long the most important schedular country on the world scene, the bulk of overseas investment tended to be confined to countries in the French Empire or otherwise bearing a special relation to metropolitan France. Thus, the territorial exemption granted to overseas income was both an incentive to such investment and an accommodation to the revenue needs of the French overseas territories. *See* OWENS, THE FOREIGN TAX CREDIT 540–544 (1961).

13 Cook v. Tait, 265 U.S. 47 (1924) (citizen of United States, resident of and domiciled in Mexico, subject to United States tax on income from real and personal property located in Mexico).

14 WORLD TAX SERIES, TAXATION IN MEXICO 5/1.2 (1957).

15 The French source income of French citizens living abroad is subject to the individual income tax in certain circumstances in which the tax would not apply equally to foreigners living abroad and receiving like French-source income. *See* WORLD TAX SERIES, TAXATION IN FRANCE 11/3 (in preparation).

the factor of residence,[16] not citizenship. Moreover, even countries which, like the United States or Mexico, use the test of citizenship to reach the foreign income of most taxpayers, use the test of residence to reach the foreign income of resident aliens.[17]

In the case of corporations organized in the United States, the concept that the United States income tax is based on world-wide liability and reaches income from foreign as well as domestic sources is equally applicable.[18] But again, just as residence rather than citizenship is typically the jurisdictional test applied by other global countries to individuals, so in these countries the location of the seat of management rather than of the place of incorporation is typically the jurisdictional test for corporations. This is the test of "fiscal domicile" rather than "legal domicile." [19] The distinction between place of incorporation and location of actual control and management is of crucial importance. The place of incorporation rule permits foreign source income to be insulated from tax through the use of a foreign subsidiary, with the insulation or tax deferral effective until the profits of the subsidiary are declared as a dividend to the United States parent. In jurisdictional terms, the foreign profits of subsidiaries incorporated abroad are not subject to United States jurisdiction, as our rules now stand, until remitted to the United States. By contrast, the seat of management rule makes the use of a foreign subsidiary irrelevant as long as the policies of the subsidiary are controlled in the country of the parent corporation.[20]

---

16 See, *e.g.*, WORLD TAX SERIES, TAXATION IN SWEDEN 5/1.1 (1959); WORLD TAX SERIES, TAXATION IN INDIA 5/1.1 (1960).

17 I.R.C. § 871 (1954); WORLD TAX SERIES, TAXATION IN MEXICO 5/1.2 (1957).

18 *See generally*, Surrey, *Current Issues in the Taxation of Corporate Foreign Investment*, 56 COLUM. L. REV. 815 (1956). Similarly, Mexico, which uses Mexican citizenship as a jurisdictional factor for individuals, uses incorporation in Mexico as a jurisdictional factor for corporations, taxing such entities on income from both Mexican and foreign sources. WORLD TAX SERIES, TAXATION IN MEXICO 5/2.1, 5/2.2 (1957).

19 See, *e.g.*, WORLD TAX SERIES, TAXATION IN THE UNITED KINGDOM 5/2.2 (1957): "The place of incorporation or of registration, the location of offices or physical facilities, and the place where business activity is conducted are all immaterial in determining the residence of a corporation. A corporation's residence is at the place where 'the central control and management actually abide.' " The test is worded differently in other countries but amounts to the same thing. In France, it is the place where the real head office (*siège social effectif*) is located, "the place where the actual management is carried on." WORLD TAX SERIES, TAXATION IN FRANCE 5/2.2 (in preparation).

20 Under taxpayer pressure to match the United States deferral approach with respect to the income of foreign subsidiaries, the United Kingdom acted in 1957 to relieve its corporations of some of the consequences of this rule by adopting the device of the Overseas Trade Corporation. These are United Kingdom corporations which are not taxed on foreign

JURISDICTION OVER NON-RESIDENTS

To this point we have been discussing the taxation of residents, recognizing that in some cases the test is citizenship rather than residence, and the scope of tax jurisdiction over resident individuals and corporations. Now we turn to non-residents. Whatever jurisdictional approach a country adopts toward residents—whether, in short, it applies a world-wide test of unlimited liability to tax on all income, foreign and domestic, or whether it applies only a test of limited liability to tax on income deemed to have its source within the country of residence—all income tax countries assert jurisdiction to tax income from sources within the country, even when it accrues to non-residents. Whatever its rules as to foreign source income, an income tax system will reach the income of non-residents from sources within the country, treating the factor of source as a sufficient connection with the country to warrant the assertion of its tax jurisdiction. The United States is a convenient example.[21]

DOUBLE TAXATION

International double taxation may arise in one of two ways. The jurisdictional connections used by different countries may overlap, or the taxpayer or his income may have connections with more than one country. In either case there may be double taxation. The taxpayer, for example, may be a resident of a country which taxes all his income wherever it arises. If some of that income arises in another country, it will be taxed there as well. No rules of international law forbid international double taxation, as we saw at the outset. Sweden, for example, taxes residents on income from all sources, foreign and domestic. Until 1951, foreign income taxes, levied on foreign source income payable to Swedish residents, were not even deductible, let alone creditable, by Swedish residents, except to the

---

business income until that income is remitted to the United Kingdom. *See* WORLD TAX SERIES, TAXATION IN THE UNITED KINGDOM 11/6.1 (Supp. 1959).

21 OWENS, THE FOREIGN TAX CREDIT 520–521 (1961): "In terms of jurisdictional contacts, the United States income tax is based on two independent factors: the status of the taxpayer and the source of income. With respect to the individual income tax, citizens of the United States, whether resident in the United States or outside the United States, and alien residents of the United States are taxed on world-wide income. Either United States citizenship or residence of the individual taxpayer is a basis for United States jurisdiction over his income from all sources. Nonresident aliens, on the other hand, are taxed only on income derived from sources in the United States. The jurisdictional contact in this instance is the source of the income. Corporations are similarly divided into two groups. Domestic corporations, i.e., United States corporations created or organized in the United States under federal or state law, are taxed on world-wide income. Foreign corporations, on the other hand, are taxed only on income derived from sources in the United States."

extent the foreign taxes were withheld at the source.[22] In most countries the domestic income tax is not deductible as an expense. This is the rule in Sweden, and foreign income taxes were not thought to stand on any better footing. The rule of non-deductibility, resulting in full double taxation, was not considered to violate international law.[23]

But the fact that no principles of international or even constitutional law require relief to be given does not mean that relief is generally denied. The necessities of commercial and fiscal co-existence and a decent self-restraint, often grounded in considerations of administrative convenience, have led the nations of the world voluntarily to limit the scope of their tax jurisdiction. Some of these restrictions are unilateral; some are bilateral; in time they may even become multilateral.

Unilateral Relief from Double Taxation

Especially since the rise in income tax rates that followed World War I, unilateral relief has become fairly common.[24] Most countries now have some accommodations in their internal tax law to take account of the tax liabilities borne, or presumably borne, by their taxpayers in the countries in which their foreign source income originated.

Unilateral methods of relief generally fall into either of two classes, depending largely on whether the tax system is schedular or unitary. For the most part, countries that now have or formerly had a schedular system follow the exemption method. France, for example, exempts the income earned by its corporations in permanent establishments located abroad; the exemption relates both to the income as earned abroad and as remitted to France.[25] Whether the income is actually subject to tax abroad—presumably it is so taxed—

---

22 World Tax Series, Taxation in Sweden 11/3.3c (1959).

23 To this day, New Zealand, which follows a rule of world-wide liability, allows neither a credit nor (except Commonwealth income) a deduction for foreign income taxes. The New Zealand individual or corporation with income from foreign, non-Commonwealth, sources "has to pay tax twice to the full extent even though the tax levied in both countries may exceed the amount actually earned." Lau, *Nouvelle-Zélande*, 44 Cahiers de Droit Fiscal International 203, 205 (1961).

24 *See* Federation of British Industries Taxation Studies, *Unilateral Relief of Double Taxation* 2 (2d ed. 1960). This pamphlet describes the systems of relief available in 13 European countries. For a tabular statement of the relief provisions available in 64 countries, *see* Avoidance of Double Taxation, *op. cit. supra* note 11, at 26–35. For a detailed, recent study of the unilateral reliefs available in 20 countries, *see* 44 Cahiers de Droit Fiscal International (1961).

25 World Tax Series, Taxation in France c. 11 (in preparation).

is immaterial. Australia, by contrast, applies an exemption to all foreign income other than dividends, but only if the income has been subject to tax in the country of source.[26]

In the countries using unitary rather than schedular systems, on the other hand, the tax credit method is the more typical method of unilateral relief. In Europe it is often referred to as the "Anglo-Saxon" system as against the "Continental" exemption method. Its chief adherents are the United States, the United Kingdom, Canada, and, in recent years, West Germany.[27] There are influential forces on the Continent which much prefer the exemption method of unilateral relief, with its outright exemption of foreign income regardless of the extent, if any, to which it bore tax abroad, to the subtle complexities of the foreign tax credit.[28] But the tax credit method assures that one tax or the other, the foreign or the domestic, must be paid.

It might be said that the tax credit method divides the tax, while the exemption method divides the taxable matter. In practice, the latter process of division, *i.e.,* determining what is foreign source income under the exemption method, involves complexities that may exceed those of the tax credit system. Despite some dissent, the exemption method is regarded as increasingly inappropriate for modern economic activity.[29] The recent adoption of the foreign tax credit system by Germany, a dominant power in the tax thinking of the Common Market, and its use by such developing countries as India, Pakistan, and Israel, suggest that the tax credit system will not readily be abandoned.

---

26 WORLD TAX SERIES, TAXATION IN AUSTRALIA 11/3.2 (1958). The exemption arose "largely for the reason that there were virtually no Australian taxpayers who received an income from investments or business abroad." SELIGMAN, DOUBLE TAXATION AND INTERNATIONAL FISCAL COOPERATION 47 (1928).

27 Other countries using the tax credit method to give unilateral relief from international double taxation include Greece, India, Israel, Japan, Mexico, Pakistan, the Philippines, and Turkey. OWENS, THE FOREIGN TAX CREDIT 20 n.30 (1961).

28 See, *e.g.*, AVOIDANCE OF TAXATION, *op. cit. supra* note 11.

29 THE FISCAL SYSTEM OF VENEZUELA 157 (Shoup, ed. 1959); SELIGMAN, *op. cit. supra* note 26, at 30. After careful appraisal of the arguments pro and con, rejection of the exemption method by the United States is supported by SMITH, FEDERAL TAX REFORM 274–282 (1961). This is true despite the fact that the usual alternative, the foreign tax credit, is also an "extremely liberal" method of relief; "[m]any other countries are far less generous." *Id.* at 269. Seligman years ago suggested that a unilateral tax credit, "making a present of the revenue to the other countries" is indeed generous, and quite possible for a wealthy country like the United States, "[but] too generous for general adoption." SELIGMAN, *op. cit. supra* note 26, at 135, 173. *Cf. Issues in Iraq Oil,* 200 ECONOMIST 1278, 1279 (1961), indicating that the fifty-fifty arrangement in international oil is supported by Western tax credits.

Two other methods of unilateral relief from international double taxation should be mentioned. One is the reduction method, whereby income realized (and, at least in principle, taxed) abroad is taxed at preferential rates. In Belgium, a leading exponent of this method, the rate is one-fifth the normal rate for some income taxes.[30] A device which attracts considerable international attention is that used by the Netherlands. Like the United States, the Netherlands applies in the first instance a world-wide test of unlimited liability, computing tax on the total of income from foreign and domestic sources. If income from a foreign permanent establishment has borne tax abroad, the total tax due is reduced in the proportion which the foreign income bears to the total income. In other words, the Netherlands income is taxed at the progressive rate applicable to the total income, and the progressive nature of the income tax is not impaired.[31]

Another method of unilateral relief arises out of the treatment which the United States and some other countries apply to foreign subsidiaries. Leaving to one side for later consideration the tax-haven legislation proposed by the Treasury in July, 1961, it has generally been "our jurisdictional tax rule that the profits of a foreign subsidiary are not subject to the United States tax until remitted to the United States parent corporation as dividends." [32] The United States tax rate applicable to the income of the foreign subsidiary is zero. Unless and until dividends are paid, there is no problem of double taxation, and relief is complete. For the United States, "the availability of tax deferral on the income of foreign subsidiaries has already provided the most useful tax encouragement which can be given." [33] Perhaps we can better judge the impact of the rule of tax deferral by considering its results in a country other than the United States, where the mere statement of the rule sometimes arouses emotional reactions. Sweden, for example, a most active overseas investor, operates quite successfully abroad without a foreign tax credit; its major source of unilateral relief is the recognition which Sweden gives to the form of foreign subsidiaries.[34] This, in turn, is supported by a comprehensive network of international tax treaties.

---

[30] van Hoorn and Wright, *Taxation*, 2 AMERICAN ENTERPRISE IN THE EUROPEAN COMMON MARKET 343, 360 (1960).

[31] For an example showing the actual operation of this *progressionsvorbehalt, see* van Lawick, *Pays-Bas,* 44 CAHIERS DE DROIT FISCAL INTERNATIONAL 211, 214 (1961).

[32] Surrey, *supra* note 18, at 826.

[33] SMITH, FEDERAL TAX REFORM 282 (1961).

[34] WORLD TAX SERIES, TAXATION IN SWEDEN 11/3.2c (1959).

BILATERAL RELIEF FROM DOUBLE TAXATION

The bilateral relief afforded by tax treaties is for many countries a major method of lifting the burdens of international double taxation. This is especially the case in those countries which, like Sweden but unlike the United States, do not provide generous unilateral relief. Tax treaties have become increasingly important since World War II.[35] There are now several hundred general income tax conventions, to say nothing of many more special agreements on such matters as shipping or air transport.

Like unilateral relief measures, bilateral treaty relief typically takes one of two forms. The treaty may involve the exemption method, whereby tax jurisdiction over specified categories of income is assigned exclusively to one of the contracting nations, and the other agrees to exempt that category of income from tax, or, to put it in jurisdictional terms, to refrain from exercising its jurisdiction to tax the particular income in question. Income from a permanent establishment is a good example. Under the exemption method, the country of source in which the establishment is located is assigned exclusive jurisdiction to tax the profits of the establishment, and the country of residence, the country in which the owner of the establishment resides, agrees in turn to refrain from exercising its jurisdiction to tax the owner on those profits.

Alternatively, the treaty may provide relief from international double taxation by reducing the tax ordinarily due in one or both of the contracting nations on that income which is subject to double taxation. For example, the country which is the source of a dividend often agrees to reduce the withholding rate normally applicable to dividends paid to non-residents, and the country of residence agrees to give a tax credit or similar relief for the tax nevertheless paid to the country of source. In such a case both countries exercise jurisdiction to tax while mutually agreeing to adjustments which either eliminate or at least reduce the burden of international double taxation on the income in question.

A confusing element in the treaty picture is that many treaties combine both methods of relief. This is especially true of treaties between a country which uses the tax credit system as its unilateral method of relief, and a country which does not. A typical example is our oldest tax treaty, that with Sweden. In form and on its face,

---

[35] *See generally* Lachmann, *International Tax Treaties and Their Effect on Double Taxation,* THE TAXATION OF BUSINESS INCOME FROM FOREIGN OPERATIONS 183 (AMA Management Rep. No. 2, 1958).

that treaty appears to follow the exemption method, allocating income from particular sources to one country or the other for tax purposes. Income from real property is said to be taxable only in the country in which the property is located, for example, while interest is taxable only in the country in which the recipient resides. But after these and similar provisions allocating particular items of income to one country or the other, a key article of the treaty provides that in computing the income of its citizens, residents, and corporations, the United States may nevertheless take into account income from all sources, including income allocated to Sweden by the treaty, "as though this Convention had not come into effect," and then shall provide relief by application of its foreign tax credit in the usual course. Sweden, on the other hand, provides relief by unilaterally exempting from tax certain income deemed by the treaty to be United States source income.[36]

On the United States side, it is difficult to see what relief such a treaty gives to our taxpayers that is not already available to them under our foreign tax credit.[37] This may have some effect in limiting our bargaining power in the treaty negotiation field. The existence of broad unilateral relief provisions in the United States may limit the desire of other contracting nations to give much relief to United States taxpayers; treaty relief may redound to the benefit of the United States Treasury rather than to the benefit of the already-relieved United States taxpayer.

Non-tax Treaties

No discussion of treaty relief from international double taxation can be complete without mention of the effect of treaties other than tax treaties. There is that widely overlooked congeries of conventions known as treaties of friendship, commerce, navigation, establishment, and the like. These sometimes have unexpected tax consequences. There is no tax treaty between France and Spain, for

---

[36] *See* World Tax Series, Taxation in Sweden 11/5.1b (1959). The same dual approach may be noted in other tax treaties in which one party is a tax credit country and the other is not. *Id.* n.101.

[37] United States tax treaties make no substantial change in United States rules governing the taxation of the foreign source income of United States citizens, residents, and corporations. They serve the primary functions (1) of reducing the United States tax on income from United States sources going to non-resident aliens and foreign corporations and (2) of reducing the tax of the other contracting nation on income coming from sources in that country to United States citizens, residents, and corporations. Owens, The Foreign Tax Credit 9/2B (1961).

example. But in 1862 the two nations signed a treaty of establishment. It provides, among other things, that nationals of one country established in the other shall not be subject to any war levy, forced loan, or "other extraordinary tax" enacted as a result of "exceptional circumstances." [38] During World War I, France enacted an excess profits tax to meet its special revenue needs. Spaniards in France contended that this tax, although of general application, was inapplicable to them under the 1862 treaty. When the French rejected this claim, the issue went to arbitration before President Ador of the Swiss Confederation. By a determination of June 15, 1922, he upheld the Spanish view.[39] In reliance on this interpretation of the 1862 agreement, Spaniards again sought relief from the burden of French taxes during World War II. By a supplemental accord dated May 18, 1949, France agreed to exempt Spanish nationals from the World War II excess profits tax and to give certain other tax concessions as well.[40] During the inflationary period of 1957 and 1958, France once again resorted to temporary excess profits taxes. Spain today contends that these are "exceptional" taxes, inapplicable to Spanish nationals under the 1862 agreement; France denies the claim.[41] The issue remains a live one between the two governments.

And the issue is not limited to Spain. The commercial and maritime treaty of February 28, 1882 between France and Great Britain has a provision substantially similar to that of the 1862 Spanish treaty.[42] On a number of occasions British taxpayers have sought from France the same kind of relief which Spaniards have enjoyed; to date they have been rebuffed by the French courts.[43]

Moreover, the situation is complicated by the existence of most-favored-nation clauses in treaties with third countries. Under the France-Switzerland treaty of establishment, for example, Swiss citizens in France are entitled to treatment no less favorable than

---

38 Treaty of Madrid, 7 Jan. 1862, art. 4 (Harvard Law Library, *Diplomatic & Consular Laws & Regulations of Various Countries*, Volume P—U, 1929).

39 *France Contre Espagne, Affair de L'Impot Sur Les Bénéfices de Guerre*, 1 U.N. Rep. Int'l. Arb. Awards 301 (1948).

40 II Lefebvre, Feuillets de Documentation Pratique (I.D.) para. 8 (Série Conv. Int'l, Espagne, 1960).

41 Direction Générale des Impots, Bulletin Officiel des Contributions Directes, 475, 1958–II–618. A number of cases and rulings deal with the exact scope of the Spanish exemption. As early as 1921 it was held that it did not extend to war-time increases in ordinary income tax rates. C.E. 2 Dec. 1921, No. 66,865, R.O. 4773.

42 Treaty of Paris, 28 Feb. 1882, art. XI, 8 de Martens, Traités de Droit International 659, 666 (2d s. 1883).

43 *See*, for example, C.E. 24 Feb. 1926, No. 88,307, Lebon, 207; Arret Cass. Civ. 2 Feb. 1954, 9 May 1955, B.O.E. 1954–I–6626, B.O.E. 1955–I–7099.

that which France gives the citizens of third countries.[44] If Spaniards are then exempt from certain French taxes, why should not Swiss be equally exempt? The claim has been put forward by private parties,[45] but by common consent such clauses are usually not invoked by third countries to obtain tax benefits for their citizens.

More important than these most-favored-nation clauses may be the clauses, sometimes found in tax treaties but often in other treaties, which provide that nationals of one contracting nation shall not receive less favorable treatment from the other contracting nation than the latter's own nationals. Many tax laws deny personal exemptions, family allowances, and the like to non-resident aliens, but such a general clause, for example in a treaty of friendship or commerce, may require the nation in question nevertheless to grant these exemptions and allowances to non-residents.[46] In every case the tax adviser considering a foreign problem must look at the relevant tax treaties; it may often be necessary also to look at treaties other than tax treaties for the full scope of relief from international double taxation.

Prevention of Evasion

There is another aspect of the tax treaty picture that requires mention. Tax treaties have two functions. One is to relieve taxpayers from double taxation. The other is to ensure that while the same income is not to be taxed twice, it should at least be taxed once. This

---

[44] Treaty of Paris, 23 Feb. 1882, 9 de Martens, Traités de Droit International 95, 96 (2d s. 1884).

[45] Lenz, Les Conventions Suisses de Double Imposition 18 (1951).

[46] There is no tax treaty between France and Japan, for example, but there is a commerce and navigation treaty of August 19, 1911, containing a most-favored-nation clause specifically applicable to taxes as well as to other matters. 8 de Martens, Traités de Droit International, art 1, § 8, 867, 869 (3d s. 1915). As a result, France extends to Japanese nationals the same right to personal allowances and reliefs which it extends by tax treaty to nationals of other countries. Note, D.G., 13 Dec. 1957, B.O.C.D. 1957–II–271.

For a discussion of the tax consequences of United States treaties of friendship, establishment, and commerce, *see* Bittker and Ebb, Taxation of Foreign Income 393 (1960). *See also* U.S. Council, Int'l Chamber of Commerce, Rights of Businessmen Abroad under Trade Agreements and Commercial Treaties (1960).

The new treaty of establishment between France and the United States (signed Nov. 25, 1959, effective Dec. 21, 1960) has detailed provisions calling for equality of tax treatment between nationals of the two contracting states, but reserves to each state the right to apply special provisions to non-residents, as well as the right to accord special tax advantages by virtue of tax treaties with third countries. Agreement with France, Nov. 25, 1959, art. IX, T.I.A.S. No. 4625. A uniform tax treaty clause somewhat to the same effect has been proposed by the OEEC Fiscal Committee. OEEC Fiscal Committee, The Elimination of Double Taxation, First Report 37, 62 (1958).

second side of the coin, stressed by the League of Nations in the twenties,[47] seems in recent years to have receded into the background. It may now be coming back into the foreground. In the course of her 1959 tax reform, France, for example, changed her rules of jurisdiction to adopt a new blanket provision: notwithstanding any contrary provision of the Tax Code, all income the taxation of which is attributed to France by a tax treaty shall be taxable in France.[48] The purpose was to see to it that income exempt in the other treaty nation did not also escape tax in France through the operation of certain self-imposed French jurisdictional limitations.[49] Double exemption is as much to be avoided as double taxation. Italy has adopted a similar rule.[50] Indeed, the drive to ensure that international income pays tax at least once may be the force of the future in international taxation.[51]

Trends of the Future

Let us then look at the future. Are there any trends we can see in the realm of jurisdiction to tax and relief from international double taxation? Let us consider first the world scene in general, then the United States scene in particular.

On the world scene, there may be little to expect by way of additional unilateral relief. On the contrary, for reasons we shall see later in connection with the United States, one might even expect a tightening of present jurisdictional rules.

But on the treaty side as distinguished from the unilateral side, signs point to a continuing increase in relief from international double taxation, coupled with a simultaneous effort to improve international fiscal discipline. For years it has been observed that tax treaties are commonly made between two developed countries and only rarely between a developed country, on the one hand, and a

---

[47] That international incomes be prevented from escaping taxation altogether is as desirable as that the same income shall not be taxed by several different countries. Committee of Technical Experts on Double Taxation and Tax Evasion, Double Taxation and Tax Evasion 23 (League of Nations 1927).

[48] Loi No. 59–1472, 28 Dec. 1959, art. 3–III, codified in the Code Général des Impots, arts. 4 *bis* 2° and 165 *bis* (individual income tax), 204 *bis* 2 (complementary tax), and 209 (corporation income tax).

[49] Projet de loi portant Réforme Fiscale, Assemblée Nationale, No. 227, 8 (1959).

[50] Testo unico delle leggi sulle imposte directe, N. 645, arts. 82(f), 133(c) (29 Jan. 1958).

[51] After alluding to "international shenanigans," Smith, for example, states that "[i]nternational tax evasion is as reprehensible as purely domestic evasion; perhaps one might even regard it as doubly reprehensible." Smith, *The Functions of Tax Treaties*, 12 Nat'l Tax J. 317, 327 (1959).

developing country, on the other. Slowly this is beginning to change. Looking only at treaties in effect and not at the many treaties under negotiation or not yet effective although signed or initialed, there are such recent steps as the United States treaty with Pakistan, the United Kingdom and Swedish treaties with Israel, and the Swedish treaties with India, Pakistan, Ghana, and Malaya.

Treaties and Tax-Sparing

Of special importance in the tax relations between the developed and the developing countries is the matter of tax-sparing. Under the typical tax-sparing arrangement, a developed country gives a tax credit—normally by treaty—not merely for taxes paid to a developing country, but also for taxes forgiven or waived by the developing country as a result of a tax concession or incentive law designed to encourage investment in the latter country. This is not relief from double taxation; it is "something which, if conceded, stands apart as a relief without exact analogy." [52] A tax-sparing provision included in the United States-Pakistan treaty as submitted to the Senate was eliminated before ratification.[53] But tax-sparing appears again in the proposed United States treaties with India and Israel, signed in 1959 and 1960, respectively, but not yet ratified.[54] Moreover, the idea has been adopted elsewhere. Sweden's new treaties with Israel and Ireland, for example, both provide for tax sparing.[55] India, Pakistan, and Singapore have signed treaties with Japan calling for tax-sparing.[56]

Perhaps even more significant, the United Kingdom recognized the principle of tax-sparing by treaty in the Finance Act of 1961. Following a 1953 recommendation,[57] the Act provides that subject to the inclusion of an appropriate clause in a tax treaty, the British

[52] Royal Commission on the Taxation of Profits and Income, First Report, Cmd. No. 8761, para. 55 (1953).

[53] For the history of this episode, *see* Bittker and Ebb, *op. cit. supra* note 46, at 454.

[54] Indian Treaty, art. XII, CCH Tax Treaties ¶ 3815 (1959); Israel Treaty, art. XV, CCH Tax Treaties ¶ 4218 (1960).

[55] Ireland-Sweden Treaty [1959] art. XXIII(2)(a), IX U.N.I.T.A. No. 44 (Supp. No. 3); Israel-Sweden Treaty [1959] art. XVII(2)(a), *id.* No. 45. Greece uses an ingenious device. It offers tax concessions only to residents of those countries which will take the concessions into account in computing tax on the resident's world-wide income. Tsingris, *Grèce*, 44 Cahiers de Droit Fiscal International 112 (1961).

[56] India-Japan Treaty [1960] art. XI(3)(b), IX U.N.I.T.A. No. 46 (Supp. No. 3); Pakistan-Japan Treaty [1959] IX U.N.I.T.A. No. 19 (Supp. No. 1), as amended by Protocol of June 28, 1960, art. III (Tax Agreements with Japan 80, 83 (Japanese Ministry of Finance, 1960)); Singapore-Japan Treaty, April 11, 1961, art. XIV(3).

[57] Royal Commission on the Taxation of Profits and Income, First Report, Cmd. No. 8761, paras. 58, 59 (1953).

tax credit will be available for a tax remitted or spared by a foreign country, with a view to promoting industrial, commercial, scientific, educational, or similar development.[58] In appropriate circumstances this relief may be retroactive to 1947. Negotiations may soon open between the United Kingdom and Israel, for example, to modify their existing tax treaty to take account of the new legislation. The preliminary draft of a treaty now under negotiation between France and Israel also provides for tax-sparing. If, for example, Israel, under its laws for the encouragement of investment, waives its tax on dividends to residents of France, France will nevertheless give a credit for the Israel tax so spared. A similar provision is expected in a treaty now being negotiated between Italy and Israel.

As this may suggest, Israel, as an intellectual leader among the developing countries,[59] is one of the most active proponents of tax-sparing. Israel has recently suggested that the developed country should agree to grant a standard credit, perhaps at the rate of 25 per cent, for income from sources in the developing country, even if tax on that income has been waived or remitted by the developing country as a tax incentive.[60] Some such device may appear in the tax treaty now under negotiation between Germany and Israel.

Whether these tax-sparing developments will reduce the opposition which the idea has generated in this country [61] remains to be seen. Tax-sparing seems likely to increase in international importance, regardless of the position of the United States.

Impact of the Common Market; the OEEC Fiscal Committee

But the most important developments in the area of jurisdiction to tax and international double taxation are those which reflect the impact of the European Common Market and other regional economic arrangements. These are the days of political fragmentation and economic integration. The same forces that are bringing about economic integration are also helping to create fiscal integration.

Indeed, Article 220 of the Common Market treaty, the Treaty of Rome, contemplates an eventual treaty "for the elimination of double taxation within the Community." [62] Up to now the basic

---

58 Finance Act, 1961, 9 & 10 Eliz. 2, c. 36, § 17. There was a somewhat similar clause in an early version of the Boggs Bill. H.R. 5, 86th Cong., 1st Sess. § 6 (1959).

59 *See* Galbraith, *A Positive Approach to Economic Aid*, 39 Foreign Affairs 444, 447 (1961).

60 Gal-Edd, *Israel*, 44 Cahiers de Droit Fiscal International 143, 161 (1961).

61 See, *e.g.*, Surrey, *The United States Taxation of Foreign Income*, 1 J. L. & Econ. 72, 84 (1958).

62 Treaty of Rome, Mar. 25, 1957, 298 U.N.T.S. 3, 87 (1958).

spade-work has been done less at the six-country Common Market level than in the wider context of the Organization for European Economic Cooperation. The OEEC is the agency set up by the Treaty of Paris in 1948 to administer Marshall Plan aid and to coordinate the restoration of the economy of Europe.[63] In the Treaty of Paris the eighteen contracting countries agreed to strengthen their economic links by all appropriate means. As a step in that direction, the OEEC set up a Fiscal Committee to consider the elimination of double taxation. The Committee has relied on the tax treaty device, recommending uniform articles for inclusion by the member states in their bilateral income tax treaties. To date, twenty-five uniform articles have been recommended in four separate reports.[64]

Representatives of the United States have attended Fiscal Committee meetings from the beginning. On September 30, 1961, in what may prove to be an important step in United States tax history, the OEEC was reconstituted into the OECD, the Organization for Economic Co-Operation and Development, with the accession of the United States and Canada. These two countries must now accept, reject, or file reservations to the uniform articles already proposed. When this has been done and additional articles established, the Committee will be able to propose a complete uniform tax treaty for consideration by OECD members. The target date is July 1, 1963. In the meantime a number of new or revised tax treaties already incorporate some of these uniform clauses. Anyone familiar with the variety of clauses and language used in the treaties of any one country—the United States will serve as an example [65]—can only hope for more progress. The end result, the OEEC hopes, may be a multilateral treaty among some or all of the member countries.[66]

Multilateral Treaties and Supra-National Tax Authority

Indeed, there already is precedent for multilateral treaties with important tax consequences.[67] Under the multilateral Treaty of

---

[63] Convention for European Economic Cooperation (Dep't State Pub. No. 3145 (1948)).

[64] OEEC Fiscal Committee, The Elimination of Double Taxation, First Report (1958); Second Report (1959); Third Report (1960); Fourth Report (1961).

[65] Staff Report, Joint Committee on Internal Revenue Taxation, A Topical Comparison of United States Income Tax Conventions (1960).

[66] OEEC Fiscal Committee, First Report, *op. cit. supra* note 64, at 16, 17. Three member countries, Norway, Denmark, and Sweden, have already harmonized their treaties. OEEC Fiscal Committee, Second Report, *op. cit. supra* note 64, at 10.

[67] As far back as 1922, a multilateral tax treaty for Central Europe was signed by

Paris of 1951, the European Coal and Steel Community levies a tax—"the first European tax"—within the member countries.[68] The European Economic Community, the Common Market, has some authority to tax under another multilateral treaty, the Treaty of Rome.[69] Some day we may all be "super-taxpayers of a super-state."[70]

In principle, the Treaty of Rome retains the concept of the independent fiscal sovereignty of each of the six Common Market countries, but this is true only so long as their tax rules do not discriminate against taxpayers of other member countries. Already the Common Market has demonstrated its authority to restrict national tax sovereignty by supervision of national income tax rules. In 1959, France enacted a temporary special depreciation allowance for certain machine tools, provided they were of French manufacture. The limitation to tools made in France caused a protest to the Commission of the European Economic Community that this was fiscal discrimination in violation of the Treaty of Rome.

The Commission agreed and requested France to withdraw the discriminatory rule, and France complied.[71] Here we have an instance of supra-national supervision of national income taxation, a supervision that will presumably become more important as treaty-based regional arrangements like the Common Market increase in number and grow in importance.

INTERNATIONAL CONTROL OF TAX EVASION

This supra-national activity may also have an impact in accelerating the trend toward more administrative assistance and coop-

---

Austria, Hungary, Poland, Italy, Roumania, and Yugoslavia (largely the succession states of the old Austro-Hungarian empire); only two of these ratified the treaty, which hence became bilateral. CHRÉTIEN, A LA RECHERCHE DU DROIT INTERNATIONAL FISCAL COMMUN 83 n.4 (1955). Seligman long ago advocated multilateral tax treaties. SELIGMAN, *op. cit. supra* note 26, at 170.

68 Treaty of Paris, April 18, 1951, art. 49, 261 U.N.T.S. 140, 177 (1957). The Coal and Steel Community tax has been in effect since the year 1952–1953. For the calendar year 1960, the Community collected $32,530,000 through a tax of 0.35 per cent on taxable production of coal and steel amounting to about 9 billion dollars. Collections went up 19 per cent over 1959. EUROPEAN COAL AND STEEL COMMUNITY, FINANCIAL REPORT 1960, 7.

69 Treaty of Rome, March 25, 1957, Protocol on the Privileges and Immunities of the European Economic Community, art. 12, 298 U.N.T.S. 3 (1958).

70 CHRÉTIEN, PROBLÈMES FISCAUX DES COMMUNAUTÉS EUROPÉENES, LES PROBLÈMES JURIDIQUES ET ECONOMIQUES DU MARCHÉ COMMUN 255, 301 (1960).

71 For a detailed account, with citations to the relevant documents, *see* Norr, *Depreciation Reform in France*, 39 TAXES 391, 394 (1961). This supervision of national tax policies extends to indirect taxes as well. As a result, Italy has recently withdrawn the buy-Italian provision of a 1949 measure exempting buyers of new cars from the national road tax if the car was made in Italy. EUROPEAN COMMUNITY, BULL. 8 (Oct. 1961).

eration between tax departments. International administrative assistance based on treaty is already extensive. An individual in country *A,* to take a current example, recently made the public claim that he had realized large profits in the stock market. When the tax officials of country *A* asked whether these had been reported for tax, he replied that at the time he had been a resident of country *B.* Country *A* then asked country *B* whether the individual had filed tax returns in that country, and what claims as to residence he had made. The number of such cases increases as international trade and investment increase. Eventually international administrative assistance, like relief from international double taxation, may be put on a multilateral basis. A European tax official has suggested that since all countries have a common interest in fiscal discipline, the proliferation of branches, subsidiaries, and international transactions generally may require an international tax enforcement agency—interfisc, for example, along the lines of Interpol, the international law enforcement agency.

Thus the Common Market and similar regional arrangements open rather different roads into the future so far as the assertion of jurisdiction to tax is concerned. On the one hand, they threaten a new level of jurisdiction on top of existing national, provincial, and local levels; on the other hand, they hold out the hope of substantial tax benefits. First, they promise to facilitate the treaty process and thus to ease the problem of conflicting jurisdictional claims while improving enforcement. Second, the case of the French depreciation rule suggests that these new supra-national agencies may increasingly exercise jurisdiction to bar national tax policies hindering the free flow of international commerce. Within the Common Market, for example, a doctrine of "interstate commerce" of the Six may evolve, with the Community's Commission or its Court of Justice perhaps occupying a position comparable to that of our own Supreme Court.

Harmonization of Tax Structures

To this point in our discussion of the impact of the Common Market and similar arrangements, we have been dealing with its institutional aspects. Far more important than the institutions is the idea of integration, economic, fiscal, even political, that underlies them. The Common Market treaty does not require the member countries to harmonize their income tax systems. Nevertheless, the Common Market countries increasingly eye each other's tax systems and select the best from each other in a process of cross-fertilization. As the tax systems grow closer together, problems of inconsistent jurisdictional concepts tend to diminish. In its major tax reform of 1959, for example, France adopted for individuals a basically unitary system to replace what had been a basically schedular system. The change brought French direct taxation into closer harmony with the German.

In the field of business taxation, to take another example, France adopted new depreciation and inventory rules modeled after the German.[72] Germany's split-rate system for distributed and undistributed profits is exercising an almost irresistible attraction for French and Netherlands business men, even though Germany is considering giving it up. Belgium is planning to replace its archaic schedular tax system with a unitary system on the Luxembourg model; that in turn grows out of the German. If this suggests that the Common Market fiscal system will speak with a German rather than a French accent, the suggestion may be well taken, unless the proposed adhesion of Great Britain changes the balance of industrial and intellectual power within the Market. In October, 1961, the directors general of taxation in the six Common Market countries met together to discuss, for the first time in their history, the harmonization of their direct taxes.[73] Whether the end product is French, German, English, or perhaps a new European mosaic of all, the trend is toward fiscal harmonization.

Now let us suppose the idea of the Common Market continues to develop and that it grows into a wider European community and then into an Atlantic Economic Community. The very possibility suggests that the time has come for us to rethink the whole problem of jurisdiction to tax in the light of modern conditions. Tax deferral dates back to 1913; the foreign tax credit back to 1918; and its origins in the British and Dutch treatment of colonial income are still older. These ideas were developed when rate schedules and international economic conditions were different from the present ones. Are these ideas of forty and fifty years ago necessarily appropriate in the very different world of today? As conditions change here and abroad, should the United States tax law change with them? There is nothing sacred about the rules of tax jurisdiction; like war and diplomacy, these rules are merely expressions of national policy.

---

[72] Norr, *supra* note 71, at 396. Indeed, the whole French tax reform of 1959 has been described as the first stage in the process of aligning the tax systems of the Common Market. NORTCLIFFE, COMMON MARKET FISCAL SYSTEMS (1960).

[73] *Du Nouveau Chez Les Six: Vers Une Harmonisation Des Impots Directs,* La Vie Francaise, Oct. 20, 1961, p. 21.

As policy changes, so might tax rules. Certainly there has been an enormous expansion of world trade and investment and an enormous change in the world economic and political position of the United States since 1913.

THE TREASURY'S TAX-HAVEN PROPOSAL

It is in this context that we must consider a major proposal to change United States rules of tax jurisdiction—the Treasury's proposed tax-haven legislation of July 28, 1961. Let us recall at the outset that a tax haven or a foreign-base company generally "means a foreign corporation which pays little or no tax in the country of its incorporation." These companies have been made possible "because of the definition of a foreign corporation in our tax law and the limited tax jurisdiction asserted by the United States on such corporations." [74] The Treasury's proposal raises the question whether the United States is bound for the future to such limited tax jurisdiction. How far, in other words, may the United States, historically an adherent of the place-of-incorporation test rather than the control-and-management test, assert jurisdiction to reach a United States shareholder's proportionate share in the undistributed profits of a controlled foreign corporation, foreign in the sense that it is formally incorporated abroad?

At the outset we can dismiss any problems of international law; there are no rules of international law which would be violated by this assertion of United States jurisdiction over United States shareholders.[75] There remains the constitutional question: does the United States Constitution restrain this assertion? Specifically, would the Treasury's draft bill to impose income tax on United States taxpayers deemed to be deriving tax-haven profits through controlled foreign corporations be constitutional if enacted in its proposed form? [76] This article will not go into detail on the legal

---

[74] Wender, *Problems of Foreign Base Companies* in 1960 PROCEEDINGS OF NAT'L TAX ASSOCIATION 501.

[75] *See* notes 1 and 2 *supra*. The Treasury Department states that none of the countries of Western Europe have objected to its recent proposals. *Hearings Before the House Committee on Ways and Means on the Tax Recommendations of the President Contained in his Message of April 20, 1961*, 87th Cong., 1st Sess. 3533 (1961).

[76] The bill in question is the draft released by the Treasury on July 28, 1961. The bill is summarized in part in the Treasury's press release as follows:

"Under the suggested legislation income tax would apply to a U.S. shareholder owning 10 per cent or more of the stock of a foreign corporation which is controlled by five U.S. shareholders or fewer. A controlled foreign corporation would be one in which these U.S. shareholders owned more than 50 per cent of the stock....

"Only those profits of a controlled foreign corporation would be taxable to the U.S.

issues involved; the opinion of Robert H. Knight, General Counsel of the Treasury Department, that legislation of this kind is constitutional under both the taxing power and the power to regulate foreign commerce, is persuasive.[77]

UNITED STATES PRECEDENT

But there are some special points which deserve further discussion here. First, there is United States precedent, in fields other than taxation, for the proposed new jurisdictional rule. In considering limitations on the exercise of jurisdiction in non-tax fields, the tentative draft of the *Restatement of the Foreign Relations Law of the United States* makes this comment: [78]

> (1) the nationality of the owners or controllers of a corporation, as well as the technical nationality of the corporation at its place of incorporation or *siège social* will be taken into account, to the end that the true nationality of the basic economic interests involved may be determined;
> (2) the nationality of a complex consisting of a corporation and its subsidiaries is that of the parent.

The Reporter's note adds: [79]

> Under United States cases and diplomatic practice, differentiations based on the place of incorporation are disregarded and the enterprise is treated as having the nationality of its owners or controllers, individual or corporate.

A controlled foreign corporation is thus within United States jurisdiction. As the *Restatement* draft says elsewhere: [80]

> . . . A state which has jurisdiction over the persons who own or control a corporation incorporated in another state may, in effect, prescribe and en-

shareholders which arise out of tax haven transactions. . . . In general, tax haven transactions are those between related enterprises in which one of the parties to the transaction derives its income from sources outside the country in which it is created. A foreign corporation which engages in manufacturing activity abroad would not be considered as engaging in tax haven transactions.'' Treasury Dep't Release, July 28, 1961, 7 CCH ¶ 6479 (1961).

77 *Hearings, supra* note 75, at 313, 314.

78 RESTATEMENT, FOREIGN RELATIONS LAW OF THE UNITED STATES, § 30, comment *e* at 85 (Tent. Draft No. 2, 1958).

79 Reporter's Note, *United States Practice Regarding Nationality of Corporations, id.* at 85. *See also* BITTKER AND EBB, TAXATION OF FOREIGN INCOME 49 (1960).

80 RESTATEMENT, FOREIGN RELATIONS LAW OF THE UNITED STATES § 13, comment *a* (Tent. Draft No. 2, 1958). For a comprehensive discussion of criteria of corporate nationality in United States law, *see* Vagts, *The Corporate Alien: Definitional Questions in Federal Restraints on Foreign Enterprise,* 74 HARV. L. REV. 1489 (1961). Professor Vagts remarks that the state-of-incorporation test seems ''intolerably naive'' and inappropriate today, although proper enough in the nineteenth century; he points out that ''[m]ore recent congressional definitions have largely turned from the place of incorporation as a sole test, though often retaining it as one requirement.'' *Id.* at 1526, 1527.

force rules governing the conduct of the corporation through the exercise of its jurisdiction over such persons.

Congress, indeed, has already acted against tax havens in a non-tax context. It recently amended the Export-Import Bank Act of 1945 "... to make sure [that the Bank's export guarantee and financing program] ... will not be used to benefit tax haven corporations either directly as beneficiaries of guarantee or insurance contracts or indirectly through guarantee or insurance of sales to tax haven corporations." [81]

Foreign Precedent

There is also foreign precedent for the Treasury proposal in the established practice of other nations. In considering the tax treatment of foreign subsidiaries, how do they, in the American Law Institute phrase, determine "the true nationality of the basic economic interests involved"? The Treasury draft of July 28, 1961 related only to "controlled foreign corporations." Here is British practice: [82]

> In general, business income has its source wherever the "control and management" of the business is situated. Consequently, the business income of a resident, whether derived from domestic or foreign operations, is generally considered to be entirely from a domestic source, even though all transactions are consummated abroad and the control and management of the business within the United Kingdom amount to no more than "passive oversight and tacit control."

The control-and-management test is not limited to the United Kingdom; it is widely followed, having been adopted in Germany, for example,[83] and especially in countries which are or formerly were under British influence.[84] In effect, these countries already go

[81] Pub. L. 87-311, 75 Stat. 673 (1961), 12 U.S.C.A. § 635(c) (Supp. 1961), amending 67 Stat. 28 (1953). The amendment provides that the Bank's guarantee and insurance program "shall be . . . for the benefit of United States exporters and foreign exporters doing business in the United States." The explanation in the text is Congressman Multer's in reporting the bill. 107 CONG. REC. 18059 (Sept. 13, 1961).

[82] WORLD TAX SERIES, TAXATION IN THE UNITED KINGDOM 11/2.2a (1957). For a discussion of the control and management test, *see* American Thread Co. v. Joyce, 6 Tax Cas. 1 (K.B. 1911), *aff'd*, 6 Tax Cas. 163 (H.L. 1913), and the note thereon in BITTKER AND EBB, TAXATION OF FOREIGN INCOME 47 (1960).

[83] Oldman, *United States Tax Law and Treaties Affecting Private Foreign Investment*, 19 FED. B.J. 342, 351 (1959). Some Swiss cantons also use the control and management test, especially where inter-cantonal tax problems are involved. LENZ, LES CONVENTIONS SUISSES DE DOUBLE IMPOSITION 74 (1951).

[84] As to the control and management test of residence in India, see, *e.g.*, WORLD TAX SERIES, TAXATION IN INDIA 5/2.3 (1960).

farther than the United States proposes to do. They tax the income of a foreign corporation if the corporation is managed and controlled in the country in question, while the United States proposes to tax certain United States shareholders on their aliquot shares of the tax-haven income of certain controlled corporations, but not to tax the corporations themselves.[85]

There is other foreign precedent, perhaps of special interest because it involves Switzerland. If a foreign corporation is doing business in France, France exercises jurisdiction to tax an aliquot portion of the corporation's home office dividends, even to non-resident shareholders,[86] on the theory that that portion of the dividend is derived from French sources. In the French-Swiss treaty of 1953, the Swiss obtained the concession from the French that if a Swiss corporation can show that more than three-quarters of its shares are owned by persons domiciled in Switzerland, the portion of the Swiss dividend taxable in France must be proportionately reduced.[87] Switzerland thus recognizes that it is appropriate for another country to give preferential tax treatment to a Swiss corporation which is Swiss-owned as against a Swiss corporation which is not Swiss-owned. The new French treaty with Germany similarly provides that in comparable circumstances a German-owned German corporation shall receive more favorable tax treatment from France than a foreign-owned German corporation.[88] Thus, for a country to condition its exercise of tax jurisdiction on the residence or domicile of the shareholders of a foreign corporation is not without precedent.

An Accounting Precedent

Moreover, the Treasury proposal would seem to have precedent in the accounting practices of some major United States corporations. They include, not for tax purposes but in income reported to shareholders, the unrepatriated earnings of foreign subsidiaries

---

85 The United States *rapporteur* for the International Fiscal Association takes the view that even a tax on the income of the controlled foreign corporation itself would be constitutional. Wilkenfeld, *États-Unis*, 44 Cahiers de Droit Fiscal International 63, 69 (1961). *See also* Surrey, *Current Issues in the Taxation of Corporate Foreign Investment*, 56 Colum. L. Rev. 815, 827 (1956).

86 Code Général des Impots art. 109.2. Section 861(a)(2)(B) (1954) treats as income from United States sources dividends paid to non-resident aliens by foreign corporations drawing more than fifty per cent of their gross income from sources within the United States. Similar tax provisions exist in India, Australia, Canada, and elsewhere.

87 French-Swiss Treaty, 31 Dec. 1953, art. 6, VI U.N.I.T.A. 59 (1956).

88 French-German Treaty, 21 July 1959, ratified 4 Oct. 1961, published by Décret No. 61-1208, 31 Oct. 1961, J.O. 8 Nov. 1961, art. 8(1).

after deducting taxes that would be due on repatriation.[89] The increasing discrepancy between tax income and book income in the United States is a matter of growing concern.[90]

That other countries do not do precisely what the United States proposes to do is hardly an answer to the Treasury proposal. Our problem is not theirs; ours is of a different magnitude.[91] It is the United States which is the great exporter of capital, the country with over 50 billion dollars invested abroad, 5 billion dollars in 1960 alone.[92] Nor is it answered by the observation that our treatment of foreign income has scarcely changed in forty years and should not be changed now. Two-thirds of our base-company subsidiaries were established in the last five years.[93] The English have a maxim that the Chancellor does not close a loophole until the abuse becomes too flagrant; this is our situation today, as distinguished, for example, from 1913.[94]

---

89 *See* REPORT OF 53D ANNUAL MEETING OF GENERAL MOTORS SHAREHOLDERS, WILMINGTON, DELAWARE, MAY 19, 1961 19, 20: "In reply to a further question from the same shareholder on the taxation of overseas profits before repatriation, Mr. Donner said that General Motors for the past 15 or 20 years has included in its reported net earnings only that net amount earned abroad after making provision for any taxes that would become payable when paid as a dividend, whether it is taxed when the dividend is paid or when earned. Accordingly, the proposed legislation would make no difference in the amount of net profits currently reported in the annual statement."

90 SMITH, FEDERAL TAX REFORM 178, 182 (1961). In France and many other countries, income as reported for tax purposes must generally coincide with income as recorded on the books. See, *e.g.*, WORLD TAX SERIES, TAXATION IN SWEDEN 6/2.4 (1959).

91 The number of known United States subsidiaries in Switzerland, for example, considerably exceeds the number known to have been established by the nationals of other industrialized countries. *Hearings*, *supra* note 75, at 3522, 3532. For an indication that there are in addition many American-owned Swiss base companies which "owe their escape from [United States] foreign personal company taxation only to the fact that their status has not—or not yet—been discovered," *see* BIANCHI AND WALTER, SWISS TAX SHELTER OPPORTUNITIES FOR U. S. BUSINESS 25 (1960). That the growth of tax havens would bring corrective action has been anticipated. See, *e.g.*, Wender, *supra* note 74, at 501: "As the early '40s was the heyday of the family partnership, the last five years may well have been that for the foreign base company. I suspect with the Treasury's organization of an International Operations Division we shall see as much litigation in connection with foreign base companies as we did in the family partnership area. Ultimately, I expect there may be legislation regulating their use."

92 *See* note 4 *supra*.

93 NATIONAL INDUSTRIAL CONFERENCE BOARD, ORGANIZING FOREIGN-BASE CORPORATIONS 9 (1961). The Board states that "the underlying reason for incorporating in a tax-haven jurisdiction is almost always one of tax advantage."

94 Brewster puts the point with more elegance: "The jurisdictional reach of our law to citizens may grow according to the seriousness of the impact upon the United States." BREWSTER, ANTITRUST AND AMERICAN BUSINESS ABROAD 333 (1958). Viscount Simonds puts it with more vigor: "... neither comity nor rule of international law can be invoked to prevent a sovereign state from taking what steps it thinks fit to protect its own revenue laws from gross abuse. ..." Collco Dealings, Ltd. v. Inland Revenue Commissioners, [1961] 2 W.L.R. 401, 410 [1961] All E.R. 762, 765 (H.L.).

AVAILABILITY OF TREATY RELIEF

Excessively generous unilateral limitations of national fiscal sovereignty are not necessarily in a country's best interests. They reduce a country's bargaining power in international negotiations, for it has no further concessions to offer tax treaty partners.[95] Thus the very broad application employed by the British authorities with respect to the Income Tax Act of 1919 led the Swiss promptly to make a double tax treaty with the United Kingdom.[96] Extension of our jurisdictional rules to permit us to reach United States shareholders of tax-haven corporations may lead at least the more responsible tax-haven countries to make reasonable bilateral accommodations with the United States. This may be especially true of those tax-haven countries which already have treaty relations with the United States—Switzerland, for example, and the Netherlands with respect to the Antilles—and which may as a result seek to modernize these treaties to take account of the new United States jurisdictional rule.[97]

THE IMAGE OF THE UNITED STATES

Winston Churchill pointed out that countries are judged by their national performance. In the tax field our national performance is not everywhere well regarded. The effect of anti-tax-haven legislation on the American image abroad may be salutary. We must recognize that there is an image abroad of the American as tax-avoider. Last summer the writer got out of a car at Sodom on the Dead Sea with two British tax lawyers and a Swedish national. Looking at the panorama of ancient desolation, one Englishman whispered to the other: "Good place for Americans to set up a base company." [98]

---

95 Dan Throop Smith, an experienced treaty negotiator, says this of the United States: "In a sense it is too bad that both deferral and the credit for foreign taxes are given by statute. If they could be given by treaty, it might be possible to work out some effective arrangement for lower taxes on retained earnings in the countries seeking capital or other desirable provisions. As it is, we have given away by statute what might be two very effective bargaining points in negotiations." SMITH, FEDERAL TAX REFORM 280 (1961). The European view is the same. LENZ, LES CONVENTIONS SUISSES DE DOUBLE IMPOSITION 9 (1951).

96 LENZ, *op. cit. supra* note 95, at 14.

97 None of our existing income tax treaties is violated by the proposed new rule. *Cf.* Head Money Cases, 112 U.S. 580 (1884); Whitney v. Robertson 124 U.S. 190 (1888); I.R.C. § 7852(d) (1954).

98 For another expression of the British view, see, *Privileged Dollars*, 200 ECONOMIST 40 (1961): "The existing [United States] law makes possible the establishment of a subsidiary in a low-tax or 'tax-haven' country for the exclusive purpose of evading United States taxation; these so-called subsidiaries often amount to no more than a printed

The Swiss acknowledge "illegitimate" United States base-company operations there.[99] They refer to "letter-box domicile," *briefkastendomizil,* and to "evasion by proxy." Europeans take malicious joy in the story of the mortician and his yacht,[100] and I heard a meeting of French tax officials break into laughter at the single word "safari."[101] Indeed the French, tired of what they regard as our sanctimonious attitude toward what we regard as tax fraud in France, devote chapters to the proposition that the United States is no better.[102] Thus, the proposed legislation would seem to be not only constitutional, but would seem to be desirable in the national interest as well.

The proposal would adopt, in this limited area, the test of economic rather than political allegiance as the criterion of tax jurisdiction. Taken in conjunction with our foreign tax credit, the proposal would not require international income to suffer taxation twice; it would ensure only that tax is paid once.

Effect on Other Countries

Moreover, the proposed legislation may have another effect in encouraging the other industrialized countries to take parallel steps against similar behavior by their own taxpayers. Secretary Dillon has pointed out that the Common Market countries, far from objecting, ". . . have urged action such as that proposed by the Treasury."[103] Foreign tax officials make the same point in private conversations.

To learn why this is so France may be employed as an example.

---

letterhead. Alternatively, companies which are conducting business abroad can juggle their finances (by transferring patent rights, management fees and so on) so as to accumulate profits in the foreign subsidiary instead of in the parent company, where they will be taxed." Still another British view may be found in Ellis, *On First Looking Into J. K. Lasser's "Your Income Tax,"* The New Yorker 50 (April 8, 1961).

99 Bianchi and Walter, Swiss Tax Shelter Opportunities for U. S. Business 7–8 (1960).

100 *Hearings, supra* note 75, at 177, item 8.

101 Sanitary Farms Dairy, Inc., 25 T.C. 463 (1955). This is not to suggest that the problem of personal expenditures by business firms is limited to the United States. France barred the deduction of hunting, fishing, and resort expenses by business firms in the course of her extensive 1959 tax reform (Code Général des Impots, art. 35.4). The Finance Bill of 1962, recently submitted to the French Parliament, proposes further restrictions on business expenses. The British imposed restrictions on automobile expenses in the Finance Act [1961] 9 & 10 Eliz. 2, c.36, § 23; the French now propose to copy these.

102 Lauré, Traité de Politique Fiscale 368 (1956).

103 *Hearings, supra* note 75, at 3522, 3533. See *T-Men Eye Overseas Havens,* Business Week 32 (Dec. 24, 1960): "Some foreign countries also are privately concerned about U.S. manufacturing operations overseas, particularly where profits are siphoned to other countries and no, or little, taxes are paid to the host country."

If a royalty is due from a French licensee to a licensor in a country with which France has no tax treaty, the French fisc is entitled to income tax withheld at the rate of 24 per cent on the gross royalty as reduced by a deduction of 20 per cent for expenses, and to the tax on services, a form of turnover tax, at the rate of 8.5 per cent.[104] But if the licensor is a Swiss corporation, neither of these taxes is due to France under the French-Swiss treaty and related arrangements.

What is a "Swiss" corporation for this purpose? Suppose that a corporation is organized under the laws of Switzerland by persons who are residents of a country with which France has no treaty, and that the "Swiss" corporation engages in no business in Switzerland, has no connection with Switzerland other than the formal one of incorporation, and pays the royalties over to the original owners of the patent involved in such a way that not even Swiss tax is due. Is this a "Swiss" corporation entitled to be recognized as such by the various countries involved? The French-Swiss treaty states at the outset that its purpose is to "protect taxpayers of the two States against double taxation." [105] There are cases pending in which such situations are under investigation by countries other than the United States. The Fiscal Committee of the OEEC, of which Switzerland is a member, recognizes that in these cases it may be appropriate to provide for denial of treaty exemptions to base companies.[106] When the tax directors of the six Common Market countries met for the first time to consider the harmonization of direct taxes within the Market, a first step was to set up a working party to consider the tax aspects of investments within the Market by third-country holding companies and base companies.[107]

Switzerland herself recognizes the problem and may apply what is called the "shovel" test: if the so-called Swiss licensor "shovels" the money out of Switzerland, tax-free, as fast as it comes in, it will not be regarded as Swiss for treaty purposes. If it shovels out only half, the result is unclear; no specific line would be drawn for fear that would induce licensors to "shovel" as far as that line.

Such a step alone will not solve the tax-haven problem, but plainly something of consequence is involved when Switzerland regards

104 For a description of turnover taxes as applied to royalties by France and other Common Market countries, *see* van Hoorn and Wright, *Taxation*, 2 AMERICAN ENTERPRISE IN THE EUROPEAN COMMON MARKET 375, 439 (1960).

105 *See* note 87 *supra*, art. I-1.

106 OEEC FISCAL COMMITTEE, FOURTH REPORT, *op. cit. supra* note 64, at 63.

107 *Du Nouveau Chez Les Six: Vers Une Harmonisation Des Impots Directs*, La Vie Francaise, Oct. 20, 1961, p. 21.

itself and its legitimate taxpayers as abused by purely formal incorporation in Switzerland.[108]

Conclusion

The change in our jurisdictional rules involved in the Treasury's tax-haven proposal thus seems both useful and necessary. But the problem of jurisdiction to tax is a larger one. To answer the question posed at the outset, the growth of international transactions has brought us to the time when we do need a modern Grotius to prepare international rules of tax jurisdiction, of tax war and peace. The first step should be taken by the United States, the country with the largest share in world trade and investment. Our treatment of foreign income in a changing world, indeed in a world that has already changed drastically since we adopted our present rules nearly two generations ago, requires reconsideration. Not many lawyers or legislators would regard a fifty-year old statute regulating divorce, or trustee investment, or security issues and stock exchanges, as particularly appropriate to 1961. Perhaps our prewar rules of jurisdiction are obsolescent too.

We need the same flexibility and the same modernity in these areas of public law that have made us so outstanding in such private law areas as corporations, trusts, or securities. The United States should launch a full-scale study of the whole problem of jurisdiction to tax and the extent to which it should properly be exercised. Double exemption as well as double taxation requires study—the problem of relieving taxpayers from international double taxation and the problem of relieving governments from international fiscal avoidance. Such a study would involve a scrutiny of our tax treaty program as well. Legislation apart, to what extent should a tax treaty require the United States to recognize a corporation to be entitled

108 "Evidences of changed attitudes in such recognized tax-haven jurisdictions as Venezuela, Canada, and Switzerland" are reported by the NATIONAL INDUSTRIAL CONFERENCE BOARD, ORGANIZING FOREIGN-BASE CORPORATIONS 22 (1961). In its 1959 budget Canada, for example, withdrew the right to set up new base companies, "foreign business corporations," under the Income Tax Act § 71. In supporting this change in Canadian jurisdictional rules, the Finance Department offered testimony to show that many base companies did not even pay tax once; their "profits paid tax neither to Canada nor to any other country." Koerner, *Canadian Taxation of Foreign Income: The Past Pattern and its Recent Development* in 1959 PROCEEDINGS OF NAT'L TAX ASSOCIATION 339, 349. About 150 foreign business corporations organized before that time may continue to serve as base companies; some of these are said to have changed hands since at prohibitive prices. Canada's action and the proposed Swiss step may reflect a broader current of thought: "the trend of contemporary legal development is towards the elimination or limitation of all types of immunity." JENKS, INTERNATIONAL IMMUNITIES 169 (1961).

to its benefits whose only connection with the other country is the formal fact of incorporation there? [109] The question should be investigated not with the purpose of achieving double taxation, but with the purpose of inquiring whether United States-controlled income should be taxed once, whether it is being so taxed, and if not, how best such taxation might be accomplished. The argument here is not for any specific program; the argument is that the problem of jurisdiction to tax international income requires fresh thought, having regard to the principle that income should not be taxed twice, but that it should be taxed once.

A major study by the United States would almost inevitably be followed by similar studies in other countries. Eventually, perhaps under United Nations auspices, a multilateral study to prepare international rules might evolve, like the Geneva conferences on the law of the sea, for example.[110] Under either public or private auspices the United States equivalent of a British Royal Commission [111] or a Swedish expert tax committee should be convened.[112] The work of the two Hoover Commissions and more recently the report of the Commission on Money and Credit offer precedent.[113] Such a group, composed of private lawyers and accountants, representatives of the State and Treasury Departments, of university representatives and others who may be interested, could be established to consider the whole problem, not solely from the point of view of whether company *A* or subsidiary *B* would pay more tax, or whether the interests of this tax haven or that would be hurt, but from the point of view of the total interests of the United States, its allies and treaty partners, and its taxpayers.

---

109 For statistics as to the extent to which base companies maintain only formal connections with the country of incorporation, *see* NATIONAL INDUSTRIAL CONFERENCE BOARD, ORGANIZING FOREIGN-BASE CORPORATIONS 91 (1961). Many of our tax treaties already provide that an enterprise, although formally incorporated in the other treaty country, will not be regarded as an enterprise of that country unless it actually carries on activities there. WORLD TAX SERIES, TAXATION IN SWEDEN 11/5.4a (1959); STAFF REPORT, JOINT COMMITTEE ON INTERNAL REVENUE TAXATION, A TOPICAL COMPARISON OF UNITED STATES TAX CONVENTIONS 17a–17e. The Treaty of Rome setting up the Common Market, in its articles governing the right of corporations of one member country to establish themselves in another, reserves the right to corporations actually carrying on activity; mere incorporation in one member country is not alone sufficient to require welcome by another (arts. 52, 58, 298 U.N.T.S. 37, 40 (1958)).

110 *See* Dean, *The Second Geneva Conference on the Law of the Sea: The Fight for Freedom of the Seas,* 54 AM. J. INT'L L. 751 (1960).

111 WORLD TAX SERIES, TAXATION IN THE UNITED KINGDOM 1/2.2a (1957).

112 WORLD TAX SERIES, TAXATION IN SWEDEN 1/3.3 (1959).

113 COMMISSION ON MONEY AND CREDIT, MONEY AND CREDIT (1961).

*

Chapter X

REVENUE SHARING

In recent years there has been widespread interest in using federal funds to assist states and municipalities. The selection which follows indicates the variety of forms such assistance may take. The subject has assumed new importance in view of President Nixon's message to Congress proposing grants to states with required further allocations of each state's grant to local government units. See 115 Cong.Rec. H 7389 (daily ed. Aug. 13, 1969). For a further discussion, see Heller, et al., Revenue Sharing and the City (1968).

A long-familiar method by which the federal government provides financial assistance to state and local governments is through exemption of interest on state and local bond issues from the federal income tax. This is discussed in Chapter II of these materials.

WEIDENBAUM, FEDERAL AID TO STATE AND LOCAL GOVERNMENTS: THE POLICY ALTERNATIVES

2 Revenue Sharing and its Alternatives: What Future for Fiscal Federalism?
Subcommittee on Fiscal Policy, Joint Economic Committee,
90th Cong., 1st Sess. 651–65 (1967).

INTRODUCTION

This study of the policy mix of Federal aid to State and local governments attempts to achieve two objectives: (1) to examine the case for increased Federal financial assistance to State governments and their subdivisions and (2) to analyze as objectively as possible the major alternative ways of distributing the aid.

The size and composition of Federal aid to State and local governments in the coming years will be strongly influenced by two interrelated factors: (1) the public policies adopted to utilize the resources made available by a post-Vietnam military cutback; and (2) the growing public awareness of the "fiscal mismatch" between Federal financial resources and State and local governmental program responsibilities.

These two factors are closely related because Federal programs designed to reduce the fiscal mismatch also represent possible alternative ways of offsetting the deflationary impacts of a reduction in military spending.

NATURE OF A LIKELY POST-VIETNAM ENVIRONMENT

At this point in time, it is extremely difficult to speculate as to the precise nature of a cutback in U.S. defense spending following peace in Vietnam. If the general dimensions correspond to the Korean experience, it would be expected that spending would decline substantially after the cessation of hostilities, but not down to the level prior to the conflict. As Vietnam outlays are now running at over $20 billion a year, a reduction of about $15 billion in U.S. military demand might be anticipated during the 12- to 24-month period following the cessation of hostilities. The new level of military spending would still be in excess of $50 billion a year and continue to require a substantial industrial base to support it.

The replacement of the $15 billion of military demand would represent the basic task of post-Vietnam economic adjustment. The major alternatives that can and are being considered in the Federal Government's current exploratory planning were listed in the January 1967 Economic Report of the President.[1] The general types of actions are

[1] *Economic Report of the President, January 1967*, p. 24.

(1) tax reduction, (2) adjustment of monetary and financial policies, (3) expansion of Government spending programs, and (4) Federal financial support to State and local governments.

The specific and essentially short-term question of the economic adjustments to the cessation of hostilities in Vietnam also involves many longer run and perhaps more fundamental considerations of social, political, and economic policy, of which aid to State and local governments is just a part. For example, there are various methods of reducing taxes and thereby pumping additional purchasing power into the economy. Prior to the Vietnam buildup there had been some public discussion of focusing the next round of tax adjustments on the lower income brackets. Such action would be more than a short term policy to offset the deflationary impact of the military cutback. It could also have an important influence on income redistribution. It also would constitute a decision to emphasize consumption at the expense of investment insofar as the lower income groups spend an above average share of their income for current consumption items and save proportionately less.

Important policy choices will be made both within as well as between the major categories of post-Vietnam economic adjustment actions. The choice between tax reduction and Government expenditure increase is not likely to be an either/or one, but some combination of the two. Hence, the public sector is not likely to contract by the full amount of the military cutback (which would be the result of complete reliance on tax reduction) but some tendency in that direction would result from most of the likely combinations of tax reduction and Government spending increases.

Limiting the short-term post-Vietnam adjustment efforts either to expansion in direct Federal operations or to general tax reductions would lessen the ability of the Federal Government to embark on the block grant or similar long-term efforts which have been proposed to aid State and local governments in their fiscal problems. However, the availability of such "discretionary" revenues of the Federal Government may become a long-term phenomenon.

THE FISCAL MISMATCH

For a considerable period of time, students of public finance have been impressed by the tendency of Federal Government revenues from existing tax rates (during a cold war period) to rise faster than the gross national product or even then the expenditure requirements for existing programs.[2] This situation comes about essentially because of two factors.

The first is the primary reliance by the Federal Government on an income tax with a generally progressive rate structure. As a result, Federal revenues tend to increase along with the Nation's economic growth, but at a more rapid rate.[3] The second factor is the dominance of Federal spending by military programs. Hence, during periods of

[2] Cf. Gerhard Colm and Manuel Helzner, "Financial Needs and Resources Over the Next Decade: At All Levels of Government," in National Bureau of Economic Research, *Public Finances: Needs, Sources, and Utilization,* Princeton, Princeton University Press, 1961, pp. 3–21.

[3] Cf. Otto Eckstein, *Trends in Public Expenditures in the Next Decade,* New York, Committee for Economic Development, 1959, p. 46.

peacetime or even cold war, when defense spending is relatively stable, total expenditures for existing Federal Government programs do not tend to rise as fast as the yield of the progressive tax structure (even though individual civilian programs may be growing at a rapid rate). Table 1 contains an estimate of the magnitude of the "potential" excess of revenues from existing rates over expenditure requirements of currently authorized programs.

TABLE 1.—*Projections of the gross national product and the Federal budget*

[Fiscal years; in billions of dollars]

Category	1955	1965	1975 projected
GNP (projected at 3¾ percent real annual growth rate)	378.6	648.7	990.3
Federal revenues (projected at present rate structure)	67.8	119.7	202.7
Revenues as percent of GNP	17.9	18.5	20.5
Federal expenditures (projected for current programs and cold war)	70.5	122.4	172.0
Expenditures as percent of GNP	18.6	18.9	17.4

Source: M. L. Weidenbaum, *Prospects for Reallocating Public Resources* (forthcoming).

Most examinations of State and local government budgets reveal a relationship between revenues and expenditures which is fundamentally different than the Federal one. The bulk of State and local revenues is obtained from regressive or proportional taxes (primarily on property and retail sales) which are generally estimated to yield revenue increases at rates equal to or less than the growth in GNP.[4]

In contrast, the requirements for existing State and local expenditure programs, notably education and welfare, tend to rise more rapidly than either the revenues from existing tax rates or the GNP.[5] For example, the Advisory Commission on Intergovernmental Relations has pointed out that in recent years State and local spending has been rising at the rate of 8–9 percent a year, strikingly faster than the growth in the GNP. The Commission believes that the recent rate of increase in expenditures of State and local governments can be expected to persist, at least for some years, because the forces that produced it continue to be operative and additional ones are developing.[6]

Hence, the fiscal outlook for State and local governments tends to be one of "potential" deficits—on the basis of existing tax rates and expenditure programs. In practice, of course, the actual Federal surpluses are "used up" and the actual State and local deficits are narrowed.

Under these conditions, the Federal Government is continually expanding civilian programs, adding new ones, and occasionally reducing tax rates, as the revenue growth permits. Hence, the projected "ex ante" gap between Federal revenues computed on the basis of

---

[4] A comprehensive tabulation of the elasticities of major categories of State general revenue is contained in Advisory Commission on Intergovernmental Relations, *Federal-State Coordination of Personal Income Taxes*, October 1965, p. 42.

[5] Cf. Joseph A. Pechman, "Financing State and Local Government," in American Bankers Association, *Proceedings of a Symposium on Federal Taxation*, New York, 1965, p. 76; Selma J. Mushkin and Robert F. Adams, "Emerging Patterns of Federalism," *National Tax Journal*, September 1966, pp. 236–240. For a contrary view, see Elsie M. Watters, *Fiscal Outlook for State and Local Government to 1975*, New York, Tax Foundation, Inc., 1966, 128 pp.

[6] Advisory Commission on Intergovernmental Relations, *op. cit.*, p. 3.

existing tax laws and Federal expenditures estimated on the basis of continuation of current programs mainly signifies the amount of discretion that may be exercised by policymakers in the future. On an "ex post" basis, past experience indicates that it is most unlikely that an entire decade will go by without important changes in either tax legislation or governmental program authorizations.

Moreover, recent economic analysis has pointed out the adverse effects of a large potential surplus in the Government budget under certain conditions. Such potential net inflow to the Federal Government may be self-defeating if it exercises a depressive influence on the level of economic activity, thus reducing governmental revenues from their potential, and preventing the realization of a large actual budget surplus.[7]

The actual responses of State and local governments to their potential deficit positions customarily take a variety of forms. They are almost continually raising tax rates, utilizing new tax sources, raising property assessment ratios, deferring desirable programs, and taking similar actions to stay within the limits of their income and of their authorized debt structures.

Each of the existing sources of funds will continue to be utilized to the extent that they can be, but some of them have severe restrictions. Further increases in debt are often limited or prevented by constitutional debt ceilings and similar legal restraints. The imposition of new taxes and raising the rates on existing sources appear to encounter increasing voter resistance and accentuate problems of interstate competition.

It seems clear that Federal aid in the form of specific grants-in-aid to States or their subdivisions will continue to expand. However, it is unlikely that existing Federal grant programs will increase sufficiently to enable State and local governments to bridge the gap between revenues from existing taxes and the rising expenditure requirements of established functions.

Hence, one basic assumption underlies the subsequent analysis: the Nation will begin to solve its long-term governmental budget problems if it links its actions on the potential Federal surpluses with the anticipated deficits in State and local budgets.

In the absence of a national decision to embark upon a major new effort of Federal aid to the States in the post-Vietnam period, there may be considerable possibility of not obtaining anything close to an optimum allocation of public resources in the United States. The possibility certainly exists that the Nation may use up potential increases in national revenues for "worthwhile" but relatively lower priority Federal programs, while State and local governments are forced either to defer relatively more worthwhile projects for lack of funds or to increase taxes which have adverse effects on economic stability and growth or on distributional equity. Hence, simply reacting to specific program demands, as the savings from peace in Vietnam are realized, may result in losing an important opportunity for reallocating public resources; a deliberate decision to use Federal funds

[7] Cf. Michael Levy, *Fiscal Policy, Cycles and Growth,* New York, National Industrial Conference Board, 1963, 141 pp.

to strengthen State and local governments may succeed in raising the aggregate level of public services or avoiding or reducing the need to expand the overall level of taxation.[8]

FEDERAL AID TO THE STATES

The general concept of distributing available Federal funds to the States goes back to early American history. In his second inaugural address, President Thomas Jefferson suggested a general program of Federal aid to the States, to be used for such purposes as "rivers, canals, roads, arts, manufactures, education, and other great objects within each States."[9]

Because of constitutional objections, President James Madison vetoed legislation which would have distributed to the States the dividends on the Federal subscription to the second national bank. Finally, in 1837 the Congress did vote to distribute surplus funds on an approximately per capita basis. The $37 million so allocated was more than double the annual Federal budget in those days. Some States used the 1837 distribution to capitalize the State banks; others devoted the money to local debt repayment or public works construction. Apparently, the greater part was devoted to education.[10] Considerable interest in distribution of Federal funds to the States arose again in the 1880's but did not result in any congressional action.

"Tied" or program grants to the States date back to the original land grants for higher education in Ohio in 1803.[11] In more recent years,[12] highways and welfare, along with education, have come to represent the bulk of Federal grants-in-aid.

Numerous other proposals have been made for Federal aid to the States. The Eisenhower administration attempted to shift a few Federal tax sources to State governments. That proposal was not adopted, in part, because it was linked with a shift of some program expenditures to the States. The proposal offered the enticement that the revenues to be shifted were to exceed the expenditures shifted.

More recently the Heller-Pechman plan [13] for relatively unrestricted block grants to the States has received considerable public attention and numerous variations have been introduced in the Congress. The Advisory Commission on Intergovernmental Relations has recommended a credit toward the Federal personal income tax be given for a portion of State and local income taxes paid.

Other "tax sharing" proposals have been made.[14] Some would give

---

[8] An earlier version of this argument appears in M. L. Weidenbaum, "Federal Resources and Urban Needs," in Samuel B. Warner, editor, *Planning for a Nation of Cities*, Cambridge, MIT Press, 1966, pp. 61–78.

[9] For historical details, see Edward G. Bourne, *The History of the Surplus Revenue of 1837*, New York, G. P. Putnam's Sons, 1885.

[10] Chester W. Wright, *Economic History of the United States*, second edition, New York, McGraw-Hill, 1949, pp. 401–402; Bray Hammond, *Banks and Politics in America, From the Revolution to the Civil War*, Princeton, Princeton University Press, 1957, p. 451.

[11] Paul B. Trescott, "Federal-State Financial Relations, 1790–1860," *Journal of Economic History*, September 1955, p. 236.

[12] "Federal Aid to State and Local Governments," *Special Analysis, Budget of the United States, Fiscal Year 1967*, Washington, U.S. Government Printing Office, 1966, p. 137.

[13] Pechman, *op. cit.*, pp. 80–84; Walter W. Heller, *New Dimensions of Political Economy*, New York, W. W. Norton & Co., 1967, pp. 139–155.

[14] Maureen McBreen, *Federal Tax Sharing: Historical Development and Arguments for and Against Recent Proposals*, Washington, D.C., Library of Congress, Legislative Reference Service, Jan. 30, 1967, 42 pp.

each State a fixed percentage of the Federal taxes collected within its borders. Other would be more indirect. For example, it is reasoned that reductions in Federal tax rates would enable State and local governments to raise their taxes without increasing the aggregate tax burden of the average taxpayer. Others would lighten the burdens on State and local governments by greater Federal assumption of civilian public sector programs.

A great deal of descriptive and interpretive material has been developed about these plans and their public policy implications. This study attempts, rather, to set up some relatively objective and measurable criteria for comparison and then proceeds to evaluate the extent to which the various alternatives meet the criteria.

ALTERNATIVE METHODS OF FEDERAL AID

The alternatives examined are (1) shared revenues, (2) tax credits, (3) direct Federal operations, (4) program grants, (5) straight block grants, and (6) block grants with an equalization feature.

The criteria for evaluation are (1) income distribution: the extent to which funds are distributed in favor of the low-income States and regions of the United States, (2) resource allocation: the effect on allocation of Government funds among programs and levels of government, and (3) stabilization: the influence on stability of economic activity in the United States.[15]

Tax sharing.—A fixed portion of Federal personal income tax revenues would be distributed to the States on the basis of the State in which the taxes were paid. The State governments would be left free to determine the uses to which they wish to put the funds they receive. To some extent, tax sharing would give the States a vested interest in the current high rates of Federal income taxation.

The Federal Government historically has shared with the States revenues from certain relatively small tax sources. These include sharing internal revenue collections with the Virgin Islands, sharing customs receipts with Puerto Rico and the Virgin Islands, and sharing a variety of national resource-type receipts with the States in which these resources (land, wildlife, power) are located.[16]

Tax credits.—The Federal tax structure currently provides credits for two types of State taxes: a limited credit for State death taxes against Federal estate tax liabilities, and 90 percent credit against Federal payroll levies for similar payments into State unemployment compensation systems.

A tax credit, such as the 40 percent income tax credit recommended by the Advisory Commission on Intergovernmental Relations,[17] differs from tax sharing substantially. The collection and administration of the State income tax is left in the hands of the State governments. Hence, they would only benefit to the extent that the Federal credit enables them to institute or raise income taxes above the levels otherwise politically acceptable.

---

[15] These criteria are very roughly modeled after the three branches of the fiscal department of what has come to be Richard Musgrave's not so imaginary state. Richard A. Musgrave, *The Theory of Public Finance*, New York, McGraw-Hill, 1959, pp. 3–27.

[16] "Federal Aid to State and Local Governments," *Special Analysis, Budget of the United States, Fiscal Year 1967*, Washington, U.S. Government Printing Office, 1966, pp. 138–143.

[17] Advisory Commission on Intergovernmental Relations, *op. cit.*, pp. 18–19.

Expansion of programs carried on at the Federal level.—Potential increases in Federal revenue, over and above those required for financing continuing programs, could be assigned to new or expanded domestic civilian operations which the Federal Government would carry on in each of the 50 States. Examples of such new programs of an interstate character could include the construction and operation of mass transportation or environmental control facilities.

This approach would result in the largest amount of direct Federal intervention in the economy of any of the policy alternatives examined here, since there would be no State or local government participation. To some extent, there would be State and local benefits, since facilities would be provided which otherwise might not be available or would have to be financed locally.

Federal grants limited to specific program areas.—The Federal Government could increase the volume and number of conditional or program grants to State and local governments. This type of Federal aid is limited to specific functions, such as hospital construction and interstate roadbuilding, where the Federal agency administering the program sets detailed standards for the approval of individual State and local projects.

This alternative would avoid direct Federal operation of the public activities to be financed. However, it would increase further the impact of Federal decisionmaking on State and local policies and practices. A number of studies have shown that Federal grants influence the allocation of the recipients' own funds.[18] This of course is hardly surprising. A 50–50 grant for public school construction, for example, would reduce the local price of a $2 million building to $1 million. Assuming some elasticity of demand in response to such a price reduction, the result is almost inevitable.

Most Federal grants are awarded directly to State government. However significant precedents exist for the National Government bypassing the States and dealing directly with localities. Examples of such grant programs include housing and urban renewal, Federal aid to airports, and aid to mass transportation systems. In the aggregate, $9.9 billion of Federal aid payments were made to the States in the fiscal year 1965, and $1.2 billion directly to local units.

Straight block grants.—Block grants have been widely utilized in other nations, notably Great Britain and Canada. The basic concept of block grants is one under which the Federal aid to the States would be completely unconditional. The most straightforward method of distribution would be on a straight per capita basis. One approach is to set up a permanent trust fund to distribute a fixed portion of the Federal income tax base among the States each year regardless of the level of program grants or the State of the Federal Budget.

Some observers maintain that, unlike the other suggested forms of Federal aid, block grants would go to the root of the fiscal dilemma plaguing State and local governments. This method would provide a revenue source that would grow rapidly as the national economy

[18] Governmental Affairs Institute, *Impact of Federal Grants-in-Aid on South Carolina*, A Report to the Commission on Intergovernmental Relations, Washington, 1954, pp. 1–4; McKinney and Company, *The Impact of Federal Grants-in-Aid in the State of Washington*, San Francisco, 1954, pp. 1–3.

expands and incomes rise. It would help free States from the compulsion to look over their shoulders at what adjacent States are doing to attract industry before undertaking their own spending programs. Also, long-term planning by States and localities would be facilitated since the regular flow of funds would eliminate the uncertainties which are characteristic of the annual appropriations process. A major criticism, however, is that block grants would divorce the responsibility for collecting taxes from decisions on their use.

Block grants with equalization.—Most of the block grant bills introduced in the Congress contain an equalization feature. The bill that has received perhaps the most attention was introduced by Senator Jacob K. Javits and cosponsored by Senators Hartke, Scott, and Mundt.[19] It provides for establishing a trust fund in which an amount equal to 1 percent of total taxable personal income would be deposited into the Treasury each year. Under present conditions, this would amount to $2½ to $3 billion a year and would increase as the tax base expands. In effect a major portion of the growth in Federal revenues would be disbursed to the States; the absolute amount of revenue available for direct Federal operations would continue to grow, but at a slower rate than otherwise. The Javits plan is somewhat more restrictive than the original block grant concept, however, as the funds could only be used in the broad categories of health, education, and welfare.

Payments from the trust fund would be made under the following formula: (1) 80 percent would be distributed on the basis of population; this amount would be increased or decreased depending on the State's own tax effort, which would be measured by the ratio of the total revenues derived by the State to total personal income of the State's residents, as compared with the national average, and (2) 20 percent of the fund would be paid each fiscal year to the 13 States with the lowest per capita income; this would be distributed according to the population of the States involved.

The States, in turn, would be required to distribute an "equitable" portion of their allotments to local governments, which must be at least the average of the distribution of their own revenues to local governments over the previous 5 years.

COMPARISONS AMONG THE ALTERNATIVES

Effect on income distribution.—A major theme underlying many of the proposals for Federal aid to State and local governments is the desirability of reducing the inequality of incomes among the various States and regions of the United States. This would particularly enable the poorer areas to support a higher level of public services, more nearly approximating that of the Nation as a whole. The externalities often accompanying State and local government activities—benefits enjoyed by those outside of the taxing jurisdiction—are cited as a crucial reason for enabling the poorer States to provide a higher level of services than they could finance from their own resources.[20] Such externalities arise, for example, when persons reared and educated in one region move to and produce income in another.

---

[19] *Congressional Record,* Oct. 11, 1965, pp. 25616–25617.
[20] George Break, *Intergovernmental Fiscal Relations in the United States,* Washington, The Brookings Institution, 1967, pp. 62–76.

Table 2 contains a summary analysis of the State shares of the six alternative aid proposals considered in this study. It is apparent that block grants with equalization would channel far more funds into the low-income areas than any of the other alternatives. It is also interesting to note that existing Federal program grants to State and local government are more income equalizing (in a geographic sense) than would be block grants distributed on a simple per capita basis. It also can be seen that direct Federal programs, as measured by the wages and salaries of civilian government employees, do not particularly favor low-income areas. As would be expected, tax credits and tax sharing provide the smallest amounts to low income States.

TABLE 2.—*State shares of Federal aid alternatives*

[Percent]

State grouping	Tax sharing	Tax [1] credits	Direct [2] Federal programs	Existing program grants	Per capita block grants	Block [3] grants with equalization
17 States with highest per capita incomes [4]	65.8	61.1	57.2	46.5	49.6	39.0
17 middle income States	19.9	23.2	23.2	24.7	25.2	20.2
17 States with lowest per capita incomes	14.4	15.7	19.3	28.8	25.0	40.6
Total	100.0	100.0	100.0	100.0	100.0	100.0

[1] Based on a credit for State income taxes equal to 7 percent of Federal individual income tax liability.
[2] Measured by the State-by-State distribution of Federal civilian wages and salaries.
[3] S. 2619, 89th Congress.
[4] 16 States and the District of Columbia.

NOTE.—Detail may not add to totals shown due to rounding.

Source: Appendix table 1.

This same rank order holds when the shares of the high income States are examined. They would receive the largest amounts under the tax sharing method, followed closely by tax credits and then by direct Federal programs. These States would obtain more funds from straight block grants than from the "status quo," as represented by their current shares of program grants-in-aid. These high-income States, of course, would receive the smallest proportions of a block grant program with a strong equalization feature.

Effect on major program areas.—It is the very nature of the block grant, tax credit, and tax sharing approaches that predictions cannot be made in advance as to how the funds will be distributed among the various program or functional areas. However, an exploratory effort is made here at just such a projection. It is based on one major assumption: that the States will follow the same pattern in distributing the Federal funds among the various program areas that they followed over the past decade in allocating revenue increases from their own sources.

That is, if a State's expenditures from its own revenues increased $2 million between 1955 and 1965, and its expenditures from its own funds on education rose $1 million, it is assumed that the State has a tendency or propensity to allocate 50 percent of new revenues to education. Precisely such "marginal propensities" were computed for each State for each of the major functional areas of State government expenditure.[21]

[21] This methodology is based with modifications upon James L. Plummer, "Federal-State Revenue Sharing," *Southern Economic Journal*, July 1966, pp. 122–124. The marginal propensities estimated here exclude expenditures from Federal grants-in-aid.

The crudeness of this effort is apparent when it is realized that the allocations among programs during the decade 1955–65 were strongly influenced by the matching provisions of various Federal grant programs which specified the minimum amounts that each State had to devote to a program from its own funds in order to receive the Federal funds. Also, there may have been considerable States effort to "catch up" in certain program areas, such as education, which would result in different "marginal propensities" in the coming decade.

Nevertheless, it is hoped that this analysis helps to convey the point that the selection of tax sharing or block grants or any of the other Federal aid alternatives may contain an implicit choice in emphasis in favor of education or health or highways or welfare, etc. because of the different State propensities to allocate funds among the various functions and the variation in individual State shares among the various alternatives. Table 3 contains the highlights of this analysis.

TABLE 3.—*Hypothetical utilization of Federal aid funds, based on State allocations of their own funds, 1955–65 (percentage distributions)*

FEDERAL AID ALTERNATIVE

Program area	Tax sharing	Tax credits	Per capita block grants	Block grants with equalization
Education	53.1	51.8	52.1	52.5
Public welfare	7.3	7.3	6.7	6.1
Highways	8.9	10.0	11.1	12.1
Health and hospitals	8.9	8.8	8.5	8.1
Natural resources	3.1	3.4	3.4	3.5
All other	18.7	18.7	18.2	17.8
Total	100.0	100.0	100.0	100.0

NOTE.—Detail may not add to totals shown due to rounding.

Source: Appendix table 2.

It can be seen that, under each of the four alternatives examined here, the States would allocate the bulk of their funds to education (between 52 and 53 percent). However, significant differences are noticeable in the case of other program areas. Given the assumptions made in this analysis, tax sharing and tax credits would result in larger shares of the funds going to "people-oriented" areas, such as welfare and health, than the block grant proposals (16 percent versus 14 to 15 percent), and less to the physical capital areas, such as highways and natural resources (12 to 13 percent versus 14 to 16 percent). To some extent, the investments in "human" capital may be more oriented to lower income classes than the highway and resource programs. Hence, the income equalizing characteristics—in a geographic sense—of the block grant approaches may be offset in part by the reverse tendency in an income-class sense.

Effect on local governments.—One of the major questions concerning the distribution of Federal funds without strings—via the tax sharing, tax credit, and block grant approaches—is the extent to which the States will "pass through" some of the funds to local government units. The concern on the part of the cities, which traditionally believe that they receive less than "fair" shares from the State legislatures, is evidenced by proposals that they have made for block grants directly from the Federal Government, which would completely bypass the States.[22]

Some of the revenue sharing bills introduced in the Congress do have a "pass through" provision. Most of these would penalize States that give local governments a smaller share of the Federal funds than they receive of State money. Although some observers contend that this would mererly maintain past and current inequities, the supporters of block grants count heavily on reapportionment for redressing the balance.[23]

An analysis of the extent to which States share funds with their local governments was performed similar to that for major program areas, on the assumption that the States would share the new Federal funds with their subdivisions in the same proportions that they shared their own funds during 1955–65. No significant differences emerged among the various Federal aid plans. The States as a whole are estimated to share between 45 and 47½ percent of the funds with local subdivisions.

These calculations do not take account of any mandatory "pass through" provisions which may be contained in legislation enacting any of the aid alternatives. Hence, the figures merely illuminate the large extent to which the States have in the past shared funds with their local governments. Differences in the marginal "sharing" propensity were substantial among the various States.

Effect on economic stability.—Little if any attention has been given to the relationship of the alternative aid proposals to economic stability. Nevertheless, significant differences emerge from even the crudest analysis. Table 4 contains a ranking of the six alternatives, without any numerical values. Some explanations may be helpful.

TABLE 4.—*Stabilizing effectiveness of Federal aid alternatives*

Rank:	
1	Direct Federal programs.
2	Program grants.
3 to 4	Block grants. Block grants with equalization.
5 to 6	Tax credits. Tax sharing.

The major empirical study of the stabilizing effectiveness of Federal Government programs was made by the staff of the Bureau of the Budget in the middle 1950's.[24] The study showed the variety of expenditure programs that would increase with declines in the gross national product (and presumably vice versa). For example, unemployment insurance, old-age and survivors insurance, and related trust fund payments would be expected to increase because of the greater number of persons who would become eligible and who would apply for benefits under existing laws.

More veterans would be expected to apply for education benefits or to qualify for compensation and pensions, which are determined in part by their income.[25] It was estimated that total veterans expendi-

[22] A recent example is City of University City, Mo., *Proposed Tax Sharing Plan for All U.S. Cities Over 50,000 Population,* March 1967 (processed).
[23] Heller, *op. cit.*, pp. 159–161.
[24] Samuel M. Cohn, "The Stabilizing Effectiveness of Budget Flexibility: Comment," in National Bureau of Economic Research, *Policies to Combat Depression,* Princeton, Princeton University Press, 1956, pp. 90–100.
[25] Supplemental appropriations might be required, but these have been virtually automatic under such circumstances, in view of the strong moral and legal commitment of the government.

tures in 1955 would rise from $5.1 to $6 billion, a 17.6-percent increase, under the recessionary conditions postulated in the study. Also, the rising benefit levels would increase the workload of and demand for governmental administrative employees.

The findings on the stabilizing effectiveness of grants-in-aid were less clear. It was assumed that a relatively small ($100 million) increase would occur in public assistance grants as recessionary conditions increased the number of persons becoming eligible for the payments. Perhaps less certain was the belief that, to a small degree, some Federal grants to States would be reduced as the objectives could be achieved at lower cost on account of the price declines accompanying the recessionary conditions.[26]

An earlier analysis by James Maxwell seems to be generally consistent with the Budget Bureau study. He concluded that public assistance grants demonstrate "only slight built-in flexibility."[27] He reasoned that in prosperity a modest decline in number of recipients would be offset by larger average payments attributable to a rise in living costs during periods of prosperity. However, Maxwell stated that one may not safely conclude that the average public assistance payment is sensitive to a decline in prices during depression. "The historical trend toward higher welfare standards and the belief that subsistence payments should be maintained will operate against it."[28]

On the basis of the foregoing, table 4 has been prepared on the assumption that direct Federal operations do tend to be anticyclical; that is, that such Federal expenditures rise with declines in GNP, and that Federal program grants are also, on balance, anticyclical but not so markedly.

The differences in cyclical effects of block grants, tax credits, and tax sharing primarily arise from the different bases on which the amount of Federal funds to be disbursed would be determined. The block grant proposals generally have provided for allocating a percentage of personal taxable income to the States, while tax sharing provides for allocating a portion of personal income tax collections. Tax credits, of course, would provide a more indirect benefit to the States.

The various studies that have been made of the income elasticity of the Federal individual income tax conclude that it is substantially in excess of unity. Pechman estimated the elasticity at 1.6 percent between the fall of 1951 and the end of 1953.[29] Eckstein used an estimate of 1.4 percent for his projections.[30] Of course, these ratios underscore the stabilizing effectiveness of the Federal tax structure. However, a distribution of State aid funds keyed to fluctuations in Federal tax collections, which is the essence of the tax sharing proposal, would itself be destabilizing insofar as the funds available for distribution to the States would decline during recessionary conditions and rise rapidly during inflationary periods.

The studies of the variability of the tax base indicate greater

---

[26] *Ibid.*, p. 98.
[27] James A. Maxwell, *Federal Grants and the Business Cycle*, New York, National Bureau of Economic Research, 1952, p. 38.
[28] *Ibid.*, p. 38.
[29] Joseph A. Pechman, "Yield of an Individual Income Tax During a Recession," in National Bureau of Economic Research, *Policies to Combat Depression*, Princeton, Princeton University Press, 1956, p. 124.
[30] Eckstein, *op. cit.*, p. 46.

stability, as would be expected for a progressive tax structure.[31] Hence, it would be expected that block grants—tied to the tax base—would be somewhat destabilizing, but not as much as tax sharing payments which are based directly on Federal revenue collections.

Although the cardinal (numerical) relations are subject to more conjecture, the ordinal or ranking relationships seem clear: existing Federal programs—both direct and grants-in-aid—on balance tend to demonstrate mild anticyclical characteristics. Block grants, either with or without equalization provisions, tend to contain mild destabilizing (procyclical) features. Tax sharing and indirectly tax credits tend to show up poorest in terms of effect on economic stability (see table 4).

Summary and Conclusion [32]

As might be expected, the foregoing analysis does not come up with a clear cut answer as to which single Federal aid approach is most desirable. Block grants with an equalization feature yield the greatest amount of income redistribution in favor of the low-income areas. However, tax credits and tax sharing, on the basis of the recent allocation patterns of State budgets, might tend to result in larger expenditures for welfare, health, and similar investments in human capital with an especial emphasis on the groups at the lowest end of the income class distribution. Yet, in terms of a stabilization objective, all of these proposals tend to show mildly destabilizing characteristics. In contrast, the existing programs, both direct Federal operations and program grants, seem to possess desirable anticyclical tendencies which would assist economic stabilization efforts.

Perhaps this analysis just provides a more objective basis for the essentially subjective and political task of decisionmaking. That is, if equalization of fiscal resources is the primary objective—a sort of fiscal federalism variation of the war on poverty—block grants with a strong equalization feature show up best.

If the concern, rather, is with emphasizing investments in human resources, tax sharing and program grant mechanisms both would rate highest. However, if the constraint is introduced that the new aid plan should have few if any controls over the State allocation of the funds, then the tax sharing approach would seem to be superior.

Hence, the choice among the various alternative means of channeling Federal aid to the States primarily becomes a matter not of examining the intrinsic merits of each alternative but rather of determining the relative emphasis to be placed on such basic objectives as income distribution, resource allocation, and economic stabilization.

Perhaps almost any of the alternative ways of strengthening State and local governments would be an acceptable "second best" solution. That is they might be superior, in terms of the overall needs of the Federal system, to merely devoting funds to new direct Federal programs or, worse still, to obsolescent programs firmly imbedded in the Federal Budget.

---

[31] Heller prefers the tax base rather than the tax yield as the basis for block grants because "taxable income is somewhat more stable than revenues." Heller, *op. cit.*, p. 146. The ratio of the change in taxable income to the change in adjusted gross income on Federal personal income tax returns was estimated to vary between 0.59 and 0.62 during the period 1949–53. Leo Cohen, "An Empirical Measurement of the Built-In Flexibility of the Individual Income Tax," *American Economic Review*, May 1959, p. 535; Wilfred Lewis used the assumption of unit GNP elasticity of personal income in an illustrative ten-year projection of Federal receipts. Wilfred Lewis, Jr., "The Federal Sector in National Income Models," in National Bureau of Economic Research, *Models of Income Determination*, Princeton, Princeton University Press, 1964, p. 242.

[32] More detailed analyses are contained in a forthcoming study by the author, *Prospects for Reallocating Public Resources*.

APPENDIX TABLE 1.—*State shares of alternative methods of Federal aid*

[Percent of total Federal outlays for the purpose]

State	Tax sharing	Tax credits	Direct Federal programs	Existing program grants	Per capita block grants	Block grants with equalization
(1)	(2)	(3)	(4)	(5)	(6)	(7)
High-income group	(65.8)	(61.1)	(57.2)	(46.5)	(49.6)	(39.0)
Delaware	.9	.4	.2	.2	.2	.2
Nevada	.2	.2	(1)	.4	.2	.2
Connecticut	1.7	2.1	.6	.13	1.5	.9
New York	17.7	13.1	8.5	7.4	9.3	8.2
California	9.4	11.1	12.2	9.5	9.4	8.7
Illinois	7.9	7.6	4.0	4.5	5.5	3.6
New Jersey	3.1	4.5	2.6	2.0	3.5	2.3
Alaska	.1	.1	.8	1.0	.1	.1
Massachusetts	2.9	3.3	2.7	3.2	2.8	2.0
Maryland	2.3	2.7	12.7	2.6	2.2	1.5
Michigan	8.6	4.7	1.9	3.7	4.3	3.5
Washington	1.2	1.8	2.1	2.0	1.6	1.4
Ohio	6.0	5.9	4.3	4.3	5.3	3.6
Hawaii	.3	.3	1.0	.5	.4	.4
Colorado	1.2	1.0	1.6	1.4	1.0	.9
Missouri	2.3	2.3	2.0	2.5	2.3	1.5
Middle-income group	(19.9)	(23.2)	(23.2)	(24.7)	(25.2)	(20.2)
Oregon	.7	1.0	.9	1.6	1.0	.8
Pennsylvania	6.3	6.9	5.2	4.9	6.0	4.1
Wyoming	.1	.2	(1)	.6	.2	.2
Indiana	2.3	2.4	1.4	1.7	2.5	1.9
Rhode Island	.6	.5	.5	.6	.4	.3
Wisconsin	1.8	2.0	.8	1.6	2.2	2.0
Nebraska	.6	.7	.6	.9	.8	.6
Iowa	.8	1.3	.8	1.4	1.4	1.2
Minnesota	1.6	1.6	1.0	2.0	1.8	1.7
New Hampshire	.2	.3	(1)	.4	.3	.2
Kansas	.7	1.1	.9	1.2	1.2	1.0
Montana	.2	.3	(1)	.8	.4	.3
Arizona	.4	.6	.9	.9	.9	.8
Florida	1.6	2.1	2.2	2.6	3.0	2.6
Utah	.3	.4	.1	.8	.5	.5
North Dakota	.1	.2	.2	.7	.3	.4
Virginia	1.6	1.6	7.7	2.0	2.3	1.6
Low-income group	(14.4)	(15.7)	(19.3)	(28.8)	(25.0)	(40.6)
Texas	3.8	4.5	5.0	5.0	5.4	4.2
Vermont	.1	.1	(1)	.4	.2	.2
Maine	.2	.4	(1)	.6	.5	.4
Oklahoma	1.0	.9	.2	2.2	1.3	1.1
Idaho	(1)	.3	.3	.6	.3	.7
New Mexico	.2	.4	1.0	.9	.5	1.2
South Dakota	.1	.2	.4	.7	.4	.8
West Virginia	.4	.7	(1)	1.1	1.0	1.8
Georgia	1.3	1.3	2.4	2.5	2.2	4.3
North Carolina	2.4	1.2	1.2	2.0	2.5	4.8
Louisiana	.8	1.2	1.0	2.8	1.8	3.9
Kentucky	1.6	1.0	1.2	2.1	1.6	3.1
Tennessee	.9	1.2	1.6	2.2	2.0	3.8
Alabama	.6	1.0	2.7	2.0	1.8	3.4
South Carolina	.4	.5	1.0	1.0	1.3	2.5
Arkansas	.3	.4	.6	1.4	1.0	1.9
Mississippi	.3	.4	.7	1.3	1.2	2.5

NOTES TO APPENDIX TABLE 1

1 Less than ½ of 1 percent.
Detail may not add to totals shown due to rounding.

SOURCE NOTES

Col. (1): States are arrayed in descending order of average per capita income during the years 1962–64. Figures for Maryland include the District of Columbia. Rankings are taken from Sophie R. Dales, "Federal Grants, 1964–65," Social Security Bulletin, June 1966, p. 12.

Col. (2): Based on Federal tax collections for 1964. "1964 Annual Report, Commissioner of Internal Revenue," Washington, U.S. Government Printing Office, 1965, p. 73.

Col. (3): Percentages are derived from estimates of a credit for State income taxes of 7 percent of Federal individual income tax liability in 1958, as computed in James A. Maxwell, "Tax Credits and Intergovernmental Fiscal Relations," Washington, Brookings Institution, 1962, pp. 184–185.

Col. (4): Wages and salaries of Federal civilian employees cover the calendar year 1963. Survey of Current Business, August 1964, pp. 18–21.

Col. (5): Actual distribution of Federal grants-in-aid to the States in the fiscal year 1964, "Annual Report of the Secretary of the Treasury on the State of the Finances for the Fiscal Year 1964," Washington, U.S. Government Printing Office, 1965.

Col. (6): Distribution based on State population figures for 1964. "Statistical Abstract of the United States, 1966," Washington, U.S. Government Printing Office, 1966, p. 11.

Col. (7): Estimates are for the Javits bill, S. 2619, 89th Cong. Congressional Record, Oct. 11, 1965, p. 25608.

APPENDIX TABLE 2.—*State incremental spending patterns: allocation of general expenditure increases among program areas, 1955–65*

[Percentage distribution]

States ranked by 1962–64 average per capita income	Education	Public welfare	Highways	Health and hospitals	Natural resources	All other	Total
Delaware	58.8	5.0	12.7	4.8	2.8	16.0	100.0
Nevada	47.0	4.2	17.5	3.9	0	27.2	100.0
Connecticut	34.1	9.3	24.4	3.9	2.3	26.0	100.0
New York	58.6	7.2	0	9.1	1.8	22.8	100.0
California	42.4	10.9	12.8	6.9	6.9	20.1	100.0
Illinois	47.6	13.1	8.7	15.4	2.4	12.7	100.0
New Jersey	50.2	9.6	0	11.1	6.0	22.9	100.0
Alaska [1]	41.9	5.7	6.2	3.8	0	42.1	100.0
Massachusetts	26.1	10.0	8.3	14.1	1.9	39.7	100.0
Maryland	44.0	5.1	7.2	14.2	1.7	27.7	100.0
Michigan	67.0	6.7	2.3	6.7	2.3	15.1	100.0
Washington	62.6	5.7	12.7	0	4.9	14.1	100.0
Ohio	56.0	11.5	0	9.4	2.5	20.5	100.0
Hawaii [1]	38.5	7.6	0	0	0	52.4	100.0
Colorado	57.4	4.1	9.3	13.0	4.0	12.2	100.0
Missouri	51.9	4.4	20.9	10.4	3.2	9.2	100.0
Oregon	53.9	5.6	14.4	5.8	5.4	14.9	100.0
Pennsylvania	52.7	7.0	14.8	9.8	2.3	13.5	100.0
Wyoming	61.0	1.8	18.6	7.1	10.4	0	100.0
Indiana	66.7	.8	12.7	6.7	2.1	10.9	100.0
Rhode Island	45.0	8.8	12.5	11.1	.7	21.8	100.0
Wisconsin	39.1	3.6	8.8	6.1	3.0	39.3	100.0
Nebraska	33.8	6.1	26.5	8.7	11.7	13.3	100.0
Iowa	40.5	6.2	28.1	8.2	2.9	13.9	100.0
Minnesota	59.7	3.4	13.1	8.4	3.4	12.1	100.0
New Hampshire	39.5	5.3	13.1	9.6	4.1	28.4	100.0
Kansas	55.7	4.4	12.1	12.1	6.2	9.5	100.0
Montana	63.7	0	16.6	2.8	4.0	12.8	100.0
Arizona	56.2	2.9	8.8	3.4	2.7	25.9	100.0
Florida	52.9	2.9	18.3	6.9	3.7	15.3	100.0
Utah	72.8	2.7	10.6	4.9	2.6	6.3	100.0
North Dakota	43.8	1.4	18.4	3.3	1.3	31.8	100.0
Virginia	45.6	2.0	19.4	11.8	4.1	17.1	100.0
Texas	65.9	3.3	13.4	5.4	1.3	10.7	100.0
Vermont	52.1	3.3	13.1	8.3	5.2	17.9	100.0
Maine	57.8	6.8	0	7.7	6.6	19.1	100.0
Oklahoma	41.5	13.2	19.0	6.1	4.1	16.0	100.0
Idaho	55.6	1.0	7.7	8.0	10.1	17.6	100.0
New Mexico	67.4	4.8	12.4	2.0	3.3	10.0	100.0
South Dakota	52.7	3.9	22.3	3.6	10.0	7.5	100.0
West Virginia	50.7	7.6	17.0	7.5	5.6	11.5	100.0
Georgia	59.6	5.2	8.7	6.7	5.5	14.3	100.0
North Carolina	59.9	1.6	8.7	7.7	3.0	19.1	100.0
Louisiana	48.4	4.8	17.2	8.4	2.7	18.5	100.0
Kentucky	49.4	2.9	19.4	8.0	2.7	17.7	100.0
Tennessee	51.1	.8	22.8	9.6	2.9	12.8	100.0
Alabama	52.5	7.7	20.2	6.9	2.3	10.3	100.0
South Carolina	38.1	.9	19.0	7.8	0	33.3	100.0
Arkansas	49.0	5.9	20.3	8.8	6.6	9.4	100.0
Mississippi	58.0	7.9	13.0	5.7	2.3	13.1	100.0

[1] Estimates were based on the period 1962–65.

NOTE.—Detail may not add to totals shown due to rounding.

Source: U.S. Department of Commerce, Bureau of the Census, "Compendium of State Government Finances" (Issues for 1955, 1962, and 1965).

†